International Directory of
COMPANY
HISTORIES

International Directory of

COMPANY HISTORIES

VOLUME 60

Editor
Tina Grant

ST. JAMES PRESS®

Detroit • New York • San Diego • San Francisco • Cleveland • New Haven, Conn. • Waterville, Maine • London • Munich

THOMSON

TM

GALE

International Directory of Company Histories, Volume 60

Tina Grant, Editor

Project Editor
Miranda H. Ferrara

Editorial
Erin Bealmear, Joann Cerrito, Jim Craddock,
Stephen Cusack, Peter M. Gareffa,
Kristin Hart, Melissa Hill, Margaret
Mazurkiewicz, Carol A. Schwartz,
Michael J. Tyrkus

Imaging and Multimedia
Randy Bassett, Lezlie Light

Manufacturing
Rhonda Williams

LIBRARY OF CONGRESS CATALOG NUMBER 89-190943

ISBN: 1-55862-505-4

BRITISH LIBRARY CATALOGUING IN PUBLICATION DATA

International directory of company histories. Vol. 60
I. Tina Grant
33.87409

Printed in the United States of America
10 9 8 7 6 5 4 3 2 1

CONTENTS

Company Histories

PREFACE

The St. James Press series *The International Directory of Company Histories (IDCH)* is intended for reference use by students, business people, librarians, historians, economists, investors, job candidates, and others who seek to learn more about the historical development of the world's most important companies. To date, *IDCH* has covered over 6,300 companies in 60 volumes.

Inclusion Criteria

Most companies chosen for inclusion in *IDCH* have achieved a minimum of US$25 million in annual sales and are leading influences in their industries or geographical locations. Companies may be publicly held, private, or nonprofit. State-owned companies that are important in their industries and that may operate much like public or private companies also are included. Wholly owned subsidiaries and divisions are profiled if they meet the requirements for inclusion. Entries on companies that have had major changes since they were last profiled may be selected for updating.

The *IDCH* series highlights 10% private and nonprofit companies, and features updated entries on approximately 45 companies per volume.

Entry Format

Each entry begins with the company's legal name, the address of its headquarters, its telephone, toll-free, and fax numbers, and its web site. A statement of public, private, state, or parent ownership follows. A company with a legal name in both English and the language of its headquarters country is listed by the English name, with the native-language name in parentheses.

The company's founding or earliest incorporation date, the number of employees, and the most recent available sales figures follow. Sales figures are given in local currencies with equivalents in U.S. dollars. For some private companies, sales figures are estimates and indicated by the abbreviation *est.* The entry lists the exchanges on which a company's stock is traded and its ticker symbol, as well as the company's NAIC codes.

Entries generally contain a *Company Perspectives* box which provides a short summary of the company's mission, goals, and ideals, a *Key Dates* box highlighting milestones in the company's history, lists of *Principal Subsidiaries, Principal Divisions, Principal Operating Units, Principal Competitors,* and articles for *Further Reading.*

American spelling is used throughout *IDCH*, and the word ''billion'' is used in its U.S. sense of one thousand million.

Sources

Entries have been compiled from publicly accessible sources both in print and on the Internet such as general and academic periodicals, books, annual reports, and material supplied by the companies themselves.

Cumulative Indexes

IDCH contains three indexes: the **Index to Companies**, which provides an alphabetical index to companies discussed in the text as well as to companies profiled, the **Index to Industries**, which allows researchers to locate companies by their principal industry, and the **Geographic Index**, which lists companies alphabetically by the country of their headquarters. The indexes are cumulative and specific instructions for using them are found immediately preceding each index.

Suggestions Welcome

Comments and suggestions from users of *IDCH* on any aspect of the product as well as suggestions for companies to be included or updated are cordially invited. Please write:

The Editor
International Directory of Company Histories
St. James Press
27500 Drake Rd.
Farmington Hills, Michigan 48331-3535

AB	Aktiebolag (Finland, Sweden)
AB Oy	Aktiebolag Osakeyhtiot (Finland)
A.E.	Anonimos Eteria (Greece)
AG	Aktiengesellschaft (Austria, Germany, Switzerland, Liechtenstein)
A.O.	Anonim Ortaklari/Ortakligi (Turkey)
ApS	Amparteselskab (Denmark)
A.Š.	Anonim Širketi (Turkey)
A/S	Aksjeselskap (Norway); Aktieselskab (Denmark, Sweden)
Ay	Avoinyhtio (Finland)
B.A.	Buttengewone Aansprakeiijkheid (The Netherlands)
Bhd.	Berhad (Malaysia, Brunei)
B.V.	Besloten Vennootschap (Belgium, The Netherlands)
C.A.	Compania Anonima (Ecuador, Venezuela)
C. de R.L.	Compania de Responsabilidad Limitada (Spain)
Co.	Company
Corp.	Corporation
CRL	Companhia a Responsabilidao Limitida (Portugal, Spain)
C.V.	Commanditaire Vennootschap (The Netherlands, Belgium)
G.I.E.	Groupement d'Interet Economique (France)
GmbH	Gesellschaft mit beschraenkter Haftung (Austria, Germany, Switzerland)
Inc.	Incorporated (United States, Canada)
I/S	Interessentselskab (Denmark); Interesentselskap (Norway)
KG/KGaA	Kommanditgesellschaft/Kommanditgesellschaft auf Aktien (Austria, Germany, Switzerland)
KK	Kabushiki Kaisha (Japan)
K/S	Kommanditselskab (Denmark); Kommandittselskap (Norway)
Lda.	Limitada (Spain)
L.L.C.	Limited Liability Company (United States)
Ltd.	Limited (Various)
Ltda.	Limitada (Brazil, Portugal)
Ltee.	Limitee (Canada, France)
mbH	mit beschraenkter Haftung (Austria, Germany)
N.V.	Naamloze Vennootschap (Belgium, The Netherlands)
OAO	Otkrytoe Aktsionernoe Obshchestve (Russia)
OOO	Obschestvo s Ogranichennoi Otvetstvennostiu (Russia)
Oy	Osakeyhtiö (Finland)
PLC	Public Limited Co. (United Kingdom, Ireland)
Pty.	Proprietary (Australia, South Africa, United Kingdom)
S.A.	Société Anonyme (Belgium, France, Greece, Luxembourg, Switzerland, Arab speaking countries); Sociedad Anónima (Latin America [except Brazil], Spain, Mexico); Sociedades Anônimas (Brazil, Portugal)
SAA	Societe Anonyme Arabienne
S.A.R.L.	Sociedade Anonima de Responsabilidade Limitada (Brazil, Portugal); Société à Responsabilité Limitée (France, Belgium, Luxembourg)
S.A.S.	Societá in Accomandita Semplice (Italy); Societe Anonyme Syrienne (Arab speaking countries)
Sdn. Bhd.	Sendirian Berhad (Malaysia)
S.p.A.	Società per Azioni (Italy)
Sp. z.o.o.	Spólka z ograniczona odpowiedzialnoscia (Poland)
S.R.L.	Società a Responsabilità Limitata (Italy); Sociedad de Responsabilidad Limitada (Spain, Mexico, Latin America [except Brazil])
S.R.O.	Spolecnost s Rucenim Omezenym (Czechoslovakia
Ste.	Societe (France, Belgium, Luxembourg, Switzerland)
VAG	Verein der Arbeitgeber (Austria, Germany)
YK	Yugen Kaisha (Japan)
ZAO	Zakrytoe Aktsionernoe Obshchestve (Russia)

$	United States dollar	KD	Kuwaiti dinar
£	United Kingdom pound	L	Italian lira
¥	Japanese yen	LuxFr	Luxembourgian franc
A$	Australian dollar	M$	Malaysian ringgit
AED	United Arab Emirates dirham	N	Nigerian naira
B	Thai baht	Nfl	Netherlands florin
B	Venezuelan bolivar	NIS	Israeli new shekel
BD	Bahraini dinar	NKr	Norwegian krone
BFr	Belgian franc	NT$	Taiwanese dollar
C$	Canadian dollar	NZ$	New Zealand dollar
CHF	Switzerland franc	P	Philippine peso
COL	Colombian peso	PLN	Polish zloty
Cr	Brazilian cruzado	PkR	Pakistan Rupee
CZK	Czech Republic koruny	Pta	Spanish peseta
DA	Algerian dinar	R	Brazilian real
Dfl	Netherlands florin	R	South African rand
DKr	Danish krone	RMB	Chinese renminbi
DM	German mark	RO	Omani rial
E£	Egyptian pound	Rp	Indonesian rupiah
Esc	Portuguese escudo	Rs	Indian rupee
EUR	Euro dollars	Ru	Russian ruble
FFr	French franc	S$	Singapore dollar
Fmk	Finnish markka	Sch	Austrian schilling
GRD	Greek drachma	SFr	Swiss franc
HK$	Hong Kong dollar	SKr	Swedish krona
HUF	Hungarian forint	SRls	Saudi Arabian riyal
IR£	Irish pound	TD	Tunisian dinar
ISK	Icelandic króna	VND	Vietnamese Dong
J$	Jamaican dollar	W	Korean won
K	Zambian kwacha		

International Directory of
COMPANY
HISTORIES

After Hours Formalwear

After Hours Formalwear Inc.

4444 Shackelford Road
Norcross, Georgia 30093
U.S.A.
Telephone: (770) 448-8381
Toll Free: (800) 594-8897
Fax: (770) 449-6707
Web site: http://afterhours.com

Wholly Owned Subsidiary of The May Department Stores
Company
Founded: 1946
Employees: 1,000 (est.)
Sales: $110 million (2001 est.)
NAIC: 532220 Formal Wear and Costume Rental

A subsidiary of The May Department Stores Company, After Hours Formalwear Inc. is America's largest tuxedo rental and sales retailer, operating more than 330 stores in 27 states and Washington, D.C. After Hours stores are open seven days a week and evenings, providing formal wear for weddings, proms, and other social occasions. In addition to an After Hours private label formal wear line, the company offers exclusive tuxedo styles from such labels as FUBU, Tommy Hilfiger, Chaps Ralph Lauren, Claiborne, and Perry Ellis. Beyond tuxedos, After Hours carries other types of formal jackets, such as cutaway, tailcoat, waistcoat, stroller, and dinner jackets, plus such accessories as shirts (in a range of colors), bow ties, four-in-hand ties, cummerbunds, jewelry, shoes, and vests. Most of the stores are found in malls and average about 1,000 square feet in size, the boutique units carrying a limited supply of in-store items and making the balance of After Hours' inventory available through catalogs. The company maintains strategically located cleaning and distribution centers to supply the chain. Rental prices run the gamut, including a package as low as $49.95 for the budget conscious. Sizes range from small boys to Big & Tall.

1940s Origins

The origins of After Hours date back to 1946 to Charlotte, North Carolina, when D.Q. Mitchell and his wife Arzelle decided to complement their florist business by renting tuxedos. Rentals proved so successful that the couple ultimately left the flower business and devoted all of their attention to tuxedos. In the mid-1950s, they launched a small chain of stores in the South, and in 1970 the company moved its headquarters to Atlanta. At this stage, the chain comprised 17 stores. In 1974, D.Q. Mitchell died, and Robert Beaty, who started with the company in 1957 as a truck driver, took charge. The business remained family owned, with Arzelle Mitchell known to visit the outlets to keep tabs. Over the next 11 years, the Mitchell's chain grew steadily, so that by 1985 it totaled 92 stores located in 11 southeastern states, making it the largest company-owned chain in the industry. (Gingiss Formalwear, a Chicago-based chain, numbered more than 200 stores, but they were franchised operations.) To support the outlets, Mitchell's maintained eight service centers to sort, inspect, clean, and restock the chain's inventory of tuxedos. Of the 92 stores, 22 were located in Florida, compared to 12 in the company's home state of Georgia. In addition, Mitchell's owned and operated two stores aimed at women, Arzelle's Brides and Formal, named after D.Q. Mitchell's wife and co-founder.

The prospects for Mitchell's in the mid-1980s were bright, prompting management in install a new computer system. Much of that promise was due to a resurgence in the popularity of formal wear, which had fallen out of favor in the late 1960s and 1970s. Actors such as Robert Wagner, known for wearing tuxedos, licensed their names and faces to tuxedo labels. In addition, after Ronald Reagan became president in 1981, Washington, D.C., placed a greater emphasis on formal events, leading to a larger number of black-tie affairs around the country. The formalwear industry was highly fragmented, especially on the rental side. According to statistics provided by the American Formalwear Association, the industry was comprised of 1,200 companies and 7,000 individual formal wear shops. There was clearly an opening to build a national brand, but Beaty was hesitant to grow the Mitchell's chain beyond its southeastern

---
Company Perspectives:

Depend on After Hours Formalwear for tuxedo rentals for your wedding, prom, college formals, and black tie affairs. Count on a wide variety of formal wear styles and convenience for the grooms, groomsmen, prom dates, and black tie invitees.
---

base, opting instead to backfill stores in the company's current markets.

New Ownership in the 1990s

The Mitchell's chain stalled around the 100 store mark. In 1996, the Mitchell family decided to sell the business to a group of investors led by three members of management: Joe Doyle, who had been with the company for 22 years, along with Dick Weir and Wayne Griner. From the outset, the new owners were determined to grow Mitchell's into a national brand. They sold the bridal business and focused all of their resources on men's formalwear, launching a re-branding effort, changing the names of the stores to After Hours by Mitchell's, as well as making efforts to beef up the company's infrastructure and hire executive talent. In addition, in 1999 the chain added its own private label and became the first to offer the Tommy Hilfiger Formal Wear line of tuxedos and accessories. Mitchell's was able to enjoy double-digit growth in revenues, but to become a major consolidator in the industry it still required an experienced capital partner. In early 1999, with 115 stores located in 64 cities, Mitchell's hired Robinson-Humphrey Co., an Atlanta securities firm, to help it find a suitable backer. In September, Mitchell's settled on New York City-based Desai Capital Management Inc., a management buyout and leveraged acquisition firm which then acquired a 51 percent interest in a recapitalization of the company. Doyle and his team retained a significant stake and continued to run the business. Desai had been in operation since 1984 and managed institutionally funded investment partnerships, giving it access to the funds necessary to turn Mitchell's into the national player the chain's management envisioned. To ensure that Mitchell's had the necessary borrowing capacity to complete the acquisitions necessary to grow the business, Desai designed the transaction to be conservatively capitalized.

Desai also contributed operating partners to Mitchell's new board, people with experience in both retail and consolidation efforts. These board members were able to offer their expertise in helping management shape the company's strategy and help evaluate acquisitions. With Desai's involvement, Mitchell's completed a series of acquisitions, the opening stage of a five-year plan to grow the chain to around 500 units. In March 2000, it acquired Nationwide Formalwear Inc. of West Chester, Pennsylvania, operators of the 70-unit Small's chain. Small was spawned from a single store founded by Bill Glah in Upper Darby, Pennsylvania, in the late 1940s. His son, Bill Glah, Jr., took over the business and concluded that in light of the consolidation trend taking place in the formal-wear industry, either the chain would have to expand to keep pace with the competition or merge with a larger player. He had talked to Mitchell's for four

years before agreeing to the sale. The Small's chain was an ideal fit for Mitchell's. Only in one Virginia mall did both chains have competing stores. As a result, Mitchell's was able to expand into the mid-Atlantic and northeastern states and top the 200 level in total units. In addition, Mitchell's picked up the Nationwide wholesale division, which provided formalwear to some 600 businesses that in turn rented the apparel in smaller markets. Again, Nationwide served the Mid-Atlantic and northeastern regions, complementing Mitchell's wholesale business that catered to the southeastern United States. In early April 2000, Mitchell's made a more modest buy, adding the three-unit formalwear business of Master's Tuxedos, located in Mobile, Alabama. A third acquisition was announced in December, the purchase of Sempliner's/Tuxedo World, a Bay City, Michigan, chain of 34 stores located in Michigan, Ohio, and Indiana. As with the Small's acquisition, this transaction added new markets to Mitchell's, helping the company gain an even greater national presence, although management was reluctant to move west of the Mississippi. Also of note in 2000, Mitchell's moved into a new headquarters in the Atlanta suburb of Norcross and began a store remodeling effort, embracing a masculine aesthetic featuring "warm wood" as the decor and men's fragrances in the air. Due to its rapid growth, the company, for the first time in its half-century of existence, hired a chief operating officer.

2000 and Beyond

Under Desai's ownership, Mitchell's posted strong increases in revenues, which grew from $48 million in 1998 to $56 million in 1999 and $99 million in 2000. In 2001, Mitchell's changed its name to After Hours Formalwear Inc., and Desai saw a chance to not only provide the formalwear chain with an opportunity for even greater growth but also to realize a healthy profit on its investment. In December 2001, the business was sold for approximately $100 million in cash to St. Louis-based The May Department Stores Company, one of the largest department store operators, which generated more than $13 billion each year in revenues. May folded After Hours into its new bridal division.

Not only did it have deep pockets, but May also boasted a rich history. The company was founded in 1877 by German immigrant David May, who opened a clothing store in the silver-mining boom town of Leadville, Colorado, after failing as a miner. Eleven years later, he expanded to Denver, and in 1892 he and his three brothers-in-law bought The Famous Clothing Store in St. Louis, followed by the 1898 purchase of a Cleveland department store which they renamed The May Company. Their headquarters was relocated to St. Louis, and the business was incorporated in 1910. It was taken public a year later and became listed on the New York Stock Exchange. Over the ensuing decades, May steadily added department stores around the country: Baltimore's Bernheim-Leader department store in 1927, Pittsburgh's Kaufmann's in 1946, Denver's The Daniels & Fisher Stores Company in 1957, and Hecht's, with locations in Washington, D.C., and Baltimore, in 1959. Starting in the late 1980s, May became an aggressive player in the consolidation of the department store industry, acquiring the varied assets of Associated Dry Goods Corporation, ten Hess's stores in Pennsylvania and New York state, 14 Wanamaker stores and 13 Strawbridge & Clothier stores in the Philadelphia area, and a number of other purchases.

In 2000, May paid $436 million for David's Bridal, a 150-unit chain founded in 1950 with a single store in Fort Lauderdale, Florida. David's grew into a bridal salon chain that did business all along the East Coast. May's addition of After Hours to David's made sense on a number of levels. There was obvious potential for synergy between the operations: male members of a bridal party who were being outfitted by David's could be steered towards After Hours for their formalwear. Perhaps of more importance was the expectation that the combination of David's and After Hours gave May an opportunity to tap into a younger demographic, the growing number of the so-called "echo boomers" who were unaccustomed to shopping in department stores. In many cases, their first interaction with a department store were through bridal registries. After Hours, in effect, became a small part of a greater strategy to use the bridal experience to create new department store customers. May added the company to the mix in January 2002, at the same time fulfilling a goal to become the largest wedding store chain in America when it acquired Priscilla of Boston for an undisclosed amount of cash. Priscilla added a more upscale clientele to May's burgeoning bridal business.

May also took steps in 2003 to grow the After Hours business, opening two dozen new stores and making several acquisitions. In June 2003, May paid an undisclosed amount of cash for the 25-store Modern Tuxedo chain, a Chicago area operation that generated about $12 million in annual sales. Later in the year, After Hours added the seven stores of Tyndall's Formal Wear, operating in North Carolina's Triangle and Triad regions. Furthermore, After Hours picked up Tyndall's wholesale tuxedo business. In September 2003, May bought the 66 stores of Desmonds Formalwear, which generated annual sales in the $20 million range and operated in ten states, including Kansas City, Kansas, and Omaha, Nebraska, representing After Hours first move west of the Mississippi. Finally, in November 2002, After Hours paid $23 million to buy 125 stores from the Gingiss Group, its longtime competitor. Gingiss, a 236-store chain, filed for bankruptcy simultaneous to selling a bulk of its assets and the rights to the names "Gingiss Formalwear" and "Gary's Tux Shop" to After Hours. With no major rival on the horizon, and the backing of a heavyweight corporate parent, After Hours was well positioned to become a serious consolidator in the estimated $1 billion a year men's formalwear industry.

Principal Competitors

Federated Department Stores, Inc.; The Men's Warehouse, Inc.

Further Reading

DeGross, Renee, "Mitchell's Expects to Rent More Than a Million Tuxes," *Atlanta Constitution*, May 5, 2000, p. F1.

Kwok, Chern Yeh, "May Department Stores Plans to Buy Atlanta-Based After Hours Formalwear," *St. Louis Post-Dispatch*, December 20, 2001, p. 1.

Lawrence, Calvin, Jr., "Mitchell's Formal Wear Has Just About Outgrown Its Market Britches," *Atlanta Constitution*, September 19, 1985, p. C2.

Lloyd, Brenda, "Mitchell's Formalwear Set to Go National," *Daily News Record*, May 5, 2000, p. 10.

Weitzman, Jennifer, "May Co. Buys After Hours Formalwear," *Daily News Record*, December 24, 2001, p. 3.

—Ed Dinger

Alaska Railroad Corporation

327 West Ship Creek Avenue
Anchorage, Alaska 99501
U.S.A.
Telephone: (907) 265-2300
Fax: (907) 265-2312
Web site: http://www.arrc.com

Government-Owned Company
Incorporated: 1914
Employees: 644
Sales: $105.7 million (2002)
NAIC: 482110 Line-Haul Railroads; 487110 Scenic and
    Sightseeing Transportation, Land

The Alaska Railroad Corporation (ARRC) operates passenger and freight trains from Seward, a major port on the Gulf of Alaska, to Fairbanks. ARRC, which has been owned by the state of Alaska since 1985, played a significant role in the development of Alaska, and the company's fortunes continue to be tied to the economic well-being of the state it serves. A significant portion of ARRC's freight business comes from hauling gravel and coal for export to Asia, as well as oil from the North Pole Refinery. On the passenger side of its business, ARRC has always served as a lifeline to the communities through which it passes. In recent years, the company has stepped up its efforts to draw more tourists. ARRC runs special trains for cruise ship passengers traveling between Seward and Anchorage.

Building the Alaska Railroad: 1902–23

The Alaska Railroad Corporation was the product of a massive federal project that sought to complete what earlier, private railroads in Alaska had failed to do—open up the resource-rich but rugged and isolated Alaskan territory to development and settlement. In the 1890s and early 1900s, gold strikes in the Yukon and at Fairbanks and Nome vindicated the purchase of what was once derisively called "Seward's Folly," as did the discovery of rich coal fields in northern Alaska. However, it was nearly impossible to transport men and equipment from the relatively accessible, ice-free ports of the Gulf of Alaska to the Alaskan heartland.

In 1902, a group of Seattle businessmen invested $30 million to build one of the earliest Alaskan rail routes, the Alaskan Central Railroad, which was to lead to the Klondike, Fairbanks, and Nome gold fields. The Panic of 1907 and the high cost of building and maintaining the railroad forced the Alaskan Central into receivership in 1908. The company reorganized and renamed itself Alaska Northern Railroad Co. and by 1910 had laid 51 miles of track. However, funds ran out again as the Alaska Northern continued to be plagued by construction difficulties and limited market potential.

In 1912, Congress passed the Alaska Territorial Act, which included a provision establishing a commission to survey Alaska's transportation network. The commission concluded that a trans-Alaska railroad would need the full resources of the federal government to be successful. Following the commission's report, Congress passed legislation in 1914 that empowered President Woodrow Wilson to construct and operate a railroad in the Alaska territory. The bill restricted the railroad to 1,000 miles in length and a $35 million budget, and required it to connect a port with the lucrative coal mines of the interior. The Alaska Engineering Commission (AEC) was created to recommend routes, and it offered two to the president. Wilson opted for the so-called western route, which incorporated the defunct Alaska Northern line and extended from Seward to Fairbanks. Construction began in 1915, and AEC soon purchased Alaska Northern's track for $16,000 per mile.

"The Government Railroad," as the endeavor was dubbed, was like no other railroad project that had come before it. It would ultimately take eight years and $60 million to complete. In 1917, at the peak of its construction, over 4,500 workers labored along the lengthening miles of track. The project required an unprecedented amount of logistical oversight and infrastructure development. Some materials were brought on a 2,000-mile journey from the mainland, and equipment was shipped from as far away as Panama (where it had previously been employed in the construction of the Panama Canal). In effect, AEC had to build its operations from the ground up. It logged and processed lumber for railroad ties. It ran barges to

Company Perspectives:

Building a Great Railroad in a Great Land: to be profitable by focusing on safe, high quality service to our freight, passenger, and real estate customers and to foster the development of Alaska's economy by integrating railroad and railbelt community development plans.

transport equipment. It lured hundreds of workers into the Alaskan heartland. It constructed telephone and telegraph lines, built terminal facilities and ocean docks, opened coal mines and smelters to fuel its locomotives, selected town sites to house workers, and operated schools and hospitals in the towns it created. Alaska's largest city of Anchorage was founded in 1915 when AEC selected the site as a construction camp and its headquarters.

In 1923, President Warren Harding drove the final golden spike into the track at Nenana, and the Alaska Railroad was declared complete. The main line was 470 miles long; bridges spanned eight of these miles. In addition to the main line from Seward to Fairbanks, ARRC included numerous branch lines, the longest of which was almost 38 miles. The railroad brought immediate changes to the Alaskan hinterlands. Trains delivered mail to the fledgling communities along the line, transported mining equipment, and allowed the residents of the small towns it served to travel between communities.

Early Years: 1920s to World War II

Even though ARRC revolutionized life along the line, it did not immediately generate profits. A combined population of 54,000 people in Seward, Anchorage, and Fairbanks—the three largest towns along the railbelt—was simply not enough to make the railroad a lucrative operation. Moreover, the railroad took constant and costly maintenance.

Ironically, the stock market crash of 1929 and the ensuing Great Depression brought better economic times to Alaska and new opportunities for ARRC. One of President Franklin Roosevelt's relief projects was the Matanuska Valley colony project, which relocated impoverished midwestern farmers to Alaska. The bulk of these settlers moved along ARRC's railbelt, generating new freight and passenger business for the railway.

The World War II era was another boon to ARRC's fortunes. Fears of Japanese aggression in the Pacific led the U.S. military to build new bases in Fairbanks and Anchorage in the late 1930s. The construction spurred a dramatic increase in ARRC's haulage and led to the company's first profitable year in 1938. The territory's population grew by one-third during the war years, and this influx of military personnel and support services during the war created more business for the railroad.

However, the demand for construction materials to build new bases and for infrastructure to support the population boom created a massive backlog at Seward, ARRC's one deep-water port. To address this problem, the U.S. Army began building a 12.4-mile branch line to Whittier in 1941. The Whittier Cutoff, as the new route was christened, opened in 1943. The Army

routed all of its traffic through the new port and the Cutoff for the remainder of the war, while commercial vessels continued to use Seward. (It was not until 1960 that the Army finally relinquished all control of Whittier and turned the port and the Cutoff over to ARRC.)

Challenges in the Postwar Era

The postwar years brought new opportunities and new challenges to ARRC. In the late 1940s, Congress approved and launched a $100 million rehabilitation program that enabled ARRC to upgrade its operations. Despite this sudden influx of funding, ARRC struggled to find its role in a changing Alaska. The cessation of hostilities spelled an end to the era when ARRC could count on military freight to prop up its bottom line.

Just as its business tapered off, the railroad faced new competition. Federal dollars had also flowed to improve the territory's road system. Better highways directly competed with ARRC for Alaska's freight business. Moreover, new air service eroded ARRC's passenger market. By 1953, competition had forced ARRC to discontinue its Seward passenger service. The railroad fought back. To attract more passengers, ARRC began running the streamliner AuRoRa in 1947, which upgraded passenger service between Anchorage and Fairbanks. The company also trimmed its expenses by replacing steam locomotives with more efficient diesel ones and began to establish car-barge and train-ship services, thereby linking ARRC directly with railroads in the continental U.S. The project was ultimately completed in 1962.

Developments in the 1960s–70s

ARRC's adjustment difficulties to the postwar era were insignificant compared with the effects of the Good Friday earthquake of 1964. The largest earthquake recorded in North American history wrought about $30 million of damage to the railroad. The line was shut down for nearly a month, and it took almost two years to fully complete repairs. The deep-water docks were destroyed at Seward, and much of the railroad's equipment was damaged or destroyed. At Anchorage and Whittier, several buildings were so badly damaged they had to be razed.

Buoyed by additional appropriations from Congress, ARRC survived the earthquake. However, in 1967 the railroad's place in the family of federal agencies changed when it was transferred from the Department of the Interior to a bureau of the Federal Railroad Administration in the newly minted Department of Transportation. ARRC was financed through a revolving fund into which the company's earnings were deposited and from which it could draw for capital improvements and general operating expenses. ARRC could also rely on Congress for appropriations and emergency expenditures.

Beginning in the 1970s, though, the federal government began looking for ways to shed the financial burden of maintaining ARRC. President Nixon sought to facilitate the transfer of the railroad from federal to state control, but the urgency of the matter fell away in the late 1970s when the construction of the Trans-Alaska Pipeline system boosted ARRC's earnings. The pipeline project, which was designed to move oil from the North Slope of Alaska to Valdez and was completed in 1977, relied heavily on ARRC to transport the construction material, supplies, and crews needed to build the 800-mile tube. It was the biggest bonanza for ARRC since the days of heavy freight hauling during World War II.

State Control and New Challenges: 1985 and Beyond

The Alaskan economy began to weaken in the early and mid-1980s with a precipitous drop in oil prices. As ARRC's profits slumped again, President Reagan acted to end federal responsibility for the railroad. In 1983, he signed legislation that authorized the transfer of ARRC to the state of Alaska. After intense internal debate, the state took ownership of the railroad in a ceremony held in 1985 at Nenana—the site where President Harding had nailed the railroad's final spike into place in 1923.

In its inaugural year under new management and ownership, ARRC had to withstand a series of setbacks. In March 1986, a chemical tank car began leaking formaldehyde in Crown Point and required ARRC to evacuate the local residents and spend about $650,000 in cleanup. One month later, a coal train derailed near Curry, spilling 22 carloads of coal and closing the line for three days. In October, a massive flood destroyed two major bridges and coated the tracks with mud. The line was closed for 13 days.

Although ARRC rebounded from these accidents and natural disasters, the company faced deeper problems. Decades of wavering federal commitment to the railroad had left the line in "deplorable condition," according to the February 10, 1997, *Alaska Journal of Commerce*. ARRC promptly began to upgrade stretches of decrepit track. In 1985 alone, ARRC replaced more miles of track than it had after the 1965 earthquake. By 1989, ARRC would invest $35.9 million in capital improvements.

ARRC also struggled with fluctuating business. In an effort to make hauling passengers more profitable, it spent $9 million to acquire 45 more efficient locomotives and new railcars. Stagnant freight revenues were more difficult to improve. "The

railroad is not in a position to influence business," the company's general manager told the *Alaska Journal of Commerce* on March 2, 1987. "We react and must follow along with someone else's plan." Nevertheless, ARRC sought to ramp up its involvement with the petroleum industry and to piggyback trailer service by operating overnight priority trains between Anchorage and Fairbanks. The company also reduced both personnel and pay to bring down costs.

Because business was good for ARRC's primary freight customers in the late 1980s and early 1990s, the railroad also performed well. In 1988, freight accounted for nearly 90 percent of ARRC's income. Coal was a particularly lucrative item for the company. Since 1984, ARRC had been hauling coal for the Usibelli Coal Mine from Healy to Seward. Usibelli's main customer was the South Korea-based Hyundai Merchant Marine Co. Ltd. When Asian coal prices were up, Usibelli shipped more coal to Korea—and ARRC benefited. The same business logic held true for petroleum products.

Beginning in the late 1980s, ARRC strove to counterbalance the vicissitudes of its freight business with more predictable revenue from other sectors. The company turned first to its passenger service. ARRC sought to cash in on the booming Alaskan tour business, particularly from cruise ships, which disgorged thousands of visitors at Seward every summer. In an effort to draw passengers from the port onto its line, the railroad constructed a new depot at Denali National Park in 1989. ARRC's strategy paid off. By 1992, ARRC had broken even on its passenger service. The company also leveraged its real estate holdings to encourage tourist business. In 1995, ARRC began building a recreational vehicle park and Comfort Inn on an 80-acre tract it owned in Fairbanks. It also entered into an agreement to convert its original depot in Anchorage into a microbrewery and restaurant. In 1996, the railroad had a record year when over 512,000 passengers rode its trains. In 2000, ARRC launched the Grandview passenger train specifically to serve cruise ship passengers traveling between Seward and Anchorage.

While ARRC was improving its passenger operations, the company continued to focus on drawing new freight business and maintaining its existing contracts. In 1994, ARRC scored a major victory when it successfully negotiated a 19-year contract with one of its most crucial clients, MAPCO Alaska Petroleum Inc., the largest refinery in Alaska. MAPCO had been threatening to construct its own pipeline rather than pay ARRC. By avoiding this scenario, ARRC could continue to count on MAPCO's business, which accounted for 35 percent of ARRC's revenues in 1994.

ARRC's ongoing efforts to bring more stability to its business were to some extent successful. Nevertheless, in the late 1990s and early 2000s, the railroad continued to be buffeted by the same forces that had demanded federal intervention in Alaska's transportation sector a century earlier. Maintenance costs were high in a land of long and harsh winters, and the company needed constant capital upgrades that eroded its bottom line. ARCC received a $10 million federal grant in 1996, which it used to install new railroad ties and ballast and partially fund the upgrade of its microwave communication system.

ARRC's customers—both passenger and freight—were captives of the same market forces that determined the railroad's fortunes. Economic downturns in the early 1990s and the first years of the new century prompted cruise ship tourists to stay home, which in turn adversely affected the railroad's business. Minute fluctuations in global coal, petroleum, timber, and gravel markets undercut the Alaskan companies involved in these industries. When the companies cut back, ARRC paid the price. For example, ARRC was hit hard in 2002 when the Usibelli Coal Mine lost its contract with Hyundai. The mine closed, and ARRC lost a significant customer. ARRC suffered a net loss of nearly $8 million that year.

In the late 1990s, the State of Alaska began to toy with disengaging from ARRC, motivated in no small part by the fact that the railroad did not pay state or local taxes. In 1996, Dennis Washington, the principal owner of Montana Rail Link, expressed some interest in acquiring ARRC, and the state legislature passed a bill to appraise the railroad for sale. Although Alaska's governor vetoed the bill, the threat of privatization remained. For ARRC, the company's role as a vital part of the Alaskan economy and communities was clear. "Privatization has a lot of romance to it, but you should examine what the railroad is really worth to the economy and to Alaska companies," the railroad board chairman stated in the *Alaska Journal of Commerce* for February 10, 1997. Nevertheless, future ownership of the company's remained murky, and its finances inextricably linked to the fortunes of its customers.

Further Reading

Bradner, Tim, "Railroad Honchos Reject Romance of Privatization in Juneau," *Alaska Journal of Commerce*, February 10, 1997.

Cohen, Stan, *Rails Across the Tundra*, Missoula, Montana: Pictorial Histories Publsihing Co., 1984, 144 p.

Foster, David, "Alaska Railroad Gets New Owner," *Washington Post*, January 2, 1985.

MacPherson, James, "Alaska Railroad Corp. Predicts Loss of $8 Million in 2003," *Alaska Journal of Commerce*, December 31, 2002.

Martin, Ingrid, "Montana Buyer Eyes Alaska Railroad Corp.," *Alaska Journal of Commerce*, February 12, 1996.

Nemeth, Imre, "Railroad: Down, But Still Making Money," *Alaska Journal of Commerce*, March 2, 1987.

Ragsdale, Rose, "Alaska Railroad Saved By Real Estate," *Alaska Journal of Commerce*, February 8, 1993.

Suddock, Sally, "Another Sterling Year for Alaska Railroad," *Alaska Journal of Commerce*, June 19, 1989.

—Rebecca Stanfel

Alfa Corporation

2108 East South Boulevard
Montgomery, Alabama 36191-0001
U.S.A.
Telephone: (334) 288-3900
Fax: (334) 288-0905
Web site: http://www.alfains.com

Public Company
Incorporated: 1946
Employees: 618
Sales: $587.5 million (2002)
Stock Exchanges: NASDAQ
Ticker Symbol: ALFA
NAIC: 524126 Direct Property and Casualty Insurance
   Carriers; 524113 Direct Life Insurance Carriers

With headquarters in Montgomery, Alabama, Alpha Corporation is a financial services holding company for Alfa Insurance Group (AIG). Over 50 percent of Alpha Corporation's common stock is owned by it affiliates, known collectively as the Alfa Mutual Insurance Companies. That majority holding and corporate structure guarantees that Alfa Mutual Insurance and Alfa Mutual Fire policy-holders maintain control of the company. The primary business of AIG is insurance, including property, casualty, and life. AIG writes life insurance in Alabama, Georgia, and Mississippi and property and casualty insurance in Georgia and Mississippi. Also, in Alabama, Alfa Corporation's insurance subsidiaries pool their property and casualty business with Alfa Specialty Insurance Corporation, which primarily writes nonstandard risk auto insurance. The corporation also offers non-insurance financial services, including real estate sales and investment, consumer lending, and construction. Alfa's property and casualty insurance company enjoys an A.M. Best A + + (Superior) rating and its life insurance company an A + (Superior) rating.

1946–77: From Fire Insurance to a Full Range of Protection

The Alfa Mutual Insurance Companies, the primary owners of Alfa Corporation, first entered the insurance market in 1946,

founded by what later became known as the Alabama Farmers Federation (AFF), which itself was first formed in 1921. AFF's purpose was to serve the state's farmers and the needs of the state's agribusiness, one of which was affordable insurance. Over time, it became the farmers' lobbyist, their professional society, information source, and public outreach manager. It also became a social and civic club, professional organization, and support group for farmers and their families.

As an extension of its services to its members, AFF first created Alfa Insurance to provide fire insurance for federation members, most of whom were farmers. John Tucker Harris, a prominent Lee County, Alabama, farmer who had been president of the Lee County farm organization, submitted the initial pre-insurance application, and the company was up and running.

Over the next three decades, Alfa expanded its business through diversifying the types of insurance that it underwrote and services it offered. In that period, it developed a structure of interlocking affiliates and subsidiaries which, collectively, sold most kinds of ordinary insurance, including life; home, mobile home, and farm; fire and other casualty; and preferred risk automobile policies. Subsidiaries were formed to oversee operations, including Alfa Life Insurance Corporation, Alfa General Insurance Corporation, Alfa Agency Mississippi, and Alfa Agency Georgia, Inc. Non-insurance subsidiaries evolved as well, including Alfa Financial Corporation, Alfa Investment Corporation, Alfa Builders, Inc., Alfa Realty, Inc., and Alfa Benefits Corporation. Alfa Corporation was also affiliated with the Alfa Mutual Insurance Company, Alfa Mutual Fire Insurance Company, and Alfa Mutual General Insurance Company. These affiliates, holding a 52.3 percent majority, controlling share of Alfa Corporation, made up the Alfa Mutual Group.

1978–98: Alfa Prospers under the Leadership of Goodwin L. Myrick

At the time that Goodwin L. Myrick became CEO, president, and chairman of the Alfa Corporation and Alfa Mutual Group in 1978, the companies, respectively, had total assets of $62 million and $276 million. Myrick would hold his position until his retirement 20 years later, in 1998, and oversee the growth of those assets to, respectively, $1.2 billion and $2.7 billion.

Company Perspectives:

To our family of customers, we are committed to excellence, integrity, and exceeding customer expectations in both sales and service by providing profitable multi-line insurance and other financial services. Alfa will focus on effective use of technology to enhance the productivity of our people and increase our knowledge of, and service to, our customers, while investing resources in product and geographic expansion.

Myrick, a dairy farmer who live in Etowah County, Alabama, started out with a herd of just eight cows in 1944, which over time he developed into a major cattle and dairy operation on two farms in Etowah and Talledega Counties. From 1973 until his election to the posts of chairman and president, Myrick had served as president of Alfa's subsidiaries and its affiliated companies. He also served as president of AFF.

Under Myrick's tutelage, Alfa Corporation transformed itself from a life insurance holding company into a comprehensive insurance holding company, with almost 80 percent of its insurance premium revenue coming from property and casualty insurance. One major move was made in 1987, when, effective in August, Alfa's principal property and casualty subsidiaries entered a pooling agreement designed to allow for the redistribution of income and expenses among its three subsidiary affiliates of the Mutual Group. Under the terms of the agreement, premiums, losses, and other expenses attributable to these companies' property and casualty business were pooled and reallocated among the companies. In accordance with the agreed upon terms, 65 percent of the Group's pooled business was allocated to Alfa's subsidiaries, Alfa Corporation and Alfa General Insurance Corporation. Up until the pooling agreement was made, Alfa's life insurance subsidiary was its main source of revenue, but that would quickly change.

As more and more of its income was derived from property insurance, Alfa faced increasing risks entirely outside its control, particularly severe weather, which, in its tri-state marketing area, had at times been catastrophic. In 1995, when Hurricane Opal hit eastern Alabama, it caused very extensive property damage and proved to be the costliest storm in Alfa's history. The Alfa Group processed over 31,000 claims representing over $76 million in damage. Opal had hit in the wake of another hurricane, Erin, which, with hail and other wind damage caused earlier in the year, brought the total damage claim liability for the Group to over $99 million. The result was that for 1995, Alfa failed to make a profit from its insurance underwriting for only the fourth time in a three-decade span. Prior to 1995, the greatest weather related claims liability Alfa faced totaled $22.5 million in 1979, the result of the ravages of Hurricane Frederic.

The impact of Hurricane Opal encouraged Alfa, in 1996, to amend its 1987 Pooling Agreement and restructure its catastrophic protection program. Under the terms of the new amendment, Alfa Corporation's participation in a single catastrophic occurrence or a series of lesser occurrences was limited to its $10 million pool share (65 percent) unless the loss was in excess of $249 million. The amended plan did provoke a legal

challenge three years later, when a former Alfa Mutual Fire premium holder attempted to bring suit against Alfa Corporation for liquidating Alfa Mutual Fire under the Pooling Agreement allegedly for its own benefit rather than that of policy holders. Alfa successfully fended off the class action suit.

1998 and Beyond: Newby Guides Alfa to Continued Growth and Success

In 1998, Myrick retired and was replaced as CEO and president by Jerry A. Newby, who also became president of the AFF. A native of Athens, Alabama, Newby had previously served as a vice-president and a state board member for both Alfa Corporation and the AFF. From 1990 to 1998, he had also served on the Alabama Board of Agriculture and Industries, and served also, as the treasurer of the Southeast Cotton Growers. A partner in his family's farming operation in Limestone County, for 14 years he had additionally served as president of the Limestone County Farmers Federation. His appointment continued the tradition of naming presidents with a farming heritage and long association with AFF.

Throughout the 1990s, Alfa enjoyed a steady growth in revenue. Its total income in 1991 was about $232.9 million, and by 2000 this had increased to just over $510.3 million, representing an average annual increase of over $27.7 million. Its net income in the same period grew from $28.4 to $69.5 million. Thanks largely to Hurricane Opal, the corporation's net income did drop to $22.3 million in 1995, but that was the only year in that stretch in which it fell below the 1991 figure; thus, with that exception, the decade was one of steady growth for Alfa, unlike the three years immediately preceding the period, when, between 1988 and 1990, Alfa's net income only increased from $22.8 million to $22.9 million. Moreover, its stability was confirmed by Standard & Poor's, which in September 2000 affirmed its ''AA'' credit and financial strength ratings of the Alfa Insurance Group member companies and its ''A-1 plus'' commercial paper rating of Alfa Corporation. At that point, commanding approximately 20 percent of the market share, the Alfa Insurance Group was the second largest underwriter of personal insurance in Alabama.

In 2001, Alfa's gross income from premiums and other revenue sources, including non-insurance operations, reached $546.3 million. Of that total, life insurance premiums generated close to $109.4 million in revenues (19.2 percent), while property and casualty insurance premiums brought in $427.4 million (78.2 percent). That is, the Alfa Group continued to derived about four-fifths of its revenue from property and casualty insurance and one-fifth from life insurance.

At a time when, increasingly, corporate feet have been held to disclosure fires, Alfa has had to weather some bad press. For example, in April 2003, an article in the *New York Times* disclosed that over three years Alfa Mutual Fire Insurance avoided a $58 million federal income tax assessment by taking advantage of a 50-year old provision allowing the creation of small, tax-exempt insurance companies. Its intent was to help farmers and others having difficulty finding insurance, but over time it became a loophole for large companies that needed only to limit their revenue from premiums to $350,000. However, no caveat prevented such companies from setting aside large reserves to invest tax free, which Alfa has done. It was an entirely legal accounting procedure, but critics, seeing it as a tax dodge, questioned its propriety.

Key Dates:

1946: Alfa founded by the Alabama Farmers Federation.
1978: Goodwin L. Myrick becomes Alfa's CEO, chairman, and president.
1987: Alfa Mutual Group enters a pooling agreement.
1996: Alfa amends pooling agreement for catastrophic contingencies.
1998: Myrick retires and is succeeded by Jerry A. Newby as CEO, chairman, and president.

The disclosure certainly did no serious harm to Alfa's reputation. One of the corporation's great strengths was its close identity with AFF, its ultimate roots. Farmers and related businessmen trusted the Alfa name for decades, and the symbiotic relationship of the corporation and AFF remained strong. Notably, the men who have served as CEO and president of Alfa came from farming backgrounds in Alabama and served as presidents of AFF and other farming organizations. Furthermore, the Alfa and AFF names have been closely linked in other ways, including partnered donations made to non-profit charities and agencies. For example, in 1996, in celebrating the 75th anniversary of AFF, it and Alfa made a joint $5 million donation to Auburn University. Given the fact that close to 90 percent of Alfa Insurance Group's earnings derive from the sale of personal insurance and products in Alabama, Alfa's high profile there was a tremendous marketing asset. However, it is worth noting that the Alfa Group, as reported in a *PR Newswire* in 2000, "continues to make a modicum of progress in growing its business model in Mississippi and Georgia. . . ." More expansion in these contiguous states may be necessary to offset a shrinking profit margin arising from competition and increasing loss costs in Alabama. The corporation has itself indicated that geographic expansion is a part of its mission and vision.

As major underwriters of insurance against property and casualty damage from fire and weather, the Alfa Group companies must deal with what part both nature and human error play in their annual, bottom line performance, a fact once more brought home to them when a series of spring storms in 2003 wreaked havoc in the Southeast. Total claims estimates made in May of that year were $40 million, cutting a fair way into Alfa's profit margin. Such is the business risk that Alfa and, of course, all its competitors must take. The risk is particularly troublesome for companies, like Alfa, whose business is largely limited to a particular region, and is therefore reason enough for the corporation to seek a wider geographic market.

Principal Subsidiaries

Alfa Financial Corporation; Alfa Investment Corporation; Alfa Builders, Inc.; Alfa Realty, Inc.; Alfa Agency Mississippi, Inc.; Alfa Benefits Corporation.

Principal Affiliates

Alfa Realty; Alfa Farmers Federation; Bay Point Resort Village, Marriott's Golf & Yacht Club; OFC Capital; Virginia Mutual Insurance Company.

Principal Competitors

The Allstate Corporation; American International Group, Inc.; Atlantic American Corporation; Cotton States Life Insurance Company; GEICO; Prudential Financial, Inc.; State Farm Insurance Companies.

Further Reading

"Alfa Insurance Group Catastrophic Loss Plan Attacked in Lawsuit," *Business Wire*, June 15, 1999.
Johnston, David Cay, "From Tiny Insurers, Big Tax Breaks," *New York Times*, April 1, 2003, p. 1C.
"Standard & Poor's Affirms Alfa Insurance Group 'AA' Ratings; Outlook Stable," *PR Newswire*, September 8, 2000.
Summerford, Roy, "AFF/ALFA Marks 75th Anniversary with $5 Million Gift to AU," *Auburn University News*, January 31, 1996.
"Vesta Announces Strategic Alliance with Alfa Insurance Group," *PR Newswire*, November 9, 1998.

—John W. Fiero

Alleghany Corporation

375 Park Avenue
New York, New York 10152
U.S.A.
Telephone: (212) 752-1356
Fax: (212) 759-8149

Public Company
Incorporated: 1929
Employees: 2,132
Sales: $576.9 million (2002)
Stock Exchanges: New York
Ticker Symbol: Y
NAIC: 524127 Direct Title Insurance Carriers; 524126
    Direct Property and Casualty Insurance Carriers;
    212399 All Other Nonmetallic Mineral Mining;
    531210 Offices of Real Estate Agents and Brokers;
    421710 Hardware Wholesalers

Alleghany Corporation operates as a diversified conglomerate with holdings related to insurance, industrial minerals, and steel fasteners. Three major subsidiaries—Alleghany Insurance Holdings LLC, Capitol Transamerica Corporation, and Platte River Insurance Company—oversee the company's interests in property, casualty, fidelity, and surety insurance. Alleghany's industrial minerals arm includes World Minerals Inc., Celite Corporation, and Harborlite Corporation. The Heads & Threads International LLC unit is responsible for steel fastener importing and distribution. Alleghany also owns and manages real estate in California through its Alleghany Properties Inc. subsidiary.

Origins

Alleghany was founded in 1929 by the well-known and eccentric Van Sweringen brothers of Cleveland as a holding company for their railroad investments. When Alleghany slid into receivership in 1934, control of the company passed to J.P. Morgan and others. Shares of the company floated around among a few different parties for the next few years, eventually landing in the hands of George Ball, of Ball Jar fame. Wheeler-dealer Robert R. Young bought the stock from Ball in 1937. Most of the money Young used to acquire controlling interest in

Alleghany was put up by Allan P. Kirby, Fred's son. Young became chairman of Alleghany, while Kirby remained behind the scenes as his silent partner. The centerpiece of the extensive but struggling Alleghany empire was its two million plus shares of the Chesapeake and Ohio Railroad.

Young spent his first few years at Alleghany whittling down the company's massive debt and untangling its gnarled finances. A legal victory against Ball provided much of the desperately needed cash for the task, and eventually Alleghany's books were in order. Under Young, the Chesapeake & Ohio (C&O) underwent something of a facelift. Equipment was modernized and many new conveniences were introduced in its passenger service. In 1945, Young decided to go after another railroad, the New York Central. That year, he purchased 225,400 shares of the Central for $4.2 million. Two years later, more shares were acquired. Initially, Interstate Commerce Commission (ICC) regulations prevented Alleghany from taking control of additional railroads. Several years of maneuvering followed, including the sale of most of Alleghany's C&O stock to associates. Young finally managed to wrest control of the New York Central away from its bank-dominated board of directors in a hotly contested proxy battle in 1954.

Meanwhile, Alleghany was transforming itself from strictly a railroad force into a financial force as well. In 1949, the company purchased controlling interest in Investors Diversified Services, Inc. (IDS), the world's largest mutual fund group. At the same time Young was purging the Alleghany portfolio of dozens of unwanted holdings. From 66 different securities in 1947, the company pared its collection down to less than ten a decade later. By 1957, Alleghany's investments consisted primarily of a "big four": the New York Central, now the company's main railroad project; IDS, in which Alleghany still maintained a strong position although actual control had been sold to Texan Clint Murchison, a longtime Young accomplice; the Missouri Pacific Railroad, a holdover from the Van Sweringen empire that had lingered in bankruptcy for decades; and Webb & Knapp, a real estate firm.

The Kirby Reign Begins in 1958

In 1958, Young committed suicide. Business had taken a severe turn for the worse, and some speculated that Young was

Company Perspectives:

Alleghany intends to continue to expand its operations through internal growth at its subsidiaries as well as through possible operating-company acquisitions and investments.

depressed over the possibility of his company's collapse. Whether or not Alleghany's condition was on Young's mind was never determined. Consequently, the publicity-shy Kirby was forced out of the shadows. He took over as chairman, president, and undisputed leader of Alleghany. The contrast between the two men could not have been more stark. While Young was a flamboyant operator, fond of speaking out in the press about almost anything, Kirby relished his role as silent partner. His style of doing business did not require much in the way of public exposure.

Under Kirby's guidance, Alleghany's fortunes reversed again, and by the end of the 1950s the company had returned to health. Kirby, unlike Young, was willing to delegate day-to-day operations to others, and the companies in the Alleghany fold responded positively to this new leadership approach. IDS started performing particularly well. With nearly $3 billion under management, IDS reported net income of $12.7 million in 1958, earning $1.4 million in dividends for Alleghany. It was quite possibly already the world's largest investment management company by that time.

In 1959, Kirby faced his first challenge for control of Alleghany. That year, Boston real estate speculator Abraham Sonnabend began picking up Alleghany stock in large chunks. He also managed to gain the support of Alleghany vice-president David Wallace, a close friend of Young's. Kirby responded by firing Wallace, which alienated Young's widow, also a major stockholder. Kirby emerged from the skirmish with his control of the company intact, but it was the first sign that his grip on Alleghany was vulnerable.

In his next proxy fight, Kirby was not as successful. In 1961, he lost control of Alleghany to the Murchison brothers, Clint Jr. and John, the sons of Young's former ally. At the heart of the struggle was a philosophical clash. The Murchisons were freewheeling businessmen in the Texas tradition, while Kirby conducted his affairs with an extreme degree of caution. The brothers managed to convince many shareholders that Kirby's conservatism was holding the company back, eventually gaining enough support to oust him from power. This proved to be a short-lived victory, however. With 35 percent of Alleghany still in hand, Kirby was able to block all of the Murchisons' attempts to overhaul the company. By 1962, they were ready to give up. John Murchison resigned as president of Alleghany and was replaced by Minneapolis businessman Bertin Gamble, to whom the brothers sold much of their Alleghany stock at a loss. Gamble had sold his controlling interest in IDS to Alleghany 13 years earlier, just before its stock began to skyrocket.

Like his associates the Murchisons, Gamble was also unable to work with Kirby, and in 1963 controlling interest in Alleghany was sold back to Kirby and his allies. Kirby now owned 43 percent of Alleghany's common stock, and another 16 percent belonged to his associated and friends. Kirby returned to the position of chairman, and longtime associate Charles Ireland was named company president. Control of the company has remained firmly in the hands of the Kirby family ever since.

In 1965, Fred Kirby II, Allan's son, was elected chairman of the IDS executive committee. Fred continued serving as executive vice-president of Alleghany, a position he had held since his father's return to power two years earlier. The company sold most of its shares of the New York Central in 1966, marking the end of its railroad-controlling era. In 1967, Alleghany won another legal battle, preventing a reorganization plan from taking place at Missouri Pacific that would have severely diluted Alleghany's holdings in that company. Later that year, the elder Kirby suffered a major stroke. Fred II and his brother, Allan Jr., were named guardians for their father, by then generally acknowledged to be one of the richest men in America, and Fred took over as chairman of Alleghany.

After years as Alleghany's principal legal tactician, Ireland left the company in 1968 to take a job at International Telephone and Telegraph Corporation, on whose board he had sat as Alleghany's representative since 1965. In 1970, Alleghany acquired Jones Motor Company, a motor carrier of modest size. This was done primarily in order to avoid being reclassified as a personal holding company by the Internal Revenue Service. Jones never performed as hoped, and it was sold off in 1982.

Diversification and Strategic Changes: 1970s–80s

Despite its legal classification, by 1974 Alleghany was for all practical purposes the family holding company of the Kirby family, who now held nearly half of the company's stock. That year, Alleghany took a major step in its attempt to transform itself into more of an asset management company. First, the legal wrangling over reorganization of the Missouri Pacific finally ended for good, with Alleghany trading in its shares for $42 million in cash and $7.2 million more in new common stock. Alleghany then purchased MSL Industries, a metals fabricating company, using cash from the Missouri Pacific deal. Alleghany's other involvements around this time included its 44 percent interest in IDS; a $15.5 million investment in Court House Square, a real estate development in Denver; and its holdings in Missouri Pacific, TI Corporation, USM, Pittston Company, and United Corporation.

Further cautious attempts to diversify peppered the remainder of the 1970s, with as many assets shed as added. Alleghany's last batch of Missouri Pacific shares was sold to Mississippi River Corporation in 1975. The following year, the company sold its Court House Square property for cash and acquired Allied Structural Steel Company. In 1979, Alleghany paid $198 million for the 45 percent of IDS it did not already own. By 1981, 95 percent of Alleghany's income was coming from the investment business. IDS had $6 billion worth of mutual funds under management and $11 billion of life insurance (hawked by the same 3,400-person sales team) in force. In September of that year, the company sold off the IDS Center building in Minneapolis to a Canadian development company for about $200 million, producing a huge capital gain. Another investment management company, New York's Gray, Seifert and Company, was acquired in 1983.

Alleghany undertook a major and more rapid shift in strategy in the mid-1980s. In January 1984, the company consummated a blockbuster deal initiated the previous summer in which IDS was sold to American Express Company for $800 million in cash and securities. When Consolidated Rail Corporation (Conrail) went up for sale, Kirby put in a bid to go back into the rail business using the proceeds for the IDS transaction. Instead, the government took Conrail public, and Alleghany's focus turned toward the title insurance business. Toward the end of 1984, Alleghany Financial Corporation was formed as a wholly owned subsidiary for acquiring insurance and other financial oriented concerns. Its most important acquisition in that area came in 1985, with the purchase of Chicago Title and Trust Company from Lincoln National Corporation for $60 million in cash and a six-year $68 million note. Two more insurance moves followed in the next two years. In 1986, the company acquired Shelby Insurance Company for $40 million. SAFECO Title Insurance Company, later renamed Security Union Title Insurance Company, was purchased by the Chicago Title subsidiary the following year. The acquisitions of Chicago Title and Security Union made Alleghany the nation's leading title insurance outfit, while Shelby gave the company entry into the property and casualty insurance arena.

Meanwhile, Alleghany shareholders approved a plan for liquidating the company in December of 1986. Under the terms of the plan, most of the company's nonfinancial holdings would be disposed of, and the surviving Alleghany Financial subsidiary would be renamed Alleghany Corporation. Shareholders would receive $41 cash and a share of new Alleghany Corporation stock for each old Alleghany share. One of the first things to go was most of the company's substantial holding in American Express, acquired in the IDS deal. Among Alleghany's other 1987 deals was the June acquisition of the steel and nonresidential construction business of Cyclops Corporation

from Dixons Group plc of London. These businesses were then immediately spun off to Alleghany stockholders as a new public company, Cyclops Industries Inc.

Acquisitions Continue: Late 1980s–Early 1990s

Alleghany initiated a new round of acquisitions beginning in 1989. That year the company acquired Sacramento Savings & Loan Association and two associated companies for $150 million in cash. By the end of 1992, Sacramento Savings had total assets of $2.8 billion, and deposits of $2.6 billion. In March 1991, Chicago Title acquired Ticor Title Insurance Company, a California operation that expanded Alleghany's reach in that business. Later that year, Alleghany purchased Celite Corporation, Manville Corporation's filtration and industrial minerals business, for $144 million. Shelby Insurance Company, Alleghany's property, casualty, life, and annuity subsidiary, was sold to The Associated Group for cash at the end of 1991. For 1991, Alleghany had net income of $64 million on $1.42 billion in revenue.

Fred Kirby II stepped down as chief executive officer of Alleghany in 1992 at the age of 72. He retained his position as chairman of the board, as well as an active voice in company affairs. Kirby's hand-picked replacement as CEO was John Burns, Jr., who had been with the company since 1968 and served as president since 1977. Burns was the first CEO at Alleghany from outside the Kirby family since 1957. In the early 1990s, Alleghany increased its participation in both the insurance and minerals industries. In November 1992, the company acquired Harborlite Corporation, a producer of the volcanic material perlite. Underwriters Reinsurance Company was purchased in 1993.

Like his father, Fred Kirby II was about as secretive about business as the head of a public corporation can be. The Institutional Voting Research Service in Belmont, Massachusetts once called Alleghany "the most heavily insulated company we have ever analyzed." The company has been historically mistrustful of the press and not at all eager for publicity. In spite of these characteristics, Alleghany and the Kirby family have not been able to avoid the spotlight of controversy at times. Bitter disagreements between Fred Kirby II and his siblings have threatened the kind of unity that gives family-owned businesses the advantage of long-term planning. Several family members resented Kirby's autocratic control of the company and questioned the legitimacy of that control.

Mid-1990s and Beyond

Nevertheless, Alleghany appeared to be well managed as it made several key moves in the 1990s that strengthened its business portfolio. The company's interest in the railroad was reborn in 1994 and 1995 when it acquired a stake in Santa Fe Pacific Corporation, which was fending off a hostile takeover attempt by Union Pacific Corporation. With the support of Alleghany, Santa Fe instead merged with Burlington Northern to become one of the largest railroad networks in North America.

At the same time, change and consolidation in the title insurance industry prompted the company to restructure its Chicago Title & Trust (CT&T) unit. In June 1998, the company spun off its title insurance businesses under the holding company Chicago Title Corporation. Burns, Jr. commented on the strategy in a 1997 National Mortgage News article, claiming that the "establishment of CT&T's title insurance business as an independent company will enhance its ability to focus on operating efficiencies and strategic initiatives required to respond to a changing marketplace." Chicago Title was listed on the New York Stock Exchange and eventually merged with Fidelity National Financial Inc.

Alleghany continued to restructure its business holdings into the new century by making several significant divestitures in an attempt to shore up profits. In 2000, the firm sold its Underwriters Re Group Inc. to Swiss Re America Holding Corporation in a deal worth approximately $660 million. The company exited the financial services sector in 2001 through the $825 million sale of Alleghany Asset Management Inc. to a subsidiary of ABN AMRO North America Holding Company. The high costs related to the September 11th terrorist attacks on the United States prompted the company to take its sell-off plans one step further: the company sold Alleghany Underwriting Holdings Ltd., a company involved in the global property and casualty insurance and reinsurance business at Lloyd's of London.

During this period of streamlining, Alleghany began to look for acquisitions to that would contribute to its bottom line. As such, the company announced that it would purchase Capitol Transamerica Corporation, a profitable Wisconsin-based insurance holding company, along with Nebraska-based Platte River Insurance Company. Both deals were completed in January 2002. The company added Royal Specialty Underwriting Inc. to its arsenal in 2003.

As a diversified conglomerate, Alleghany's position was unique in that many of its subsidiaries—in very unrelated industries—held leading market positions. For example, its Minerals unit operated as world's largest producer of filter-aid grade diatomite, a silica-based mineral consisting of the fossilized remains of microscopic freshwater or marine plants. Unpredictable world economies, consolidation, the ever-changing characteristics of the insurance industry, however, promised to keep the company on its toes in the years to come. Indeed, Alleghany planned to focus on internal growth while making selective investments and purchases to bolster its financial position. With a history full of significant merger and divestiture activity, the company's future would no doubt be marked by additional changes to its operating portfolio.

Principal Subsidiaries

Alleghany Insurance Holdings LLC; Capitol Transamerica Corporation; Platte River Insurance Company; World Minerals Inc.; Celite Corporation; Harborlite Corporation; Heads & Threads International LLC; Alleghany Properties Inc.

Principal Competitors

Atlas Minerals Inc.; The Chubb Corporation; Eagle-Picher Industries Inc.

Further Reading

"Allan Kirby Cleared on Murchison Fraud Charge," *New York Times,* January 14, 1965, p. 49.

"Alleghany Completes Purchase of Investors Diversified Services," *Wall Street Journal,* May 11, 1979, p. 39.

"Alleghany Completes Sale to Swiss Re," *Journal of Commerce,* May 16, 2000, p. 10.

"Alleghany Spinning off Largest Title Insurer," *National Mortgage News,* December 29, 1997, p. 1.

"Biding His Time on Rails," *Business Week,* January 21, 1950, pp. 27–28.

Blumstein, Michael, "The Power behind the Alleghany Deal," *New York Times,* July 17, 1983, p. F6.

"The Corporate Marine," *Time,* January 5, 1968, p. 71.

Cowan, Alison Leigh, "Kirby Keeps Control over Foundation," *New York Times,* June 6, 1991, p. D4.

——, "Promise into Peril: The Kirby Fight," *New York Times,* June 10, 1990, p. F1.

Elliott, J. Richard, Jr., "Switch for Alleghany?," *Barron's,* February 4, 1957, p. 3.

"Fred M. Kirby Succeeds Father as Alleghany Corp. Chairman," *New York Times,* September 15, 1967, p. 69.

Fritz, Michael, "Chicago Corp. Woes a Red Flag for ABN AMRO in Latest Deal," *Crain's Chicago Business,* November 20, 2000, p. 28.

Gores, Paul, "New York-Based Alleghany to Acquire Madison, Wis.-Based Insurance Company," *Milwaukee Journal Sentinel,* July 21, 2001.

"Hands Untied," *Forbes,* August 15, 1964, pp. 16–17.

Kaufman, Larry, "Alleghany Corp. A Seasoned Veteran of Railroad Battles," *Journal of Commerce,* October 19, 1994, p. 2B.

"Kirby's Luck," *Forbes,* February 1, 1959, p. 29.

"Kirby vs. Sonnabend," *Forbes,* December 1, 1959, pp. 15–16.

"Lloyd's-Alleghany Sale Accelerates Post-September 11 Reshuffle," *Lloyd's List,* November 7, 2001, p. 2.

"New Man at Alleghany," *Time,* December 21, 1962, p. 68.

"$930 Buys $1,250," *Business Week,* April 19, 1941, pp. 67–68.

"Practicing What Papa Preached," *Forbes,* March 1, 1974, pp. 60–61.

Rudnitsky, Howard, "Polishing the Family Jewels," *Forbes,* December 7, 1981, pp. 77–78.

Tannenbaum, Jeffrey A., "Alleghany Chief Kirby Transfers Post to J. Burns," *Wall Street Journal,* June 18, 1992, p. B3.

"Texas on Wall Street," *Time,* June 16, 1961, pp. 80–84.

"Tired of Railroading?," *Business Week,* November 23, 1946, pp. 80–86.

"Winner by a Knockout," *Time,* July 12, 1963, p. 88.

"Young's Empire: The Seeds He Sowed Bear Fruit," *Business Week,* February 14, 1959, pp. 108–16.

—Robert R. Jacobson
—update: Christina M. Stansell

Allen Foods, Inc.

8543 Page Avenue
St. Louis, Missouri 63114
U.S.A.
Telephone (314) 426-4100
Toll Free: (800) 888-4855
Web site: http://www.allenfoods.com

Wholly Owned Subsidiary of Royal Ahold NV
Founded: 1901 as L. Allen & Sons Company
Employees: 450
Sales: $245 million (2002 est.)
NAIC: 422490 Other Grocery and Related Products
Wholesalers

Based in the St. Louis area, Allen Foods, Inc. is a subsidiary of Dutch supermarket giant Royal Ahold NV. Allen is a small part of Ahold's U.S. Foodservice operation—the second largest food service distributor in the United States, trailing only SYSCO Corporation. Allen is a wholesale distributor to restaurants, hotels, shopping mall food courts, riverboat casinos, high schools and colleges, military bases, and prisons in a six-state territory located within a 300-mile radius of St. Louis. The largest distributor in the St. Louis market, Allen serves communities as far east as Terre Haute, Indiana, and as far west as Topeka, Kansas. The company does a limited amount of international business, all of which is related to its longtime military contracts. Allen's 300,000-square-foot warehouses stock more than 13,000 different items. Its delivery fleet and 122 full-time drivers average 90 routes per day, and the company employs a computerized routing system, "Roadnet," and GPS tracking. To insure product integrity, Allen is converting to trailers with three compartments, each of which will be capable of maintaining temperatures appropriate for different types of products.

Origins and Growth

Allen Foods was founded by Louis Allen, who immigrated to St. Louis from Poland in the 1890s at the age of 23. Impoverished, he left behind his wife, who soon gave birth to a son, Harry. The family would not be reunited until four years later, when Allen was finally able to send for them. His was truly a rags-to-riches story, an embodiment of the American dream. He started out as a peddler of clothing and small household goods, at first on foot. Because competition was greater in the city, he decided to try his luck in the countryside. According to the O'Fallon Historical Society, Allen had just 50 cents in his pocket after buying his merchandise from the city's wholesale houses on his first day in business. He hauled his wares on his back across the Eads Bridge that spanned the Mississippi River until he reached the Relay Depot in East St. Louis, Illinois. Having no idea which of the outlying communities would offer the best opportunity, he simply asked the clerk how far 50 cents would take him by train. The answer was the village of O'Fallon, Illinois. However, once he arrived, Allen faced an unexpected complication—the local marshal demanded that he pay $1.75 for a peddler's license in order to business in the area. Since he had no money, the marshal and the town clerk decided not to jail the young man. Instead, he was allowed him to peddle his goods in hopes that he would be able to pay for his license, thus enriching the town's treasury without incurring the expense of feeding a prisoner. O'Fallon turned out to be a fortunate choice for Allen. At the end of the day, he was able to pay for a three-month license.

For four years, Allen walked his country route in the small communities surrounding O'Fallon: Lebanon, Shiloh, and Summerfield. He was successful enough to bring his family to the United States from Poland. He was also able to take the next step in his career and buy a horse and wagon from which to do business. In 1901, Allen and his three sons—Harry, Ben, and Al—established the L. Allen & Sons Company general store, taking over a former barbershop in O'Fallon and selling groceries and other merchandise. As he had done before, Allen built upon success. By 1904, he and his family were able to move to a larger location. Because they needed only half of the space, they adding clothing to their product mix. (In 1929, according to the O'Fallon Historical Society, the Allens opened a clothing store in Chicago. Launching a new business on the dawn of the Depression proved to be unfortunate timing, and the venture was ultimately sold.) The profitability of this store then led to the family opening a retail grocery store in O'Fallon in 1912. Over the next 30 years, this operation grew into a regional grocery store chain, with locations added in such Illinois communities as Belleville, Breese, and East St. Louis. The company also developed a grocery delivery service and during World War I found customers in the officers and their families living at a military facility now known as Scott Air Force Base, located near Belleville, Illinois. In 1917, "Scott Field"—named after Corporal Frank S. Scott, the first enlisted man to die in an air accident—opened to train pilots.

Postwar Focus on Distribution

World War II proved to be a turning point for the Allen family business. In 1941, the company received its first federal contract to supply large quantities of food to the Scott air base. In addition, Al Allen began to sell canned good to other bases as well as to other large institutional customers. From his tailor shop, brother Ben made uniforms for the troops stationed at Scott. By war's end, L. Allen & Sons food distribution business was so successful that the family eased out of retail groceries to concentrate on its growing institutional food operations. In addition to supplying Scott, the company also began to supply restaurants in the postwar years. As the business expanded, Ben Allen decided to close the tailor shop and went to work for the family company, taking over buying. By the end of the decade, the distribution operation outgrew the O'Fallon facility, and the Allen family elected to move to St. Louis, taking over a much larger warehouse.

Renamed Allen Foods, the family business entered the 1950s and embarked on a new era. A moment that marked this passage, and severed the family's business ties to O'Fallon, came on May 23, 1953, when the drygoods store the Allens had run since 1904 was destroyed by fire. They decided against replacing the store, and Harry Allen, who had been running the operation, joined his brothers Al and Ben at Allen Foods. Operating out of St. Louis, the food distribution business expanded, leading to the company to relocate to larger accommodations on Gustine Avenue. Another major step taken during the 1950s was the acquisition of Halben Foods Manufacturing Company, which began the transformation of Allen from a food distributor to a "broadliner" able to manufacture its own products. Under the brand name "Lasco" (drawing on the initials of the company's original name, L. Allen & Sons Company), Halben would ultimately provide food service operators with a range of more than 300 food and beverage products, including a complete line of cocktail mixes and other beverage mixes, salad dressing, gravy and sauce mixes, ready-to-use sauces, and dessert mixes. In addition to Lasco products, Halben also developed a private label and custom design product program that could create items to customer specifications as well as offer the services of its own research and development staff to formulate new products.

In 1968, Allen made another advance in its evolution when it added frozen foods to its inventory. The company then moved into restaurant equipment and furnishing, as well as restaurant design, accomplished by the 1972 Allen acquisition of Bensinger's Inc. The growth of the company was so strong that it soon outgrew its warehouse capacity once again. In 1972, Allen moved into a new warehouse located in the St. Louis community of Overland. It had been built in 1969 for the Bettendorf supermarket chain, but when Bettendorf was subsequently acquired by Schnuck Inc. the warehouse went unused for three years. Allen continued to utilize its old Gustine Avenue facility, converting it to use by Halben for food manufacturing.

In the 1980s, a third generation of the Allen family took over leadership of the company when, in 1982, 42-year-old Stanley Allen was named president. He had been working for the family business since graduating from college in 1962. He was joined in the running of the company by other family members of his generation: Rick Allen, Joel Allen, and Louis Cohen. Allen Foods enjoyed exceptional growth during the 1980s. Stanley Allen told the *St. Louis Post-Dispatch* in 1996, "Our company profited from the industry boom in the 1980s. . . . As more women went into the work force, the novelty of eating out grew like crazy." To take further advantage of that trend, Allen once again expanded its operations, adding fresh produce in 1986. A year later, this segment was bolstered with the acquisition of Marske Produce Company, a Soulard, Missouri, company. During this period, Allen attempted to expand internationally, hoping to build on the overseas business it conducted through military contracts (essentially the sale of Lasco cocktail lemon and lime concentrates at military PXs and general stores). The company worked with the Missouri Department of Economic Development as well as with U.S. Senator John Danforth of Missouri to gain access to countries such as Germany and Japan. In the end, however, Allen was confronted with a number of protective measures that thwarted its attempts to break into these markets. On the domestic front, Allen looked to secure new business by turning 6,000 square feet of its warehouse into a quasi-supermarket where, on a cash-only basis, individuals could buy the same bulk products the company supplied to large restaurant customers. These offerings, under both the Lasco and brand-name labels, included 50-oz. cans of soup, gallon containers of mustard, and large bags of meatballs. Primarily, the idea was to find a way to fend off new competition like Sam's Wholesale Club, which sold a limited selection of institutional-sized food products.

Last of Founder's Sons Dies in 1995

During the 1990s, Allen expanded its range of institutional customers to include gambling riverboats and prisons. As Stanley Allen told the *St. Louis-Post Dispatch* regarding the trend the company was responding to, "What are we building? Prisons, sports stadiums and gambling riverboats." For a wholesaler operating out of St. Louis, finding new outlets was important because, as he commented, "It's pretty flat in this market now. We also happen to be in a region that's not growing in population. Our business has to come at the expense of our competition, it appears." Moreover, the entire food service industry was undergoing a period of extreme consolidation with a few deep-pocketed companies swallowing up smaller companies. Able to take advantage of their sheer size to better control costs and undercut their rivals on price, these mega-concerns

Key Dates:

1901: L. Allen & Sons Company is founded.
1912: The family opens a retail grocery store.
1941: The company receives its first military contract for food distribution.
1949: The company's headquarters are moved to St. Louis.
1968: Frozen foods added to the company's inventory.
1972: Bensinger's Inc. is acquired.
1987: Marske Produce is acquired.
2002: Royal Ahold NV acquires Allen Foods.

continued to grow larger, while regional, family-owned-and-operated companies like Allen Foods were fast becoming relics. Ben Allen, the last of the Allen brothers who founded the business with his father finally quit working at the company in 1995. Two years later, at the age of 92, he died as the result of a lengthy illness. He left the business in the hands of third- and fourth-generation members of the family, but Allen Foods, like so many other family businesses, was soon destined to become part of a corporate giant.

In December 2002, Royal Ahold acquired Allen Foods for an undisclosed amount that analysts pegged to be around $100 million. Not included, however, was Halben, which the Allen family retained and would continue to operate. Stanley Allen remained as president of Allen Foods, and cousin Richard Allen continued to serve as an executive vice-president. During the 1990s, Netherlands-based Ahold had been one of the more aggressive players in the food industry, primarily by acquiring supermarket chains. In the previous three years, it expanded into the food distribution business. The first step was the 2000 acquisition of U.S. Foodservice, followed by a number of smaller purchases involving regional food distributors such as Parkway Food Service, PYA Monarch, and Alliant Foodservice. Earlier in 2002, Ahold acquired Lady Baltimore Foods Inc., an Allen rival in the Kansas City market. Although Wall Street seemed unimpressed with Ahold's purchase of Allen Foods, it was apparent that the Dutch firm was committed to growing U.S. Foodservice by continuing to roll up regional businesses.

Less than a year after becoming part of the Ahold family, Allen Foods lost its direct ties to the family that gave the company it name and nurtured it for a century. Both Stanley Allen and Richard Allen left the company in September 2003, leaving Allen Foods with no members of the family involved in its leadership for the first time in its history.

Principal Competitors

Performance Food Group Company; SYSCO Corporation.

Further Reading

Eubanks, Ben, ''Allen Foods Looks out for the Little Guy,'' *St. Louis Business Journal*, November 28, 1988, p. 8A.

Hanuska, Karl Emerick, ''Ahold Buy of Allen Foods Confuses Srategy,'' *Reuters News*, December 5, 2002.

Karlen, Josh, ''Royald Ahold Strikes Again,'' *Daily Deal*, December 6, 2002.

Lee, Thomas, ''Dutch Grocery Giant Buys Allen Foods,'' *St. Louis Post-Dispatch*, December 6, 2002, p. C14.

—Ed Dinger

Amalgamated Bank

Amalgamated Bank is the only bank in the United States wholly owned by a labor union. Located chiefly in New York City, but with branches in California, the District of Columbia, and New Jersey as well, Amalgamated Bank offers free checking accounts, no minimum balance on savings accounts, low monthly fees, low rates on mortgages and auto loans, and low or no fees on ATM transactions. In addition to its full line of commercial and individual banking services, Amalgamated Bank provides trust, investment advisory, custodial, and benefit remittance services for employee benefit plans.

Working-Class Financial Institution: 1923–63

The Amalgamated Bank of New York was founded in 1923 by the Amalgamated Clothing Workers of America (which later became the Amalgamated Textile and Clothing Workers Union, and, still later, the Union of Needletrades, Industrial and Textile Employees–UNITE). The first labor bank in New York, it was also said to be the first bank in the city to operate on a profit-sharing basis with the depositors. Amalgamated Bank was originally located on East 14th Street in Manhattan but took a lease in 1925 on the five-story Tiffany Building adjoining Union Square, where its headquarters remain to this day. By this time, the number of its depositors had grown from 1,900 to 12,000.

Amalgamated Bank of New York—and its sister bank in Chicago, the Amalgamated Trust and Savings Bank—were among the 36 union-backed banks founded in the United States during the 1920 (22 in the first four years of the decade alone). Most of them failed to survive the Great Depression because they were run by union officials who made poor investments and often put ideology before prudence—for example, by financing strikes and making unsecured loans to union members and supporters.

The Amalgamated Bank of New York, founded with $300,000 in capital, offered such services as low-interest loans to workers and debt-consolidation services to police and firemen. Because many of the parent union's members were immigrants, Amalgamated was the first to introduce a foreign-exchange transfer service allowing them to send remittances safely to their relatives in Europe, payable in dollars rather than local currency. Within three years, over 400,000 individuals and 200 banks were using this service, and during the first 20 years more than $50 million was sent to 1,273,931 distressed persons abroad. Amalgamated also established a travel agency for the same reason. In 1924, it was the first New York City bank to offer unsecured instalment loans based on the borrower's employment history and future earnings potential. It also financed the first union-supported housing project in the United States, in New York City's borough of the Bronx. Eventually the program grew to three cooperative projects—the other two in lower Manhattan—providing low-cost housing for 2,536 families and serving as a model for much larger housing developments financed by big insurance companies.

Amalgamated Bank of New York had prepared itself beforehand for what proved to be the panic period of the Depression by selling securities for cash and liquidating loans, even at a loss, until its holdings were all in cash and short-term federal Treasury bonds. As a result, it was always able to reimburse depositors closing their accounts and was one of the first banks allowed to reopen following the bank holiday declared by Franklin D. Roosevelt following his presidential inauguration in March 1933.

During the next 30 years, Amalgamated Bank of New York provided loans for workers who wanted to buy apartments in its three housing cooperatives. It started managing trust funds for

---

Company Perspectives:

Our mission is to bring affordable banking and investment services to working men and women and to serve as a strong financial ally to unions.

---

other unions in the early 1960s and extended banking hours for the convenience of workers. The bank also established professional investment counseling for the managers of the union's growing pension and welfare funds. By 1963, when Amalgamated Bank celebrated its 40th anniversary, it was—along with the sister bank in Chicago and a Kansas City, Kansas, institution—the only survivor of the many fully owned union banks that had been founded in the 1920s. The institution's assets came to $115 million (compared to $1.44 million at the end of its first year). Amalgamated's rates for auto and personal loans were the lowest in New York City. It had a customer base of about 30,000 depositors and borrowers in 1965.

Remaining True to Its Origins: 1973–98

Amalgamated Bank of New York began offering checking accounts in 1973, becoming the first in the metropolitan area not to charge a fee either for the service or for checks without requiring a minimum balance. Also in 1973, it created a division for trust and investment services to serve employee benefit plans, providing trust, investment advisory, custodial, and benefit remittance services. A tradition of special help to labor and liberal groups continued into the 1970s and 1980s. Amalgamated Bank of New York once opened its vault on a Saturday in order to provide $300,000 in bail for pickets arrested the night before. The National Association for the Advancement of Colored People received $800,000 to post a cash bond within 24 hours. In 1973, bank officials worked all weekend to come up with bail checks so that striking Philadelphia teachers could stay out of jail. Nine years later, Amalgamated gave the striking National Football League Players Association a $200,000 loan even though the association did not have a bank account.

Since Amalgamated Bank of New York had no private shareholders—the parent union remained sole owner—it felt no pressure to abandon its conservative way of doing business in order to increase earnings. "We're probably the most liquid bank in the country," Edward M. Katz, the bank's president and chief executive officer, told Mario A. Milletti of the *New York Times* in 1978. Over 90 percent of its assets were in cash, temporary loans to other banks, and government and municipal securities. Amalgamated made practically no commercial or industrial loans, and its mortgage loans were only up to a maximum of five years. In all, loans came to only 15 percent of assets, compared to about 52 percent for non-labor banks of comparable size. Amalgamated encouraged thrift among its small customers by allowing pooling of funds to buy U.S. Treasury securities, so that a depositor with only $500 to invest could buy a certificate with a maturity of as little as nine months, yet receive 7 percent in interest. The bank had four offices and $720 million in assets at the end of 1977.

Amalgamated Bank of New York's practice of concentrating its investments in short-term securities was a wise policy during the inflation-ridden 1970s and early 1980s, when interest rates rose into the double digits. Its fully discretionary pension assets grew from $365 million in mid-1978 to $500 million in mid-1980. Amalgamated was managing pension funds for 93 unions by late 1983, almost entirely in the New York metropolitan area. Although it also had a few such nonunion accounts, none were personal trusts or estates, corporate employee-benefit accounts, charitable trusts, or state or local retirement funds. "We're selective as to who we take on," Katz told Cathy Capozzoli of *Pensions & Investments*. "We don't accept funds with stipulations about equity or long-term investments."

In 1980, as Japanese-made automobiles were flooding the U.S. market, Amalgamated offered purchasers of domestic cars a half-percentage-point discount on 24-to-36-month auto loans. "We just think it is important to help the American worker get back on the job," Katz told the *New York Times*. "It is important to give a helping hand." In 1982, after the *New York Times* quoted a Citicorp officer as saying, "A person with $200 or $300 in savings shouldn't be in a bank," Amalgamated took out an ad in the *Times* expressing outrage. Katz told Alice Arvan of *American Banker* that the statement was "philosophically inconsistent with the spirit of good community banking," adding that "in fact, one of the reasons labor banks were founded was to provide banking services to people not considered acceptable to other banks." Speaking to Lawrence Van Gelder for a 1985 *Times* profile, Katz summed up what he saw as the bank's philosophy in these words: "What differentiates a labor bank from any other bank is that while we are a profit-making institution, we feel that some portion of our profits should go into areas where you don't always have to maximize your earnings. . . . In a sense we have become the conscience of the banking community."

When sharply lower inflation rates belied Katz's belief that the annual cost of living increase would never drop below 5 percent, Amalgamated Bank of New York found itself deprived of the higher yields that other investors had locked in from long-term corporate bonds and Treasuries. Nevertheless, the bank continued to make steady profits and few mistakes. In 1986, it charged off only $195,000 in bad loans out of its portfolio of $313.5 million. Only 11 out of 13,034 auto loans were 30 days or more delinquent, perhaps because Amalgamated's interest rate was the lowest offered by any bank in the city. The annual yield on its money-market rates was higher than the average paid by ten big institutions tracked. Amalgamated also charged no fees on savings accounts with a $5 minimum. In 1992, the bank initiated what it called a unique equity index mutual fund that it said would push for enhanced shareholder value by encouraging business boards to pursue sound governance policies and hold managements accountable to high social and corporate citizenship.

Expanding beyond New York: 1998–2003

Amalgamated Bank of New York opened its seventh branch—and its first outside the city—in 1998, in Washington, D.C., the home of AFL-CIO headquarters and to more than 40 labor unions. Bank officials said that, as in New York, they would offer free checking accounts with no minimum balance. Almost a year and a half later, however, Amalgamated had brought in only $35 million in deposits, inspiring a letter from consumer advocate Ralph Nader chiding local union leaders for

---

Key Dates:

1923: The bank is founded by the Amalgamated Clothing Workers of New York.

1925: Amalgamated Bank of New York moves to 15 Union Square, which is still its headquarters.

1933: The bank is one of the first to reopen following panic withdrawals of the early Depression era.

1962: Amalgamated Bank of New York's assets reach $115 million.

1973: Amalgamated begins offering checking accounts.

1977: The bank has four branches and $720 million in assets.

1998: Amalgamated opens a branch in Washington, D.C.

2002: The bank opens a branch in Pasadena, California.

---

ignoring the bank, which was reported to be taking measures to attract Hispanic customers.

Also in 1998, Amalgamated acquired an 81 percent stake in the First Trade Union Trust Company. The name of this Los Angeles-based institution was changed to Amalgamated Trust Company. Amalgamated Bank of New York shortened its name to Amalgamated Bank in 2000.

In 2002, Amalgamated Bank became the first plaintiff to take legal action against Enron Corp. managers for securities fraud in relation to the failure of the giant corporation in the previous year, and it was a member of the class-action lawsuit against the company. The bank also led litigation by shareholders opposing Unocal Corp.'s investments in Myanmar, challenged what it called excessive compensation for executives of General Electric Corp. and other firms, and opposed initiatives by some U.S. companies to relocate in Bermuda in order to avoid federal taxation.

Amalgamated opened a branch in Lyndhurst, New Jersey, and expanded into California in 2002, when it opened a branch in Pasadena. A UNITE executive told Dave Melendi of the *San Garbriel Valley Tribune* that ''A lot of banks have been pulling out of California, especially Southern California. We think that creates a need. We think with banks pulling out there's a lot of low-wage workers and hard pressed working people in Southern California.'' In 2003, Amalgamated opened a branch in uptown Manhattan's West Harlem neighborhood.

Besides its headquarters and its Washington, Lyndhurst, and Pasadena branches, Amalgamated Bank had, in 2003, three Manhattan branches, two Bronx branches, and one in Queens.

Total assets came to $3.28 billion at the end of 2002, total deposits to $1.81 billion, and net income to $11.15 million. The bank's deposit options included checking, savings, and money-market accounts, certificates of deposit, and direct-deposit payments. It also offered bank cards and online banking. Automobile, home equity, home improvement, mortgage, and personal loans were available. The bank also offered personal lines of credit and health-care financial services.

Principal Competitors

Astoria Financial Corporation; New York Community Bankcorp Inc.; Independence Community Bank Corporation; Washington Mutual, Inc.

Further Reading

Andrejczak, Matt, ''New York's Amalgamated to Court Hispanics in D.C.,'' *American Banker*, October 6, 1999, p. 6.

——, ''New York Union-Owned Bank Establishes an Outpost in D.C.,'' *American Banker*, May 15, 1998, p. 5.

Arvan, Alice, ''Amalgamated Takes Out Ad to Decry Citicorp Official's Remarks on Saving,'' *American Banker*, March 3, 1982, p. 2.

Capozzoli, Cathy, ''Amalgamated Portfolios 'Short Term','' *Pensions & Investments*, July 21, 1980, p. 38.

''Clothing Workers' Bank Twenty Years Old Today,'' *New York Times*, April 14, 1943, p. 38.

''Incentives Offered on U.S. Cars,'' *New York Times*, August 12, 1980, p. D4.

Koshetz, Herbert, ''Amalgamated Bank to Reduce Charges for Special Checking,'' *New York Times*, September 14, 1965, pp. 49, 56.

''Labor Bank Fetes Its 40th Year,'' *Business Week*, May 25, 1963, pp. 67–68.

''Labor Bank Leases Tiffany Building,'' *New York Times*, August 3, 1925, p. 27.

Melendi, Dave, '' 'Labor Bank' Opens Branch in Pasadena, Calif.,'' *San Garbriel Valley Tribune*, August 31, 2002, p. 1.

Milletti, Mario A., ''Amalgamated: Cautious Bank with Union Label,'' *New York Times*, July 1, 1978, pp. 23, 31.

Paz, Peter, ''N.Y. Bank Opening Branch on K Street,'' *Washington Post*, May 13, 1998, p. C11.

Peterson, Leroy, ''Twenty-Two Labor Banks Organized in Four Years,'' *New York Times*, April 10, 1924, Sec. 8, p. 12.

Rose, Robert, ''How a Union Survives in Banking by Pushing Services Over Profit,'' *Wall Street Journal*, December 14, 1987, pp. 1, 18.

Tyson, David O., ''Union-Owned Amalgamated Bank Manages Pensions by Matching Rates,'' *American Banker*, October 25, 1983, pp. 24–23.

Van Gelder, Lawrence, ''A Banker Who Began at 60 Cents an Hour,'' *New York Times*, April 21, 1985, Sec. 21, p. 2.

—Robert Halasz

Ameren Corporation

One Ameren Plaza
1901 Chouteau Avenue
St. Louis, Missouri 63103
U.S.A.
Telephone: (314) 621-3222
Fax: (314) 554-3801
Web site: http://www.ameren.com

Public Company
Incorporated: 1922 as Union Electric Light and Power
    Company
Employees: 7,422
Sales: $3.84 billion (2002)
Stock Exchanges: New York
Ticker Symbol: AEE
NAIC: 221112 Fossil Fuel Electric Power Generation;
    221113 Nuclear Electric Power Generation; 221122
    Electric Power Distribution; 486210 Pipeline
    Transportation of Natural Gas; 221210 Natural Gas
    Distribution

Ameren Corporation provides a variety of energy services to over 2.2 million customers in Missouri and Illinois with a generating capacity of approximately 14,500 megawatts. The company's major subsidiaries include AmerenCILCO, responsible for providing electricity and natural gas to customers in Illinois; Ameren CIPS, which oversees electric and natural gas services to over 323,000 retail customers; and AmerenUE, the largest electric utility in Missouri. Nearly 95 percent of Ameren's revenues stem from its electric sales, with natural gas sales shoring up the remainder. Ameren was born out of the 1997 merger of Union Electric Company and CIPSCO Inc. and operates as one of the leading energy services firms in the United States.

Early History

Union Electric was incorporated in Missouri in 1922 as Union Electric Light and Power Company, a successor to a company of the same name incorporated in May 1902 as a result of the merger of Imperial Electric Light, Heat, and Power Company; Citizens Electric Lighting and Power Company; and Missouri Edison Electric Company. An early task for Union Electric Light and Power was providing power for the St. Louis World's Fair of 1904. Through its Ashley Street Plant, the company controlled 12 megawatts of power, enough to light the fair and make clear that electricity was readily available.

As more individuals and businesses began to rely on electricity, Union Electric Light and Power sought out additional generating sources. In 1913, the company began buying power from the Keokuk dam, 150 miles north of St. Louis. Union Electric later bought the dam, providing power carried over a longer distance than had ever been achieved before.

During World War I, the company expanded to serve rural areas. With the addition of a plant in Cahokia, Illinois, Union Electric Light and Power progressed through the 1920s, acquiring smaller light and power companies in Missouri and Illinois.

In the early 1930s, the Great Depression notwithstanding, Union Electric Light and Power completed construction of Bagnell dam in Missouri's Ozark mountains and organized Lakeside Light & Power Company in 1931 for residents in the surrounding area. In 1937, the company changed its name to Union Electric Company of Missouri. Its Illinois operations became a subsidiary, Union Electric Company of Illinois, with subsidiaries in Iowa renamed Iowa Union Electric Company. In 1940, the company proceeded with further corporate simplification, merging several Missouri subsidiaries into the parent. By 1945, surrounding Illinois and Iowa properties were merged into one subsidiary, Union Electric Power Company. In March 1945, Union Electric made the significant acquisition of Laclede Power & Light Company, a former competitor controlling 15 percent of the electric business in St. Louis.

Postwar Growth

With some delay in construction due to World War II, the company completed a new plant in Venice, Illinois, in 1950, bringing the total company capacity to 1,000 megawatts. Acquisitions continued. The company acquired Missouri Power & Light Company in 1950, following up with the 1954 addition of

Missouri Edison Company to its roster. In February 1955, the company absorbed its holding company, North American Company, and in August 1955 purchased all properties and on-going businesses in Illinois and Iowa of the subsidiary Union Electric Power Company. Following this consolidation, Union Electric Company of Missouri became simply Union Electric Company in 1956. The company made one more electric company acquisition in southeastern Iowa in 1958.

Reacting to such growth, Union Electric recognized the need to organize the generation and storage of power at its various plants. In a program begun in the early 1950s, the company built inter-company transmission lines, establishing power pools that any unit connected to the system could access. Soon outside companies joined the power pool; the total number of utilities reached 17.

Union Electric constructed the Merramec plant, with a capacity of 900 megawatts, in 1961, while launching construction for a plant at Taum Sauk, 90 miles southwest of St. Louis. The Taum Sauk plant was the world's first and largest pumped storage facility, more powerful than any yet built. The system was designed to pump up to five million tons of unused water from a lower to an upper reservoir. The water would then flow downhill during peak periods, funneled into two water wheels that would in turn drive turbines and other equipment to produce electricity. Major advantages of the plant were its automation—it required only 15 maintenance employees—and its cost, $50 million, in contrast to $67 million for a comparable steam facility. Completed in 1963, the plant drew visiting engineers from the United States and Europe.

Approximately 75 percent of Union's business was providing electricity to St. Louis. The company benefited from the modernization of the metropolitan area; in the 1960s the city was adding a new expressway, civic center, sports stadium, riverfront memorial park, and a number of office and apartment complexes as well as industrial plants. In the early 1960s, the company negotiated a contract with the city to redesign the street lighting. Using all mercury vapor fixtures, Union Electric in 1964 installed in St. Louis the brightest business district lighting of any city in the United States.

Another boon to the electric utility business in general came with the reduction of natural gas rates in 1964. The U.S. Supreme Court ordered the Federal Power Commission to extend the benefits of lower wholesale costs to the customers in the form of rate reductions, but due to the difference in federal and state regulations, not all rate cuts were mandatory. For those utilities whose earnings were below the allowed rate of return—and Union Electric was one of these—savings did not have to be passed along to the customers.

Power Pools and New Plants: Mid-1960s to Mid-1970s

In 1965, Union Electric extended its reach in generation, transmission, and interconnection by joining six other utilities in Mid-Continent Area Power Planners to pool resources. Member area reached from St. Louis north to St. Paul, Minnesota. The company enlarged its scope further when it joined with a group of 12 utility companies to form the largest power pool in the United States, the Mid-America Interpool Network. Connecting ten states, from Michigan and Missouri east to Virginia, the group would increase its number of high voltage power lines to nearly 4,000 within six years. The interconnection would further reduce costs through the coordinated planning of power plants.

Union Electric continued building its own plants as well as joining power pools. The first section of its Sioux Plant in St. Charles County, near St. Louis, went into operation in 1967 and the second in 1968. The two units' combined capacity was 1,000 megawatts. The company added three smaller plants in Missouri in 1967. The Venice, Kirksville, and Viaduct combustion-turbine plants had a combined net capability of 62,000 kilowatts. The four-unit Labadie plant was launched in 1970, with one unit added each year. Labadie was by far the company's largest generating plant, with a total capacity of 2.22 million kilowatts. In July 1973, Union Electric announced its intention to build Missouri's first nuclear plant in Callaway County, approximately 100 miles west of St. Louis.

The 1970s brought environmental issues to the focus of U.S. civic and business organizations in a number of ways. In February 1977, the company announced its withdrawal from plans to generate electricity from solid waste, a scheme that had been in the works since 1972. The Environmental Protection Agency (EPA) had contributed $800,000 and Union Electric $600,000 to build a prototype waste-processing plant. By 1974, Union Electric was ready to set the station in motion, collecting trash from four sites in St. Louis and processing up to 2.5 million tons of garbage at the Labadie plant. One of the four sites was not approved by community residents, forcing Union Electric to buy another site, which also was not approved. The issue then went to court, at which time Union Electric decided to cancel the entire project.

Delays in Nuclear Expansion: Late 1970s–Early 1990s

The decision to discontinue the trash recycling plan coincided with Union Electric's plan to delay construction on its nuclear plant. Charles Dougherty, president, attributed the delay of its nuclear plant to a reaction to a 1976 referendum prohibiting Union Electric from including anticipated construction costs in its current utility rates.

Another event contributing to a delay in Union Electric's nuclear plant plans was the March 1979 accident at the Three Mile Island nuclear plant near Harrisburg, Pennsylvania. Due to failure of valves in the water cooling system, water levels in the reactor temporarily fell, unshielding nuclear radiation. The accident spurred public opposition to the construction and operation of nuclear plants. Union Electric waited for further information to apply to its own design and personnel training for the Callaway plant.

Key Dates:

1922: Union Electric Light and Power Company is incorporated in Missouri.
1931: Lakeside Light & Power Company is organized.
1937: The company changes its name to Union Electric Company of Missouri.
1945: Laclede Power & Light Company is acquired.
1956: The company adopts the name Union Electric Company.
1961: Construction is launched for a plant at Taum Sauk.
1970: The Labadie facility begins operations.
1984: The Callaway nuclear plant goes online.
1997: Union Electric and CIPSCO Inc. merge to create Ameren Corporation.
2003: Ameren acquires CILCORP Inc.

In August 1979, the Missouri Public Service Commission advised suspension of the company's nuclear plant construction permit. As a condition of a rate increase granted in 1978, the commission had been investigating Union Electric's generation-facility expansion program and found the company's load forecasts beyond peak demand levels. Union Electric held that its generation amounts had been leveling off, but the company also anticipated demand for electric power to increase, since other sources such as oil and natural gas were less available.

By November 1979, Union Electric made final arrangements for fuel financing sources including commercial paper and letters of credit, for its Callaway plant. The following December the company reached a settlement with Westinghouse Electric, which Union Electric had sued, charging failure to fulfill a 1975 uranium-supply contract. Union Electric stood to gain from the settlement $200 million in cash, uranium, and various other goods and services over a 20-year period.

In April 1980, Union Electric named president Charles Dougherty chairman, a position unoccupied since 1973. W.E. Cornelius, former director of corporate planning and more recently executive vice-president, was elected president at age 48. Company stockholders agreed to increase the number of common shares available to 100 million, up 25 percent. In November, the company increased the estimated costs of the first unit of the Callaway plant to $1.58 billion, $260 million more than previous estimates, while the second unit was priced at $1.72 billion, an increase of $54 million. The company cited inflation, financing, costs of meeting regulatory requirements, and two spring 1980 labor strikes as causes.

A respite for the company came with the July 1981 approval of a $50 million rate increase. September, however, brought announcement of further delays and higher estimates for the Callaway plant. Union Electric stated that complex testing and installation procedures postponed start-up of the first Callaway unit and would raise costs, although by how much was unknown. The company also was considering canceling the second unit at a possible loss of $7 million, which it would seek to regain via rate increases. By October, Union Electric canceled the second unit, increased projected costs of the first unit to $2.1 billion, and

consulted with state regulators regarding a time plan to write off the investment expenses. The company considered other means of power generation to replace, if necessary, the more than one million kilowatts lost in the second unit cancellation.

Investment rating services lowered ratings on Union Electric bonds and preferred stock as a result of the utility's August 1982 announcement of a further delay in the Callaway nuclear plant. Originally scheduled for completion in April 1983, the plant operation was set for late 1984 or early 1985. The estimated cost increased to $2.85 billion. Union Electric cited continuing design changes required by the Nuclear Regulatory Commission and additional skilled labor costs as the major factors for the increase. Union Electric received a rate increase of 9 percent from Missouri regulators to help defray expenses, but the amount was not enough to keep industry investors from considering the company financially weakened. Union Electric requested a 16.8 percent rate increase for its 70,000 Illinois customers, a proposal that the Illinois attorney general opposed. The company offered 6.5 million common shares of stock in December 1982, and sold a total of $220 million in various bond issues to help offset the short-term debt caused by the nuclear plant construction delay.

In October 1984, the Callaway nuclear plant finally went on-line, producing enough power for one million customers. In November, the company was granted a full-power operating license from the Nuclear Regulatory Commission. Full commercial operation commenced at the Callaway plant on December 19, 1984. The plant produced more electricity in its first year of operation than any other U.S. nuclear power plant.

In the spring of 1985, the Missouri commission significantly cut the amount that Union Electric attempted to charge its customers in rate increases to pay for Callaway-related expenses. The commission called the rate increase request a result of inefficiency and unreasonable or unexplained costs. The commission okayed a six-year phased-in rate increase designed to gain Union Electric a total of $455 million. Union Electric denied the commission's charges, commenting that the Callaway plant cost one-fifth less than nuclear plants under construction during the same time period. The company planned to appeal the Missouri decision and pursue further rate increases in Iowa and Illinois to recover costs.

By the end of April, it was clear that the Missouri commission opposed Union Electric's appeal to include all Callaway-related construction costs in rate increases. Outstanding costs amounted to $384 million; after taxes, the amount was $250 million, which the company would post as a one-time loss. Utilities, formerly able to list construction costs expected to be regained in rate increases as profit, were under review by the financial accounting standards boards. Union Electric stated, however, that its 1985 net income would be reduced by only $50 million. Also during 1985, Illinois and Iowa granted phased-in rate increases, similar to the Missouri plan.

The year 1986 provided good news; sales of electricity to commercial and residential customers increased, while Union Electric's fuel costs decreased as a result of reduced generation. During 1987 and 1988, Moody's Investors Service and Standard & Poor's Corporation upgraded Union Electric's credit ratings, as the company regained its solid financial footing. The unusually hot summer of 1988 prompted extra use of electricity for air conditioning, boosting Union Electric sales to double the normal level.

Following a 15-month review of the Callaway nuclear plant, in mid-1988 the Nuclear Regulatory Commission concluded that Union Electric management was aggressive in responding to safety concerns and granted the company a license to increase power generation at the plant. By the end of 1988, Callaway generated one-fourth of total electricity for Union Electric.

While much attention had been centered on the company's Callaway nuclear plant, coal continued to be Union Electric's chief source of fuel. Burning coal transformed water to steam, the steam powered generators, which in turn produced more than 70 percent of the utility's electric energy needs. The advantage of using coal was that the supply was plentiful and relatively inexpensive; a disadvantage was that the use of coal caused noxious emissions. Union Electric, however, reduced emissions by 33 percent from the mid-1970s to 1989. The company's Keokuk and Osage hydroelectric plants, while dependent on weather conditions, continued to provide power dependably and at low cost.

At the close of the 1980s, Union Electric concentrated on increasing productivity and reducing its work force; by 1989, staff decreased by 16 percent in fossil-fuel and hydroelectric operations. To stay competitive in customer services the company introduced a new electronic telephone system, Braille billing, and home-weatherizing programs. Other projects stressing energy efficiency included an all-electric apartment complex designed jointly with residential developers.

In 1990, the U.S. Congress approved amendments to the Clean Air Act. The amendments required a two-thirds reduction, by 2000, of sulfur dioxide emissions as well as a decrease in nitrogen oxide output. The amendments did allow utility companies flexible means of compliance. Also in 1990, the company was named a potentially responsible party for five hazardous waste sites. Costs for cleaning up the sites, however, were not expected to reduce earnings significantly.

Union Electric appeared to be streamlining in the early 1990s. The work force at the time was decreasing at the rate of 100 people per year. The Callaway nuclear plant's performance had been consistently superior. Production costs were half that of the company's coal-based plants and refueling took half the time comparable nuclear plants need. An agreement with the Missouri Public Service Commission to reduce rates and not seek an increase until 1993 freed both parties from rate-related disputes. Ensuing rate reductions, while reducing company revenue by $30 million a year, were anticipated to spur commercial and industrial development. In addition, although implementation of the requirements of the Clean Air Act could cost up to $300 million through the 1990s, fuel prices were expected to decrease by a similar amount. Union Electric, with no apparent need for new construction necessary, seemed financially fit for the future.

Changes in the Mid-1990s and Beyond

During the latter half of the decade, however, deregulation threatened to dramatically shakeup the utilities industry throughout the United States. As such, major utilities began to revamp their business strategies in order to better position themselves for competition in an open market. This held true for Union Electric, and in 1995 the company announced that it planned to merge with Illinois-based CIPSCO Inc. The firm's president and CEO Charles W. Mueller offered his take on the deal in a 1995 company press release claiming, "The merger combines two financially strong, low-cost energy providers with common visions and strategies and highly compatible operations and managements. This transaction allows us to spread the cost of advanced energy delivery systems over a larger base, while keeping our rates low and enhancing our reliability and service quality." In addition, Mueller stated that the union would "enable us to take full advantage of the changing industry landscape to capitalize on our financial strengths, our service-oriented cultures and our lean organizational structures. By doing so, we will be well positioned to continue to provide superior shareholder returns and customer benefits, both now and into the next century."

The $1.3 billion transaction—expected to save the firm approximately $759 million over a ten-year period—was eventually completed in December 1997 after undergoing scrutiny by several regulatory commissions. A new company, Ameren Corporation, was created to act as a holding company for Union Electric's operations, which were folded into AmerenUE, and CIPSCO, which became known as AmerenCIPS. Upon completion of the deal, Ameren ranked 11th in the United States in terms of generating capacity.

In its first year of operation, Ameren began to prepare for future deregulation in the electricity industry. In 1999, the company's large commercial customers were allowed to choose energy suppliers, which forced it to seek out major contracts with powerful industrial concerns, including Archer Daniels Midland—Illinois' largest electricity customer. Additionally, the company focused on expanding its generating capacity, providing its customers with a variety of new services and branching out into nonregulated ventures. In 2000, Ameren restructured its holdings, transferring five of its AmerenCIPS power plants to a newly created subsidiary, AmerenEnergy Generating Company.

In the early years of the new century, Ameren continued to pursue growth in its energy production and delivery markets. At the same time, the company became embroiled in a rate dispute with the Missouri Public Service Commission (MPSC). In 2001, the MPSC set forth a proposal of an electric revenue reduction of over $300 million per year. According to the company, Ameren had not raised its rates in Missouri in over 15 years and had provided over $1 billion in rate reductions and consumer credits since the early 1990s. With rates already 14 percent below the national average and 10 percent below 1987 levels, the company was concerned that the new proposal set forth by the MPSC would hinder the company's ability to make future infrastructure investments in Missouri's energy sector. As such, Ameren and the MPSC hammered out a new deal in July 2002 that called for a rate freeze until June 30, 2006, $110 million in rate reductions, and a pledge to pursue energy conservation and energy infrastructure improvements.

In early 2003, Ameren acquired Illinois-based CILCORP Inc. The $1.4 billion deal positioned Ameren as Illinois' second-largest utility and added 400,000 customers to its arsenal. While Ameren battled a weak economy and a downturn in the energy sector, the company remained dedicated to its core strategy of pursing growth, controlling costs, and providing top notch service to all of its customers.

Principal Subsidiaries

AmerenCILCO; Ameren CIPS; AmerenUE; AmerenEnergy; AmerenEnergy Resources; Ameren Services; CIPSCO Investment Company; CILCORP Investment Management; CILCORP Energy Services Inc.

Principal Competitors

Aquila Inc.; Exelon Corporation; Great Plains Energy Inc.

Further Reading

"Ameren Completes CILCORP Acquisition," *Public Utilities Fortnightly*, March 1, 2003, p. 23.

"Cilcorp Sold for $1.4 Bil," *Crain's Chicago Business*, May 6, 2002, p. 58.

Corey, Andrea, "Ameren, Others Vow to Pursue Deregulation," *St. Louis Business Journal*, May 15, 2000, p. 10.

Desloge, Rick, "Ameren's Profit Odyssey," *St. Louis Business Journal*, January 19, 1998, p. 3A.

"Union Electric Company of Missouri and CIPSCO Incorporated of Illinois Sign Definitive Merger Agreement," *PR Newswire*, August 14, 1995.

Union Electric Company: Service to People, St. Louis: Union Electric Company, 1986.

VandeWater, Judith, "UE Clears CIPSCO Buyout Hurdle," *St. Louis Post-Dispatch*, October 16, 1997, p. 1C.

—Frances E. Norton
—update: Christina M. Stansell

American Civil Liberties Union (ACLU)

125 Broad Street, 18th Floor
New York, New York 10004-2400
U.S.A.
Telephone: (212) 549-2500
Fax: (212) 549-2646
Web site: http://www.aclu.org

Not-for-Profit Company
Incorporated: 1920
Employees: 170
Sales: $42.2 million (2002)
NAIC: 813310 Social Advocacy Organizations

The American Civil Liberties Union (ACLU) is a New York City-based nonpartisan, not-for profit corporation dedicated to the preservation and extension of constitutional liberties. Often controversial, the ACLU works through the legal system to forward its mission, initiating test cases and becoming involved in cases initiated by others. All told, the organization takes part in about 6,000 cases each year, primarily divided into three general areas: freedom of expression, equality before the law, and due process of law for everyone. Moreover, the ACLU runs nine ongoing national projects devoted to specific areas of civil liberties: AIDS, capital punishment, drug policy, litigation, lesbian and gay rights, immigrants' rights, prisoners' rights, reproductive freedom, voting rights, and women's rights. With a base of nearly 400,000 members and supporters, the organization employs some 300 staff people. In addition, it is assisted by thousands of volunteers, many are whom are attorneys working pro bono. In addition to its Manhattan headquarters, the ACLU maintains a legislative office in Washington, D.C., and a Southern Regional Office in Atlanta, Georgia, dedicated to voting rights and race discrimination. The ACLU also has 57 independently run affiliates that are active in every state as well as in Washington, D.C., and Puerto Rico. The organization is governed by an 83-member Board of Directors that includes a member from each state plus at-large members. The ACLU, which receives no government money, is funded by annual dues and contributions from members, as well as individual donations and grants from private foundations.

Key Founder Born to Wealthy Family in 1800s

The person most responsible for the founding and rise of the ACLU was Roger Nash Baldwin, the oldest child of a prominent Boston, Massachusetts-area family, whose heritage could be traced back to at least two people who came to America on the *Mayflower*. His father was a wealthy leather merchant, his mother, Lucy Cushing Nash, was an early feminist, and many of his relatives were active in social causes in keeping with the sense of noblesse oblige that permeated the upper classes of the day. As a teenager, he was involved in efforts at social reform through the Unitarian Church, to which his and other aristocratic families belonged. Baldwin enrolled at Harvard University in 1901, where he soon became a believer in the Progressive Movement that was taking place across America. After earning degrees in anthropology in 1905, Baldwin turned for career advice to his father's lawyer, Louis D. Brandeis, who would one day become a Supreme Court justice. It was Brandeis who convinced Baldwin to forego a business career in favor of devoting his life to social service.

In 1906, Baldwin moved to St. Louis on a twofold mission: to create a sociology department at Washington University, where he would also teach courses, and to head Self Culture Hall, a settlement house. During the next several years, Baldwin earned a national reputation as a social worker and became exposed to such influential political activists as Emma Goldman, who furthered the process of chipping away at his uppercrust sensibilities. For a time, he was even engaged to radical activist Anna Louise Strong. He gained national prominence in 1910 by being named the president of the St. Louis Civic League, which was instrumental in bringing "clean" government to St. Louis. When World War I broke out in Europe in 1914 and soon threatened to envelop the United States, he opposed his country's entry. After America joined the war on the side of Great Britain and France, Baldwin moved to New York City in March 1917 to become secretary of the American Union Against Militarism (AUAM), founded two years earlier by such well-known social activists as Jane Addams, Florence Kelley, and Lillian Wald.

In May 1917, the U.S. Congress passed the Selective Service Act that established a military draft, and Baldwin was named to

---

Company Perspectives:

The ACLU's mission is to fight civil liberties violations wherever and whenever they occur.

---

head AUAM's Civil Liberties Bureau (CLB), which would take on the plight of conscientious objectors and opponents to the war. At this stage, Baldwin still believed that he could draw on his upper-class connections to influence government officials and work cooperatively to come to reasonable accommodations, hoping to employ the CLB as an intermediary between authorities and conscientious objectors. Cordial relations between Baldwin and the government, however, gradually eroded. He condemned the harsh treatment to which conscientious objectors were often subjected, and he was very much opposed to the threat to free speech that came with the passage of the Espionage Act (later known as the Sedition Act). The legislation also caused division within the leadership of AUAM, concerned that CLB's work might put AUAM in violation of the law. In order to provide some insulation, a Civil Liberties Committee was formed in July 1917, and the break was finalized in October of that year when Baldwin and Crystal Eastman established the National Civil Liberties Bureau (NCLB).

By now, from the perspective of many U.S. officials, Baldwin was nothing less than a menace. He was spied on by Military Intelligence and NCLB's offices were raided in August 1918. The following month he was indicted for refusing to comply with the new Selective Service Act. In a celebrated trial, he was sentenced to a year in prison, which proved to offer little hardship for Baldwin. While working as a cook and a gardener, he established a reading and writing program for inmates, a prisoner's welfare league, and even a dramatic society and glee club, relying heavily on the political influence of sympathetic socialites.

ACLU Emerges in 1920

Baldwin was released from prison after ten months and, rather than immediately resume his duties at the NCLB, he decided to taste the working life for several weeks. He performed stints as a day laborer before becoming a scab at the Homestead Steel Mills, where he briefly operated as a spy for the striking union before being found out and fired. He returned to the NCLB during the final weeks of 1919, at a time when a "Red Scare" led to the government passing new sedition laws that allowed participants in "un-American" activities to be arrested without a warrant and held without trial. It was also a time of considerable labor unrest. To help refocus the mission of the NCLB away from conscientious objectors to the championing of labor rights, Baldwin felt it was necessary to change the name of the organization. The name he chose was the American Civil Liberties Union, which succeeded the NCLB in January 1920 following a reorganization. It was co-directed by Baldwin and NCLB attorney Albert DeSilver. The ACLU attempted to operate on funds raised from annual dues of $2, and even though it boasted 1,000 members by the end of its first year, the organization was strapped for cash. A key benefactor of the early years was Charles Garland, a rich Bostonian who donated money that was used to establish the American Fund for Public Service, which then financed legal defense cases and supported other efforts at social reform.

When the ACLU launched its activities, civil liberty violations took place on a number of fronts in America, as exemplified by a sampling of the incidents that caught the organization's attention in its first year: two organizers of the Nonpartisan League were forced by a mob to tar themselves in Kansas; an Oregon mayor refused to allow muckraking journalist Lincoln Steffens to lecture at a public meeting that was deemed to be un-American; seven people in Washington state were jailed for two months for selling a union newspaper; a man in Massachusetts was denied citizenship because of his religious stand as a conscientious objector; and, in Alabama, union coal miners were denied the right to meet for any purpose. In the first several years of its existence, the ACLU was especially devoted to keeping tabs on the activities of the Ku Klux Klan, whose members number one million in 1921. At the time, the Justice Department made little effort to monitor the Klan. In keeping with the ACLU's mission to protect the rights of those individuals that government leaders might disagree with, the ACLU also represented the KKK, supporting the group's right, in the words of Baldwin, "to parade in their nightgowns and pillowcases, and their right to burn fiery crosses on private property." In some cases, the ACLU took the side of the KKK over the NAACP.

"Monkey Trial" of 1925 Puts ACLU on the Map

The case that first brought widespread notoriety to the ACLU was the 1925 "Monkey Trial" that became the basis for the play, and later film, *Inherit the Wind*. In this case, the ACLU was looking to make a "friendly challenge" to a Tennessee law that prohibited the teaching of Charles Darwin's theory of evolution. The ACLU openly advertised in the state for a teacher willing to participate. The greater purpose, however, was to construct a case that could then be taken to the U.S. Supreme Court. The man induced to help was John T. Scopes, who coached football and taught physics on a part-time basis. He was talked into participating in the test case by a local booster who thought the community might benefit from the publicity. Scopes barely qualified for his role, since he never actually taught evolution, but he had once used an evolution textbook to help some students prepare for a test. As it turned out, the friendly challenge drew international attention, setting the standard for all modern media circuses to follow, due in large part to the men who stepped forward to argue the case. Representing Scopes was famed criminal attorney Clarence Darrow, who made his reputation representing labor leaders. On the other side was William Jennings Bryan, who was famous for his unsuccessful presidential campaigns and skills as an orator. When the case was stripped down, the question presented to the jury was simple: did Scopes violate the Tennessee law or not. In the end, Scopes was convicted and fined $100, but the subsequent appeal thwarted the ACLU's larger plans. The Tennessee Supreme Court reversed Scopes conviction on a technicality but upheld the statute, leaving the ACLU with nothing to appeal. The Tennessee law stood for another 40 years. Moreover, many textbook publishers, in light of the Scopes trial, chose to simply drop Darwin's theory of evolution from their textbooks rather than face legal complications. As a consequence, the ACLU's most celebrated case was perhaps its greatest defeat.

Key Dates:

1915: American Union Against Militarism (AUAM) formed.
1917: AUAM forms National Civil Liberties Bureau.
1920: AUAM is reorganized as ACLU, headed by Roger Baldwin.
1925: Scopes "Monkey Trial" takes place.
1949: Baldwin retires from active involvement.
1981: Baldwin dies at the age of 97.
1988: ACLU gains notoriety in U.S. presidential campaign.
1996: ACLU wins a case before the U.S. Supreme Court that gains civil rights for gays and lesbians.

Over the course of its first 25 years, the ACLU was involved in other noteworthy cases. It fought the U.S. Customs Service ban on the sale of James Joyce's novel *Ulysses,* lifted in 1933. The organization was successful in its arguments before the U.S. Supreme Court in 1939 when it opposed a Jersey City ban on political meetings held by union organizers. During World War II, the ACLU took the highly unpopular stand of opposing the internment of more than 100,000 Japanese-Americans, an act for which the U.S. Congress would formally apologize 50 years later. It was also during the war years that Baldwin and the ACLU ended a dalliance with communism, prompted by the Nazi-Soviet pact that Joseph Stalin and Adolph Hitler signed in 1939. Baldwin led the move to purge communist members from the ranks of the ACLU, an act which many in the organization considered a major breach in principle and almost resulted in splitting the organization in two.

Baldwin was involved in a number of outside causes that adversely affected the ACLU's operation. In 1949, when he turned 65, he retired as executive director, after which he played an elder statesman's role, devoting much of his time to the subject of international civil liberties. He enjoyed robust health and was quite active until his early 90s. He died on August 26, 1981 at the age of 97. In his biography of Baldwin, Robert C. Cottrell reflected on Baldwin's achievements: "During the six-decade span of his involvement with the modern civil liberties movement, Baldwin witnessed expanded protection of key portions of the Bills of Rights. . . . The ACLU leaders, guided by their long-time executive director, waged public relations wars, undertook groundbreaking litigation, and wrestled with public officials, while demanding an expansive interpretation of the Bill of Rights. Consequently, by the close of Baldwin's life, First Amendment provisions involving freedom of speech, the press, assemblage, and religion had been brought closer to actuality than at any point in American history."

The ACLU after Baldwin

In the postwar years, during the height of the Cold War, the ACLU fought against loyalty oaths that federal workers were enjoined to swear and state laws that required schoolteachers to avow they were not members of the Communist Party. The ACLU furthered its commitment to racial justice by involving itself in the cause of school desegregation in the 1950s (in

particular the U.S. Supreme Court decision in *Brown v. Board of Education*) and the Civil Rights movement of the 1960s. Also during the 1960s, the ACLU opposed the criminal prohibition of drugs, and thereafter opposed the on-going "war on drugs." Reproductive rights came to the forefront in the early 1970s with the landmark 1973 U.S. Supreme Court decisions *Roe v. Wade* and *Doe v. Bolton*, which extended the right to privacy to include the right of a woman to choose abortion. With the reinstatement of the death penalty in 1976, the ACLU opposed the "ultimate sanction" on grounds that it constituted cruel and unusual punishment and disproportionately affected minorities and the poor.

In 1988, the ACLU became swept up in national politics when Republican George H.W. Bush made Democrat Michael Dukakis's ACLU membership an issue in the presidential campaign. While the Republicans were successful in vilifying the ACLU with a large section of the American public, the attention that came to the organization also led to a surge in memberships and fund raising. The ACLU's reputation among conservatives was further hardened in 1989 when it was successful in having the U.S Supreme Court invalidate a Texas law that made flag desecration a punishable offense. The ACLU then succeeded in having the Supreme Court recognize the civil rights of gays and lesbians as a result of the 1996 case *Romer v. Evans*. Over the years, the ACLU has also riled people on the left. The most celebrated example was its 1978 defense of a neo-Nazi group to march through Skokie, Illinois, an act that led to a decline in ACLU membership.

Critics from both the left and the right have contended that the ACLU altered its mission over the final 30 years of the 20th century. In a 1988 article in *The New Republic*, Mark S. Campisano wrote, "The ACLU has strayed very far from its old agenda of civil liberties and civil rights. A new agenda of exotic leftwing causes now occupies most of the Unions time and energy." In the words of Christopher Clausen, writing for *The New Leader* in 1994, "The organization is obsessed with abortion." A second area of undue focus, in his opinion, was the organization's "dogged support for the discriminatory forms of affirmative action." The ACLU also faced questions from within its own ranks. A 1993 *Time* magazine article reported: "One essential conflict is between strict libertarians, for whom individual rights are as sacred as Moses' tablets, and new-breed egalitarians who favor minority and feminist causes and are more willing to see civil liberties give ground in the name of justice and equality." *Time* also noted that "Insiders disagree on whether the shifting views are fostered by the A.C.L.U's in-house affirmative-action plan that requires the board, formerly dominated by white males, to be at least 50 percent female and 20 percent minority. Whatever the reason, old soldiers like Harvard law professor Alan Dershowitz . . . asserts that the 'A.C.L.U. is a very different organization today.' To him, the key tenet of the A.C.L.U. faith is support for free-speech rights for 'causes that you despise.' Without that, 'all you are is a political activist.' " Opposed to this old guard thinking were ACLU board members like "gay activist Tom Stoddard, who says the absolutists are seeking 'otherworldly vindication on one constitutional right without recognizing that all rights have value and can be reconciled.' To him, both equality and liberty must be weighed and many rights enshrined.'' Ever controversial, the ACLU entered a new century continuing to play its role as a national gadfly.

Further Reading

Campisano, Mark S., ''Card Games: The ACLU's Wrong Course,'' *New Republic*, October 31, 1988, p. 10.

Carlson, Margaret, ''Spotlight on the A.C.L.U.,'' *Time*, October 10, 1988, p. 36.

Clausen, Christopher, ''Taking Liberties with the ACLU,'' *New Leader*, August 15, 1994, p. 12.

Cottrell, Robert C., *Roger Nash Baldwin and the American Civil Liberties Union*, New York: Columbia University Press, 2000, 504 p.

Garey, Diane, *Defending Everybody*, New York: TV Books, 1998, 240 p.

Ostling, Richard N., ''A.C.L.U.—Not All That Civil,'' *Time*, April 26, 1993, p. 31.

—Ed Dinger

The Anderson-DuBose Company

6675 Davis Industrial Parkway
Solon, Ohio 44139
U.S.A.
Telephone: (440) 248-880
Fax: (440) 248-6208

Private Company
Incorporated: 1991
Employees: 102
Sales: $197.3 million (2002)
NAIC: 424410 General Line Grocery Merchant
　　Wholesalers

The Anderson-DuBose Company is a distributor for more than 270 McDonald's restaurants in northeastern Ohio, western Pennsylvania, and northern West Virginia, as well as more than 75 McDonald's restaurants in South Africa. The company purchases about 575 products from approved vendors for distribution to McDonald's franchise owners in its territory. Products include hamburger, chicken, and fish patties, French fries, condiments, paper and plastic products, cleaning supplies, ''Happy Meal'' toys for kids, and promotional items. Distribution centers are located in Solon, Ohio, and Johannesburg, South Africa. The company operates a beer distributorship in Oklahoma City as well. Anderson-DuBose is among the largest businesses to be owned by African-Americans in the United States.

Apprenticeship with McDonald's

Warren E. Anderson and Stephen DuBose formed The Anderson-DuBose Company in November 1991 for the purpose of purchasing majority ownership in a McDonald's distributorship from Martin-Brower Company. This event is noteworthy for two reasons. First, the distributorship operated profitably, with a strong cash flow and an assured customer base, raising the question of why Martin-Brower would sell. As the largest distributor for McDonald's Corporation, and the largest restaurant chain distribution company nationwide, Martin-Brower served 40 percent of McDonald's restaurants in the United States through 16 regional distributorships. Martin-Brower sold

its Solon, Ohio-based distributorship to foster positive relations with McDonald's, opening the way for future business opportunities with the company. Selling the profitable distributorship to Anderson and DuBose helped McDonald's to fulfill its commitment to building minority involvement with the company. Hence the second reason the sale to Anderson-DuBose is noteworthy—the company became the first distributor for a major fast food chain to be owned by African Americans.

Anderson provided the impetus for the pursuit of a business opportunity with McDonald's. Before buying into the business, he had built a career in broadcast journalism, working as general sales manager for WFSB-TV, the Hartford, Connecticut, affiliate of CBS. Like many entrepreneurs, Anderson learned that his independent spirit often conflicted with the standpoint of his boss. After being fired from WFSB-TV, he lived off of investments and began exploring entrepreneurial opportunities. In his work at WFSB-TV, Anderson often interacted with McDonald's managers and franchise owners and thought highly of how the company operated. Anderson conferred with managers at McDonald's about opportunities and decided that operating a distribution center would be a promising enterprise. A regional purchasing specialist for McDonald's encouraged Anderson to contact the corporate office in Oakbrook, Illinois.

Anderson shared his idea with DuBose, then manager of international business acquisitions for GE Capital Corporation in Stamford, Connecticut, bringing DuBose's financial expertise into the business. The idea of entrepreneurship had appeal within a certain framework. Anderson and DuBose felt that a service company better suited their capabilities than a manufacturing operation. Furthermore, a distribution company was easier to finance than other service companies because an acquisition involved material assets, such as a building and delivery trucks. In deciding to pursue an association with McDonald's, they considered that the acquisition of a large business would involve the same level of involvement as the acquisition of a small business.

Anderson and DuBose encountered two problems on the path to entrepreneurship. First, they found that no McDonald's distributorships were available for purchase. Second, they had no

Key Dates:

1990: Anderson and DuBose begin their apprenticeship at a distributorship for products used by the McDonald's restaurant chain.
1991: Anderson-DuBose purchases a 51 percent stake in McDonald's distributorship from Martin-Brower Company.
1993: Anderson-DuBose is ranked number five on *Black Enterprise* magazine's list of 100 largest black-owned businesses.
1995: Company becomes sole owner of the distributorship and begins operating a joint venture in South African.
2002: Warren Anderson is named Male Entrepreneur of the Year by the U.S. Department of Commerce's National Minority Business Development Agency.

experience in distribution, a circumstance that McDonald's officials were quick to observe. The second problem was resolved when McDonald's offered to provide an apprenticeship through its Minority Business Development Program that would teach Anderson and DuBose all aspects of distribution operations. Finding a distributorship remained unresolved, however.

McDonald's modeled the apprenticeship on its program for franchise owners, which involved hands-on training. Through on-the-job experience, Anderson and DuBose learned all aspects of operating a distribution center, including truck-loading, warehousing, customer service, accounting, and budgeting. Anderson worked for a distributor in Whitewater, Wisconsin, serving McDonald's restaurants in Wisconsin, Minnesota, and Illinois, while DuBose worked for a Toledo distributor. Also, they found a mentor in Michael Gilman, director for U.S. purchasing for McDonald's. Initially set for eight months, the apprenticeship extended to 18 months as Anderson-DuBose searched for a distributorship to buy. They worked without pay, demonstrating a commitment to McDonald's but risking their high-paying careers without a guarantee that a distribution opportunity would be available.

Acquiring a McDonald's Distributorship in 1991

In search of a business to buy, Anderson and DuBose spent several months writing to McDonald's officials, attending conventions, and meeting with distributors and purchasing managers. Corporate officials acted as intermediaries as well, eventually introducing Anderson and DuBose to Herbert Heller, president of Martin-Brower. Martin-Brower proved to be the right match, and the company agreed to sell its northeastern Ohio distributorship, based in Solon, Ohio, southeast of Cleveland. Anderson and DuBose liked the location both for its business potential and for the fact that the company was situated in an area with a substantial African-American population. The distributorship served 229 McDonald's restaurants and employed 90 people at a 60,000-square-foot distribution center. In 1991, the company recorded slightly over $100 million in revenues.

Anderson and DuBose sold their homes, liquidated investments, and obtained financing to purchase a 51 percent interest

in the business. Anderson acquired a 40 percent interest and DuBose acquired an 11 percent interest, becoming president and vice-president, respectively. Martin-Brower assisted with financing the sale and retained a 49 percent stake in the distribution center; however, the contract involved a mechanism that returned ownership to Martin-Brower if Anderson-DuBose did not meet the stringent standards that McDonald's requires of its business associates.

While Anderson and DuBose had complete control of the management of the company, they were new faces to employees and franchise owners. The two men addressed employee concerns by meeting with employees on the job. Through the formation of an advisory committee comprised of warehouse workers, drivers, and managers, Anderson and DuBose initiated improvements in communication and teamwork. Cross-training employees in different aspects of distribution improved operating efficiency by combining job responsibilities. The company acted to improve cost efficiency as well, obtaining, for instance, a maintenance contract at lower cost.

To introduce themselves to franchise owners and address customer concerns, Anderson and DuBose distributed a customer service survey which inquired about the timeliness of delivery, the courtesy and knowledge of sales representatives, and other service issues. One problem uncovered by the survey involved franchise operators not receiving enough advance notice on special promotions to order goods appropriately. Anderson-DuBose initiated a monthly newsletter that provided restaurant owners with notice of promotional campaigns and how to prepare for them, as well as other valuable information.

After one year in business, Anderson-DuBose increased sales by 7 percent, to $110 million in 1992. The following year, *Black Enterprise* magazine ranked the company as fifth on its list of top-grossing black-owned industrial/service businesses; the company remained among the top ten for the next three years. Also, Anderson-DuBose ranked as the largest black-owned business in the state of Ohio.

Ownership of the company changed quickly and unexpectedly. First, DuBose sold his 11 percent interest in the company to Anderson in 1993. Then Anderson became the sole owner of the company in March 1995. Though Anderson had planned to purchase Martin-Brower's 49 percent stake in five to seven years, advantageous lending rates and operational efficiencies allowed him to acquire full ownership much sooner. Anderson-DuBose retained its original name.

Company revenues increased as the distributorship expanded to serve 259 McDonald's franchises by the end of 1995, including stores in western Pennsylvania and northern West Virginia. With a staff of 85 employees, including six managers, the company recorded sales of $118 million in 1995.

South Africa Opportunity Arises in 1994

After the dismantling of apartheid and the institution of democratic elections in South Africa in 1994, McDonald's decided to make franchise opportunities available there and hired Anderson to act as consultant for developing distribution in South Africa. (Anderson had spent several years in Nigeria, Tanzania, and Zambia, where his parents taught for a private education company.) In South Africa, he found that no existing distributor could handle the distribution needs of McDonald's, which required warehouses and delivery trucks that could accommodate different temperatures for dry, frozen, and chilled products.

Anderson decided to pursue the distributorship through a joint venture with local investors. He formed AD South Africa, which owned one-third of the venture, while Spar, a white-owned trucking company, and Thuthuka Investments, a black-owned firm, each owned a third of the business. The venture, ASP Distributors Ltd., used the existing infrastructure at Spar but modified it to suit the requirements of McDonald's. Managers from Anderson-DuBose's Ohio facility traveled to South Africa to assist with organizing the distribution center. ASP made its first delivery in October 1995, in time for the first store opening in Johannesburg on November 1st. With only two major fast food competitors, Kentucky Fried Chicken and Wimpy's, a British hamburger chain, sales at the McDonald's store quadrupled projections.

Despite this initial success, business operations in South Africa at this time encountered a number of challenges. High unemployment and uncertain social change fed a high crime rate, and thieves armed with machine guns hijacked delivery trucks out of the country. Though unemployment was high, the company had difficulty finding people willing to work nights and weekends, when deliveries are made. Also, after AD South Africa transferred money into the country, the value of the rand declined, resulting in a 20 percent loss in the value of funds.

Another major problem involved warehousing and distribution itself. Spar had difficulty maintaining McDonald's standards for operation, and Anderson had to buy his partner's interest and invest in a new distribution center. In addition to hiring staff and purchasing office and delivery equipment, Anderson had to build a warehouse at a capacity far beyond what the market's revenues could carry. By the end of 1999, the distribution center was supplying food products to only 25 McDonald's restaurants in Johannesburg and Capetown, although it had the means to serve 300 stores.

Stability and Steady Growth in the New Century

While business operations in South Africa became stable as the country matured, Anderson-DuBose continued to operate successfully in the United States. In 1997 sales reached $137 million. That year, the Ohio facility ranked as the third most productive distributorship of 40 McDonald's distributors in North America, in contrast to a rank of 30 when the business was acquired in 1991. In the United States, the company grew slowly, adding less than a dozen McDonald's restaurants to its Ohio distribution and acquiring a beer distributorship in Oklahoma City. In South Africa, distribution expanded quickly as 50 McDonald's restaurants opened throughout the country between 2000 and mid-2003.

Anderson was recognized for his success by several business institutions. In February 1999, Dun and Bradstreet and *Entrepreneur* magazine placed Anderson at number one on a list of ten Minority Entrepreneurs of the Year. In 2002, Anderson was named Male Entrepreneur of the Year by the U.S. Department of Commerce's National Minority Business Development Agency and Ohio Minority Supplier Firm of the Year by the Ohio Statewide Minority Business Development Center. Anderson-DuBose remained the largest black-owned business in Ohio and maintained positions among the top 20 of *Black Enterprise* magazine's list of 100 top-grossing black-owned businesses. In 2002, Anderson-DuBose listed at number 17 based on 2001 revenues of $177 million.

Principal Subsidiaries

AD South Africa, Inc.

Principal Competitors

Golden State Foods Corporation; J.R. Simplot Company; Martin-Brower Company, LLC.

Further Reading

Canedy, Dana, ''Taking the Plunge; Partners' Big Gamble Pays Off,'' *Cleveland Plain Dealer*, June 1, 1993, p. 1D.

Flint, Troy, ''Minority Entrepreneurs Began Journey with Hope, Risk-Taking,'' *Cleveland Plain Dealer*, November 19, 1998, p. 1C.

Neely, Anthony, ''Fast Success in Fast Foods,'' *Black Enterprise*, June 1992, p. 33.

Payne, Melanie, ''S. Africa Challenge for U.S. Firms/Solon-Based Businessman Finds Maintaining Operation in Country in Transition Is Difficult,'' *Akron Beacon Journal*, November 11, 1996, p. D1.

Pledger, Marcia, ''African-American Firms in Ohio Make Leaders List,'' *Cleveland Plain Dealer*, May 28, 2002, p. C1.

——, ''McEntrepreneur; McDonald's Distributor Makes Burgers His Business from Solon to S. Africa,'' *Cleveland Plain Dealer*, February 17, 1996, p. 1C.

Stella, Phillip J., ''Gamble Pays McDividends: McDonald's Distribution Rookies off to Quick Start,'' *Crain's Cleveland Business*, October 12, 1992, p. 19.

Thompson, Kevin D., ''The Freshman Class of '93,'' *Black Enterprise*, June 1993, p. 131.

—Mary Tradii

Ansell Ltd.

Level 3, 678 Victoria Street
Richmond, Victoria 3121
Australia
Telephone: (03) 9270-7270
Fax: (03) 9270-7300
Web site: http://www.ansell.com

Public Company
Incorporated: 1920 as Dunlop Rubber Company of
  Australia Ltd.
Employees: 12,013
Sales: A$1.29 billion ($880 million)(2003)
Stock Exchanges: Australia New Zealand London
Ticker Symbol: ANN
NAIC: 313320 Fabric Coating Mills; 315299 All Other
  Cut and Sew Apparel Manufacturing; 315999 Other
  Apparel Accessories and Other Apparel; 339113
  Surgical Appliance and Supplies Manufacturing;
  326999 All Other Rubber Product Manufacturing

Ansell Ltd. operates as a multinational company that manufactures, distributes, and markets protective products and services related to professional, occupational, and consumer healthcare. The firm's product line includes surgical and examination gloves, industrial hand protection, household gloves, and condoms. Ansell underwent a major reorganization in the late 1990s and into the 2000s, selling off a host of businesses unrelated to its healthcare-related product group. The firm adopted its current corporate moniker in April 2002, changing its name from Pacific Dunlop Ltd.

Early Roots: Late 1800s

The roots of Pacific Dunlop reach back to Belfast, Ireland. It was there that John Boyd Dunlop based his prosperous veterinary practice. In the course of his work, Dunlop traveled throughout the countryside on often bumpy roads. In order to suffer the "unsprung weight" of his bicycle less and thus ease his travels, Dunlop attached pneumatic tires to his tricycle in 1889. In July of that year, he applied for a patent. Dunlop was soon approached by two businessmen who expressed an interest in forming a company. They purchased the rights to Dunlop's patent and asked William Harvey Du Cros, the president of the Irish Cyclists Association, to serve as president of the new company. He agreed, providing that he could "assume complete control, appoint the directors, write the prospectus, and make the issue to the public."

In November 1889, the Pneumatic Tyre Company and Booth Cycle Agency of Dublin was created with £25,000. Dunlop was allotted 3,000 shares and £500 and was named to the board of directors. Uncertain of the venture's future, however, Dunlop soon returned 1,500 shares.

To the surprise of the newly formed company, Dunlop's patent application was refused—the principal of a pneumatic tire had been patented in 1845, although it remained unused. The name of the company was changed to the Dunlop Pneumatic Tyre Company Ltd. of Dublin, but the business soon moved from Dublin to Coventry, England, and eventually to Birmingham, England. By 1892, the company had offices in Europe and North America.

In 1893, a branch office and factory of the Dunlop business was established in Melbourne, Australia. Semi-assembled tires were sent to the factory, where they were completed. The manager of the factory was 18 years old, and Dunlop's general manager for Australasia was 19 years old. In 1896, the Melbourne factory gained a contract for making hand-assembled pneumatic tires for the Thomson steam car. The offices in England did not see any future in making tires for automobiles, however.

By 1899, the parent company's financial speculation as well as the decline of bicycling popularity led the parent company to sell off its interests in North America and Australasia. In August of that year, the Dunlop Pneumatic Tyre Company of Australasia Ltd. went public on capital of £170,000; 80,000 shares priced at one pound each were offered to the general public. Only 23,000 shares were sold, however, and the unsold stock was purchased by one of the company's backers. The company was registered on August 31, 1899, and was listed on the stock exchanges at Melbourne, Sydney, and Adelaide.

Growth in the Early 1900s

The company grew as the popularity of the automobile grew, and Dunlop expanded its production facilities. In 1906, the company changed its name to the Dunlop Rubber Company of Australasia Ltd. With the coming of World War I, there was a new demand for Dunlop products.

On August 20, 1920, the company was incorporated in Victoria, Australia. By 1927, Dunlop U.K. took a 25 percent equity in its Australasian relative when it purchased 500,000 shares and was given a position on the board of directors. (The equity was reduced over time, however, and the relationship was completely severed in 1984.) Dunlop continued to expand. In 1929, it merged with the Perdriau Rubber Company, a manufacturer of general rubber products that was based in Sydney. That company was founded in 1888 after Henry Perdriau was contracted to supply rubber parts to the railroads of New South Wales. Because of an incorrect invoice, he was sent five times the amount of rubber he had ordered. Perdriau quickly opened a retail store to sell the surplus, and in 1904 he took the business public with £40,000 in capital. By the time it merged with Dunlop, the Perdriau Rubber Company had expanded into a large venture valued at A$3 million. The newly formed company was named Dunlop Perdriau Ltd.

Dunlop Perdriau quickly acquired a controlling interest in Barnet Glass Rubber Company Ltd. Barnet, founded in 1876, originally manufactured waterproof clothing. It expanded to produce other rubber products, and in 1910 it began to make automobile tires. In 1941, Barnet Glass became a wholly owned subsidiary of Dunlop, which again changed its name to Dunlop Rubber Australia Ltd.

Postwar Expansion

After World War II, the company expanded its range of consumer goods in an effort to profit from increased postwar demand; for example, in 1948 Dunlop opened a factory to produce footwear. During the 1960s, the company initiated a continuing effort to diversify, and in 1967 it was renamed Dunlop Australia Ltd. By the end of the decade, it had branched into the manufacture of clothing, textiles, footwear, bedding, and other rubber products. Like many other manufacturers, Dunlop began to move some of its operations offshore. Its first such venture was the Dunlop Papua New Guinea Pty. Ltd., which was established in 1969.

Also in 1969, Dunlop made an acquisition that would later prove to be of central importance to its operations when it purchased the Ansell Rubber Company. Ansell had been founded in Richmond, Australia, in 1905 by a former Dunlop employee, and its first products were balloons and condoms. In 1925, Ansell started to make household rubber gloves, and by 1945 Ansell had created an automated process that could turn out 300 dozen pairs of gloves every eight hours. Ansell actively sought clients in North America and Europe. The advent of disposable surgical gloves in 1964 proved to be a boon for Ansell, and the company's profits soared. Ansell won an export award in 1967 from the Australian Department of Trade and Industry.

During the 1970s, the company consolidated many of its burgeoning operations and streamlined its corporate structure. These moves readied it for another major expansion program that took place throughout the 1980s. In 1980, Dunlop Australia Ltd. renamed itself Dunlop Olympic Ltd. after it acquired Olympic Consolidated Industries Ltd. for A$92.5 million. Olympic, like Dunlop, was a major tire manufacturer in Australia with its own chain of tire stores; the company also made other industrial products. Founded in 1922 and incorporated in 1933 (as the Olympic Tyre and Rubber Company Pty. Ltd.), Olympic started producing tires in 1934 and had expanded to other industrial products by 1949. By the time of its merger with Dunlop, Olympic held 169 tire-store outlets and its post-tax profit had reached A$10.2 million. The tire stores would later come together under the name Beaurepaires for Tyres.

Along with Olympic Consolidated Industries came a 50 percent interest in Olex Cables Ltd.; Dunlop Olympic acquired the remaining 50 percent in 1981 for A$56.8 million. Olex had been founded in 1940 in an effort to meet the wartime demand for insulated cable.

Dunlop Olympic continued to grow when in 1984 it acquired Dunlop New Zealand Ltd. (which manufactured tires, industrial products, and sporting goods) and Olex Canzac Cables, New Zealand's second largest cable manufacturer. By the end of the year, the company had severed its ties with Dunlop U.K. and the technical agreements that had been in effect since 1899 were halted.

A Name Change in 1986

In 1986 Dunlop Olympic Ltd changed its name to Pacific Dunlop Ltd., thus reflecting the company's region-wide aspirations. The company's stock began trading on the London Stock Exchange on December 31st of that year. Pacific Dunlop entered into a joint venture with Goodyear Tire and Rubber Company in 1986 that consolidated the two companies' tire manufacturing, marketing, and retail operations in Australia, New Zealand, and Papua New Guinea under the name South Pacific Tyres. However, the brand names Dunlop, Olympic, and Goodyear were still used, and the tire services—Beaurepaires for Tyres and Goodyear Tyre, Brake, and Clutch Service—continued to be operated independently. In February 1987, shares of Pacific Dunlop Ltd began to be traded on the Tokyo Stock Exchange.

Also in 1987, the company acquired clothing and textile manufacturers and marketers Bonds Industries, which brought under the Dunlop wing many brand names well-known in Australia, including Chesty Bond, Grand Slam, and Gotcha. Pacific Dunlop then acquired a 60 percent interest in GNB Batteries, which was to become a division of the company. Dunlop had first manufactured batteries in 1949, and in 1985 it had acquired the Chloride Group PLC, which had operations in the United States, Canada, Mexico, New Zealand, and Australia, as well as its own manufacturing facilities. With the purchase of GNB

Key Dates:

1889: John Dunlop applies for a patent for pneumatic tires.
1899: Dunlop Pneumatic Tyre Company of Australasia Ltd. goes public.
1906: The company changes its name to the Dunlop Rubber Company of Australasia Ltd.
1929: Dunlop merges with the Perdriau Rubber Company and adopts the name Dunlop Perdriau Ltd.
1967: As part of its diversification effort, the firm changes its name to Dunlop Australia Ltd.
1969: Ansell Rubber Company is acquired.
1980: Dunlop renames itself Dunlop Olympic Ltd. after its purchase of Olympic Consolidated Industries Ltd.
1986: The company becomes Pacific Dunlop Ltd., thus reflecting its region-wide aspirations.
2001: As part of a major restructuring effort, the firm divests its automotive distribution and Pacific Brands clothing businesses.
2002: Dunlop changes its name to Ansell Ltd.

Batteries, Dunlop became one of the world's largest manufacturers of automotive, traction, and stationary batteries. In 1989, it acquired the U.S. battery manufacturers Standard Batteries and Southern Batteries.

Furthering its diversification program, the company in 1988 purchased Nucleus Ltd. and also Telectronic Holdings Ltd., a manufacturer of such health care products as pacemakers and hearing aids. The company went on to acquire a controlling or complete interest in a vast array of manufacturers, including Repco Automotive Parts, Repco Leisure Cycles, Red Robin Industries, Mates Healthcare Ltd., Derby Bicycles, and Slumbertime Bedding. Also in 1988, the company created a manufacturing facility in Colombo, Sri Lanka, to make gloves and condoms, and started construction of a balloon-manufacturing plant in Thailand—examples of the company's efforts to move production offshore.

In 1990, Pacific Dunlop and Goodyear entered into a second joint venture, forming Tecbelt Pacific to manufacture steel-cord conveyor belting. By 1991, Dunlop's Ansell division had become the world's largest producer of medical, industrial, and household gloves. Dunlop diversified further that year by entering the food-manufacturing business when it acquired Petersville Sleigh Ltd., a leading Australian food company, for A$374 million. Petersville Sleigh carried with it many well-known brand names, including Edgell-Birds Eye, Peters Ice Cream, Herbert Adams Bakeries, and Socomin International. Dunlop named its new food division the Pacific Brands Food Group. The following year the company restructured its food division to better position it in the international market—its strategy being to enter growing markets armed with strong brand names on high-profit items. The company also sold a string of Petersville assets. (For example, Pacific Dunlop sold off Eastman, the U.S. stationary and furniture concern, for $142 million in December 1992.)

Dunlop quickly added to its stable of food products. In July 1992, it purchased a 75 percent interest in Pasta House and took 100 percent ownership of International Se Products. In July 1993, Dunlop purchased the Plumrose food-products business in Australia for A$225 million. The agreement carried with it the rights to market several brand names, including Yoplait and Silhouette. At the same time the food division launched its arrival in the Japanese premium ice cream market when, in a partnership with a Japanese company, it sent a shipment of ice cream to Japan worth A$5 million. Dairy and pasta products were examples of upper-end items with high export value.

The company signaled its intention to become a force in the Pacific region when it created the Pacific Rim Advisory Board—which was mandated to seek ways to take advantage of the burgeoning Pacific Rim economy—in 1991. By 1992, Dunlop had investments of more than A$400 million throughout the region, and its total exports were A$144 million.

A major element of Pacific Dunlop's strategy was to strengthen and expand its presence in Asia from A$500 million in 1992 to A$1 billion in the year 2000. A significant component of its Asian gambit was China, where in 1992 its investments totaled A$120 million. Olex Cables held two factories in China that produced cable for its own exploding market as well as for export. In May 1992, Olex Cables won a A$22 million contract to supply optical-fiber cable to link the cities of Chengdu, Xi'an, and Zhengzhou. The next year, it won a A$70 million contract to supply 3,150 kilometers of optical-fiber cable between the Chinese cities of Lanzhou and Yining in northwestern China. By 1993, its factory in the Shenzen economic area, which had started production in 1992, was manufacturing near capacity—nearly 2,500 kilometers of cable daily.

In May 1993, Pacific Dunlop registered a holding company in China—Pacific Dunlop Holdings (China). The Shanghai-based entity was at that time only the third foreign company that had earned the approval to do so. The holding company was created to oversee Pacific Dunlop's investments in that country, which then comprised nine factories. The company sought at least a controlling 51 percent interest in its Chinese ventures. It looked to its Chinese partners to secure the land to build its factories, staff them, and procure orders for them.

By the mid-1990s, Pacific Dunlop Ltd was one of the 20 largest companies in Australia. Its operations spanned more than 20 countries. In 1993, Pacific Dunlop reported sales of A$6.3 billion for the year ending June 30. The company's profits climbed to A$260.4 million, up from A$185.6 million.

During this time period, the company was comprised of eight divisions. The Pacific Brands division focused on consumer products such as footwear (with names such as Grosby, Candy, Pro-Sport, Dunlop, and Hollandia); sporting goods (Dunlop, Repco, Speedwell, Raleigh, and Slazenger); clothing (Chesty Bond, Red Robin, Baby Gro-Wear, Grand Slam, Berlei); and bicycles (Tuf, Adidas, Jockey, Dunlop, Speedwell, Raleigh, and Holeproof).

Pacific Brands Food Group, the food products division, manufactured and marketed products with brand names such as Edgell-Birds Eye, Plumrose, Big Sister, Four 'n Twenty, Leggo, Vitari, and Herbert Adams. Food products were distributed in Australia, New Zealand, and other Pacific Rim nations.

The Distribution division distributed a wide range of electrical products (such as cables) and industrial goods (such as transmission and rubber products). The Medical Group—the health care division—produced pacemakers, implantable defibrillators, and ultrasound equipment. Ansell International produced latex products such as condoms, balloons, and household and medical gloves.

South Pacific Tyres, the automotive division, manufactured and marketed tires under the names Dunlop, Goodyear, Kelley, and Olympic. Tires and other automotive parts were sold through Beaurepaires for Tyres and other outlets. GNB Batteries manufactured and marketed batteries under the brand names Chloride, Dunlop, Masse, Marshall, and Exide in Australia and New Zealand and the Champion, National, Stowaway, and Marshall brands in North America. Industrial Foam and Fibre, the division that manufactured products to be used in building and construction, made industrial rubber products as well as plastics, transmission hoses, foam and fiber products, and bedding (including the Sleepmaker, Serta, and Slumberland brands).

Dramatic Changes in the Late 1990s and Beyond

As a multinational conglomerate, Pacific Dunlop faced challenges in the late 1990s and into the 2000s due to burgeoning debt and faltering profits. While the company continued to bolster certain divisions into the late 1990s, it began to sell off businesses that were not related to its core operations in an attempt to remedy the aforementioned issues. The firm made a move to divest its food business in 1995, along with its RMax, Plastic Group, and Dunlop Flow Technology holdings. In 1996, the company sold its industrial footwear division, its Telectronics Pacing Systems, and its share of its adidas International joint venture.

As the company strengthened the position of its Ansell business unit through strategic acquisitions, Pacific Dunlop began a significant divestiture program that proved to dramatically change the company's structure. In 1998, the firm began to sell off its communications cables business. A leveraged buyout group purchased the company's Olex Cables division in 1999 for A$300 million. Pacific Dunlop also planned to unload its GNB Technologies Battery group that year—the group had been involved in costly litigation in the United States related to the Accufix pacing lead. The deal fell through, however, when Quexco Inc. failed to meet the requirements of the contract.

Pacific Dunlop entered the new century with additional restructuring on the horizon. The company found a buyer for its battery business and in 2000 sold it to Exide Corporation for $333 million. At the same time, management began to set plans in motion to separate its Ansell business—whose product line included surgical gloves, industrial and household protective gloves, and condoms—from its other businesses in an attempt to restore profits. In order to control costs, most of Ansell's manufacturing operations were moved from the United States to Mexico and Asia.

In 2001, the company posted a loss of A$139.4 million, due in part to the deteriorating value of the Australian dollar, problems in the tire industry related to an influx of low-cost imports, and slow growth in many of its business segments. The company's shareholders continued to push for additional changes, since by this time the company's market capitalization had fallen by nearly $4 billion from the mid-1990s.

As such, Pacific Dunlop made several important moves that would position it with one core business revolving around its Ansell Healthcare business unit. By the time the divestiture dust had settled, the company was rid of its Pacific Automotive division, its Pacific Brands unit, and its specialty hose division. The firm opted, however, to retain its investment in the South Pacific Tyres joint venture.

Signaling its commitment to its Ansell holdings, the company officially adopted Ansell Ltd. as its new corporate moniker in April 2002. Harry Boon was elected CEO of the company that year. Under his leadership, the firm implemented a strategic program entitled Operation Full Potential, a directive designed to bolster operations within its three business divisions: Professional Healthcare, Occupational Healthcare, and Consumer Healthcare.

During fiscal 2003, the company's restructuring showed signs of paying off. Ansell reported a profit of $29.3 million, a substantial improvement over the previous year's loss of $60.5 million. While the long-term effects of the firm's strategy remained to be seen, Ansell management was confident that its rebirth positioned it for profitable growth in the years to come.

Principal Divisions

Occupational Healthcare; Professional Healthcare; Consumer Healthcare.

Principal Competitors

MedPointe Inc.; Playex Products Inc.; SSL International plc.

Further Reading

"Ansell Turns Loss into Profit in Major Turnaround," *AsiaPulse News*, August 14, 2003.

"Australia's Pacific Dunlop to Split Operations and Spin Off," *Futures World News*, May 17, 2001.

Foley, Brett, "Dividend Handouts Fits Shareholders Like a Glove," *Australian Financial Review*, August 15, 2003, p. 54.

Jacques, Bruce, "Pacific Dunlop Sells Eastman Stake to U.S.," *Financial Times*, December 8, 1992, p. 23.

"Major Australian Food Groups Map Plans for Stagnant Market," *South China Morning Post*, June 29, 1993, p. 9.

McNulty, Mike, "Shifting Gears; Ansell Emerges From Restructuring with Tight Focus," *Rubber & Plastics News*, December 16, 2002, p. 15.

"New Name and New Focus for Pacific Dunlop," *European Rubber Journal*, May 2002, p. 7.

"Pacific Dunlop Pushes up Profit," *South China Morning Post*, September 11, 1993, p. 2.

"Pacific Dunlop Renamed Ansell," *BERNAMA*, April 13, 2002.

Walker, Tony, "Firm Chinese Foothold for Pacific Dunlop," *Financial Times*, May 8, 1993, p. 24.

Wright, Chris, "Pacific Dunlop Prefers to Issue Little and Often," *Corporate Finance*, August 1999.

—C. L. Collins
—update: Christina M. Stansell

Arnold Clark

Arnold Clark Automobiles Ltd.

134 Nithsdale Drive
Pollokshaws
Glasgow
Lanarkshire G41 2PP
Scotland
Telephone: (+44) 1414-222-700
Fax: (+44) 1414-222-790
Web site: http://www.arnoldclark.co.uk

Private Company
Incorporated: 1954
Employees: 6,000
Sales: £1.4 billion ($2.24 billion)(2003)
NAIC: 532111 Passenger Cars Rental; 441110 New Car Dealers

Arnold Clark Automobiles Ltd. is the leading automobile dealer in Scotland, and the fourth largest in the entire United Kingdom. With more than £1.4 billion in sales in 2003, the company is also Scotland's largest private company. Led by founder Arnold Clark, the company has established a network of nearly 120 new and used car dealerships. Most of the company's showrooms are in Scotland, although England, with nearly 20 showrooms, represents the group's fastest growing territory. Arnold Clark holds franchises from some 20 different car manufacturers; yet the company's large size enables it to offer its own insurance and financing services, in addition to those often imposed by auto makers. The company also owns the property to all of its showrooms. In addition to insurance and financing, the Arnold Clark empire extends to one of Scotland's largest suppliers of automobile parts and accessories; motorcycle and scooter sales; accident and automotive repair services; and car and van rentals. In the latter category, Arnold Clark has been recognized as one of the United Kingdom's leading hire services. Founder Clark, at 76 years of age, shows no signs of letting up (much of the group's growth has come since the late 1990s) nor any intention of stepping down as head of the company. Nonetheless, Clark is supported by a large family, with five of his children taking active roles in the company.

An Honest Car Dealer in the 1950s

Glasgow, Scotland-born Arnold Clark left school at the age of 14 and started his working career as a shoe designer—he designed the tops of shoes—for a retail group known simply as Co-Op. That job enabled the thrifty Clark to save up some £160 before he was called up for military service at the age of 17, joining the Royal Air Force in the late 1940s. During his four years with the RAF, Clark, who later claimed that he did not know how to drive, was trained as a motor mechanic, earning the rank as an NCO Motor Mechanic Instructor.

Upon leaving the army at the age of 21, Clark sought employment in the automobile industry. Clark quickly discovered that he was overqualified for a simple mechanic's position, yet lacked the experience and finances to set up his own business, despite the £160 in savings he had kept throughout his military service. As Clark told the *Sunday Times:* "I had no job and I was petrified. I was technically skilled and determined to get into the car business, but needed to get work to earn some money."

Clark turned to family friend and pub owner Robert Sunderland, who agreed to allow Clark to use Sunderland's drinks license in order to organize dances and other catering functions in the region's Masonic halls and other establishments. For this, Clark put together a traveling bar, and soon had enough business to begin hiring temporary staff. Sunderland, as Clark explained it, remained a major figure in the young Clark's early career, acting as "more my mentor than a boss, teaching me the basics of business, and I taught myself management skills through the employment of casual labor."

Yet Clark remained committed to an entry into the automotive market, and continued building up his savings. By 1953, he had enough money saved to begin buying used cars, then repairing and reselling them from an abandoned shed. Clark's first purchase was a Morris Ten Four, for which he paid £70. After repairing the car himself, Clark turned around and sold it for more than double his purchase price.

Clark not only had to face competition among other car dealers, he also had to confront the decidedly poor public perception of used car dealers at the time. As Clark admitted:

Company Perspectives:

We at Arnold Clark are a committed team of caring professionals. The simple philosophy on which the company was founded in the 1950s remains the aim of the company today—to offer unrivalled value for money and create the highest possible levels of customer satisfaction.

"It was about building a good name, a sound business, and being polite and honest." Clark quickly displayed a knack for personal service, winning customer confidence. As part of that effort, Clark adopted the slogan "Promises Kept."

The Suez Canal crisis and the resulting gasoline shortages provided Clark's springboard to national success. As Clark explained: "One of my biggest breaks came with the Suez crisis, which should have been my downfall. Petrol was rationed and I saw this as an opportunity. I traveled up to Wick in northern Scotland and bought cars on the cheap because demand was low due to petrol shortages, and I sold them for full value in Glasgow where petrol was not so short. I made enough money to open my first showroom."

That showroom opened on Park Road, in Glasgow, in 1956, the first to boast the Arnold Clark signage that shortly was to capture the leading share of the Scottish automotive market. The original Clark showroom remained opened into the next century, despite becoming a money-loser for the company, for sentimental reasons, a rare example of indulgence on the part of Clark and his company. Indeed, throughout the next four decades, Clark maintained a policy of plowing group profits back into the company, enabling it to grow strongly and weather the ups and downs of the U.K. automotive industry.

Joining the Ranks of U.K. Leaders

Clark's growing car sales enabled him to branch out at the end of the 1950s and into the 1960s. In 1959, the company gained its first new car concession, starting sales of Morris automobiles. Two years later, as sales started to climb, the company opened its second showroom. As Clark told *Scotland on Sunday*, "It was very hard to make the first £1000. After that it gets easier."

Clark continued adding new showrooms and franchises at the beginning of the 1960s, and by 1963 the company boasted five showrooms and two new makes, Daimler and the period's hottest car maker, fast-growing Jaguar. Clark was aided by the reluctance of new car dealers to offer used cars at their own showrooms, providing a steady source of new vehicles for Clark's growing automobile empire.

Working six days a week, 12 to 14 hours per day, Clark continued to plow profits back into the business, enabling the group to expand without taking on any significant long-term debt. This allowed the company to expand its network, in part by taking advantage of down cycles in the U.K. economy to buy up struggling car dealerships. By the beginning of the 1990s, Clark's network numbered some 40 dealerships, including most of the major automotive brands.

A strong part of the group's success was its willingness to branch out into a range of extended automotive services. During the 1970s and 1980s, the group began adding new components, including accident towing and body repair services, as well as full-scale automotive repair and maintenance operations. The company also began a parts and accessories service, becoming the largest dealer in that segment in Scotland. Later, Clark developed its own automotive rental service as well. In a related market, the company launched its own motorbike and scooter showrooms. Meanwhile, in the late 1980s, the company decided to take over its advertising and marketing operations, launching its own advertising department to prepare its ads, which generally featured Arnold Clark himself.

Another integral part of the group's success was its willingness to help in customer financing, with Clark himself often putting up funds to back purchases. This led the company into developing its own financing component. From financing, the group entered the insurance market, offering not just automobile insurance, but home and fire insurance policies as well. These latter services, coupled with the group's policy of owning its showroom properties, did not always sit well with a number of automotive manufacturers. The group's growing portfolio of car brands topped 20 makes by the end of the 1990s. Nonetheless, several major names, including upscale brands such as Mercedes and BMW, remained absent from the group's showrooms. Another notable gap was the group's lack of a Ford dealership, despite the brand's strong position in the U.K. market.

By the middle of the 1990s, Clark's empire had topped 45 showrooms throughout Scotland, generating sales of nearly £350 million. Yet the company, which for a time had held a spot among the top ten U.K. car dealers, had slipped down in the national ranks. From about 1996, however, Clark, by then 70 years old, put his business into overdrive. The company started a new, more aggressive dealership campaign, culminating in September of that year with the £7 million purchase of Ewarts of Iverness, which operated four dealerships in Scotland. The deal brought the group's dealership total to 55, as sales soared past £460 million for the year, firmly establishing the company once again among the U.K. top ten.

Clark had set his ambitions higher; by mid-1998, the group's network topped 70 showrooms and included the £6 million purchase of ten dealerships from two Aberdeen-based groups, Corners and Harpers. These acquisitions also helped the group plug a gap in its franchise portfolio, adding Clark's first Ford dealerships.

By 2000, Arnold Clark had cracked the U.K. top five, boasting 90 dealerships, and a growing number of showrooms in England as well. The company's sales had risen accordingly, nearly doubling over the previous three years as the group gunned its engines for the £1 billion sales mark, which would enable it to claim the number one position among privately held Scottish firms.

Clark nearly met its billion-pound goal at the end of 2001. Instead, the company had to wait for the following year, when its sales raced past that mark to top £1.2 billion. Already Scotland's largest dealer, with more than a 15 percent market share, the company stepped up its expansion, building its network to

Key Dates:

1954: Arnold Clark buys his first car, repairs it, and makes his first sale.
1956: Clark establishes his first showroom in Glasgow.
1959: Company receives its first new car franchise, for Morris automobiles.
1963: Company opens a fifth showroom.
1996: Ewarts of Iverness is acquired, boosting dealership network to 55 showrooms.
2003: Annual sales at Clark top £1 billion with 120 show-rooms in Scotland and England.

more than 120 shops by 2003, including nearly 20 in England. With sales of more than £1.4 million, the company had also moved up a notch, taking the number four spot in the entire United Kingdom.

In the meantime, Arnold Clark remained solidly at the helm of the company he'd founded nearly 50 years before. In excellent health, Clark had no plans for retiring soon. With nine children—including five taking part in the company's operations—Clark appeared committed to maintaining the company's privately owned status, and to his own place as sole decision-maker.

Nonetheless, as Clark admitted to the *Evening Times:* "It's a good position to be in, but there are times you feel a little bit lonely and you'd like to ask someone else's advice."

Principal Competitors

Pendragon plc; C D Bramall plc; Reg Vardy plc; RAC plc; Jardine Motors Group plc; Dixon Motors plc; Lookers plc.

Further Reading

Bain, Simon, "Arnold Clark Moves Up a Gear," *Herald* (Glasgow), August 30, 2001, p. 21.
Bowker, John, "Arnold Clark in the Fast Lane as 1bn Pound Turnover Passed," *Scotsman*, February 26, 2003, p. 19.
Calder, Colin, "Arnold's Broken Pounds 1 Billion Barrier," *Evening Times* (Glasgow), February 27, 2003, p. 5.
Darroch, Valerie, "Still a Few Miles to Go On the Clock," *Sunday Herald* (Glasgow), March 30, 2003, p. 4.
——, "The Driving Ambition of Arnold Clark," *Scotland on Sunday,* August 6, 2000, p. B9.
Hamilton, Sheila, "Why Arnold Won't Take His Foot Off the Pedal," *Evening Times* (Glasgow), July 12, 2000, p. 16.
Russell, Scott, "A Family Affair," *Evening Times* (Glasgow), May 2, 1997, p. 69.
Steiner, Rupert, "Car Dealer Hit Road to Top with Traveling Bar," *Sunday Times* (London), March 16, 1997, p. 12.

—M.L. Cohen

ASBURY

AUTOMOTIVE GROUP

Asbury Automotive Group Inc.

Three Landmark Square, Suite 500
Stamford, Connecticut 06901
U.S.A.
Telephone: (203) 356-4400
Fax: (203) 356-4450
Web site: http://www.asburyauto.com

Public Company
Incorporated: 2002
Employees: 7,900
Sales: $4.48 billion (2002)
Stock Exchanges: New York
Ticker Symbol: ABG
NAIC: 44111 New Car Dealers; 44112 Used Car Dealers;
   441229 All Other Motor Vehicle Dealers

Asbury Automotive Group Inc. is the fifth largest automobile retailer in the United States. Its ten regional "platforms," or groups of dealerships, work to achieve economies of scale on such items as newspaper advertising. The company markets 36 different brands of new cars; luxury cars and mid-line imports accounted for a little less than two-thirds of sales. The company operates approximately 100 dealerships in ten states (Arkansas, California, Florida, Georgia, Mississippi, Missouri, North Carolina, Oregon, Virginia, and Texas) and is looking to continue its growth by acquiring more multi-location dealers in booming metro areas.

Origins

Tom Gibson, a former president of Subaru of America Inc., formed Asbury Automotive Group in January 1995. The venture, which was backed by the Toronto investment group Onex Corporation, was a means to build a chain of "megadealers," or automobile retailers with annual sales of $150 million or more. Onex's holdings were diversified and included Sky Chefs, Purolator Courier, and three leading auto suppliers (Automotive Industries, Dura Mechanical, and R.J. Tower Corporation). Asbury was originally based in Conshohocken, Pennsylvania.

Asbury allowed the owners of the dealerships it bought to keep an equity share (between 30 and 49 percent) of the businesses while they continued to manage them. It also sought to identify their "best practices" and share them with its other dealers. "By Merging Visions," according to the company's online vision statement, "we're all better off." Asbury's offers had appeal for retiring owners whose dealerships were too large to sell to local competitors. Asbury sometimes bought single stores to add to its existing chains, buying all the shares of these units.

In February 1995, Asbury formed a joint venture with Jim Nalley Auto Group, which owned 11 dealerships in the Atlanta area. The purchase of Plaza Motors, a luxury auto mall in St. Louis, followed the next month. In August, Asbury acquired a 70 percent interest in the David McDavid Auto Group, a $500 million business in Dallas with 14 dealerships and 17 branches. This brought Asbury's annual sales to $1.3 billion. McDavid Auto, which was officially renamed Asbury Automotive of Texas Ltd. after the acquisition, had been formed in Houston in 1936 and had been family-owned for three generations.

Later in 1995, Timothy Collins, the investment manager in charge of Asbury at Onex Corporation, formed his own company, Ripplewood Holdings L.L.C. (later named Ripplewood Investments L.L.C.), bringing Asbury with him. Asbury's CEO Tom Gibson owned a minority interest in the company; leveraged buyout firm Freeman Spogli & Company Inc. also invested in the business in 1997. Asbury sold 12,000 new cars that year.

By February 1998, Asbury had added deals to buy two leading Florida car dealers, Coggin Automotive Group of Jacksonville and Courtesy Automotive Group of Tampa. Arkansas's McLarty Automotive Group (later renamed North Point), North Carolina's Crown Automotive, and Oregon's Thomason Auto Group were also acquired during the year.

Gibson told *Automotive News* that Asbury was building infrastructures called platform groups as a basis for achieving economies of scale on things such as newspaper advertising in local markets. The shared costs allowed the company to consider acquiring dealers with margins as small as 1 percent, versus the typical 4 percent.

Kendrick Becomes President and CEO in 1999

Brian E. Kendrick was named president and CEO of Asbury Automotive Group in November 1999. He had previously led

Company Perspectives:

Asbury Automotive Group is about more than selling cars—much more. It's about getting and keeping "Customers for Life" by redefining the automotive buying and service experience. We're building long-term relationships by giving car buyers a fair deal and satisfying all of their automotive needs, from financing and insurance to maintenance and repair . . . and then, their next car. Asbury's strategic goal can be summed up as "the best dealers in the best markets with the best brands." Ultimately, though, Asbury is about Merging Visions—the perspectives and industry know-how of hundreds of veteran car dealers, the business savvy of world-class automotive and retailing executives, and even the aspirations and philosophies of successful dealers we'd like to acquire. By Merging Visions, we're all better off—including our customers and our stockholders.

Key Dates:

1994: Asbury Automotive Group is formed with backing from Onex Corporation.
1995: An Onex portfolio manager forms Ripplewood Holdings L.L.C., which includes Asbury Automotive.
1997: Freeman Spogli invests in Asbury.
1999: Former luxury goods executive Brian Kendrick succeeds Tom Gibson as CEO.
2000: Asbury Automotive's corporate structure is streamlined.
2002: Former Limited Inc. COO Kenneth Gilman is named CEO; Asbury goes public.

DFS Group Limited, a luxury goods distributor controlled by LVMH Moët Hennessy Louis Vuitton. He had also been chief operating officer of Sak's Holdings during that company's initial public offering (IPO). Gibson remained on as Asbury's chairman.

Automotive News ranked Asbury the country's second largest dealer chain in 1999. It was the 39th largest private company in the United States. Asbury added four stores in 2000 for a total of 84, reported *Automotive News*. It sold 154,422 new and used cars in that year for revenues of $4.03 billion, up from $1.08 billion the previous year. Profits of $28 million were more than nine times the $3 million the company netted in 1999.

Corporate Structure Streamlined in 2000

In April 2000, Asbury streamlined its corporate structure from eight individual companies to just one, as the Oregon platform changed its name to Asbury Automotive Group, L.L.C. and became the parent company. A depressed stock market led Asbury to keep its plans for an IPO, always considered an eventual possibility, on hold.

Two dealerships in the Jackson, Mississippi, market, Gray-Daniels Ford and Metro Mazda-Hyundai-Suzuki-Isuzu, were added in the first half of 2001. Asbury created its ninth regional platform to include these with its nearby Mark Escude dealerships, which had previously been part of the Arkansas platform. The Jackson dealers were re-branded under the Gray-Daniels Auto Family name. Tom Wimberley Auto World was added later in the year. Asbury also acquired Kelly Pontiac-GMC of Jacksonville, Florida, in late 2001; it became part of the Coggin Automotive Group.

The threat of car lots losing business to Internet auto retailers was perceived as less of a threat after the collapse of tech stocks. In August 2001, Asbury's leadership felt the time was right to bring their shares to market. It was the first IPO from a brick-and-mortar car dealership since 1998. Company executives described the auto dealer business as resistant to down cycles in the economy, since they also provided auto repairs, parts, and used cars for people concerned with saving money.

Asbury's own online marketing strategy emphasized individual web sites for its dealers, rather than a unified national brand. Features such as searches of inventories and Blue Book values were shared, however. Asbury hired one web developer to oversee all its dealers' web sites.

Going Public in 2002

Kenneth B. Gilman, former chief operating officer at The Limited Inc., became Asbury's president and CEO in January 2002. On March 14, Asbury's initial public offering finally arrived on the New York Stock Exchange. The company then had 91 dealerships in nine states (Arkansas, Florida, Georgia, Mississippi, Missouri, North Carolina, Oregon, Virginia, and Texas). Asbury was the nation's third largest dealership group.

One of Asbury's selling points was the vast, untapped market controlled by private car dealers. The 100 largest groups accounted for less than 10 percent of the $1 trillion new car market in the United States. Asbury posted net income of $43.8 million on revenues of $4.3 billion in 2001.

Twenty-one percent of the company's shares were offered, priced at $16.50. The IPO raised $127 million. Most of the proceeds went to insiders selling shares, while some were earmarked for paying down the company's $550 million credit line. The company's total debt load was $987.1 million. Share price rose only slightly in the first day of trading, reflecting a lackluster stock market in general. Ripplewood and Freeman Spogli each owned slightly more than a quarter of shares after the offering.

Operationally, Asbury was embracing customer relationship management (CRM), a series of practices designed to encourage repeat business by following data about customers' buying habits. It was much cheaper to retain a customer than to recruit a new one, reported *Ward's Auto Business*.

Another unique marketing effort was the opening of five used car lots at Wal-Mart Supercenters near Houston, Texas. Under the name Price 1 Auto Store, the lots were meant to capture some of the large amount of foot traffic that visited the giant department stores every day. However, Asbury found that not enough of these patrons were interested in lingering to consider an automobile purchase, and the venture was closed down after a year.

Asbury sold 96,000 new vehicles in 2002 for revenues of $4.5 billion. This ranked it fifth in an *Automotive News* survey of the top dealership groups in the United States. According to *Automotive News,* in spite of the downturn in car sales in 2002, publicly held dealer groups like Asbury had a more difficult time finding owners willing to sell their dealerships. However, Asbury was able to enter the California market by acquiring a half-dozen dealerships from Bob Baker of San Diego for $88 million in cash and stock. This deal was amended to drop one Bob Baker store which sold Ford cars after Ford voiced objections to the sale. This deal was not closed until 2003.

In 2003, Asbury built its holdings in North Carolina, adding dealerships in High Point and Charlotte to its Crown Automotive Company platform. It entered the robust Charlotte market through the acquisition of LaPointe Honda/Mitsubishi, the oldest Honda dealer in the Carolinas. Honda was the best-selling of the 36 brands of car Asbury's dealers sold. Asbury was on track to add $300 million per year to its revenues through acquisitions.

Principal Operating Units

Bob Baker Auto Group; Coggin Automotive Company; Courtesy Dealership Group; Crown Automotive Company; David McDavid Automotive Group; Gray-Daniels; Nalley Automotive Group; North Point; Plaza Motor Company; Thomason Auto Group.

Principal Competitors

AutoNation Inc.; Group 1 Automotive Inc.; Hendrick Automotive Group; Sonic Automotive Inc.; VT Inc.

Further Reading

Banks, Cliff, "Dealership Group Tests the CRM Waters . . . Cautiously," *Ward's Dealer Business*, August 2002, p. 12.

Box, Terry, "Dallas-Area Auto Businessman Leaves Corporation That Bought His Dealerships," *Dallas Morning News*, August 2, 2003.

Crabtree, Penni, "Sale of Auto Chain Is Flagged Again," *San Diego Union-Tribune*, June 11, 2003, p. C3.

Craver, Richard, "High Point, N.C. Auto Dealership Gets New Ownership," *High Point Enterprise,* November 5, 2002.

——, "Auto Dealership Grows in High Point, N.C., Again," *High Point Enterprise*, January 2, 2003.

Egbert, Dan, "Stamford, Conn.-Based Asbury Automotive Group Raises $127 Million in IPO," *News & Observer* (Raleigh, NC), March 15, 2002.

Eldridge, Earle, "Auto Dealer Groups Have Cash to Grow," *USA Today*, February 26, 2002, p. 6B.

Gebolys, Debbie, "Ex-Limited Exec to Lead Automotive Group," *Columbus Dispatch* (Ohio), January 4, 2002, p. 1F.

Harris, Donna, "Gibson to Buy Megadeals: Canadians Backing Ex-Subaru Chief," *Automotive News*, January 23, 1995, p. 1.

——, "Chain Thinks Nationally, Acts Locally," *Automotive News*, October 16, 2000, p. 3.

——, "Stakes Are Higher for Auto Retailing IPOs," *Automotive News*, March 18, 2002, p. 4.

——, "Buyers Want Stores, But Dealers Aren't Selling," *Automotive News*, October 14, 2002, p. 4.

——, "Asbury Has Second Chance to Buy Baker Chain; 'Ticked Off' Dealer Says He Will Exclude Ford Store from Deal," *Automotive News*, August 11, 2003, p. 4.

Henry, Jim, "Acquisitions Alter Retail Landscape," *Automotive News*, August 4, 1997, p. 6.

——, "Depressed Market Makes IPO Decision Easy for Asbury," *Automotive News*, December 4, 2000, p. 30.

Herzog, Boaz, "Well-Known Portland, Ore. Automobile Pitchman Resigns from Post," *Oregonian*, December 5, 2002.

Keenan, Tim, "Megadealers High on the List Use the Hometown Approach Despite Their Size," *Ward's Dealer Business*, May 2001, p. 9.

Krebs, Michelle, "Dealer Says Staying Private Has Some Advantages," *Automotive News*, February 9, 1998, p. 60.

Lee, Wendy, "Wal-Mart, Car Dealer Part Ways in Texas," *Houston Chronicle*, July 11, 2003.

Moore, Heidi, "Asbury Automotive Trades Up Slightly in IPO," *Daily Deal*, March 14, 2002.

Musero, Frank, "Asbury Auto Puts Pedal to Metal, Races Toward IPO," *IPO Reporter*, August 6, 2001.

Plume, Janet, "Ranking Slipped; It Was a Wakeup Call," *Automotive News*, February 8, 1999, p. 38.

Renteria, Melissa, "West Orange, Texas Used Car Lot Has Strong Sales for First Four Months," *Beaumont Enterprise*, September 19, 2002.

Sawyers, Arlena, "Groups Map Strategies to Buy Dealer Chains," *Automotive News*, August 28, 1995, p. 8.

——, "Size Does Matter to Dealers: Public Groups Rule; Big Deals Get Bigger," *Automotive News*, April 20, 1998, p. 1.

Smith, David, " 'Megadealerships' Shape New Car Market in Arkansas," *Arkansas Democrat-Gazette*, March 27, 2001.

—Frederick C. Ingram

Association of Junior Leagues International Inc.

132 West 31st Street, 11th Floor
New York, New York 10001
U.S.A.
Telephone: (212) 951-8300
Fax: (212) 481-7196
Web site: http://www.ajli.org

Nonprofit Organization
Incorporated: 1901 as the Junior League for the
Promotion of Settlement Movements
Sales: $20 million (2002 est.)
NAIC: 813319 Other Social Advocacy Organizations

The Association of Junior Leagues International Inc. is the umbrella group for close to 300 local chapters of one of the nation's oldest and best-known women's volunteer organizations. Junior Leagues operate in cities across the United States, with half the members concentrated in southern states and the rest spread through other regions of the country. In addition, the group has chapters in Canada, Mexico, and in the United Kingdom. Junior League members are involved in a host of different charitable activities, many specifically benefiting women and children. Many Junior Leagues are active particularly in issues relating to children's health and education, including the financing of a children's hospital in Nashville and the running of a special school for children with speech problems in Atlanta. Junior League projects are quite various, and are carried out independently by local chapters. Some core concerns of the Junior League are family literacy, transitional housing, affordable and accessible daycare, caregiver education, and breast and ovarian cancer prevention, among others. All Junior League work is carried out by volunteers, often in association with other charitable groups such as the Red Cross. The group is financed by member dues, by fundraising activities such as charity balls, and by individual and corporate donations. Membership is open to women who commit to a certain amount of training and volunteer hours. Total Junior League membership is more than 190,000 women.

Founding in the Aftermath of a Ball

The Junior League was founded in New York City in 1901 by 19-year-old Mary Harriman. Harriman was from an extraordinarily privileged background. Her father, Edward H. Harriman, had made a fortune in railroads. Harriman's brother Averill went on to become governor of New York. While Mary Harriman was a freshman at Barnard College, she had her traditional "coming out" ball, a fancy dress affair that left her the next day aswim in bouquets of roses presented by her admirers. Harriman was apparently agitated by the waste of the flowers, which would soon fade, and she organized a group of friends to distribute the bouquets to patients in hospitals. Harriman soon formalized a group of 80 or so of her friends into what she named the Junior League for the Promotion of Settlement Movements. The settlement movement had gotten its start at the end of the 19th century with Jane Addams. Addams encouraged women to work to solve the problems of poverty in the cities, and settlement houses provided services such as daycare for working mothers. Harriman's group took the epithet "Junior" because the founding members were young. Later the group lost the specific association with the settlement movement and became simply the Junior League, though social work continued to be the focus of the group's activities.

Harriman's Junior League seemed to provide a needed outlet for young women in New York. Harriman wrote in the group's 1906 annual report, "It seems almost inhuman that we should live so close to suffering and poverty, that we should know of the relief work that exists within a few blocks of our home, and bear no part in this great life." Women like Harriman, who were wealthy and educated, were not expected to hold paying jobs, but it was acceptable to volunteer. The New York Junior League helped to find housing for young working women, brought dental care to children, and taught classes in art and music for poor children. Eleanor Roosevelt, one of six Junior League members to become First Lady, joined the Junior League in 1903, and taught dance and exercise classes. The Junior League quickly spread to other cities. Boston opened a chapter in 1907, and in 1910 Brooklyn, New York, and Portland, Oregon started Junior Leagues. By the early 1920s, there were more than 80 chapters spread across the United States.

Company Perspectives:

The Association of Junior Leagues International Inc. is an organization of women committed to promoting voluntarism, developing the potential of women and improving communities through the effective action and leadership of trained volunteers. Its purpose is exclusively educational and charitable.

The focus of the early Junior Leagues varied from group to group, but most issues related to health and education. The Brooklyn Junior League was instrumental in getting its community Board of Education to provide free lunches to public school children. Other groups worked on the campaign for women's suffrage. During World War I, the groups turned to war relief. In conjunction with the YWCA (Young Women's Christian Association), some Junior League members went to Europe to support the troops. The Junior League in San Francisco started a motorized delivery service that became the model for the Red Cross Motor Corps. In 1921 the various Junior League groups were put together under the Association of Junior Leagues International, headquartered in New York. The group was truly international, as the first Canadian group had gotten its charter in Montreal a few years earlier. The first Junior League in Mexico joined in 1930.

Fighting a White Gloves Image Mid-Century

Although community action was the core of the Junior League, from its earliest days the group also was seen as a blue-blood domain, its members pampered and privileged, more interested in appearing in the society pages than in truly changing society. In most groups, prospective members had to be nominated by two existing members, and this system ensured a certain homogeneity in those who joined. For most of its early history, the Junior League was overwhelmingly white and Protestant, and the New York group, which was for a long time the largest, had a reputation for containing only upper-crust, fashionable young women. The New York group built a $1.2 million home for itself in 1929 that had a swimming pool and a squash court. It was supposed to contain a nursery for children whose parents were ill or unable to care for them, but the posh clubhouse was evidently more known for its elegant Persian Room and hair salon than for its daycare center. Other groups outside of New York were far more modest, meeting in garages or in municipal buildings.

In the 1920s, many Junior Leagues instituted children's theater groups. The Chicago chapter first tried a children's theater project, and within a few years, more than 100 Junior League chapters made this a prime activity. Junior League fundraisers often came in the form of a "Follies" night, where League members put on a musical or dramatic show. Junior Leagues in many cities also became famous for elaborate balls, put on to raise money for League charitable projects. This kind of gala event helped fix the image of the Junior League as more or less aristocratic. Meanwhile, Junior League projects were often not only needful but less than glamorous. In the 1930s, during the worst years of the Great Depression, Junior Leagues

ran soup kitchens and milk stations. Junior League volunteers also staffed or funded birth control clinics and training schools for nurses, as well as daycare centers for working mothers. In the 1930s the Junior Leagues also became more broadly politically active, forming Public Affairs committees that worked to track and influence legislation relating to public welfare policy. During World War II the Junior League was instrumental in finding women to fill civilian jobs left vacant by men who were fighting overseas. The Association of Junior Leagues International's executive director in the war years, Katherine Van Slyck, eventually became the head of the federal Office of Civilian Defense.

By the end of the 1940s, the Junior League boasted 47,000 members in 159 cities in the United States, plus several international chapters. The Junior League had many projects to be proud of, including a veterans rehabilitation center in Los Angeles, a school for speech therapy in Atlanta, a blood bank in Milwaukee, and group homes for troubled children in Detroit and St. Louis. But the Junior League was still plagued by its reputation as a haven for wealthy do-gooders; for some members, charitable work consisted of donating used clothing to League thrift shops. Other Junior League members confessed to being poorly trained for social work, or to being set tasks of dubious usefulness such as clipping photos out of magazines. In 1948 the Junior League launched a concerted campaign to refocus its energies on concrete projects, and to change its image with the press and public. The New York Junior League sold its clubhouse that year, finding that the luxurious building detracted from the message the group wanted to present. The League put out a pamphlet for its members called "How to Get Off the Society Page," and individual chapter members across the country met with newspaper editors to ask for more coverage of their charitable projects and less emphasis on their names and faces. The League also standardized its training program for new members and instituted stricter minimum requirements for how much charitable work members must take on. In addition, the group developed stricter guidelines for new groups wanting to become Junior League chapters. One national Junior League officer told the *Saturday Evening Post* (February 7, 1948) how petitioning chapters had previously been selected: "We took them in if we liked their handwriting and their stationery," she told the reporter. Starting in 1948, the group instituted a three-year process in which groups wanting to become Junior Leagues had to be inspected annually and comply with a program of community service.

Adapting to New Roles for Women: 1970s–80s

The group continued to grow strongly in the postwar years. By the early 1960s, the Junior League had more than 200 chapters and 88,000 members. However, as more and more women began working for pay in the 1960s and 1970s, the volunteer group began to seem in some cases outdated. When Mary Harriman began the Junior League, educated women had few options for a career outside the home. As professional jobs opened up to women, the Junior League had difficulty attracting new young members. One woman who became the director of the Association of Junior Leagues' Washington office in the 1990s told *Town & Country* (May 1993) that she had been ashamed to join the Junior League in the 1970s and had kept it

Key Dates:

1901: The Junior League for the Promotion of Settlement Movements is founded in New York by Mary Harriman.

1921: The Association of Junior Leagues International is formed.

1948: The New York chapter sells its luxurious clubhouse.

1978: The admissions policy is revamped.

2001: The group co-chairs the International Year of the Volunteer effort in the United States.

secret from her friends. In the 1970s the group also was forced to grapple with the fact of its homogeneous membership. Rose Kennedy, mother of President John F. Kennedy, had been denied membership in the Junior League in her day, presumably because she was Catholic. The Junior League began to accept its first African American members in the late 1960s, but these women often faced considerable opposition. In an era of heightened racial politics, the overwhelmingly white face of the Junior League did little to enhance its reputation for committed social work. In 1978, the League's national conference voted to do away with the mandatory admissions policy, which had required two current members to sponsor a prospective member. Some local groups promptly changed to an open admissions policy, letting anyone join who would devote the necessary hours to League projects. Some chapters clung to the old policy, but gradually through the 1980s the Junior League began accepting Jewish and Catholic women, African Americans, and Hispanics.

By the mid-1980s, the Junior League's membership looked rather different from what it had 20 years earlier. *Newsweek* (August 11, 1986) sweepingly declared that "most of its 163,000 members are still from well-to-do families," yet half held paying jobs. These were often professional women with demanding careers, as opposed to the earlier League image of women who defined themselves as the wives of professional men. And the group became more politically vocal in the 1980s. The stature of the Junior League was lifted to new heights when a member, Sandra Day O'Connor, became the first female justice on the Supreme Court in 1981. The Junior League maintained a full-time lobbyist in its Washington office to argue for or propose legislation to Congress. The Junior League was influential in the 1980s in helping to pass the first federal legislation dealing with domestic violence. The group also focused on child welfare issues, and began a broad campaign in the 1980s to address the problems of women and alcohol abuse. Some chapters made concerted efforts to get Junior League members elected to state and local office. Individual chapters were often powerful fundraisers. The Kansas City Junior League alone, for example, raised $525,000 in 1985, from selling cookbooks and staging a ball.

Heading into the 21st Century

By the early 1990s, the Junior League was still going strong, with 190,000 members and an administrative budget of more

than $7 million. Collectively, the Junior League chapters raised approximately $20 million annually. Some 250 Junior League members or former members held elected office, including four women in Congress. The Junior League continued to be involved in a range of community service projects, from mural painting and playground repair to teen outreach programs and the funding of children's hospitals. The group added members over the 1990s, and made strides in attracting a more diverse population. By 1999, only slightly more than 70 percent of the group's membership was Protestant. The new president of the Association of Junior Leagues International beginning in 1998 was a Cuban-American woman, Clotilde Dedecker. Dedecker flouted Junior League stereotypes. She was an immigrant whose family had fled to the United States with virtually no money. Dedecker had benefited personally from charity showered on her family when she was a child, and she was at pains to dispel the clinging perception of Junior League members as cosseted wives with time on their hands for good works.

The Junior League celebrated its centennial in 2001. The group continued to focus on issues relating to women and children, including domestic violence, rape, AIDS prevention, and community theater and arts programs. The group had established more rigorous expectations of its members. New members now received six months of training, and then were expected to commit to at least two and a half hours a week of volunteer work. The United Nations designated 2001 the International Year of the Volunteer, and the Junior League was co-chair of the United States committee for the program. The Junior League adopted a new logo in 2002 as part of a public relations campaign to burnish the image of the organization. The group's new leader, Christine Benero, began an initiative called Healthy League, aimed at helping individual chapters become more effective.

Further Reading

Amory, Cleveland, "The Junior League Gets Tough," *Saturday Evening Post,* February 7, 1948, pp. 33–34, 89.

Bumiller, Elisabeth, "Reshaping the Image of the Junior League," *New York Times,* August 24, 1999, p. B2.

Cleveland, Kathleen Parker, "A League of Their Own," *Town & Country,* May 1993, pp. 70–72, 126–128.

Conant, Jennet, et al., "No More White Gloves," *Newsweek,* August 11, 1986, pp. 42–43.

Franklin, Barry M., "Women's Voluntarism, Special Education, and the Junior League," *History of Education,* September 2000, p. 415.

Gibbs, Nancy R., "High Noon for Women's Clubs," *Time,* May 30, 1988, p. 72.

Green, Penelope, "100 Years Old and Still an Ingénue," *New York Times,* January 28, 2001, Sec. 9, p. 4.

"Junior Mrs.," *Newsweek,* May 18, 1964, pp. 70–72.

Kavelman, Buff, "The Junior League Comes of Age," *Classic American Homes,* February/March 2001, p. 20.

Lightsey, Ed, "A League of Their Own," *Georgia Trend,* August 2002, p. 25.

Logue, Ann C., "The Junior League Wants You!," *T&D,* June 2001, p. 62.

Marks, Peter, "The Gloves Are Off, Sleeves Rolled Up," *New York Times,* January 16, 1994, Sec. 9, pp. 1, 5.

—A. Woodward

Bank Leumi le-Israel B.M.

24-32 Yehuda Halevy Street
Tel-Aviv 65546
Israel
Telephone: (972) 3 514-8111
Toll Free: (800) 892-5340
Fax: (972) 3 514-8656
Web site: http://english.leumi.co.il

Public Corporation
Incorporated: 1902 as Anglo-Palestine Co. Ltd.
Employees: 11,457
Total Assets: NIS 248.2 billion ($52.38 billion) (2002)
Stock Exchanges: Tel Aviv
NAIC: 522110 Commercial Banking; 522210 Credit Card
Issuing; 522310 Mortgage and Other Loan Brokers;
523110 Investment Banking and Securities Dealing;
523120 Securities Brokerage; 523920 Portfolio
Management; 523991 Trust, Fiduciary and Custody
Activities; 525110 Pension Funds

Bank Leumi le-Israel B.M., Israel's second-largest bank, has its origins in the modern Zionist movement of the late 19th century and issued the nation's currency during its early years of independence. A full-service commercial bank, it also has subsidiaries engaged in such activities as issuing debentures, making loans for agriculture and industrial development, and offering mortgage loans, insurance, and a full range of investment, trust, and banking services, including managing portfolios and underwriting stock issues. It also invests directly in about 35 Israeli businesses and companies. Bank Leumi has five foreign subsidiaries and offices in 19 countries.

Origins and Evolution

The Jewish Colonial Trust was established in 1899 by the Second Zionist Congress with the intention to raise enough money to extend a loan to the government of the Ottoman Empire in return for a charter giving overseas Jews the legal right to settle in and develop Palestine. It was not successful in this goal but in 1902 founded Anglo-Palestine Co. Ltd., a bank

incorporated that year in London. The following year, an office of the bank was opened in Palestine. Anglo-Palestine's meager resources did not allow it to function as the investment bank envisioned but as a commercial bank only, dealing almost exclusively in short-term credit for trade, services, and handicrafts. Nevertheless, the bank had opened five more branches in Palestine by 1914 and also one in Beirut, Lebanon, the financial and commercial center of the region. It also established a network of credit cooperative societies and played an important role in financing land purchases and settlement in Haifa, Jerusalem, and what became Tel Aviv.

In the aftermath of World War I, Palestine passed from Turkish to British rule. In 1921, Anglo-Palestine established its first subsidiary, a mortgage bank. The parent company formally changed its name to Anglo-Palestine Bank in 1930. By 1936, there were 32,000 deposit accounts. The bank expanded tremendously during World War II, and by the end of the war it held about half of all bank deposits in Palestine. It founded subsidiaries for agricultural and industrial development in the latter part of the war and also an investment subsidiary to deal in securities and grant long-term loans to local authorities and institutions. Anglo-Palestine Bank helped finance the struggle for independence from the British that followed World War II. As a consequence, Palestine was expelled from the pound sterling area, and the bank issued its own fully backed notes as currency. When Israel became independent in 1948, Anglo-Palestine retained the exclusive right to issue notes and was made the new government's sole banker and financial agent, remaining so until 1954, when a central bank, the Bank of Israel, was created. Since Anglo-Palestine was a foreign chartered company, a new Israeli-based one, Bank Leumi le-Israel B.M., was incorporated in its place in 1954.

Bank Leumi grew from 14 branches in 1948 to 53 at the end of 1954, when it also had representatives in New York, London, and Zurich. These cities subsequently became headquarters for foreign subsidiaries of the bank. A French subsidiary bank, headquartered in Paris, was founded in 1972 and one in Luxembourg in 1994. By the end of 1975 Bank Leumi had 307 branches, of which 293 were within Israel. This expansion was partly the result of acquiring other banks and credit cooperative societies, including the Union Bank of Israel, the Arab-Israel Bank, and Bank Kupat-Am. Bank Leumi issued its first credit card in 1978.

The following decade was an extremely difficult one for Bank Leumi, during which it lost its position as Israel's largest bank to Bank Hapoalim B.M. Israeli bank shares accounted for more than half of the stocks traded on the Tel Aviv Stock Exchange and were said to be the backbone of the national economy. The leading Israeli banks had greatly enhanced the value of their shares by buying their own stock. In October 1983, however, stockholders, fearing an imminent devaluation of the shekel—Israel's national currency—rushed to convert their bank shares into dollars. Panic selling of these stocks resulted in a two-week suspension of trading. The government then stepped in, taking over $6.9-billion worth of bank stock and promising to pay for them, with interest, over several years. Bank Leumi lost money in only one year but angered Israelis in 1986 when its chairman negotiated a ''golden parachute'' of $5 million in severance pay plus an annual pension of $360,000. Public outrage forced the entire board of directors to resign.

In accordance with its program to privatize major bank holdings, the government sold 22.4 percent of Bank Leumi in a 1993 public offering that reduced its stake to 72.6 percent. It also sold 60 percent of Union Bank, which was jointly owned with Bank Leumi, to a group of private investors. Appointed chief executive officer of Bank Leumi in 1995, Galia Maor became the first female head of an Israeli bank and the first woman to wield so much influence in Israel since Golda Meir had been premier in the 1970s. Her program to improve the bank's slim profit margin was to emphasize corporate rather than retail banking and to invest in electronic home banking in order to reduce reliance on costly branches. Bank Leumi already had closed nearly one-third of its 67 foreign branches since 1983 and had suffered heavy losses in the United States because of bad loans. During Maor's first seven years in office, the bank staff was cut by about 15 percent.

By the end of 2002, the government had reduced its stake in Bank Leumi to 41.73 percent and was seeking—as it had for years—to dispose of the rest. Another 28.08 percent of the common stock was in public hands. The government also had weakened the grip of Israel's banks on the national economy by legislation reducing their holdings engaged in non-banking activities. Bank Leumi established a global private-banking unit, with $30 billion under its management, in 2002.

Bank Leumi in the United States: 1954–2002

Bank Leumi opened an office on New York City's Wall Street in 1954 and formed First Israel Bank and Trust Company there in

1968, receiving a state charter, with an initial $75 million in assets and $67 million in deposits. Branches were established in Manhattan's garment district in 1969 and on Fifth Avenue in midtown, only steps from the heart of the diamond-and-jewelry district, in 1971. The bank changed its name to Bank Leumi Trust Company of New York in 1973 and offered free checking for its customers.

By 1976, Bank Leumi ranked 18th in size among banks in the state of New York, with deposits of between $700 million and $800 million and loans in excess of $300 million. Financing international trade, in large part between the United States and Israel, accounted for about half its business. In that year, the bank acquired scandal-ridden American Bank & Trust Company for $12.6 million. Acquisition of the bank, which was in receivership, included four or five branches and gave Bank Leumi a foothold in the Bronx and Brooklyn. The following year, it expanded to Long Island by opening a branch in Hewlett, and in 1978 it opened another in Great Neck. The bank now also had a representative office in Toronto and offshore branches in Nassau, Bahamas, and George Town, Cayman Islands.

Bank Leumi purchased 13 city branches from Bankers Trust Company in 1980 and the following year added another in Plainview, Long Island, reaching what proved to be its maximum extent of 25 branches in the United States. By 1984, Bank Leumi Trust Company of New York had some $2.7 billion in assets. Its advertising theme, ''The Bank You Can Believe In,'' was intended to attract Jews without excluding other potential customers. ''Some people need a little help getting to the Promised Land,'' read an ad for the bank's Individual Retirement Accounts. ''If you dream of retiring to a land of milk and honey,'' it closed, ''you're going to need plenty of bread.'' Branches in heavily Jewish neighborhoods shut down early on Friday for the Jewish Sabbath and opened again on Sunday. Three other Israeli banks had subsidiaries or offices in the city, but these, unlike Bank Leumi, emphasized commercial loans rather than retail accounts. Bank Leumi was working to extend its commercial reach by targeting small and medium-sized businesses.

Bank Leumi entered Westchester County in 1986 with a branch in White Plains. By now, it was the largest of New York City's banks aimed at ethnic customers such as the Irish, Italians, or Puerto Ricans. Employing more than 100 loan officers, it was, in 1987, making a major effort to find customers in the diamond, apparel, fur, and real-estate industries, which were Jewish-dominated sectors centered in Manhattan. However, some 70 percent of these loans were below $100,000. When the U.S. economy sank into recession at the beginning of the 1990s, many of these small businesses began to fail. Bank Leumi lost $48.6 million in 1990 and by midsummer 1991 had $243 million in bad loans, nearly 10 percent of its assets. Yet another $350 million in bad loans were transferred by the parent company to a separate unit, BLN Corporation, within the U.S. holding company Bank Leumi le-Israel Corporation. These missteps were attributed to Bank Leumi's desire to keep its customers happy in a competitive environment, but in part the bank was criminally lax.

Some 30,000 small and unprofitable accounts were shed during 1992–93 as Bank Leumi essentially withdrew from retail banking, selling or closing all branches but the flagship Fifth Avenue headquarters and the one in the garment district between 1993 and 1996. Bank Leumi had, in 1991, decided on a

---

Key Dates:

1902: Anglo-Palestine Co. Ltd. is founded as a bank to serve Jews in the Holy Land.

1945: Now Anglo-Palestine Bank, it holds about half of all bank deposits in Palestine.

1948: Anglo-Palestine is the sole banker for the government of newly independent Israel.

1968: A subsidiary bank is chartered in New York.

1975: Bank Leumi—successor to Anglo-Palestine—now has 307 branches.

1983: The government takes over Israel's banks to avert a financial collapse.

1991: The U.S. subsidiary has accumulated $600 million in bad loans.

2002: The Israeli government has reduced its holding in Bank Leumi to 42 percent.

---

major shift in focus with Premier Banking, targeted to the upscale customer affluent enough to deposit a minimum of $25,000. Those prepared to deposit at least $250,000 were offered a more customized approach. Special bank teams for textiles, real estate, and diamonds and jewelry targeted companies and top executives in these industries, offering to serve their needs with loans, letters of credit, cash management, and collection services. Some of these individuals represented the second and third generations of family-owned businesses.

Only 300 employees remained when Bank Leumi Trust Company of New York changed its name to Bank Leumi USA in 1997. As part of another reorganization, Bank Leumi USA assumed control of the parent company's branches in Chicago and Beverly Hills and Encino in California. The BLN unit was liquidated in 1998. By 2001, private banking was Bank Leumi's fastest-growing area and composed more than 40 percent of its income. The bank was also serving 250 middle-market clients and had some $4 billion in assets. In 2001, it opened a branch in San Jose, California—headquarters for Silicon Valley—because many high-technology companies were trading with their Israeli counterparts. Also in 2001, the bank established Leumi Investment Services, a brokerage subsidiary. In 2002, it acquired a Miami branch of parent Bank Leumi le-Israel that collected deposits from non-U.S. citizens and added $6 million worth of assets and $23 million of deposits purchased from the failed Net First National Bank of Boca Raton, which then became the site of another branch. Bank Leumi USA saw Florida as a growth area because its parent had offices throughout Latin America and wanted to expand its trade-related business in that market from the United States.

At its Manhattan headquarters, Bank Leumi hired a new marketing director in 2002 who was charged with raising the bank's profile among all ethnic groups. "We still advertise in certain ethnic publications, but they're not just Jewish anymore," she told Ben Jackson of *American Banker*. "I've tried to make the advertising more sophisticated so it appeals across the board." Zalman Siegel, chief executive officer, said the typical bank customer was still the owner of a small business specializing in apparel or diamonds and jewelry, but these clients were not as likely to be Jewish as in the past. Segal said many of the bank's customers were Indians who often bought and sold diamonds in India. The bank even sponsored at least one conference for diamond dealers of Indian descent.

Bank Leumi in 2002

In 2002, Bank Leumi had, including its subsidiaries, close to 300 branches and offices, with some 44 of them located abroad. It was organized along four business lines. Corporate and international banking consisted of a corporate division managing the activity of the bank's large business customers and multinational companies. It also held responsibility for the international finance and foreign trade sector at the bank and financing for the diamond sector. The international division was responsible for most activity overseas. Another division managed the activity of large business customers mainly engaged in construction and real estate. The banking division managed the activity of private and small commercial customers. The commercial banking division was managing the activity of middle-market companies. The global private banking division managed the activity of affluent customers and included private banking centers in Israel, tourist branches, trust services, securities trading, and the subsidiaries in Switzerland and Luxembourg. The investments division was responsible for developing financial and investment products, research relating to the capital and money markets, and managing the bank's 16 provident funds.

Bank Leumi's own investment portfolio included holdings in a television channel, high-technology companies, real estate, office equipment, consumer products, clothing and fashion accessories, chemicals, shipping, and energy. It also owned 20 percent of one of the largest insurance groups in Israel. In all, Bank Leumi had revenues of NIS8.13 billion ($1.73 billion) in 2002 and a long-term debt of NIS10.42 billion ($2.2 billion). Its total assets came to NIS248.2 billion ($52.38 billion), of which 86 percent were in Israel and 9 percent in the United States. Bank Leumi's net profit of NIS530 million ($112 million) abroad offset a loss of NIS110 million ($23 million) in Israel, whose economy was in recession.

Principal Subsidiaries

Arab-Israel Bank Ltd.; Bank Leumi (France) SA (96%); Bank Leumi (Luxembourg); Bank Leumi (UK) plc (79%); Bank Leumi le-Israel (Switzerland, 69%); Bank Leumi le-Israel Corporation (United States); Bank Leumi USA; Leumi Mortgage Bank Ltd. (90%); Leumi Agricultural Development Ltd.; Leumi Finance Company Ltd.; Leumi Industrial Development Bank Ltd.; Leumi Leasing Ltd.; Leumi & Company Investment Bankers Ltd.; Ofek Securities and Investments Ltd.

Principal Divisions

Commercial Banking; Corporate Banking; Global Private Banking; Construction and Real Estate; Financial and Accounting Division; International Division; Investments.

Principal Competitors

Bank Hapoalim B.M.; The First International Bank of Israel ltd.; Israel Discount Bank Ltd.; United Mizrahi Bank Ltd.

Further Reading

Breznick, Alan, "Faltering Leumi Maps New Strategy," *Crain's New York Business*, July 6, 1987, pp. 1, 22.

Chira, Susan, "Leumi Appeal Not Just Ethnic," *New York Times*, May 14, 1984, pp. D1, D10.

Gabriel, Frederick, "Unbilled Twin Protects Bank Leumi's Profits," *Crain's New York Business*, October 2, 1995, p. 24.

Halevi, Nadav, et al., *Banker to an Emerging Nation: The History of Bank Leumi Le-Israel*, Jerusalem: Shikmona Publishing Company, 1981.

Isidore, Chris, "Bank Leumi's Passport to Financial Health," *Crain's New York Business*, May 18, 1998, p. 14.

"Israel Sells 22.4% Slice of Bank Leumi," *American Banker*, September 2, 1993, p. 24.

Jackson, Ben, "Leumi Casts Wider Net for Biz, Wealth Clients," *American Banker*, July 8, 2002, p. 5.

Leuchter, Miriam, "Bank Leumi Shrinking to Stanch Its Losses," *Crain's New York Business*, February 7, 1994, p. 4.

McNatt, Robert, "FBI Is Probing Bank Leumi Customer Accounts," *Crain's New York Business*, August 3, 1991, pp. 1, 22.

Merrill, Cristina, "Leumi's Bond with Diamond Trade Pays Off," *American Banker*, August 15, 1995, p. 8.

Moyer, Liz, "Bank Leumi to Link U.S. Units under One Name," *American Banker*, November 13, 1997, p. 8.

Robinson, Karina, "A Woman of Great Importance," *Banker*, April 2003, pp. 26–27.

Sandler, Neal, "A New Face for Bank Leumi," *Business Week*, August 28, 1995, p. 89.

Silk, Leonard, "Overhauling Israeli Banking," *New York Times*, May 30, 1986, p. D2.

"Stocks Fall at Israeli Reopening," *New York Times*, October 24, 1983, p. D18.

Wels, Alena, "Bank Leumi Acquires American Bank & Trust," *Journal of Commerce*, October 21, 1976, pp. 1–2.

—Robert Halasz

Ben Bridge Jeweler, Inc.

2901 3rd Avenue, Suite 200
Seattle, Washington 98121
U.S.A.
Telephone: (206) 448-8800
Fax: (206) 448-7456
Web site: http://www.benbridge.com

Wholly Owned Subsidiary of Berkshire Hathaway Inc.
Incorporated: 1912
Employees: 700
Sales: $88 million (2002 est.)
NAIC: 448310 Jewelry Stores

Ben Bridge Jeweler, Inc. is a retailer of jewelry and time-pieces with more than 70 stores scattered throughout 11 western states. Ben Bridge Jeweler ranks as the 12th largest retailer in the country. Most of the company's stores are located in shopping malls, where the company is regarded as a valuable tenant. A family-run business, Ben Bridge Jeweler is led by the fourth generation of the Bridge family. Warren Buffett, through his holding company Berkshire Hathaway Inc., owns the company.

Origins

One of the nation's largest chains of jewelry stores began with one store in 1912. Samuel Silverman, a watchmaker, opened his store in downtown Seattle, beginning a business that would endure for the remainder of the century, but not with his name on the storefront. The name of the business went to his son-in-law, Ben Bridge, who became a partner in the store's operation in 1922, the year he married Silverman's daughter, Sally Silverman. In 1927, Samuel Silverman decided to move to California for health reasons, and he offered his stake in the store to his son-in-law. Ben Bridge purchased his father-in-law's interest in the store and renamed it Ben Bridge Jeweler, starting what would become a family dynasty in the retail jewelry business.

There were two defining characteristics of the Bridge enterprise that were passed down from generation to generation.

From the start of Bridge's full ownership in 1927, a policy of promoting only from within the company was strictly adhered to, and this practice enabled the company to record one of the lowest employee-turnover rates in the jewelry industry. All management and administrative positions were filled by selecting employees who had started out on the sales floor, a rule that applied to Bridge family members as well. The other dominant trait was the company's conservative approach to expansion. Ben Bridge Jeweler eventually developed into a chain, but the company pursued expansion extremely cautiously, careful not to overextend its financial resources by expanding too rapidly.

The company's conservative approach to growth was instilled by the family patriarch. Ben Bridge's first decade of business on his own presented a crucible for survival. The debilitative economic conditions during the 1930s nearly forced Ben Bridge to declare bankruptcy, putting him in a position he never wanted to occupy again. Suppliers were demanding payment, and for a period of time Bridge was unable to meet their demands. Bridge eventually was able to pay his creditors back in full, with interest, but the pain of the experience did not disappear after he had escaped the ravages of the Great Depression. "He never wanted to owe anybody again," his grandson, Ed Bridge, remarked in an August 1, 2003, interview with *National Jeweler*.

Fiscal prudence and conservative growth were leadership attributes inherited by Ben Bridge's sons, Herb Bridge and Robert (Bob) Bridge. The brothers were actively involved in the family business when it took its first step outside downtown Seattle. In 1950, the company opened its second retail outlet, establishing a store in nearby Bremerton, Washington. Bob Bridge managed the Bremerton store while his brother and father ran the flagship store. At first, the new store fared well, replicating the success of the Seattle store during its first two years of business. After the initial success, however, sales dropped and never returned to their previous level. Later, the Bridges realized they lacked the expertise required to orchestrate the planning for a multi-store operation, but at the time of the Bremerton's flagging sales there were more pressing, personal problems afflicting the family business.

Company Perspectives:

At Ben Bridge, we're proud of our 90 years of serving our communities with the very best in jewelry values with special attention to personal, caring service. Our commitment to professionalism means that we have more Registered Jewelers and Certified Gemologists of the American Gem Society than any other jeweler in North America. We want you to think of us not just as a jewelry store, but as your personal jeweler, and we look forward to assisting you with all of your fine jewelry needs. Please accept our invitation and consider yourself welcome in any of our over 70 retail store locations or our online store. Experience the pleasure of receiving the kind of true personal service that you deserve from people who really care at Ben Bridge Jeweler.

For a family renowned for its unity, the tensions that cropped up during the early 1950s represented an unusual moment of discord. In Bremerton, Bob Bridge felt too far removed from the excitement of the Seattle store. At the Seattle store, Herb Bridge was experiencing his own feelings of frustration. He and his father were at odds over the management of the store, unable to agree on the day-to-day decisions related to its management. Herb Bridge's frustration grew to a point that prompted him to search for a job elsewhere. In 1955, he informed his father that he was moving to Denver, where the retail jeweler Zale had offered him a position. Upon learning of his son's intention to leave, Ben Bridge called a family meeting and, as Ed Bridge recounted in his August 1, 2003 interview with *National Jeweler,* "laid his keys on the table and said, 'Boys, I'm out.' And he walked out." In an earlier interview, Ed Bridge remarked, "Ben didn't want to be the one to drive the family apart," as quoted in the July 17, 1992 issue of the *Puget Sound Business Journal.* "He wanted the family business to be a unity venture."

Expansion Begins in the Late 1960s

After Ben Bridge's decision to hand the business over to the younger generation, Herb and Bob Bridge jointly led the retail firm. Under their control, the company revisited the idea of expansion, although it would be more than a decade before they made their first move. The problems with the performance of the Bremerton store made the brothers especially cautious about establishing a new location, but their reluctance faded somewhat after they gained confidence from an encouraging experience during the 1960s. Early in the decade, department store retailer J.C. Penney asked the Bridge brothers to manage the jewelry departments in the company's Seattle-area stores. The Bridges agreed, and for the next several years they gained first-hand knowledge of J.C. Penney's policies and practices relating to chain-store management. The brothers also were introduced to the intricacies of the operating in a shopping mall environment, where the bulk of Ben Bridge Jeweler's expansion would take place during the ensuing decades.

After honing managerial skills related to administrating a multi-store operation, the Bridges were ready to expand again. They opened their next store in 1968, establishing it in the Southcenter Mall, located between Seattle and Tacoma, Washington. Over the course of the next ten years, Ben Bridge Jeweler developed into a small chain, becoming a six-store operation by the time the next generation of Bridges joined the company.

The third generation of Bridges consisted of cousins Ed and Jon Bridge, who would guide the company into the 21st century. Ed Bridge, the son of Bob Bridge, was the first to officially join the company, although both Ed and Jon Bridge spent their childhood and teenage years helping out with the family business. Ed Bridge, for example, swept the floors and polished the silver at the company's flagship location in downtown Seattle. After his graduation from the University of Washington with a degree in business administration and accounting, Ed Bridge began working on the sales floor in 1978, just before the company was scheduled to open its sixth store in Olympia, Washington. He spent only a few months on the sales floor before the prospect of promotion arrived unexpectedly. In December 1978, the company's chief financial officer announced his retirement, without warning, after 29 years of service. Bob Bridge asked his 22-year-old son to take charge of Ben Bridge Jeweler's finances. After serving several years as the company's chief financial officer, Ed Bridge assumed responsibility for the company's merchandising activities in 1981. His duties as chief financial officer were handed to his cousin Jon Bridge, the son of Herb Bridge, who joined the company in 1981 after serving in the military.

Although their fathers remained in control of the company, Ed and Jon Bridge assisted in a decade of prolific expansion for Ben Bridge Jeweler. The company opened its first out-of-state store in 1980, when an outlet debuted in Portland, Oregon. In 1982, the company entered the California market, opening a store in San Mateo. Although industry pundits continued to note the company's conservative approach to expansion when the 1980s were over, the growth achieved during the decade greatly increased its stature. The chain grew from seven stores in 1980 to 39 stores in 1990. The bulk of the company's expansion was achieved in California, where it had 20 stores in operation by the beginning of the 1990s, a juncture that also marked the succession of control from Herb and Bob Bridge to Ed and Jon Bridge.

In September 1990, daily management of Ben Bridge Jeweler officially passed to Ed and Jon Bridge, the fourth generation of family leadership when Silverman's tenure at the company was included. When the Bridge cousins took over, the company's stores were located throughout Washington and into Oregon, California, Alaska, and Hawaii, representing a regional chain of distinction. According to industry estimates cited in the October 22, 1990, issue of the *Puget Sound Business Journal*, the company's 1,400-square-foot stores each generated between $1.2 million and $2 million in annual sales, adding up to a chain that was collecting at least $45 million in annual sales. Expansion plans for the first five years of the decade called for adding between three and four stores annually, but only if market conditions and prospective locations were ideal. "Our biggest challenge in the 1990s," Ed Bridge explained in a July 17, 1992 interview with the *Puget Sound Business Journal,* "is going to be saying 'No.'"

Ben Bridge Jeweler eyed expansion assiduously during the 1990s, but the company's cautious approach did not impede it from adding a substantial number of new stores during the decade. Ed and Jon Bridge rejected roughly six prospective

Key Dates:

1912: Samuel Silverman opens a jewelry store in Seattle.
1922: Ben Bridge becomes a partner in the jewelry store.
1927: Ben Bridge acquires full ownership of the Seattle store.
1950: A second store, located in Bremerton, Washington, opens.
1955: Ben Bridge's sons take control of the company.
1980: The company's first out-of-state store, located in Portland, Oregon, opens.
1982: Ben Bridge Jeweler enters the California market.
1990: Ben Bridge's grandsons assume responsibility for daily management of the company.
2000: Warren Buffett's Berkshire Hathaway acquires Ben Bridge Jeweler.

locations for each new store they established, yet presided over a 56-store chain spread throughout nine states by 1998. Looking ahead from this point, expansion plans called for adding between 30 and 40 new retail outlets in as many as three new geographic markets during the ensuing decade.

New Ownership in the 21st Century

By the end of the 1990s, Ben Bridge Jeweler operated 62 stores in 11 states, having achieved 15 percent annual revenue growth during the previous 15 years. Financially, the company was performing admirably, but there were concerns weighing on the minds of the company's top executives. The concerns were related to the succession of leadership, estate transfer issues, and inheritance taxes that had the potential to cripple the company. Like their fathers and grandfather, Ed and Jon Bridge took the long-term survival of the company seriously and wanted to ensure that the company carried on after their departure. The pair discussed a range of solutions to the problems the company faced, including the idea of converting to public ownership, but Ed Bridge eventually followed the advice of a colleague in the jewelry industry and made a telephone call in December 1999. On the other end of the line was multi-billionaire investment legend Warren Buffett.

When Ed Bridge made the telephone call in December 1999, he was hoping Buffett would be interested in acquiring Ben Bridge Jeweler. He saw Buffett's intervention as his best course of action primarily because of Buffett's preference to let the existing management of his acquisitions operate with little interference. To Ed Bridge's surprise, Buffett was interested in his proposal, attracted by Ben Bridge Jeweler's record of profits and growth and seeing the company as an ideal complement to Borsheim's Jewelry Company and Helzberg's Diamond Shops Inc., two other jewelry chains he owned. The deal was completed in May 2000, when Buffett's holding company, Berkshire Hathaway Inc., became the new owner of the 88-year-old enterprise.

Ben Bridge Jeweler celebrated its 90th anniversary in 2002 as a firmly footed, respected name in the jewelry industry. In the wake of its acquisition by Buffett, much remained the same at the family-run enterprise, with the Bridge family's dedication to stability and careful expansion underpinning the company's strength. By 2003, the company operated 71 stores in 11 western states, with its most recent expansion program carving a presence in Texas, home to eight Ben Bridge Jeweler outlets. The company also had begun marketing a branded diamond, selling the Ben Bridge Signature diamond in 2002, which was followed by a Canadian diamond brand, the Ikuma. "I believe in brands," Ed Bridge explained in his August 1, 2003 interview with *National Jeweler*, "but they have to be meaningful brands. I still want the two most important brands we promote to be our store name and the name of the sales associate standing across the counter."

Principal Competitors

Zale Corporation; Helzberg Diamonds; Whitehall Jewellers, Inc.; Signet Group plc.

Further Reading

Gomelsky, Victoria, "Ed Bridge: Best in the West," *National Jeweler*, August 1, 2003, p. 58.
Prinzing, Debra, "A Local Business That Slays Jewelry Giants: Ben Bridge," *Puget Sound Business Journal*, October 22, 1990, p. 5.
Virgin, Bill, "Buffett Firm to Acquire Ben Bridge Jeweler," *Seattle Post-Intelligencer*, May 19, 2000, p. D1.
Volk, David, "Building a 'Bridge' that Lasts," *Puget Sound Business Journal*, July 17, 1992, p. 18.

—Jeffrey L. Covell

The Bing Group

11500 Oakland Avenue
Detroit, Michigan 48211
U.S.A.
Telephone: (313) 867-3700
Fax: (313) 867-3897
Web site: http://www.binggroup.com

Private Company
Incorporated: 1980 as Bing Steel, Inc.
Employees: 1,139
Sales: $344 million (2002)
NAIC: 331221 Rolled Steel Shape Manufacturing;
336370 Motor Vehicle Metal Stamping; 336360
Motor Vehicle Seating and Interior Trim
Manufacturing; 336399 All Other Motor Vehicle Parts
Manufacturing

The Detroit-based Bing Group shapes steel, stamps parts, assembles components, and performs other tasks through a combination of wholly owned and joint venture subsidiaries. Bing Group customers include the Big Three American automakers and several Japanese transplants, as well as manufacturers of appliances and office furniture. Founder and owner Dave Bing, a former Detroit Pistons star and basketball Hall of Fame member, serves as the company's chairman. The company is one of the largest African-American-owned firms in the United States.

Beginnings

The Bing Group traces its roots to 1980, when Bing Steel, Inc. was founded by recently retired basketball player Dave Bing. After growing up in Washington, D.C., where his father, a bricklayer, had started a construction company, Bing had been an all-American at Syracuse University and also studied business and economics. He was the second player chosen in the 1966 National Basketball Association (NBA) draft, and his outstanding first-season play with the Detroit Pistons earned him NBA Rookie of the Year honors. In nearly a decade with the team, he set many club records, and he was named to the league's all-star team several years running.

During the off-season, Bing worked for National Bank of Detroit, where he moved from teller to branch manager over a seven-year span, and then later participated in the Chrysler dealership training program. These jobs helped him learn the respective trades as well as supplementing the relatively modest wages he earned from basketball in the pre-free agent era.

In 1978, after Bing had finished out his playing career with short stints as a Washington Bullet and Boston Celtic, he began to look for a new job back in Detroit. Rejecting the familiar but no longer inspiring fields of banking and auto sales, he examined an offer from Pistons owner Bill Davidson to work as a public relations representative for Paragon Steel, a company Davidson co-owned. The steel business intrigued Bing, and he convinced Davidson to let him train at Paragon to learn every aspect of it. After working for two years in a wide variety of different departments, he left with plans to found his own company. Although the U.S. steel industry was in a depressed state at this time, Bing felt the downturn represented an opportunity for growth.

Taking $80,000 from his own savings and a $250,000 loan that he had arranged through his banking contacts, he formed Bing Steel, Inc. to purchase steel from U.S. mills and then cut, bend, and shape it to order for customers, who would use it to fabricate their own products. Given its location in Detroit, there was much potential for sales to the auto industry, and 80 percent of revenues would eventually come from this sector.

Starting with just four employees, Bing Steel did $1.7 million in business in its first year of operations. It quickly expanded, and revenues increased to $40 million by 1985. At this point, the firm had 63 employees and two manufacturing facilities and was trucking shipments of steel to 53 customers that included General Motors, Ford, and Deere & Company. Dave Bing's success was recognized by President Ronald Reagan, who named him National Minority Small Business Person of the Year. By this time, he had also founded Heritage 21, a construction company that specialized in renovations.

Bing took pride in giving back to his community and outlined his business philosophy to the Detroit News. "If people are employed," he stated, "they don't have all that idle time on their hands to go out and do the things they're doing now. If

---

Company Perspectives:

The Bing Group, formed in 1980 by Dave Bing, a prominent Detroit area entrepreneur, is a diversified base of manufacturing companies that provides superior products to our customers in the automotive, appliance, and office furniture industries through vertical integration. We have an outstanding reputation for providing our customers with exceptional quality and outstanding value. Our versatility allows us to accommodate the ever-changing customer demands of various industries with optimum efficiency and minimum costs. Our full-service business units provide extensive capabilities to our customers in the areas of steel processing, metal forming, and interior and exterior systems. All of the Bing Group companies are ISO 9000 and QS 9000 certified. The Bing Group is a certified Detroit-based minority business enterprise dedicated to uplifting our community. We are strongly committed to providing employment opportunities to area residents and ongoing support of efforts that improve the overall quality of life in the city of Detroit.

---

they're properly educated, then they've got some options of what to do with their lives. What I want to do is offer young people in this area an option. I may never get to be a Fortune 500 company, but if I can employ a couple of hundred people, I will have made a positive impact on my city.''

Superb Manufacturing Founded in 1985

Despite Bing Steel's rapid growth, its profits were low because margins in the steel service industry were razor-thin. In 1985, the firm began to work with Ford Motor Company's minority vendor program, which linked small minority-owned businesses with larger white-owned ones that could serve as mentors. This led to the formation of Superb Manufacturing, of which Bing would own 60 percent and Toronto-based Magna International 40 percent. Magna, which had annual revenues of $1.7 billion, was a major supplier to the auto industry. The newly created Superb would make stamped underbody parts such as hinges, brackets, and gas tank pans. Because of Magna's fears about locating in the depressed, high-crime city of Detroit, Bing found a plant in the northern suburb of Sterling Heights. Once in operation, Superb recorded first-year sales of $2.4 million. By 1989, its revenues had grown to $20 million.

At this juncture, Bing had convinced Magna to allow him to move Superb to a new $5 million, 56,000-square-foot plant in Detroit. It would form one of the cornerstones of North Industrial Park, which was located on property he owned or had the option to buy. Unfortunately, the move came just as the bottom was dropping out of the automobile market, and this had a tremendous impact on small industry suppliers like Superb and Bing Steel. As their losses mounted, the two firms began to edge close to bankruptcy.

In the summer of 1990, Magna sold its stake in Superb to tool and die specialists L&W Engineering, Inc. of Belleville, Michigan, and Southgate, Michigan-based ASC, Inc., a leading maker of convertible tops, which split Magna's 40 percent stake. The deal had been brokered by Bing's lenders, Manufac-

turer's Bank, and they insisted that he take over Superb's management, a job he had previously left to others. After taking control, he was able to significantly reduce its losses.

The summer of 1990 also saw Dave Bing form a money management firm called Alpha Capital Management in association with television executive Bob Warfield and Pistons star Isiah Thomas. With the latter Bing had earlier founded a fiberglass-distribution company called Bing-Thomas, Inc. The busy Bing, who had recently been inducted into the Basketball Hall of Fame, also helped form an association for retired players and led a campaign to raise money to restore school programs cut by Detroit's Board of Education. For 1990, The Bing Group, as the combined Superb Manufacturing, Bing Steel, and Heritage 21 Construction were now known, was voted eighth on *Black Enterprise* magazine's list of the top twenty black-owned industrial and service companies in the United States.

In the early 1990s, The Bing Group's financial stress eased, and revenues climbed upward from an estimated $61 million in 1990 to $64.9 million in 1991 and then $77.6 million in 1992. In 1994, Chrysler President Robert Lutz urged his largest suppliers to buy 5 percent of their materials from minority-owned firms, and his lead was soon followed by Ford, General Motors, and the major Japanese carmakers that had manufacturing facilities in the United States. To meet the 5 percent figure, purchases from firms like The Bing Group would have to double.

Bing Manufacturing Created in 1994

While the move toward greater minority supplier participation was unfolding, carmakers were also trying to reduce the total number of suppliers they dealt with, which caused a number of smaller ones to consolidate so they could improve their chances in the market. During 1994, Bing approached his friend William Pickard, owner of Regal Plastics, Inc., to discuss the possibility of combining forces. Regal was a maker of injection-molded auto interior parts with $23.5 million in annual sales. Deciding against a merger, in early 1995 they made plans to form a new entity called Bing Manufacturing, Inc. as a joint venture between Bing, Pickard, and former Chrysler Acustar division president Forest Farmer. Financial assistance would come from Textron Automotive Interiors, a major industry supplier which would also take an equity stake.

Bing Manufacturing was set up to build more complicated component systems such as seating frames and instrument panels, and over time the company came to specialize in such tasks as adding color and detailing to bumpers and attaching cloth or leather to seat covers. The operation would be housed in a new $2.5 million, 40,000-square-foot plant that was located in North Industrial Park, which was in a federal ''empowerment zone'' that offered tax breaks and other incentives. Bing would be CEO and chairman, while Pickard was named vice-chairman and Farmer president and chief operating officer.

In 1996, Dave Bing formed another new company as a joint venture with the Lear Corporation called Detroit Automotive Interiors. Lear was one of the top three seat manufacturers in the world, with $7 billion in revenues. That same year, Bing also formed a joint venture with foam producer Woodbridge Ventures to create Trim Tech, which would make foam for automo-

Key Dates:

1980: Former basketball star Dave Bing founds a steel company in Detroit.
1985: A joint venture with Magna International creates Superb Manufacturing.
1995: Bing and William Pickard found Bing Manufacturing, Inc.
1996: Joint ventures Detroit Automotive Interiors and Trim Tech are formed.
1997: Bing Blanking is founded in partnership with Rouge Industries.
1998: Bing teams with Ford to build a non-profit industrial training center.
2000: Bing sells his stake in the Blanking venture.
2002: Dave Bing leads an initiative to build 40 new homes near the company's headquarters.
2003: The firm announces new acquisition plans and projects $1 billion in sales by 2008.

tive arm- and headrests. November 1997 saw the formation of a third new company, Bing Blanking LLC, in association with Rouge Industries, Inc. Bing had also acquired full ownership of Superb by this time.

Bing's rapidly-growing operations employed more than 700 and were taking in $183 million in revenues. $111 million of this amount was from the Big Three automakers, led by Ford with $67.2 million and Chrysler with $32.8 million. Other important customers included appliance and office furniture manufacturers. In June 1998, The Bing Group's success was recognized by *Black Enterprise* magazine, which named the firm its Company of the Year. Dave Bing's three daughters were now working for him, with the eldest, Cassaundra, serving as vice-president in charge of materials.

In the summer of 1999, Bing and Ford teamed up to build the Detroit Manufacturing Training Center, a nonprofit facility that would help prepare individuals to work for minority-owned automotive suppliers. The center would offer free eight-week training sessions in areas like welding, injection molding, and computers, with 400 students per year expected to enroll. Bing donated land near the firm's headquarters, while the Ford Motor Land Development Corporation supplied funding to construct the $3 million facility and supply it with equipment.

On August 13, 1999, a fire started in the 60,000-square-foot Bing Steel plant, causing extensive damage to the facility. Investigators ruled it had been deliberately set, possibly by a disgruntled employee. In December, a second fire occurred at Detroit Automotive Interiors, this time destroying more than a quarter of the 135,000 square foot plant where workers had relocated from the facility burned in August. Despite these setbacks, the company had a record year in 1999, with revenues estimated at $304 million. The Bing Group now employed more than 1,100.

Bing/Lear Venture Adds Mirrors Unit in 2000

In June 2000, the company's automotive interiors venture with Lear Corporation, now renamed Bing-Lear Manufacturing

Group, acquired Lear's exterior mirror production operations in Berne, Indiana. Lear had recently acquired the mirror business, which generated more than $50 million in annual sales and employed 350, as part of a larger deal. The expanded unit was later renamed Bing Assembly Systems.

August saw another joint venture formed between Columbus, Ohio-based Worthington Industries and the Bing Metals Group, which consisted of the former Bing Steel, now known as the Steel Processing Division, and the former Superb, now known as the Stamp & Assembly Division. Worthington was a leading metal processing company with $2 billion in annual sales, and the venture would utilize its Taylor, Michigan, plant. Later in the year, Bing pulled out of the Bing Blanking venture with Rouge Industries, which was not performing up to expectations.

In the summer of 2002, Dave Bing became involved with another initiative to give back to his community. In partnership with Corinthian Developments, Inc. and National City Community Development Corporation, his Dogwood Ventures LLC group would build 40 single-family homes near North Industrial Park as the first phase in a larger re-development program. The three-bedroom homes, which were planned for families making $25,000 to $30,000 per year, would fill in vacant lots in an area that was dotted with older occupied homes.

The Bing Group had also recently resolved serious quality control issues that surfaced in 1999, at which time the company had undergone a large amount of job turnover. After General Motors reported an unacceptably high defect rate of 2,200 parts per million, GM supplier development engineers worked with Bing to lower the total to just 37 per million in 2002, and then to 17 per million for the first half of 2003. As a result of this improvement, General Motors named The Bing Group one of its suppliers of the year in both 2002 and 2003.

Late in the summer of 2003, Dave Bing announced new expansion plans for The Bing Group. Two acquisition deals were reportedly in the works, one in the South and the other near Detroit, which would potentially double the firm's workforce. The Assembly Systems unit was also making efforts to enter the instrument panel manufacturing business at this time. Bing projected annual revenues of $1 billion by 2008, nearly triple the $344 million his companies had earned in 2002.

The Bing Group had grown over nearly a quarter-century into a major auto industry supplier and one of the leading African-American-owned companies in the United States. Owner Dave Bing had earned a position of high esteem in Detroit for both his entrepreneurial skills and his many efforts to improve the lives of those less fortunate than himself. With new acquisitions on the horizon, The Bing Group looked to be on track for continued growth.

Principal Divisions

Bing Metals Group; Bing Assembly Systems.

Principal Competitors

Kasle Steel Corporation; Trianon Industries Corporation; Dana Corporation; Johnson Controls, Inc.; Magna International, Inc.

Further Reading

Aldridge, David, "Dave Bing's Smooth Transition; After NBA, Succeeding in Big Business," *Washington Post*, May 22, 1989, p. B1.

Armstrong, Julie, "Bing Group Poised to Buy," *Automotive News*, September 1, 2003.

Blood, Katherine, "Steel Star," *Forbes*, February 25, 1985, p. 162.

Garsten, Ed, "Bing Ties Success to Teamwork," *Detroit News*, August 26, 2003.

Goodin, Michael, "Bing, Pickard Eye First Plant," *Crain's Detroit Business*, October 31, 1994, p. 1.

——, "Bing: Work Together; This May Be City's Last Chance," *Crain's Detroit Business*, February 13, 1995, p. 1.

Green, Leslie, "The Bing Group," *Crain's Detroit Business*, May 1, 2000, p. 21.

Henderson, Tom, "Dave Bing's Best Turnaround," *Corporate Detroit Magazine*, October 1, 1991, p. 37.

Holland, Meegan, "Ex-Pistons Great Bing Keeps Eye on Business, Politics," *Grand Rapids Press*, February 6, 1994, p. C1.

King, Angela, "Bing Adds NBA Star as Investor, Expands," *Crain's Detroit Business*, August 10, 1992, p. 1.

Kosdrosky, Terry, "Bing-Led Group Plans Detroit Homes," *Crain's Detroit Business*, August 5, 2002, p. 7.

McCracken, Jeffrey, "Worker May Have Set Bing Blaze," *Crain's Detroit Business*, September 20, 1999, p. 12.

Miel, Rhoda, "Lear, Bing Expand Venture into Mirror Biz," *Plastics News*, June 12, 2000, p. 5.

Robertson, Scott, "Worthington-Bing Linkup Targets Motor City Market," *AMM*, August 24, 2000, p. 1.

Sherefkin, Robert, "The Big Stories: Two Auto Suppliers Moved Black-Owned Business to a Higher Level," *Crain's Detroit Business*, February 27, 1995, p. 75.

Smith, Eric L., "Motor City's Man of Steel," *Black Enterprise*, June 1, 1998, p. 124.

—Frank Uhle

Blackfoot Telecommunications Group

1221 North Russell Street
Missoula, Montana 59808
U.S.A.
Telephone: (406) 514-5350
Toll Free: (800) 649-4108
Fax: (406) 541-5333
Web site: http://www.blackfoot.net

Cooperative
Incorporated: 1954
Employees: 200
Sales: $40 million (2002 est.)
NAIC: 513310 Wired Telecommunications Carriers;
    513322 Cellular and Other Wireless Communications;
    514191 Internet Service Providers

Blackfoot Telecommunications Group, a customer-owned cooperative, serves over 20,000 consumers in eight counties in Montana and Idaho. A single telephone cooperative for most of its history, Blackfoot now consists of four telecommunications companies. Blackfoot Telephone Cooperative provides local and long-distance telephone service, mostly to rural communities ranging across a 6,580-square-mile territory. Blackfoot Communications, a wholly owned for-profit subsidiary, offers digital PCS and mobile technology. The company's Internet arm, Blackfoot.net, provides both dial-up and DSL Internet connections. Telesphere, a joint project between Blackfoot Telephone Cooperative and GeoEconomics, is a nationally marketed software package that aids utility companies with customer care, billing, and plant management. Like other telecommunications companies, Blackfoot is still adjusting to the monumental changes brought about by the Telecommunications Act of 1996, which introduced both new opportunities and new challenges for the cooperative.

Rural Roots: 1934–54

The original Blackfoot Telecommunications Group company, Blackfoot Telephone Cooperative, was founded by residents of rural communities in western Montana. Like other rural Americans, these Montanans had been left behind by the first communications revolution of the twentieth century, which brought telephones into people's homes. While residents of America's cities and towns could count on having access to a phone in every home (if they could afford one), rural dwellers enjoyed only limited access to the new technology. In the small communities of western Montana, many towns collectively shared a single phone line.

Market forces were largely responsible for this communications gap between rural and urban America. In the early twentieth century, large telephone companies rushed to serve cities, where population density balanced the costs of installing expensive communications infrastructure. However, Ma Bell often ignored rural areas, where low population density and the vast distances between communities made service provision prohibitively expensive.

This unfulfilled need for basic telephone service spurred many small communities to try to take matters into their own hands by banding together into cooperatives in order to finance, develop, and build their own telephone systems. However, the astronomical costs of such enterprises made them unfeasible for the majority of communities.

In the 1930s, Congress moved to address this divide and enacted the Communications Act of 1934. The act was intended to "make available, so far as possible, to all the people of the United States a rapid, efficient nationwide, and worldwide wire and radio communication service with adequate facilities at reasonable charges." To accomplish this goal, the act created a Universal Service Fund (USF), which was financed by assessing charges on interstate long distance carriers and which was used to subsidize telephone service in rural, high cost communities. The USF helped ease the financial burden for telephone companies to bring telephone lines to the backwoods of America. Another significant shift in federal telecommunications policy took place in 1949, when Congress amended the Rural Electrification Act to broaden the scope of the Rural Electrification Administration (REA) so that it could offer loans to finance rural telephone systems.

Buoyed by these changes that brought the possibility of cost-effective telephone service within reach, the residents of Arlee and Dixon, Montana (two small communities in the western part of the state), began to meet and develop plans for phone service in the early 1950s. With the assistance of the local REA agent, the residents formed a cooperative. They collected $50 from each community member, $10 of which was used for membership in the cooperative and the rest for equity to obtain a loan from the REA to establish full-fledged telephone service. By 1954, the cooperative had raised sufficient capital and was incorporated as the Blackfoot Telephone Cooperative.

Expanding Service: 1950s–1970s

The new cooperative began providing phone service in Arlee and Dixon in May of 1957. A month later, residents of Clinton had telephone service as well. By October of that year, service was initiated in Elliston, Avon, Ovando, and Potomac. In 1958, Blackfoot made its first acquisition when it bought the existing system in Charlo, which had been owned by a mini-cooperative. In 1961, Seeley Lake and Condon joined the Blackfoot family, and in 1973 the cooperative brought service to the Powell, Idaho, ranger station, just on the far side of the western border of Montana. In 1979, the town of Alta was added to the Blackfoot family. This steady expansion of service required a significant addition of capacity. Between 1954 and 1964, the number of Blackfoot's access lines grew from zero to over one thousand. By 1975, that number had doubled again.

Although Blackfoot expanded its service range from the 1950s through the 1970s, the cooperative operated primarily in a survival mode for its early history. It did not make a profit for a number of years. Moreover, like most other telephone companies and cooperatives of that time, Blackfoot functioned as a utility. In other words, the company operated in a highly regulated environment that mandated that its mission primarily was to bring basic telephone service into local communities rather than turn profits or accelerate growth.

Yet despite working from a limited fiscal base, Blackfoot was able to make key service improvements in the 1970s. In 1973, the cooperative began to upgrade all its lines from four-party and multiparty to one-party service. Two years later, Blackfoot began offering direct (rather than operator assisted) long distance dialing. Beginning in 1978, Blackfoot made a significant capital investment to start converting its electromechanical switches to digital ones. (Digital switches had the advantage of providing both faster and higher fidelity call transmission.) The cooperative was only the second company in Montana to install a digital switch, which it accomplished a full ten years ahead of the regional Bell company.

Developments in the 1980s

In 1980, the cooperative purchased the exchange for the St. Ignatius community from Continental Telephone, which was withdrawing from Montana. This acquisition nearly doubled the number of Blackfoot's access lines. Nevertheless, by 1987 Blackfoot had installed digital switches on all its lines. More technological improvements followed. Between 1988 and 1994, Blackfoot invested between $1.6 million and $2.9 million annually in upgrades. Blackfoot began to install a fiber optic network in 1989. Within the next five years, 96 percent of the cooperative's customers came to be served by that improved system.

Even though it had invested heavily in making improvements, Blackfoot maintained the same rates for local service that it had had in place since one-party lines were installed in 1973. The cooperative was able to accomplish this feat because, like other cooperatives in rural areas, Blackfoot derived steady revenue from three sources: regulated rates it charged its customer members, access charges it was entitled to levy on long distance companies for connecting to local networks, and funds from the Universal Service Fund, which continued to subsidize communications in rural areas. Because of this stable funding base, Blackfoot had been able to remain a "small, rural telecommunications company with a parochial view of the world," as Earl Owens, who assumed the helm of the cooperative in 1989, later told *Rural Communications*. Within the next several years, however, the status quo at Blackfoot would undergo a complete transformation.

New Directions in the 1990s

This shift began in 1994, when Blackfoot acquired nine new exchanges from U.S. West, Inc. (now Qwest Communications International Inc.). U.S. West was pulling out of rural markets in Montana and sold off a total of 60 exchanges to six Montana cooperatives. With the addition of these exchanges in Alberton, Superior, St. Regis, Haugan, Plains, Thompson Falls, Noxon, Drummond, and Philipsburg, Blackfoot doubled in size. The purchase cost Blackfoot about $21 million (the cooperative raised $2 million of its own funds and borrowed the remaining $19 million from the Rural Telephone Finance Corporation). Blackfoot planned to operate its nearly 6,000 new access lines as a wholly owned subsidiary, Clark Fork Telecommunications.

While the switch from U.S. West to Blackfoot was barely noticed by the customers affected, it brought considerable challenges to the cooperative. Not only did Blackfoot have to absorb a business nearly its own size, but the acquisition necessitated major and costly improvements to U.S. West's outdated technology. U.S. West's physical assets, which were necessarily included in Blackfoot's purchase of U.S. West's exchanges, were less than ideal. "The switching machines that are there right now—that technology was developed in the early part of the century," Owens told the *Missoulian* (February 20, 1994). "You can hear the noise." Within two years, though, Blackfoot fully upgraded the system.

U.S. West's exit from rural Montana was a product of significant shifts in the telecommunications industry as a whole. The former Baby Bell had already sold off rural exchanges in Utah and was planning a similar exit from Wyoming. Once it had shed its rural exchanges, U.S. West sought to focus on its larger—and more lucrative—urban markets. This change in strategy was driven by the pressure U.S. West was feeling from new competitors—not only phone companies but also providers of cable, cellular, and fiber technologies. By jettisoning its less

Key Dates:

1954: Blackfoot Telephone Cooperative is incorporated.
1980: The company purchases St. Ignatius exchange.
1994: Blackfoot acquires nine exchanges from U.S. West.
1996: U.S. Congress passes landmark Telecommunications Act.
1998: Blackfoot creates Blackfoot Communications and TeleSphere.
1999: The company forms Blackfoot.net Internet Services.

profitable rural operations, U.S. West could keep what the *Missoulian* (October 3, 1993) referred to as "the cream—the bigger cities, with their efficiencies and their business customers." Under federal utility regulation, U.S. West was required to charge the same basic rate for telephone services for all its Montana residential customers, whether they lived in Alberton (population 350) or Billings (population nearly 90,000). Because serving its Alberton customers cost so much more, U.S. West subsidized its rural residential business by charging its urban business customers more. This cost-shifting strategy had worked fairly well in the past, but growing competition meant that urban business customers could choose other cheaper telecommunications providers.

These tectonic shifts taking place in the industry escalated into a veritable earthquake of change when Congress passed the Telecommunications Act of 1996. This landmark legislation strove to introduce greater competition and increased consumer access to new technologies in the telecommunications field at all levels—local and long distance telephone service, Internet access, and mobile telephony. The act provided unprecedented opportunities for savvy telecommunications companies, as well as a myriad of pitfalls and new challenges for the unprepared.

Blackfoot was directly impacted in a number of ways by the Telecommunications Act of 1996. The act had a two-fold mission that on its face seemed contradictory: it promised to introduce greater competition at the same time that it renewed its commitment to universal funding. In an effort to implement these two aims, the Federal Communications Commission (FCC) sought to alter aspects of the USF. First, the FCC changed the funding mechanism of universal service by expanding the types of companies contributing to the USF. Starting in 1998, universal service was supported by all telecommunications carriers that provided service between states, including long distance companies, local telephone companies, wireless telephone companies, paging companies, and pay phone providers. Second, in an effort to impose greater competition in local telephone service, the FCC tried to create a system with incentives for new providers to enter USF areas.

The radical overhaul imposed by the Telecommunications Act and the subsequent FCC changes meant that Blackfoot could face new competition—also with the benefits of federal subsidies—in its rural territory. As a Blackfoot executive told the *Missoulian* (November 6, 1997), "It's a new era for communications. Big, big changes. In the end, who will win? It's

going to be the company that provides the most value—the best service, the best price."

Rather than wait passively for the competition to arrive, Blackfoot, under the leadership of Earl Owens, opted to enter the telecommunications fray more forcefully in search of new opportunities. Owens told *Rural Telecommunication* in 2000 that to be one of the "survivors" in the "competitive landscape," the cooperative had to "evolve" to become a "full service provider [of] voice, highspeed data, long distance, video, Internet access, and related services." In keeping with this strategy, the cooperative decided to compete head to head with U.S. West in 1997 when it began offering local telephone service in Missoula, one of Montana's three largest cities. That same year, Blackfoot started offering long distance service. Blackfoot also recognized that remaining competitive in the brave new world of telecommunications would involve more than offering phone service. The cooperative had already begun to offer dial-up Internet access in 1995. (In fact, it was the first Montana company to offer a local dial up number to Internet users in rural areas). In the late 1990s, Blackfoot continued to expand its Internet service, and in 1999 established a separate subsidiary, Blackfoot.net Internet Services. In 2001, Blackfoot.net first offered DSL (digital subscriber line) to its customers, and by 2003 the cooperative had over 1,000 DSL subscribers.

Blackfoot also maneuvered to enter the lucrative and fast-growing wireless market. Wireless service had the potential to undermine Blackfoot's hold on local telephone markets in western Montana as the expanded reach of wireless networks began to free rural customers from exclusive dependence on land lines. In response, Blackfoot purchased a wireless license when the FCC made new licenses available in 1998 and began providing service, including PCS (personal communications system) later that year. The cooperative launched a subsidiary, Blackfoot Communications, to handle its wireless business.

In 1998, in an effort further to broaden the range of services it provided, Blackfoot formed TeleSphere, a software package that targeted telecommunications and other utility companies, as a joint venture with GeoEconomics, Inc. Blackfoot marketed the software, which it had developed initially for its own customer care, plant management, and billing needs, to other utilities.

By the time Owens retired from Blackfoot in 2003 and was succeeded by Joan Mandeville, the cooperative looked to be well on its way to achieving the goal of diversifying its operations. The new CEO told the *Missoulian* (July 20, 2003) that "the move from a traditional telephone company to an enterprise meeting the future communications needs of rural customers is paramount to the company's growth." While Blackfoot strove to become a more competitive company, though, it also remained in touch with its roots as a rural cooperative. Over the life of the company, it had returned over $10 million in dividends back to the communities it served.

Principal Competitors

Bitterroot Wireless; Cellco Partnership; Qwest Communications International Inc.; Sprint Corporation; Western Wireless Corporation.

Principal Subsidiaries

Blackfoot Communications; Blackfoot.net Internet Services; Blackfoot Telephone Cooperative, Inc.; TeleSphere.

Further Reading

Holien, Mick, "Beyond the Dial," *Missoulian*, July 20, 2003.

Lakes, Greg, "Deal Would Double Blackfoot Telephone Cooperative's Size," *Missoulian*, October 3, 1993.

Ludwick, Jim, "Homes and Businesses in Missoula Will Soon Be Able to Choose the Phone Company That Provides Local Service," *Missoulian*, November 6, 1997.

——, "Phone Exchanges Change Hands," *Missoulian*, February 20, 1994.

Mandeville, Joan, "Will Proxy Models Bring Rural Consumers Access to Better Telecommunications Services at Affordable Rates?," *Rural Telecommunications*, November 1, 1998.

Shultz, Paul, "Hitting the Ground Running: A Profile of Earl Owens," *Rural Telecommunications*, May 1, 2000.

Wipplinger, Gary, "Montana Calling," *Concrete Products*, June 30, 1999.

—Rebecca Stanfel

Bluefly, Inc.

42 West 39th Street
New York, New York 10018
U.S.A.
Telephone: (212) 944-8000
Fax: (212) 354-3400
Web site: http://www.bluefly.com

Public Company
Incorporated: 1991 as Pivot Corporation
Employees: 83
Sales: $30.6 million (2002)
Stock Exchanges: NASDAQ
Ticker Symbol: BFLY
NAIC: 454111 Electronic Shopping

Bluefly, Inc. operates an Internet outlet store (bluefly.com) for designer apparel and upscale home accessories that the company claims to sell at prices as much as 30 to 75 percent cheaper than retail. The New York City-based company offers more than 350 brands of designer apparel, including such prominent labels as Prada, Ralph Lauren Collection, Tod's, Diesel, Michael Kors, Dolce & Gabbana, Diane Von Furstenberg, Gucci, and Versace. In 2002, Bluefly sold close to 70,000 different types of items. Although the site sells menswear, Bluefly caters primarily to women customers around 30 years of age. Houseware offerings include such merchandise as bedding, bath, dinnerware, drinkware, flatware and table linens, picture frames, and pillows and throws. Bluefly is 90 percent-owned by money manager George Soros.

1991 Origins as a Golf Apparel Retailer

Bluefly was incorporated in 1991 as Pivot Corporation by E. Kenneth (Ken) Seiff. He grew up in the affluent community of Scarsdale, located in Westchester County, north of New York City. After graduating from the Wharton School of Business, he took a job on Wall Street with Lorne Weil, Inc., a strategic planning and corporate development consulting firm, where he worked from 1986 to 1988. He then struck out on his own for a spell, creating EKS Capital Corporation to serve as a leveraged

buyout firm. In 1989, he returned to the corporate fold, taking a job with Founders Equity, another New York-based buyout specialist. It was while he was looking into a acquisition candidates for Founders that Seiff, who had never played golf, became familiar with golf apparel. Many of his friends were golfers, and he soon became aware that they were not enamored with the traditional garb featuring garish colors and decidedly un-hip plaids. Even older golfers were known to change at the golf course rather than wear such clothing in public. However, younger golfers, including Seiff's friends, could not afford to maintain a separate golf wardrobe. From these seeds, Seiff conceived of a line of golf-inspired sportswear, clothing that, in his words, was suitable for "the front nine and the backyard." Moreover, rather than sell the apparel in golf pro shops, he wanted his line to be available where his target customer shopped—department specialty stores. Thus, in April 1991, he quit Founders and co-founded Pivot Corporation, serving as chairman, treasurer, and chief executive officer.

Seiff's co-founder was designer Courtney Taylor. They were the only two employees of the company in the early days and were responsible for everything from design to selling. According to Seiff, they worked every day of the week from early in the morning until midnight or later. In the first year, he estimated he took off no more than three or four weekend days. As the clothing line became established, Seiff hired a longtime friend, James Hilford, to help out. Hilford had an advertising background but quit his job at BBD Needham to take off a summer to play golf. Because Pivot had a trade show coming up and it was too early in the year to play golf, Hilford agreed to work the show, after which he began to fill a number of other functions in the office, including typing and even some cleaning. He never did take his golfing holiday, staying on at Pivot to head sales and ultimately to take over as president so that Seiff could focus on the big picture for the company. Hilford's brother, Andrew, who held a Ph.D. in cognitive psychology, was enlisted to write the company's ad copy, which was then placed by CMG Advertising. Andrew Hilford was credited with creating the company's advertising tag line: "Pivot Rules. Clothes You Can Play a Round In."

In 1994, Pivot Corporation became Pivot Rules, Inc., and in December of that year the company's original unnamed inves-

Company Perspectives:

Bluefly strives to be the store of first resort for fashion by offering the most compelling combination of selection, value, service, and convenience.

tors sold out to Seiff and his management team. At this stage, Pivot managed to place its clothing line in such department stores as Bloomingdales and Macy's despite Seiff's lack of retail experience. Seiff's goal was to build Pivot into a lifestyle brand along the lines of Nautica, Polo, and Tommy Hilfiger. As he explained to the *Daily News Record* in 1995, "Nautica doesn't require you to sail to wear their clothes and Polo doesn't require you play polo to wear their clothing, just like we don't require that you play golf. If we can properly capture the lifestyle and convey that to the consumer, which is something Tommy does extremely well with his young American approach, I think there's room for another brand. These things don't happen overnight, much to our frustration, but I certainly think it's achievable in the long run." In addition to the company's original golf-inspire menswear, Pivot added women's clothing, tested a boys' line, and looked to include a lower-priced tier of men's golfing clothes. The company also delved into licensing, including as a neckwear deal with Robert Stewart.

Company Goes Public in 1997

Pivot went public in May 1997, raising $7.5 million, $3 million of which was earmarked for an advertising campaign to help the clothing line move from upper-moderate to moderate prices. Filings associated with the offering indicated that revenues grew from $2.2 million in 1992 to $8.6 million in 1996, when the company recorded a net profit of $135,000. Nevertheless, despite an increase in sales and the rising popularly of golf-lifestyle apparel, Pivot faced serious challenges from both designer labels and retailer's private brands. Pivot's answer was to shift its focus to the moderate-priced segment, selling to higher-volume department stores, sporting goods stores, catalogs, and even discounters—the opposite approach to what had made Pivot initially successful. In 1996, the company also decided to eliminate its women's sportswear collection, which accounted for less than 13 percent of total sales, although it continued to sell some women's clothing on a contractual basis.

In September 1997, Pivot moved its corporate headquarters and showroom to a larger space in midtown Manhattan. "It's an exciting time in our history," Seiff declared. "The move is a reflection of the company's continued growth and future goals." Within a matter of months, however, Seiff decided to exit the golf apparel business entirely and dramatically shift the focus of his company. Supposedly frustrated after spending a day of outlet shopping, during which he was forced to sort through disorganized bins only to find out-of-date designer clothing, Seiff had a moment of inspiration: why not use the power of the Internet to create a virtual outlet store that could carry up-to-date fashions from a wide range of labels? In May 1998, Pivot announced its intention to form a new division to market brand-name discounted apparel on the Web. Clothing companies, to this point, had been reluctant to embrace the Internet, but when online sales

enjoyed a significant bump during the 1997 holiday season, Seiff was not alone in targeting the Internet for future growth. Establishing an online presence was of such great importance that Seiff and his staff worked virtually around the clock, so that by September 1998 Pivot launched its ecommerce site, bluefly.com. The origin of the name, according to company literature, was pinned to the image of a fly—a creature that was nimble and quick to change directions. "Blue" was added because it conveyed a friendly personality. The creation of Bluefly could not have come at a more opportune time for Seiff. The change to the moderately-priced market for its apparel failed to work, and the company was unable to reestablish its department store connections. In 1997, the company lost $381,000. Thus, in late June 1998, Pivot elected to discontinue is golf sportswear line. The company sold the Pivot Rules brand and trademarks, and in October 1998 changed its name to Bluefly, Inc.

When the Bluefly web site opened for business on September 8, 1998, it offered items from 40 designers, including apparel from such well-known brands as Ralph Lauren, Tommy Hilfiger, J. Crew, and Donna Karan. In that first month, the company shipped a mere 96 orders, but just three months later, in December, Bluefly shipped more than 2,700 orders. Traffic to the site also increased dramatically, growing from 28,000 unique visitors to some 660,000. Registered users also grew from 1,572 at the end of September to 26,048 at the end of 1998. The company also established a key alliance with the Yahoo shopping site, creating a co-branded store that resulted in a 40 percent surge in the price of Bluefly stock. In addition, Bluefly also established a strategic marketing deal with another prominent Internet portal, Lycos. For the year, Bluefly lost $3.7 million, due in large part to costs involved in launching the site.

Losses in the Late 1990s

Business would grow in 1999, but spending, mostly for marketing, kept pace, contributing to further losses. For the time being, at least, the company had little difficulty in acquiring additional funds. In February 1999, Bluefly raised $10.2 million through the exercise of warrants and underwriter options connected to the Pivot Rules' initial public offering of May 1997. Another $10 million came from Soros Equity Partners, led by billionaire financier George Soros, who received a 19.5 percent equity and voting stake in the company. The second largest shareholder was Seiff with a 10.4 percent interest. In 1999, Bluefly also continued to add major brands and labels, so that by the holiday season of 1999 it boasted some 150 brands and 200 labels. It also struck additional portal deals with American Online, MSN, Excite, Netcenter, Go Network, and Tripod, and established deals with a number of leading magazines—including *Harper's Bazaar, Esquire, Marie Claire,* and Metropolitan Home—to provide original trend content to the site. In addition, the company improved its infrastructure, adding several new computer servers to handle the increasing volume of activity on its site. By the end of 1999, Bluefly was the number-three apparel retail site in terms of sales. It posted net sales just short of $5 million, but like so many Internet startups its burn rate of money greatly exceeded its ability to generate sales. Bluefly in 1999 recorded a net loss of nearly $13.2 million.

While Bluefly struggled to establish itself as a profitable business, it was certainly better off than two off its main Internet rivals, Cybershop and Outletmall, both of which went out of business. Despite the departure of competition, as well as a growing customer base and increasing sales, Bluefly remained in a challenging financial position, so that early in 2000 the company indicated it was shopping for a financial investor. However, with venture capital drying up for ecommerce, in mid-April the company shifted its focus to a search for a "strategic investor," although Seiff denied that the company was for sale. Investors, in the meantime, were pressing Bluefly to prove it could be a profitable business. Although Seiff maintained that the company could simply "turn the switch and move to profitability" if it no longer plowed revenues into marketing and infrastructure needed to grow the business, Wall Street remained unconvinced. The price of Bluefly stock, which traded at $20 at its peak in 1998, dipped below $2 per share in August, at which point the press reported that management was beginning to seriously consider selling the company. In spite of speculation that Bluefly was running out of money, Seiff maintained that the company had enough cash on hand to last through the year. Announcements of an expanded relationship with America Online's shopping site and new funding from Soros helped to stop the company's decline in the equity markets. Bluefly stock rebounded to the $3.50 range. In October 2000, Soros reaffirmed his faith in Bluefly, or at least moved to shore up his position in the struggling business, by arranging to have Soros Private Equity Partners acquire a controlling interest in a deal that could bring $25 million in financing to Bluefly. For the year, net sales improved to $17.5 million, but the company nonetheless lost another $21.1 million and the price of its stock continued to decrease, falling in December 2000 to below $1.

Bluefly started off 2001 facing negative publicity, as *Barron's Online* ranked the firm as number two on its "Burn Victims," a list of companies with the highest cash burn rate.

Seiff took public umbrage at the designation, but there was no doubt that at the very least Bluefly faced a challenge in its effort to turn a profit and achieve stability. Again, Soros came to the company's aid, committing another $10 million through his funds. However, with the company's future increasingly tied to his backing, Soros began to exercise more of a direct hand in the running of the business. In June 2001, Bluefly fired one-third of its staff, 32 jobs, and cut its marketing budget, part of a plan to reach profitability by the end of 2002. The company did manage to significantly reduce its year-end losses, recording a net loss of $6.5 million on sales of $30.6 million.

In January 2003, Soros invested another $1 million in Bluefly through companies he controlled. New management was also installed in 2003, when the former president and CEO of Spiegel Catalog, Inc., Melissa Payner-Gregor, was brought in to fill the newly created position of president. She reported directly to Seiff and was responsible for merchandising, marketing, and e-commerce groups. Payner-Gregor had 23 years of retail experience. While at Spiegel, she oversaw Spiegel's catalog, Internet, and outlet stores and was successful in cutting costs while growing Spiegel's online business. In October 2003, Soros pledged another $2 million, his total investment in Bluefly now totaling $55 million.

Principal Subsidiaries

Clothesline Corporation.

Principal Competitors

Filene's Basement Corporation; Loehmann's Holdings, Inc.; The TJX Companies, Inc.

Further Reading

Dillon, Nancy, "Tycoon Shores up Failing Discount E-Tailer with $2 million Cash Infusion," *New York Daily News*, October 21, 2003.

Hakim, Danny, "Soros Group Said Ready to Take Over Bluefly," *New York Times,* October 13, 2000, C7.

Owens, Jennifer, "Pivot Rules Files for IPO to Raise about $8.4 Million," *Daily News Record*, March 14, 1997, p. 2.

Salfino, Catherine, "Pivot Rules Prospers by Making up Some Rules of Its Own," *Daily News Record*, October 9, 1995, p. 10.

Thilmany, Jean, "Bluefly.com: The Pains and Gains," *WWD*, July 28, 1999, p. 25.

Welling, Deanna, "Investors Have Said 'Shoo Fly' to Bluefly," *Apparel Industry Magazine*, August 2000, p. 56.

—Ed Dinger

British Sky Broadcasting Group plc

6 Centaurs Business Park
Grant Way
Isleworth, Middlesex TW7 5QD
United Kingdom
Telephone: (44) 1-20-7705-3000
Fax: (44) 1-20-7705-3030
Web site: http://www.sky.com

Public Company
Incorporated: 1988 as SkyTV and British Satellite
    Broadcasting
Employees: 9,083
Sales: £2.7 billion ($4.25 billion) (2002)
Stock Exchanges: London New York
Ticker Symbol: BSY
NAIC: 513120 Television Broadcasting; 513220 Cable
    and Other Program Distribution; 513340 Satellite
    Telecommunications

With nearly 17 million viewers, digital satellite television operator British Sky Broadcasting Group plc, better known as BSkyB, stands as the United Kingdom's top pay television provider. The company shuttered its analog service in 2001, making it the world's first digital-only service provider. Since its launch in 1998, Sky digital has flourished, growing from 225,000 customers to nearly seven million in 2003. BSkyB's cutting-edge service allows subscribers to access 400 channels related to sports, movies, entertainment, and news. Sky digital also enables viewers to perform a wide variety of interactive tasks ranging from sending email, shopping, betting, and banking. News Corporation—headed by Rupert Murdoch—owns approximately 36 percent of BSkyB.

British Satellite Birth Pains in the 1980s

The 1990 merger of bitter satellite rivals SkyTV and British Satellite Broadcasting to form BSkyB caught the U.K. television industry by surprise, but the company's roots already reached back to the early 1980s. In 1983, Rupert Murdoch's

News International set up Sky Channel, a European-based satellite-to-cable broadcaster providing a mix of English-language sports and entertainment programming to much of Europe's cable television systems. Sky Channel proved less than successful, however, generating under $20 million per year in advertising revenues, and by the mid-1980s Murdoch was already looking to evolve the Sky concept toward the newly emerging direct satellite broadcasting technology and to focus the television subsidiary on the British market. Rather than paying for the rights to beam Sky's single-channel signal to cable providers, which in turn supplied the channel's programming to subscribers, direct satellite broadcasts presented the opportunity of providing multichannel programming directly to subscribers' homes via small satellite dish and decoder packages.

Satellite television represented a significant step in British television history. By law, broadcast television was restricted to just four channels—the two license-fee backed BBC channels and two advertiser-supported channels, ITV and Channel 4. Cable television, meanwhile, was nonexistent in the United Kingdom (the country's cable infrastructure would be completed only toward the mid-1990s). If the Australian-born Murdoch, who had already become a dominant player in the British newspaper market, as well as a key figure in the U.S. newspaper and television market (taking on U.S. citizenship to satisfy FCC television network ownership requirements for the nascent Fox network), hoped to step into the British television market, satellite appeared his sole opportunity. However, when regulators handed out the satellite broadcasting license, Murdoch's SkyTV concept, wholly owned by his News International Corporation, was denied due to British law, which limited foreign ownership in television networks to 20 percent. Instead, the exclusive British satellite license was awarded to British Satellite Television, a consortium launched by media giants Reed, Pearson, Granada, and Chargeurs.

BSB, as it was known then, was established in 1988 and announced plans to begin broadcasting in mid-1989. Rather than making use of existing satellites, the company determined to build and launch its own satellites, dubbed Marco Polo, and to broadcast using a new technology, called D-MAC, to a Philips-designed receiver dish known as a "squarial." BSB

Company Perspectives:

Our overall objective is to increase our revenues by growing our subscriber numbers. And to increase subscriber numbers, we strive to improve the service we deliver by enhancing the quality and diversity of our programming and ancillary services.

proposed five channels, including a premium movie channel supplied through exclusive rights for more than 2,500 films from such major distributors as Paramount, MCA, MGM/UA, Columbia Pictures, and Orion Communications, purchased at premium flat-rate prices totaling £500 million. Technical problems with the system delayed BSB's launch for more than nine months, until April 1990; even after starting up, BSB was confronted with a shortage of squarials. By then, however, BSB no longer had an exclusive on the British satellite market.

Murdoch had not abandoned his British satellite designs. Denied the British license, and rebuffed in an attempt to join the BSB consortium, Murdoch pushed ahead with his SkyTV concept. By renting space on the Luxembourg-based Astra satellites, Murdoch circumvented British ownership laws. Formed in 1988 and using the existing PAL broadcast technology, SkyTV began broadcasting four channels of programming in 1989, including an upgraded version of the original Sky Channel, called Sky One; Eurosport, a joint-venture between the European Broadcast Union and News International; Sky Movies, a fee-based all-film channel; and Sky News, a 24-hour news channel. Start-up costs reached £122 million; losses for its first year of operations were £95 million.

By the time BSB finally launched its service in April 1990, SkyTV had already placed 750,000 satellite dishes. Six months later, SkyTV had extended its reach into more than 1.5 million homes, against BSB claims of 750,000—figures that included cable-based subscribers. Actual sales of satellite dishes told a different story, with nearly one million SkyTV dishes sold compared to fewer than 120,000 of the BSB squarials. Both services were hurt, however, by consumer reluctance to commit to satellite dish purchases (at £650 per unit) before a standard was reached between the two competing—and incompatible—satellite receiver systems.

Meanwhile, engaged in a bitter rivalry for the home satellite market, both companies were hemorrhaging badly. Murdoch's investment in SkyTV already totaled some £400 million, while the satellite company was losing more than £2.2 million per week. Nevertheless, with a break-even point of three million households expected to be reached in 1992, SkyTV still appeared in better shape than BSB. That service had already spent some £800 million by November 1990, with a break-even point projected for 1993 at the earliest. That point seemed more and more unlikely as the weeks went by, given that each week was costing the BSB partners more than £8 million. Nonetheless, it was still the early days of the British satellite market, with its television viewing potential of more than 20 million households, and despite SkyTV's initial subscriber lead, BSB held the financial edge, with its powerful parent companies prepared to plow as much as £1.3 billion into the company—compared to Murdoch's growing struggles to meet the interest payments on News International's debts of more than £4.5 billion. In the end, Murdoch's financial problems determined the next phase of the British satellite television industry.

The two companies caught the British television industry by surprise when they announced their intention to merge in November 1990. Talks between the services had begun informally in July of that year during a dinner meeting between Murdoch and Read CEO Peter Davis. Without reaching any agreement—Murdoch was uninterested in selling, given SkyTV's early lead and its good chances of reaching its break-even point—but the pair agreed to keep in touch. As pressure from Murdoch's banks mounted, however, the pair met again in October. This time, Davis and Murdoch sketched out a merger agreement, which was finalized by the beginning of November after two weeks of intensive, secret meetings.

The newly merged company, now known as British Sky Broadcasting, or BSkyB, represented a 50–50 ownership between Murdoch and the four BSB investors. The two sides agreed to put up £100 million in working capital, with the BSB side contributing £70 million and Murdoch adding the remainder. The agreement also included a scale of dividend payments: after reaching profitability, News International would receive 80 percent of the first £400 million in dividends, which would then be split 50–50 for 12 years until 2008, at which point BSB would receive 80 percent of the next £400 million. The merger was met with resistance from Britain's television regulators, an issue again subverted by plans to broadcast the new BSkyB from the Astra satellite group—and later mooted altogether by a redrafting of the British Broadcasting Act. The company would abandon the BSB D-Mac technology—and its two satellites—and convert its combined subscriber base of 2.3 million wholly to the SkyTV receiver system. The combined nine channels would be narrowed to just five, including two premium-fee movie channels, one each from BSB and SkyTV. Within the company itself, the former SkyTV staff quickly dominated the workforce, virtually replacing all of the former BSB managerial and other staff.

Reborn in the 1990s

Perhaps the most significant change for the newly merged company, however, was the appointment of Sam Chisholm as the broadcaster's CEO. Born to a well-to-do farming family in New Zealand, Chisholm started his career as a floor wax salesman. Moving to Australia at the age of 25, Chisholm joined that country's Channel 9, where, as a protégé of the station's founder, he worked his way up the ladder, finally becoming its CEO at the age of 35, making him the youngest chief executive in Australia's television history. Chisholm remained at Channel 9 for 15 years, building it into the country's largest and most profitable television station, while establishing a reputation as an aggressive, sometimes abrasive personality, an uncompromising but effective leader, and a lavish spender. Recruited by Murdoch in September 1990, Chisholm was placed in charge of repairing the damages at the merged company, which posted a loss of £14 million in its first week of operations. These losses would continue for some six months, forcing Murdoch and partners to arrange a refinancing package, worth some £700 million, to keep the company afloat.

Key Dates:

1983: Rupert Murdoch's News International sets up Sky Channel.
1988: A consortium of media giants establishes British Satellite Broadcasting (BSB); Murdoch creates SkyTV.
1989: SkyTV is launched with four channels of programming.
1990: BSkyB is formed out of the merger of SkyTV and BSB.
1993: Sky Multi-Channels, a fee-based multi-channel concept, is launched.
1995: BSkyB goes public.
1998: Sky digital, the United Kingdom's first digital television service, is established.
2001: The company shutters its analog service.

Chisholm pushed through an extensive series of cost-cutting procedures, which included firing most of the former BSB staff—total staff dropped from 4,500 to just 1,000—and returning the BSB's fleet of luxury cars, managing to reduce the company's losses to just £1.6 million per week by the summer of 1991. Chisholm next turned his attention to BSkyB's programming. His first step there was to renegotiate the expensive film rights contracts the company had inherited from BSB—the rivalry between the two former companies had resulted in both companies bidding as much as £1 million for the rights to a single film—releasing BSkyB from the flat-rate fee structure and instead linking fees to subscriber levels, thus effecting immediate savings of some £100 million per year. Next, Chisholm scored a programming coup when, with BBC backing, he offered £304 million, outbidding rival ITV, for the exclusive rights to broadcast the plum Premier League's live football (soccer) matches. With these broadcasts added to its sports lineup, Chisholm converted this channel to a premium, subscription-backed, scrambled broadcast—a gamble that quickly proved successful, generating more than one million subscribers within months after implementation, while also attracting new subscribers to the satellite service.

By March 1992, BSkyB was showing its first operating profits, of £100,000 per week, fully a year ahead of schedule. Subscription revenues reached £3.8 million weekly, while advertising revenues added another £1 million each week. The company continued to post operating profits through the year, and by the end of the company's 1993 fiscal year BSkyB was posting an operating profit of nearly £186 million. A large part of the company's rise in fortune was Chisholm's and Murdoch's decision to convert the company to an entirely fee-based, multichannel concept. Launched in September 1993, Sky Multi-Channels initially featured 14 channels (and would grow to 40 channels), including Sky One, Sky News, Bravo, Discovery, BBC-owned the Children's Channel and UK Gold, the Family Channel, U.K. Living, Nick at Nite, VH-1, and MTV, as well as the Viacom-BSkyB joint venture Nickelodeon U.K. and a BSkyB partnership with the QVC home shopping network.

As BSkyB expanded its multichannel offerings, often accompanied by subscription fee increases, the company's virtual

monopoly on the British satellite television market continued to bring in new subscribers, passing the critical three million mark in 1993 and topping 3.5 million households by mid-1994. It was at this point that Chisholm—by then leading Asia's StarTV satellite network, 64 percent of which Murdoch had purchased for $525 million in 1993—prepared to lead BSkyB into a public offering. Completed in January 1995, the offering of 20 percent of the BSkyB's shares valued the company at £4 billion. The stock flotation, which reduced Murdoch's holding to 40 percent, raised £825 million, cutting the company's debt in half. Taking the company public also proved enormously profitable to Chisholm, who saw himself become one of the world's most highly paid television executives.

Going Digital in the Late 1990s and Beyond

While BSkyB's fortunes continued to rise—with revenues topping £1 billion and pre-tax profits of £257 million by year-end 1996—the company also hastened to join the next, and perhaps greatest, revolution in television history: digital broadcasting. With the capacity of offering as many as 500 channels, as well as interactive services such as video on demand and telephony applications, the dawn of digital broadcast technology was quickly making BSkyB's analog equipment appear obsolete. BSkyB first announced its intention to join a consortium with European media giants Bertelsmann of Germany, and CanalPlus and Havas of France, to form a digital television alliance. When that fell through, BSkyB next attempted to form a joint-venture partnership with Germany's Kirch Gruppe. This deal, too, fell through. Finally, in May 1997, BSkyB announced the formation of British Interactive Broadcasting (BIB), an independent company owned by BSkyB and British Telecom (each with 32.5 percent), Midland Bank (20 percent), and Matsushita Electric (15 percent). With initial funding of £265 million, BIB promised to bring BSkyB—and the United Kingdom—firmly into the new era of interactive digital television and telephony services.

Indeed, the launch of BSkyB's digital service in 1998 was enormously successful. Sky digital, the United Kingdom's first digital television service, easily carved out a leading position in the industry with its offering of 140 channels. In just 30 days, the company sold over 100,000 digiboxes and secured its position as the fastest-growing digital platform in the world. This growth continued at a rapid clip and was bolstered by the company's decision to give away free digiboxes, or set-top boxes, and minidishes. Within ten months of the promotion, Sky digital had gained 1.2 million new subscribers. In 1998, the company also launched several interactive services, including Sky Sports Extra—which allowed viewers access to instant replays, match statistics, and highlights—and Open, an interactive shopping channel.

The *Economist* explained the frenzy surrounding digital television in a May 2001 article, claiming that "digital brings many features, among them a clearer picture and the ability to squeeze more channels into the box. But the main reason why British pay-TV broadcasters, with their continental counterparts, are in breathless pursuit of this costly conversion is that digital TV promises interactivity: the ability of viewers to 'talk' to the telly. Interactive TV, it is said, will animate couch potatoes, tempting them to spend money ordering anything from pizzas to package holidays, all at the press of a remote-control button." According to the article, research group Jupiter Media Metrix claimed that by 2004 interactive commerce and research would rise to $8.1 billion in Europe, while climbing to $5 billion in the United States.

As such, BSkyB entered the new century ahead of the game in the U.K. digital arena. The company introduced the first interactive advertising campaigns in 2000 and rolled out Sky News Active, the world's first interactive television news service. It also launched Sky+, a fully-integrated personal video recorder. By 2001, the firm's digital subscriber base had surpassed five million. That year, BSkyB shuttered its analog signal, becoming the world's first nationwide provider to rely solely on digital service.

By 2002, Sky digital programming was broadcasted into a quarter of all British households. The company developed Freeview that year, offering customers three channels through digital terrestrial television (DTT). The firm defined DTT as television channels using digital signals delivered to homes through a conventional aerial and then converted through a digibox or set-top box. In 2003, BSkyB expanded into music television with the launch of three new channels. The company signed its seven millionth subscriber in October of that year.

Since his appointment in 1999, BSkyB CEO Tony Ball had overseen the company's successful foray into the digital television industry. Over a five-year period, the company had transformed itself into a digital powerhouse, garnering respect from its international peers as well as industry acclaim. Ball announced his intentions to leave his post in October 2003, causing many to speculate about the company's future leadership. In November, Murdoch appointed his 30-year-old son, James Murdoch, to the position. While the younger Murdoch had industry experience heading up News Corp.'s Asian satellite network, certain shareholders opposed the appointment based on the belief that he lacked the necessary experience to run BSkyB's burgeoning digital network.

Principal Competitors

British Broadcasting Corporation; NTL Europe Inc.; Telewest Communications plc.

Further Reading

Beale, Claire, "BSkyB to Turn off Analogue in 2002," *Campaign*, May 7, 1999, p. 1.

"BSkyB Prepares for Life after Ball's Departure," *Satellite News*, October 6, 2003.

Clarke, Steve, "BSkyB: The Second Coming," *Campaign*, April 26, 1991, p. 24.

Fallon, Ivan, "How They Kept the Secret of TV Deal," *Sunday Times*, November 4, 1990.

Groves, Dan, "BSkyB Takes Sky-High Gamble with Pay TV," *Daily Variety*, September 6, 1992, p. 23.

"How to Skin a Potato; Interactive TV, Inactive Viewers," *Economist*, May 26, 2001, p. 5.

Lynn, Matthew, "BSkyB Partners Play Shrewd Flotation Game," *Sunday Times*, October 4, 1994.

"Murdoch Faces Wrath of BSkyB Dissenters," *Birmingham Post*, November 14, 2003, p. 22.

"The Odd Couple; Digital Television," *Economist*, July 6, 2002.

Reed, Stanley, "Murdoch's British Sky Is Looking Brighter," *Business Week*, February 24, 1997, p. 16.

Snoddy, Richard, "Day of the Dish for BSkyB," *Financial Times*, August 22, 1996, p. 17.

——, "Sky Bruiser Who Relishes the Fray," *Financial Times*, September 11, 1995, p. 10.

Thomson, Richard, "Thunder Behind the Blue Sky," *Independent*, November 20, 1994, p. 8.

Thynne, Jane, "Murdoch Aims for the Sky and His Press Rivals," *Daily Telegraph*, September 2, 1993, p. 4.

"Will Sky Ever Be an All-Rounder?," *Marketing*, February 6, 2003, p. 22.

—M.L. Cohen
—update: Christina M. Stansell

Burdines, Inc.

22 East Flagler Street
Miami, Forida 33131
United States
Telephone: (305) 835-5151
Fax: (305) 577-2234
Web site: http://www.burdinesflorida.com

Wholly-Owned Subsidiary of Federated Department Stores Inc.
Incorporated: 1925
Employees: 9,000
Sales: $1.36 billion (2002)
NAIC: 452110 Department Stores

Burdines, Inc., a subsidiary of Federated Department Stores, operates more than 50 upscale department stores, providing designer clothing, shoes, cosmetics, and home accessories to residents and tourists throughout the state of Florida. Known as The Florida Store, Burdines differentiates itself from other department stores by incorporating elements of Florida culture in the design and decor of its stores. The retailer stocks spring and summer clothing during the winter months and emphasizes Florida's sunny, tropical atmosphere by integrating tropical colors and motifs and sculpted palm trees into each store's interior design. With locations in Fort Lauderdale, Tampa, Gainesville, Tallahassee, Daytona Beach, Melbourne, Fort Meyers, and other areas, the retailer is perhaps best known for its flagship Miami Dadeland store, which is considered one the best suburban department stores in the United States. With 640,000 square feet of retail space in two buildings, including the Burdines Home Gallery, the Dadeland Burdines is the largest suburban department store in the country. In 2003, as part of a plan to consolidate its holdings, parent Federated announced plans to begin converting the Burdines name to that of Macy's.

From Frontier Trading Post to Modern Department Store

After a winter freeze destroyed his citrus crop in 1895, retired Confederate Army General William Burdine turned his attention to the dry goods retail business. He opened a small store in central Florida, and in 1898, he and his son moved the operation to Miami, then a small fishing village that had just received its first railroad line and incorporated as a city. When Burdine opened Wm. Burdine & Son in Miami, the town had a population of less than 1,200. Funded with $300 capital and housed in a 1,250 square-foot building at Avenue D and 12th Street (now Miami Avenue and Flagler Street), the dry goods store resembled a frontier trading post. Burdine & Son offered a limited selection of shoes, clothing, fabrics and sewing notions, lace curtains, table linens, and umbrellas. Burdine catered to local construction workers, soldiers, and natives from the Miccosukee and Seminole tribes, who bought foods with money obtained from the sale of alligator and otter skins.

The city of Miami and Burdine & Son matured together during the early 1900s. The store's product offering expanded, and by 1912 the store had evolved into a full-scale department store, with all of the modern merchandise available in large northern cities. During this time Miami had become a luxury resort destination for wealthy northerners escaping the cold winters, and Burdine & Son configured itself to meet the needs of this clientele. Roddey Burdine, who became manager of the store after his father's death in 1911, shaped Burdine & Son into a fashion-savvy store with an identity that reflected its tropical location. He coined the name "Sunshine Fashions" in reference to the clothing styles, colors, and fabrics appropriate to Miami's warm climate and casual atmosphere. Burdine & Son stocked high-quality European clothing in the latest fashions and began to display them in fashion shows in 1914. Excellent customer service became a hallmark of the store as Burdine awarded bonuses to employees at every level. Burdine & Son became the largest volume retailer south of Washington, D.C. and east of New Orleans, earning Roddey Burdine the moniker Merchant Prince of Miami.

Burdine & Son attained a reputation in northern states as a fashionable place to shop and dine. The company advertised the store in national magazines, urging potential customers to travel with empty trunks that could be filled with merchandise found only at Burdine & Son. One advertising slogan referred to Florida as the place "Where Summer Spends the Winter."

Company Perspectives:

Through and through, Burdines is "The Florida Store." We're palm trees, tropical colors, dolphins and sunshine—the imagery and the mindset that makes Florida a place like no other. Our customers are Floridians of multiple dimensions—full-time residents employed in the state's fast-growing economy ... young families who want the excitement and unique lifestyle of seaside communities ... snowbirds seeking sun and warmth when it's cold up north ... new immigrants from across Latin America and around the world ... tourists thirsty for entertainment experiences ... retirees relocated to enjoy the slower pace of life near the beach. Because Burdines operates in Florida—and only in Florida—we uniquely mold and reflect the state's unique sense of style and fashion.

Because the store offered warm-weather clothing all year long, Burdine & Son proved to be an excellent test market for manufacturers' lines of spring and summer clothing before delivery to department stores in northern states.

The company simplified its name to Burdines, Inc., in conjunction with the first public sale of stock in November 1925. Proceeds from the stock offering were used to fund expansion and as working capital. During the 1920s, Miami experienced an economic boom, and Burdines found it necessary to expand the store, by then a six-story, 138,000 square foot structure. A six-story addition provided another 70,000 square feet of retail space. Burdines opened new stores in West Palm Beach in 1925 and in Miami Beach in 1928.

As a promotional device, Burdines launched a radio show in 1928, hosted by "Enid Bur" (derived from reshaping the letters in the name Burdine). In addition to presenting fashion news and guides to shopping at Burdines, the show provided household hints and played classical music. In promoting Burdines as a prominent Florida store, Roddey Burdine commissioned an exclusive fabric design, called Moon over Miami for the popular song of the same name, available only as clothing sold at the store. In 1936, the year Roddey Burdine died at the age of 49, company sales reached $5.6 million, earning net profit of $500,000.

Mid-20th Century: Success, Failure, and Expansion

Burdines struggled through the Great Depression, but expanded again during the 1940s. The company closed the West Palm Beach store during the 1930s, but opened a store at another location in that city in 1941. Burdines also opened its fourth store in the growing city of Fort Lauderdale. Capitalizing on the patronage of wealthy Latin American tourists, the company launched a mail-order catalog to serve customers in Latin American countries. Customers included American military personnel stationed in Cuba, who sent a supply ship to Miami every six months to place and fill orders at Burdines. The company developed a Teen Board to consult on clothing selection, insuring that store merchandise appealed to a new generation of shoppers. In 1950 sales reached $27.8 million, garnering net profit of $1.1 million.

During the early 1950s Burdines experienced financial difficulties which constricted cash flow and would lead to its sale to Federated Department Stores. By November of each year, the company's credit line was exhausted, forcing buyers to hold orders until after the Christmas shopping season. In summer 1954 Burdines refinanced debt with a 20-year, $5.5 million loan and arranged for a sale and leaseback of a new store in West Palm Beach. The situation worsened, however, as competition from a new Jordan Marsh store diminished Burdines' prevailing market share. Jordan Marsh offered shoppers an elegant new shopping environment, while the buying power of the parent company, Allied, allowed the store to stock a wider selection of merchandise. After several years of resisting Federated's offers to acquire Burdines, in 1956 the company accepted. A stock swap valued at $18.5 million completed a merger in May.

The second-largest department store group after Allied, Federated provided capital investment which significantly improved the merchandise mix at Burdines and enabled Burdines to expand with new stores. Operating in one the fastest-growing areas in the nation during the 1960s, Federated located new Burdines department stores with demographic growth projections in mind. For instance, the company opened two stores in Hialeah, a sparsely populated area northwest of Miami. Burdines acquired 100- to 200-acre parcels of land and sold the land surrounding the stores to mall developers. Thus the two stores in Hialeah eventually became part of shopping centers, specifically Dadeland Mall and Westland Mall, and residential development followed commercial development. In 1971 the Dadeland Mall store became the largest volume suburban department store south of New York City.

Burdines expanded throughout the state of Florida, initially in the greater Miami area. During the late 1970s the company expanded outside of southeast Florida for the first time. New stores opened in Orlando and the Tampa Bay area, the latter including Sarasota, St. Petersburg, and Clearwater, and Tampa. New stores opened during the early 1980s included locations in Daytona Beach and Gainesville. Burdines opened stores in Ft. Meyers, in southwest Florida, and Melbourne, along the central Atlantic coast. Locations in near Miami in southeast Florida included Boca Raton, Hollywood, and Cutter Ridge. In 1984 Burdines opened a specialty store at the fashionable Mayfair Shops in Miami's Coconut Grove neighborhood, selling men and women's fashions and accessories, cosmetics, and consumer electronics. Between 1977 and 1985, Burdines expanded its chain from 14 stores to 29 stores, ranging in size from 50,000 square feet to more than 200,000 square feet. In 1985 sales reached $757.5 million.

Burdines refined its image as it grew during the 1970s and 1980s. As population growth in Florida attracted other department store chains to the state, Burdines developed "the Florida Strategy" to differentiate the company from the competition. Identified as "The Florida Store," Burdines highlighted the unique product offerings attributable to its experience and knowledge of Florida's tropical climate. When competing department stores from northern states offered dark colors and winter clothing, Burdines stocked merchandise suitable to Florida weather. Winter merchandise included shorts, bathing suits, cotton sweaters, and linen clothing, but few winter coats.

Burdines' attention to demographics also extended to the needs of individual stores. Buyers selected merchandise in styles appropriate to the Palm Beach socialite or the Midwesterner living on the Golf Coast, depending on the location of the store. Burdines provided an extended line of junior clothing for college students in the Gainesville area and petite-sized clothing for the Hispanic customers and Latin American tourists at the Dadeland store. As hip-hop style clothing became popular in the 1990s, the North Miami store served the African-American community with designer clothing from Karl Kani.

Burdines designed store interiors to fit the tropical atmosphere of Florida as well as the location of the store. Designer Kenneth Walker applied tropical hues, such as coral, turquoise, and white, as well as beachside motifs, such as the ocean, dolphins, and palm trees. In Gainesville, home of the University of Florida, columns around the escalators resembled the school's alligator mascot. The Mayfair store in upscale Coconut Grove exuded elegance, with mirrored ceilings, marble flooring, and columns in lacquered pastel colors. The stores featured atriums and skylights or ceilings painted sky blue with clouds. Plaster palm trees became an informal trademark of the company's identity as The Florida Store. Officials at Burdines considered expanding to nearby states or Puerto Rico during this time, but ultimately decided to limit expansion to Florida, so as not to dilute the Burdine's brand identity.

Change in Ownership in the 1990s

While new store expansion continued in the mid-1980s, growth came to halt in 1988 when Campeau Corporation acquired Federated through a leveraged buyout. The high level of debt forced Federated and Allied, acquired by Campeau in 1986, into Chapter 11 bankruptcy in 1990. In the course of bankruptcy proceedings Federated and Allied merged. Federated closed four stores and sold 17 stores, mostly Jordan Marsh and Maas Brother stores previously owned by Allied.

This eliminated stores with low profits as well as direct competition, as most stores were sold to mid-range department store chains such as Mervyn's, Montgomery Ward, and J.C. Penney. Another 17 Jordan Marsh and Maas Brothers stores were merged with Burdines. When Federated emerged from bankruptcy, Burdines thrived as a streamlined company of 44 stores with profit margins at 12 percent, compared to 8 percent in 1986. Sales had declined under Campeau's ownership, attributed to lower quality, lower-priced merchandise meant to stimulate cash flow through high sales turnover. Burdines revamped its product offerings and sales surpassed $1 billion in 1992. The Dadeland store alone garnered $30 million in profits.

Burdines' attention returned to growth and expansion during the early 1990s. A new department store opened in Pembroke Pines in 1992, and the company launched a new store concept, Burdines Home Gallery. These stores offered furniture, home accessories, fine china, silverware, glassware, housewares, electronics, gifts, and floor coverings. In addition to small home stores, in November 1993 Burdines opened a 215,000 square-foot home furnishings store in the building once occupied by Jordan Marsh at Dadeland Mall. Home merchandise was relocated from the Burdines department store at Dadeland to the Home Gallery, allowing the department store to double its clothing line; Burdines then added significantly to the home furnishings line to fill the large new store.

The Burdines Home Gallery offered an extensive line of high-quality home merchandise on three floors. The glassware selection featured crystal designed by Gianni Versace and Paloma Picasso, and the store dedicated an entire room to Waterford crystal. Electronics included the Oster line of 1950s retro style kitchen appliances. Burdines promoted the Home Gallery through 60 full-page advertisements on television, billboards, and in certain regional editions of *The Miami Herald*. Direct mail advertising to Burdines charge card customers involved a 44-page catalog. The store's bridal registry alone required a staff of 15.

In 1994 Federated purchased Macy's Department Stores, raising questions about the possibility of changing Burdines to the Macy's brand. In May 1996 Federated issued catalogs that were essentially the same; since both chains offered much of the same merchandise, Federated saved the expense of advertising by offering the same catalog with the different brand names on the cover. Burdines became Federated's most profitable division during the 1990s, even more profitable than Macy's and Bloomingdales. Questions about a possible name change faded for the time being as Burdines continued to expand as The Florida Store.

2000 and Beyond

During the late 1990s Burdines introduced several new stores, including those at Florida Mall in Orlando, Citrus Mall in Tampa (replacing a store closed nearby), and the upscale Oviedo Marketplace northeast of Orlando. In July 1999 Burdines celebrated the grand opening of a department store at Aventura Mall, considered one of the company's flagship stores with 226,000 square-feet of retail space. Burdines promoted the store with an elaborate bus advertising campaign; the fully-painted exterior of 33 public buses which stopped at Aventura mall featured cooperative product advertising with Liz Claiborne, Ralph Lauren, and other designer brands. In 2001 Burdines opened a new store at The Mall at Wellington Green.

With the opening of its eighth furniture gallery, in Clearwater, in 2001, Burdines applied unusual merchandising techniques, as the store featured more home accents to create drama and glamour. For instance, a wall of Natuzzi chairs highlighted leather covers in bright colors. The floor plan combined with merchandise display to lead customers to various sections of the store where they encountered different styles and moods. The company applied these techniques at existing stores as well as at Burdines Fort Lauderdale Furniture Gallery, which opened in July 2002.

In 2001 Burdines' initiated store renovations which launched a sophisticated, contemporary look to reflect the international, refined taste of the company's customer base, while maintaining the store's Florida identity. Burdines began with the store at Aventura Mall. The company's identifying palm trees were recomposed in cast resin for a more elegant look. Tile flooring was custom-designed with embedded seashells and sparkling flecks of mica. New lighting and sculptured palm trees on either side of the main entrance enhanced the store's exterior. Burdines remodeled stores in Hialeah, Miami, and Orlando in 2002, and the company authorized a $50 million renovation of the Dadeland store as well, to occur in phases over three years. Improvements at Dadeland included the addition of a parking garage at the front of the store, wider aisles for ease of movement while shopping, a babysitting area, and a day spa.

As the national economy slowed, Burdines experienced a decline in sales, prompting the company to initiate several programs to attract customers. Burdines sought to attract young women by stocking hip styles in junior clothing and remodeling fitting rooms for comfort, with more space and the addition of lounge chairs. As discount mass merchandisers, such as Wal-Mart and Target, began to sell clothing in fashion-forward styles, parent Federated suggested several strategies to compete with the discount chains. At two test stores Burdines provided shopping carts and price-check scanners and moved cash registers from each department to a central check-out area near the store exits.

Customers at test stores did not like the new system, however, complaining that it was more difficult to find a sales clerk to assist them in store departments; Burdines halted the test program after five months. Burdines sought new ways to improve on service, for instance, by testing the use of palm-pilots in the shoe department. A sales clerk could check stock and request an item to be brought to the customer by a stock clerk without the sales clerk having to leave the customer.

In May 2003 Federated announced plans to convert Burdines to the Macy's nameplate. Beginning in February 2004, Burdines' 56 stores would operate under the name Burdines-Macy's. Seven Macy's stores in Florida operated under the dual name as well. At a later date the stores would be switched to the Macy's name. Since Macy's and Burdines maintained several stores at the same malls, industry specialists speculated that Federated would close some stores or convert them to home furnishing stores.

Principal Competitors

Dillard's Inc.; The May Department Stores Company; Saks Inc.

Further Reading

Altaner, David, ''A South Florida Original Burdines Succeeds Where Most Others Have Failed,'' *Sun-Sentinel*, December 9, 1991, p. 4.

''Burdines at Aventura Mall Radiates Visual Magnetism,'' *Display & Design Ideas,* May 2001, p. 31.

''Burdines Borrows $5.5 Million,'' *Wall Street Journal*, August 3, 1954, p. 11.

''Burdines Launches E-Commerce Site in Partnership With Miami Herald Online,'' *Business Wire,* February 4, 1999.

''Burdines of Florida Is Planning To Join Federated Store Chain,'' *New York Times,* May 4, 1956, p. 33.

Chabot, Lucy, ''Burdines Wraps Up Grand Opening,'' *South Florida Business Journal,* July 23, 1999, p. 6.

''Federated Department Stores and Allied Stores Receive Offers to Purchase Jordan Marsh and Burdines Stores,'' *Business Wire,* July 2, 1991.

''Federated Department Stores to Buy Burdines With 4 Florida Units,'' *Wall Street Journal,* May 4, 1956, p. 9.

''Florida Reflects on Rich History of Burdines Department Store,'' *Knight Ridder/Tribune Business News,* May 23, 2003.

''Florida Retailer Burdines to Combine Operations with Macy's,'' *Knight Ridder/Tribune Business News,* May 23, 2003.

Geran, Monica, ''Three Burdines Stores by Walker-Group Inc.,'' *Interior Design,* February 1985, p. 204.

Gingold, Oliver J., ''Abreast of the Market,'' *Wall Street Journal,* April 3, 1945, p. 15.

Heimlich, Cheryl Kane, ''Burdines Unplugged,'' *South Florida Business Journal,* October 4, 1996, p. 1.

Hersch, Valerie, ''Making Up for Lost Time,'' *Florida Trend,* November 1991, p. 54.

Kane, Cheryl, ''Burdines Readies Super Furniture Store,'' *South Florida Business Journal,* November 5, 1993, p. 3.

McQuade, W., ''Making a Drama Out Of Shopping,'' *Fortune,* March 24, 1980, pp. 104–07.

Morgan, Roberta, *It's Better at Burdines,* Coconut Grove: Pickering Press, 1991.

Sloan, Carole, ''Burdines Give Home Accents Big Billing in New Location,'' *Home Accents Today,* March 2001, p. 54.

Walker, Elaine, ''Miami-Based Retailer Burdines Celebrates 100 Years of Growth, Change,'' *Knight Ridder/Tribune Business News,* September 27, 1998.

''William Burdine, Founder of the Florida Store,'' *Palm Beach Post,* December 19, 1999, p. 70.

—Mary Tradii

Burlington Coat Factory Warehouse Corporation

1830 Route 130 North
Burlington, New Jersey 08016
U.S.A.
Telephone: (609) 387-7800
Fax: (609) 387-7071
Web site: http://www.coat.com

Public Company
Incorporated: 1972 as Burlington Coat Factory Warehouse
Employees: 23,000
Sales: $2.69 billion (2003)
Stock Exchanges: New York
Ticker Symbol: BCF
NAIC: 452110 Department Stores

Burlington Coat Factory Warehouse Corporation operates as a leading national department store chain with 335 stores in 42 states. Along with outerwear, the company offers apparel for the entire family; shoes; accessories; a complete baby and toddler line of clothing, furniture, and toys; home décor; linens; and gifts—all at discounted prices. Burlington Coat also oversees Cohoes Fashions, a five-store chain offering upscale label fashions in Connecticut, New York, Rhode Island, and New Jersey. Founder Monroe G. Milstein and his family own a majority interest in the firm.

A 20th-Century Family of Retailers

Belying its enormous size, Burlington Coat was essentially a family owned and operated business in the new millennium, as it was more than 30 years earlier, when Monroe G. Milstein, the patriarch of the Milstein family, opened the first Burlington Coat store in 1972. Over the ensuing 30 years, the family's grip on the operation of Burlington Coat was maintained by successive generations of Milsteins, led by Monroe Milstein and his wife, Henrietta, who succumbed to cancer in 2001.

Monroe's father, Abe, first linked the Milstein name to retailing when he opened a wholesale outerwear business in 1924. Nearly 50 years later, his son was drawn to the same type of business, selling outerwear at discount prices, but in a much different era, that would witness the rise in popularity of a particular breed of retailers and launch the Milstein name toward prominence in the U.S. retailing industry. Monroe Milstein acquired the first Burlington Coat facility in 1972, a coat factory located in Burlington, New Jersey, with an attached retail outlet. Initially, Burlington Coat specialized in selling winter overcoats, a product line whose sales were heavily dependent on the weather, peaking in the winter and dropping off during the summer months as temperatures rose. Although first-year sales reached $1.5 million, Monroe Milstein was wary of the company's reliance on the vagaries of the thermometer, and quickly realized that substantial growth could not be predicted on unpredictable climatic variations.

Milstein diversified into other apparel niches, thus laying the foundation for Burlington Coat's further growth. In its first few years, the company had assumed characteristics that would dictate its future success. The company's first facilities, the coat factory and the adjoining retail outlet, were purchased as existing properties, not constructed specifically for Burlington Coat, a practice the company would employ throughout its history, leasing existing retail spaces, rather than constructing its own. This strategic flexibility enabled Burlington Coat to expand rapidly when economic conditions were favorable and quickly halt expansion when conditions soured, an enviable ability in a frequently capricious retail market. Another precedent set in the first few years was the decision to display the company's merchandise in sparsely decorated surroundings, giving Burlington Coat outlets a bare, "warehouse" feel, while enabling prices to be discounted 30 to 40 percent. The diversification of the company's product line also would prove to be a linchpin to its future success, lessening Burlington Coat's dependence on a particular market niche within the retail clothing industry and expanding the company's inventory outside apparel into furniture and linens.

Success Beginning in the Mid-1970s

These hallmarks of Burlington Coat's existence—leased, sparsely decorated stores offering a wide assortment of merchandise—were established policies by 1975, a benchmark year for discount retailers. Prior to 1975, manufacturers were allowed to fix their prices in collusion with the more entrenched, conventional retailers, such as department stores, that sold their merchandise at standard prices. Essentially left on the sidelines, discounters frequently could not stock the same products as their higher-priced competitors, and the merchandise they were able to obtain from manufacturers could not be offered to the public at prices low enough to attract their business. Under such an arrangement, manufacturers and the higher-priced retailers prospered while discount retailers were forced to traffic in inferior quality products. When federal antitrust legislation in 1975 made the agreements between manufacturers and retailers illegal, the door was opened to discount retailers, spurring their ascent to the top of the retail industry. For Burlington Coat, federal intervention arrived just as the company was gaining momentum and provided the defining difference between the two eras in which the father Abe and the son Monroe had hoped to succeed in the retail industry. For the son, it appeared the opportunity for success was now more readily attainable.

Success came, but at a moderate pace, at least in comparison with the rate of growth the company would realize later. By 1983 annual sales had climbed to nearly $300 million, and the company was becoming a giant in the retail industry. It went public that year, with the Milstein family purchasing a majority of Burlington Coat's stock and the company's name changing from Burlington Coat Factory Warehouse to Burlington Coat Factory Warehouse Corporation.

Two Supreme Court rulings in the early 1980s took much of the strength away from the 1975 decision that had essentially put an end to price fixing between manufacturers and traditional retailers. The new decision put the onus of proving vertical price fixing on the accuser, which invariably was the discounter. This greatly diminished the ability of discount retailers to mount a serious threat against the more established partnership between manufacturers and department stores; once a manufacturer terminated a contract with a discounter, the discounter was left with little recourse except to engage in lengthy and costly litigation. Perhaps more disturbing to discount retailers, such as Burlington Coat, was a shift in fashion trends toward high-priced merchandise, a potentially deleterious development that stifled growth throughout much of the decade. During the early 1980s, when consumers developed an affinity for high-priced, designer labels, Burlington Coat recorded modest sales growth, as the once bright prospects for discount retailers noticeably dimmed.

Evolving into a Retail Empire: Late 1980s–Early 1990s

While sales growth was slow, it was better than average during these lean years for discounters nationwide. Sales barely eclipsed $300 million in 1984, then inched upward, climbing to $480 million by 1987. This lull in business, however, was only temporary, for in the next five years Burlington Coat's sales volume would more than double, as the company evolved into a retail empire. Several of the reasons for this exponential growth were attributable to strategic decisions made by Burlington Coat's management, but others were attributable to changing conditions within the retail industry that brought Burlington Coat and other discount retailers to the fore.

Efforts toward diversification were intensified, as the number of linen stores within Burlington Coat stores rapidly increased, growing from 55 in 1989 to more than 140 by 1991. Men's apparel, particularly men's suits, became an important contributor to company sales, and stores began to offer merchandise entirely beyond the scope of many apparel retailers, including such items as children's furniture. Perhaps the most important contributor to Burlington Coat's dramatic growth was a recession in the late 1980s and early 1990s that arrested consumer demand for expensive designer apparel. As the economy suffered and many consumers were left with significantly less discretionary income, discount retailers flourished. Burlington Coat, still continuing to lease its retail space, moved to take advantage of the situation, quickly increasing the number of its stores.

As Burlington Coat's sales figures spiraled upward, the company made two key moves to increase the efficiency of its operation. Burlington Coat improved inventory controls and took advantage of economies of scale by constructing a 438,000-square-foot national distribution center in 1990. Located a mile and a half from the company's original coat factory and store in Burlington, the distribution center was supported by a new computer system Burlington Coat had instituted in 1988 in anticipation of the new distribution center. The computer system enabled Burlington Coat to process as many as 125,000 pieces of merchandise each day at its distribution center and helped position the company to continue to grow during a period that saw many other businesses fail.

Annual sales flirted with the $1 billion mark in 1992, then reached $1.2 billion the following year. There were 185 Burlington Coat stores in 1993, ranging in size from 16,000 square feet to 133,000 square feet, and plans were in place to continue expanding throughout the mid-1990s. Typical Burlington Coat stores offered 10,000 to 20,000 garments from as many as 300 different manufacturers at a 35 percent to 40 percent discount. In 1993, Burlington Coat signed an agreement with Mexican retailer Plaza Coloso S.A. de C.V., an operator of supermarkets and department stores, to open a Burlington Coat store in Juarez, Mexico, the company's first store outside the United States. The following year, after purchasing a ten-store discount chain called Mid-Island, Burlington opened an experimental freestanding men's store that offered men's outerwear, sportswear, and tailored clothing, a service not offered by many discount retailers.

Diversification Paying Off: Mid-1990s and Beyond

As the company entered the mid-1990s expecting to open 25 to 30 stores between 1994 and 1996, an emphasis was placed on its men's apparel segment, particularly men's suits. Men's apparel increased its importance to the company during the early 1990s, in large part because fewer and fewer retailers were offering men's formal attire. By the mid-1990s, men's apparel accounted for 35 percent of Burlington Coat's total sales, a substantial portion that nearly matched the sales garnered from outerwear. With this emphasis on men's apparel and another segment, children's furniture, which, it was hoped, would cultivate Burlington Coat customers at a younger age, the company positioned itself for further growth.

Indeed, success continued into the late 1990s due in part to the company's diversification efforts and its aggressive growth strategy. Bolstered by the past success of moving into new product lines, Burlington Coat continued to add new items to its marketing mix and by this time had morphed into one of the most successful discount department stores in the United States, selling not just outerwear but family apparel; shoes; infant and children's clothing, furniture, and toys; linens; and home décor. By 1998, slightly more than 20 percent of revenues stemmed from coat sales. To spark interest in its new product categories, the company launched a new $48 million television advertising campaign sporting the tagline, ''We're more than great coats.''

Founder Monroe Milstein commented on obstacles Burlington Coat had overcome in becoming more than just a ''coat'' company in a 2000 *WWD* article. ''Early on, when we just had coats or mainly coats, it would have destroyed us to have the warm winters like we've had the last few years.'' Milstein continued, ''It took a long time, especially in the North, for people to get over the perception that we aren't just coats. What we found when we opened in the South in the last ten years is that we don't have that heavy coat perception because we came with a full complement, a full line of clothes.''

For the most part, Burlington Coat was lauded throughout the industry for its success in the retail sector. The company did have to deal with several instances of bad press, however, including several bouts with employees claiming the company used discriminatory practices when hiring and promoting. Then in 1998, the Humane Society of the United States informed the company that it was selling parkas trimmed with dog fur from China. In an effort to control the negative publicity a situation like this could bring from animal activists, Burlington Coat immediately recalled the parkas and returned them to the vendor.

These instances did not deter Burlington Coat from pursuing additional expansion. During 1999, the company opened 27 new stores, remodeled 15 locations, and relocated five units. The company continued to bolster its store count into the new millennium and by 2003 had opened its 335th store. Along with its namesake Burlington Coat stores, the company operated five Cohoes Fashions stores; seven Decelle stores, slated to be shut down in fiscal 2004; four Luxury Linens locations; one Totally 4 Kids unit; one Baby Depot; and ten MJM Designer Shoe stores.

The company's revenues had grown steadily since the early 1990s, reaching $2.7 billion in fiscal 2003. Burlington Coat appeared to flourish despite the weak retail operating environment that threatened many of its competitors. Management believed that its business strategy—superior selection and great brands at low prices—would propel the company's growth well into the future. With a history of success behind it, Burlington Coat appeared to be well positioned for expansion in the years to come.

Principal Subsidiaries

Burlington Coat Factory Realty Corporation; Burlington Coat Factory Warehouse Inc.; Monroe G. Milstein Inc.; LC Acquisition Corporation; C.L.B. Inc.; C.F.B. Inc.; C.F.I.C. Corporation; Burlington Coat Factory Direct Corporation.

Principal Competitors

Bed Bath & Beyond Inc.; Ross Stores Inc.; The TJX Companies Inc.

Further Reading

Arlen, Jeffrey, ''Burlington Coat Factory: Original Off-Pricer,'' *Discount Store News,* March 16, 1992, p. A10.
''Burlington Coat in Pact to Open Store in Mexico,'' *Women's Wear Daily,* October 11, 1993, p. 2.
''Burlington Coat Purchases 11 Locations,'' *DSN Retailing Today,* July 9, 2001, p. 4.
''Burlington Coat's Decelle Chain to Close,'' *WWD,* May 5, 2003, p. 16.
''Burlington Coat Sees Record Expansion,'' *HFN,* December 9, 1999, p. 3.
''Burlington Recalls 340 Parkas Trimmed with Dog Fur from China,'' *Plain Dealer* (Cleveland, Ohio), December 16, 1998, p. 1C.
Butler, Stacey, ''Retail Industry Divided Over Bill to Protect Discounters,'' *Baltimore Business Journal,* May 27, 1991, p. 6.
''Coat Factory Takes Honors,'' *Chain Store Age Executive,* February 1994, p. 44.
''Henrietta Milstein, 72,'' *WWD,* August 20, 2001, p. 15.
Palmer, Jay, ''Pipe-Rack Recovery,'' *Barron's,* March 23, 1992, p. 20.
Peres, Daniel, ''Burlington Coat to Open Experimental Men's Store,'' *Daily News-Record,* March 3, 1994, p. 2.
Salfino, Catherine, ''Burlington Coat Pins Star on Men's Suit Business,'' *Daily News-Record,* March 26, 1993, p. 8.
Troy, Mike, ''Burlington Sheds Old Coat, Goes for Brighter, Homier Look,'' *DSN Retailing Today,* November 6, 2000, p. 4.
Von Bergen, Jane M., ''Burlington Coat's Founder Credits Success to Cold Cash,'' *Houston Chronicle,* November 8, 1998, p. 8.

—Jeffrey L. Covell
—update: Christina M. Stansell

Callanan Industries, Inc.

1245 Kings Road
Albany, New York 12212
U.S.A.
Telephone: (518) 374-2222
Fax: (518) 756-8587
Web site: http://www.callanan.com

Wholly Owned Subsidiary of Oldcastle Inc.
Incorporated: 1895 as Callanan Road Improvement
    Company
Employees: 250
Sales: $140 million (2002)
NAIC: 212312 Crushed and Broken Limestone Mining
    and Quarrying

A subsidiary of Oldcastle Inc., Callanan Industries, Inc. is an Albany-based supplier of paving materials and construction services in New York State. In turn, Oldcastle is a subsidiary of CRH plc, an international company with its headquarters in Dublin, Ireland, specializing in building materials and value-added products, serving both the construction and do-it-yourself markets. Callanan is involved in four product areas. The aggregates segment includes crushed sandstone, limestone, and dolomitic limestone, produced by the company's quarry operations. Callanan provides aggregates in standard New York State approved sizes and is also able to custom manufacture to customer specifications. Callanan's asphalt products are produced at computer-controlled plants and meet the highest standards set by the federal government, New York State, and special agencies. Callanan also provides construction services, specializing in paving jobs ranging in size from small parking lost to major state highway projects. In addition, Callanan participates in the readymix concrete business through subsidiary Clemente Latham Concrete, the top supplier in New York's Capital District, which includes the cities of Albany, Try, and Schenectady.

19th-Century Origins

The man behind the Callanan name was Peter Callanan, a successful hay farmer who lived in South Bethlehem, New York. On part of his property located in Albany County were exposed limestone rock ledges, ideal for use as a quarry. In 1883 Callanan saw an opportunity to take advantage of this natural resource to supply ballast to the Buffalo and Weehawken Railroad, then under construction in the state. (Railroad ballast was crushed stone laid down as a bed beneath the tracks to provide drainage, track stability, and support for especially heavy loads.)

In addition to being a savvy businessman, Callanan was also a visionary. At a time when the automobile was little more than a drawing board creation, he foresaw the need for a system of state roads to facilitate commerce, replacing the rudimentary town and country roads that were in use at the time. These roads, of course, would need crushed stone.

To supply both ballast for the railroads and prepare for a future of road building projects, Callanan gathered a group of local investors to establish what would become Plant No. 1. His partners were Christian Scharbauer, a South Bethlehem shopkeeper who several years later moved to Texas, where the family grew rich through cattle and oil; John Newton Briggs, owner of several ice houses; and a local physician named Davidson. Supervised by Callanan, who retained a controlling interest, the quarry operation in these early days was a crude affair, involving considerable manual labor. Steel points driven into the stone by sledge hammers created holes just large enough to accommodate an explosive charge. The debris that resulted from the blast was then screened and loaded by hand. Not even shovels were used.

Peter Callanan also found time to champion his belief in better roads, advancing a way to pay for a system of state roads. He spoke to numerous town and county governmental bodies and in 1889 published a 40-page pamphlet entitled ''Roads and Road Making'' that laid out his beliefs. In this ''practical treatise,'' Callanan maintained that America's network of roads were ''inferior to those of any other civilized country.'' He also estimated that the delays in hauling agricultural and manufactured products caused by poor roads cost the state of New York more than $15 million a year.

In the meantime, his quarry prospered by providing railroad ballast. A steam-driven crusher and mill were added. In 1895 the business was incorporated as the Callanan Road Improvement Company. One year later, however, Peter Callanan died of a heart attack, leaving his wife, Hannah Whitbeck Callanan, to raise their six children and keep the company running. His brother John J. and cousin Olin, both non-stockholders, took charge of the quarry operations.

Highway Act of 1898 Spurs Callanan's Growth

Peter Callanan's persistence and belief in a state highway system would pay off two years after his death. The Highway Act of 1898, passed by the New York State Legislature, established a Highway Commission. The first contract was awarded to the Callanan Road Improvement Company to build a two-mile road leading out of Albany. With roadbuilding adding to its business, Callanan was able to pay off debts incurred in expanding the operation, and by the end of 1902 the company was debt free and on the verge of profitability.

However, on December 28, 1902, misfortune again struck: the crushing plant was completely destroyed by fire. Although some minority shareholders urged her to sell the company, Hannah Callanan decided to rebuild the plant. Part of her reason to carry on the business was that her son John Hoyt Callanan showed promise as its future leader. Both he and his brother Charles learned the quarry business from childhood and as young adults were able to manage the operation on their own, prompting their uncle, John J. Callanan, to move to Whiteplains, New York, to open his own quarry. Again, the company thrived and soon paid off the loans taken out to rebuild the stone crushing mill, and once more tragedy befell the Callanan family. On May 12, 1909, an explosive charge, a ''big shot,'' went off early, killing 23 out of a 24-man crew. The only survivor was a man working on top of the ledge being blasted. Included among the dead were both John Hoyt and Charles Callanan. The grieving Hannah Callanan, having lost her husband and two sons, was once more urged to sell the company. She refused. Instead, she called upon her brother-in-law, John J. Callanan, to step in and make the quarry operational again.

A younger son, Reid Callanan, started working for the company in 1916. (He would later emerge as the company's long-time president.) In that same year the quarry business saw a significant change in technology with the purchase of a steam-powered shovel, which took a crew of nine men to operate: a crane man, fireman, engineer, and a six-man gang to reposition track on which the shovel operated. In 1919 Callanan added a second steam shovel. In addition, sledges and steel points were replaced by steam, and later compressed air drills. The new equipment helped the company to cut its costs, especially helpful during a price war that ensued when a second stone company, Albany Crushed Stone, was launched. There was simply not enough business in the market to support both companies. The price war lasted until 1929, when Albany Crushed Stone sold out to Callanan. Although the victor, Callanan was wounded and it took some time before the company regained its fiscal health. Also during this period, other family members joined the company: Keith Callanan in 1924 and Harry Battin in 1927.

Callanan operated the Albany Crushed Stone quarry for just three years, until, at the height of the Great Depression, management decided to shutter the operation. The equipment, however, would soon find good use at a new quarry Callanan opened in 1937 in Kingston, New York. The stone produced from this operation was then barged down the Hudson River to serve the New York market. The quarry supplied the heavy fill needed to make Flushing Meadows suitable to host the 1939 World's Fair.

In the 1940s and 1950s, as government spending during World War II spurred the U.S. economy, Callanan grew even more prosperous. In 1947 it formed a joint venture with Republic Steel, creating Callanan Slag & Materials Co., Inc., to process the slag produced by Republic's blast furnaces located in Troy, New York. In addition, Callanan supplied Flux stone to the Troy blast furnaces. Nevertheless, it was highway building, as Peter Callanan envisioned several decades earlier, that would become the lifeblood of the company.

During the Cold War years of the 1950s, the U.S. highway system was built as part of a program of national defense. In New York, one of those arteries was the New York State Thruway, running 67 miles from Albany to New York City. Callanan supplied more than 1.5 million tons of materials used to pave the length of the Thruway, plus 31 miles of access roads, six interchanges, and various bridges. By the end of this period, Callanan was operating three crushed stone facilities and five blacktop plants. In addition to supplying materials, the company provided construction services. Also of note in the 1950s, Hannah Callanan died in November 1952, two weeks short of her 97th birthday. Her husband may have provided the vision that launched the company, but it was her dedication to his vision, in spite of painful adversity, that was indispensable to Callanan's longevity.

Callanan Family Sells Company in 1967

A major project of the 1960s was the Empire State Plaza, a massive urban renewal project in Albany that in its day was the largest construction project in the world. Callanan supplied over 2.5 million tons of stone used in the construction of several public buildings. Ownership of the company passed out of the hands of the Callanan family in 1967 when Penn Dixie Cement acquired it. It was during this 15-year period of ownership that the company changed its name to Callanan Industries, a name more in keeping with the company's activities beyond road building.

Penn Dixie encountered financial problems in 1980 and was forced to reorganize under Chapter 11 of the U.S. Federal Bankruptcy Code. Although Callanan was not a party to this reorganization, two years later the company was sold to M&S Resources Inc. for $14.1 million in order to allow the parent company, renamed Continental Steel Corporation, to fund its core steel business. M&S was a partnership headed by A.J. ''Doc'' Marcelle, Callanan's CEO during the period of Penn Dixie owner-

---

Key Dates:

1883: Peter Callanan and partners establish a limestone quarry on Callanan's property.
1895: Callanan Road Improvement Company is incorporated.
1896: Peter Callanan dies.
1898: New York Highway Act leads to growth at Callanan.
1909: Explosion at the plant kills 23 men, including the founder's sons.
1929: Callanan purchases its chief competitor, Albany Crushed Stone.
1937: A quarry in Kingston, New York, is opened.
1967: Penn Dixie Cement acquires the company.
1985: CRH plc, through subsidiary Oldcastle Inc., acquires Callanan.
1993: Clemente Latham Concrete is acquired.

---

ship. Although Callanan operated under management-led ownership for less than two years, the company enjoyed significant growth by acquiring construction material companies. Callanan bought Troy-based Fitzgerald Brothers; Crushed Rock and Asphalt Stone Products, with operations in Schenectady and Pattersonville, New York; and Oxbow Stone and Asphalt, based near Canastota, New York.

Callanan changed hands again in 1985, when CRH plc (Cement Roadstone Holdings) of Dublin, Ireland, through its U.S. subsidiary Oldcastle Inc., bought the company. CRH was established in 1970, the product of a merger of two public Irish cement companies: Cement Limited, founded in 1936, and Roadstone Limited, founded in 1949. The resulting company produced all of Ireland's cement and was a major supplier of aggregates, concrete products, and asphalt. Not content with dominating Ireland's relatively small market, CRH set its sights on international expansion. In 1973 the company made its first acquisition on the European continent. The initial foray into the United States came in 1978 when CRH bought Utah-based Amcor, maker of concrete products. However, it was the acquisition of Callanan that formed the nucleus for Oldcastle Materi-

als, formed in 1985, which would grow into a major revenue stream for its Irish parent company.

CRH invested the necessary resources to grow Oldcastle's "New York Group." In 1986 King Road Materials and two blacktop plants were acquired. In 1993 Oldcastle added Clemente Latham Concrete and Valente Gravel, which ran five ready mix plants as well as sand and gravel operations. A year later the group picked up two quarries and four blacktop plants through the acquisitions of Sullivan Materials. In 1995 Fane Asphalt and Fane Concrete was acquired, adding two more ready mix plants and another quarry. Acquisitions in 1998 included Ritangela Construction and Maybrook Materials, which brought with them a highway construction and paving company, plus a blacktop plant and quarry located in Orange County. Then, in 2000, the Rochester-based Dolomite Group of companies were bought, adding nine aggregate facilities, eight blacktop operations, and six readymix plants. The future need for Callanan's products remained strong, and the company's ability to provide the necessary materials would not be an issue for many years. Callanan's South Bethlehem Quarry, already mined on a continuous basis for more than 100 years, contained estimated reserves of another 100 years.

Principal Divisions

Readymix Concrete; Aggregates and Asphalt; Construction Services.

Principal Competitors

APAC, Inc.; Hanson plc; Rinker Materials Corporation.

Further Reading

Drake, Bob, "Operations at a Crossroads Takes New Path to Profits," *Pit & Quarry,* October 1993, p. 24.
Hency, Richard, "Callanan Industries Serving Upstate New York for 199 Years," *North American Quarry News,* July 2003.
Phelan, Thomas, and P. Thomas Carroll, *Hudson Mohawk Gateway: An Illustrated History,* Sun Valley, Calif.: American Historical Press, 2001.

—Ed Dinger

Carma Laboratories, Inc.

5801 West Airways Avenue
Franklin, Wisconsin 53132-9111
U.S.A.
Telephone: (414) 421-7707
Fax: (414) 421-0737
Web site: http://www.carma-labs.com

Private Company
Incorporated: 1937
Employees: 71
Sales: $50 million (2002 est.)
NAIC: 325620 Toilet Preparation Manufacturing

Based near Milwaukee in the town of Franklin, Wisconsin, Carma Laboratories, Inc., is a one-brand, family-owned company that manufactures Carmex lip balm. Founder Alfred G. Woelbing was at the helm of Carma Labs until the age of 96, at which time his son Don and grandsons Paul and Eric assumed management responsibilities.

Carma Labs uses custom equipment to produce Carmex products. For many years Carmex was available in only one formula, which was sold in tiny white opal glass jars with yellow metal lids. However, Carma Labs began offering the product in squeezable tubes during the late 1980s, followed by a stick version containing sunscreen. By the early 2000s, a peppermint formula was added to the company's product lineup.

Carma Labs prides itself on adhering to ethical business practices with customers, suppliers, and employees. "I am proud of my position," says Paul Woelbing. "It's very rare for a family business to survive into the third generation. My job is one of stewardship. Many customers, our long-time employees and my family all depend upon the continued success of Carma Laboratories, Inc. I was an art teacher for ten years prior to joining the family business, and teaching was the best training for the business world; business is pretty basic once you have an established and successful running company. It's the ethics and people skills that really make the difference in the long-time health of an organization."

With regard to pricing Carmex, Carma Labs takes a somewhat old-fashioned approach by printing prices directly onto containers. "This comes from my grandfather's belief that a customer should know their cost for a product," says Woelbing. "We sell Carmex for the lowest price possible, which allows us to make a reasonable profit. From another standpoint, I believe that it makes sense for us to continue to put the price on the container in that we tend to be amongst the lowest priced products on the market. Because we buy ingredients and packaging in such large quantities and because I pay every bill every week . . . we get materials for very good prices. Because of this, we pass our good prices on to our customers."

This philosophy of honesty and integrity is ingrained in the very fabric of Carma Labs' culture. The company's web site talks about the organization's friendly and homey atmosphere and includes the following simple statement from Don Woelbing: "We want people to come to work and enjoy it."

Humble Beginnings: 1930–56

Carma Labs' origins are closely linked to the Great Depression years of the early 1930s, when Alfred Woelbing lost his job as a buyer for Schuster's Department Store in Milwaukee. Woelbing's experience buying cosmetics, toiletries, and pharmaceuticals led him to develop his own lip balm called Lyptone—not the Carmex brand that brought him so much success in later years. Woelbing produced Lyptone from his home and marketed the product for a quarter.

Eventually, Woelbing sold Lyptone to a New Jersey firm for the then handsome price of $2,500. His entrepreneurial spirit led to the development of Shynebright, a silver polish that he also produced independently. Woelbing sold Shynebright to department stores, grocers, and jewelers in Chicago and Milwaukee. Other products Woelbing invented included a silver polish called Maid of Honor and Blue Flame lighter fluid. Although Shynebright was his primary source of income, in 1937 Woelbing developed Carmex, a new lip protection formula, for his own personal use. Carmex provided relief from both cold sores and chapped lips, and Woelbing started selling to product to others.

In the November 10, 1986 issue of the *Milwaukee Journal,* Woelbing told Gerald Koss: "I wanted something for my own cold sores, so I mixed up a batch in a kettle and tried it on myself. Then I made the rounds of drugstores, leaving a dozen jars at each place. I'd tell the proprietor, 'This is for you. If you sell out, here's my card and you can re-order. If you don't sell 'em, just throw 'em out.' Well, you know how it is—whatever the man sold was clear profit, so he sold out, all right. The rest was word of mouth. And that's how it worked. My wife and I did all the mixing and jar-filling and label-pasting ourselves at home, and it got so that's all we seemed to be doing. We almost hated it when a big order came in."

When the United States entered World War II during the 1940s, a wide variety of manufacturing companies faced shortages of the raw materials needed to produce their products. Carmex was no exception. According to the company, a shortage of lanolin—which the military used for greasing equipment and stopping rust—placed limitations on the amount of Carmex that could be produced. Fuel shortages also served to restrict growth. While Woelbing was too old to serve in the military during these difficult years, he went to work for a company called Allis-Chalmers. There, he served in the purchasing department and had some involvement in the Manhattan Project, which led to the development of the atomic bomb.

However, these wartime challenges were only temporary. Production eventually was allowed to continue unhindered, albeit in a primitive manner. As Carma Labs explains on its web site: "After the war, Alfred and his wife continued production of Carmex from their home, pouring the mixture by hand into its little glass jars, from a 12-quart kettle they kept warm on a hot plate. Alfred sold the product himself from the trunk of his car."

Expansion and Modernization: 1957 and Beyond

During the postwar boom of the 1950s, positive word-of-mouth led to the healthy growth of the Carmex brand. Woelbing remained the product's sole spokesman and salesperson, and no advertising was used. By 1957, this success eventually prompted Woelbing to move production from his home to modest, rented manufacturing space on West State Street in the western Milwaukee suburb of Wauwatosa.

Simple production techniques continued to be employed at Carma Labs throughout the 1960s and into the early 1970s. It was not until 1973 that an assembly line approach was used in the manufacture of Carmex. The transition from hand-pouring Carmex into glass jars occurred when Alfred Woelbing's son, Don, joined the company. The younger Woelbing previously worked in the masonry field. After joining Carma Labs, he purchased used assembly line equipment in nearby Chicago and reconfigured it for the manufacture of Carmex.

Strong, steady growth continued at Carma Labs during the 1970s. In 1972, success allowed Alfred Woelbing to stop making sales calls. Prior to that time, he made rounds to prospective buyers in Wisconsin, Illinois, and portions of Indiana. After operating for almost 20 years in Wauwatosa, Carma Labs relocated to a new facility in Franklin, Wisconsin, in 1976.

For almost 50 years, Carmex was distributed primarily in the Midwest. Exceptions included California, Texas, and locations in the Rocky Mountains where skiing was a popular pastime. However, this changed during the 1980s. By mid-decade, Carma Labs had begun to extend its reach to additional markets. In 1988, the first major change to Carmex occurred when the company installed a tube filling and sealing line and began offering the product in squeezable tubes. According to the May 1994 issue of *Packaging Digest,* this change was implemented based on feedback from consumers who wanted an alternative to "finger dipping" Carmex from glass jars. Initially, the company encountered leakage problems associated with the tubes, which were sealed with heat. A solution was found in ultrasonic sealing equipment. Shortly after tube production began, two additional filling and sealing lines were added in only four short years, due to increased demand.

After 53 years of steady sales increases, Carma Labs sold an estimated $10 million worth of Carmex in 1990, or more than 11 million jars and tubes of product. At this time, 89-year-old Alfred Woelbing still headed up the company he started, driving to work from his home 46 miles away in a Ford Festiva and working more than eight hours per day. Amazingly, the company had managed to grow without the use of advertising and had never accumulated any debt. It counted celebrities like Charlton Heston among its base of faithful consumers and received positive feedback from customers in the form of letters, poems, and even a country song. The company also had contracts in place with the Pentagon to supply soldiers in Operation Desert Storm with Carmex in order to protect their lips.

Despite its success, Carma Labs continued to operate under relatively simple conditions until 1991. At this time, the company was preparing to expand its plant for the fifth time. It still kept records on paper instead of using computers and had no fax machine. Humorously, in the January 26, 1991 issue of the *Milwaukee Journal,* Alfred Woelbing remarked: "There's more stress than there needs to be. We're always rushing. They always tell me to get a fax machine because it speeds things up. What in the hell are we speeding things up for? We're going to reach the end of the road fast enough." Continuing, Woelbing remarked on his amazing longevity with the company, explaining: "Work is the best therapy I can think of. It's a lot better than doing nothing and waiting for the undertaker."

In 1993, Carma Labs held an estimated 9 percent share of the U.S. lip balm market, according to the October 11, 1993 *Milwaukee Sentinel.* The following year, the company reported that more than 80 percent of its employee base, which then ranged from 25 to 30 workers, was hired through leading temporary services like Manpower, Inc. and Olsten Staffing Services.

Around this time, Carma Labs had performed another upgrade to its packaging equipment in order to keep pace with rising demand. In the May 1994 issue of *Packaging Digest,* Don

Key Dates:

1937: Alfred Woelbing develops Carmex, a new lip protection formula, for his own personal use.

1940s: Fuel and ingredient shortages the hinder production of Carmex during World War II.

1950s: Positive word-of-mouth leads to healthy growth of the Carmex brand.

1957: Woelbing moves the production of Carmex from his home to a manufacturing in the western Milwaukee suburb of Wauwatosa.

1973: Founder's son, Don Woelbing, joins Carma Labs and introduces an assembly line approach to the manufacture of Carmex.

1976: Carma Labs relocates to a new facility in Franklin, Wisconsin.

1988: Carmex is sold in squeezable tubes, marking the product's first packaging change.

1993: Carma Labs holds an estimated 9 percent share of the U.S. lip balm market.

2001: President and founder Alfred Woelbing dies at the age of 100.

Woelbing explained how the upgrade was in line with the company's simple, straightforward approach to doing business, commenting: "We want the best packaging machinery and materials we can get for our investment dollars. But we don't want machines that are difficult to run and maintain, nor those loaded with electronics. Such machines require considerable training. They also pose a difficulty for us in that there aren't many technicians in our area that can repair them. We believe our business is efficient because of its simplicity. That includes packaging. We've found that by making a good product and selling it at a reasonable price, people have beaten a path to our door."

By the early 2000s, Carma Labs had expanded distribution of Carmex to include every state. In addition, the company had expanded internationally, marketing its products in Australia and some areas of Europe.

In 2001, Carma Labs bid a final farewell to its president and founding father. Sixty-seven years after starting the company, Alfred Woelbing passed away at the age of 100. Until the age of 95, Woelbing had continued to drive to the office every day by

himself from his home in Rubicon, Wisconsin. After suffering a stroke in 1997, he continued to visit the office about once a week.

By October 2002, a survey reported in several newspapers, including the *Chicago Tribune,* revealed that lip balm sales at pharmacies, supermarkets, and discounters—excluding retail behemoth Wal-Mart—had increased 8 percent over the previous year, reaching $281 million. As the lip balm market grew, so did rumors that popular lip protection products like Blistex, Carmex, and Chap Stick were addictive. Responding to rumors that it included fiberglass and other irritants in its lip balm to create dependency, Carma Labs posted a disclaimer on its web site negating such claims. In the March 11, 2003 issue of the *Pittsburgh Post-Gazette,* Richard Chin concluded that so-called lip balm addiction was "an urban legend, an Internet myth and utter fallacy, at least according to manufacturers and doctors."

With its evolution from Alfred Woelbing's kitchen stovetop to status as a leading, family-owned American enterprise, Carma Labs is an amazing success story. Given the rapid growth of the Carmex brand through word-of-mouth testimonials, as well as a strong retail market, the company's future appears to be secure.

Principal Competitors

Blistex, Inc.; Wyeth Consumer Healthcare.

Further Reading

Chin, Richard, "Smear Campaign Lip Balm Addiction: Menace or Modern Myth?," *Pittsburgh Post-Gazette,* March 11, 2003.

Dresang, Joel, "Carmex a Balm to Soldiers," *Milwaukee Journal,* January 26, 1991.

"Filling/Sealing Soothe Carmex Tube Demand," *Packaging Digest,* May 1994.

Kiley, David, "Going It Alone: One-Brand Companies," *Adweek's Marketing Week,* November 26, 1990.

Kloss, Gerald, "A Factory Full of Unchapped Lips," *Milwaukee Journal,* November 10, 1986.

Romell, Rick, "In Songs and Poems, Fans Glorify Carmex," *Milwaukee Sentinel,* October 11, 1993.

Rubin, Bonnie Miller, "Lip-Balm 'Addicts' Just Can't Lick Habit," *Chicago Tribune,* March 12, 2003.

Silvers, Amy Rabideau, "Creator of Carmex Found a Lip-Smacking Success," *Milwaukee Journal Sentinel,* May 22, 2001.

—Paul R. Greenland

Chas. Levy Company LLC

1200 North North Branch Street
Chicago, Illinois 60622
U.S.A.
Telephone: (312) 440-4400
Fax: (312) 440-7414
Web site: http://www.chaslevy.com

Private Company
Incorporated: 1883
Employees: 8,500
Sales: $725 million (2002 est.)
NAIC: 422920 Book, Periodical, and Newspaper
  Wholesalers

The Chas. Levy Company LLC is one of the top four distributors of magazines in the United States, and the leading distributor of books to mass retailers. The company's operating units include Chas. Levy Circulating Co., which sells magazines to grocery, drug, and large retail stores, and Levy Home Entertainment, which distributes books to the likes of Wal-Mart and Target. The firm is owned by board chairman Barbara Levy Kipper, the granddaughter of its founder.

Beginnings

The Chas. Levy Company traces its roots to the year 1883, when 15-year-old Chicago newsboy Charles Levy won a horse and cart in a raffle and decided to put them to use distributing papers. His first assignment was hauling copies of the *Chicago Mail* to the stockyards, and he soon found his niche as a middleman distributing papers to newsboys and newsstands on the city's West Side, handling major publications of the era like the *Times,* the *Chronicle,* and the *Inter-Ocean.* As his workload increased brothers Joseph, Ben, and Max joined him in the enterprise.

In the early 1900s the Levys began purchasing gasoline-powered trucks to make deliveries, hiring union drivers to cover their growing network of delivery routes. By this time Charles Levy had come to focus on promoting the business and main-taining good relations with newspaper publishers, while Joe Levy handled the day-to-day management chores.

In 1910 the company began distributing magazines, starting with Curtis Publishing Company titles like the *Saturday Evening Post,* the *Ladies Home Journal,* and the *Country Gentleman.* As their popularity grew, in particular that of the *Post,* Levy started to buy up other magazine distributors in the Chicago area until the firm was the sole Curtis distributor for the city. The company subsequently made deals with other magazine publishers like Crowell and Macfadden to distribute their titles in Chicago as well.

During the 1910s and 1920s the Chicago newspapers established their own distribution systems within the city, and Levy redirected its efforts to the outlying areas. The company's routes expanded to service towns up to 100 miles away, including Elgin, Rockford, and Joliet, Illinois, as well as the suburbs that were beginning to spring up around Chicago, starting in 1923. Levy would truck newspapers directly to a publisher's suburban branch, which would handle distribution door-to-door. The firm also continued to deliver magazines to local businesses like newsstands, pool rooms, hotels, and candy and cigar stores.

Late 1940s: Adding Paperbacks

Following World War II a new opportunity presented itself in the form of paperback books, which had become popular through their use by servicemen fighting overseas. In the late 1940s the company started distributing the inexpensive books, which at that time cost between 25 and 50 cents each.

In 1952 Levy purchased one of its main competitors, the J.O. Stoll Company. Each firm controlled approximately 30 percent of magazine distribution to newsstands in the Chicago area, with Levy handling the titles of four large publishers and Stoll those of 11 smaller ones. Afterward the number of magazines Levy carried increased from 150 to 750, while annual book and magazine sales doubled to $5 million. With this surge in business Charles Levy's son Charles, Jr. ("Chuck"), who was now running the company, hired his friend Herbert Fried to oversee the integration of Stoll. Among the changes made at this time were the centralization of distribution operations and the trans-

---

Company Perspectives:

Chas. Levy Company is a leading distributor of books and magazines and provider of related services. By delivering quality service, flexibility, innovative marketing and customized support programs, we meet the needs of our business partners consistent with their perception of value. We will maintain our leadership position through the use of advanced technology, constant process improvement and continuous cost reduction. We will continue to seek growth opportunities. We will expand our primary businesses through internal growth and acquisition. We will leverage our core competencies into other related areas and pursue opportunities outside our traditional lines of business. We will provide both a challenging and rewarding environment for our employees and a fair return to our shareholders. The Company is privately held and believes strongly in actively contributing to the public interest and giving back to the communities in which we live and work.

---

fer of magazine distribution from independently owned routes to company-owned ones, which made the delivery drivers full-time Levy employees.

The 1950s also saw Levy's newspaper business grow at a rapid rate as the suburbs expanded. The firm was handling the out-of-Chicago trucking for the city's three major papers, the *Tribune,* the *Sun-Times,* and the *American,* with delivery runs made as far away as Milwaukee, Wisconsin to the north and South Bend, Indiana to the east. Nearly 70 trucks were utilized to deliver up to one million papers per night.

To ensure that the business grew in a healthy manner, Levy began to hire professional management personnel, as well as training the firm's existing staff in modern business techniques through the use of seminars and classes. The company also instituted a profit-sharing plan to encourage productivity. Levy was one of the first in its industry to take this approach, in contrast with many magazine and book distribution firms that were still small, family-run organizations.

The late 1950s saw Chuck Levy found the Council of Independent Distributors, a trade organization that promoted the interests of companies like his own. In 1962 Levy began distributing hardcover books, and by 1965 the company's annual revenues had reached an estimated $14 million.

In 1968 the firm created a new unit, Computer Book Services (CBS), which helped retailers select titles based on computer analyses of sales data. Herb Fried, who was now serving as president of the company, chose former Bantam Books executive David Moscow to run the division. Taking advantage of emerging computer technology, the company placed punch-cards in each book, which retailers could return to generate a new order. CBS was targeted toward mass merchants, and soon began working with retail giants like Sears, Montgomery Ward, and Penney's. The chains were able to consolidate most of their purchases with Levy rather than dealing with different distributors around the country, which saved them time and money. The initiative helped Levy become the largest paperback book dis-

tributor in the United States during the decade. This era also saw the company ship books overseas to developing nations in association with the Books USA program, as well as to troops serving in Vietnam.

Parallel growth was occurring in Levy's magazine division, through innovations like the Family Reading Center, a supermarket fixture that organized and expanded the number of magazines displayed and also offered space for children's books and paperbacks. Initially used in some Chicago area Jewel food stores, the idea caught on and was soon adopted in many locations. Levy subsequently brought out a checkout counter rack that could hold as many as 15 different publications, nearly four times the amount previously displayed.

Distributing Videos and Software in the 1980s

In 1976 Herb Fried stepped down as president. His place was later taken by David Moscow, who began to formulate aggressive expansion plans. Seeking new ways to take advantage of the company's existing delivery routes, he added items like computer software, which debuted in 1984. That same year, at a time when home videocassette recorder sales were rapidly taking off, the company began to distribute videos through the purchase of Detroit-based Video Trend, a fast-growing regional tape distributor with $11 million in sales. Video Trend had outlets in several markets, and in early 1985 added one near Chicago. Levy soon bought a second video distribution company in Tampa, Florida, and then acquired a third in 1986 in Seattle, Washington that had four West Coast locations.

The firm had also recently launched a series of humorous greeting cards called "Chicago Breezes," which lampooned subjects like politicians and sports teams. The line gave Levy entrée into the card sections of drug stores and supermarkets, and over the next several years the company took on distribution chores for six other greeting card makers.

In 1986 Charles "Chuck" Levy, Jr., passed away at the age of 73, having worked for the company for 51 years. His daughter Barbara Levy Kipper, a former *Chicago Sun-Times* reporter, took over the chairman's job.

The following year the company recorded sales of more than $360 million, driven in large part by the growth of video. Video Trend was now the third largest distributor of tapes in the United States, with revenues of $143 million. The company's Chicago-centered magazine division, in contrast, accounted for just $77 million in sales.

In 1990 Levy entered another new category, buying Mid-Michigan Music Co. of Grand Rapids, Michigan, for an estimated $2 million. Mid-Michigan distributed cassettes and compact discs to 175 stores in 26 states.

In early 1991 Levy president and CEO David Moscow was dismissed due to philosophical differences with owner and board chairman Barbara Levy Kipper. He was immediately replaced by Carol Kloster, age 42, who had joined Levy in 1974 as a personal assistant and then risen through the ranks. With the owner's blessing Kloster set about shoring up Levy's magazine business, buying United News Co. of Philadelphia during the year to give the company a larger geographical presence in this category.

<table>
<tr><td colspan="2">**Key Dates:**</td></tr>
<tr><td>1883:</td><td>Charles Levy begins distributing newspapers in Chicago.</td></tr>
<tr><td>1910:</td><td>Levy adds magazines, including *Saturday Evening Post.*</td></tr>
<tr><td>1923:</td><td>The first newspaper deliveries are made to Chicago suburbs.</td></tr>
<tr><td>1952:</td><td>The acquisition of J.O. Stoll Co. doubles the firm's magazine distribution business.</td></tr>
<tr><td>1968:</td><td>The Computer Book Services unit is formed to serve mass-market retailers.</td></tr>
<tr><td>1984:</td><td>The company begins to distribute computer software; the company buys Video Trend.</td></tr>
<tr><td>1990:</td><td>Mid-Michigan Music Co. is purchased.</td></tr>
<tr><td>1991:</td><td>United News Co. of Philadelphia is acquired.</td></tr>
<tr><td>1994:</td><td>Newspaper distribution ends; the Levy Music & Video unit is sold.</td></tr>
<tr><td>1999:</td><td>The merger with Unimag to form the second largest distributor fails.</td></tr>
</table>

Abandoning Newspaper and Video Distribution in 1994

Over the years Levy's newspaper distribution business had tapered off, and it ultimately became unprofitable. On April 30, 1994 the company halted distribution of the remaining handful of papers it carried, which included the *New York Times* and *Investor's Business Daily.* Earnings from video wholesaling also were dropping sharply, and later the same year the firm sold its video and music division, whose annual revenues had shrunk to approximately $50 million. The unit was purchased by the Handleman Co. of Troy, Michigan, a leading distributor of music, video, software, and books. Several years later Handleman sold Levy its book distribution arm, which had sales of $54.1 million. By now Levy Home Entertainment was the largest distributor of books to mass-market retail accounts in the United States. Over the next several years it would add capacity with new distribution centers in Salem, Virginia and Clearfield, Utah.

During this same period the firm's magazine business continued to grow. In 1996 Levy began a three-year run of distributorship acquisitions that would bring a total of nine new companies into the fold. A wave of industry consolidation was now taking place, which left 50 firms at the end of the 1990s from a total of 300 in 1995. The shakeout was caused by a change in policy at the major retail chains, which had begun forcing distributors to bid on contracts to serve many or all of their stores. This saved money for the retailers but wreaked havoc with distributors, who had to lower prices and offer new incentives to remain competitive.

In late 1998 plans were announced for Levy's largest acquisition to date, the purchase of Dublin, Ohio-based United Magazine Co., or Unimag. The merger between the two companies, which were similar in size, would create the second largest magazine distributor in the United States with 18 percent of the market. As the closing date approached, the struggling Unimag saw its debt climb dangerously high, which forced a revision of the deal. In April the Kroger Co. dropped its Detroit and Cincinnati contracts with Unimag, reportedly over concerns about the distributor's unpaid bills, and this proved a death blow to the agreement. In May it was officially abandoned, and in September Unimag went out of business.

Levy's operations continued to grow after this disappointment, and by 2003 the Chas. Levy Circulating Co. had more than 6,500 sales and support staffers, operated more than 600 delivery vehicles, and had nine distribution centers and 42 transportation centers that handled both magazines and books. Levy Home Entertainment kept more than 2,000 busy in the field doing in-store merchandising, and also employed specialists in marketing and inventory to keep customers like Best Buy, Target, and Wal-Mart in 48 states stocked with books. The two divisions' combined revenues had grown to an estimated $725 million.

After 120 years the Charles Levy Co. LLC had evolved into a leading distributor of magazines and books. While it no longer handled newspapers or the videos that once drove profits in the 1980s, it had staked out a strong position in its respective markets.

Principal Subsidiaries

Chas. Levy Circulating Co.; Levy Home Entertainment, LLC.

Principal Competitors

Anderson News LLC; The News Group; Hudson News Co.; Ingram Industries, Inc.

Further Reading

Borden, Jeff, "Chas. Levy Delivers New Strategy, CEO," *Crain's Chicago Business,* May 6, 1991, p. 1.
——, "Michigan Buy Gives Chas. Levy Entrée to Music Distribution Biz," *Crain's Chicago Business,* April 23, 1990, p. 16.
Harvey, Mary, "Chas. Levy Abandons Plans to Buy Unimag," *Folio,* July 1, 1999, p. 13.
Kuczynski, Alex, "The Media Business: 4 Big Magazine Wholesalers Face Federal Inquiry," *New York Times,* October 19, 2000, p. 1.
"Media Distributor Drops Newspapers," *Crain's Chicago Business,* March 7, 1994, p. 46.
"Midwest Newsstand Distribution Stand-Off Winds Down," *Circulation Management,* August 30, 1999.
Milliott, Jim, "Handleman Selling NBC to Chas. Levy," *Publishers Weekly,* June 15, 1998, p. 13.
Owens, Jennifer, and Teresa Ennis, "Latest Wholesaler Merger Shrinks Major Players to Four," *Folio,* February 1, 1999.
Waldstein, Peter D., "Chas. Levy Goes Hollywood: Video Magic Boosts Vendor," *Crain's Chicago Business,* October 5, 1987, p. 1.
Wisby, Gary, "Herbert B. Fried, Business Leader," *Chicago Sun-Times,* December 15, 2001, p. 58.

—Frank Uhle

CHS

CHS Inc.

5500 Cenex Drive
Inver Grove Heights, Minnesota 55077
U.S.A.
Telephone: (651) 355-5151
Toll Free: (800) 232-3639
Fax: (651) 355-4554
Web site: http://www.chsinc.com

Public Company
Incorporated: 1998 as Cenex Harvest States Cooperatives
Employees: 8,000
Sales: $7.85 billion (2002)
Stock Exchanges: NASDAQ
Ticker Symbol: CHSCP
NAIC: 311119 Other Animal Food Manufacturing;
    311211 Flour Milling; 311991 Perishable Prepared
    Food Manufacturing; 311830 Tortilla Manufacturing;
    311823 Dry Pasta Manufacturing; 311941
    Mayonnaise, Dressing, and Other Prepared Sauce
    Manufacturing; 324110 Petroleum Refineries

CHS Inc. is a leading regional agricultural cooperative in the United States. Its 325,000 members are concentrated in the Midwest and Northwest. The co-op processes and sells grain and soybean products on behalf of its farmer members and sells them petroleum, fertilizer, and other farming inputs. CHS was formed when Cenex Inc. and Harvest States Cooperatives were combined in June 1998. By such moves as acquiring tortilla factories and developing close ties with pasta makers, the co-op has extended its involvement in finished consumer products in order to offset lower prices for agricultural commodities in the face of increasing global competition. The co-op has operations in 24 states.

Origins

CHS Inc. traces its origins to a number of individual cooperatives that operated in the Northwest and Midwest. The oldest of these organizations was North Pacific Grain Growers, Inc. (NPGG), a regional cooperative formed in Lewiston, Idaho, in

December 1929. NPGG relocated to Portland, Oregon, in 1938. It would merge with another cooperative to form Harvest States Cooperatives in 1983.

Cenex was formed as Farmers Union Central Exchange on January 15, 1931 in St. Paul, Minnesota, by about two dozen local oil cooperatives. According to the *Star-Tribune,* the venture was founded with a $25,000 loan from the precursor to Harvest States Cooperatives. Farmers Union opened its own warehouse, oil blending plant, and headquarters in 1935.

The Farmers Union Grain Terminal Association (GTA) opened in St. Paul in June 1938 with the support of 121 local coops. GTA acquired Rush City, Minnesota-based Amber Milling Company in 1942, entering the wheat milling business. The next year, it acquired three elevator lines and some lumberyards.

Cenex was making investments in petroleum refining. In 1942, the co-op began marketing feed, seed and fertilizer. Cenex built a new headquarters building in St. Paul in 1957.

Expansion in the 1960s and 1970s

Cenex, GTA, and NPGG continued to expand in the 1960s and 1970s, which were a period of growth for the farming industry and agricultural cooperatives. Cenex expanded in the Pacific Northwest in 1971. The purchase of Northern Cooperative Services brought Cenex into transportation in 1972. "Where the customer is the company" became Cenex's motto in 1973. In 1976 and 1977, Cenex added 80 more local co-ops in Utah, Washington, Oregon, and Idaho. Sales to members exceeded $1 billion in 1979. At the time of its fiftieth anniversary in 1981, Cenex had 1,500 member co-ops in 15 states. That year, Cenex became a top ten propane supplier with the acquisition of Solar Gas.

Harvest States Formed 1983

Harvest States Cooperatives was formed in 1983 by the merger of GTA with NPGG. The 1980s saw a contraction of the farming industry in the United States, and the number of large co-ops fell due to bankruptcies and consolidation. In 1977, GTA had made an important acquisition, that of Wisconsin-

Company Perspectives:

At CHS, we believe success is not just measured by the numbers we report on the bottom line for a single year. Real success occurs over an extended time. Real success is about the values and vision held deep within our organization. Amid the business environment of the past year, CHS directors and management recognized the need to take a close look at what we do and how we do it. The results build confidence that this member-owned company operates at the highest standards every day and for the long term. What do we mean by that? We mean our relationships with customers, owners and employees, and business partners must be conducted with utmost trust and integrity. We are commixed to growing this system for its stakeholders with a deliberate and thoughtful approach that some may consider conservative, but one we believe will support the system's ability to add lasting value for its owners and customers. In all decisions, we must balance the competing needs of our current infrastructure with embracing appropriate opportunities for growth and providing our member-owners with sufficient return on their investment. And we must always focus on our first priority: maintaining the investment-grade financial health essential for the long-term success of this company.

based Holsum Foods. Its processed foods business would be an important cushion against falling grain prices in the coming years.

Cenex began the 1980s with earnings of $32 million a year. However, it posted a pretax profit of just $426,000 on sales of $1.4 billion in 1985, while Harvest States logged sales of $2.3 billion and a pretax profit of $12.1 million.

Petroleum accounted for two-thirds of Cenex's revenues in the mid-1980s. At the time, Land O'Lakes and Cenex were ranked two and three behind Harvest States Cooperatives in the Midwest region.

In 1986, Cenex teamed with Land O'Lakes to manage certain of their operations jointly. Cenex directed petroleum operations, Land O'Lakes managed feed and seed, and the two companies jointly managed their fertilizer and chemical businesses through a joint venture called Cenex/Land O'Lakes Ag Services.

Cenex faced some of its most difficult years in the mid-1980s as the price of its two main commodities, petroleum and fertilizer, fell. Cenex lost $12 million in 1986, resulting in layoffs and a scaling back of facilities in Cenex's 13-state territory.

Adding Value in the 1990s

Processed food accounted for $459 million of Harvest States' annual sales in fiscal 1991. The company was expanding in this area to make up for declining margins in the grain trading business, acquiring Great American Foods of Chicago, Lewis Albert & Sons of Omaha, and Private Brands of Philadelphia. Honeymead Products, which processed soybean oil for salad dressing, and the Amber Milling pasta unit were star performers of the processed foods division. Total annual revenues were about $3 billion a year in 1990 and 1991, when the co-op handled a record 740 million bushels of grain.

By the early 1990s, Cenex had seen a complete turnaround and was distributing record disbursements to its member cooperatives. It refunded $52.8 million based on fiscal 1992's $64 million profit on sales of $1.8 billion.

In the early 1990s, Cenex invested $80 million in an upgrade of a refinery in Laurel, Montana, which had been operating since 1930. By this time, Cenex served 1,800 local cooperatives in fifteen states. It supplied farmers with automotive accessories and tires as well as petroleum products and fertilizer. A subsidiary of Cenex acquired Rockford Gain Growers Inc., a small co-op based near Spokane, Washington, in 1994.

Harvest States formed a canola oilseed joint venture with Mitsubishi's SeedTec International unit in 1992. In the same year, it formed a pet and dairy food venture with Farmland Industries, using an existing extrusion feed mill Harvest States owned in Owatonna, Minnesota.

In 1992, Harvest States' Holsum Foods Division acquired Portland-based Gregg Foods. Holsum produced salad dressings and oils. In 1994, the division expanded into California with the purchase of Los Angeles-based Saffola Quality Foods.

Harvest States formed another joint venture with another Japanese-owned company, Mitsui & Company's Wilsey Foods Inc. unit, to acquire a Pennsylvania salad dressing plant from H.J. Heinz in 1995. In addition to expanding Harvest States' value-added foods business (it already owned a smaller dressings plant), the venture, eventually called Ventura Foods, LLC, was designed to increase the co-op's prospects for food sales in the Far East.

John Johnson became CEO of Harvest States in January 1995. He had joined the co-op 19 years earlier as a feed consultant. While the co-op's three previous CEOs had come from a grain merchandising background, Johnson's marketing experience was particularly important to Harvest States at that time as it embraced the value-added mantra, reported the *Star Tribune*. Johnson replaced CEO Allen D. Hanson, who retired at the end of 1994.

In the mid-1990s, Harvest States' member co-ops represented 125,000 farmers. Harvest States was building flour mills in Kenosha, Wisconsin; Houston, Texas; and Mount Pocono, Pennsylvania. In 1998, American Italian Pasta Company built a factory next to the Kenosha plant, which was originally constructed to supply bakery flour to commercial baking customers in the Chicago-Milwaukee area. Harvest States was also supplying Kraft with flour for its macaroni.

Harvest States invested $2.5 million in Minnesota-based tortilla producer Sparta Foods Inc., attaining an 18 percent stake in the company. The *Star Tribune* reported the tortilla market was growing between 10 and 15 percent a year, and the co-op supplied Sparta with its main ingredients: flour, corn and oil.

United in 1998

CENEX, Inc. and Harvest States Cooperatives merged in June 1998, forming Cenex Harvest States Cooperatives (CHS). Combined, they had annual revenues of $10 billion. This was less than massive companies like Cargill; however, the size of the new company did help its member farmers deal with a market that was seeing more global competition. CHS aimed to build a vertically integrated organization that would provide farmers with supplies and consumers with value-added specialty foods.

In 1999, CHS officials held talks with Farmland Industries Inc., a cooperative based in Kansas City, about combining their grain-handling operations. This led to merger talks. They were roughly equal in size. Officials said a merger would allow the combined firms to save $100 million a year.

CHS shareholders barely failed to approve the merger by the required two-thirds majority of its 44,000 farmer-owners. Dissidents cited management incentives as a stumbling point. Other issues were a potential tax liability, which was resolved in Farmland's favor, and Farmland's dependence on the declining nitrogen market.

Partnering in 2000 and Beyond

CHS bought two Minnesota tortilla businesses in June 2000: Sparta Foods Inc. and Bec-Lin of Perham, Inc. Rodriguez Festive Foods of Fort Worth, Texas, was added in 2001. The Harvest States Foods division began building a new tortilla plant in Newton, North Carolina, in 2002.

The main ingredients in tortillas were wheat flour and vegetable oil derived from soybeans, both of which CHS already processed. The co-op saw such vertical integration as the best chance for its members to be profitable as agriculture markets consolidated and prices for a variety of commodities such as grain, livestock, petroleum, and flour reached record lows.

CHS partnered with Farmland and Land O'Lakes, Inc. in Agriliance, LLC, a joint venture created in 2000 to deliver agronomic inputs to farmers. At the same time, CHS was joining Cargill Inc. and DuPont in developing an e-commerce site for farmers called Rooster.com. The *Wall Street Journal* reported that analysts thought the agriculture business was an excellent candidate for online success, since geographically isolated farmers were facing fewer options for acquiring supplies in their local markets. Rooster.com was envisioned as a kind of online shopping mall, with the three founders as anchor tenants. They aimed to attract hundreds of other merchants. Farmers could sell crops as well as buy supplies at Rooster.com.

CHS revenues reached $7.85 billion in fiscal 2002. The co-op would return $56.5 million, or 45 percent of earnings, to its members.

CHS Cooperatives—the name had been streamlined in 2000—officially became known as CHS Inc. in mid-2003.

CHS continued to seek better efficiencies of scale by partnering with other companies. It teamed with Cargill, Inc. in a wheat milling joint venture called Horizon Milling, LLC.

Principal Subsidiaries

CHS Holdings, Inc.; CHS-Agri Valley; CHS-Chinook; CHS-Connell, Inc.; CHS-Crookston; CHS-Devils Lake; CHS-Edgeley; CHS-Garrison; CHS-Glasgow; CHS-Grangeville, Inc.; CHS-Highmore; CHS-Jasper; CHS-Kalispell; CHS-Kindred; CHS-Lewistown; CHS-Madison; CHS-Philip; CHS-Richey; CHS-Salol/Roseau; CHS-Sioux Falls; CHS-Stevensville; CHS-Tracey/Garvin; CoGrain (54.5%); Cooperative Business International, Inc.; Country Hedging, Inc.; Front Range Pipeline LLC; HSC-Edmore; HSC-Herman/Norcross; HSC-Minot, N.D.; Ventura Foods, LLC (50%).

Principal Divisions

Grains and Foods; Crop Inputs; Services to Cooperatives and Producers.

Principal Competitors

Archer Daniels Midland Company; Bunge Ltd.; Cargill, Inc.; ConAgra Foods, Inc.; Farmland Industries, Inc.

Further Reading

Aehl, John, "How CENEX Grew to a Giant," W*inston-Salem Journal*, February 23, 1992.
Backmann, Dave, "Pasta Factory to Open," *News* (Kenosha, Wis.), July 8, 1998, p. C6.
Brandt, Steve, "Cenex and Land O'Lakes Approve Joint Venture," *Minneapolis Star and Tribune*, December 2, 1986, p. 7B.
——, "Cenex Loses $12 Million; Sales Drop to $1.1 Billion," *Minneapolis Star and Tribune*, February 4, 1987, p. 1M.
——, "Moseson Resigns as Cenex Chief: Co-Op Moves Quickly to Fill Surprise Vacancy," *Star-Tribune* (Minneapolis-St. Paul), August 7, 1987, p. 9B.
——, "Puny Profits Push Giant Co-Ops Together: Cenex-Land O'Lakes Venture Seeks to Head Off Trouble," *Star-Tribune* (Minneapolis-St. Paul), January 12, 1987, p. 1M.
"Cenex Co-Ops Will Share $16 Million," *Billings Gazette*, March 21, 1993, p. D6.
DiGiovanni, Joe, "Elevator, Mill Largest in the Country," *News* (Kenosha, Wis.), May 22, 1994, p. B1.
Fedor, Liz, "Ag Giants Create Online Mall; Rooster.com Is Venture of Cargill, Cenex and DuPont," *Star Tribune* (Minneapolis), March 2, 2000, p. 1D.

Gardner, Steven, "Local Farm Stores to Close Up," *Columbian* (Vancouver, Wash.), February 13, 2002, p. E1.

Howard, Tom, "Cenex Works on Reducing Sulfur," *Billings Gazette*, May 20, 1992, p. A1.

Jones, Grayden, "Farm Co-Ops Establish Canola Joint Venture," *Spokesman Review*, January 30, 1992.

——, "Grain Co-Op Purchased by Midwest Firm," *Spokesman Review*, July 28, 1994, p. A14.

Kennedy, Tony, "Harvest States CEO Had Fruitful Timing," *Star Tribune* (Minneapolis), April 17, 1995, p. D1.

Kilman, Scott, "Business Spins Onto the Web: Cargill, DuPont, Cenex to Form Site for Farmers," *Wall Street Journal*, March 2, 2000, p. A12.

Kram, Jerry W., "CHS Looks to Buy Cargill Elevators," *Grand Forks Herald*, April 10, 2002, p. B1.

Levy, Melisssa, "Cenex Plans to Take Another Stab at a Farmland Merger," *Star Tribune* (Minneapolis), December 3, 1999, p. 1D.

Merrill, Ann, "Harvest States Invests $2.5 Million in Private Sparta Foods Placement," *Star Tribune* (Minneapolis), February 26, 1998, p. 1D.

——, "Merger Shows Cenex Harvest States Is Hungry for Growth," *Star Tribune* (Minneapolis), January 16, 2000, p. 1D.

Zaslow, Jeffrey, "The Changing Face of Agriculture," *Wall Street Journal*, November 9, 1984.

—Frederick C. Ingram

Chugach Alaska Corporation

560 East 34th Avenue
Anchorage, Alaska 99503
U.S.A.
Telephone: (907) 563-8866
Toll Free: (800) 858-2768
Fax: (907) 563-8402
Web site: http://www.chugach-ak.com

Private Company
Incorporated: 1971
Employees: 5,000
Sales: $354 million (2002)
NAIC: 561210 Government Base Facilities Operation
    Support Services; 611710 Educational Support
    Services; 236220 Construction Management,
    Commercial and Institutional Building; 561310
    Employment Placement Services

Chugach Alaska Corporation (CAC) is one of the most successful of the 12 Alaska Native Regional Corporations that were formed in 1971 as part of the Alaska Native Claims Settlement Act. The company, whose shareholders are 2,000 Native Alaskans of the Aleut, Eskimo, and Indian peoples, controls about 900,000 acres of mostly coastal land in the Chugach region of Alaska (south-central Alaska and Prince William Sound). Since emerging from bankruptcy in 1991, CAC has followed a new corporate plan. Rather than focus exclusively on developing its rich natural resources of timber and fisheries, the company has become a leading provider of government services contracts, ranging from managing U.S. military bases to employment services to telecommunications. Through its six subsidiaries and numerous joint ventures, CAC now oversees 51 such projects in 21 states and six foreign countries.

ANCSA and the Creation of CAC: 1971

In 1971, the U.S. Congress broke with established federal Indian policy when it enacted the Alaska Native Claims Settlement Act (ANCSA) to resolve aboriginal land claims in Alaska.

For over a century, Native Alaskans had sought the return of their lands, which had been illegally confiscated by Russians in the eighteenth and nineteenth centuries and then sold to the U.S. government. Little progress was made until 1968, when oil was discovered in Alaska's Prudhoe Bay. Recognizing that the pipeline needed to transport the 9.6 billion barrels of oil out of Alaska would have to cross disputed land, the oil industry pushed Congress to settle the land claims once and for all.

Congress, with the approval of the majority of Alaska Natives, chose to break with the reservation system it had used with Native Americans in the Continental U.S. for over a century. Instead, Congress applied a corporate model to solve the problem in Alaska. ANCSA returned $962 million in cash and 44 million acres of land to the 12 regional native corporations (and nearly 200 village corporations) it created. Native Alaskans were made shareholders in these corporations. ANCSA's radical innovation was to break with the trusteeship model of federal Indian policy and, instead, have the corporations, and thus the indigenous Alaskans, use the land itself as the foundation from which they could build an economic and political future.

Transition to a Corporate Model: 1970s to the Early 1980s

With nearly 2,000 shareholders, Chugach Alaska Corporation (CAC) was the second smallest regional corporation formed by ANCSA. CAC was promised $11.5 million and 930,000 acres in the coastal areas of south-central Alaska, a region rich in fish and timber. Like the other regional corporations, CAC had a difficult transition to make. ANCSA had instantly transformed rural—and often subsistence-level—Alaskans to shareholders in major corporations. Few of CAC's shareholders or managers had significant business experience. "We didn't know what we were doing," a shareholder in another regional corporation told the *Seattle Times*. "We were taken out of a village culture and put into a corporate culture that we didn't understand." Moreover, the structure imposed by ANCSA was somewhat artificial. Unlike in the "real" business world, where people form corporations to fulfill a specific business need or make a specific product, the Native regional corporations were launched, endowed with federal dollars, and then charged with discovering a business purpose.

CAC followed what seemed a sensible course, investing in the local resource industries (fishing and timber) that it knew best. Unfortunately, CAC's start-up difficulties were compounded by ongoing legal battles. The actual conveyance of lands promised under ANCSA stalled. CAC sued the U.S. government in 1975, but the matter was not resolved until 1982, when Congress passed the Chugach Natives, Inc. Settlement Agreement, which finally transferred the land and awarded the corporation an additional $12 million to make up for lost opportunities. However, the monetary settlement could not wholly undo the lost years. In the intervening period, global markets for CAC's staple businesses had plummeted. A worldwide salmon glut proved particularly harmful to the fisheries-dependent CAC. A fire at one of its canneries in Prince William Sound and a botulism scare at another in 1982 also hurt the company.

Despite these problems, CAC's strategy for most of the 1980s remained centered on its local resource-base industries. At the same time, CAC also looked to profit from other resources on its lands. The Bering River Field on CAC's properties near Cordova had the potential to produce nearly 59 million tons of coal. To explore the field, CAC formed the Bering Development Corporation, a joint venture with a consortium of Korean companies called KADCO to explore and extract coal, which was destined primarily for export markets. However, as the *Alaska Journal of Commerce* noted in 1996, mining was subject to the same pitfalls as fishing and timber. All three were "extremely volatile businesses influenced by market events far beyond the influence of the corporation's managers."

New Challenges: Mid-1980s and Early 1990s

CAC's debts mounted in the mid-1980s as global salmon and timber markets remained saturated. Like its compatriot regional Native corporations, CAC cast about for a way to remain afloat in a shifting business climate it was just beginning to understand. In 1985, two Native corporations failed and were forced into bankruptcy. In response, Congress changed the tax code in 1986 to allow Native corporations to sell net operating losses to private firms seeking tax breaks, which provided CAC and other Native corporations a much-needed infusion of cash and helped return them to profitability. CAC obtained $54 million in 1986 from the sale of its net operating losses.

At the same time, CAC benefited from a marked improvement in its resource-based businesses. For the first time since its inception, CAC paid a dividend to its Native shareholders. Nineteen eighty-six was "a year in which the mistakes and losses of the past were corrected and reversed but not forgotten," CAC's president and CEO Michael Chittick told the *Alaska Journal of Commerce* in 1988. CAC's fisheries sector led the company-wide turnaround. Seafood product sales alone

accounted for 89 percent of the company's corporate revenues in 1986. Hoping to capitalize on the positive trends in this sector, CAC purchased another cannery in 1987 on Kodiak Island. This new acquisition increased CAC's fish processing capacity by 30 percent and gave the corporation access to lucrative new salmon runs.

CAC also began to exploit its timber assets more thoroughly. In 1986, the company made plans to begin harvesting timber on its land on the remote Montague Island. This sale garnered the company $2.3 million in 1987. CAC formed a new subsidiary, Chugach Forest Products, to oversee its timber-related operations. In 1988, CAC approved construction of a new sawmill, which had the capacity to produce kiln-dried dimensional lumber, in Seward. The $22 million project used computer-controlled lasers to scan logs to make the most efficient cuts.

CAC suffered a huge setback in 1989 when the *Valdez*, an Exxon oil tanker, ran aground in Prince William Sound, spilling 11.7 million gallons of crude oil into the pristine waters where CAC carried out its commercial fishing. The economic catastrophe not only threatened the traditional way of life of the Alaska Natives living in the area and sullied the spectacular beauty of the region, but it also threatened to destroy CAC's fragile financial success. Nearly 85 percent of CAC's profit-making operations were in the area. The spill ground commercial fishing activity to a halt and jeopardized the company's three canneries in the area. Although CAC eventually reached a settlement with Exxon, CAC's condition did not improve. "The *Exxon Valdez* is what in many people's minds put us over the side," CAC's president would remark in 2001 to the *Alaska Business Monthly*. "It's hard to put a number on the impact of the spill, but it was certainly devastating on fishing."

CAC's debts began to mount once again. The Valdez catastrophe compounded underlying business-cycle problems that had plagued the company since its inception. Fishing prices plummeted in the early 1990s, and CAC's top-of-the-line sawmill in Seward encountered a host of difficulties. The Alaska housing boom of the 1980s tapered off, shrinking a major market for the mill's dimensional lumber. Furthermore, the mill had an inadequate power supply and was too far from other markets to realize its full potential.

After disastrous fiscal performance in 1990, when the company posted net losses of $25.3 million on revenue of $46.9 million, CAC entered bankruptcy proceedings in 1991. As part of its reorganization, the company moved away from the volatile fishing and timber sectors and to became a smaller organization rooted in less capital-intensive industries. As the Seward mill's losses continued to mount, CAC closed it in 1991, briefly reopened it as part of a joint venture in 1993, and then closed it again soon thereafter. The company emerged from bankruptcy in 1992 and appointed Michael E. Brown as president and chief executive officer in 1993.

A New Direction in the Mid-1990s

CAC's new leadership immediately involved CAC in a series of diverse enterprises that required less risk and lower capitalization than the big resource-oriented projects the company had taken on in the past. These new ventures positioned CAC as a service provider, focusing on facility management, services for the oil industry, personnel and computer services, and tourism.

CAC's new strategy began to pay off in 1994, when the company won two contracts with the U.S. government. The first paid CAC $1.2 million annually to maintain family housing units at the Adak Navy base in Alaska. The second provided CAC $4.5 million a year to provide an array of base services operations for the King Salmon Airforce Base in Alaska. CAC performed both contracts successfully and was eager to win more. To do so, the company formed a subsidiary, Chugach Development Corporation (CDC), which qualified for bid preferences in government services contracts under the Small Business Administration's Section 8(a) program. "This is what shaped our life after bankruptcy," a company executive stated in the *Alaska Journal of Commerce* for August 12, 2001. After landing a base operations contract in Wake Island, Alaska, in 1996, CDC was awarded a multi-year contract worth $18 million to oversee base maintenance and operations at the U.S. Navy base on Whidbey Island, Washington.

CAC moved into other new areas as well. In 1996, the firm entered a four-way partnership with a Nebraska telecommunications company called MFS Network Technologies Inc. and two other Alaska Natives regional corporations to form Kansas Telecom Inc. Kansas won a contract from Alyeska Pipeline Service Co. to build and operate a $100 million fiber optics communications system along Alyeska's 800-mile trans-Alaska oil pipeline corridor. The project, which was slated to take over two years to complete, was intended to provide state-of-the-art digital and voice communications systems for Alyeska and to upgrade operations control along the pipeline. CAC held a 25 percent stake in Kansas and appointed one of its own corporate vice-presidents as Kansas' first chief executive. (After the project's completion in 2000, Alyeska terminated its contract with Kansas; CAC reduced its stake in the venture to 5 percent). Also in 1996, CAC joined with North Employment Services to form another subsidiary, Chugach North Technical Services, which provided temporary contract personnel services to private employers in Alaska and the Pacific Northwest.

CAC's post-bankruptcy strategy was hugely successful. The company returned to profitability in 1994 and gross revenues

rose from $32 million in 1994, to $35.5 million in 1995, to $52.5 million in 1996. By 1996, CAC had paid down its debts to $4 million and had a backlog of $300 million in contracts. Although its debt prevented CAC from paying its Native shareholders a dividend, CAC's numerous base contracts throughout the Northwest provided much-needed jobs to Chugach shareholders living both in Alaska and Washington.

While CAC spent much of the mid-1990s de-emphasizing its resource-based operations, the company still hoped to exploit the natural resources, particularly timber, of its land. Beginning in 1996, CAC sought to complete a process that it had begun in its 1982 settlement with the U.S. government. ANCSA had transferred to CAC timber-rich land in the Carbon Mountain Tract of the Copper River Delta east of Cordova, Alaska. This property was completely encircled by United States Forest Service (USFS) and Bureau of Land Management (BLM) land, though, and CAC wanted to build a road that gave it access to its property. Under the terms of ANCSA and the 1982 settlement, CAC was guaranteed an easement across USFS land to access its property, but the easement still had not been granted by 1996, despite CAC's compliance with applicable environmental prerequisites.

In response, CAC twice turned to the U.S. Congress in 1998 and 1999 for legislative solutions that would allow for the road. Both efforts failed. CAC was under considerable pressure from environmental groups and administration officials to give up on the planned road and future logging and instead negotiate a conservation easement and a settlement. However, CAC was resolute, viewing the matter as one of sovereignty rather than payment. "What this is really about is the federal government keeping its promises," CAC's Brown told *National Wildlife* in 1999. After a flurry of negative publicity, CAC was eventually granted its easement in 2000. Given the state of global timber markets, however, the company postponed any work on the road.

Despite the media's attention to timber, CAC continued to focus primarily on its post-bankruptcy enterprises, particularly government service contracts. Michael Brown left his post in 1999 and was ultimately replaced by Barney Uhart, who continued his predecessor's business plan. In 1999, another of CAC's government services-oriented subsidiaries, Chugach Management Services (CMS), won a base maintenance contract at Kirtland Air Force Base in Albuquerque, New Mexico, worth $170 million. That same year, CMS moved even further from its home territory when it was awarded a $500 million contract to manage base facilities at MacDill Air Force Base in Tampa, Florida.

Success in the 21st Century

CAC won its most significant government services contract in 2002, when it teamed with Lockheed Martin and Bechtel to provide support services for the missile-testing site on the island of Kwajalein in the Marshall Islands. The total procurement for the three companies was worth over $2 billion and allowed CAC to hire 1,200 new employees.

In the late 1990s, the company continued to diversify its operations. Through its subsidiary Chugach Telecommunications & Computers, Inc. (CT&C), CAC won a contract to operate a worldwide seismic network used to enforce the Nuclear Test Ban Treaty. CT&C also validated software for the Navy's Tomahawk missile program and tracked space debris for the Naval Space Command. Another subsidiary, Chugach Support Services, ran Job Corps facilities in Alaska, San Francisco, and Roswell, New Mexico. CAC's Ship Escort Response Vessel System escorted oil tankers into and out of Prince William Sound. In 2002, CAC bought the Fairbanks, Alaska-based McKinley General Contractors, which it converted into a new subsidiary, Chugach McKinley Corporation. In 2003, Chugach McKinley won a five-month contract to take over construction operations at Midway Atoll National Wildlife Refuge.

CAC's success was apparent in the early years of the new century. In 2000, the company paid out a dividend to its shareholders for the first time in 11 years and increased the dividend payment annually thereafter. Revenues for 2002 topped $355 million, a jump of 28 percent from the previous year. The company's future looked bright. "There are a lot new things on the horizon," Uhart told the *Alaska Journal of Commerce* in 2003. "Actually business couldn't be better. There's really not a lot to complain about."

Principal Subsidiaries

Chugach Development Corporation; Chugach Industries Inc.; Chugach McKinley Inc.; Chugach Telecommunications and Computer Inc.; Chugach Systems Integration, LLC; Chugach Management Services, Inc. (51%); Chugach Support Services, Inc. (51%).

Principal Competitors

Satellite Services, Inc.; EMI Services; Del-Jen, Inc.; Piquniq Management Corporation.

Further Reading

"Alaska Native Regional Corporations," *Alaska Business Monthly*, September 1, 2001.

Bauman, Margaret, "Chugach Alaska, in Chapter 11, Plots Reorganization," *USA Today*, April 18, 1991.

Begley, Sharon, "Will This Wilderness Stay Wild?," *National Wildlife*, April 1, 1999.

Bennett, Ed, "Service Contracts Bring Chugach Alaska Back From the Brink," *Alaska Journal of Commerce*, August 12, 2001.

Bradner, Tim, "Chugach Alaska Inc.," *Alaska Journal of Commerce*, October 28, 1996.

Bukro, Casey, "Stakes High for Native Alaskans," *Chicago Tribune*, March 15, 1990.

"Chugach Makes Most of Seafood Biz," *Alaska Journal of Commerce*, June 6, 1988.

Gwinn, Mary Ann, "Profitable Chugach Corporation May Face Economic Devastation," *Seattle Times*, April 17, 1989.

King, Pat, "Government Land, Money Manager Chugach Alaska Corp. Expects Continued Growth," *Alaska Journal of Commerce*, May 25, 2003.

Moffat, Tim, "Chugach Looks for Outside Help to Reopen Its Seward Sawmill," *Alaska Journal of Commerce*, November 4, 1991.

Patty, Stanton, "Native Groups Are Developing Plans for Tourism Projects," *Seattle Times*, March 13, 1988.

Ragsdale, Rose, "Alyeska Upgrades Communication Network With Alaska Partnership," *Alaska Journal of Commerce*, July, 1996.

Stricker, Julie, "Chugach Alaska Corp.," *Alaska Business Monthly*, December 1, 2001.

Wells, Ken, "Endangered Again: A Year After the Spill, Prince William Sound Faces a Forest Crisis," *Wall Street Journal*, March 30, 1990.

Williams, Marla, and Ross Anderson, "From Villagers to Boardrooms," *Seattle Times*, September 22, 1991.

—Rebecca Stanfel

Compagnie Financière Sucres et Denrées S.A.

20-22, rue de la Ville l'Eveque
75008 Paris
France
Telephone: (+33) 0 1 5330 1234
Fax: (+33) 0 1 5330 1212
Web site: http://www.sucden.com

Private Company
Incorporated: 1952
Employees: 1,212
Sales: EUR 2.2 billion ($2.23 billion)(2001)
NAIC: 424490 Other Grocery and Related Product Merchant Wholesalers; 424450 Confectionery Merchant Wholesalers; 424590 Other Farm Product Raw Material Merchant Wholesalers; 424720 Petroleum and Petroleum Products Merchant Wholesalers (Except Bulk Stations and Terminals)

Compagnie Financière Sucres et Denrées S.A. (Sucden), is one of the world's leading sugar trading houses, controlling some 15 percent of the world sugar market. Each year, the company is responsible for the trade of over five million tons of both raw and white refined sugar. Yet Sucden, a privately held company based in Paris, France, remains more or less unknown. The company acts as a go-between among sugar-producing countries, often at a government level, and sugar refining markets, again at a government level, but also directly to major sugar-based industrial companies. Sucden supports its operations through an internationally operating subsidiary network, with its primary sugar trading offices in the United States, Russia, Switzerland, and Brazil. The company's Miami, Florida-based Amerop is one of Sucden's largest subsidiaries, handling 1.5 million tons of sugar per year, chiefly for the North and South American markets. Amerop is also present in Chile, Mexico, and the Philippines, and handles trading among the Central and South American market countries as well. The company also operates a dedicated Brazilian subsidiary, which handles some 25 percent of that country's total sugar output. Sucden's early entry into the liberalized Russian market has

given the company a leading industry position in that country, one of the world's largest sugar processing and consumer markets. Sucden has also long operated a trading subsidiary in the United Kingdom, Sucden UK, which is one of that country's leading commodity and futures brokerage houses. Sucden's UK operations also include Comfin—which targets the sugar markets in the African, Caribbean, and Pacific regions—and Genoc Chartering, which acts as a chartered shipbroker for the international trade in sugar and other dry commodities. The private company's annual revenues are estimated at more than EUR 2 billion ($2 billion) per year. Sucden is led by chairman Serge Varsano, son of the company's founder.

Cuban Connection in the 1950s

Maurice Varsano founded a small sugar-trading business in the 1952 at a time when the international sugar trading market was undergoing profound changes. Sugar, which had long been an important commodity, became even more integral for the developing food processing industry, which relied on sugar for both for its flavoring and food preservation properties.

The end of World War II had also brought about the end of the colonial era, as former colonies claimed or gained their independence. At the same time, the new countries regained control over their natural resources, which had formerly been exploited for the benefit of the colonial occupiers. This situation opened the opportunity for a new generation of trading houses to establish itself on the world sugar scene.

Sugar quickly became an important economic and political liaison, linking both sugar producing countries—predominantly in the developing world—and sugar processing and consumer markets, especially in the West. Varsano recognized that the new governments would seek the help of traders to market their countries' sugar production on the world markets and positioned his company as a middle man, buying up contracts for a specified amount of sugar, which he then resold to sugar refiners and processors.

By the beginning of the 1960s, Varsano had already positioned his company, Compagnie Financière de Sucres et Denrées, or Sucden, as a major player on the worldwide sugar

Company Perspectives:

For half a century, the name of Sucres and Denrées and that of Varsano have been synonymous with worldwide expertise in the trading of sugar. Sucres et Denrées S.A. is a private company founded by Maurice Varsano, who ran the company until 1980, when his son Serge Varsano succeeded him. Serge Varsano controls the Sucres et Denrées Group as the major shareholder of the holding company. Since it was founded, the Sucres et Denrées Group has consistently ranked amongst the world leaders in the sugar trade. In a very competitive environment, the Sucres et Denrées Group has reinforced its position as the foremost sugar trading firm over the last five years. Between 1997 and 2001 the financial turnover and tonnage traded have significantly increased.

market. Varsano's moment had come with the Cuban revolution and the rise to power of Fidel Castro at the end of the 1950s. In 1959, Varsano correctly recognized that Castro required a new trading partner in order to sell the country's important sugarcane crop—a primary source of Cuban income. Yet Castro was unable to find buyers for the country's sugar crop, which until the revolution had been controlled by U.S. interests. Varsano stepped in, offering to sell Cuban sugar to Japan and North Africa. The move not only helped preserve Castro's regime but also established Sucden as a force in the sugar industry. In 1961, Sucden established a subsidiary, Amerop Sugar Corporation, bringing it closer to the Latin and North American market.

Sucden's success with Cuban sugar led the company to adopt a policy of political neutrality, a position that was to encourage *Forbes* magazine later to describe the company as the "despots' best friend." Indeed, into the 1970s, the company continued to play the role of lifeline for a number of politically unstable—and unpopular—countries. Yet Sucden's strategy differed markedly from that of its English and American rivals, which typically sought quick profits, since the company developed long-term relationships with its government customers. At the same time, Sucden often received backing from the French government, as Sucden's commercial operations often coincided with the country's political ambitions. Nonetheless, as *Le Monde* reported, when asked by Fidel Castro which side he was on, Maurice Versano was quoted as saying: "I am on the side of sugar."

Maurice Varsano had become an important figure on the international commodities scene by the early 1970s, leading the company to expand beyond its focus on sugar to trade in a variety of other commodities. The creation of the European Common Market led to new opportunities, and in 1973 Sucden opened a subsidiary in the United Kingdom after that country joined the European Community. Sucden UK developed into a diversified commodities and futures brokers which, through subsidiary Comfin, also established in 1973, spearheaded Sucden's sugar brokerage interests in the Africa, Caribbean, and Pacific regions that remained under British influence.

Sucden's success as a trader encouraged its industrial ambitions as well. The company's investments led it into the growing agro-industrial market, and by the mid-1980s Sucden had emerged as one of France's leading food producers, particularly through its holding of Sogelait, a dairy products broker and distributor, and Sogeviandes, which, through its Charal brand, became the number one French beef products producer.

Sucden's transformation into an agro-industrial group took on steam after Maurice Varsano's death in 1980. The company's leadership was then transferred to a "trustee" management team under Max Benhamou, Benjamin Coriat, and Jacques Bachelier, who had been instrumental in helping Varsano build up the business. Yet majority control of the company rested with the Varsano family, in particular with Serge Varsano, who was just 24 at the time of his father's death.

Sucden's acquisition of chocolate maker Cacao Barry in 1982 thrust it to the forefront of the French agro-indusrial sector. Barry had originally been founded in England in 1842 and launched a cacao processing arm in Meulan, France, in 1920. By the 1960s, Barry had ceased production of processed chocolates and instead focused on operating as a cocoa processor, becoming the wold's largest by the 1980s.

Focused Sugar Trader in the 21st Century

Sucden's rising food processing operations came to represent the majority of the group's sales, which reached the equivalent of $7.5 billion by the end of the 1980s. Nonetheless, the company still remained a key player in the international trading market. Once again, Sucden displayed a willingness to take political risks, acting as a broker in Nicaragua in 1984 and slightly later adding contracts in El Salvador. The company's brokerage activities took it beyond sugar as well, and in the 1980s the company became a major rice broker operating in such markets as Laos and Vietnam. The company also entered the market for fertilizer, coffee, and other commodities during this time.

The arrival of Serge Varsano as head of the company took Sucden into a new era. By 1988, the younger Varsano had succeeded in gaining control of 85 percent of the group. He quickly imposed his own management team on the company and now sought to replicate his father's talent for large-scale contracts. Cuba once again became a primary market for Sucden, which acted as a middle man between that country and the Soviet Union in a transaction involving some 1.8 million tons of sugar in 1988.

Varsano decided to take on the cocoa market as well. In 1988, the Ivory Coast, the world's largest cocoa producer, was under pressure to repay its foreign debt. Varsano offered to purchase some 400,000 tons of cocoa, representing some 20 percent of the country's crop, which was then placed it in storage. The deal brought Sucden into the headlines and also into a head-to-head confrontation with the cocoa market's longtime leader Phillip Bros., based in the United States.

Varsano next turned to the petrol market, buying up 17 percent of Germany's Marimpex, which enjoyed contacts in the Iranian and Libyan oil markets. By 1990, Sucden had gained majority control of Marimpex and had begun negotiating its first Iranian oil contracts in a bid to become a major player in that market as well. Yet a slump in worldwide cocoa prices, which forced the company to sell short on its cocoa holdings, led to a quick unraveling of its empire.

Key Dates:

1952: Maurice Varsano founds Compagnie Financière Sucres et Denrées (Sucden) as a sugar trading firm.

1959: Sucden acts as broker for Cuban sugar after Castro revolution.

1961: Amerop Sugar Corporation is established in the United States for the company's North and Latin American brokerage operations.

1980: Maurice Varsano dies.

1982: Sucden acquires Cocoa Barry and becomes a world-leading processor of cocoa.

1988: Serge Varsano takes over Sucden management.

1991: After heavy losses, Sucden is rescued by its bank creditors and re-focuses as a sugar trading group.

1993: The company establishes subsidiary operations in Russia.

1994: A Brazilian subsidiary, Sucden do Brasil, is created as part of the company's Latin American expansion.

2003: The company announces plans to step up operations in the Asian sugar market.

By 1990, Sucden suffered losses of more than FFr476 million, the first loss in the company's history. Unable to pay off its debt, the company initially hoped for a government bailout. Yet the French government refused to come to the rescue of the private company, and instead Sucden was forced to submit to the control of its bank creditors. Serge Varsano remained with the company, although he shifted to a more titular position as company chairman. Instead, Max Benhamou and other former company heads returned to Sucden's leadership to negotiate a rescue plan.

Sucden's banks agreed to loan the group as much as FFr700 million (approximately $120 million). In exchange, Sucden proceeded with the sell-off in 1993 of its industrial holdings, including Cacoa Barry—which ultimately became part of the Barry Callebaut group—and Sogeviandes.

Sucden then moved to streamline its trading operations, narrowing its focus once again to the international sugar market. In support of that activity, the company turned to the newly liberalized Russian market, establishing a subsidiary there. Sucden's early entry into the market enabled the company to become one of the most prominent brokers for Russian sugar by the turn of the 21st century.

Sucden also expanded its operations in South America, founding a subsidiary in Chile under Amerop. In 1994, Sucden, which had long been active in the Brazilian sugar market, formed a new subsidiary there as well, Sucden do Brasil. Into the new century, Sucden expanded into other Latin American markets, including the Dominican Republic, Argentina, and Uruguay.

The Asian markets, which saw steady increases in sugarcane production in the 1980s and 1990s, became another important market for Sucden, which added operations in India and Indonesia. The company had also become a major figure on the Thai sugar market, accounting for more than one million tons of that country's raw sugar exports. In 2003, the company announced its intention to step up its position in the Asian sugar market and extend its trading activities into Malaysia and South Korea. With more than 15 percent of the world's free market sugar under its control, Sucden planned to remain a major trading force in the new century.

Principal Subsidiaries

Amerop Mexico; Amerop Philippines; Amerop Sugar Corporation (United States); Comfin (United Kingdom); Genoc Chartering Ltd (United Kingdom); Sucden (UK) Ltd.; Sucden do Brasil; Sucres et Denrées Russia.

Principal Competitors

Cargill Inc.; Eridania Beghin-Say S.A.; Groupe Louis Dreyfus S.A.; Tate & Lyle plc.

Further Reading

Fottorino, Eric, "Serge Varsano, PDG de Sucres et Denrées: Un négociant monté en graine," *Le Monde*, July 1, 1989.

——, "Sucres et denrées, de la régence à la gestion," *Le Monde*, October 25, 1991.

Fuhrman, Peter, "Despots' Best Friend (Serge Varsano)," *Forbes*, February 5, 1990, p. 178.

"Sucden Eyes Bigger Sugar Market Share in Asia," *Reuters*, November 26, 2003

"Sucden Reappointed on Cocoa and Sugar Futures," *Trade Finance*, February 2003, p. 8.

"Sucden Sweetens Russian Business," *Trade Finance*, March 2002, p. 3.

—M.L. Cohen

Continuum Health Partners, Inc.

555 West 57th Street
New York, New York 10019
U.S.A.
Telephone: (212) 523-7195
Toll Free: (877) 420-4209
Fax: (212) 523-7885
Web site: http://wehealny.org

Private Company
Incorporated: 1997
Employees: 16,000
Operating Revenues: $1.92 billion (2002)
NAIC: 622110 General Medical and Surgical Hospitals;
622310 Specialty General Medical and Surgical
Hospitals; 551112 Offices of Other Holding
Companies

Continuum Health Partners, Inc. is the holding corporation for four New York City hospitals: Beth Israel Medical Center, St. Luke's-Roosevelt Hospital Center, Long Island College Hospital, and New York Eye and Ear Infirmary. Founded in 1997, Continuum is attempting to coordinate the operations of its members in such a way as to control costs and keep the hospitals financially solvent in an era of increased competition for patients and for payments by government programs and managed-care organizations.

St. Luke's and Roosevelt: 1850–1997

Founded in 1850 by an Episcopalian minister, Rev. William Augustus Muhlenberg, St. Luke's Hospital is the oldest of the Continuum hospitals. It opened in 1858 on Fifth Avenue between 54th and 55th streets. A school of nursing was added in 1888. St. Luke's moved in 1896 to the rapidly developing neighborhood of Morningside Heights in upper Manhattan, where a building had been constructed on the block between West 113th and 114th streets and between Amsterdam Avenue and Morningside Drive, just north of the site where the Episcopalians were building the Cathedral of St. John the Divine, the world's largest cathedral. A new wing, or pavilion, completed in 1906, provided space for additional wards as well as private

rooms for the 30 percent of St. Luke's patients able to pay in full for their care. By 1930, seven pavilions had been added to original French Renaissance building.

St. Luke's merged with nearby Women's Hospital in 1952, thereby providing obstetrical services for the first time. New buildings were completed in 1954 and 1957, and another opened in 1965 for Women's Hospital, filling in the last space available on St. Luke's city block. By this time, St. Luke's was a teaching hospital for Columbia University's College of Physicians and Surgeons.

Roosevelt Hospital was established by the bequest of James Henry Roosevelt, a wealthy New Yorker who died in 1869 and left an estate of close to $1 million. It opened in 1871 on the block bordered by West 58th and 59th Streets and Ninth and Tenth Avenues in Manhattan. Many of the early staff of Roosevelt Hospital held faculty appointments at Columbia's medical school, which for a time was located across the street from the hospital. Roosevelt Hospital established an ambulance service in 1877 and an outpatient department in 1881. The Syms Operating Pavilion, highly advanced for the time, was completed in 1892. In the 19th century, hospitals were generally regarded as only fit for the poor, and it was quite common even to perform operations in the home. Roosevelt's Private Patients' Pavilion, erected in 1896, was established to provide service equivalent to the finest hotels of the day, together with the advantage of full hospital facilities. It proved highly lucrative for Roosevelt. By 1951, only the four-story administration building of 1871 and its annex remained from the early complex. The nine-story Tower Building, with its entrance on Ninth Avenue, opened in 1953. It connected with the nine-story Ward Building, opened in 1923.

Mired in deep financial trouble, Roosevelt merged in 1979 with St. Luke's—which had lost $4 million the previous year—to form St. Luke's-Roosevelt Hospital Center. Like other metropolitan hospitals, the two were suffering from overcapacity. The consolidation was intended to drop 100 beds from the total of more than 1,300, achieve economies of scale, and unify more than 1,100 physicians, 1,000 nurses, and about 4,000 other employees under an administration serving an area of nearly 500,000 people on Manhattan's West Side, parts of which were classified by federal and state health agencies as medically under-served. In addition, the new hospital center also authorized large sums for the largest hospital development project in the United States, completed in the early 1990s at a cost of about $500 million. A new hospital on the Roosevelt campus replaced the antiquated facilities on Ninth Avenue. Uptown, St. Luke's built a facility north of its complex and extensively renovated its existing buildings.

One way that St. Luke's-Roosevelt planned to save money was by consolidating duplicated services, such as shifting St. Luke's obstetrics, pediatrics, and neonatal intensive care to Roosevelt. The change was opposed by uptown community activists and only partially effected. St. Luke's-Roosevelt lost $12 million in 1993 and $12.5 million in 1994. The hospital shed 450 of its 7,150 jobs in 1995 and began to cast eyes on a merger with Beth Israel Hospital Center, which had a reputation for superior financial management.

Beth Israel: 1890–1997

Beth Israel Hospital Association was incorporated in 1890 by Orthodox Jews, with each of the 40 founders contributing 25 cents. "They did it because the city hospitals at the time wouldn't take patients who hadn't been residents for over a year," Beth Israel's director told Nicholas Pileggi of *New York* in 1983. "Also the newly arrived Russian- and Polish-Jewish immigrants of that day didn't feel welcome uptown at the German-Jewish ... Mount Sinai Hospital." Not yet able to support a hospital, they opened a storefront dispensary on Manhattan's Lower East Side, the center of immigrant Jewish life. Within a year, Beth Israel Hospital had opened, with accommodations for 20 patients. It was the only Manhattan hospital conducted in accordance with Orthodox Jewish religious principles. The building leased quickly proved too small, and in 1892 the association rented two buildings from the Hebrew Free School.

Beth Israel was able to move into its own newly erected building in 1902, with 115 beds. Nevertheless, many people had to be turned away for lack of space. In 1929, a new 13-story building, with about 500 beds, opened adjacent to Stuyvesant Square at East 16th Street. It grew into a complex that included a school of nursing, a clinic building, and a pavilion for private and semi-private patients and stretched from First to Second Avenues between East 15th and 18th Streets. Beth Israel purchased Manhattan General Hospital, its neighbor across Stuyvesant Square, in 1964, and changed its name to Beth Israel Medical Center the following year.

By the 1980s, Beth Israel long had ceased to be a hospital for predominantly Jewish patients and was serving, in southern Manhattan, one of the most ethnically diverse communities in

the world. The 174-bed Bernstein Institute had been serving as a detoxification hospital for alcoholics and drug addicts since 1961, when it was still part of Manhattan General Hospital. By 1988, Beth Israel was operating the largest network of heroin-treatment clinics in the United States, with nearly 7,500 patients and 23 facilities. It was also a pioneer in care for AIDS patients, many of them heroin addicts infected by dirty needles. At about the same time, it became the first nonprofit hospital in New York to advertise on television, dramatizing its alcohol- and drug-treatment services for private clients at Stuyvesant Square.

Beth Israel acquired Doctors Hospital on the Upper East Side in the early 1990s; bought DOCS Physicians, a major suburban network of primary-care clinics, in 1993; expanded to Brooklyn by purchasing Kings Highway Hospital Center in 1995; and opened an outpatient center on Union Square, not far from Stuyvesant Square. Its health-care system now included two long term care institutions and four primary care and physicians' groups, presiding over an extensive system of clinics, doctors' offices, and affiliate hospitals in an untiring hunt for patients. DOCS, for example, was serving more than 150,000 patients who were now referred almost exclusively to Beth Israel for surgery or other advanced care. Beth Israel welcomed doctors with high-volume practices and delivered more babies than any other hospital in New York. It also expanded its programs in a number of fields, including neurosurgery, pain medicine, and cardiology in a bid for recognition as one of New York's elite teaching hospitals.

Continuum Health Partners: 1997–2003

The merger of St. Luke's-Roosevelt and Beth Israel in 1997 united the main Manhattan West Side medical institution with one on the borough's East Side. It also eased pressure on both parties because Beth Israel was thought able to shoulder St. Luke's-Roosevelt's heavy debt load, while the latter had a wealth of space to relieve the former's cramped operation. A holding company, Continuum Health Partners, Inc., was established to govern both hospitals, but it had no assets of its own. Beth Israel received six of Continuum's ten board seats and was given management of joint finances. St. Luke's-Roosevelt remained a major teaching hospital for Columbia University's medical college, while Beth Israel retained its primary affiliation with the Albert Einstein College of Medicine, a unit of Yeshiva University.

The new alliance ran into financial difficulties from the outset, with St. Luke's-Roosevelt nearly doubling its operating loss, to $27.7 million, in 1997 and Beth Israel's operating profit turning into a $2.2-million loss in the same year. Continuum sustained these losses even though the merger saved $33 million by integrating 13 administrative functions and eliminating hundreds of physicians. St. Luke's-Roosevelt and Beth Israel agreed on a single chairman of radiology, and Beth Israel agreed to surrender most of its pediatric services to St. Luke's. Continuum also established HealthWorks as a purchasing subsidiary to buy supplies for its member hospitals in the belief that such a group could apply significant leverage on prices. HealthWorks also began inviting other hospitals in the region to join, promising them lower prices, cheaper delivery, and the ability to sell medical and personal-care products directly to patients through catalogues distributed in each member facility.

Key Dates:

1858: St. Luke's Hospital opens.
1871: Roosevelt Hospital opens.
1891: Beth Israel Hospital opens.
1964: Beth Israel purchases neighboring Manhattan General Hospital.
1979: St. Luke's and Roosevelt merge to form St. Luke's-Roosevelt Hospital Center.
1988: Beth Israel's network of heroin-treatment clinics is the largest in the United States.
1996: Beth Israel acquires two more hospitals and opens an outpatient center.
1997: Continuum is created in a merger of St. Luke's-Roosevelt and Beth Israel.
1999: Continuum adds Long Island College Hospital and New York Eye and Ear Infirmary.

In spite of its money problems, Continuum established an institute for neurology and neurology, expanded efforts in cancer care, and lured department heads from other local hospitals with lucrative contracts. It also added Long Island College Hospital to the corporation in 1998, even though this Brooklyn institution was itself in poor financial health. This hospital was founded in 1858 as a medical college—the Long Island College of Medicine—as well as a hospital. After the medical college became part of the State University of New York system in 1954, it remained the hospital's primary teaching affiliate. Long Island College's addition brought Continuum's ranks to more than 3,000 beds, 3,800 doctors, and 17,000 employees, with an operating budget of $1.8 billion. Continuum again expanded in 1999, when it added New York Eye and Ear Infirmary, a 103-bed hospital on East 14th Street in Manhattan affiliated with New York Medical College. It had been the last specialty hospital in the city to remain independent. Founded in 1820 as a two-room clinic in downtown Manhattan by two graduates of Columbia's College of Physicians and Surgeons, New York Eye and Ear Infirmary was said to be the oldest hospital of its kind in the Western Hemisphere. In recent years, it had contended with the same financial problems as bigger institutions as many of its services shifted to outpatient settings.

By 2000, Continuum's hospitals—like most in New York—were in even worse financial shape than before as a result of reductions in government reimbursements and the growth of cost-conscious managed-care networks. Beth Israel ended 1999 with an operating loss of $46 million and only $41 million in cash on hand—the equivalent of 17 days' worth of expenses. By the following summer, the hospital only had enough cash to fund seven days of expenses, impelling its 80-member board to contribute $26 million to avert a financial crisis. Beth Israel cut employment by 620 with the intention of reducing its payroll by $40 million a year, but its bonds remained ranked below investment grade. Nevertheless, the hospital assumed the management and medical care of 48,000 Health Insurance Plan (HIP) subscribers in a five-year contract with the managed-care group. The agreement was expected to generate $95 million a year for Beth Israel, but the hospital thereby assumed full financial

risk. Meanwhile, Continuum closed a unit, run by St. Luke's-Roosevelt, to provide nursing and other home-care services to 1,200 New Yorkers. Continuum also announced in 2000 that it would slash 800 to 900 jobs.

Beth Israel had more beds in 2002 than other hospital in New York City except New York-Presbyterian Hospital. Its operating revenue came to $910.2 million (second only to New York-Presbyterian), while St. Luke-Roosevelt's amounted to $701.3 million, Long Island College's to $261.9 million, and New York Eye and Ear's to $50.7 million.

Principal Subsidiaries

HealthWorks.

Principal Competitors

Mount Sinai Medical Center; New York University Medical Center; NewYork-Presbyterian Hospital.

Further Reading

Agovino, Theresa, "Beth Israel's Heroin Solution," *Crain's New York Business*, August 8, 1988, pp. 3, 29.

Becker, Cindy, "Almost Broke Beth Israel Welcomes HIP," *Modern Healthcare*, July 24, 2000, p. 12.

Benson, Barbara, "2 Big Hospitals in Talks, *Crain's New York Business*, October 23, 1995, pp. 1, 35.

——, "Beth Israel Gains Clout in Merger with St. Luke's," *Crain's New York Business*, December 9, 1996, pp. 3, 39.

——, "Health Network Big, Not Better," *Crain's New York Business*, June 29, 1998, pp. 3,

Fein, Esther B., "Managed Care Leads to Marketing Strategies as Hospitals Compare," *New York Times*, April 29, 1995, pp. 1, 25.

"Infirmary Will Join Continuum Health," *New York Times*, June 22, 1999, p. B6.

Levitan, Tina, *Islands of Compassion: A History of the Jewish Hospitals of New York*, New York: Twayne, 1964, pp. 89–106.

Lipowicz, Alice, "Hospital Giants Splinter Area Purchasing Groups," *Crain's New York Business*, April 26, 1999, pp. 19–20.

"Merger Approved for Two Hospitals," *New York Times*, November 19, 1952, p. 30.

Messina, Judith, "Trustees Buy Beth Israel Time," *Crain's New York Business*, October 16, 2000, pp. 3, 95.

"The New Wing at St. Luke's Hospital," *New York Times*, October 21, 1906, Sec. 4, p. 4.

Oser, Alan S., "From a Hospital Project Comes Housing," *New York Times*, April 15, 1990, Sec. 10, pp. 3, 6.

Pileggi, Nicholas, "A New Life," *New York*, April 18, 1993, pp. 196, 199–201.

The Roosevelt Hospital 1871–1957, New York: The Roosevelt Hospital, 1957.

Steinhauer, Jennifer, "At Beth Israel, Lapses in Care Mar Gains in Technology," *New York Times*, February 15, 2000, pp. B1, B4.

——, "Health Care Leader to Retire as Consortium Chief," *New York Times*, May 24, 2000, p. B8.

——, "Hospital Mergers Stumbling As Marriages of Convenience," *New York Times*, March 14, 2001, pp. B1, B4.

——, "To Cut Costs, Continuum Closes Its Unit For Home Care," *New York Times*, December 19, 2000, p. B6.

Sullivan, Ronald, "Emergency Room Operation Merges St. Luke's, Roosevelt," *New York Times*, September 23, 1979, Sec. 4, p. 6.

—Robert Halasz

David Jones

David Jones Ltd.

86-108 Castlereagh Street
Sydney NSW 2000
Australia
Telephone: (+61) 2 9266 5544
Fax: (+61) 2 9267 3895
Web site: http://ww.davidjones.com.au

Public Company
Incorporated: 1920
Employees: 9,883
Sales: A$1.71 billion ($1.13 billion)(2003)
Stock Exchanges: Sydney
Ticker Symbol: DJL
NAIC: 452111 Department Stores (Except Discount Department Stores)

Sydney, Australia-based David Jones Ltd. stakes the claim as the world's oldest continuously operating department store; the company's original store opened at its George Street location in 1838. The company is also Australia's third-largest department store company, with revenues of A$1.7 billion in 2003. David Jones operates more than 30 stores across Australia, although the bulk of its operations are located on the country's eastern seaboard. Nonetheless, the group has regained a presence in western Australia, with the purchase of Perth-based Aherns in 1999. David Jones no longer owns most of its properties, having disposed of the real estate in sale-leaseback agreements, a move which gave the company cash needed for a vast store renovation drive. After an attempt to broaden its reach into the mass-market in the 1990s, the company has returned to its historic focus as a decidedly upscale retailer, stocking some 120 high-end fashion brands. In addition to apparel, the company also has strong sales in furniture and home furnishings. A launch at the beginning of the 2000s of a chain of gourmet grocery stores under the Foodchain name was abandoned in 2003, at which time the company took steps to reposition its online retail venture, David Jones Online, which offers retail sales of perfume, jewelry, and other gifts.

Pioneering Success in the 19th Century

David Jones, born in Wales, arrived in the young city of Sydney, Australia, and in 1838 opened a general store catering not only to the growing population in town but also to the increasing numbers of people who chose to settle in the city's outlying areas. Jones chose the store's location wisely: a busy corner of Georges Street, directly across the street from the town's General Post Office. From the start, Jones emphasized textiles. At the same time, the store's emphasis on "the best and most exclusive goods" made it a favorite among Sydney's growing upper classes.

Jones retired, turning over the store to his business partners. Yet the new owners lacked Jones's retail touch, and the store was eventually taken over by its creditors. Jones himself came out of retirement, borrowing money and taking on new business partners in order to rebuild the store. Joining the store at this time was Jones's son Edward, who had spent some time abroad, where he discovered the newly developing European-styled "department store." Under Edward Jones, the George Street store was remodeled and expanded, and in 1887 he introduced the department store retail format to Sydney. The new store featured furniture and other household furnishings over several floors—and boasted Sydney's first hydraulic elevator. The new building also featured the company's growing mail order business, as the fame of the David Jones name spread throughout Australia.

David Jones had long relied on imports in order to stock its shelves, and boasted of items and fashions from all over the world. At the end of the century, however, the company decided to move against the high cost of imports, and in 1899 founded its own factory, on Sydney's Marlborough Street. Then one of the largest manufacturing plants in Australia, the new site supplied a wide range of goods to the store, including David Jones branded clothing. At the same time, however, the store remained one of the Australian gentry's main sources of goods and fashions from the United Kingdom and elsewhere.

The success of that operation and the company's growing retail and mail order sales led it to go public in the new century, as David Jones Ltd. In the 1920s the company began preparations to build a new store, buying a site spanning an entire block of in Sydney's Hyde Park neighborhood—a move criticized by

100

Company Perspectives:

Moving forward, we are focusing on leveraging our core department store strengths into ongoing value and returns for shareholders. Our objective is to restore the investment fundamentals of the Company by positioning David Jones as a well-defined and brand oriented retail department store which delivers consistent, strong yields and steady growth.

some, given the location's remoteness from the city's main shopping district.

Construction went ahead, however, under Charles Jones, grandson of the founder, and the new store on Elizabeth Street opened in 1927. A far larger site, the new store was to remain the company's flagship store throughout its years of expansion. The opening of the site quickly attracted other retailers to the area, and before long, the Elizabeth Street store formed the core of the city's new retail center.

Postwar Fashion House

David Jones opened a third store in 1938, on Market Street around the corner from the Elizabeth street store. Such was the company's stature that then Prime Minister Billy Hughes presided over the new store's grand opening. This did not prevent the government from requisitioning the Market Street site for the Ministry of Munitions at the outbreak of World War II, however. The company continued operations at its other sites for the duration, despite rationing and the loss of a number of personnel to the war effort.

The postwar period marked a new era in the retail industry with the introduction of a new style of high fashion. David Jones soon became the fashion center of Australia, organizing its own runway shows to highlight the latest European fashions. The company's status among the fashion world was highlighted in 1948 when it brought over Christian Dior's famed "New Look" collection.

Australia's economic boom brought new fortune for David Jones, which became a key part of the Australian retail fashion industry in the 1950s. The company's growing sales, including its strong catalog sales, inspired it to expand into new regions of the country, and by 1959 the company boasted nine stores.

Initially sticking close to its New South Wales base, David Jones continued to grow during the ensuing decades, aided by the country's continued economic expansion in the 1960s. By the 1980s, the company had added stores in Queensland, Victoria, South Australia, and elsewhere. Not all of the group's expansions were successful, however. An attempt to move into western Australia, and especially the Perth region, failed in the 1970s. Faced with competition from such local stalwarts as Aherns, David Jones was forced to exit Perth at the end of the 1970s.

Nonetheless, at its height, the David Jones retail empire boasted more than 30 stores, and the company claimed the title as Australia's leading department store group. Adding to the group's growth was its acquisition of two rival chains: Georges

and, more importantly, John Martins, which, centered on the Adelaide region, was acquired by David Jones in 1985.

The 1980s marked a new period of expansion for the group, as the social mood changed from the exclusivity of the 1970s to a new, more blatant focus on consumerism. Guiding that growth in the 1980s was Rod Mewing, who joined the company as director of operations in 1981. With Mewing, then just 33 years old, named managing director in 1986, David Jones underwent a new boom, becoming a magnet for a new breed of brand-conscious shoppers amid a generalization of the luxury goods market.

During the decade, David Jones began refurbishing its stores, especially the Elizabeth Street flagship store, which opened its famed seventh floor designer boutique. The company also rolled out new in-store retail concepts, such as food halls, in the 1980s. The emphasis on high-end, high-quality (and high-margin) goods in the 1980s made David Jones one of Australia's fastest-growing retailers.

It also brought the company to the attention of empire builder John Spalvins. One of a host of a new-breed of Australian tycoons, which included Rupert Murdoch, Alan Bond, and the Kerry family, Spalvins went on his own buying spree in the late 1980s, cobbling together a vast and extraordinarily diversified collection of businesses. In 1990, Spalvins orchestrated a merger among his company, Adelaide Steamship, and David Jones, Tooth & Co. and Industrial Equity Ltd. The resulting company, known as Adsteam, became one of Australia's largest businesses, with interests in a variety of industries, including the retail market; in addition to David Jones, the company controlled Australia's leading food retail group, Woolworths.

Financed by debt and pummeled by a global recession, Adsteam began to teeter from the outset. By 1992, as its losses neared A$750 million ($500 million), Spalvins had been removed from the company, and Adsteam had been taken over by its creditors. Adsteam then began selling off its assets, including the Woolworth chain, which was floated in one of Australia's largest-ever public offerings in 1993.

Focused Department Store Group in the New Century

Despite the tribulations at its parent company, the David Jones arm prospered at the beginning of the decade, continuing to outpace rival retailers. Part of the group's success was due to Mewing's decision to expand the David Jones brand range, which enabled the company to generate a new image for itself as a high-value retailer—a move that brought the company high margins as well. By 1993, David Jones's revenues had risen to A$1.3 billion.

Mewing left the group in 1994 as Adsteam prepared to spin off David Jones as public company. In Mewing's place came Chris Tideman, a retailing veteran brought in from England. Tideman brought David Jones through its well-publicized public offering (IPO), an event that included wrapping the Elizabeth store in the company's trademark houndstooth fabric. Valuing the company's 33 stores, including a number of John Martins stores, at some A$750 million, the company's stock was priced at A$2 per share. Shares were marketed in part as an opportunity for the country's "mum and dad" investors to grab a piece of Australian retailing history.

Key Dates:

1838: Welsh immigrant David Jones sets up a general store in Sydney's Georges Street.
1887: Under son Edward Jones, the Georges Street store is expanded, introducing the department store format to Australia.
1899: David Jones builds a factory to produce goods under its own name.
1920: Company goes public as David Jones Ltd.
1927: Charles Jones, grandson of the founder, opens a new flagship store on Sydney's Elizabeth Street.
1938: A third store is opened on Market Street.
1947: Paris-style runway shows are introduced.
1959: David Jones expands to nine department stores.
1978: Company withdraws from the Perth market.
1985: The John Martins department store chain is acquired.
1990: David Jones becomes part of Adelaide Steamship Company (Adsteam).
1995: After the financial collapse of Adsteam, David Jones is spun off as public company.
1997: Company begins a sale-leaseback program in order to finance renovation of store chain.
2000: Company diversifies into gourmet food retail with launch of Foodchain stores; acquires TheSpot.com.au and launches an e-commerce web site.
2003: Foodchain operation is shuttered and the e-commerce site is restructured.

Into the mid-1990s, David Jones continued to shift its offerings in order to attract a broader clientele. However, this move toward mass-market offerings only served to confuse customers—failing to bring in mass-market consumers, while alienating the group's traditional high-end customer base. By 1997, as Australia dove into its deepest retailing crisis in some three decades, the company's profits—and shareholder patience—were running out. In that year, Tideman stepped down and was replaced by Peter Wilkinson, who had formerly led the Just Jeans retail chain.

Under Wilkinson, David Jones revamped its offerings, returning to its emphasis on high-end and branded items, and reducing its range of house brand items. The company also began revitalizing its store mix, selling off five John Martins stores in 1997 and re-branding the remainder under the David Jones name by the end of the decade. Another feature of the company's new strategy involved a chain-wide refurbishment program, calling for the renovation of up to four stores each year. Financing that drive was a sell-off of the group's properties in a series of lucrative sale-leaseback arrangements.

As part of its revitalization effort, David Jones returned to the Perth market in the late 1990s. The company had begun scouting sites as early as 1998, then, in 1999, found a platform for its re-entry through the acquisition of the Aherns department store group. One of the most prominent department store groups in the region, and one of the last in the country remaining under its founding family's ownership, Aherns gave David Jones five new stores in western Australia. The company converted some of these to the David Jones signage but maintained the flagship Aherns store under its original name.

David Jones had also begun exploring other retail formats. In 1998, the company launched a test store for a new format, a factory outlet site for its old and overstock goods. By 2000, however, the group had opted instead for two different directions. The first extended the David Jones shopping experience to the Internet, with the acquisition in June 2000 of TheSpot.com.au, which gave the company the technology infrastructure, as well as support operations, including a call center and logistics and warehousing support, for the launch of David Jones Online. Rather than offering the full product range of the group's departments stores, the web site limited itself to sales of perfumes, cosmetics, and related gifts. The site got off to a good start, with the signing of a number of major cosmetics and fragrance companies, including Lancôme and Estee Lauder.

The year 2000 also saw the company attempt to expand its in-store food halls into a full-fledged retail concept. Under the somewhat uninspiring name Foodchain, the new concept was meant to reduce the group's reliance on its department store format, positioning the group in a gourmet supermarket category. The company quickly opened four Foodchain stores. However, the format failed to attract shoppers, and after years of losses was finally shut down in June 2003. At the same time, the limited success of the group's e-commerce site led it to restructure that operation as well, ending the group's online shopping experiment.

The collapse of the group's diversified retailing strategy brought down Wilkinson, who was replaced at the end of 2002 by Mark McInnes. By the end of the group's 2003 fiscal year, chairman Dick Warburton announced his decision to step down as well. With a renewed focus on its core department store operations, David Jones turned toward the future with fresh optimism.

Principal Subsidiaries

Aherns Holding Pty Ltd.; Akitin Pty Ltd.; Helland Clse Pty Ltd.; David Jones Credit Pty Ltd.; David Jones Financial Services Ltd.; Speertill Pty Ltd.

Principal Competitors

Coles Myer Ltd; Howard Smith Pty Ltd; Warehouse Group; Nuance Global Traders; Harvey Norman Holdings Ltd.; Harris Scarfe Holdings; Spotlight Stores; Brazin; Sussan Corporation.

Further Reading

"Chairman to Leave DJs Helm," *Advertiser*, June 4, 2003, p. 2.
Jimenez, Katherine, "David Jones Glosses Loss," *Australian*, September 24, 2003, p. 37.
——, "DJs Counts on Sales Spike Despite Hike," *Australian*, November 6, 2003, p. 21.
Moran, Jonathan, "DJs Boss Ready to Improve Fortunes," *Daily Telegraph* (Australia), September 24, 2003, p. 49.
Murdoch, Scott, "David Jones Lifts Sales to Impress Critical Market," *Courier-Mail*, November 6, 2003, p. 30.
"Retailer Keeps Up with the Joneses," *Herald Sun*, October 12, 2000, p. 30.

—M.L. Cohen

DC Shoes, Inc.

1333 Keystone Way, Unit A
Vista, California 929801-8311
U.S.A.
Telephone: (760) 599-2999
Fax: (760) 597-2511
Web site: http://www.dcshoeusa.com

Private Company
Incorporated: 1993 as Circus Distribution, Inc.
Employees: 150
Sales: $100 million (2003 est.)
NAIC: 315299 All Other Cut and Sew Apparel
   Manufacturing; 316219 Other Footwear
   Manufacturing

DC Shoes, Inc. produces footwear for extreme sports, specifically skateboarding, snowboarding, surfing, motocross, and BMX. Two million pairs of DC shoes were produced in 2001. The company also sells shirts, pants, jeans, shorts, jackets, caps, backpacks, and other accessories. DC Shoes experienced explosive growth during the mid-1990s and remained one of skateboarding's top brands. It has been able to successfully gain nationwide, mall-based distribution while keeping hard-core skateboarders loyal by offering exclusive designs through skate shops only.

Origins

In 1989, at the age of 22, Ken Block, a snowboarder, began creating a line of screen-printed T-shirts that would become the Eightball brand. He honed his computer design skills at Palomar Community College in San Marcos, California, where he met a skateboarding schoolmate, Damon Way, in an algebra class a few years later. Way helped find stores to sell Eightball clothes. Way's brother, Danny Way, became one of the first pro skateboarders to endorse the line.

Block's parents had loaned him $10,000 to expand Eightball, according to *Agents of Change: The Story of DC Shoes and Its Athletes,* enabling the operation to move into a rented 750-square-foot warehouse. Way and Block contracted another fellow student, Aaron Lovejoy, to screen-print T-shirts.

Eightball's unique designs proved instantly popular with skate shops. They turned to a friend's father, Clay Blehm, for advice in financing their explosive growth. Blehm was then an unemployed accountant who had launched several businesses during his career. These included a childcare center and Christmas tree business. As the company grew, Blehm was named chief financial officer. Block was the company's president and CEO.

The success of Eightball led to the creation of the Droors ("drawers") brand of jeans in 1992. Eightball/Droors moved into a 3,300-square-foot facility in Carlsbad, California in January 1993. On October 3, 1993, the business was incorporated as Circus Distribution, Inc. Revenues for the year were more than $1.5 million. The Eightball brand was retired (at least in the United States) after someone else claimed ownership of the name in 1993.

DC Shoes Launched 1994

In 1994, Way launched a footwear line, DC Shoes, named, according to one version of the story, after the first initials of Danny Way and that of another pro, Colin McKay (another version has it standing for "Droors Clothing Shoes"). The company contracted Vans, then Etnies to produce the first shipments of shoes before settling on a Korean manufacturer, the Samil Tong Sang Company.

Yet another brand, Dub, was introduced in the fall of 1994 on a line of weatherproof outerwear for snowboarding. Snowboarding was a natural extension. Half of skaters snowboarded, according to a survey by market research firm Board-Trac cited by the *San Diego Tribune,* and 40 percent rode BMX bikes.

In October 1994, the business moved to a still-larger, 16,000-square-foot facility. Blehm became a partner in the company with Block and Way in January 1995. Revenues were about $7 million in 1995, more than double the previous year's. The company had about 35 employees. Circus ended 1996 with 50 employees and revenues of $21 million.

DC Shoes was one of the first skateboard shoe companies to make extensive use of professional endorsements. In 1996, DC's skateboarding team had grown to eight pros who went on a world tour in 1997. Motocross and surf teams were assembled by the end of the year.

DC garnered tremendous coverage from its promotional events designed to showcase its pro's talents. One of the most notable was when Danny Way jumped ten feet from a helicopter to a ramp adorned with DC Shoes logos. The growth of extreme sporting events such as the X Games further increased DC's exposure.

Droors and Dub were sold off in 1997, eclipsed by the DC Shoes brand's triple-digit growth in the mid-1990s. In 1998, Circus Distribution was renamed DC Shoes, Inc.

DC produced its first television advertising in the summer of 1999. A line of children's shoes debuted in the fall of 1999. Revenues dropped slightly to $43 million for the year but rose again to $60 million in 2000.

A Hot Property in 2000 and Beyond

The DC brand was a hot property. During 2000, the company settled a lawsuit against an alleged counterfeiter and closed a dealer it said had resold products to unauthorized stores. At the same time, DC was offering graphics kits in conjunction with One Industries for labeling dirt bikes with the DC logo.

The number of skate shoe brands proliferated from six to 30 during DC's first six years, reported *Sporting Goods Business*. By this time, DC was shipping product across the globe. Its shoes were already being marketed in mall-based stores. Many footwear companies found to their peril that their core consumers frowned on brands becoming too mainstream or reaching too many non-skaters. However, DC Shoes was able to successfully expand its distribution in the late 1990s to chains such as Pacific Sun, Copeland's Sports, and Nordstrom. As the *San Diego Union-Tribune* noted, DC kept hardcore skaters happy by reserving certain styles for mom-and-pop skate stores and regional surf and skate chains.

Giant footwear companies such as Nike and Reebok were attempting, with limited success, to enter the skate shoe market. As the *Los Angeles Times* noted, DC had itself looked to the athletic footwear industry for design and marketing inspiration.

By 2002, DC's administration and distribution facilities in California encompassed 150,000 square feet of space. DC had

built an indoor training facility, called Vista TF, for its skateboard team in 2001. The company also constructed a training and testing center for snowboarding, the DC Mountain Lab, near Park City, Utah.

Australian surfwear manufacturer Billabong International Ltd. offered to buy DC Shoes in 2002. However, the deal fell through. Along the way, Blehm was terminated; he then sued DC and Billabong, claiming age discrimination. DC countersued, alleging breach of fiduciary responsibility on Blehm's part. The company was also enduring an IRS audit at the same time.

The film *DC Video* celebrated the aerial exploits of DC's two original endorsers, Danny Way and Colin McKay. It took three years to make and was released in July 2003. Footage included Way's record 75-feet-long and $23\frac{1}{2}$-feet-high jumps. After years of involvement with the company, Danny Way and Colin McKay received equity stakes in DC Shoes in September 2003.

DC's celebrity endorsements extended beyond professional extreme athletes. The company developed a signature shoe with the rock group Linkin Park. It had also sponsored musical tours like Sno-Core. DC's Artist Projects produced limited runs of shoes designed in collaboration with artists such as Shepard Fairey, Thomas Campbell, and Phil Frost. In the early 1990s, DC featured hip-hop DJs in its print ads.

DC-branded skate-oriented outerwear was introduced in 2002. DC launched a new brand of shoes, Fallen, with popular pro skateboarder Jamie Thomas in October 2003. Fallen shoes reflected the edgier fashions preferred by core skaters, as opposed to the more general skateboarding market targeted by the DC Shoes brand. A line of girls' clothing was developed for spring 2004.

DC collaborated with Yamaha to develop the DC/Yamaha SXViper Mountain snowmobile. The vehicle was designed specifically to take snowboarders to backcountry powder, that is, to climb steep terrain faster than stock snowmobiles. DC had become acquainted with Yamaha through motocross events.

Many municipalities frowned on skaters' use of rails, benches, and other urban props. However, the skate plaza concept encouraged skateboarding in a town square setting. The

Rob Dyrdek-DC Shoes Foundation was created to promote the construction of skate plazas, beginning with one in Kettering, Ohio, the hometown of DC Shoes endorser Rob Drydek. In October 2003, the foundation granted the town $250,000 to fund half the cost of building the first skate plaza of its kind.

What can account for DC's explosive growth in the mid-1990s, and its durability as one of the most popular brands in action sports? (According to Board-Trac, DC Shoes was the favorite brand of skateboarders, snowboarders, and surfers in 2002.) DC's close association with top pros has certainly been a factor, as has its knack for staging promotional events. However, the company also creatively met challenges in design, production, distribution, and financing. As one industry insider put it in *Agents of Change:* "DC was the first skate shoe company to really fire on all cylinders."

Principal Competitors

Globe International; Skechers U.S.A.; Sole Technology, Inc.; Tare7; Vans Inc.

Further Reading

Blehm, Eric, ed., *Agents of Change: The Story of DC Shoes and Its Athletes,* New York: Regan Books, 2003.

Clodfelter, Joanne, "Kettering Skate Plaza Gets Go-Ahead Funding," *Dayton Daily News* (Ohio), October 23, 2003.

"DC Shoes Announce New Shareholders," *Transworld Skateboarding,* September 30, 2003.

"DC Shoes Launches Its First Ever TV Commercial," *Transworld Skateboarding,* July 21, 1999.

Dougherty, Conor, "Ken Block, President, DC Shoes," *San Diego Union-Tribune,* October 5, 2003, p. N4.

——, "Street Credibility; In Fickle Teen Market, DC Shoes Appeals to Skaters and Beyond," *San Diego Union-Tribune,* August 27, 2003, p. C1.

"Fallen Footwear Is Born," *Transworld Skateboarding,* October 28, 2003.

Gellene, Denise, "DC Shoes Following Giants' Steps," *Los Angeles Times,* July 26, 2000, p. 1.

Johnston, Eric, "Australia's Billabong Identified in US$140 Mln Lawsuit," *Dow Jones International Wires,* December 9, 2002.

Kristensen, Ken, "Skateboarding Stays in the Grind," *SGB: Sporting Goods Business,* February 1, 2000, pp. 73+.

"Skateboard Shoes—Good Gear; For the Citizens of Phat City, Looks Are (Nearly) Everything. But Are These Sneakers as Good as They Look?," *Independent on Sunday* (London), December 2, 2001, Sports Sec., p. 26.

Stein, Charles, "Can They Stay Cool?," *Your Company,* October/November 1998, pp. 34+.

Vrana, Debora, "Audit, Lawsuit Trip Up DC Shoes' Smooth Ride," *Los Angeles Times,* December 26, 2002, p. C1.

—Frederick C. Ingram

DEMCO, Inc.

4810 Forest Run Road
Madison, Wisconsin 53704
U.S.A.
Telephone: (608) 241-1201
Toll Free: (800) 962-4463
Fax: (608) 241-1799
Web site: http://www.demco.com

Private Company
Incorporated: 1905
Employees: 130
Sales: $50 million (2002 est.)
NAIC: 322130 Paperboard Mills; 323118 Blankbook,
   Loose-leaf Binder and Device Manufacturing; 334310
   Audio and Video Equipment Manufacturing

DEMCO, Inc. is a Madison, Wisconsin-based supplier of school and library products. The company offers supplies in a large number of different categories, including audiovisual (AV) equipment, AV packaging and supplies, boards and easels, computer supplies, facilities management, library supplies, office supplies, security, and signage. In addition to supplies, DEMCO sells many different kinds of children's, computer, library, office, and school furniture. The company also markets learning materials related to arts and crafts, library skills, and reading enrichment, among other areas. Finally, DEMCO's Periodicals Subscription Service makes subscription management easier for librarians by enabling them to search hundreds of titles in approximately 50 different subject classes ranging from archaeology, boating, and chemistry to economics, genealogy, and writing. This service also allows librarians to evaluate periodicals by grade level or recommending source.

A Quiet Start: 1905–67

DEMCO's roots stretch back to 1905, when the company was a division of the Democrat Printing Co. At that time, its primary role was printing forms for the University of Wisconsin-Madison Library. However, Norman D. "Smiley"

Bassett, who purchased DEMCO in 1931, has been credited as DEMCO's founding father.

Born in Minneapolis on Nicolet Island, Bassett graduated from the University of Wisconsin in 1914 after attending the Jefferson School in Charlottesville, Virginia, and New Jersey's Lawrenceville Preparatory School. He served in the U.S. Navy and Air Corps during World War I and then pursued a successful business career.

After buying the DEMCO division from Democrat Printing, Bassett established it as an independent enterprise, and the former parent company reorganized as Webcrafters, Inc. As DEMCO's president and chairman, Bassett led the company for many years. The April 29, 1980 issue of the *Wisconsin State Journal* explained that Bassett "built the firm from a small mail-order company in the early 1930s to one of the country's three leading national suppliers of materials to school, public, academic, private, and professional libraries."

Despite its ascension to a position of leadership within the library market, DEMCO historically kept a relatively low profile. The company's first four decades were marked by quiet, steady growth. However, a number of important developments occurred during the 1950s and 1960s. The first of these milestones came in 1950, when DEMCO moved to a facility located at 2120 Fordem Avenue in Madison, from which it would operate until the late 1980s.

In 1965, DEMCO obtained what eventually would grow into a 176,000-square-foot warehouse and production facility in DeForest, Wisconsin. In 1967, the company strengthened its international reach through an affiliation with Toronto, Ontario-based McLean Stationers. By forming Demco-Mclean Co., Ltd., DEMCO was able to offer library and school supply products throughout Canada.

Growth and Expansion: 1968–89

One of the most important developments in DEMCO's history occurred in 1968, when John E. Wall was named president. He would provide valuable leadership to the company for many years. Born in Chicago on April 17, 1926, Wall served in the U.S. Navy Air Corps during World War II and earned an undergraduate philosophy degree from Xavier University in 1950. His professional management career began that same year at Inland Steel Co. in Indiana Harbor, Indiana. Wall's career path then took him to a number of manufacturing firms in the Chicago area, including Cook Electric.

After joining DEMCO, Wall invigorated the company in a number of ways. Despite a burgeoning education market during the 1960s, DEMCO's growth had been sluggish because of a culture that downplayed risk taking. According to the May 1993 issue of *In Business*, Wall "wandered around, asked people questions, and gave them the go-ahead to try new ideas. He had employee luncheons and set up quarterly 'state-of-the-company' meetings with managers and year-end meetings with all employees. Another step Wall took early on was to set up a board of outside directors."

As the 1960s drew to a close, DEMCO was growing in sophistication. The company changed its name from Demco Library Supplies, Inc. to Demco Educational Corp. It offered approximately 3,000 different products—including some carrying the DEMCO brand name—to customers from several warehouse/office locations. These included sites in DeForest, Wisconsin; Fresno, California; and Hamden, Connecticut. In May 1969, DEMCO hired John Willert, a manager of marketing and business planning who President John Wall said would "serve as the company's 'nervous system' and provide for future company growth by identifying market and business opportunities and developing long-range strategy," according to the May 19, 1969 issue of the *Capital Times*.

When the 1970s arrived, DEMCO had truly secured its position as an industry leader. Processing as many as 800 orders each day, the company offered thousands of different items, including book cards, pockets, and jacket covers; devices for storage and filing; magazine binders; and close to 2,000 multimedia selections (slides, overheads, tapes, records, and filmstrips). DEMCO also offered a microfilm cataloging service to aid librarians with book circulation. The company, which employed approximately 75 to 80 workers, produced about half of its total product offerings at the facility in DeForest, Wisconsin.

The 1970s also were a time of considerable change at DEMCO. In 1972, Norman Bassett retired as chairman, and the company became a wholly owned subsidiary of Menasha, Wisconsin-based George Banta Co., Inc., one of the nation's leading printers of educational materials. DEMCO's sales for fiscal year 1971 totaled $5.8 million, while the larger Banta had recorded sales of nearly $40 million in the first three quarters of calendar year 1971.

In August 1972, DEMCO announced that construction was underway on a 37,000-square-foot addition to its 50,000-square-foot DeForest facility. The new space was intended to provide more warehouse and shipping capacity. Completed in 1973 at a cost of $250,000, the finished structure included new shipping and receiving docks, as well as space for storing finished products and assembling furniture. It also was in 1972 that DEMCO's sales reached record levels, driven by a product offering that had grown to include some 25,000 items. With 160 employees, DEMCO had extended its market reach to include all 50 states and 20 foreign countries.

DEMCO furthered its expansion in 1973 by acquiring Paramus, New Jersey-based American Library and Educational Services Co. (Alesco). With annual sales of $6 million and 150 employees, Alesco was a distributor of periodicals, hard cover books, and other instructional materials that mainly served elementary and secondary schools, according to the October 1, 1973 issue of the *Milwaukee Journal*. Alesco was founded in 1961 as the Missionary Society of St. Paul.

An important development occurred in 1978, when an Alabama firm offered to buy DEMCO from Banta. Along with William Erickson, vice-president of operations; Greg Larson, vice-president of marketing; and Lawrence Sobyak, vice-president of finance, President John Wall made a successful counteroffer and purchased DEMCO. However, significant challenges remained. These included a loan that carried an interest rate of 25 percent, as well as a debt-to-equity ratio of 11 to 1. DEMCO's Alesco subsidiary also was struggling financially. In the May 1993 issue of *In Business*, Wall said: "There were 24 people at the closing downtown, including all the vice-presidents from Banta, and they were saying, sotto voce, down at the end of the table, 'They'll never make it. They'll go bankrupt in six months.'" Although the buyout put a strain on DEMCO's resources until the mid- to late 1980s, Wall and his executive team were successful in keeping the company afloat and guiding it to more prosperous times.

In 1980, DEMCO lost its founding father when Norman D. Bassett died in April at the age of 89. Bassett left a charitable gift totaling $4.5 million, which was dispersed to a number of different organizations. At the time, this was the largest charitable contribution in Madison's history.

As the 1980s progressed, DEMCO continued to find success. In 1987, the company's warehouse in DeForest underwent another expansion, increasing in size to 133,000 square feet. The facility stocked approximately 25,000 different items worth more than $4 million. The following year, sales reached levels of more than $30 million—fueled by annual growth of approximately 15 to 18 percent—and the company's employee base numbered almost 250. By this time, about 35 percent of DEMCO's sales were attributable to schools. Another 20 percent of sales came from the library market, while colleges and universities represented 18 percent. The remainder of DEMCO's revenues came from businesses and other specialized markets. While the company still manufactured some of its own branded products, it mainly purchased items from other manufacturers and repackaged them under the DEMCO name.

Key Dates:

1905: DEMCO is established as a division of the Democrat Printing Co.
1931: Norman D. "Smiley" Bassett purchases DEMCO.
1965: A warehouse and production facility is established in DeForest, Wisconsin.
1968: John E. Wall is named president.
1971: Sales reach $5.8 million.
1972: Norman Bassett retires as chairman, and DEMCO becomes a wholly owned subsidiary of Menasha, Wisconsin-based George Banta Co., Inc.
1978: President John Wall leads a successful leveraged buyout of DEMCO.
1980: Norman Bassett dies at the age of 89.
1989: Greg M. Larson is named president, and John Wall becomes chairman and CEO.
1993: DEMCO expands internationally by acquiring Library Furnishing Consultants, a British company that supplies shelving and other furniture items to libraries.
1998: Ed Muir is appointed as DEMCO's president.
2001: Bill Stroner is named president of DEMCO.
2003: DEMCO acquires Gaylord Brothers' library supplies and furniture division, as well as the Gaylord brand name.

It also was in 1988 that DEMCO was preparing to relocate its headquarters from the location on Fordem Avenue to a new, two-story, 42,000-square-foot facility at Forest Run and Hayes Roads. DEMCO was committed to staying in Madison and to remaining independent. As John Wall explained in the July 13, 1988 issue of the *Capital Times:* "I hope to do what we are doing a little better each year. That's my philosophy. Selling the business and taking the money would not be good for the company's viability. Nor is going public. I like the ability to focus on the long term rather than quarterly updates for the shareholders." Continuing, Wall praised DEMCO's workforce, stating: "I can't stress enough about the quality of our workers. What they say about the Wisconsin work ethic is true. We try to keep everyone happy. We have profit-sharing and supervisors meet monthly with their staffs. Also, my door is always open."

In March 1989, DEMCO announced that Greg M. Larson was its new president. With Larson's appointment, Wall became the company's chairman and CEO. Larson, who had served DEMCO for five years as vice-president of marketing, earned an undergraduate business degree from the University of Wisconsin-Whitewater in 1972, followed by an MBA from the University of Wisconsin-Milwaukee in 1981.

Preparing for a Second Century: 1990–2003

In 1993, DEMCO expanded internationally by acquiring Library Furnishing Consultants, a British company that supplied shelving and other furniture items to libraries. It was around this time that the company made a decision to move its computer operations from an old Groupe Bell mainframe to a system comprised of IBM AS/400s and 40 PC terminals de-

voted exclusively to its customer service application. By 1996, DEMCO's computer system also included some 200 traditional PCs that employees used to access productivity software like word processing and spreadsheet applications.

While DEMCO once developed all of its software in-house, after moving to the new computer system the company purchased a number of software applications from other vendors to handle many traditional business functions, including inventory and payroll. These applications included a database program called Showcase Vista that enabled DEMCO to perform sophisticated analysis of its marketing initiatives. Following the adoption of Showcase Vista, the response rate to DEMCO's catalog mailings doubled. Plans also were made to enter more specialized niche markets, such as legal libraries, assisted by the ability to quickly analyze product offerings and adapt to customer feedback.

Despite these third-party software purchases, DEMCO continued to write its own customer service software, given the importance it placed on customer relationships. The application DEMCO developed for its new computer environment had a positive impact on the firm. Prior to its creation, customer service functions were split among different employees and systems. The new program enabled any employee to address virtually every concern a customer had, from order processing and accounts receivable to product returns. The amount of time required to fulfill orders fell significantly, from as many as four days to only one day.

In 1997, DEMCO strengthened its audio book program when it found that libraries were doubling or tripling their budgets for such media. The company partnered with Rezound Media, Inc., an audio book rental company, to offer its 13,000 library customers some 300 titles via a biannual, 24-page catalog. While the titles offered were mainly abridgements, some unabridged audio books were also included.

As the 1990s came to a close, DEMCO had evolved considerably. The company's DeForest warehouse had grown to occupy 176,000 square feet, and its main catalog spanned 900 pages. Indeed, an article in the January 10, 1999 issue of the *Wisconsin State Journal* revealed that DEMCO's offerings included "items such as steel book supports in dragon and giraffe designs, eight-headset student listening centers, carpets depicting the four seasons, whale-shaped lounging chairs, and curriculum supplements with posters, games, costumes and maps on subjects like ancient Egypt and colonial America." DEMCO's customers included such prestigious institutions as the Library of Congress, and its employee base numbered 344.

Sales were expected to exceed $60 million in 1998—a double-digit jump from the previous year. That year, Ed Muir was appointed as DEMCO's president. While he was new, his philosophy mirrored the culture that Chairman John Wall had done much to shape over the years. "We know who our customers are and we service them well," he remarked in the January 10, 1999 issue of the *Wisconsin State Journal*. "We've not tried to be who we aren't."

By the early 2000s, sales had declined slightly from levels seen in the late 1990s. However, DEMCO was still a strong company. This was especially true considering the weak economic climate that negatively impacted library and school budgets. By 2003, sales totaled approximately $50 million, and employees numbered 130. In June of that year, DEMCO acquired Gaylord Brothers' library supplies and furniture division, as well as the Gaylord brand name. The acquisition strengthened the foothold DEMCO had established on the library market during nearly 100 years of operation. Led by President Bill Stroner, who was appointed in July 2001, DEMCO appeared to be positioned for success in a second century of operations.

Principal Competitors

Highsmith, Inc.

Further Reading

"Company Information," DEMCO, Inc., October 5, 2003. Available from http://www.demco.com.

Corcoran, Cate T., "Demco Looks to AS/400 for Its Client/Server Picture," *InfoWorld*, February 19, 1996.

"Demco Buys Library Services Firm," *Wisconsin State Journal*, October 14, 1973.

"John Willert," *Capital Times*, May 19, 1969.

Leslie, Gay, "If You Read, You Know Demco," *Wisconsin State Journal*, April 26, 1970.

Molvig, Dianne, "On to New Chapters," *In Business*, May 1993.

Newman, Judy, "Demco Has a Read on Library Demands," *Wisconsin State Journal*, January 10, 1999.

Parkins, Al, "Demco Quietly Pulls in Big Bucks," *Capital Times*, July 13, 1988.

"Philanthropist, Businessman Norman Bassett Dies," *Wisconsin State Journal*, April 29, 1980.

"Rezound to Supply Audios to Demco," *Publishers Weekly*, October 6, 1997.

Rogers, Michael, "Gaylord Revamps: Blauer Out, Demco Buys Supplies Biz," *Library Journal*, June 15, 2003.

—Paul R. Greenland

Dresdner Kleinwort Wasserstein

20 Fenchurch Street
London EC3P 3DB
United Kingdom
Telephone: (207) 623-8000
Fax: (207) 623-4069
Web site: http://www.drkw.com

Wholly Owned Subsidiary of Dresdner Bank AG
Incorporated: 1961
Employees: 6,500
Total Assets: EUR 413.4 billion ($424.5 billion)(2002)
NAIC: 523110 Investment Banking and Securities
Dealing; 523999 Miscellaneous Financial Investment
Activities

Dresdner Kleinwort Wasserstein (DrKW) operates as the investment banking arm of Germany's Dresdner Bank AG. The company offers its corporate, government, and institutional clients a variety of capital markets products and services, including short-term products and treasury, equity products, rates, credit products, foreign exchange debt origination, sales and marketing, research, risk management, and tax services. The firm was formerly known as Kleinwort Benson until Dresdner Bank acquired it in 1995. In 2001, Dresdner Bank acquired Wasserstein Perella & Co. and folded it into Dresdner Kleinwort's operations. DrKW became a member of the world's fourth-largest financial institution later that year when Dresdner Bank merged with the Allianz Group.

Early History

Kleinwort Benson was formed in 1961 when the firm of Kleinwort, Sons & Company merged with Robert Benson, Lonsdale & Company Limited. Both houses were British merchant banks of long standing. Kleinwort could trace its roots to 1838, when a Hamburg shipping clerk named Alexander Kleinwort immigrated to Cuba and joined a Havana trading company run by James Drake. Kleinwort relocated to London in 1855. He quickly became the dominant partner, and by 1883 he and his sons were in sole control of the company and had given it their

family name. Kleinwort also shifted its focus from trade to merchant banking during these years.

World War I caused trouble for British merchant banks by disrupting foreign trade, and Kleinwort, which relied considerably on business in Germany, was among the hardest hit. Nonetheless, the firm suffered no permanent damage from the war, and even had slightly more capital in 1918 than it did in 1913. However, the merchant banks' traditional business of raising money for foreign ventures never fully recovered after the armistice, due to informal restrictions on foreign trade and increased competition from banks in New York and other up-and-coming financial centers.

In response, Kleinwort joined the industry-wide trend toward raising money for domestic industry in the 1920s. It did so under the guidance of Herman Andrae, Alexander Kleinwort's grand-nephew, who had become a partner in 1907 and whose influence in the firm waxed as that of his aging uncles waned. Kleinwort took on more domestic underwriting business than it had in the past, but it also embarked on unsuccessful forays into shipbuilding, cotton manufacturing, and fire insurance. In the first two cases, the firm found itself with unprofitable investments in failing companies that it was also forced to manage; in the third, it loaned money to insurance entrepreneur Clarence Hatry, only to lose all of it when Hatry was convicted of fraud in 1929. Kleinwort's profitable activities in precious metals and foreign currency trading during this decade helped offset these fiascos.

The Depression proved disastrous for many British merchant banks, slowing foreign trade to a virtual standstill. Even worse for Kleinwort, the German government declared a moratorium on the repayment of foreign loans in the wake of that nation's bank crisis of 1931. In response, foreign bankers with loans outstanding in Germany declared that they would grant no more credit to German interests. Because of its traditional reliance on trade with Germany, Kleinwort was hit harder than most of its competitors by the crisis. Nevertheless, Kleinwort survived the Depression, while other merchant banks either folded or needed a handout from the Bank of England.

The German debt problem continued to dog Kleinwort after the outbreak of war in 1939. At the time, it had £4.4 million in

Company Perspectives:

Our ability to excel in such a variety of transactions reflects the importance we place on combining sector, country, and product specialization expertise with strong client relationships to ensure our clients receive the best quality solutions and advice.

German, Austrian, and Hungarian bills outstanding. It tried to recover its money through foreign courts but without success. After 1945, the destruction of the German economy, the loss of prewar loan records, and the fact that Soviet Union did not want to see money repaid to Western bankers from its zone of occupation complicated the matter of settling the debts. In 1951, the West German government and the banks reached an accord whereby the banks would end the credit freeze, and German companies would repay their debts, figured at a 4 percent annual rate from 1939 to 1953. By 1959, Kleinwort had recovered £2 million.

The Benson family came from the Lake District and were of Quaker stock. By the 1780s, they had gone into business in Liverpool as cotton merchants. The firm moved to London in 1852 and gradually began to specialize in investment banking. By the end of the century, the Bensons had scored a major prestige coup by providing capital for the railroad construction boom in the American West. In 1948, Robert Benson & Company Limited merged with Lonsdale Investment Trust, whom it had served as bankers, to form Robert Benson Lonsdale.

In 1958, Robert Benson Lonsdale became embroiled in what became known as Britain's Great Aluminum War. The fracas started when Reynolds Metals, in cooperation with the relatively new British investment firm Tube Investments, made an unfriendly bid to take over British Aluminum, which was then considering a friendly offer from Alcoa. A syndicate of 14 old-line merchant banks, which was led by Hambros and Lazard Brothers and included Robert Benson Lonsdale, came to the aid of British Aluminum. However, S.A. Warburg, another London banking house of long standing, sided with Reynolds, producing a bitter and divisive rupture in London's merchant-banking fraternity. Reynolds finally won, acquiring 80 percent of British Aluminum stock by early 1959. The Great Aluminum War altered merchant banking by turning mergers and acquisitions into a high-profile, high-profit business.

Diversification after the Merger

When Kleinwort and Robert Benson Lonsdale merged in 1961, *The Economist* described it as "a marriage of essentially complementary partners." Kleinwort had strong overseas connections thanks to its history of involvement in foreign trade but was weak in corporate finance and investment banking. Robert Benson Lonsdale's strengths lay in corporate finance and underwriting, but it had done little business in more traditional areas of merchant banking. The resulting Kleinwort Benson Lonsdale held assets of £60 million. Its new-found size and strength stood it in good stead for the hectic times to come.

The 1960s and 1970s were years of fierce activity for merchant banks, marked by increased competition both from for-

eign firms and from domestic rivals spurred on by a 1971 Bank of England policy statement encouraging looser regulation of British financial institutions. As a result, merchant banks had to diversify and shuck their traditional specialist status. By 1977, Kleinwort Benson had become involved in unit and investment trusts, factoring, leasing, insurance brokering, venture capital, tax planning, executor and trustee services, property development, commodity dealing, and bullion brokering and dealing, among other services.

In 1965, Kleinwort Benson entered the oil and gas business when its subsidiary Kleinwort Benson Energy began drilling on the continental shelf. Two years later, Kleinwort Benson entered a consortium with 17 other partners, including Barclays and the Bank of Scotland, to form Airlease International, a company specializing in aircraft leasing. In 1986, it entered the domestic life insurance business by buying Transinternational Life from Transamerica Corporation and, even more importantly, prepared itself for the impending deregulation of the British financial markets known as the Big Bang by acquiring the securities brokerage Grieveson Grant.

Kleinwort Benson's 1984 annual report spoke of the firm forming a "global chain." In fact, its international expansion had actually been underway for over a decade. In 1967, it opened an investment bank in New York, using its strong reputation in the Eurobond market to get underwriting business. In 1970, it opened an office in Tokyo which, combined with its subsidiaries in Thailand and Hong Kong, gave it a stronger presence in Asia than any other British merchant bank.

In 1984, anticipating the new opportunities that the 1986 deregulation of the financial markets would bring and aware of the increasing interdependence of the world's financial markets, Kleinwort Benson redoubled its efforts, making several major acquisitions in the United States. In New York, it bought ACLI Government Securities Incorporated, a U.S. government securities dealer, from the investment bank Donaldson, Lufkin & Jenrette, renaming it Kleinwort Benson Government Securities (KBGS). The deal made Kleinwort Benson the first foreign bank to own a government securities firm that dealt directly with the Federal Reserve Bank of New York. In Chicago, it acquired the institutional and funds operations of Virginia Trading Corporation, a futures brokerage. In Los Angeles, it purchased the services of a group of brokers specializing in interest-rate swaps and renamed it Kleinwort Benson Cross Financing. Also in 1984, Kleinwort Benson Australia acquired a 50 percent interest in Australia Gilt Company Group, a dealer in Australian government securities.

Some of these moves worked well; others did not. Kleinwort Benson Cross Financing proved to be a consistent moneymaker, while KBGS disappointed its parent's expectations. Kleinwort Benson had made the acquisition in order to acquaint itself with price trends and auction techniques in the American treasuries market. However, KBGS seldom participated in auctions, nor was its familiarity with the demand for treasury securities as strong as had been hoped. In 1988, Kleinwort Benson sold a 25 percent interest in KBGS to Fuji Bank. In addition, Kleinwort Benson's Australian banking and securities operations were sold to Security Pacific in October 1989.

Key Dates:

1883: Alexander Kleinwort and his sons gain sole control of a merchant banking company and give it their family name.

1948: Robert Benson & Company Ltd. merges with Lonsdale Investment Trust to form Robert Benson Lonsdale.

1961: Kleinwort, Sons & Company merges with Robert Benson, Lonsdale & Company.

1971: The Bank of England calls for looser banking regulations; the company continues to diversify its holdings.

1986: Britain's financial markets are deregulated.

1995: Dresdner Bank AG acquires Kleinwort Benson; the new company adopts the name Dresdner Kleinwort Benson (DKB).

2001: Wasserstein Perella & Co. is purchased, and its operations are folded into DKB; the new company is called Dresdner Kleinwort Wasserstein.

Overcoming Problems in the Late 1980s

In 1986, *The Economist* called Kleinwort Benson the "great white hope of British merchant banking," stating that Kleinwort Benson and S.A. Warburg were the only British merchant banks poised to become world-class financial institutions. As it turned out, however, the year of the Big Bang was not entirely kind to Kleinwort Benson. The worldwide slump in bond prices, a decrease in mergers and acquisitions activity in Britain, and problems with Kleinwort Benson's settlement system all hurt its financial performance and left it in need of capital. Before the year was out, the house had sold a 4.9 percent interest to American Can, which sold its shares to Morgan Stanley International several months later. Late in 1987, Kleinwort Benson sold a 1.5 percent stake to Sumitomo Life Insurance, and Consolidated Gold Fields bought a 50 percent interest in Kleinwort Benson Energy. In 1988, American International Group acquired a 5.3 percent interest in Kleinwort Benson.

Thanks to the integration of the world's financial markets, the American stock market crash of 1987 was felt around the world. Nonetheless, Kleinwort Benson survived the crisis in better shape than its competitors. It was one of the few British securities firms that made a profit on equities dealing in late 1987 and early 1988. It also disclosed in its 1987 annual report that its treasury division chalked up "record operating income" due to volatility in the dollar and interest rates.

Kleinwort Benson did not fare as well in the second half of 1988. Its securities business lost more than £45 million, reducing the bank's overall pre-tax profits to £17.7 million that year as compared to £51.6 million in 1987. Thanks to this poor performance, its stock price neared a four-year low in the spring of 1989. Kleinwort Benson nevertheless remained committed to securities. Jonathan Agnew, who succeeded Michael Hawkes as chief executive of the Kleinwort Benson Group in 1989, staked the firm to the prospect of becoming an integrated investment bank based on the conviction that a strong securities business would help market the products generated by the bank's other activities. Such an attitude was not surprising, coming from a man who was elevated to chairman of Kleinwort Grieveson Securities in 1987, following the acquisition of Grieveson, Grant and Company, in an effort to give the former Grieveson Grant younger and more aggressive leadership.

Nonetheless, Kleinwort Benson's share of the British equities market remained at 5 percent in 1989, not enough to put it in the front ranks of Britain's securities firms. Corporate finance continued to account for a large share of its revenues and, according to *The Economist,* it also had "the biggest banking book of any British merchant bank, with some £3 billion of loans outstanding."

With its place in the securities industry somewhat uncertain, the future of Agnew's vision of Kleinwort Benson as a fully integrated investment bank appeared equally up in the air. Traditionally, merchant bankers had to live with uncertainty as an inherent fact of business life. No matter what its future held, Kleinwort Benson deserved credit for its ambitious program of expansion and diversification in the 1970s and 1980s, which recalled the golden age of the British merchant banks. Back then, the influence of the merchant bankers extended to the far corners of the world as they provided the money that built the empire. Kleinwort Benson recognized early on that the future of merchant banking also lay over the seas. By 1989, it boasted of offices and subsidiaries in ten countries and four continents—a small empire of its own.

Changes in the 1990s and Beyond

The company's fortunes took a tumble once again in the early 1990s due in part to its attempts to diversify its holdings. The strategy proved to be both costly and damaging to its reputation in the industry. Rumors began to fly that the once mighty and prestigious merchant bank would be forced to dissolve. By 1995, however, the firm had rebounded through the implementation of a new management plan that focused company efforts on corporate finance and origination and distribution of domestic and international equities.

Despite its turnaround, Kleinwort Benson continued to face increased competition from its larger U.S. and European counterparts. As such, the company agreed to be acquired by Dresdner Bank AG, Germany's second-largest bank at the time. Both parties eyed the $1.6 billion purchase as being highly beneficial. Through Kleinwort Benson, Dresdner would gain a foothold in international investment banking. At the same time, Kleinwort Benson expected to expand under the leadership of a strong bank, giving it solid footing for a secure future.

The company operated as Dresdner Kleinwort Benson (DKB) after the 1995 acquisition. Its amalgamation into Dresdner proved to be the first of many changes for the firm in the upcoming years. The European banking sector as a whole began to experience a wave of merger activity in the late 1990s and into the 2000s. Dresdner followed suit, engineering an enormous $30 billion deal with Deutsche Bank. The merger fell through, however, after it became apparent that DKB would be carved up as a result of the deal.

Undeterred, Dresdner continued to look for opportunities to bolster its holdings, especially for its investment banking arm.

In 2000, the company began courting Wasserstein Perella & Co., an American investment bank founded in the late 1980s by the infamous dealmaker Bruce Wasserstein in conjunction with Joseph Perella. The two companies ironed out the terms of the agreement, completing the $1.4 billion transaction in January 2001. The combination created Dresdner Kleinwort Wasserstein (DrKW), the seventh-largest corporate merger advisor in the world.

Dresdner became involved in yet another deal later that year. Allianz AG, a large German insurance group, made a $22 billion play for Dresdner, adding it to its arsenal in late 2001. The union created the world's fourth-largest financial group, leaving Dresdner in an enviable position. On the other hand, the merger left the future of DrKW in question. Its recent financial performance had been faltering and, to top it off, Dresdner did not appear as adamant as it had in the past for keeping its investment unit intact now that it had a rich parent. *The Economist* summed up the company's problems in an August 2002 article, stating, ''In the past year almost one-fifth of Dresdner's revenues have crumbled away. The trouble lies in Dresdner's 'corporates and markets' division, which includes Dresdner Kleinwort Wasserstein.'' The article went on to report, ''As equity markets have weakened and mergers-and-acquisitions business has dried up, trading revenues have fallen by more than half, and fees and commissions have dropped by more than one-eighth.''

In response to the challenging business environment, DrKW implemented a series of cost-cutting strategies in order to shore up its bottom line. Its internal restructuring efforts appeared to pay off, and by September 2003 DrKW had reported three consecutive quarters of growth. Its ability to overcome hardships and the market downturn had secured it a short-term future with Allianz. The financial giant pledged to hold onto the unit for two years before considering a sale, giving DrKW and its employees some breathing room for the next 24 months.

Principal Competitors

Allen & Company Inc.; Credit Suisse First Boston Corp.; Lazard LLC.

Further Reading

Astbury, Kate, ''Allianz Still Half in Love,'' *Euromoney*, September 2003, p. 10.

Channon, Derek. *British Banking Strategy and the International Challenge*, London: Macmillan Press Ltd., 1977.

''Dresdner Buys Kleinwort,'' *Global Investor*, July/August 1995, p. 4.

''Finance and Economics: Death of a Deal,'' *Economist*, April 8, 2000, p. 81.

''For Better, For Worse; Allianz and Dresdner Bank,'' *Economist*, August 17, 2002.

Hobday, Nicola, ''Whither Dresdner Kleinwort Wasserstein,'' *Daily Deal*, March 29. 2001.

Jenkins, Patrick, ''DrKW Aims to Recapture Past Glory,'' *Financial Times*, September 23, 2003, p. 26.

Kerr, Ian, ''Can Kleinwort Elude the Vultures,'' *Euroweek*, February 24, 1995, p. 43.

Merrell, Caroline, ''Allianz Signals Disposal of DKW,'' *Times* (London), May 17, 2003.

A Short History of the Kleinwort Benson Group, London: Kleinwort Benson Group, 1988.

Stevenson, Richard W., ''Dresdner Will Pay $1.6 Billion for Kleinwort Benson,'' *New York Times*, June 27, 1995, p. D6.

''Wasserstein's Acquisition Completed by Dresdner,'' *Wall Street Journal*, January 5, 2001, p. 1.

—update: Christina M. Stansell

E✳TRADE
FINANCIAL

E*Trade Financial Corporation

4500 Bohannon Drive
Menlo Park, California 94025
U.S.A.
Telephone: (650) 331-6000
Toll Free: (800) 387-2331
Web site: http://www.etrade.com

Public Company
Incorporated: 1982 as TradePlus Inc.
Employees: 3,500
Sales: $1.325 billion (2002)
Stock Exchanges: New York
Ticker Symbol: ET
NAIC: 523110 Investment Banking and Securities
Dealing; 523120 Securities Brokerage; 523999
Miscellaneous Financial Investment Activities; 523910
Miscellaneous Intermediation

E*Trade Financial Corporation operates as a diversified financial services holding company. Considered a pioneer in the online trading world, E*Trade was forced to expand its services when the dot-com bubble burst—an event that left many pure play online companies scrambling to shore up revenues and profits. As such, the firm not only offers online investing and trading to its four million customers but a host of other financial services related to wealth management and banking. E*Trade touts its products and services to retail, corporate, and institutional customers. Its clients can access account information online and through E*Trade Centers and automated teller machines located throughout the United States. Christos Cotsakos led the company through its stellar growth period in the late 1990s but stepped down in 2002. Mitchell H. Caplan was named his replacement and is leading the charge to transform E*Trade into a multi-faceted financial services concern. In 2003, the company changed its name from E*Trade Group Inc. to E*Trade Financial Corporation.

Fomenting the Brokerage Revolution in the 1980s

When William Porter formed TradePlus with $15,000 in startup capital in 1982, the online investment revolution was already underway. The first online service, called Tickerscreen, was initiated in May 1982 by Max Ule, as a division of Rosenkrantz, Ehrenkrants, Lyon & Ross, Inc. A bulletin-board system, Tickerscreen enabled customers to place orders after the markets were closed, which would then be transacted by the brokerage house when the markets opened again the next day. Porter, who had held management positions with General Electric and Textron, after earning an MA in physics at Kansas State College and an MBA in management from the Massachusetts Institute of Technology, saw an opportunity to take online investment services further—by automating the full transaction process.

Porter's TradePlus ''vision'' combined two emerging trends. Already trading under his own account, Porter also looked at cutting the cost of trading. By then, a new breed of discount brokers, such as Charles Schwab, had arisen to challenge the full-service brokerage houses. By the mid-1980s, discount brokers amounted to 9 percent—up from 2 percent at the start of the decade and rising—of all stock transaction commissions. Porter, however, believed that he could cut the cost of trading even deeper than the discount brokers, who still charged as high as $100 per transaction. The second trend was the appearance of the first personal computers in the early 1980s. Porter immediately recognized the potential of this new electronic market, foreseeing that personal computers—equipped with their own modems—would soon become commonplace office and home equipment.

In 1982, TradePlus contracted with C.D. Andersen & Company to create a computerized order entry system. That system went online in July 1983. TradePlus enabled its customers to access market information and conduct trades during market hours, while offering 24-hour-per-day portfolio management capability. By paying a premium on the basic service charge, customers could also receive real-time stock pricing and portfolio updates; otherwise, they received information after a 20-minute delay. Customers paid a sign-up fee, ranging up to $195, and monthly subscription fees of $15, which gave them one-hour of connect time per month. Use of the service beyond that cost $24 per hour during market hours and $6 per hour when the markets closed. For the premium, real-time service, nonprofessional customers paid $75 per month and professional investors paid $135 per month, fees established by the National Association of Securities Dealers.

By 1984, C.D. Anderson counted some 500 TradePlus customers, who contributed as much as 12 percent of the firm's commissions. In that year, the Anderson's exclusive agreement with TradePlus ended, and Porter began marketing the company to other discount brokers, signing on Fidelity Brokerage Services, of Boston, and Texas Securities, Inc., of Fort Worth, by the middle of the year. By then, TradePlus was not alone: several other discount brokers had begun to offer their own online services. Nevertheless, TradePlus continued to build, in 1985 signing Quick & Reilly, then the nation's third-largest discount broker, to offer TradePlus through the Compuserve Information Network. The following year, TradePlus services were also added to another large database service of the time, Dialog Information Retrieval Service. The concept of online investment transactions was catching on, although individual investors were still burdened by monthly subscription charges. Toward the late 1980s, that changed when Donaldson, Lufkin & Jenrette introduced its PC Financial Network, which was incorporated into the standard services of such online businesses as America Online and Prodigy. TradePlus's primary customers, meanwhile, included a growing number of discount brokerage houses, conducting their activities via the TradePlus system.

Online trading continued to build momentum. By the summer of 1987, TradePlus reported that its servers were in use nearly every minute, often by several people at once, 24 hours per day, including a large number of international customers as well as domestic customers. By then, in addition to Quick & Reilly and C.D. Anderson, two banks began offering TradePlus as a brokerage gateway. Bank of America's Home Banking service gave customers access to Charles Schwab & Company using TradePlus's computers, while Chemical Bank's Pronto customers could place orders through TradePlus to Quick & Reilly. Electronic trading seemed on its way to becoming a competitive force in the investment community. Then, in October 1987, the market crashed. Trade volume contracted, and the online trading services, TradePlus included, withered.

Reborn in the 1990s

Trading picked up only slowly as the 1990s began, crippled by a national recession and then by the U.S. entry into the Gulf War. In 1991, however, Porter, still active with TradePlus, again showed his visionary side. With several hundred thousand dollars of startup capital from TradePlus, Porter established a new company, E*Trade Securities, Inc., providing deep-discount brokerage services. Instead of the monthly fees charged by TradePlus, E*Trade offered flat-rate trading and free information services via the online services, including America Online and Compuserve. By the following year, Wall Street had recovered from its slump, entering the bull market of the 1990s.

At the same time, interest in the online services began to build, while advances in modem technology and falling prices among computer equipment in general, were providing faster access to a widening range of people.

E*Trade quickly dominated this new investors market. As trade volumes continued to build, interest in investing—particularly among the Baby Boom generation—was also rising. By the mid-1990s, more than 20 percent of the nation's population was investing in stock, compared with less than 5 percent the decade before. By 1992, combined revenues at TradePlus and E*Trade neared $850,000. The following year, revenues—based on E*Trade's $40 per transaction charge—topped $2 million. The company also turned profitable, posting $100,000 in net earnings. The new availability of investment information, accessible by the online services' customers 24 hours per day, added to the popularity of investing, and particularly self-directed investing by the growing numbers of computer-literate customers. Both America Online and Compuserve were undergoing their own growth boom during this period. By 1994, the two companies counted some two million customers between them. In less than three years, America Online alone would count more than eight million customers.

The year 1994 proved significant for E*Trade as well: revenues exploded, nearing $11 million, making TradePlus and its E*Trade subsidiary the fastest-growing private company in the country. E*Trade quickly outpaced its parent, and the company would eventually be reorganized as the E*Trade Group, with E*Trade Securities remaining its principal subsidiary. The company, which counted 44 employees in 1994, scrambled to keep up with its own growth, adding more than 200 employees in one year and expanding its office space from 4,800 square feet to more than 20,000 square feet in 1994. By the end of 1995, however, E*Trade was forced to move again, to new quarters with some 48,000 square feet.

By 1995, the new American information revolution was firmly underway. The appearance of so-called multimedia PCs, which bundled sound, video, and—particularly important for E*Trade—modems into relatively inexpensive and easy to install packages, brought a whole new wave of people to computers and online services. E*Trade soon found itself joined by competing online investment services, forcing it to drop its transaction rate to $19.95. However, the company had already taken the lead among the growing home investors community, which was also served by such popular online services as America Online's Motley Fool investment information area. E*Trade found its system overloaded with customer calls, and in the summer of 1995 was forced to quadruple its systems. By the end of that year, the company's revenues had doubled again, reaching $22.3 million and generating a net income of $2.6 million.

The online services proved merely a taste of things to come. By the end of 1995, the Internet—and more specifically its graphical World Wide Web interface—had become the buzzword of the country. A new range of service providers sprang up, countering the hourly charges of the online services with unlimited access at flat-rate monthly fees. E*Trade quickly set up shop on the World Wide Web as well. Within weeks after the company's entry on the Web, the Internet accounted for more than 13 percent of the company's sales.

Key Dates:

1982: William Porter forms TradePlus.
1987: The market crashes in October; online trading services wither.
1991: Porter establishes E*Trade Securities Inc.
1994: With revenues of nearly $11 million, TradePlus and E*Trade operate as the fastest-growing private company in the United States.
1996: Christos Cotsakos is named president and CEO; E*Trade goes public.
1999: Revenue increases by 134.2 percent.
2000: Telebanc Financial Corporation and Electronic Investing Corporation are acquired.
2002: E*Trade adds Tradescape Corporation to its arsenal.
2003: Cotsakos steps down; the company changes its name to E*Trade Financial Corporation.

Riding the Dot-Com Wave in the Late 1990s

In early 1996, E*Trade began preparing its own initial public offering (IPO). Porter stepped aside, bringing in Christos Cotsakos to lead the company. Cotsakos, a son of Greek immigrants from Paterson, New Jersey, had been a decorated Vietnam veteran—a volunteer awarded the Congressional Medal of Honor for his actions during the Tet Offensive—before joining the early 1970s startup Federal Express. Beginning at an hourly wage of $3.50, Cotsakos worked his way up the Federal Express ranks over nearly 19 years before becoming president and CEO of Nielsen. With Porter as chairman, Cotsakos was named president and CEO in April 1996 and led E*Trade into its IPO that summer.

E*Trade was adding some 500 customers and as much as $10 million in assets per day; by May 1996, the huge increase in trading volume—in the first half of that year alone volume had tripled, from 50 million shares traded to more than 170 million—proved too much for the company's system, crashing the company's computers and leaving its customers stranded for some two hours. For that two-hour period, the company paid out $1.7 million to cover its customers' losses. A second, more limited glitch occurred in July. By then, however, the company had already begun to prepare for such an event, having leased a 53,000-square-foot space in Sacramento, California, to install a redundant hardware and customer service facility. The growth of its competitors, including the arrival of Schwabs' e.schwab service, forced E*Trade to cut its transaction rate again, to as low as $14.95.

E*Trade's growth pace continued, seeing revenues more than doubling again to near $52 million for 1996. The company also began expanding its services, offering investors the opportunity to buy shares in IPOs and purchase equity in private offerings. Trade volume continued to grow, reaching 8,000 transactions per day, with the Internet accounting for more than a quarter of all transactions. The company also formed a subsidiary, E*Trade Online Ventures, to search for other directions in which the company could expand. One such expansion was the company's agreement with Versus Brokerage to extend the E*Trade brand name to Canada's financial market. A similar agreement would bring the company to Australia in May 1997. In June 1997, E*Trade and leading World Wide Web search engine Yahoo!, which recorded some ten million "hits" per day, announced an agreement which added a direct link to E*Trade's Web site from the Yahoo! site.

With an estimated 40 million Americans online by mid-1997, and a total online community of some 60 million worldwide, E*Trade's future appeared electric. Analysts expected the online investment market to grow from 1.5 million in 1997 to ten million or more by 2000. E*Trade looked forward to becoming the top brand name of this new investment era.

Indeed, during the latter half of the 1990s E*Trade continued its upward climb. The company expanded its services to customers in Australia, Germany, Israel, and Japan. In 1999, revenues increased by 132.4 percent over the previous year to $662.3 million. Despite E*Trade's success, Cotsakos was not satisfied and continued to pursue growth options. Adding to its strong presence in online trading, E*Trade began setting its sights on becoming the world's first digital financial media company. An August 1999 *Fortune* article reported that "Cotsakos wants every piece of every financial transaction, and he wants it done without any human interaction. He wants E*Trade to tell you how to invest, what it means to invest, and where to invest, and then take a cut from both you and the market maker. He wants to take your company public, insure your car, manage your employees' options, and sell you books about golfing."

True to form, Cotsakos set his sights on acquiring Telebanc Financial Corporation, the largest online bank. Cotsakos met with Telebanc CEO Mitchell Caplan in 1999 and shortly thereafter announced that E*Trade would acquire the bank in a $1.8 billion deal. The transaction was completed in January 2000. That same year, the firm added Electronic Investing Corporation to its arsenal. Cotsakos' strategy appeared to pay off as revenues surpassed $1.36 billion.

Overcoming Hardships in the New Century

By this time, however, the dot-com frenzy of the late 1990s was starting to show signs of deterioration. In fact, in just one short year, E*Trade saw its revenues drop and profits plummet, with the company posting a loss of $241.5 million in 2001. By 2002, the company's stock was trading at $8 per share, down from nearly $63. To make matters worse, E*Trade and its formidable leader Cotsakos took center stage in a public relations disaster in April 2002 when the company disclosed that its CEO had been paid $77 million in 2001. In an attempt to appease angry shareholders who believe he had been paid an exorbitant amount, Cotsakos returned $21 million to E*Trade and signed a renegotiated contract that eliminated a base salary in favor of a bonus structure based on performance.

Despite the challenging business environment, E*Trade forged ahead with its expansion and diversification plans. To lure new customers, the company opened small financial zones in 26 Target stores and larger financial centers in New York, Boston, Denver, San Francisco, and Los Angeles. The firm also branched out into automated teller services, staking its claim on the third-largest ATM network in the United States. In June

2002, the company acquired Tradescape Corporation in a move that nearly doubled the number of its brokerage transactions.

Cotsakos resigned in January 2003, leaving Caplan to take the helm. That same year, the company adopted E*Trade Financial Corporation as its new corporate moniker, a sure sign that the company's strategy of focusing on brokerage, banking, and lending was alive and well. While the company continued to battle a weak economy, it appeared to have weathered the dot-com fallout better than most and seemed to be on track for future growth. In a 2003 *Money* magazine interview, Caplan was asked if people recognized that E*Trade was more than just a broker. He responded, "That's one of the things I'm going to work on. I'll be happy the day I die if people refer to us as a diversified financial services company."

Principal Subsidiaries

ATM Ventures, LLC; BRE Holdings, LLC; CCS (Canada), Inc.; Canopy Acquisition Corporation; Capitol View, LLC; ClearStation, Inc.; Confluent, Inc.; Converging Arrows, Inc.; Dempsey & Company LLC; Deutsche Recreational Asset Funding Corporation; E TRADE Systems India Pte. Ltd.; E*TRADE Access, Inc.; E*TRADE Advisory Services, Inc.; E*TRADE Asia Ltd.; E*TRADE Asset Management, Inc.; E*TRADE Australia Ltd.; E*TRADE BBH, Inc.; E*TRADE Bank; E*TRADE Bank AG (Germany); E*TRADE Bank A/S; E*TRADE Benelux SA (Netherlands); E*TRADE Brokerage Holdings, Inc.; E*TRADE Business Solutions Group, Inc.; E*TRADE Canada Securities Corporation; E*TRADE Capital, Inc.; E*TRADE Capital Holdings, Inc.; E*TRADE Clearing LLC; E*TRADE Europe Holdings B.V. (Netherlands); E*TRADE Europe Holding Ltd.; E*TRADE Europe Securities Ltd.; E*TRADE Europe Services Ltd.; E*TRADE Financial Corporation; E*TRADE Germany Communications GmbH; E*TRADE Global Asset Management, Inc.; E*TRADE Global Research Ltd.; E*TRADE Insurance Services, Inc.; E*TRADE International Equipment Management Corporation; E*TRADE International Holdings Ltd.; E*TRADE Italia S.r.l. (Italy); E*TRADE Japan K.K. (36%); E*TRADE Korea Company Ltd. (10%); E*TRADE Mortgage Corporation; E*TRADE National Holdings, Inc.; E*TRADE Nominees Ltd.; E*TRADE Nordic AB; E*TRADE Online Ventures, Inc.; E*TRADE Professional Trading, LLC; E*TRADE Re, LLC; E*TRADE SARL; E*TRADE Securities Corporation; E*TRADE Securities Ltd.; E*TRADE Securities LLC; E*TRADE Svierge AB; E*TRADE Systems Holdings Ltd.; E*TRADE Technologies Corporation; E*TRADE Technologies Group, LLC; E*TRADE UK (Holdings) Ltd.; E*TRADE UK, Ltd.; E*TRADE UK Nominees Ltd.; E*TRADE Web Services Ltd.; E-TRADE South Africa (Pty) Ltd.; eAdvisor; EGI Canada Corporation; Electronic Shares Information Ltd.; Engelman Securities, Inc.; ETRADE Asia Services Ltd.; ETRADE Finance (Hong Kong) Ltd.; ETRADE Securities (Hong Kong) Ltd.; ETRADE Global Services, Ltd.; ETRADE Securities Ltd.; GVR Company LLC; Ganis Credit Corporation; Momentum Securities Partners, LLC; Telebanc Capital Trust I; Telebanc Capital Trust II; Telebanc Servicing Corporation; Telebanc Mortgage Funding Corporation; Thor Credit Corporation (50%); TIR (Australia) Services Pty. Ltd.; TIR (Holdings) Ltd.; TIR (Holdings) Brazil Ltda.; TIR Securities (UK) Ltd.; Tiresome Nominees Pty. Ltd.; Tirade Nominees Pty. Ltd.; TM1 Funding LLC; TM2 Securitization LLC; TM2 Securitization QSPE LLC; TradePlus Brokerage, Inc.; Tradescape Momentum Holdings, Inc.; Tradescape Securities, LLC; Tradescape Technologies, LLC; Tradescape Technology Holdings, Inc.; Tradescape Trading, LLC; U-2 Dynamics, Inc.; VERSUS Brokerage Services (U.S.) Inc.; Web Street, Inc.; Web Street Securities, Inc.; Webstreet.com, Inc.; W&L Aviation, Inc.

Principal Competitors

Ameritrade Holding Corporation; The Charles Schwab Corporation; TD Waterhouse Group Inc.

Further Reading

Bills, Steve, "To Broaden Itself, E-Trade Buys Tradescape Assets," *American Banker*, June 27, 2002, p. 12.

Byron, Christopher, "Money Talks: Flame Your Broker!," *Esquire*, May 5, 1997.

"E*Trade: CEO Pay Isn't the Only Problem," *Businessweek*, May 17, 2002.

Hoffman, Thomas, "Online Brokers Drive Industry Changes," *Computerworld*, April 14, 1997, p. 77.

Heylar, John, "At E*Trade, Growing Up is Hard to Do," *Fortune*, March 18, 2002, p. 88.

Iwata, Edward, "Trading Up," *San Francisco Examiner*, March 17, 997, p. C1.

Kerr, Deborah, "Number One: A Second-Thought Success," *Business Journal*, October 23, 1995, p. S8.

Krampf, Allison, "Booting the Bear: E*Trade Is Poised for the Bull's Return," *Barron's*, August 25, 2003.

Lee, Jeanne, "E-Trading Places," *Money*, June 1, 2003, p. 58.

Lee, Louise, "Did E*Trade Just Trade Up?," *Business Week*, February 10, 2003.

Marjanovic, Steven, "E-Trade Merger to Create 'One-Stop' Web Venture," *American Banker*, June 2, 1999, p. 1.

McCarroll, Thomas, "Investors Rush the Net," *Time*, June 3, 1996, p. 54.

Roth, Daniel, "E*Trade's Plans for World Domination," *Fortune*, August 2, 1999, p. 95.

Tyson, David O., "The TradePlus Innovation: Latest Prices and Automated Orders in Market Hours," *The American Banker*, August 16, 1984, p. 1.

Weinberg, Neil, "After the Bubble," *Forbes*, October 1, 2001, p. 60.

Wyatt, John, "Etrade: Is This Investing's Future?," *Fortune*, March 3, 1997, p. 190.

—M.L. Cohen
—update: Christina M. Stansell

EMCOR Group Inc.

301 Merritt Seven Corporate Park
Sixth Floor
Norwalk, Connecticut 06851
U.S.A.
Telephone: (203) 849-7800
Fax: (203) 849-7900
Web site: http://www.emcorgroup.com

Public Company
Incorporated: 1966 as Jamaica Water Supply Company
Employees: 26,000
Sales: $3.968 billion (2002)
Stock Exchanges: New York
Ticker Symbol: EME
NAIC: 235110 Plumbing, Heating, and Air-Conditioning
Contractors; 235310 Electrical Contractors; 235950
Building Equipment and Other Machinery Installation
Contractors

EMCOR Group Inc. operates as one of the world's leading specialty construction and facilities services firms. The company installs and maintains mechanical, electrical, plumbing, communications, and various other systems for both domestic and international organizations. Through its network of over 70 subsidiaries, EMCOR has been involved in many different construction projects, ranging from certain casinos in Las Vegas, to interstate highways, to London's underground rail system. Formerly known as JWP Inc., the company adopted is current moniker after emerging from bankruptcy in 1995. Over the next eight years, EMCOR recorded 32 consecutive profitable quarters.

Origins

JWP Inc.—EMCOR's predecessor—was launched in 1966 as the Jamaica Water Supply Company and, for much of its early history, was the primary provider of water to Nassau County, Long Island, and Queens, New York. The company thus functioned for many years as a regulated monopoly, with low but stable profits and regulated prices. The company began to branch out in the mid- to late 1960s and henceforth was exposed to the instabilities of the marketplace. As it diversified its product lines, JWP experienced many ups and downs in its bottom line.

Instability in the 1960s and 1970s

The company changed its name often between 1966 and 1986, the year it adopted the name JWP Inc. This 20-year period was marked by extreme instability, and not in name only. From 1966 to around 1970, Jamaica Water Supply expanded by buying up other water companies. For example, in 1966 the firm acquired the entire capital stock of Sea Cliff Water Company. In 1968, they acquired most (80 percent) of Orbit International Inc. of San Juan, Puerto Rico.

With this accumulation through acquisition of other water companies, the firm was ready to make its first significant move out of the water business. Founder Martin Dwyer expressed the frustration with the water business at the time, stating, ''Private companies have no place in an urban area.'' Limited by public regulation, he sought to diversify into specialized construction, utility type operations, telephone systems, and electric lighting. In support of this shift in business focus, the company's most significant move was its 1971 acquisition of the Welsbach Corporation, a Philadelphia-based electrical contracting concern. Welsbach also installed street lighting and traffic control systems. Welsbach was merged into Jamaica Water, and the company took on the name Welsbach in 1974. Welsbach had a profit of $659,000 in 1969, and thus helped push Jamaica's bottom line out of the red. Jamaica's acquisitions throughout the late 1960s also led the firm to take on an increasingly expanding stock of debt, and, with interest rates rising, the company's cash flow was severely threatened. Combined with the severe recession of 1973 and 1974, Jamaica went from a stable water utility company to near bankruptcy in the mid-1970s.

In 1978, Andrew T. Dwyer, the son of founder Martin Dwyer, was put in charge of the ailing company. It took Dwyer and his associates several years to fend off complete collapse. They restructured the cost structure of the company to increase cash flow, and in the process they lessened some of the debt that was dragging down the company's growth prospects. To begin with, Dwyer sold off many of the money-losing ventures, including many of the non-utility holdings. He also began a complete retrenchment of the water utility component of the company, which at the time comprised 50 percent of the company's business, and set his sights on diversification, offering Jamaica's sophisticated and technologically advanced plumbing and piping systems technology for other applications.

Dwyer's stated goal at the time was to transform the company once again, this time using its already developed strengths in developing large computer systems, equipment, and office maintenance as a base. He started development of heating ventilation and air conditioning systems maintenance and other systems involved in operating high rise buildings in New York City. "The technologies needed to merge," Dwyer said, and his company set up building systems whereby one box could control fire, alarm, energy management, and security systems. By the mid-1980s, in New York City, Jamaica maintained everything from electric signs in Times Square to printing presses at the *New York Times.*

Success in the 1980s

This general strategy continued to yield positive results as the company adapted existing technologies to diverse applications. As Dwyer reflected in November 1991: "We tried to identify those markets where there was a need for sophisticated equipment." The result was phenomenal growth for the company in the 1980s, as the company once again completed a fundamental, and profitable, shift in its focus. Dwyer's first specific target was the fastest growing segment of the economy in the 1980s, the financial services sector. He aimed at providing all the technical services support required to create high tech and efficient trading rooms for Wall Street giants such as Merrill Lynch & Co, Inc., including installation and maintenance of air conditioning, telephones, wiring, cables, and computers. Clients also included Morgan Stanley, Goldman Sachs, and Salomon Brothers. From here, the company branched out further, installing energy management systems for Sears and computer rooms for Hewlett-Packard.

In the wake of these very successful endeavors, Dwyer's company won big contracts with DuPont and also began providing services to hospitals and utilities, including Illinois Bell. One of the largest deals was a six and one half year, $468 million contract to convert New York City's sludge to fertilizer pellets to be marketed nationally. From solid waste management and conversion plants, the company developed and marketed security systems and electrical networks. The company expanded overseas during this time as well.

By now known as JWP Inc., the company grew not only in the rapidly expanding market for technical services and the decentralized management style implemented by Dwyer, but

also through smartly managed acquisitions. Dwyer acquired Forest Electric in 1986 and Dynalectric in 1988 to broaden the company's electrical services repertoire. The acquisition of University Industries in 1988 got them into the West Coast mechanical services market. To crack the international market, JWP acquired Drake & Skull Holdings, a British electrical and mechanical services company. Dwyer's JWP gobbled up two dozen companies from 1984 to 1987, generating scale economies out of mergers and getting a jump on the competition in the high tech end of the technical services industry. "We are continually migrating to the higher technology side of the business," Dwyer remarked. "That's where the margins are better, the growth greater, and the competition a lot smarter."

The successes of these acquisitions were phenomenal. In fact, from 1980 until the end of 1991, JWP enjoyed 48 quarters of uninterrupted growth. The company grew from 400 employees working out of five offices in 1980 to over 21,000 employees in 195 offices in 1990. Successful diversification went hand in hand with the company's move away from water sales as its dominant market. The stable water sales, which made up over 50 percent of the company's total revenues in 1980, declined to less than 2 percent in 1990, while total net income grew from a loss of $495,000 in 1980 to $59.3 million profit in 1990. At the start of the 1980s, JWP was a $40 million water utility that had lost money for eight straight years and was on the brink of bankruptcy. By 1990, the company was a $3 billion technical services company. Compound growth from 1985 through 1989 was 179 percent, and JWP became the dominant maintenance firm in New York. Sales from 1981 to 1986, for example, went from $42 million to $379 million, and net income rose from $1.7 million to $13.5 million.

With the company's expansion into high tech applications, JWP was increasingly getting into the business of setting up computer systems. Thus, it was a natural outgrowth of the company to begin selling the computers to its clients. In 1990, this new avenue of growth for JWP meant the purchase of Neeco, Inc., a desktop computer systems sales company which operated out of Canton, Massachusetts. In its most important recent acquisition to date, the firm bought Businessland in early 1991, a move that was considered a natural extension of the firm's experience in selling electrical systems. This deal pushed total revenues from $744.6 million to $944.9 million. From the Businessland acquisition, Dwyer created JWP Businessland Inc., a division of JWP Information Services, which had sales of $1.8 billion worldwide and which operated through its own retail outlets.

Restructuring and Bankruptcy in the Early to Mid-1990s

While the 1980s were a decade of unprecedented growth, the early 1990s saw near bankruptcy and collapse. Contributing to the decline of JWP was a commercial construction slump, price wars, intensified competition in the personal computer component of the business, and the burden of servicing a huge debt accumulated during the boom years of acquisition in the 1980s. JWP's high debt-equity ratio in particular (1.2 to 1) caused great concern. Profits fell to around $40 million for 1990 and 1991 as the company struggled through the recession that plagued those years. By the fourth quarter of 1992, however, losses were as great as $265 million.

The company's highly leveraged position threatened its very existence, prompting some drastic action to restructure the company's debt. Meanwhile trouble brewed elsewhere. In April 1992, in their water business, complaints about high rates charged for water were lodged against JWP's water subsidiary, Jamaica Water Supply Company, which still served homes in Queens and Nassau County. JWP planned to sell the unit as part of the corporate restructuring and not, they said, in response to the consumer complaint controversy. The company put those plans on hold, however, in 1993.

In October 1992, David Sokel presented to the board evidence of what were alleged to be widespread accounting improprieties, confirming the charges of shareholders, and then resigned as president of the company. More restructuring decisions led to the sale of ten or more businesses, including the sale of four environmental businesses to Wheelabrator Technologies Inc. for about $69 million, in order to raise $250 million as the company focused on its traditionally more lucrative mechanical and electrical services. These moves helped raise needed cash to deal with the heavy debt load, which at one point was said to be as large as $485 million.

As a major debt restructuring move, in July 1993 JWP sold its Information Services subsidiary to an investment group in a deal releasing JWP from about $210 million of the company's more than $300 million in outstanding debt. In 1993, Andrew Dwyer resigned as chairman of the board of JWP, and Edward Kosnik was elected to the post.

Expansion continued, notably on the international front; international operations generated about $1 billion in revenue in 1992. Coupled with the debt restructuring, long-term growth prospects brightened. In 1991, JWP acquired Comstock Canada, the largest Canadian electrical and mechanical services firm, with 12 offices in Canada and $200 million in sales. Furthermore, the Businessland project did business in Canada, the United Kingdom, Germany, and France, selling its interactive personal computer system integrated to complement its international facilities management. JWP also expected growth in new markets in transportation projects, pharmaceutical, and

biotechnology facilities. The most promising general source of demand for JWP's services lay in the fact that, in general, businesses found it increasingly cheaper to outsource the kind of services that JWP provided.

Despite its demonstrated resiliency, JWP announced in October 1993 that it would file for Chapter 11 bankruptcy protection, after nearly a year of negotiating a financial restructuring with its creditors. Under the proposed debt restructuring and capitalization plan, JWP's creditors, a group of 50 bankers, insurance companies, and equity funds, exchanged $484 million of the company's debt for $180 million of new debt and 100 percent control of JWP's equity. The new debt was to be paid from the proceeds of asset sales.

Renewed Success in the Mid-1990s and Beyond

By early 1995, JWP had emerged from bankruptcy under the leadership of newly elected chairman, president, and CEO Frank T. MacInnis. The company changed its name to EMCOR Group Inc. to signal its focus on key business segments related to its electrical and mechanical construction services. (EMCOR is a fusion of the words electrical, mechanical, and core.) Company headquarters were moved from Rye Brook, New York, to Norwalk, Connecticut. In 1996, the firm sold its Jamaica Water Supply unit, leaving behind the company that had originally provided the backbone for the business in the 1960s.

EMCOR indeed turned over a new leaf with its reorganization and immediately began to reap the benefits of its new, leaner, business structure. Over the next several years, the company secured its position as a world leader in its market segments by diversifying its customer base in both the public and private sectors as well as taking a conservative, long-term approach to business decisions. From 1995 to 2003, the company recorded 32 consecutive quarters of profits, a remarkable feat for any company, especially one emerging from bankruptcy protection. According to a 2003 *Fairfield County Business Journal* article, much of the company's success could be attributed to MacInnis, who "saved it from going bust, and transformed it from an underdog to the number-two player in the industry—shifting the company's primary business from water utility to electrical and mechanical construction and facilities management."

EMCOR bolstered its holdings in 2002 with the purchase of 19 companies from Comfort Systems USA, which gave it a foothold in the midwestern U.S. construction and services industry. A second purchase followed in December when the firm added Virginia-based Consolidated Engineering Services Inc. to its arsenal. The deal secured EMCOR's position as the leading facilities management concern in the United States. By now, the company's turnaround from the mid-1990s and its overall success had garnered industry attention. In 2003 alone, EMCOR was named one of "America's Most Admired Companies" by *Fortune* magazine, ranked 37 on *Barron's* "Top 500 Best Performing Companies" list, and awarded the Frost & Sullivan Competitive Strategy Award for its expansion efforts in the facilities management services market.

The soft economy that continued into 2003, however, threatened to challenge the company's financial achievements. Nevertheless, MacInnis and his management team remained confident that EMCOR was on a path for success for years to come. Through its "growth through diversity" strategy—which focused on broadening company services, branching out into new geographical areas, and moving into new markets sectors—EMCOR appeared to be well positioned for future growth.

Principal Subsidiaries

Aircond Corporation; BALCO; Betlem Service Corporation; Building Technology Engineers Inc.; Combustioneer Corporation; Commonwealth Air Conditioning & Heating Inc.; Consolidating Engineering Services Inc.; Duffy Mechanical Corp.; Dynalectric Companies; EMCOR Energy & Technologies Inc.; EMCOR Facilities Services Inc.; F & G Mechanical Corporation; Forest Electric Corporation; Gotham Air Conditioning Service Inc.; Heritage Mechanical Services Inc.; J.C. Higgins Corporation; Labov Mechanical Inc.; Mandell Mechanical Corporation; Meadowlands Fire Protection Corporation; New England Mechanical Services Inc.; North Jersey Mechanical Contractors Inc.; Penguin Air Conditioning Corporation; Poole & Kent Northern Operations; Poole & Kent Southern Operations; R.S. Harritan & Company Inc.; Trimech Corporation; Tucker Mechanical; Welsbach Electric Corporation; Comstock Canada Ltd.; EMCOR Drake & Scull Group Inc. (U.K.).

Principal Competitors

Integrated Electrical Services Inc.; Quanta Services Inc.

Further Reading

"Accord Is Signed to Sell Information Services Unit," *New York Times*, July 17, 1993.

Chartock, David S., "EMCOR Group Focuses on Three Market Sectors," *Colorado Construction*, May 2001, p. 35.

Cook, James, "If at First You Don't Succeed," *Forbes*, June 29, 1987.

"EMCOR Acquires Facility Manager," *Fairfield County Business Journal*, January 27, 2003, p. 2.

"EMCOR Group Moves from Bust to Boom," *Fairfield County Business Journal*, April 7, 2003, p. 1.

"EMCOR to Sell Jamaica Water Unit for $178.8 Million," *New York Times*, February 13, 1996, p. D4.

Emmett, Arielle, "JWP: Lean, Mean Business Machine," *Computerworld*, June 15, 1992.

Gilpin, Kenneth N., "JWP's Bankruptcy Plan Will Put the Creditors in Control," *New York Times*, October 12, 1993.

"Jamaica Water Agrees to Acquire Welsbach for About $10.2 Million," *Wall Street Journal*, May 28, 1969.

"Jamaica Water Links With Welsbach; to Get 49% It Doesn't Own," *Wall Street Journal*, October 15, 1970.

"JWP Completes Sale of Four Businesses for about $69 Million," *Wall Street Journal*, October 19, 1992.

Lueck, Thomas J., "Private Owner to Sell L.I. and Queens Water Utility," *New York Times*, April 21, 1992.

Pacey, Margaret D., "Thirst for Acquisitions: Investor-Owned Water Works Grow by Swallowing Municipal Ones," *Barron's*, February 15, 1971.

Pollack, Andrew, "JWP Gains Control of Businessland," *New York Times*, August 6, 1991.

Quickel, Stephen W., "By Leaps and Bounds," *Business Month*, March, 1989.

Schriener, Judy, "EMCOR is Turning Around," *Engineering News-Record*, November 27, 1995, p. 7.

——, "JWP is Reborn as EMCOR," *Engineering News-Record*, January 16, 1995, p. 12.

Steinberg, Jacques, "Water Utility of a Thousand Faces," *New York Times*, November 2, 1991.

Zweig, Jason, "Roller Coaster: JWP Sold Just Water until Andy Dwyer Arrived," *Forbes*, August 3, 1992.

—John A. Sarich
—update: Christina M. Stansell

Findel plc

Burley House
Bradford Road
Burley-in-Wharfedale
Ilkley
West Yorkshire LS29 7DZ
United Kingdom
Telephone: (+44) 1943-864-686
Fax: (+44) 1943-864-986
Web site: http://www.findel.co.uk

Public Company
Incorporated: 1955 as Fine Art & Philately
Employees: 2,732
Sales: £368.2 million ($579.6 million)(2002)
Stock Exchanges: London
Ticker Symbol: FDL
NAIC: 454113 Mail-Order Houses; 322232 Envelope
  Manufacturing; 322233 Stationery, Tablet, and
  Related Product Manufacturing; 424120 Stationery
  and Office Supplies Merchant Wholesalers

The United Kingdom's Findel plc operates through three primary divisions: Home Shopping, Education, and Findel Services. Home Shopping represents the company's largest division, at more than 50 percent of sales, and is centered on the company's core Express Gifts Ltd. mail order business. The Express Gifts catalogs, Studio and Ace, reach a customer base of more than one million nationwide, with a focus on the 25- to 45-year-old female with children demographic. Through Express Gifts, Findel sells a variety of clothing, home furnishings, gardening, and other items, and offers Europe's largest "personalization" service. The company also operates online, through web sites linked to its two catalog titles. Since its takeover of Novara plc in 2001, Findel is also the leading independent specialist in educational supplies in the United Kingdom. Under this division, the company manages nine distinct brand ranges under the names Davies Sports, Galt, Hope Education, NES Arnold, Percussion Plus, Philip Harris Education, Step by Step, UNILAB, and, in Northern Ireland,

EDCO. In addition to its sales to schools and institutions, as well as to the U.K. government, the Education division also operates in retail sales channels, through its Galt brand, which is distributed in more than 5,000 stores throughout the United Kingdom. Findel's third division, Services, provides fulfillment and logistics support services, ranging from call center operations to product development to pickup and delivery services to mail order and catalog companies, and Internet and television-based marketers. Services represented more than 25 percent of Findel's sales of £368 million ($580 million) in its 2003 year. The company, listed on the London Stock Exchange, is headed by CEO D.A. Johnson and chairman Keith Chapman.

Merging Family Businesses in the 1950s

Three small, family-owned companies joined together to create a greeting card company in 1955. That company, called Fine Art & Philately, published and distributed greeting cards, and also operated a business-to-business mail order house, supplying retailers in the United Kingdom. The three companies were TE Webb & Co, which published greeting cards and sold them via mail order; Ivory Cards, which specialized in fund raising and charitable services based on greeting cards sales; and Joseph Arnold & Co., which acted as supplier to the other two. Following the formation of Fine Art & Philately, the company focused its greeting card and mail order operations under the TE Webb name.

Fine Art set its sights on growth at the start of the 1960s, and in 1961 took a listing on the Birmingham stock exchange. The following year, the company made its first major expansion, when it agreed to merge with Foxhill Christmas Card Company. Under terms of that deal, the Foxhill brand operations were transferred to TE Webb, while Foxhill shareholders gained a 50 percent stake in the newly enlarged company. Following the merger, Fine Art & Philately changed its name, to Fine Art Developments plc.

Fine Art's expansion continued into the mid-1960s, as the company added retail operations under subsidiary Findel Stores Ltd. The company also expanded its manufacturing facilities, placed under subsidiary Foxhill Group, and by 1967 produced more than 95 percent of the cards sold through its growing number of greeting cards subsidiaries. These included Miller Greetings, Collisons Ltd., and Studio Cards, a specialty Christmas card producer. The company had also ventured onto the European continent, taking an 80 percent stake in a joint-venture, Editions Ivoire, based in Paris.

By the end of the decade, Fine Art had added subsidiaries in West Germany, the United States, and Ireland. The company also switched its listing to the London Stock Exchange, then entered Australia at the beginning of the 1970s through mail order subsidiary Bell & Howell.

Fine Art developed strongly through the 1970s, notably through acquisitions, such as that of A. Vivan Mansell & Co., a fine art color printer, in 1970. The company also acquired mail order greeting cards company Leswyn Cards that year. Then, in 1971, Fine Art paid £650,000 to British Publishing Company to acquire its greeting card operations, including the companies W. Barton, British Greeting Cards, Raphael Tuck & Sons. Also acquired that year was greeting card company Delgado & Mowbray. At the end of 1971, Fine Art's sales neared £8.4 million.

By the middle of the 1970s, Fine Art was already Europe's largest manufacturer of greeting cards. Yet the company itself had shifted the focus of its revenue growth from its greeting card business to its mail order operations. The company began expanding its product ranges, adding lines of stationery, games, and toys, but also perfume, jewelry, and home furnishings and equipment. By 1976, more than 70 percent of the group's £26 million in sales came from its non-greeting card mail order operations.

Fine Art's revenues grew strongly into the 1980s, rising to £58 million by 1980. In that year, the company added greeting card group Wilson Bros to is holdings, paying £4.3 million for its long-time rival. Yet by the following year, Fine Art ended a 25-year run of revenue and profit, as its sales started to slip, sinking the group into the red by 1982.

Retail became the bright spot for the group, particularly after its acquisition of educational retailer Early Learning. Fine Art began a rapid expansion of the chain, doubling the number of stores to more than 40 by the end of 1983, and to more than 90 by the end of 1984, including its first international stores. In 1985, however, the group sold off the Early Learning chain, to the John Menzies group.

Fine Art then returned its focus on its mail order and greeting cards businesses, which took a new step forward in 1984 when it acquired Selective Paper Group Ltd. That purchase, at a cost of £13 million, helped boost Fine Art's turnover to nearly £100 million. Also in that year, future chairman and CEO Keith Chapman joined the company.

Triple Focus in the New Century

Despite the sale of Early Learning, Fine Art had not abandoned retailing. Instead, the group developed a new retail concept, closer to its greeting card base, called Papertree. Fine Art invested heavily in building that business, opening some 100 stores by the beginning of the 1990s. Yet the company, already suffering from the dismal economic climate, found it difficult to find profits through its Papertree arm. The company sold off a number of other operations, including its stake in the Bell & Howell mail order firm in Australia, and its attempt to enter the direct mail market, Venture Marketing.

By the mid-1990s, Fine Art's long-time combination of greeting cards and mail-order businesses, including a newly developing educational supplies business, no longer seemed a viable match. Instead, in 1997, Fine Art decided to split itself into its two halves, spinning off the greeting cards business as Creative Publishing. That business was subsequently acquired by U.S. greeting card giant Hallmark in 1998.

Fine Art was now focused in three primary areas: home shopping, including mail order; educational supplies; and fund-raising, which produced catalogs for charitable organizations. At the same time, Fine Art recognized the growth of a new sales channel—the Internet. In 1999, the company joined a partnership to launch a charity-based Internet service provider, Care4Free, which promised to donate 70 percent of its profits to charities of the subscriber's choice. In another move, echoing the group's former life as Europe's leading greeting card group, Fine Art launched a new web site, www.say-it-with-ease.com, which allowed customers to send electronic greeting cards.

At the same time, Fine Art sought new outlets for its long-time expertise in mail order distribution services, and at the turn of the century decided to step up providing services to third-party customers, such as discount fashion retailer Matalan, for whom Fine Art launched a home shopping catalog in 2000. In that year, Fine Art announced a decision to exit the charity and fund-raising business, a move completed in 2001 through a management buyout. By then, Fine Art had changed its name, to Findel plc.

Findel plc now embarked on a three-prong strategy for the new century. The company restructured into three divisions: Home Shopping, which included the group's core catalog and Internet-based operations; Findel Services, for its fast-growing third-party distribution services operations; and the group's fast-growing Educational Supplies operations. The latter appeared to have high hopes, particularly after the U.K. government promised a new £1.5 billion schools spending initiative through 2005.

Educational supplies took on a still greater focus for the group when it launched a takeover of rival group Novara. Formed in 1997 through the merger of two prominent U.K. educational supply companies, Nottingham Group and Philip Harris, Novara boasted a range of prominent brands, including segment leaders such as NES Arnold and the Philip Harris brand itself. Yet merging the two companies proved difficult for Novara, and by 2000 the group's profits and share price had slumped, while group sales had fallen by more than 50 percent, leaving the company vulnerable to takeover.

Key Dates:

1955: Three family-owned companies merge to form greeting card and mail-order company Fine Art & Philately.
1961: Company is listed on Birmingham stock exchange.
1962: Company merges with Foxhill Christmas Card Company and name is changed to Fine Art Developments.
1964: Collisons greeting card company is acquired.
1971: Fine Art pays £650,000 to acquire W. Barton, British Greeting Cards, Raphael Tuck & Sons.
1976: Focus on mail-order operations is stepped up, especially non-greeting card business.
1984: Selective Paper Group is acquired for £13 million.
1999: Fine Art enters Internet and e-commerce market, joining partnership to launch Care4free Internet access service.
2000: Fine Art announces plans to sell off fundraising division, and changes its name to Findel plc.
2001: Findel becomes the United Kingdom's leading independent educational supplies group.

Despite an attempt by Novara's management to take over the company through a management buyout, Novara's shareholders agreed to Findel's offer for the company, worth some £57 million. The integration of Novara's brands into Findel's educational supplies division placed the company as the United Kingdom's leading independent supplier to the education market. Findel set out to restructure the newly enlarged operation, shutting down a number of facilities, and by 2002 the division had become profitable.

Findel's hopes for stronger growth in its education division were dashed, at least in the short term, by a crisis in the United Kingdom's educational budget in 2003, as the promised funding for supplies was instead shifted toward paying teacher salaries. Findel itself, however, appeared to have no difficulties in weathering the drop in the educational supplies market, in large part because of strong growth in its core home shopping division. With the launch of two new web sites supporting its core catalogs, Findel had also begun a program of boosting its year-round sales, reducing its reliance on the core year-end holiday season. These moves enabled the division to double its sales by the end of 2003. Findel's three-prong strategy seemed a strong foundation for continued growth in the new century.

Principal Subsidiaries

Express Gifts Ltd.; Findel Education Ltd.; Home Farm Hampers Ltd. (60%); James Galt & Co. Ltd.; Findel Europe B.V. (Netherlands); Fine Art Developments (Far East) Ltd. (Hong Kong).

Principal Competitors

Argos Ltd.; NEXT plc; Waitrose Ltd.; Littlewoods Ltd.

Further Reading

Blackwell, David, "Fine Art Poised for E-Commerce," *Financial Times*, May 23, 2000, p. 28.
Cassidy, Siobhan, "Home Shopping Sales Growth Lifts Findel," *Financial Times*, May 23, 2003, p. 27.
"Findel Fine Despite School Cash Squeeze," *Birmingham Post*, October 16, 2003, p. 21.
"Findel Gets its Sums Right as School Funding Crisis Bites," *Yorkshire Post*, May 22, 2003.
"Findel Gets Out of Charities Business," *Yorkshire Post*, April 12, 2001.
Kiphoff, John, "Findel Optimistic on Purchase of Novara," *Financial Times*, December 7, 2001, p. 26.

—M.L. Cohen

Firmenich International S.A.

Route de La Plaine 45
CH-1283 La Plaine, Geneva
Switzerland
Telephone: (+41) 22-780-22-11
Fax: (+41) 22-754-14-73
Web site: http://www.firmenich.com

Private Company
Incorporated: 1895
Employees: 4,500
Sales: CHF 1.9 billion ($1.28 billion) (2002)
NAIC: 325188 All Other Inorganic Chemical
   Manufacturing; 311930 Flavoring Syrup and
   Concentrate Manufacturing; 325620 Toilet Preparation
   Manufacturing

Family-owned Firmenich International S.A. is the world's largest privately held manufacturer of fragrances and flavorings for the perfume, food, cosmetics, cleaning products, and related industries. In terms of the total market, Firmenich claims third place, behind the American company International Flavors and Fragrances and fellow Swiss company Givaudan (formerly part of Roche). Firmenich develops and supplies more than 45,000 different fragrances, aromas, and speciality chemicals components, including a list of some 800 patented chemicals. Headquartered in Geneva, Switzerland, Firmenich operates sales and manufacturing sites in 50 countries worldwide, including major sites in New York City and New Jersey, as well as locations in Europe, South America, and Asia. India and China also represent two important production sectors. Firmenich's client list includes the world's largest food, beauty, household care, and fabrics companies, although its behind-the-scenes work for the world's leading perfume names remains a major part of the group's activity. Indeed, the company has created a number of the most prominent contemporary perfumes, including CK One and Jean-Paul Gaulthier. In 2003, Firmenich was hired by retailing giant Walgreens to create its C'est Moi perfume. Research and development has played a key role in Firmenich's steady success—an early R&D director, Leopold Ruzicka, was awarded the Nobel Prize in 1939—and the company continues to spend approximately 10 percent of its revenues on R&D operations. These efforts have helped the company more than triple its sales since the early 1990s. By 2003, the group posted about CHF 2 billion ($1.3 billion) in sales. The company is led by Partick Firmenich, who took over as CEO in 2002.

Synthesizing Success at the End of the 19th Century

In the closing years of the 19th century, Young chemist Philippe Chuit set up a small workshop in Geneva's Servette neighborhood in order to develop and synthesize chemicals for the growing perfume industry. Backed by businessman Martin Naef, who provided the capital for launching the business in 1895, the partnership began producing its first product, Vanillin, using a new synthesis technique developed by Chuit. In 1897, Chuit & Naef bought land for the construction of a new site at La Queue d'Arve, and the following year the business moved to its new quarters, known as La Jonction. In that year, the company, which had already grown to 20 employees, reincorporated as a limited partnership, Chuit, Naef & Cie.

The original partners were joined by Chuit's brother-in-law, Fred Firmenich, in 1900. Firmenich soon took over the group's sales and distribution operations, while Chuit remained the guiding force behind the company's growing list of products, which included the launches of Violettone and Dianthine in 1902, Iralia in 1903, and Cyclosia in 1908. Two years later, Chuit sold out his share of the company to Firmenich, who became majority partner in the business. Yet Chuit remained active within the company for another two decades.

Chuit remained the head of the group's research and development efforts into the early 1920s. In 1921, however, Chuit convinced friend Leopld Ruzicka to join the company as its R&D director. Ruzicka, a native of Hungary and a naturalized Swiss citizen, later earned the Nobel Prize for Chemistry in 1939, in part for his work at Firmenich. Ruzicka's work led to the development of the first synthetic musk.

During the 1920s, Firmenich launched a number of new products, including Nerol and Nerolidol in 1922 and the evocatively named Exaltolide in 1925. The company also began working with the designer market, developing perfumes components and entire recipes for its customers.

Chuit retired in 1931, followed by Naef in 1933. In the latter year, the company came under the full control of the Firmenich family, taking on the name Firmenich & Cie. Fred Firmenich took over as the group's top manager, while Ruzicka remained at the head of the group's research and development program and led Firmenich into the development of the first synthesized raspberry ketone in 1938. The success of that effort brought Firmenich into a new product group for the first time, that of food flavorings.

By 1945, the group had begun developing citrus and strawberry flavorings as well, and the company created a new, dedicated Flavors division for its growing operations in that sector. By 1946, the group had successfully developed the first strawberry flavoring and the Tetraromes series of citrus flavors. The development of these and other food flavoring agents were to revolutionized the food industry, creating the basis for the food technology sector. In particular, the development of synthetic flavorings enabled the growing industrial food sector to replace more expensive natural ingredients with lower-cost synthetic alternatives and also to restore food flavors lost during the increasingly intensive food production process.

Firmenich expanded in the early 1950s through its acquisition of rival Usines de l'Allondon in 1952. That purchase brought the company a new manufacturing complex, known as the La Plaine site, which became the group's primary production plant in 1962. The company's research and development efforts, meanwhile, resulted in the synthesis of a major new chemical, Hedione, in 1959. Launched commercially in 1971, the chemical, a volatile molecule extracted from jasmine flowers, quickly became one of the most widely used base ingredients for the international perfume industry.

The company's work in the flavorings sector had by then also resulted in the launch of Furaneol, described by the company as a "sweet, cotton-candy like molecule key to red fruit, tropical fruit, and roasted flavors." In the fragrance sector, Firmenich achieved a new breakthrough in the mid-1970s with the launch of its synthetic rose ketones, including Dorinia and Damascenia in 1975 and two damascones in 1978. The company had changed its name to Firmenich SA in 1972, and Fred-Henri Firmenich took over as CEO the following year. In 1976,

Firmenich added a new production facility, a compounding plant, in Geneva's Meyrin-Satigny.

International Leader in the 21st Century

Firmenich released a new rose ketone, damascenone, in 1982, as well as citrus-scented Citronova. Continued research efforts were to result in a number major new products, such as Polysantol in 1985 and Firanova in 1988. The company also began branching out into a number of new fragrance categories, adding, for example, the first 100 percent synthetic amber product, Ambrox, in 1989.

In the meantime, the company's major clients—particularly the perfume and food industries—had began a steady consolidation which was to lead to creation of a smaller of number of large-scale, multinational companies. In order to match this development, Firmenich itself turned toward international expansion in the mid-1980s, starting with its 1986 acquisition of Chem Fleur, located in Newark, New Jersey, which formed the basis of the group's operations in the crucial United States market.

Firmenich's international growth became even more vital to its interests in the early 1990s, after Fred-Henri Firmenich stepped up to the chairman's seat of the group. Brother Pierre-Yves Firmenich had taken over as group CEO in 1989, seconded by Jean-Pierre Linder, who took charge of the group's fragrance development. The following year, the company reorganized under a new holding company, setting the stage for a new era of growth. In 1990, also, the company opened a new, 7,000-square-foot office in New York city, complete with laboratory, which became the center of much of the group's fragrance development in the 1990s.

The team of Pierre-Yves Firmenich and Jean-Pierre Linder took the relatively small Firmenich, which had sales of approximately CHF 400 million at the beginning of the 1990s, and transformed it into one of the world's top three fragrance and flavors specialists—and the number one privately held company in the sector. Part of the group's success was due to the expansion of its international network, which enabled it to create flavors and fragrances for specific cultural markets. In this way, the company opened subsidiaries in a number of key foreign markets, including China, India, and Malaysia in 1994, Thailand in 1995, and Vietnam in 1996.

Much of the company's international growth was spurred on by its flavorings division, which alone accounted for nearly 15 new manufacturing plants into the 2000s. In the meantime, the group saw enormous success on the fragrance front as well, especially with the launch of such company-developed perfume successes as CK One in 1995 and designer perfumes for Jean-Gaultier, Hugo Boss, and Tommy Hilfinger, among many others.

Acquisitions played a key part in the group's growth as well. In 1995, the company entered South Africa with the purchase of Darryl Gunther (Proprietary) Ltd. In 1997, the company purchased two new factories, one in Poland and the other in Japan, and the following year acquired or built facilities in France, the United Kingdom, Mexico, the United States (Florida), and China. Other new operations at the turn of the 21st century included a research and development laboratory that specialized in body care products in Germany and a manufacturing facility

Key Dates:

1895: Philippe Chuit and Martin Naef found a fragrance chemicals company in Geneva and launch of their first product, Vanillin.

1898: The company incorporates as a limited partnership, Chuit, Naef & Cie.

1900: Fred Firmenich, brother-in-law of Chuit, joins the partnership.

1910: Chuit sells his share of the business to Firmenich.

1921: Leopold Ruzicka, future Nobel Prize winner, joins as chief of research and development and leads the company toward synthesizing the first food flavorings.

1934: After Chuit and Naef retire, the company takes on name of Firmenich & Cie.

1945: A dedicated Flavors division is created.

1952: Swiss rival Usines de l'Allondon is acquired.

1959: Hedione, which becomes a major base ingredient for perfume industry, is developed.

1972: The company changes its name to Firmenich SA.

1986: The New Jersey-based firm of Chem-Fleur is acquired.

1989: Pierre-Yves Firmenich becomes CEO and leads the company on a growth drive, tripling revenues by 2000.

1994: The company steps up international expansion, opening subsidiaries in China, India, Malaysia, and elsewhere.

1995: The company enters South Africa with the acquisition of Darrly Gunther.

1997: Factories in Poland and Japan are purchased.

2001: Construction of a new Food & Flavors Expertise Centre in Geneva begins.

2002: Patrick Firmenich becomes CEO.

2003: Innovaroma joint-venture is launched.

in India in 1999, followed by the opening of a new chemical plant in Port Newark, New Jersey.

A major development for the group's Flavors division came in 2001, when the company began development on a new, Geneva-based Food & Flavors Expertise Center. Completed at the end of 2002, the new facility offered more than 8,600 square meters of operating space and included state-of-the-art ventilation and odor-removal systems—crucial for the development of new flavor products.

By then, Firmenich had reached another milestone when the next generation of the family, represented by Patrick Firmenich, son of Fred-Henri, took over as company CEO in May 2002. With both a law degree and an MBA, Firmenich joined the company at the beginning of the 1990s and had largely taken over for Linder in the middle and later years of the decade. The younger Firmenich quickly led the group on its next expansion drive, joining the battle to acquire Bayer's flavor and fragrances division, Haarman & Reimer, with bidding expected to top $1.5 billion. At this point, Firmenich sales had topped CHF 2 billion ($1.3 billion).

In the meantime, Firmenich continued to seek out new growth opportunities. In 2002, the company acquired Norway's Bjorge Biomarin A/S, founded in 1988 and a specialist in the production of natural seafood extracts. At the beginning of 2003, Firmenich expanded again, forming Innovaroma, a joint-venture partnership with Agan Aroma, a unit of Makhteshim Agan Industries Group. Simultaneous with its latest acquisitions campaign, Firmenich continued to score major new customers, leading to triumphs such as the October 2003 launch of a new fragrance, C'est Moi, developed by Firmenich to be sold as the house brand of the retailing giant Walgreens. As Firmenich entered its second century as a company, its future never seemed more promising.

Principal Subsidiaries

Firmenich and Companhia Ltda. (Brazil); Firmenich Asia Pte Ltd. (Singapore); Firmenich de Mexico S.A. de CV; Firmenich et Cie. (France); Firmenich GmbH (Germany); Firmenich Inc. (U.S.A.); Firmenich S.A. (Argentina); Firmenich S.A. (Colombia); Firmenich UK Ltd.

Principal Competitors

International Flavors and Fragrances Inc.; Givaudon SA.; Imperial Chemical Industries PLC.

Further Reading

Brookman, Faye, "Walgreens Designs Its Own Fragrance," *WWD*, October 31, 2003, p. 9.

Eastwood, Colin, "The Cost of Perfume," *Observer*, September 2, 2001, p. 5.

Firn, David, and Klaus Max Smolka, "Firmenich Joins Bayer Arm Bids," *Financial Times*, May 24, 2002, p. 32.

Floreno, Anthony, "Firmenich Marks 100th, Looks Ahead to Next 100," *Chemical Marketing Reporter*, October 23, 1995, p. 28.

Hall, William, Naomi Mapstone, and Ruth Sullivan, "Firmenich to Lead Family Firm," *Financial Times*, May 22, 2002, p. 11.

Larson, Soren, "Firmenich: Story of a Streak," *WWD*, July 7, 1995, p. 6.

Naughton, Julie, "Firmenich Passes the Torch," *WWD*, May 24, 2002, p. 5.

—M.L. Cohen

Flanigan's Enterprises, Inc.

5059 Northeast 18th Avenue
Fort Lauderdale, Florida 33334
U.S.A.
Telephone: (954) 377-1961
Fax: (954) 377-1980
Web site: http://www.flanigans.net

Public Company
Incorporated: 1959
Employees: 359
Sales: $28.3 million (2002)
Stock Exchanges: American
Ticker Symbol: BDL
NAIC: 722110 Full-Service Restaurants; 445310 Beer,
    Wine and Liquor Stores; 533110 Owners and Lessors
    of Other Non-Financial Assets; 551112 Offices of
    Other Holding Companies; 722410 Drinking Place
    (Alcoholic Beverages)

Flanigan's Enterprises, Inc. operates a chain of retail liquor stores under the banner "Big Daddy's Liquors" and a chain of full-service restaurants under the name "Flanigan's Seafood Bar and Grill." Flanigan's Enterprises' properties are located in South Florida except for an entertainment club located in Atlanta, Georgia, that is operated by another company under a management agreement. The company owns two restaurants, four retail liquor stores, and four units that house both restaurants and liquor stores. Flanigan's Enterprises, through joint venture investments, also maintains interests in six franchised units.

Origins

In a March 1988 article in *Florida Trend,* reporter Bradley Sterz wrote: "Students by the hundreds of thousands have flocked to Florida's beaches from the North, and for two decades Joe "Big Daddy" Flanigan stood as their toastmaster." Joseph G. Flanigan played a colorful role as one of the chief suppliers of alcohol to the annual gatherings of students spending their spring-break vacations in Florida. Known for his ability to drink more than a case and a half of beer in a 12-hour span, Flanigan reveled in his role: "I was the king," he said in Sterz's article. "I had it all. We were big time. We were nationwide. I would go out to dinner, and people wouldn't leave me alone. I was in the spotlight, famous or infamous."

The success of Flanigan represented the success of his company, Flanigan's Enterprises, but the early professional career of the entrepreneur did not suggest either fame or infamy as a bar owner. Flanigan attended the University of Pennsylvania's Wharton School of Business, where he helped pay his expenses by working as a campus bar manager. In his interview with Sterz, Flanigan explained the genesis of his professional career: "Right after I got married I walked into an Eastman Dillon, Union Securities & Co. office to sell $1,400 worth of stocks so I could go on a honeymoon. Just before I left, the broker asked me if I wanted a job with his firm. Well, I looked around and saw that everybody working there was 70 to 80 years old and thought I'd be able to move up quickly. Sure enough, within a year-and-a-half I'd become sales manager."

Flanigan excelled at Eastman Dillon. He became involved in brokering increasingly bigger deals, earning the esteem of the firm's clientele. Flanigan's reputation was sufficient to earn the business of a prominent Philadelphia family named McManus. During the late 1950s, the McManus family sold Crown Cork & Seal Co., a firm that produced bottle caps, and turned to Flanigan to invest the proceeds from the sale. Flanigan chose to invest in bars in Florida, one of the few states that allowed the ownership of multiple liquor licenses. The investments served as the foundation for "Big Daddy's," a chain of small cocktail lounges and package liquor stores that was founded in 1959.

As they evolved, Flanigan's Big Daddy's liquor lounges became the most popular gathering spots for legions of students on spring-break in South Florida. Bikini contests and drinking competitions were seductive draws, as was the availability of 38-cent drinks at Big Daddy's lounges. Flanigan, who stood six-feet tall and weighed more than 230 pounds, held sway over the annual festivities, embodying the drunken rowdiness that made South Florida famous as a spring-break Mecca. Within ten years, Flanigan's Enterprises was generating $15 million in annual revenue, with the lack of capital representing virtually the only

Company Perspectives:

Flanigan's has become a South Florida legend due to the almost insatiable urge of our customers to consume our juicy, tender "meat falls off the bone" baby back ribs. These flame broiled, hickory smoked beauties outnumber the sales of the rest of our menu items by about three to one, and we currently sell approximately one million pounds of ribs a year! When it comes to food (or anything else), Joe Flanigan thinks big, and all of our portions are generous, like Flanigan's full rack of baby back ribs, which weighs in at a whopping $1\frac{3}{4}$ pounds! We take pride in having "something for everyone" and maintain a wide assortment of items like unique pasta dishes, enormous salads, gargantuan ten ounce burgers, U.S.D.A. choice steaks, and a variety of fresh seafood!

impediment to further growth. In 1969, Flanigan sought to resolve the company's financial shortcomings by taking it public, but he was able to do so only after convincing the American Stock Exchange that his business had no ties to organized crime. Once he dispelled this suspicion, and the company completed its initial public offering of stock, the proceeds were used to finance expansion. During the next several years, he opened Big Daddy's lounges throughout Florida and related lounges in Los Angeles, Philadelphia, Atlanta, Nashville, Tennessee, and Mobile, Alabama. By 1972, four years after registering $15 million in sales, Flanigan's Enterprises generated $38 million.

Bad Decisions in the 1970s

As Flanigan expanded his chain, the need for further capital became a persistent problem. The proceeds from the public offering provided enough funds for the company's initial growth spurt, but more was needed. Consequently, Flanigan began to borrow heavily, using bank loans to build a financial operating base for national expansion. Bankers were reluctant to lend Flanigan as much as he wanted, however, so he was forced to search for other ways to raise cash. The solution to the problem ended up being the worst business decision Flanigan ever made.

To raise cash, Flanigan turned into a real estate broker of sorts. He decided to use his own real estate assets to provide a source of capital. During the 1970s, he sold the properties that housed his bars and liquor stores, then leased back the buildings from the properties' owners. His failure stemmed from the type of arrangement he brokered with the acquirers of the real estate assets. Flanigan pegged his long-term leases not to the amount of revenue each location generated but to the inflation rate. In his March 1988 interview with *Florida Trend*, Flanigan explained the nature of his error: "We were getting crushed because I didn't foresee the big rise in inflation." As the inflation rate skyrocketed during the mid-1970s, Flanigan's lease-back scheme backfired. "Our rents doubled in a five-year period," he said. "We figured the bad leases were costing us $5,000 a day."

Flanigan's once-burgeoning business empire began to fall to pieces. The escalating lease payments drained the company's cash flow, delivering the exact opposite effect as intended. To make matters worse, Flanigan's Enterprises suffered from other

mistakes during the period as well. In the late 1970s, the company tried to capitalize on the pervasive discotheque trend. Flanigan ordered the construction of giant, three-story nightclubs that featured delicatessens, dancing, and packaged liquor for carry-out. The business failed primarily because the discotheque fad faded just as Flanigan's three-story nightclubs were opening their doors. Flanigan also tried to capitalize on another trend: he built an expensive racquet club in Atlanta, hoping to reap rewards from the popularity of the fitness movement. The foray failed in 1979 when a patron at the Atlanta club was electrocuted as he sat in an improperly grounded Jacuzzi.

By the end of the 1970s, the effect of the lease-back scheme was evident on Flanigan's Enterprises' balance sheet. After losing $1.5 million in 1979, the company recovered slightly the following year by posting a negligible profit, but by then Flanigan and his management team were aware that the inflated lease payments they were paying represented a ticking bomb. Back in 1975, Flanigan ordered the closure of the company's package liquor store operations except for those in four counties in southern Florida: Dade, Broward, Palm Beach, and Monroe. The divestitures were not enough to alleviate the financial weight of the bad lease arrangement, however. By 1982, the development of new nightclubs was restricted to joint ventures through limited partnership entities. In March 1985, financial constraints led the company to begin franchising up to 26 of its package liquor stores and lounges in South Florida. Under the terms of the franchise agreement, a franchisee acquired the liquor license, furniture, fixtures, and equipment of a particular unit and entered into a sublease for the business premises, which gave the franchisee a license to use the "Big Daddy's Liquors" and "Big Daddy's Lounges" servicemarks in the operation of the business. The cost-saving measures were not enough to save the company from another financial loss for the year. Flanigan's Enterprises lost a record $1.9 million in 1985, by which time the company already had taken a major step to cure its financial ills.

Flanigan faced the collapse of his business in 1985. Through a franchisee, he learned of a possible escape route from his financial problems, and in November 1985 his company filed to reorganize under Chapter 11 of the Federal Bankruptcy Code. Declaring bankruptcy offered salvation to Flanigan for his mistake in devising the lease-back scheme, but many of his friends and business associates—the majority of the individuals who had participated in the lease-back arrangement—were angry. Under federal bankruptcy laws, a debtor was able to cancel lease agreements by paying 15 percent of the lease value during a period of one to three years. By using the provisions in the federal bankruptcy code, Flanigan was able to nullify nearly 50 lease agreements, which netted his company nearly $3 million.

A Transition to Restaurants in the 1990s and Beyond

Flanigan's Enterprises was officially discharged from bankruptcy in late December 1987, and its strategic orientation had changed as a result of its financial problems. Flanigan emerged as different person as well, replacing his garish attire of the previous decade with more conservative wear. Instead of driving a shamrock-green Excalibur that matched his green jackets and slacks, Flanigan wore oxford shirts and drove a black minivan. In his late 50s when his company emerged from bankruptcy,

Key Dates:

1959: Flanigan's Enterprises is founded.
1969: The company completes its initial public offering of stock.
1985: The company files for bankruptcy.
1987: Flanigan's Enterprises emerges from bankruptcy.
1995: The company begins to franchise its restaurant concept.

Flanigan had stopped drinking alcohol, replacing nights of consuming beer by the case with Alcoholics Anonymous meetings. At Flanigan's Enterprises, the look was also different. By the time the company was discharged from bankruptcy, it already had begun to convert its lounges into full-service restaurants initially named "Flanigan's Conch Key Joe's." The five restaurants in operation by December 1987 became part of the company's new chain, which would be recast as "Flanigan's Seafood Bar and Grill," restaurants that featured a nautical decor. For the first time in its history, Flanigan's Enterprises would rely on food sales as a major source of revenue.

Flanigan operated his business under three names during the 1990s. The lounges operated under the name "Big Daddy's Lounges." The package liquor stores operated under the name "Big Daddy's Liquors." The restaurants operated under the name "Flanigan's Seafood Bar and Grill." The company continued to restructure after emerging from bankruptcy, primarily by shuttering underperforming locations. After four years of annual losses, the company posted a profit of $865,000 in 1992, a gain that was attributable to either the sale or the closure of ten locations. As it progressed in its new guise, Flanigan's Enterprises was a fraction of its former size. By the mid-1990s, there were slightly more than a dozen properties under its control, all in Florida. A decade earlier, the company had operations in 62 locations in Florida, California, and Pennsylvania. Annual revenues, which were nearly $40 million in the early 1970s, were less than $20 million in 1995.

By the beginning of the 21st century, Flanigan's Enterprises was financially stable, although its financial health fell short of being characterized as vibrant. In 2002, the company recorded $1.38 million in profits, a 10 percent decline from the total registered in 2001. Sales were up, however, reaching $28 million, a total generated by seven company-owned restaurants, four combination units that featured both a restaurant and a package liquor store, and five retail liquor stores. As the company prepared for its future, the halcyon years of the 1960 and 1970s were far behind it. The promise of a return to the electrifying growth that had once typified the company seemed remote. In the years ahead, industry onlookers could expect to watch the progress of a more reserved enterprise, a company whose growth was expected be moderately paced, mirroring the more staid lifestyle of its septuagenarian founder.

Principal Subsidiaries

Flanigan's Management Services, Inc.; Flanigan's Enterprises, Inc. of Georgia; Seventh Street Corporation; Flanigan's Enterprises, Inc. of Pennsylvania; CIC Investors #13 LP (50%); CIC Investors #60 LP (42%); CIC Investors #70 LP (40%); CIC Investors #80 LP (25%); CIC Investors #95 LP (28%).

Principal Competitors

Delhaize America, Inc.; Landry's Restaurants, Inc.; Shells Seafood Restaurants, Inc.

Further Reading

"Flanigan's Enterprises, Inc.," *South Florida Business Journal*, April 2, 1990, p. 25.

"Flanigan's Enterprises Sees 4th-Q Gain of $54K," *Nation's Restaurant News*, January 22, 1996, p. 12.

"Flanigan's FY '02 Restaurant Sales Increase 6% to $16.4 m," *Nation's Restaurant News*, January 13, 2003, p. 12.

"Return on Equity," *Florida Trend*, July 1993, p. 58.

Sterz, Bradley, "Big Daddy Goes Another Round," *Florida Trend*, March 1988, p. 66.

—Jeffrey L. Covell

FosterGrant, Inc.

500 George Washington Highway
Smithfield, Rhode Island 02917
U.S.A.
Telephone: (401) 231-3800
Fax: (401) 231-4120
Web site: http://www.fostergrant.com

Wholly Owned Subsidiary of AAi.FosterGrant, Inc.
Incorporated: 1919 as Foster Grant Co.
Employees: 2,000
Sales: $200 million (est.)
NAIC: 339115 Opthalmic Goods Manufacturing

FosterGrant, Inc. is the leading U.S. marketer of moderately priced sunglasses, and one of America's most recognized brand names. The company also manufactures reading glasses. The company was the first to popularize sunglasses, which had their initial vogue in the 1930s. Foster Grant was well known for its long-running advertising campaign, "Who's behind those Foster Grants?," which it revived in the late 1990s. The company passed through many different owners since the 1970s. It is now a subsidiary of Aai.FosterGrant, Inc. Aai, formerly Accessories Associates, Inc., purchased the company in 1996 and moved its headquarters to Rhode Island. Foster Grant maintains sales and marketing facilities as well as warehouses in Rhode Island. Its manufacturing facilities are located in Rhode Island and overseas in Asia and Africa. Foster Grant sunglasses are sold through many mass-market outlets in the United States, including Target, Wal-Mart, and the Sports Authority. The company also sells its sunglasses in Mexico, Canada, England, and Germany, and is expanding into other European markets and into South America as well.

From Health Aid to Fashion Must During the Depression

Sunglasses were not popular until the 20th century, but they were invented far earlier. The mastermind behind tinted lenses was a London inventor and instrument maker, James Ayscough. Ayscough specialized in manufacturing microscopes, and also made spectacles. In 1752 he devised glasses with green or blue-tinted lenses, because he thought plain lenses created a harsh glare. In ensuing years, people with weak or delicate eyes wore tinted lenses. These early sunglasses were far from considered fashionable, as they were associated primarily with invalids. The glamour we now associate with sunglasses came from the spectacles the Foster Grant Company began selling in the seaside resort town of Atlantic City, New Jersey in 1929. The Foster Grant Co. was founded in 1919 in Leominster, Massachusetts, by Sam Foster and Bill Grant. The two men went into business together to manufacture women's hair accessories. The company apparently did well at first, but then ran into trouble in the mid-1920s when women's hair styles changed from long to short. Foster Grant was a pioneer in plastic injection molding. Leominster eventually became a plastics manufacturing mecca, and now holds the National Plastics Center and Museum. But Foster Grant may have been a little ahead of its time in the 1920s, and it took a while before the company had a viable product. In 1929 Foster and Grant sold a half-interest in their firm to Goody Products, a New Jersey manufacturer of hair ornaments and accessories. That year, Foster Grant began selling sunglasses at the Woolworth's store on the famous Boardwalk of Atlantic City. Foster Grant was able to produce sunglasses cheaply at its Leominster plant. Although it displayed the dark glasses with other medical aides at Woolworth's, these were the first sunglasses sold as an over-the-counter consumer item. Previously, people wanting sunglasses had to have them made to order by an optometrist.

Foster Grant sunglasses became popular among fun seekers in Atlantic City, and the fad spread quickly. Very soon, movie stars like Greta Garbo were wearing them. The king of Egypt sported a pair. The image of sunglasses changed completely. No longer were they for people with weak eyes. They offered an air of luxury and mystery to men and women alike. Steve Ainsworth, writing on the history of sunglasses in *Optician* (March 14, 2003), claims it is significant that sunglasses became popular during the depths of the Great Depression. "Sunglasses spelt glamour and wealth in years which had precious little of either," he writes. Foster Grant glasses gained wide popularity, though the company soon had other significant competitors. Foster Grant's Leominster factory also turned out a variety of other injection-molded plastic goods. By 1938, the company

---

Company Perspectives:

AAi.FosterGrant, based in Smithfield, RI, owns one of the leading brands of sun and reading glasses in the United States and is also a leading designer of costume jewelry. The FosterGrant brand provides the consumer with eyewear representing exceptional styling, quality and features at competitive prices.

---

owned more than 100 injection molding presses, and it made barrettes, curlers, and combs as well as sunglasses.

Postwar Growth

During World War II, the Foster Grant factory was refitted for defense work. It continued to make and sell sunglasses, and it did very well immediately after the war. Its parent company, Goody, was not as profitable, and Goody frequently borrowed against its Foster Grant stock. In 1965 Foster Grant initiated an advertising campaign that became a 20th century classic: ''Who's behind those Foster Grants?'' The ads, which ran both on television and in print media, featured celebrities of the day wearing Foster Grant sunglasses. The campaign was created by the Geer DuBois agency, and used the faces of film stars like Woody Allen, Raquel Welch, Peter Sellers, and Anthony Quinn, all trendy and rising young actors of the era. The Foster Grant name gained wide exposure with its celebrity ads. Although the rich and famous wore Foster Grants in its advertising, the company sold its glasses at mass marketers like Woolworth's and Walgreens. Foster Grants were moderately priced. Although by 1976 the company had some higher-end glasses that sold for $15, most of the line retailed for between $2 and $10.

The company spent about $1 million annually on advertising in the mid-1970s, and sponsored the World Series of baseball. Foster Grant's success did not go unnoticed. Goody had continually raised money for itself by using its Foster Grant stock as collateral. In 1970, Goody's chairman Len Goodman was informed by his bankers that United Brands, a large conglomerate, had bought up a significant stake in Foster Grant from the estate of one of the founders. United Brands was known as an aggressive speculator, and Goody's bankers were worried that it was planning to wrest Foster Grant away from its parent. This situation continued uneasily for some years. Then in 1974, United Brands suffered a major blow when a hurricane wiped out its banana plantations in Honduras. To raise cash, United Brands sold its stake in Foster Grant to the U.S. subsidiary of the German pharmaceutical firm Hoechst A.G. Goody decided to sell Hoechst its stake as well, so Foster Grant had entirely new ownership after 1975.

Changes of Ownership in the 1980s–90s

Foster Grant retained a 35 percent share of the drugstore sunglasses market through the mid-1980s, but conditions in the industry became increasingly competitive. Warner-Lambert, which manufactured another popular moderately priced line of sunglasses under the Cool Ray brand name, quit the sunglasses business in 1980. Warner-Lambert claimed that cheap imports

were making it increasingly unprofitable to manufacture sunglasses domestically. Makers of more expensive sunglasses had only sluggish sales. Foster Grant reported sales of $150 million for 1980, with roughly a 10 percent increase over the year previous. Despite this good year, overall market conditions worsened in the early 1980s. Consumer demand for sunglasses dropped by close to 15 percent from 1981 to 1983. By 1983, some 80 percent of all sunglasses sold in the United States was imported. Foster Grant remained a large player in a very fragmented market, and so fared better than some competitors. In 1980 it introduced a line of reading glasses it called SparePair. These became the second best sellers in the reading glasses market. But in 1983 the company dropped a higher-priced designer sunglasses line, which had not done well, to concentrate on its basic line, which sold for around $12. As the cheaper end of the market picked up over the next several years, Foster Grant's sales and market share began to fall.

In 1986, Foster Grant was bought out by a private investment firm called Andlinger & Co. Andlinger was headed by Gerhard R. Andlinger, an Austrian businessman who had worked for the conglomerate ITT until the mid-1970s. In 1976 he and other ITT executives formed Andlinger & Co., and specialized in picking up undervalued businesses for cheap. Foster Grant seemed to be just the kind of company Andlinger liked. Although it had strong brand name recognition, its sales were declining. Foster Grant had discontinued its signature ad campaign in 1984, and in the mid-1980s was advertising primarily in car and motorcycle magazines. In 1987, Foster Grant changed its advertising agency and initiated a new, more fashion-oriented campaign.

But this was apparently not enough to rescue Foster Grant. Its sales continued to decline, from $60 million in 1985 to $50 million in 1989. Sales had been three times that a decade earlier. Imports from Asia skewed the market heavily toward sunglasses that retailed for less than $5. Foster Grant, which had moved some of its manufacturing facilities to Arizona and Mexico, could not compete in the lower tier of the market. Andlinger had planned to move Foster Grant into a more upmarket mode, but this did not happen. The company had very heavy debt stemming from Andlinger's buyout, and it could not afford to advertise. By mid-1990, Foster Grant had let half its employees go. With $43 million in debt, the company filed for bankruptcy in September 1990.

Shortly after it filed for Chapter 11 (a type of bankruptcy proceeding that allows the company to continue operating), the Dallas, Texas-based Bonneau Company made an offer of $9 million for Foster Grant. Bonneau quickly revised its offer downward, and Foster Grant eventually went for only $4.9 million. The sale excluded the company's technical products division, based in Leominster, which sold goods to the automotive and computer industries. Bonneau had been in the sunglasses business for some time, and in 1986 it acquired Pennsylvania Optical, a maker of reading glasses. Pennsylvania Optical had doubled its sales under Bonneau's leadership.

Bonneau itself was acquired three years after it bought Foster Grant. Benson Eyecare Corporation, a new consolidator in the market, paid $21 million for Bonneau in 1993. Benson was run by Martin Franklin, a young British-born investor. In 1992 Franklin began acquiring optical companies, aiming to be a big player in a market filled with many small companies. By 1994, Benson Eyecare had revenues of $169 million, and it owned roughly a dozen sunglasses brands in addition to Foster Grant. Like Gerhard Andlinger before him, Martin Franklin hoped to have a sleeping giant in the undervalued Foster Grant. "The Foster Grant brand has languished," Franklin told *Fortune* magazine (April 17, 1995), "but we're counting on its tremendous name recognition to revive it." Benson turned its attention to advertising, and revived the famous "Who's behind those Foster Grants?" tagline in 1995.

But Foster Grant continued to be a poor performer. In 1996, Benson Eyecare sold some of its assets and changed its name to BEC Group. BEC consisted of the Foster Grant Group and Benson's other nonprescription eyewear businesses. BEC blamed a loss for the fourth quarter of 1995 on high returns from Foster Grant customers. Two quarters later, BEC posted a drop in net income of more than 50 percent from a year previous, again attributing the loss to a poor showing by Foster Grant. At that point, BEC put Foster Grant up for sale. Benson claimed revenues of $90 million from the Foster Grant Group for 1995. American Greetings Corp., a $2 billion greeting card manufacturer based in Cleveland, Ohio, offered to take Foster Grant off BEC's hands for a sum believed to be about $45 million. But this deal was quickly canceled. A few months later, BEC announced that a management group was going to buy Foster Grant. This deal also did not come off, and in December 1996 BEC sold its Foster Grant Group to a jewelry and accessories distributor called Aai for $29 million. Aai, formerly Accessory Associates, Inc., was based in Smithfield, Rhode Island. The company distributed costume jewelry, hair ornaments, and small leather goods to mass-market vendors like Target, Ames, and Wal-Mart. Most of its business came in the first six months of the year. It hoped to find a good fit with Foster Grant, whose business came principally in the second half of the year. Aai moved Foster Grant's headquarters to Smithfield. The subsidiary lost the space in its name and became FosterGrant, Inc. The parent company then changed its name to Aai.FosterGrant.

New Marketing Push in the Late 1990s

Aai.FosterGrant spent $3 million on new facilities for its corporate headquarters and a large new warehouse and distribu-

tion center. The company closed FosterGrant's operations in Canada and Georgia, and consolidated the business in Rhode Island. The new parent worked quickly to revive FosterGrant's advertising. FosterGrant came out with a new athletic line of sunglasses, its Ironman Triathlon line, in 1998. Association with the Ironman, a triple race of swimming, biking, and running, had been a good selling point with Timex, the watch brand, and Aai hoped the same would hold true for FosterGrant. Aai's most signal move, however, was to sign up model Cindy Crawford as the celebrity spokeswoman for the Foster Grant brand. The company wanted to build on its "Who's behind those Foster Grants?" theme, but with one recognizable figure who would appeal to a broad market base. Crawford was picked because she appealed to young and old alike. She had a long track record, but had a lot of exposure to younger consumers through appearances on the music television network MTV.

By the late 1990s, the sunglasses market overall was showing strong growth, and FosterGrant seemed to be in a unique position. FosterGrant's marketing director, Bill Potts, told *Supermarket Business* (July 1999) that his company had "the only brand name out there for sunglasses priced under $30." The company put some $3 million to $5 million into advertising worldwide, and seemed to get fast results. Sales per retailer increased markedly. The two models Crawford wore in the FosterGrant ads became the first and second best-selling sunglasses of 1999. The company found thousands of new retail outlets for its line, and FosterGrant began to look to international markets.

In 2002, the company was able to swap some $52 million of its debt for equity in FosterGrant. The company built up the sporty side of its image by signing on another celebrity spokesperson, champion Nascar driver Jeff Gordon. Cindy Crawford continued to appear in FosterGrant ads. FosterGrant seemed to be part of a trend of comeback brands in the sport and fashion industries. Other revived brands from the 1960s and 1970s included OP (Ocean Pacific), PF Flyers, and Pony. These all did well in the 2000s after losing steam earlier. By the early 2000s, FosterGrant seemed to have done what many of its previous owners had hoped for, and finally capitalized again on the tremendous name recognition it had built up in its early years.

Principal Competitors

Luxottica Group S.p.A.; Marchon Eyewear, Inc.

Further Reading

"Aai Shines with Foster Grant Acquisition," *Discount Store News,* December 9, 1996, p. A55.

Adams, Valerie, "No Rose-Colored Glasses at Foster Grant," *Advertising Age,* July 12, 1976, pp. 84–86.

Ainsworth, Steve, "Shades of History," *Optician,* March 14, 2003, p. 1.

"Andlinger & Co. Acquires Foster Grant from Firm," *Wall Street Journal,* March 25, 1986, p. 1.

"BEC Group Inc: Net Plunges 52%, Affected by Foster Grant Results," *Wall Street Journal,* August 1, 1996, p. B4.

"Company Revives '60s 'Who's Behind Those Foster Grants?,' " *Marketing News,* March 15, 1999, p. 12.

"Court Oks the Sale of Foster," *Chain Drug Review,* January 14, 1991, p. 22.

Ebenkamp, Becky, "Cindy Crawford Is Behind Foster Grant's '99 Push," *Brandweek,* November 23, 1998, p. 5.

——, "Fostering a Grant Tradition," *Brandweek,* January 24, 2000, pp. 26–29.

"Fifty-Year Foster Grant Veteran Iacoboni Dies," *Plastics News,* September 23, 1996, p. 24.

Flax, Steven, "The Cost of Staying Private," *Forbes,* February 15, 1982, pp. 102–06.

"Foster Grant Corp.: Firm Agrees to Sell Assets to Dallas Eyewear Concern," *Wall Street Journal,* October 19, 1990, p. A4.

"Foster Grant Is Putting Focus on Fashion," *New York Times,* April 27, 1987, p. D12.

Fraust, Bart, "Eyes on Benson," *Wall Street Journal,* February 13, 1996, p. B7.

Fried, Lisa I., "Ag Close to Foster Grant Buy," *Drug Store News,* September 23, 1996, p. 51.

Gormley, Brian, "Foster Grant Targets New Market," *Providence (Rhode Island) Business News,* June 28, 1999, p. 16.

Griffin, Cara, and Leand, Judy, "Back by Popular Demand," *Sporting Goods Business,* July 2002, pp. 46–47.

Hammonds, Keith H., "Foster Grant Runs for the Shade of Chapter 11," *Business Week,* September 3, 1990, p. 44.

Mendelson, Seth, "Through the Looking Glass(es)," *Supermarket Business,* July 1999, pp. 75–76.

O'Brien, Timothy L., "The Building of Benson Eyecare Got Started with Only a Vision," *Wall Street Journal,* May 13, 1994, pp. B1, B2.

Rattner, Steven, "Sales Turn Soft for Sunglasses," *New York Times,* July 28, 1980, pp. D1, D4.

Rudolph, Bar, "Shades of Discontent," *Forbes,* July 18, 1983, p. 50.

Serwer, Andrew E., "A Man with a Vision Consolidates the Eye-Care Business," *Fortune,* April 17, 1995, p. 205.

Sloane, Leonard, "New President for Foster Grant," *New York Times,* July 11, 1980, p. D2.

—A. Woodward

GARMIN.

Garmin Ltd.

5th Floor, Harbour Place
103 South Church Street
George Town, Grand Cayman
Cayman Islands
Telephone: (345) 946-5203; (913) 397-8200 (U.S.)
Fax: (913) 397-8282
Web site: http://www.garmin.com

Public Company
Incorporated: 2000
Employees: 1,575
Sales: $465.14 million (2002)
Stock Exchanges: NASDAQ
Ticker Symbol: GRMN
NAIC: 334220 Radio and Television Broadcasting and
    Wireless Communications Equipment Manufacturing;
    334511 Search, Detection, Navigation, Guidance,
    Aeronautical, and Nautical System and Instrument
    Manufacturing

Garmin Ltd. is a leader in Global Positioning System (GPS) navigation products. Once found mostly in specialized equipment for aircraft and boats, GPS technology has been adapted for use in a variety of handheld and wristwatch units for users such as hikers, athletes, sportsmen, and automobile drivers. Garmin has sold five million units in its first dozen years. Its product line has proliferated into 50 different items marketed through a network of 2,500 dealers, distributors, and partners in 100 countries around the world. While the parent company is registered in the Cayman Islands, Garmin has manufacturing and sales operations in the United States (Kansas) and Taiwan and a marketing office in the United Kingdom.

Origins

The U.S. Department of Defense began developing the Global Positioning System (GPS) in the mid-1970s, eventually spending $15 billion to put two dozen satellites into orbit. GPS receivers could determine their coordinates by comparing signals from different satellites. Like the first computers, the first commercially available GPS units were large and expensive, costing up to $10,000.

Garmin Corporation was formed in Taiwan in January 1990 by two electrical engineers, Gary Burrell and Dr. Min Kao. (The company's name is derived from the first names of the founders.) Burrell and Kao had been employed by Kansas-based King Radio Corporation, a maker of radios and aircraft navigation equipment, which was acquired by Allied Corp. (later Allied Signal) in 1985. Burrell displayed in interest in integration early on and is credited with designing the first combination navigation/communications radio for general aviation while at King Radio.

Garmin introduced its first product, the GPS 100AVD, in January 1991. Aimed at boaters and pilots of small planes, it was about the size of a paperback book and sold for about $1,000. By 1992, GPS devices were a $100 million-a-year market.

Garmin subsequently introduced another GPS unit for pilots called the GPS 95. This one, which sold for $1,795, incorporated a display of the plane's position on a moving map, as well as nearby airports and radio beacons. It could also backup the aircraft's built-in instrumentation with groundspeed, heading, and altitude readings.

Sales reached $102 million in 1995, producing net income of $23 million. Garmin International, the U.S. unit, moved to a new $8 million, 100,000-square-foot headquarters in early 1996. Its offices had previously been housed in four separate buildings.

Locating Drivers in the Late 1990s

Garmin turned its attention to the automotive market in the late 1990s with two hand-held units. GPS III, introduced in late 1997, incorporated a map of major roads in the Americas. This device displayed the position of the driver and destination on the map. Garmin brought out the StreetPilot in March 1998. It retailed for $700 and replaced more detailed mapping programs requiring a laptop computer.

Garmin's next project was a waterproof mobile phone with a GPS receiver and map display built in called NavTalk. The

---

Company Perspectives:

Technology that touches people. Our customers around the world are loyal and take pride in having "guidance by Garmin." Our dealers and employees are likewise devoted to designing, selling, and servicing our consumer electronics. Garmin's success is not due solely to the quality of our materials and end products. We are successful because we have a simple mission: to turn complicated technology into useful products that enhance people's lives. Garmin products ... add convenience and improve the daily lives of customers. We design, we build, and we dream of products through the eyes of people who need our technology though they may not understand it. All the more reason to make our products intuitive and fun to use. In the days when GPS (Global Positioning System) technology was still in its infancy, our company founders envisioned a wide range of products that would help consumers, pilots, mariners, and industry professionals pinpoint positions and navigate to destinations.

---

company also expanded beyond GPS products in its aviation-related products, introducing a Mode C transponder (a device for communicating a plane's position to air traffic controllers) and an intercom. Sales were $232.6 million in 1999. The company soon doubled the size of its Kansas plant to 240,000 square feet. It also had manufacturing operations in Taiwan and a sales office in England.

Public in 2000

Through a process called Selective Availability, the Department of Defense limited the accuracy of commercial uses of GPS technology to prevent the devices from being used to guide weapons. However, this policy was cancelled in May 2000, improving the unit's accuracy from 100 meters to less than ten meters. This resulted in increased interest in GPS in time for Garmin's initial public offering (IPO).

Before the IPO, a Cayman Islands-based holding company called Garmin Ltd. was created in July 2000. Garmin Ltd. became a public company on December 8, 2000 with one of the best IPOs following the dot-com bust. The price of shares, offered at $14, rose 42 percent to $20 in the first day of trading. The offering raised $147 million, most of it earmarked to fund growth. Revenues rose almost 50 percent to $345.7 million in 2000, and Garmin's net margins were above 30 percent.

Flush with cash, the company continued to spend significantly on research and development and introduced two dozen new products in 2001. However, both the aviation market and the overall economy experienced a downturn following the September 11 terrorist attacks on the United States. Nevertheless, Garmin was able to open 2002 with its best first quarter results to date—net income of $26.8 million on revenues of $100.9 million.

Revenues rose 26 percent to $465.1 million for 2002 as a whole, while net income was up $38 million to $142.8 million. Consumer revenue brought in $350.6 million, while aviation

revenue accounted for $114.5 million. The company's aviation business had fallen by 9 percent in the previous year due to the FAA's restrictions on private aircraft following 9/11.

Garmin's product line had expanded considerably in the previous dozen years. It targeted a variety of users, from fishermen to commercial pilots, and its units were priced from $100 to $10,000. Consumer products then accounted for three-quarters of sales; Garmin had a new agreement to have them distributed at Target and Circuit City stores in the United States.

International sales were also very important. Garmin's first major buyer of its NavTalk GSM cell phone, which featured a GPS receiver and map, was a Chinese firm, CEC Telecom Co. Garmin had had manufacturing facilities in Taiwan for several years.

The company had also patented its "Rino" walkie-talkies (Radios Integrated with Navigation for the Outdoors) with integrated map and GPS features, including the ability to report the position of other radios on each user's map.

Co-founder Gary Burrell retired as co-CEO on August 24, 2002, his sixty-fifth birthday; he remained co-chairman and a director of the company. The company then employed 1,400 people around the world, a little less than half of them at its operating headquarters in Olathe, Kansas. According to *Investor's Business Daily,* Garmin had a 50 percent or better market share in the consumer segment of the GPS market, which accounted for three-quarters of the company's revenues. It controlled 80 percent of the aviation market and was also quite popular among boaters and hikers.

GPS for the Masses in 2003

The *Chicago-Sun Times* reported that GPS began to hit the mass market, versus the gadget enthusiasts, in 2003. This was evidenced by new offerings from Cobra Electronics Inc., a company that did much to popularize CB radios. Established GPS rivals such as Motorola Inc. and Magellan Corp. continued to develop low-priced units, and they were finding acceptance at more and more big box retailers like Best Buy and Wal-Mart.

The next step saw the combining of a handheld personal digital assistant (PDA) with GPS technology, allowing users to receive turn-by-turn directions to contacts listed in their address books. The combined handheld unit, called the iQue 3600, used the popular Palm operating system and was introduced at a January 2003 trade show. The device had "voice guidance" to give users spoken directions while driving as well as a full color map. It retailed for less than $600 and also offered traditional palmtop features such as the ability to edit word processor and spreadsheet files.

At the same time, Garmin was rolling out its first under-$100 GPS device, the Geko 101. Garmin technology was also featured in a Timex athletic training watch, enabling speed and distance calculations for runners. Garmin brought out its own training watch, the Forerunner 201, in the fall of 2003. The Forerunner's GPS included altitude capabilities and retailed for about $160.

Key Dates:

1990: Garmin Corporation is formed in Taiwan.
1991: The company's first product, GPS 100AVD, debuts.
1996: Garmin moves to new headquarters building.
1997: GPS III, Garmin's first automotive product, is introduced.
1998: StreetPilot, an auto navigation product, is introduced.
2000: The company goes public, and Garmin Ltd. is formed.
2003: Palm OS-based iQue 3600 is unveiled.

Aviation products accounted for 20 percent of revenues. Garmin continued to bring forth innovations, combining several flight instruments in its integrated avionics systems, which were selected for use in Cessna Aircraft Co. business jets and piston-engine aircraft from Diamond Aircraft Co.

Garmin International acquired UPS Aviation Technologies, Inc. from United Parcel Service, Inc. in August 2003 for $38 million. The unit, which employed 150 people producing general aviation and air cargo products, was renamed Garmin AT, Inc.

A mandate from the FCC for mobile phone companies to offer enhanced 911 service to help dispatchers locate callers—along with penetration of GPS technology into new fields, such as golf—suggested the market for GPS-related devices was still relatively untapped. The Kansas facility was slated for another expansion to be completed in 2004.

Principal Subsidiaries

Garmin (Asia) Corporation (Taiwan); Garmin (Europe) Ltd. (United Kingdom); Garmin International Inc. (United States); Garmin USA, Inc.

Principal Divisions

Aviation; Consumer.

Principal Competitors

Cobra Electronics Corporation; Magellan Corporation; SiRF Technology, Inc.; Thales Navigation, Inc.; Trimble Navigation, Ltd.

Further Reading

Angell, Mike, "Satellite Communications, Global Positioning Putting New Firms on Street's Map," *Investor's Business Daily*, May 15, 2003, p. A4.

Cronkleton, Robert A., "Electronic Maps Are Intended to Assist Motorists," *Kansas City Star*, January 5, 1998.

Davis, Mark, "Cayman Islands-Based Product Developer Makes Strong Debut on Market," *Kansas City Star*, January 16, 2001.

Eng, Paul, "A 'Moving Map' for Weekend Pilots," *Business Week*, August 2, 1993, p. 84A.

"GARMIN: Gary Burrell and Dr. Min Kao," *Ingram's for Successful Kansas Citians*, March 1, 2000, p. 41.

"Garmin to Build New Headquarters in Olathe, Kan.," *Weekly of Business Aviation*, May 22, 1995, p. 219.

"Garmin to Get into Lucrative GPS-Wireless Markets," *Global Positioning & Navigation News*, January 28, 1998.

Hayes, David, "Kansas City, Mo.-Area Marine Equipment Maker Posts Profits at First Meeting," *Kansas City Star*, June 9, 2001.

——, "Olathe, Kan.-Based Digital-Navigation Firm Posts Its Best First Quarter Ever," *Kansas City Star*, May 2, 2002.

——, "Co-Founder of Olathe, Kan., International Manufacturer to Retire as Co-CEO," *Kansas City Star*, August 22, 2002.

——, "Olathe, Kan.-Based Firm Unveils Handheld Mapping Device," *Kansas City Star*, January 9, 2003.

Hennessey, Raymond, "Traders Hope Garmin Can Point Market for Initial Offerings in a New Direction," *Wall Street Journal*, December 5, 2000, p. C22.

——, "Garmin's Attempt to Ease Pain of Lockup Expiration Faces Test," *Wall Street Journal*, June 4, 2001, p. C15.

King, Suzanne, "Olathe, Kan., Supplier of Navigation Equipment Lowers Initial Stock Price," *Kansas City Star*, November 24, 2000.

——, "Olathe, Kan.-Based Firm Reports Decline in Sales of Air Navigation Devices," *Kansas City Star*, November 2, 2001.

——, "Shares Rise 42 Percent for Olathe, Kan., Navigation Device Maker," *Kansas City Star*, December 9, 2000.

Lewyn, Mark, "Where Am I? Ask a Satellite," *Business Week*, October 26, 1992, p. 116.

Linecker, Adelia Cellini, "Tech Firm Maps out a Winning Growth Plan," *Investor's Business Daily*, February 28, 2003, p. A8.

Margolies, Jane, and Pooja Bhatia, "Let Your Laptop Do the Driving," *Wall Street Journal*, June 29, 2001, p. W4.

Pogue, David, "This Palmtop Knows Its Place," *New York Times*, July 31, 2003, p. G1.

Rash, Wayne, "GPS Receivers for the Masses," *Washington Post*, April 27, 2003, p. F7.

Richfield, Paul and Fred George, "Garmin International Goes Public," *Business & Commercial Aviation*, January 2001, p. 36.

Taylor, Paul, "Driving on Autopilot: With Voice Prompts and Automatic Routing, In-Car Navigation Has Come a Long Way," *Financial Times* (London), October 28, 2002, p. 18.

Velocci, Anthony L., Jr., "Bulls and Bears Both Tugging at Garmin," *Aviation Week & Space Technology*, May 5, 2003, p. 12.

Wildstrom, Stephen H., "A Handheld That Knows Where It Is," *Business Week*, August 11, 2003, p. 18.

Wolinsky, Howard, "GPS Finds Its Way; All Roads Lead to Mass Market for Navigation Technology," *Chicago Sun-Times*, March 10, 2003, p. 55.

—Frederick C. Ingram

Geiger Bros.

Mount Hope Avenue
Lewiston, Maine 04240
U.S.A.
Telephone: (207) 755-2001
Fax: (207) 755-2422
Web site: http://www.geiger.com

Private Company
Founded: 1878
Employees: 438
Sales: $119 million (2002)
NAIC: 323110 Commercial Lithographic Printing;
    323119 Other Commercial Printing; 323121
    Tradebinding and Related Works; 424920 Book,
    Periodical and Newspaper Merchant Wholesalers

Geiger Bros., founded in 1878, is the largest privately held company in promotional advertising and the largest manufacturer of time planners in the United States. Managed by its fourth generation of siblings, Geiger manufactures, supplies, and distributes calendars, diaries, executive gifts, and specialty advertising products. Geiger offers over 25,000 promotional items from more than 5,000 suppliers through its independent sales force in over 20 offices in the United States and Puerto Rico as well as online catalogs. Geiger's major corporate clients include Aramark, ACE Insurance, Warner Bros. Home Video, Boy Scouts of America, Princess Cruises, and Mattel. Geiger has a wholly owned direct mail promotional company called Crestline and also owns Geiger-Donnelly Marketing LLC, a promotion agency based in Boston, Massachusetts, that services large accounts. Since 1935, Geiger has been the exclusive distributor of the venerable *Farmers' Almanac,* a publication that dates back to 1818 and is the second oldest almanac in the United States. The *Farmers' Almanac* has a readership of 1.2 million through retail store sales and 4.5 million through promotional business giveaways.

19th Century Roots

In 1878, brothers Andrew and Jacob Geiger, having learned the print craft from their father Andrew, Sr., opened a small print shop in Newark, New Jersey. The brothers expanded their business through their pioneering efforts in specialty advertising, selling paper fans, calendars, and other paper novelty items to businesses for promotional purposes.

In 1902, Frank Geiger, Jacob's oldest son, founded the Frank A. Geiger Calendar Company, and his brother Charles joined that company in 1904. In 1907, after stewarding Geiger Bros. for 29 years, Jacob was killed in an automobile accident. Following his brother's tragic death, Andrew announced he would retire. Frank and Charles Geiger then purchased the company from their mother and Uncle Andrew, combining the two companies. Frank became company president and remained in that role until 1944.

During the second-generation tenure in the 1920s, the company greatly increased its commercial calendars business, achieving sales to position Geiger as one of the largest business calendar manufacturers in the United States. During this time period, the company also acquired H.B. Hardenburg Company and Walker Longfellow Company, two of the earliest manufacturing firms of diaries and date books in the United States.

Family Ownership Extends to Third Generation

In 1930, Frank Geiger's son Francis (Frank) joined the family business full time after graduating from Georgetown University. Two years later, in 1932, Frank's brother Raymond (Ray) joined the company after completing his degree in philosophy from Notre Dame University. Frank focused on growing Geiger's specialty advertising market by adding such goodwill products as yardsticks, pens, badges, and ashtrays. Ray looked to the *Farmers' Almanac,* a longstanding almanac that was first published in 1818, as a way to grow the business. In 1935, Ray secured a licensing agreement with the Almanac Publishing Company to publish and sell the *Farmers' Almanac* and became editor that year, a position he would fill until 1994. As a public relations giveaway that was not sold through retail channels, the *Almanac* was a natural addition to the company's other products.

The Farmers' Almanac: An American Tradition Takes Root

Not to be confused with the New Hampshire-based *Old Farmer's Almanac,* which was first published in 1792, the

Farmers' Almanac dates back to 1818, when it was founded by David Young and Jacob Mann. Young, a mathematician, followed in the tradition of Benjamin Franklin, whose popular *Poor Richard's Almanack* first appeared in 1732. Keeping with Franklin's use of the label *Philom,* derived from the Greek *philomath* (meaning "lover of learning"), Young applied the term to himself as editor, a tradition that has continued throughout the *Farmers' Almanac*'s history.

While the *Almanac* is a compendium of humor, household hints and recipes, verses, nostalgia, trivia, and more, many readers turn to it for the weather predictions. As the first editor of the *Farmers' Almanac,* Young developed a formula for predicting the weather two years in advance—a formula that is based on sunspots, the position of planets, and tidal action—that has been a closely guarded secret passed on through the generations. Upon Young's death in 1852, the editorship of the *Farmers' Almanac* passed to Samuel Hart Wright, an astronomer who calculated the weather predictions. Berlin Hart Wright succeeded his father as editor and calculator in 1875 and remained prognosticator through the early 1930s. Hart's son-in-law, Roland E. Hart, assumed the duties of prognosticator until the mid-1950s, when astronomer and schoolteacher Harry K. Buie assumed the role. After Buie's death in 1980, his widow stepped in to calculate the predictions and was then succeeded by scientist and astronomer Kenneth Franklin. Beginning in 1982, in order to guard the secret weather formula, the *Almanac*'s forecaster became known only under the pseudonym Caleb Weatherbee. When the *Almanac* debuted, farmers relied heavily on its weather predictions, since there were no meteorologists at the time. While farmers and gardeners still turn to the *Almanac*'s forecasts, modern readers more often survey the predictions to plan weddings and other outdoor events. Although there are some detractors who question the accuracy of the weather forecasts, the company maintains that the predictions have shown a 75 to 85 percent accuracy.

"The King of Cornography" Reigns

As editor of the *Farmers' Almanac,* Ray Geiger infused his brand of wry wit and a "high moral tone" to the *Almanac*'s content of homespun lore, inspirational thoughts, recipes, gags, puzzles, aphorisms, time-saving hints, and trivia. One Canadian writer dubbed him "the King of Cornography," to which Ray responded, "I'd rather be corny than porny." When Ray began as editor in 1935, the *Almanac* had a circulation of 86,000.

During World War II, brothers Frank and Ray both joined the armed services. While serving in the South Pacific for three years, Ray continued to edit the *Almanac,* even after he was wounded in the Philippines in 1944. On his way to the field

hospital, Ray stated in an interview, "As I was carried off on a stretcher I checked for two things—my dogtags and almanac material." Upon Ray's return in 1945 and Frank's in 1946, they were prepared to be the third generation to lead the family business with Ray as president and Frank as vice-president of sales. While sales of the *Almanac* had remained flat throughout the first decade of Geiger ownership, following the war the company won a large New York insurance company account. With a single order of 115,000 copies, circulation literally doubled overnight.

Ray met his future wife, Ann Hueber, after she commented to him: "I think your recipes and household hints are horrible." Taking the schoolteacher's words to heart, Ray devoted more attention to the haphazard collection of unscreened recipes included in the *Almanac.* The couple wed in 1948. Ann became co-editor of the *Almanac* and tested each recipe in her kitchen and each household hint in her home. In 1949, Ray and Ann acquired the rights to the *Farmers' Almanac* and continued its noncommercial distribution through businesses such as banks, insurance companies, and feed companies, among other outlets.

In 1951, as Ray assumed full leadership of the company as president, the cramped quarters of the Newark facility and the poor business climate there prompted him to look elsewhere to locate company headquarters. Geiger chose Lewiston, Maine, because he felt that Maine's predominantly rural character befitted the *Almanac* and believed he would find a strong, willing workforce there. In 1955, the company moved to its new 60,000-square-foot facility where Geiger employed 85 people and earned $1.2 million in sales that year. In 1961, the company added 20,000 square feet, and in 1969 it built a two-story office building. As the physical layout of the Geiger facilities expanded, sales grew steadily, doubling every six years.

Throughout his long tenure as company president and editor of the *Almanac,* Ray enthusiastically championed, with varying degrees of success, numerous pet causes. In the 1975 edition of the *Almanac,* Ray launched his first campaign. Directed at the United States Postal Service, Geiger decried the post office's decision to remove the community name on the postmark in favor of the more efficient state abbreviation and first three zip code digits. He asserted, "Efficient it undoubtedly is, but romantic it isn't—'OK740' is a far cry from the 'Broken Arrow, Okla.' of yorn." Through the national attention of his efforts, the U.S. Postal Service did, in fact, reinstate the city postmark. Other campaigns Ray waged included a pro-hug crusade in which he urged "Hugs Not Drugs," the elimination of the penny (to be supplanted by a "bit" worth 12½ cents), the abolishment of the nine-digit zip code, the discontinuation of the dollar bill (to be replaced by a dollar coin called the Columbus Dollar), moving the date of Thanksgiving to the second Monday in October to correspond more closely with the fall harvest, changing the national anthem to "America the Beautiful," and adding colors other than green to American currency.

Geiger Promotional and Specialty Advertising Prospers

Circulation of the *Almanac* continued to rise, from 86,000 in 1935 to two million in 1955 to 6.25 million by 1980. A tireless promoter of the *Almanac,* Ray traveled extensively to give newspaper, radio, and television interviews. His devotion to

Key Dates:

1878: Andrew and Jacob Geiger open Geiger Bros., a one-room print shop in Newark, New Jersey.

1907: Jacob Geiger is killed in an automobile accident and Andrew retires. Jacob's sons, Frank and Charles Geiger, purchase company.

1935: Frank's son Raymond becomes editor of *Farmers' Almanac* after obtaining licensing rights to the franchise that had been founded in 1818.

1949: Ray Geiger and wife Ann buy the rights to the *Farmers' Almanac*.

1955: Geiger Bros. moves from New Jersey to Lewiston, Maine.

1973: Ray Geiger's sons Gene and Peter join the family business, becoming the fourth generation to lead the company.

1976: Ann Geiger becomes sole owner of Almanac Publishing Co. and its trademark.

1992: President George Bush names Ann Geiger the 618th Point of Light to honor the company's community and charitable involvement with Montello Elementary School.

1994: Ray Geiger dies; Peter Geiger assumes the editorship of the *Farmers' Almanac*.

2003: Geiger celebrates its 125th anniversary.

promoting the *Almanac* brought increased sales to Geiger's specialty advertising, the much more lucrative side of Geiger's business. By 1971, Geiger had reached $10 million in sales, only 10 percent of which came from the *Almanac*. In 1979, with $18 million in annual sales, the *Almanac* garnered less than 10 percent of those sales. By 1980, the core of Geiger's business came from its success supplying 35,000 customers with specialty items. Customers ranged from small business owners to such giants as Eli Lilly, Avon, General Foods, and Westinghouse. By 1986, Geiger, with 16 offices and subsidiaries in seven states, was the fifth largest specialty advertising company in the United States. Sales had reached $38 million, with the *Almanac* representing only 10 percent of manufactured-product sales. The company distinguished itself in the industry by acting as both a distributor and manufacturer of its specialty items, with 73.3 percent of 1986 sales generated from distribution and 26.7 percent generated from manufactured products.

Ray's eldest son Gene, who was made president of the firm, attributed the company's success to its treatment of its sales representatives. As he noted in an article in the *Portland Press Herald* in 1987, "Our customers are our sales representatives. By consistently doing a good job they are taking care of our needs. We have created a climate enabling them to succeed." Another key to Geiger's success has been in the company's approach to acquisitions. Since the 1960s, Geiger has actively worked to acquire key manufacturing and distribution firms in the specialty advertising industry. With most acquisitions, Geiger operated the acquired firm under its original name. Gene maintained, "We try not to run roughshod over people." He further asserted that through this approach "very few acquisitions over the years have gone bad."

After suffering from a stroke in 1985, Ray was unable to embark on his annual promotional tour. At that point, Geiger estimated he had given 18,000 interviews. Ray's son Peter took his father's place on the promotional tour, although Ray continued as editor of the *Almanac*. By 1990, Geiger was the third largest promotional advertising company in the United States. Still very active in the company, Ray demonstrated his flair for flamboyant promotion in 1990 when he staged his own funeral for his 80th birthday. He invited family, friends, and employees to attend the unveiling of his tombstone at Mount Hope Cemetery overlooking the Geiger plant. As he greeted the 400 mourners, he intoned, "Friends, I am delighted and really quite excited that you came to this rather grave event." He also noted, "Well, when you buy a tombstone for $4,500 you should get some enjoyment out of it while you can."

The Torch Passes to the Fourth Generation

Ray Geiger died April 1, 1994, but his legacy is carried on through two of his five children. Peter, who serves as executive vice-president of Geiger, is also the editor of the *Farmers' Almanac,* having worked with his father on the publication for 15 years. With the 1995 edition, the first edition with Peter as editor, the *Almanac* became available on the retail market through bookstore and newsstand sales. The primary outlet of sales, however, continued to be businesses that purchased the *Almanac* as a promotional giveaway. Following his father's lead, Peter has raised campaigns of his own in the pages of the *Almanac,* including writing a "Patient's Bill of Rights" to combat doctors who routinely keep patients waiting and a call to change the date of traditional Halloween festivities to the last Saturday in October in order to promote a more family-oriented holiday.

Gene and Peter Geiger have steadily expanded the company and solidified its standing as an industry leader. When they joined Geiger in 1973, annual sales stood at $8 million, and the company had a sales force of approximately 75. In 2002, Geiger sales totaled $119 million, with over 400 sales representatives. The *Farmers' Almanac,* which is sold through the company's Time By Design division, represents 14 percent of that division's sale but only 0.9 percent of overall company sales. While the core of the company's business is through the marketing and distribution of promotional products, Geiger also distinguishes itself as a manufacturer. As Gene asserts on the company web site, "During the last 30 years, we developed a capacity and capability for making world-class, quality planners, diaries and calendars. In our category, we have no U.S. competitors, only European and Asian ones. We have survived and prospered because we have consistently invested in ourselves—people, equipment and product development—and have sought new markets both within our industry and beyond."

Principal Subsidiaries

Crestline; GeigerDonnelly Marketing LLC.

Principal Competitors

Old Farmer's Almanac.

Further Reading

"Almanac Editor Stages Own Funeral," *Portland Press Herald*, December 8, 1990, p. 3C.

"Almanac Publisher's Push Lost to Stroke," *Portland Press Herald*, September 18, 1985, p. 9.

Austin, Phyllis, "Old Almanac Takes Poke at Pollution," *Portland Evening Express*, September 20, 1971, pp. 1, 12.

"Farmers' Almanac: Get out Parka, Shovel," *USA Today*, August 8, 2002.

Gabriel, Angela, "Geiger Buys Holt," *Business Journal—Serving Phoenix and the Valley of the Sun*, January 21, 2000, p. 14.

"Geiger Bros. Buy Bandrich of Puerto Rico," *Portland Press Herald*, August 12, 1972, p. 2.

"Geiger Bros. Purchases NYC Firm," *Portland Press Herald*, January 9, 1980, p. 17.

Harkavy, Jerry, "Farmers' Almanac Pushing $1 Coin," *Portland Evening Express*, September 12, 1989, p. 34.

——, "Farmers' Almanac Would Retrieve Friendly Postmark," *Portland Press Herald*, September 25, 1974, p. 3.

——, "Geiger's Still 'Popping Corn,' " *Portland Evening Express*, September 28, 1983, p. 30.

——, "Hugging Definitely 'In,' " *Portland Evening Express*, September 7, 1984, p. 44.

Kinnicutt, Michael T., "King of Cornography," *Down East*, November 1980, pp. 49–52, 79–82.

——, "Oh, Say Will You Choose?," *Portland Evening Express*, September 5, 1986, p. 8.

Lukas, Paul, "The Farmers' Almanac Is Chock Full of Facts and Still Thriving in the Age of the Net," *Fortune*, June 25, 2001.

Morrison, Kenneth H., "147 Years Old, Lewiston-Edited Almanac Producing Offspring Now," *Portland Sunday Telegram*, September 26, 1965, p. 18A.

Naujeck, Jeanne A., "Farmers' Almanac Signs on as 'Opry' Sponsor," *Tennessean*, July 18, 2003, p. E1.

Scanlin, Mike, "The Calendar—An Industry All Its Own," *Portland Press Herald*, January 5, 1973, p. 17.

Smith, Jeff, "A Down-Home Big Business," *Maine Sunday Telegram*, March 22, 1987, pp. 1C, 3C.

Stevens, Emery, "Publishers Girding to Wage 'Battle of Almanacs'," *Portland Press Herald*, February 9, 1979, pp. 1, 8.

"Tired of Waiting?," *Trustee*, October 1996, p. 6.

"What's in a Name?," *Portland Evening Express*, April 20, 1982, p. 5.

—Elizabeth Henry

George P. Johnson Company

3600 Giddings Road
Auburn Hills, Michigan 43826
U.S.A.
Telephone: (248) 475-2500
Fax: (248) 475-2324
Web site: http://www.gpjco.com

Private Company
Incorporated: 1914
Employees: 1,000
Sales: $300 million (2003 est.)
NAIC: 541850 Display Advertising; 541613 Marketing
   Consulting Services

The George P. Johnson Company (GPJ) is one of the world's leading event marketing firms. The company is best known for the many eye-catching displays it has created for the North American International Auto Show in Detroit, but in recent years it has expanded internationally and gained new, nonautomotive clients like IBM and Samsung. The privately held firm has production facilities in Auburn Hills, Michigan; Torrance, California; and Stuttgart, Germany, as well as offices on both U.S. coasts and in Europe and Asia. GPJ produces more than 4,000 events each year.

Early Years

The George P. Johnson Co. was founded in 1914 by its namesake in Detroit, Michigan as a flag-making and sail-repair shop. George Johnson, age 25, had been involved with the Detroit Auto Show as early as 1910, and his new company continued to do work for the auto industry's annual exhibits of new vehicles. Over the following decades Johnson also began to produce banners, flags, and bunting for parade floats and special exhibits. As displays at the Auto Show became more and more elaborate, the company established itself as one of their leading creators.

In 1956 GPJ helped produce the first International Auto Show in New York, and in 1961 the firm introduced the first vehicle display turntable, which soon became a staple of such events. The company also had Detroit's Woodward Avenue "paved with gold" to help celebrate the auto industry's 50th anniversary.

In 1976 Johnson's grandson Robert G. Vallee, Jr., began working for the company, and two years later he was appointed head of production. In 1980, in his new job of account executive, he was assigned American Honda, one of the first foreign carmakers with which the company had worked. In 1985 the growing GPJ opened an office in Los Angeles, and with Vallee's help the new unit gained assignments from important clients like Toyota and Nissan. Because of the increasing amount of work it was doing on the West Coast, in 1989 GPJ built a second production facility there. The company was now beginning to attract clients outside of the automotive industry, and also was working to develop its consulting capabilities.

Expansion to Europe in 1995

The early 1990s saw GPJ open new offices in Boston, Chicago, and Seattle, and also win the account of Chrysler International. The latter assignment led the firm to open its first European office in Brussels, Belgium in 1995. That same year saw the formation of the Rutchik Group in Boston, which designed interiors for chain restaurants like Boston Market and Burger King. By now GPJ's annual revenues had grown to more than $100 million, and the company employed between 300 and 500, depending on seasonal needs.

The year 1996 saw many changes for the firm. In March its main headquarters and production operation were moved from Madison Heights, Michigan to a new 300,000-square-foot facility in the Detroit suburb of Auburn Hills. In addition to administrative, sales, and design offices, the new building included a 36,000-square-foot state-of-the-art paint shop and 100,000 square feet of warehouse space to store client exhibits. A few months later GPJ also opened a new office in San Jose, California to serve the growing exhibition needs of Silicon Valley. New contracts were soon won with Cisco Systems, Siebel, and Intel. Also during the year Robert Vallee, Jr., by now the firm's president, gained the additional title of CEO.

GPJ's clients now included 40 different *Fortune* 500 companies, and although 90 percent of sales was still derived from the auto industry the firm was actively seeking to diversify. Major accounts included General Motors, Chrysler, Frigidaire, Sunrise Medical Co., and Warner Brothers.

The company's highest profile activity continued to be the creation of eye-popping displays for the introduction of new vehicles, however. Carmakers traveled to as many as 150 auto shows around the United States each year, and spent $1–$3 million approximately every three years for a new display. Each one was custom-made and incorporated the latest developments in attention-grabbing technology like simulated-motion and virtual reality. The largest displays were more than 10,000 square feet in size and were constructed in modules that could be configured to fit the space in which they were assembled.

Winning IBM's Worldwide Account in 1998

In June of 1998 GPJ scored a major coup when it was selected by IBM to perform all of the computer maker's exhibition management services worldwide. IBM had worked previously with more than 50 different agencies, but, seeking to cut costs, awarded the entire account to GPJ. The $40 million assignment would add more than 1,000 business shows and events to the company's schedule. The year 1998 also saw GPJ form a strategic alliance with National Commerce Bank Services to begin designing bank branches for location inside supermarkets and retail stores.

In 1999 the company's offerings for the recently renamed North American International Auto Show (NAIAS) in Detroit included a 42,000-square-foot exhibit for Chrysler, Plymouth, and Jeep that utilized a two-tiered structure, a rotating turntable suspended above the floor, and telescopes that visitors could peer through to see cars, videos, graphics, and company awards. Subaru's GPJ-built entry depicted a Pennsylvania forest on a spring day and included trees, a waterfall, and a pond. Scent machines and sound effects completed the illusion. Other exhibits were constructed for Cadillac, Honda/Acura, Saturn, Toyota, Nissan/Infiniti, and Saab, whose display used 60 tons of ice that was kept intact for 22 days with a massive, custom-designed cooling system.

In March of 1999 GPJ bought a majority stake in Raumtechnik Messebau GmbH of Stuttgart, Germany, which was subsequently renamed Raumtechnik Messebau & Event Marketing GmbH. The newly acquired firm, which had 100 employees and $18 million in annual sales, had a long history of executing trade shows and events for clients like Bosch, DaimlerChrysler, and Zeiss. Just two months later GPJ bought a minority stake in Project Worldwide, a London-based creative

communications agency with 35 employees and $14 million in annual sales. Both of these moves were made to help the firm service its IBM account. The year also saw GPJ triple the size of its California facility in the L.A. suburb of Torrance and consolidate three separate offices there into a single 170,000-square-foot building.

For the 2000 NAIAS the firm once again built exhibits for many of the participating companies, adding Audi and Lexus to the ten it had worked for the previous year. One of the show's highlights was Chrysler's exhibit, which featured live performances by the acrobatic troupe Artistry in Motion. In April GPJ bought a large stake in Conference Planners of Burlingame, California, a 20-year-old provider of event management and web-based registration services.

The year 2001 saw the firm build an exhibit for the Camp Jeep Celebration in Virginia, which featured the largest free-flying American flag ever displayed. The 160- by 90-foot flag was suspended from a construction crane at the event, which saw the launch of the new Jeep Liberty.

Going Down Under in 2001

In September of 2001 GPJ acquired an Australian company called Designtroupe, which was the leading event marketing agency in the Asia-Pacific region. It had offices in Sydney and Singapore. Two months later the firm also reached an agreement with Shobiz, Inc. of India to form a joint venture that would serve clients in its region. By this time GPJ also had opened offices in Milan, Paris, and Tokyo.

A study sponsored by the firm in the fall found that nearly half of the companies surveyed felt that event marketing yielded a better return on investment than advertising or sales promotion. More than a third of the participants also stated that they would increase their budget in this category by an average of 23 percent the next year.

The 2002 NAIAS featured another set of dramatic displays from GPJ including Toyota's ''Mediascape,'' a multimedia show with a musical score that emphasized the firm's new ''Get The Feeling'' tagline. In July the company formed a joint venture in China with Highteam Public Relations Co. Ltd. of Beijing, an event marketing firm with 110 employees and offices in three cities. It was one of the top ten firms of its type in the country. The venture, which was named George P. Johnson - HighTeam Event Marketing Company Limited, would provide services for such clients as IBM and Nissan.

In the fall of 2002 GPJ launched a mobile marketing campaign for the new Saturn ION. Four 50-foot trailers, which contained interactive video games, vehicle displays, tenting, and inflatable marketing displays, would be deployed at events like college football games and concerts. They would spend 40 weeks touring the United States. The firm had earlier used an inflatable Dodge Ram Pickup truck at a 23-concert Aerosmith tour, and also created Jeep Liberty and Chrysler PT Cruiser dirigibles for use at other events.

In November of 2002 the company helped execute a marketing conference for Samsung at the Chateau de Versailles near Paris for which a special projection screen and stage were

Key Dates:

1914: George P. Johnson Co. is established in Detroit to repair sails and make flags.
1910s: Johnson begins doing work for Detroit Auto Shows.
1956: Johnson works on its first international auto show in New York.
1985: The company opens a new office in Los Angeles.
1989: A second production facility is added in L.A.
1992: The company wins the account of Chrysler International.
1996: A new headquarters is built in Auburn Hills, Michigan; Robert Vallee, Jr., is named CEO.
1998: Johnson wins IBM's worldwide event marketing account.
1999: The company acquires Raumtechnik of Stuttgart, Germany.
2000: A stake is bought in Conference Planners of California.
2001: Designtroupe is acquired.

installed at the historic palace. The year also saw GPJ join with others in the event marketing industry to form a trade group called the Event & Experience Marketing Council. One of its initial tasks would be the development of tools to measure the relative success of event marketing activities. By now GPJ's annual revenues had grown to top $300 million.

The 2003 NAIAS again featured a series of elaborate automotive displays from the firm, with new clients this year including Lamborghini and BMW. In April GPJ helped put on the IBM PartnerWorld conference in New Orleans for 2,500 attendees, and in June the firm's Designtroupe unit presented an Australian conference for Rotary International that featured a 131-foot projection screen and appearances by wood-chopping champion David Foster and several popular vocalists.

In June of 2003 GPJ announced a new joint event marketing venture with Mitsuya, Inc. of Japan, which would employ 50. It took the place of the firm's Tokyo office, which had been opened in April of 2000. A new survey of corporations co-sponsored by the company found that the number of events in which they participated was increasing, with this growth particularly evident in the healthcare and automotive industries. By now half of GPJ's client base was drawn from nonautomotive companies such as IBM, Siebel, MGM, Cisco Systems, and PeopleSoft. During the year the firm was named one of the top 25 marketing agencies in the world by *Advertising Age* magazine.

As it neared a century in business, the George P. Johnson Co. was experiencing its greatest growth ever. The firm's historic dependence on the auto industry had abated as new contracts were won from companies in a variety of other industries. As corporations increasingly turned to events to market their products, the company's position as one of the world's leading providers of event marketing services placed it in a strong position for continued success.

Principal Subsidiaries

Raumtechnik Messebau & Event Marketing GmbH (Germany); Rutchik Group; Juice Creative; The George P. Johnson Company—Designtroupe (Australia); George P. Johnson—HighTeam Event Marketing Company Limited (China; joint venture); George P. Johnson Japan (Japan; joint venture).

Principal Competitors

Exhibitgroup/Giltspur, Inc.; The Freeman Companies; MediaLive International, Inc.; Jack Morton Worldwide; Edelman.

Further Reading

Fitzgerald, Kate, "Event Marketing Seeks Measurement: Trade Group Formed to Discuss a System to Rate ROI for Events," *Advertising Age,* September 2, 2002, p. 6.

Fletcher, Mike, "Report Uncovers Marketing Switch to Standalone Events," *Marketing Event,* May 20, 2003, p. 6.

Gargaro, Paul, "Exhibiting Headway: Johnson Co. Plans to Rake in New Clients," *Crain's Detroit Business,* December 2, 1996, p. 3.

Geist, Laura Clark, "Event Marketing Reigns Supreme: Survey Reveals Special Promotions Reap Best Rewards," *Automotive News,* December 10, 2001, p. M2.

Johnson, Bradley, "IBM Consolidates Trade Show Duties at One Event Agency," *Advertising Age,* June 8, 1998, p. 51.

"U.S. Motor-Show Coordinator to Launch Venture with Mitsuya," *Nikkei Weekly,* June 2, 2003.

—Frank Uhle

Greg Manning Auctions, Inc.

775 Passaic Avenue
West Caldwell, New Jersey 07006
U.S.A.
Telephone: (973) 882-0004
Toll Free: (800) 221-0243
Fax: (973) 882-3499
Web site: http://www.gregmanning.com

Public Company
Founded: 1966 as The Greg Manning Company
Employees: 64 (2003)
Sales: $118 million (2003)
Stock Exchanges: NASDAQ
Ticker Symbol: GMAI
NAIC: 541990 All Other Professional, Scientific, and
    Technical Services

One of the world's most important auction houses for stamps, Greg Manning Auctions, Inc. (GMAI), is also a major auctioneer of coins, sports cards, movie posters, comic books, and other specialty collectibles. Greg Manning does business across the price spectrum but focuses on high-end specialty markets where its expertise and customer service can serve to differentiate the company from the competition. The company has a strong presence in Europe and Asia through joint ventures in Spain and China.

Origins in the 1960s

Greg Manning began collecting stamps at the age of seven, and as a teenager he sold stamps through the mail, earning, by his account, "thousands of dollars per year." After high school, he set out to learn the auction business, realizing that auctions held more potential for profit than the lower-volume retail business. James Rasdale, of the Rasdale Stamp Company, later remembered the young Manning as "very polite, aggressive, and mature," as well as a good judge of people. In 1966, at the age of 20, he held his first public auction. By 1971, he had opened an office, and ten years later his business had grown to the point that he opened a 76,000-square-foot facility in Montville, New Jersey, to house his auctions. At the same time, he was operating a venture called International Postal Marketing, which was cited in 1981 by *Inc.* magazine as the fifth-fastest-growing private company in the United States. In 1993, Manning's ventures went public as Greg Manning Auctions, Inc. (GMAI), initiating a growth spurt fueled by a rapid series of acquisitions. Purchases including Ivy, Shreve, & Mader Philatelic Auctions; Harmer Rooke Galleries; and CEE JAY Auctions. Although GMAI branched out into auctioning sports cards and other collectibles, stamps remained its focus. The company stockpiled a huge inventory and carved out a niche selling major collections in their entirety, with the quality and enormous volume of material attracting dealers from all over the world. In 1994, GMAI auctioned a collection of envelopes printed with illustrations for $330,000, which was believed to be the largest sum ever paid for an individual stamp collection sold as a whole. The company's aggregate sales for the year rose to $27 million. By 1995, GMAI had 32 employees, a new facility in West Caldwell, New Jersey, and a second office in Manhattan. Manning himself was recognized as one of the world's leading authorities on stamps.

Establishing a Presence on the Web and throughout the World

In 1998, GMAI moved into electronic auctions by purchasing Teletrade, Inc., an auction house that sold diamonds on the Web and by touchtone telephone, for $6 million. Teletrade's technology allowed customers to bid by computer or telephone keypad; their bids registered directly on the auctioneer's computer. Suddenly perceived as an Internet company, GMAI saw its stock leap from $2 to $21 per share. Within six months, Web sales accounted for more than 50 percent of GMAI revenue. In 1999, the company launched a partnership with the online auctioneer eBay. Daily auctions of GMAI goods were held on eBay's site, which boasted 3.8 million registered bidders. Unlike eBay, which bought buyers and sellers together but otherwise stayed aloof from transactions, GMAI continued to serve as a full-service intermediary for its clients, collecting payments, delivering purchases, and serving as a guarantor of authenticity. The company's offerings had expanded to include diamonds (via the Teletrade purchase), movie posters, music memorabilia, fine art, and coins.

Moving into the global market, the company held a 50 percent interest in GMAI-Asia.com, a Chinese Web auctioneer.

Key Dates:

1966: The Greg Manning Company is founded.
1981: The company opens a 76,000-square-foot facility.
1993: Greg Manning Auctions, Inc. (GMAI) goes public.
1994: Sales reach $27 million.
1998: GMAI buys Teletrade and launches an Internet presence; the company's stock price increases tenfold.
1999: GMAI announces an alliance with eBay and buys Spectrum Numismatics.
2000: GMAI's joint venture with eBay is terminated, and the company rejects a purchase offer from Take to Auction.com.
2001: GMAI re-incorporates under Delaware state laws.
2003: The company makes significant international acquisitions; sales reach $118 million.

The explosion of Web users in China served the company well: within one month, said Manning, "We had 10,000 registered users." At the same time, the Chinese market posed interesting challenges. Customers were accustomed to using cash, not credit; shipping was expensive; and shoppers were unused to making purchases sight unseen. GMAI-Asia.com worked around these obstacles by establishing kiosks where customers could place an order, then return several days later to examine and retrieve their purchases. Plans were laid for an additional partnership in Spain, to be called GMAI-Europe.com. In late 1999, GMAI acquired Spectrum Numismatics International, a leading coin wholesaler, for $25 million in stock. Spectrum Numismatics sold coins to auction houses and Internet distributors. Sales for the fiscal year rose to $39.6 million.

In early 2000, GMAI discontinued its partnership with eBay in favor of online retailer Amazon.com, citing disappointment with marketing for its eBay site and vowing to take joint responsibility for aggressively marketing the new venture to Amazon's 17 million registered customers. In August, the company received an unsolicited purchase offer from Take to Auction.com, a much smaller Web auctioneer, which offered $14 a share, or $140 million, in stock. The offer was rejected as too low by the GMAI board, which expressed optimism about its own prospects for growth. In December, GMAI announced the purchase of certain assets of World's Finest Comics and Collectibles, a dealer in comic books and art as well as movie posters and Disney collectibles. The Disney memorabilia alone was valued at $1 million.

In 2001, GMAI shareholders approved a plan to re-incorporate the company in Delaware to take advantage of the state's pro-business legal climate. In 2003, GMAI announced plans for a series of international acquisitions, including majority interests in Corinphila Auktionen of Switzerland, the Kohler group of auction houses in Germany, and Spanish auction house Auctentia Subastas. GMAI also announced its first major philatelic auction in Hong Kong.

Financial Strength as a Platform for Growth

By the end of the first quarter of fiscal year 2004 (which ended in September 2003), GMAI's aggregate sales had increased to $41.3 million for the quarter, a 41 percent increase over the previous year. Revenue was up 36 percent, to $34.5 million, and net income stood at $2.5 million, a company record. GMAI's forecast for the year's aggregate sales was pegged at $165 million, up from $118 million in 2003. Board Chairman Esteban Perez noted that GMAI's recent acquisitions had already had a decisive impact on results and revealed that the company was investigating a listing on Spain's Bolsa market in addition to its NASDAQ listing. As Perez stated, "We view fiscal 2004 as a platform for the future growth of GMAI, and as we further integrate our companies we fully expect that the synergies we have already achieved can only be beneficial to our long-term growth."

Principal Subsidiaries

Ivy and Mader Philatelic Auctions, Inc.; Greg Manning Galleries, Inc.; Teletrade Inc.; Spectrum Numismatics International, Inc.; Kensington Associates L.L.C.; Auctentia Subastas S.L. (Spain); Kohler Group (Germany); Corinphila Auktionen AG (Switzerland); GMAI-Auctentia Central de Compras, S.L. (Spain).

Principal Competitors

Matthew Bennett, Inc.; Charles Shreve Galleries, Inc.; H.R. Harmer; Robert A. Siegel Auction Galleries, Inc.; Butterfields & Butterfields Auctioneers, Inc.; Sotheby's Holdings, Inc.; Christie's Inc.; eBay, Inc.; Yahoo!, Inc.; Interactive Collector, Inc. (d/b/a iCollector.com); Collectors Universe, Inc.; Sothebys.com, Inc.

Further Reading

"An Auctioneer Rejects Takeover Offer, *New York Times*, September 13, 2000, p. C18.
"Another Venture in Art Auctions for Ebay," *New York Times*, July 15, 1999, p. C8.
Bensinger, Ken, "Take to Auction.com Offers $141 for Manning Firm," *Wall Street Journal*, August 28, 2000, p. 1.
Fitzgerald, Beth, "West Caldwell-Based Online Auctioneer Going into More Detail," *Star-Ledger* (Newark, N.J.), December 17, 1998.
——, "New Jersey-Based Auctioneer's Future Spinning on Deal with Ebay," *Star-Ledger* (Newark), July 14, 1999.
——, "Amazon.com Acquires New Jersey Partners Paying Fees for Access," *Star-Ledger* (Newark), February 8, 2000.
——, "Auction House Doing Some Buying of Its Own," *Star-Ledger* (Newark), March 25, 2003, p. 34.
Goldblatt, Dan, "Reinventing an Auction House," *Business News New Jersey*, November 29, 1999, p. 8.
"Greg Manning Auctions Inc.: ING Barings Will Explore Acquisitions and Mergers," *Wall Street Journal*, June 6, 2000, p. 1.
"Greg Manning Discusses the Market for Collectibles and the Changing Art of Auctioneering," *Business News New Jersey*, June 23, 1997, p. 11.
Jusko, Jill, "'Net Changes Stripes for China," *Industry Week*, May 15, 2000, p. 14.
Lasseter, Diana G., "A Small Postage Stamp Means Big Business," *Business News New Jersey*, September 20, 1995, p. 14.
"Take to Auction.Com Makes Offer for Greg Manning," *New York Times*, August 26, 2000. p. C3.
"$2.6 Realized at Greg Manning Auction," *Stamps*, July 31, 1993, p. 132.

—Paula Kepos

Groupe Bourbon S.A.

La Mare
97438 Sainte Marie, Réunion
Réunion Island
France
Telephone: (+262) 262-53-24-00
Fax: (+262) 262-53-24-01
Web site: http://www.groupe-bourbon.com

Public Company
Incorporated: 1948 as Sucreries de Bourbon
Employees: 7,644
Sales: EUR 940 million ($985.7 million)(2002)
Stock Exchanges: Euronext Paris
Ticker Symbol: GBB
NAIC: 488330 Navigational Services to Shipping;
    483211 Inland Water Freight Transportation; 488320
    Marine Cargo Handling; 445110 Supermarkets and
    Other Grocery (Except Convenience) Stores; 424410
    General Line Grocery Merchant Wholesalers; 424420
    Packaged Frozen Food Merchant Wholesalers; 452111
    Department Stores (Except Discount Department
    Stores); 483111 Deep Sea Freight Transportation

Former sugar cane producer Groupe Bourbon S.A. has refocused itself at the beginning of the 2000s to concentrate on two core divisions: Maritime and Retail Distribution. The group's Maritime division is rapidly becoming a major shipping force with a specialty in four areas: Towing, Offshore Towing and Salvage, Offshore Services, and Dry Bulk Transport. Towing, chiefly through subsidiary Les Abeilles, is Bourbon Maritime's largest operation, providing tug and related port services in most of France's ports as well as in the Indian Ocean and South Atlantic. Related company, Les Abeilles International, provides towing, salvage, and shore-line protection services for the offshore market, principally in the English Channel. The group's Offshore operations focus on the deepwater market in West Africa, the Gulf of Mexico, and, through Bourbon's 50 percent stake in Delba Maritime, in Brazil. The company's Dry Bulk Transport division operates under subsidiary Setaf-Saget, which has been rebuilding

its fleet to focus on 40,000-ton-plus handy-max vessels. If Groupe Bourbon intends to become exclusively a shipping company by 2010, it remains for the time being the major retail distribution group on Réunion Island, operating four Cora branded shopping malls and 15 Score supermarkets under subsidiary Vindémia. The company is also the leading retailer in Mauritius, and has a strong presence in Madagascar, Vietnam, and Mayotte. The company expects to operate more than 100,000 square meters of selling space by 2005, 50 percent of which will be outside Réunion. Nonetheless, Groupe Bourbon expects to exit the retail market and has already sold a 33 percent stake in Vindémia to French retail giant Casino, which is expected to acquire the remainder by 2007. Groupe Bourbon is led by Jacques de Chateauvieux and is listed on the Euronext Paris Stock Exchange.

Uniting Réunion's Sugar Growers in the 1940s

Prior to World War II, the sugar cane industry on Réunion Island, one of France's overseas departments, had been fragmented among a number of small, family-owned sugar-producer plantations, or "sucreries." However, the need to rebuild the cane industry's infrastructure following the war brought together a number of families, including the Hulot and de Chateauvieux families. In 1948, these families founded Sucreries de Bourbon, merging their holdings and beginning a modernization of their production facilities.

Sucreries de Bourbon remained close to its specialty, producing sugar and rum for the French market. By the late 1970s, the group emerged as the leading sugar-producer on Réunion Island. Nonetheless, with sales of just FFr44 million, Bourbon remained a tiny player in the global market. At that time, there were still some eight sugar production facilities located around the island.

Faced with heavy competition and fixed European sugar prices, Bourbon turned to Jacques de Chateauvieux, son of one of the company's founders, to lead it into a new era. Born on Réunion, educated largely in France, and holding an MBA from Columbia University, Jacques de Chateauvieux left his job at the Boston Consulting Group to take over Bourbon. The young de Chateauvieux, then just 28 years old, led the group on a

Key Dates:

1948: Several Réunion Island sugar cane producers merge to form Sucrerie de Bourbon.

1978: Jacques de Chateauvieux takes over as company head and begins restructuring, reducing the number of sugar refineries.

1989: Bourbon decides to diversify, acquiring professional fishing operations.

1991: Bourbon diversifies into retail distribution, acquiring its first supermarket in Réunion.

1992: The company enters the maritime services market by acquiring a controlling stake in Marseilles-based Compagnie Chambon; Bourbon also begins food production operations.

1994: The company begins developing international retail operations with the opening of its first store in Madagascar.

1996: Groupe Bourbon acquires French port towing and services leader Les Abeilles, which absorbs Chambon, then acquires Sociéte de Provençale; Bourbon acquires dry bulk transport specialist Setaf-Saget.

1998: Groupe Bourbon goes public with a listing on Euronext Paris Stock Exchange's secondary market.

2000: Bourbon decides to refocus on retailing and maritime services, selling off its food production businesses.

2001: Restructuring of the company continues with the sale of its last remaining sugar refinery, the acquisition of 50 percent of Brazilian deepwater offshore specialists Delba Maritime, and a move to exit retail distribution by 2007.

2002: The company enters the Gulf of Mexico market with an agreement to supply ten offshore support vessels to its partner Rigdon Marine.

restructuring drive over the next decade, shutting down six of its sugar refineries and refocusing production on two European-grade plants.

By the end of the 1980s, however, the company was caught between rising production costs on the one hand and fixed European sugar prices on the other, making it unable to compete effectively against its far larger adversaries. Instead, Bourbon decided to diversify into other industries, starting with a move into the professional fishing market in 1989 and the development of operations involving lobster fishing and line fishing for larger fish species.

The company remained focused on its Réunion Island home for its next venture as well, when it acquired its first retail operation on the island in 1991. Over the next decade, the group developed into Réunion's leading supermarket group, acquiring the franchises for the Cora and Score retail formats. By the end of the 1990s, Groupe Bourbon had opened four Cora shopping malls and 15 Score supermarkets across the island. In support of its retail growth, the group also began developing a food production component, producing a variety of foods, including dairy foods starting in 1992, for sale in its retail network.

Maritime Specialist for the New Century

International expansion, however, held increasing interest for Groupe Bourbon in the 1990s. In 1994, the company made its first venture into the International retail market, opening a Cora hypermarket in Madagascar. The company followed that successful expansion with the opening of a supermarket in Vietnam in 1995. By the end of the decade, Bourbon's retail empire had extended into Mayotte, also known as the Comoro Islands, and in 2001 the group became the leading retailer on the island of Mauritius as well. By then, the company's diversified activities overshadowed its historic sugar refining operation, and in 2001 the group sold off its last sugar refinery.

Instead, Bourbon's attention had been captured by a much different activity: maritime services. Bourbon's introduction to that market came in the early 1990s, when the group's auditor had alerted de Chateauavieux that another customer, family-controlled Compagnie Chambon, was looking for a new shareholder. Chambon had been providing towing and other port services for the port of Marseilles since 1873, adding offshore rescue and salvage services in the 1930s, and had grown largely through absorbing other Marseilles-based tugboat companies and thereby becoming one of the port's two main operators. In 1971, Chambon formed a partnership, Société de Remorquage Portuaire et d'Assistance en Méditerranée (SRPAM), with its chief rival, Société Provençale de Remorquage, founded in 1899.

Bourbon bought a majority stake in Chambon in 1992. The purchase represented the group's first venture into the mainland French market. If Bourbon's entry into maritime services had come somewhat by chance, de Chateauavieux quickly recognized the potential for growth in its new market. In addition to its Marseilles-based port activities, Chambon had also developed a small operation in West Africa, providing personnel transport and other support services for the Elf petroleum group's offshore oil platforms there. Chambon had built up a small fleet of so-called high-speed "surfer" craft, as well as supply vessels. However, as Elf prepared to venture into the deeper offshore waters, it required a new class of support vessel. Bourbon quickly met the challenge, adding three new 1,400 gt supply vessels to its fleet that were capable of providing deepwater support to the new Elf platforms.

The move gave Bourbon good early experience in the new and fast-growing deepwater offshore market, and over the next decade the company added eight more large-scale supply ships. As de Chateauavieux explained in *Europe Intelligence Wire:* "The competition is still fragmented. Everyone thinks they can become a deep offshore major but not everyone has taken the measure of what needs to be done to do this." Bourbon's early move into the market not only gave it the experience, it also led it to target the sector as one of its core growth areas for the new century.

In the meantime, Bourbon continued to build up its Maritime Division. In 1996, the company took a major step forward into its transformation to a shipping group when it acquired France's Les Abeilles. That company had originated in the northern port of Le Havre in 1864, and, through a series of acquisitions, including Union des Remorqueurs de l'Ocean and Progremar, had grown into one of France's leading port tugboat and towing services provider. Following its takeover by Bourbon, Abeilles absorbed the operations of Compagnie Chambon, then acquired SRPAM partner Société Provençale.

The new Abeilles now became France's leading towing and port services operator. At the same time, Bourbon spun off its international and deepwater offshore services operations into a new subsidiary, Les Abeilles International, and was busy integrating another new shipping acquisition, that of Setaf-Saget. Founded in 1968, Setaf-Saget represented yet another new shipping market for Groupe Bourbon, that of the dry bulk transport market.

Bourbon went public in 1998, listing on the Euronext Paris Stock Exchange's secondary market. By 2000, Bourbon's shipping revenues were growing rapidly and already represented one-third of the group's total annual sales of more than EUR 1.1 billion. In that year, however, the company undertook a strategic review with an eye toward boosting value for its shareholders, who included, in addition to the de Chateauavieux family, some 200 other Réunion-based shareholders. As a result of that review, the company decided to refocus around a dual core of retail distribution and maritime services.

By the end of 2000, the company had already sold of its dairy foods unit, with plans to dispose of the rest of that division soon after. Also to go was the group's last remaining sugar refinery, sold in 2001. Then, at the end of that year, Bourbon signaled the start of the next phase of its restructuring—an exit from the retail sector. That process was begun with the sale of a one-third stake in Vindémia to French retail giant Casino. Although Bourbon remained in control of its retail operations, and continued to expand the division not only within Réunion but internationally as well, the agreement with Casino gave Bourbon the right to exercise an option whereby Casino would acquire all of Vindémia. That step was expected to come as early as 2007.

With the sell-off of the retail group, Bourbon expected to become a pure-play shipping group. As part of its effort to take a place among the majors in the maritime services market, especially in the fast-growing deepwater sector, Bourbon acquired a 50 percent stake in Brazilian deepwater specialist Delba Maritime, expanding the company's operations into South America. That purchase also brought the company closer to the lucrative Gulf of Mexico market. In 2002, the group formed a partnership with Rigdon Marine, with Bourbon agreeing to build ten oil platform supply ships for use by Rigdon Marine in the Gulf. The company expected the first delivery phase to be completed by 2004 and the entire delivery to be fulfilled in 2005.

Groupe Bourbon continued to look for opportunities for expansion in the international maritime market. In 2002, the group took control of Norway's Island Offshore II, with a 51 percent stake. The company then acquired 25 percent (later boosted to 39 percent) of fellow Island Offshore shareholder Havilas Supply. In 2003, the group reached a further agreement with one of Havilas's institutional shareholders to acquire majority control of Havilas by 2006, thereby boosting its control of Island Offshore itself. These deals were initially meant to give Bourbon an entrance into the offshore market in the Nordic region; yet the acquisition of Island Offshore also strengthened the group's operations in the booming West African offshore market.

The refocused Bourbon group now boasted revenues of EUR 940 million, with its shipping operations accounting for 38 percent of those sales. While France (Réunion Island is considered a part of France) remained the company's core market, international operations had already reached 39 percent of the group's total sales. Bourbon continued to seek new maritime expansion activities as it set sail for a leading position in the fast-growing offshore services market.

Principal Subsidiaries

Antilles Trans; Armement Sapmer Distribution; Bourbon Brazil Participacoes; Bourbon Maritime; Chambon Offshore International; Compagnie Financière De Bourbon; Island Offshore A S (Norway); Les Abeilles International SA; Les Abeilles SA; Sapmer; Setaf Saget SA; Sonasurf (Angola); Surf SA.

Principal Competitors

Exel PLC; Kawasaki Kisen Kaisha Ltd.; Alghanim Industries; Wagenborg Shipping B.V.; Serco Group PLC; HAL Investments B.V.; Royal Boskalis Westminster N.V.; Arkhangelsk Seaport Joint Stock Co.; International Marine Services.

Further Reading

"Le Groupe Bourbon ouvre son 1ᵉʳ magasin à Hanoi," *Reuters*, October 6, 2000.
"Jumbo Score: le groupe Bourbon renforce sa présence avec un troisième hypermarché dans le sud,"
Business Mag-Online, August 27, 2003.
"The Path Less Taken Has Proved the Right Choice," *Europe Intelligence Wire*, Oct 15, 2002.
Spurrier, Andrew, "Bourbon in Plan for 10 US Platform Supply Ships," *Europe Intelligence Wire*, October 8, 2002
"Supply Boat Market Requires Investment in New Tonnage," *Offshore*, May 2003, p. 106.

—M.L. Cohen

Groupe Louis Dreyfus S.A.

87 avenue de la Grande Armee
F-75782 Paris Cedex 16
France
Telephone: (+33) 40-66-11-11
Fax: (+33) 45-01-70-28
Web site: http://www.louisdreyfus.com

Private Company
Incorporated: 1851
Employees: 10,000
Sales: EUR 20 billion ($22 billion) (2003 est.)
NAIC: 483111 Deep Sea Freight Transportation; 424490
    Other Grocery and Related Product Merchant
    Wholesalers; 424510 Grain and Field Bean Merchant
    Wholesalers; 424590 Other Farm Product Raw
    Material Merchant Wholesalers; 424690 Other
    Chemical and Allied Products Merchant Wholesalers;
    424720 Petroleum and Petroleum Products Merchant
    Wholesalers (Except Bulk Stations and Terminals);
    483112 Deep Sea Passenger Transportation; 483113
    Coastal and Great Lakes Freight Transportation;
    523130 Commodity Contracts Dealing; 424720
    Petroleum and Petroleum Products Merchant
    Wholesalers (Except Bulk Stations and Terminals);
    483111 Deep Sea Freight Transportation; 483113
    Coastal and Great Lakes Freight Transportation;
    531120 Lessors of Nonresidential Buildings (Except
    Miniwarehouses)

Groupe Louis Dreyfus S.A. is one of the world's largest, family-owned, diversified conglomerates, with interests ranging from grain and other agricultural commodities, to shipping, gas and petroleum refining and marketing, property development, and telecommunications. Commodities trading represents the group's historic core—Louis Dreyfus remains one of the world's leading grains traders—and, in addition to wheat, includes such commodities as cocoa, coffee, cotton, rice, sugar, and oilseeds. In addition to these trading interests, the group is also one of the world's leading producers of orange juice, with

operations spanning more than 25,000 acres of Brazilian orange groves, and processing facilities in Brazil and Florida. With a total orange juice concentrate production of 250,000 tons, Louis Dreyfus holds 10 percent of the global market. The company has been in the global shipping industry for some 70 years, owning and operating its own fleet through subsidiary Louis Dreyfus Armateurs, among others. At the turn of the century, the group's fleet included 26 ships and 21 floating cranes, tugs, and barges. Louis Dreyfus's entry into the gas and petroleum markets came in the early 1970s; once focused primarily on the United States, the group's interests in this business has shifted to its Wilhelmshaven, Germany, refinery, which boasts a daily capacity of more than 220,000 barrels. The group is also active in property development, controlling more than eight million square feet of primarily office space throughout North America and Europe. The group's property holdings include a share in the Four Seasons hotel in Washington, D.C. Other group holdings include a majority stake in Brazilian particleboard maker Placas and its Argentinean counterpart Faplac. One of the group's fastest-growing operations, however, is its telecommunications subsidiary LDCom Networks, which has risen to become France's number three provider of wholesale and retail telephone and broadband Internet services, through its own 11,000-kilometer fiber optic network. Louis Dreyfus remains wholly owned by the founding family, led by Gerard (William) Louis-Dreyfus and his cousin Robert Louis-Dreyfus.

Grain Trading Empire in the 19th Century

Léopold Dreyfus was born in 1833 to a farming family in Sierentz, in the French Alsace region, just a few kilometers away from Basel, Switzerland. Dreyfus began carting grain from his farm for sale in Basel when he was just 17 years old. By 1851, Dreyfus had begun trading wheat from neighboring farms as well, and in that year incorporated what is considered to be the world's first international grain trading company. Too young to work under his own name, Dreyfus originally operated under his father's, Louis Dreyfus. The younger Dreyfus later changed his surname to Louis-Dreyfus, founding one of the great French family dynasties.

The company's trading activity expanded quickly in its first decade, and in 1858 it moved its trading focus to the more

Key Dates:

1850: Léopold Dreyfus begins trading grain and incorporates the following year.

1858: Company moves trading operations to Berne, and later to Zurich.

1875: Headquarters are established in Paris following Franco-Prussian War.

1883: Futures trading begins after authorization by Liverpool Corn Trade Association.

1909: Company opens an office in Duluth, Minnesota, and begins trading durum wheat.

1911: Cotton trading begins from new operations in Brazil.

1932: A new fleet of faster ships is designed for the company.

1969: Gerard (William) Louis-Dreyfus takes over and broadens company's role from grain trader to diversified trading house.

1971: The property development market in North America and Europe is entered.

1985: Louis Dreyfus becomes one of the first to trade oil and natural gas commodities, launching Louis Dreyfus Natural Gas.

1988: Citrus plant in Brazil is acquired.

1993: Louis Dreyfus Natural Gas goes public on the New York Stock Exchange.

1996: Louis Dreyfus Citrus lists on the Paris secondary market; Louis Dreyfus Energy begins electricity commodity trading.

1998: Telecommunications subsidiary LDCom Networks is launched.

1999: Louis Dreyfus Natural Gas is sold to Dominion Resources for $1.8 billion.

2002: LDCom acquires Belgacom, 9Telecom, and KAPTECH to become one of top three French telecommunications wholesale providers.

international Berne market. From there, Louis-Dreyfus began expanding throughout Europe, buying grain in Hungary, Romania, and elsewhere in Eastern Europe to meet the fast-growing demand for wheat and other grains in Western Europe. In 1864, Louis Dreyfus (the family hyphenated the name, but the company did not) moved again, to Zurich, while extending its network of offices into France and Germany as well. The company found its permanent home a decade later, when it established its headquarters in Paris—a result of France's ceding the Alsace region to Germany after the Franco-Prussian War.

The company's expansion was further aided by a number of important developments, notably improvements in transportation with the construction of cross-continental railroad systems as well as more reliable ships. The invention of new communications methods, including the telegraph and telephone, was also an important factor in the group's growth, particularly with the deployment of the first international cables.

These developments enabled the company to grow through the use of arbitrage—buying at low prices in one area in order to sell at higher prices elsewhere—and the company proved

adept at locating new and profitable opportunities. Such was the case in 1883, after the Liverpool Corn Trade Association allowed futures trading. Louis Dreyfus became one of the first to take advantage of the ability to buy and sell simultaneously, thereby guaranteeing the company's profits.

By the turn of the century, Louis Dreyfus had grown into the world's leading grain trader, with offices throughout Europe. Russia was one of the group's primary markets, and by the outbreak of World War I, the company counted some 115 offices there. Romania nonetheless remained the group's top market, and in recognition of this the group named its first ship after the country's King Carol I.

In the years leading up World War I, Louis Dreyfus expanded beyond Europe, opening a trading office in Duluth, Minnesota, in 1909, and then establishing operations in Brazil, in 1911, where the company began trading cotton for the first time. The company also ventured into Australia, setting up an office in Melbourne in 1913. In 1915, founder Léopold Louis-Dreyfus died, turning over the family company to sons Louis and Charles. Two years later, the company faced an upheaval of a different sort, when the Soviet revolution forced the company out of Russia.

Despite its setback in Russia, the company remained the world's "King of Wheat," a position it held through the Great Depression and up to the outbreak of World War II. International expansion continued, with new markets including South Africa, where the company opened an office in 1924. At the same time, Louis Dreyfus began expanding its shipping interests. Although the company had long operated a small fleet of vessels supporting its Russian operations, the 1920s and the 1930s saw the company emerge as a major shipper in its own right. In 1932, the company traded in its fleet of eight ships for a new fleet of high-speed vessels designed and built for Louis Dreyfus under the guidance of Pierre Louis-Dreyfus, son of Charles Louis-Dreyfus. When Dreyfus died in 1940, the next generation, which also included François and Jean Louis-Dreyfus, in addition to Pierre, took over as the company's leaders.

Postwar Reconstruction

World War II devastated the company's operations, as some of the family fled to Argentina, while Pierre Louis-Dreyfus joined the Free French air force in London, flying nearly 80 missions as a tail gunner. Following the war, the group was forced to rebuild. The group once again targeted the shipping and grain trading markets. As Pierre led the reconstruction of the group's shipping fleet, adding a number of new vessels in the 1950s, Jean Louis-Dreyfus led the rebuilding of the group's grain trading operations.

The intervening years had changed the grain market, which had become much less volatile—and therefore less profitable for traders such as Louis Dreyfus. While the company's competitors, such as Continental Grain and Cargill, adapted to the changing market by adding processing and refining facilities, Louis Dreyfus clung to its image as a grain trader. As Gerard (also known as William) Louis-Dreyfus later told *Forbes*: "That was one of our major errors. We didn't expand, and it cost us our predominant place in this business. We went from being the first of the five major companies to the fifth. Our business had to be redone.''

Gerard Louis-Dreyfus, son of Pierre Louis-Dreyfus, was tapped to ''redo'' the business in the late 1960s. Raised in the United States by his American mother, the new leader of the group had adopted the American first name of William and had worked for a New York law firm since the late 1950s before being asked to join the group in 1965 by his father. In 1969, at the age of 37, William, or Gerard, Louis-Dreyfus took over as head of the company, using both his French and adopted names.

Gerard Louis-Dreyfus correctly identified his grandfather Léopold's legacy as more than just a simple grain trader—but rather an arbitrage house that should trade in a variety of commodities. Louis-Dreyfus therefore extended the group's trading activities beyond grain for the first time in 1971, with an entry into the property development market. The following year, Louis-Dreyfus took a bigger risk when he went outside the company for fresh trading expertise, hiring a team of seven commodities traders who had been working for Cook Industries, a grain and cotton trading house based in Memphis, Tennessee.

Louis-Dreyfus's gamble paid off as the company quickly expanded into new commodities areas, re-establishing itself as a leading global arbitrage house. A key feature of the ''new'' Louis Dreyfus was its ability to shift focus from markets where margins were falling—a natural consequence of the arbitrage process—to newly developing, high-margin markets. Such was the case in the mid-1980s, when the company became one of the first to launch the trading of energy products, including oil and gas, as commodities, launching subsidiary Louis Dreyfus Energy Corporation.

Diversified Conglomerate in the New Century

Louis Dreyfus's determination not to repeat the previous generation's mistakes led it on a diversification effort through the 1990s as it not only entered new trading areas, but added production operations as well. Such was the case in 1988 when the group bought an orange processing plant in Matao, Brazil. By the beginning of the 2000s, the group had expanded that business to include operations in Florida as well, with 25,000 acres of orange groves supporting processing capacity of more than 250,000 tons of orange juice concentrate per year—worth some 10 percent of the global market. Louis Dreyfus Citrus was later listed on the Paris stock exchange's secondary market in 1996. The group's diversification focus remained in Brazil, with the addition of a majority stake in Placas, a leading producer of particleboard and related lumber and forestry products and chemicals. The company added similar operations in Argentina, through its control of Faplac.

In the meantime, the company had been building a major position in the North American energy market, paying $59 million for Bogert Oil Company, based in Oklahoma, in 1990, adding an exploration and production business with proven natural gas reserves of more than 100 billion cubic feet. The company also began leasing oil storage terminals, before buying its own from Unocal in 1992, as its trading activity in that sector topped

70 million barrels per year. The rising success of the energy operations prompted management to take part of the company public, with a listing of Louis Dreyfus Natural Gas on the New York Stock Exchange in 1993. The group also sought to extend its petroleum business to the European continent, buying an unused refinery in Wilhemshaven, Germany, from Mobil for $50 million in 1990. In 2001, the company made a temporary exit from the U.S. market, selling off Louis Dreyfus Natural Gas Corporation to Dominion Resources for $1.8 billion.

In the mid-1990s, Louis Dreyfus recognized the emergence of a new commodities market, with the deregulation of the U.S. electricity market. In 1996, the group launched Louis Dreyfus Energy, becoming one of the first to trade electricity as a commodity. Three years later, the group extended its business to the rapidly deregulating European market as well, forming a commodities trading agreement with France's Electricité de France.

With annual sales routinely topping EUR 20 billion at the turn of the century, the Louis Dreyfus group was one of the few remaining family-owned dynasties that once dominated the global trading market, and the company continued to seek out new markets.

Telecommunications became one of the group's most dynamic new operational areas at the turn of the century, with the launch of LDCom Networks in 1998. LDCom began constructing its own fiber optic network in France in order to support an entry as a bandwidth wholesaler. Louis Dreyfus began considering a public offering for its new subsidiary, and in 2000 convinced another family member, Robert Louis-Dreyfus, to take on the role of LDCom's chairman in support of the proposed offering. Robert Louis-Dreyfus had long pursued his own path in the French business world, notably as head of sportswear group Adidas.

In the end, LDCom remained wholly owned by Louis Dreyfus—and protected from the dramatic crash in the telecommunications sector in 2001. By then LDCom's revenues had reached just EUR 198 million. The crash of the telecommunications sector provided LDCom with the opportunity for impressive growth as it began acquiring other businesses, including telecommunications retailers Belgacom and 9Telecom.

At the same time, LDCom continued developing its network—which reached 11,000 kilometers by 2003—financed in part by renting out new bandwidth before the actual construction began. In this way, LDCom remained debt free, and by 2003, as its sales neared EUR 1 billion, the company had claimed one of the top three spots in the French telecommunications market. In order to support the group's further growth plans, without relinquishing the Louis-Dreyfus family's ownership of the company, Louis Dreyfus launched a $100 million private placement offering through U.S. subsidiary Louis Dreyfus Corporation in November 2003. After more than 150 years in business, Louis Dreyfus's ability to reinvent itself, while clinging to its arbitrage traditions, gave it a solid foundation for the future.

Principal Subsidiaries

LDCom Networks S.A.; Louis Dreyfus Citrus S.A.; Louis Dreyfus Travocean; Louis Dreyfus Armateurs; Faplac S.A.

(Argentina); Resinfor Metanol S.A. (Argentina); Flooring S.A. (Argentina); Louis Dreyfus Property Group (U.S.); Louis Dreyfus Corporation (U.S.); Louis Dreyfus Energy Corporation (U.S.); Allenberg Cotton Company (U.S.); Louis Dreyfus Canada Ltd.; Placas do Parana S.A. (Brazil); Louis Dreyfus & Cie. GmbH (Germany); Compromex S.A. de C.V. (Mexico); Louis Dreyfus Asia Pte Ltd. (Singapore); Coffee Agency S.A. (Spain); Sungrain S.A. (Switzerland); Kopko Ltd. (Israel); Louis Dreyfus Trading Ltd. (U.K.); Louis Dreyfus Australia.

Principal Operating Units

Citrus; Commodities; Energy; Agricultural; Manufacturing; Real Estate; Shipping; Telecommunications.

Principal Competitors

ADM-Growmark Inc.; CHS Inc.; Connell Company; Korn- og Foderstof Kompagniet A/S; DeBruce Grain Inc.; Groupe Soufflet.

Further Reading

Kremer, Victor, "Louis Dreyfus Seen Turning Focus from Power to Gas Mart," *Power, Finance and Risk,* June 9, 2003, p. 1.

Levine, Joshua, and Graham Button, " 'A' is for Arbitrage: William Louis-Dreyfus Revived his Family's Faltering Business by Applying Great-Grandpa's Original Principles," *Forbes,* July 15, 1996, p. 116.

"Louis Dreyfus to Be Sold in $1.8 Billion Gas Deal," *Houston Chronicle,* September 11, 2001, p. 1.

Roberts, Adrienne, "Dreyfus Dynasty Staff in Mourning," *Financial Times,* February 6, 2003, p. 27.

—M.L. Cohen

Grupo Portucel Soporcel

Mitrena, Apartado 55
2901-861 Setúbal
Portugal
Telephone: (+351) 265 700 570
Fax: (+351) 265 700 553
Web site: www.portucelsoporcel.com

Public Company
Incorporated: 1952
Employees: 2,485
Sales: EUR 1.09 billion ($1.23 billion)(2002)
Stock Exchanges: Lisbon
NAIC: 322121 Paper (except Newsprint) Mills; 115310
   Support Activities for Forestry; 322130 Paperboard
   Mills; 551112 Offices of Other Holding Companies

Grupo Portucel Soporcel is Portugal's leading producer of wood pulp and paper and ranks among the leading European integrated pulp and paper manufacturers. Formed through the merger of paper producers Soporcel and Inapa into Portuguese government-controlled pulp producer Portucel, the company now has an output of more than 1.2 million tons of largely eucalyptus-based wood pulp each year and one million tons of paper. Portucel is one of Europe's top five manufacturers of uncoated ''woodfree'' paper, which refers to the chemical process that breaks down wood pulp to produce a higher-quality, longer-lasting paper. A pioneer of the use of eucalyptus trees in the European paper industry, Portucel directly controls more than of 180,000 hectares of forest, representing 4.5 percent of the country's total forest and roughly 2 percent of Portugal itself. Nearly 70 percent of the group's forests are planted with eucalyptus. Portucel operates from three primary pulp and paper mill sites: Cacia, the group's first mill, which produces some 260,000 tons of pulp each year, as well as decor, coated, and tissue papers; Setubal, with a capacity of 500,000 tons of pulp and 275,000 tons of paper, including high-quality writing and printing papers; and Soporcel's Figueira da Foz site, which boasts a capacity of 500,000 tons of bleached kraft pulp and a paper product line of more than 7,000 items. Publicly listed since the early 1990s, Portucel has nonetheless remained under the control of the Portuguese government, which holds a 55 percent stake in the company. Since the end of 2003, the government been seeking a buyer for up to 30 percent of Portucel in a move to edge the company toward full privatization.

Eucalyptus Pulp Pioneer in the 1950s

Portucel-Empresa de Celulose e Papel de Portugal, S.A was established in the town of Cacia, Portugal, in 1952 for the purpose of producing wood pulp for the European paper industry. By 1953, the Cacia mill was already in operation, producing raw pine pulp. Yet Portucel had already begun preparations for the launch of a new type of wood pulp based on eucalyptus trees.

Eucalyptus presented a number of advantages over traditional woods for the pulp and paper industry. Trees grew quickly and were capable of producing new trees from stumps after the original tree had been cut down, enabling a single tree to be used up to three times. Eucalyptus pulp also had shorter fibers, producing stronger and higher-quality papers. By 1957, Portucel had launched production of eucalyptus-based pulp, becoming the first company in the world to produce sulphate-bleached eucalyptus pulp for kraft paper market.

During its early years, Portucel concentrated its production efforts on the pulp market, supplying primarily European paper manufacuers. In the mid-1960s, however, the Portuguese government decided to extend its pulp operations into papermaking as well and in 1964 began construction of a mill in Setubal.

The new mill combined a pulp production unit, under Portucel, with an integrated papermaking operation placed under a new company, Industria Nacional de Papeis, later known as Inapa. Although Portucel eventually gained a shareholding of more than 35 percent of Inapa (before taking full control in 2000), the two companies remained separate businesses. Pulp production began in 1967. Paper production at the Inapa, fed through a direct connection to Portucel's pulp line, began in 1969. By 1972, Inapa had launched its first range of eucalyptus-based papers on the European market.

Portucel continued to expand and began producing other varieties of papers through subsidiary Gescartao, among others.

154

While Inapa focused on high-quality papers, Portucel's own paper production targeted other markets, especially the packaging market, with a range of bleached and unbleached papers, kraft linings, and similar materials, including its popular Portoliner-branded kraft linings. The company's packaging production was eventually brought its Gescartao subsidiary. In support of its growing range, and in order to meet the demand for its pulp from the export market, the company installed a second pulp line at its Setubal site in 1978.

By the end of the 1970s, Portucel's cellulose pulp production had topped 500,000 tons, representing some 70 percent of all wood pulp production in Portugal. While much of that targeted the export market, a rising share of the group's pulp production was by then already absorbed by its own paper production. At the end of the 1970s, Portucel's paper production, including the group's shares in other paper producers such as Inapa, included 200,000 tons of paper and 120,000 tons of packaging materials.

Privatization Process for the New Century

The Portuguese paper industry continued to expand during the 1980s. Inapa opened a second paper mill in 1980 and that year launched Portugal's first branded line of writing papers, Inacopia. The 1980s also saw the emergence of a new Portuguese paper force, Soporcel, which began construction on a pulp and paper mill in Figueira da Foz. The first phase of the site was completed in 1984, and Soporcel began pulping operations. Soporcel, half owned by the Portuguese government, also took on a major shareholder, Wiggins Teape (later Arjo Wiggins), which acquired nearly 43 percent of the young company in 1985. In 1991, Soporcel inaugurated its first paper production. Soporcel expanded its mill in 1995, reaching a capacity of 330,000 tons. With the addition of a second production line in 2000, the Soporcel site became the largest single mill on the Iberian peninsula.

Starting in 1988, Portucel launched its own upgrade program. This involved shutting down the original Setubal pulp line and boosting the capacity of the larger number two line. At the same time, the company installed new state-of-the-art waste and environmental protection systems.

On the other side of the Setubal site, Industria Nacional de Papeis was merged together with its coating subsidiary, Parel, to form Papeis Inapa in 1987. Inapa, whose operations had been brought steadily closer to those of Portucel, was also preparing to triple in size with the launch of a third paper mill, PM3, in 1990.

In this way, Portucel moved closer towards its goal of becoming a major integrated pulp and paper company in Europe. By 1990, Portucel's own paper operations claimed some 37 percent of its pulp production—the addition of Inapa's operations pushed the group's pulp integration past 50 percent. Fucling this growth was the group's emergence as a major forestry business, with more than 100,000 hectares of Portuguese forest land under its control.

Yet bigger changes lay in store for Portucel in the new decade. At the beginning of the 1990s, the Portuguese government began formulating plans to exit many of the domestic industries it controlled in order to allow them to better compete in an international market. The European Community was itself set to enter a new era in 1992, when trade barriers among member nations were scheduled to fall. The paper and pulp industry had become one of the most vibrant and vital in the Portuguese economy, making the privatization of the sector a delicate process.

Nonetheless, Portucel took the first step in the process in 1990 when it converted to private limited company status. By 1993, the company readied itself to go public, with the government listing some 13 percent of Portucel's shares on the Lisbon Stock Exchange. As part of that offering, the company's name was changed, to Portucel Industrial—Empresa Produtora de Celulose. The privatization process continued into mid-decade, as the group took on a major shareholder, Portuguese industrial group Sonae. That company became Portucel's largest single shareholder other than the government, which maintained control of some 55 percent of the company.

Commanding 14 percent of the world market for eucalyptus pulp by 1995, Portucel emerged as one of the country's largest businesses, accounting for some 2 percent of total Portuguese exports. As such, the company remained of vital importance for the country, and the Portuguese government, a situation that ultimately served to slow down the privatization process. The next step, however, was achieved at mid-decade when the company announced plans to sell off its Gescartao packaging materials operation, which represented more than 30 percent of group sales. That plan was carried out in 2000, when Spain's Europac and Sonae joined together to pay the equivalent of $48 million to acquire 65 percent of Gescartao. The remainder was spun off in a public offering.

In the meantime, the Portuguese pulp and paper industry continued to take shape. In the late 1990s, the Portuguese government flirted with a merger between Portucel and Spain's Ence, a move that would have created the largest pulp and paper group in Europe. After that deal foundered, however, the government turned its intention instead toward consolidating the domestic market. In 1998, a new holding company was created, called Papercel, combining the government's shares in both Portucel and Soporcel. In order to provide liquidity for the rest of Soporcel's shares, that company was then listed on the Lisbon Stock Exchange in 2000.

By then, Portucel at last took full control of Papeis Inapa, paying some EUR 90 million ($88 million) to take over its Setubal partner. That purchase led to the announcement in December 2000 of an offer by Portucel to acquire Arjo Wiggins' remaining 40 percent stake in Soporcel. That deal, along with a second, concurrent deal to acquire the Portuguese government's stake in Soporcel as well, was completed in 2001. Portucel then became one of Europe's largest pulp and paper operations.

Key Dates:

1952: Cacia pulp mill is opened and Portucel is founded.
1953: Portucel begins producing pine-based pulp.
1957: Eucalyptus-based pulp production is launched.
1964: A second pulp mill in Setubal is established.
1967: The Setubal mill begins pulp production; construction begins on a sister site for paper production, placed under a new company, Industria Nacional de Papeis (Inapa).
1969: Inapa begins paper production.
1972: Inapa becomes the first business to sell paper in Europe based on eucalyptus pulp.
1980: Inapa launches Inacopia brand writing paper.
1984: Soporcel pulp operations begin at Figueiro.
1991: Soporcel begins the production of paper.
1993: Portucel is listed on the Lisbon Stock Exchange as a step toward its privatization.
1995: Sonae acquires a 29 percent stake in Portucel.
1998: Papercel, a holding company for the Portugese government's stake in Portucel and Soporcel, is created.
2000: Portucel acquires full control of Inapa.
2001: Portucel acquires Soporcel, becoming one of the top five European integrated pulp and paper producers.
2003: An agreement to sell a 25 percent stake in Portucel Soporcel to a Cofina-Lecta partnership is blocked by Sonae.

The addition of Soporcel also allowed the company to shift away from its reliance on the pulp market, which had come increasingly under pressure from low-cost producers in Brazil and elsewhere. As part of that strategy, the Portucel Soporcel Group, as the company now began to call itself, launched a new line of SoporSet heavyweight papers in 2002.

The Portuguese government, reluctant to relinquish control of one of the country's major industries to foreign investors, nonetheless began accepting bids for part of its stake in 2003. By November, the government had chosen to sell 25 percent of Portucel to a partnership between Portugal's Cofina and CVC-controlled paper group Lecta. That deal would have given Portucel control of Lecta's pulp and paper operations in France, Italy, and Spain, as well as an additional 25,000 hectares of forest in Portugal owned by Cofina.

However, Portucel's other major shareholder, Sonae, opposed the sale. As one Sonae official told the *Financial Times:* "We don't understand why the government is seeking partners abroad when it could find them at home." With more than 37 percent of shareholder votes—including Sonae's 29 percent—siding with Sonae, the government was forced to return to the negotiating table in order to find a new form for Portucel's continued privatization. In the meantime, the Portucel Soporcel Group remained not only one of Portugal's premier companies but also a leader in the European pulp and paper scene as well.

Principal Subsidiaries

Aliança Florestal-Sociedade para o Desenvolvimento Agro-Florestal, S.A. (50%); Arboser-Serviços Agro-Industriais, S.A. (50%); Celpinus-Empresa de Desenvolvimento Agro-Florestal, S.A. (60%); Emporsil-Empresa Portuguesa de Silvicultura, Lda; Lazer e Floresta-Empresa de Desenvolvimento Agro-Florestal, Imobiliário e Turístico, S.A. (60%); Portucel (UK), Ltd; Portucel Florestal-Empresa de Desenvolvimento Agro-Florestal, S.A. (60%); Portucel Pasta y Papel, S.A. (Spain); Sociedade de Vinhos da Herdade de Espirra-Produçao e Comercializaçao de Vinhos, S.A. (60%); Soporcel-Sociedade Portuguesa de Papel, S.A.; Soporcel 2000-Serviços Comerciais de Papel, Soc. Unipessoal, Lda; Soporcel Deutschland, GmbH; Soporcel España, S.A.; Soporcel France, EURL; Soporcel Handels, GmbH (Austria); Soporcel International, BV (Holland); Soporcel Italia, SRL; Soporcel North America Inc. (U.S.); Soporcel United Kingdom, Ltd; Tecnipapel-Sociedade de Transformaçao e Distribuiçao de Papel, Lda; Viveiros Aliança-Empresa Produtora de Plantas, S.A.

Principal Competitors

Stora Enso AB; UPM-Kymmene Corp.; Svenska Cellulosa AB; Metsaliitto Group; Mondi Ltd.; M-real Corp.; Orkla ASA; Jefferson Smurfit Group PLC; SAPPI Ltd.; Norske Skogindustrier ASA.

Further Reading

O'Brian, Hugh, "Portucel Views a Privatized Future," *Pulp & Paper International*, October 1990, p. 81.
Wise, Peter, "Portucel details plans," *Privatisation International*, March 1995, p. 5.
——, "Rivals Square up for Portucel," *Financial Times*, July 29, 2003, p. 26.
——, "Revolt Sparks Portucel Rethink," *Financial Times*, November 3, 2003, p. 30.

—M.L. Cohen

Hale-Halsell Company

911 East Pine Street
Tulsa, Oklahoma 74115
U.S.A.
Telephone: (918) 835-4484
Fax: (918) 641-5471

Private Company
Incorporated: 1901
Employees: 4,500
Sales: $950 million (2001 est.)
NAIC: 445110 Supermarkets and Other Grocery (except Convenience) Stores; 447110 Gasoline Stations with Convenience Stores; 445120 Convenience Stores; 722310 Food Service Contractors; 422410 Grocery and Related Product Wholesalers

The Hale-Halsell Company has grown from its modest roots as a food supplier to settlers in newly opened Indian Territory in Oklahoma at the turn of the twentieth century to flourish as one of the ten largest food wholesalers in the United States and one of the 400 largest privately owned companies in the country. By following a conservative strategy of growth and acquisitions, and constantly remaining focused on the importance of high quality customer service and employee relations, Hale-Halsell has thrived amid the ever-changing landscape of the food wholesaler industry. Over the years, the company has added a dozen subsidiaries, all of which are connected to Hale-Halsell's core competency of food supply. The largest is the Git-n-Go chain of convenience stores, with over 120 outlets operating across five states.

Early Years

Hale-Halsell was the brainchild of two west Texas entrepreneurs, Tom Hale and Hugh Halsell. Hale was a successful hardware dealer who, in the late 1890s, identified the massive influx of settlers into Oklahoma as a potentially lucrative market for foodstuffs. At the time, small town merchants in frontier communities procured most of their goods from food wholesalers in west Texas. Supplies were uncertain, however, due to the unreliability of transport across the often swollen Red River. Local merchants had to tie up funds maintaining sufficient stocks of goods on hand in case of delays in resupply. Hale thought that a grocery wholesaler with a warehouse on the Oklahoma side of the river could capture the lion's share of the market, which was growing with the advent of significant coal mining operations in Oklahoma at the dawn of the twentieth century. With seed money from his old friend Hugh Halsell, Hale opened the Durant Grocery Company in Durant, Oklahoma, in 1901.

The new venture, which was incorporated as the Hale-Halsell Grocery Company in 1903, quickly blossomed, and Hale began to extend his reach across the whole of the Oklahoma Territory. In 1904, Hale-Halsell purchased the Townsend Grocery Company in McAlester, Oklahoma, which soon became the hub for the company's expanding operations. (The company's headquarters remained in McAlester until 1969, when they moved to Tulsa.) With such a wide distribution network, Hale-Halsell's merchandise soon graced the shelves of a majority of the food retailers in the Oklahoma Territory. By 1908, though, Muskogee had surpassed McAlester as the engine of Oklahoma's growth, and Hale-Halsell bought a building there to broaden its sphere of operations still further. Oil was discovered near Tulsa in 1909, leading to a tremendous population boom. To capitalize on this new market, Hale-Halsell acquired Tulsa's Harvey Wholesale Company in 1912. Hale-Halsell added additional branch offices in Holdenville in 1918, Hugo in 1920, Ada in 1922, and Okmulgee in 1926.

As the company expanded geographically, Hale-Halsell also broadened its offerings. In 1915, it renovated its McAlester headquarters to install Oklahoma's first coffee roasting plant and soon added a peanut butter factory as well. During the 1920s and 1930s, the company diversified its manufacturing operations further when it began to grind and pack spices and create flavor extracts. Hale-Halsell's products were distributed under the labels ''Hale's Pride,'' ''Hale's Leader,'' ''Choctaw,'' and ''Cowboy.''

Over the next few decades, Hale-Halsell gradually increased the orbit of its operations from its Oklahoma heartland to include parts of Texas, Arkansas, Kansas, and Missouri. After Tom Hale died in 1941, his son Elmer continued to run the company.

Growth and Innovation in the 1950s–60s

The economic boom and the demographic changes that occurred following World War II brought new pressures to bear on the grocery wholesaler industry. To position itself to compete effectively in this new environment, Hale-Halsell constructed huge, modern warehouse complexes in Tulsa in 1951 and Durant in 1953 and closed its plants in McAlester, Hugo, Ada, and Muskogee in 1954. In 1955, a third generation of Hales assumed leadership of the company when Tom's grandson, Elmer Hale, Jr., took the reins from his father. That same year, Hale-Halsell moved to develop a retail presence when it acquired Sipes Food Markets, a Tulsa-based group of grocery stores that had previously been owned by the Sipes family. This bit of vertical integration ensured Hale-Halsell a captive outlet for its wholesale goods. The company's refocusing continued in the late 1950s, as it began to exit the manufacturing sector. By 1963, Hale-Halsell had shed all of its manufacturing operations.

One of the most significant turning points in the company's history occurred in 1958, when Hale-Halsell opened its first Git-n-Go convenience store. The name was selected by Elmer Hale, Jr., who chose the moniker because the store was intended to cater to customers who would "git in there and then want to go along with their business," as Hale-Halsell CEO and board chairman Bob Hawk told *Tulsa World* (August 30, 1998). Elmer Hale, Jr. had decided to enter the nascent convenience store industry after seeing some of the early 7-Eleven stores in Texas. The original concept for the field was exactly what its name suggested: convenience, particularly for one car families who would rather pay a premium to pick up a few grocery staples close to home than brave long check-out lines at an area grocery store. The industry was in its infancy (in 1958, there were barely 500 convenience stores worldwide), but with its long history of food provision, entry into this new sector represented a logical step for Hale-Halsell.

Git-n-Go had six stores in operation by 1959. Together they generated $495,000 in sales. These outfits were set up along the lines of open-air roadside fruit stands, where customers could stop by and quickly grab a few staple items. However, they soon evolved into full-fledged retail venues, complete with air conditioning. The convenience food industry proved to be exceptionally competitive, particularly in the brutal Tulsa market, which has the highest per capita number of convenience stores in the country. To remain viable, Hale-Halsell had to adapt its Git-n-Go business plan frequently. Convenience stores made inroads on the traditional grocery retail market throughout the 1960s, but grocery stores fought back by adding express lanes and extending their hours of operation, thereby forcing convenience store owners to find new market niches.

In the late 1960s, Git-n-Go identified a new area of opportunity: gasoline sales. "We surveyed the market and realized that the old-time filling station was going by the wayside," Bob Hawk commented in the 1998 article in the *Tulsa World*. "Since the consumer needed an outlet for gasoline, we could supply that and then, when they came in to pay, they'd buy something else." Gas sales proved to be an explosive market throughout the convenience store industry. By 1998, Git-n-Go's biggest local competitor, QuikTrip Corporation, sold more gas in the Tulsa area than Philips Petroleum and Texaco Inc. combined.

Changes in the 1970s–80s

Despite the success of its Git-n-Go subsidiary, Hale-Halsell did not restrict its focus to the convenience store segment of the retail market. In 1972, the company increased its presence outside Oklahoma when it bought a partnership interest in the two-store Foodtown Supermarkets group of Rogers, Arkansas. Hale-Halsell further expanded its supermarket business two years later when it acquired a partnership interest in the 26-store United Supermarkets of Oklahoma chain. In 1976, Hale-Halsell celebrated its 75th anniversary by buying the Tulsa-based Fadler Company, which traced its own roots back to 1913 when its founder, L.F. Fadler, began selling produce from a wagon. Over the years, Fadler had continued to specialize in fruits and vegetables and later added frozen foods and institutional food service to its repertoire, serving over 300 retail customers and 500 institutional food service accounts. Hale-Halsell soon brought Fadler's retail arm in-house, allowing Fadler to concentrate exclusively on food service supply. (By 1998, Fadler had grown to serve more than 5,000 institutional customers—including hospitals, schools and restaurants—in Oklahoma, Kansas, Missouri, and Arkansas, with frozen foods accounting for roughly half the company's business.)

In the latter part of the 1970s, Oklahoma, along with its neighboring states, experienced a massive economic boom as the Arab oil embargo drove up prices for domestic oil. During this period, many businesses embarked headlong on expansion plans, extending themselves greatly and taking on vast amounts of debt. Hale-Halsell, by contrast, chose a more conservative tack, paying off its outstanding debt entirely and making only cautious investments in the five core states (Oklahoma, Arkansas, Kansas, Missouri, and Texas) in which it operated. Many industry analysts questioned the wisdom of this approach, but Hale-Halsell stuck to its guns. "When the economy was hot, we thought it was too hot and . . . elected to get totally out of debt," Bob Hawk told the *Tulsa World* (March 19, 1989). "People thought we were going broke." Hale-Halsell was vindicated when the region's economy entered a deep and prolonged slump and interest rates skyrocketed in the early 1980s. With no debt to service, the company was able to weather the storm without layoffs and was well-positioned to expand when interest rates dropped in the mid-1980s.

In 1986, Hale-Halsell's Fadler subsidiary purchased Curtis Restaurant Supply, whose operations were centered in Tulsa. Curtis was in the business of designing and equipping food service venues, which represented another logical extension of Hale-Halsell's foodstuff empire. "We complement the parent company," Curtis's president Tom Byford recalled in an interview published in a December 2001 "Advertorial Supplement"

<table>
<tr><td colspan="2">

Key Dates:

</td></tr>
<tr><td>**1901:**</td><td>Tom Hale and Hugh Halsell found the Durant Grocery Company.</td></tr>
<tr><td>**1903:**</td><td>Durant Grocery Company is incorporated as the Hale-Halsell Company.</td></tr>
<tr><td>**1915:**</td><td>Hale-Halsell begins manufacturing operations with the first coffee-roasting plant in Oklahoma.</td></tr>
<tr><td>**1941:**</td><td>Tom Hale dies; Elmer Hales takes control of Hale-Halsell.</td></tr>
<tr><td>**1958:**</td><td>Hale-Halsell opens its first Git-n-Go convenience store.</td></tr>
<tr><td>**1969:**</td><td>Hale-Halsell moves its corporate headquarters from McAlester to Tulsa.</td></tr>
<tr><td>**1972:**</td><td>Hale-Halsell expands into Arkansas with its purchase of an interest in Foodtown Supermarkets.</td></tr>
<tr><td>**1976:**</td><td>Hale-Halsell buys Fadler Company.</td></tr>
<tr><td>**1986:**</td><td>Hale-Halsell's Fadler subsidiary acquires Curtis Restaurant Supply.</td></tr>
<tr><td>**1991:**</td><td>Hale-Halsell buys ValuFare Supermarket chain.</td></tr>
<tr><td>**2000:**</td><td>Hale-Halsell establishes Forefront Petroleum Company and takes over Gro-Mor.</td></tr>
<tr><td>**2001:**</td><td>Hale-Halsell celebrates its centenary and establishes the Blue Valley Water Company.</td></tr>
</table>

in the *Shelby Report* commemorating Hale-Halsell's 100th anniversary. "We can build a restaurant, grocery store or convenience store . . . from the ground up and then we can supply the facility with food and equipment." (The addition was a wise one. Between 1991 and 2001, Curtis's annual sales jumped from $3 million to over $10 million.)

Much of the growth in the 1980s, though, was focused on Hale-Halsell's Git-n-Go subsidiary, whose range of offerings the company continued to update in order to meet and stay ahead of consumer demands. "Demographics are changing," a Git-n-Go manager told the *Tulsa Tribune* for May 26, 1989. "We used to have the 18–34 year-old male customer wanting quick sandwiches, pop, beer. Now the customer is more mature. We sell cosmetics and have fountain things." Indeed, soda fountains had been a tremendously successful innovation. Git-n-Go began installing the drink dispensers in 1984, and by 1989 fountain drinks accounted for 12 percent of the chain's $90 million in revenues. During the 1980s, the company also expanded its auto parts offerings and added touchless car washes, which proved to be very popular.

The 1980s were also a time of dramatic change in Hale-Halsell's core sector of food wholesaling. A wave of mergers and consolidations crested over the industry, driven in large part by the entry of retail giants into the food business. "Wal-Mart, Kmart and Target supercenters and wholesale clubs have changed how the entire food industry operates," Hale-Halsell CEO Bob Hawk told *the Tulsa World* for June 12, 1994. "Grocers have gone from competing just with other grocery stores to compete with lots of non-traditional food retailers." The economies of scale and technical innovations the huge retailers brought to the grocery industry forced many traditional wholesalers to scramble to keep pace. Hale-Halsell identified

the personal relationships built from a stable employee base and strong customer service as its biggest point of differentiation from such giant competitors and strove to strengthen the long-term relationships that were its hallmark. Doing so also required careful attention to customer preferences and a nimble operating style that allowed for quick adaptation to shifting consumer demands. "If we have a customer," Hale-Halsell president and chief operating officer Jim Lewis explained in a December 2001 "Advertorial Supplement" in the *Shelby Report*, "our aim is to spoil them so bad, nobody else will have them."

Expansion and Diversification in the 1990s and Beyond

In 1991, Hale-Halsell acquired ValuFare Supermarkets, a two-store outfit in Oklahoma City. That same year, the company cracked *Forbes*' list of America's top 400 privately held companies at number 300, with revenues of $607 million. The year 1992 was also a successful one for Hale-Halsell, which now led the wholesale food industry with a whopping $2,667 in sales per square foot of warehouse space, moving the company up to number 276 on the *Forbes* list. Reflecting the intense competition in the wholesale food industry, though, sales per warehouse square foot dropped dramatically the following year, to $1,313. While others in the field sought to regain lost ground by trying to spice up their warehouse outlets with ready-to-eat meals and fast food, Hale-Halsell decided to return to its core principals. "We are never going to be another Boston Market," company CEO Bob Hawk told the *Orange County Register*. "We have to get back to the basics of merchandising and selling food." By 1996, sales were up more than 72 percent over the previous year.

The 1990s were kinder to Git-n-Go, as the company opened nearly ten stores a year and expanded its presence in growing markets such as Oklahoma City. Git-n-Go also began to experiment with "junior" stores, with a 1,500-square-foot floor plan rather than its customary 3,100- to 3,200-square-foot design. These more diminutive models allowed Git-n-Gos to be built on smaller lots in more prime locations, though the majority of the company's new openings were of the larger variety.

In the mid-1990s, Git-n-Go also started incorporating fast food outlets, such as McDonald's Express, into some of its stores. The concept failed to take off, but the company was not chastened. "When you're as aggressive as we are," Bob Hawk remarked in the August 30, 1998 *Tulsa World*, "you're not going to have every experiment work." By the late 1990s, Git-n-Go was beginning to install drive-through windows in many of its stores.

By the turn of the 21st century, gas sales were accounting for nearly 65 percent of Git-n-Go's revenues. Recognizing a golden opportunity to diversify further, Hale-Halsell formed a new subsidiary, Forefront Petroleum Company, in 2000. Forefront was tasked with distributing gas to all of Hale-Halsell's convenience stores and distribution centers. The venture proved so successful that Forefront began selling to outside customers as well.

Also in 2000, Hale-Halsell acquired the Gro-Mor Company. Gro-More was in the business of building and remodeling convenience stores and had done a great deal of work with

Git-n-Go. The deal allowed Hale-Halsell to become even more vertically integrated and to establish a greater presence in the service side of the food industry. In 2001, the company celebrated its 100th anniversary and added another subsidiary, Blue Valley Water Company, a bottled water supplier. With a strong base in the wholesale food market, and with subsidiaries capable of doing everything from building, equipping, and remodeling retail and institutional food service venues, to retailing foodstuffs, to delivering gasoline and transporting inventory, Hale-Halsell was positioned for another century of success.

Principal Subsidiaries

Git-n-Go Corporation; Faydler Company; Curtis Restaurant Supply; Forefront Petroleum Company; Gro-Mor Company.

Principal Competitors

Fleming Companies; Kroger Co.; Wal Mart Stores Inc.; Quik-Stop.

Further Reading

Elson, Joel, "Hale-Halsell to Build a Low-Price Image," *Supermarket News*, April 17, 1995.

Erwin, Jane, "Git-n-Go Marks 30 Years," *Tulsa World*, June 23, 1998.

——, "Hale-Halsell Co.: A Different Approach," *Tulsa World*, March 19, 1989.

Fox, Sam, "Tulsa's Git-n-Go on the Go," *Tulsa Tribune*, May 26, 1989.

"Hale-Halsell Company," *Shelby Report* (Southwest edition), December, 2001.

"Inching Ahead," *U.S. Distribution Journal*, September 15, 1996.

Lee, Mark, "Trends Reshaping Food Industry," *Tulsa World*, June 12, 1994.

"Making up Ground," *U.S. Distribution Journal*, September 15, 1994.

Schafer, Shaun, "Fadler Shows Off Cool Addition," *Tulsa World*, March 10, 1998.

"3 State Firms Make *Forbes* List of Largest Companies," *Journal Record*, November 26, 1991.

Tiernan, Becky, "Convenience on Every Corner," *Tulsa World*, August 30, 1998.

"Wholesale Grocery Industry 1993 Report," *U.S. Distribution Journal*, September 15, 1993.

—Rebecca Stanfel

Hang Seng Bank Ltd.

83 Des Voeux Road, Central
Hong Kong
Telephone: (+852) 2198-1111
Fax: (+852) 2868-4047
Web site: http://www.hangseng.com

Public Company
Incorporated: 1933 as Hang Seng Ngan Ho
Employees: 7,200
Sales: HK$10.68 billion ($3.65 billion)(2002)
Stock Exchanges: Hong Kong
Ticker Symbol: HSNGY
NAIC: 522110 Commercial Banking

Hang Seng Bank Ltd. is Hong Kong's second-largest bank, behind the Hong Kong and Shanghai Banking Corporation, which, like Hang Seng, is majority controlled by the United Kingdom's HSBC. Hang Seng operates throughout Hong Kong, with more than 155 branches, including locations in Mass Transit Railway stations and a strong network of automated teller machines. Hang Seng provides the full range of commercial banking services for the both the retail and corporate sectors, as well as credit and debit card services, insurance policies, home mortgages and automobile loans, and investment services. With the slowing down of Hong Kong's economy following its return to Chinese control, Hang Seng has joined its compatriots in seeking new expansion opportunities on the mainland. Since the mid-1990s, the group has opened a number of branches in Chinese cities, including in Shenzhen, Shanghai, Fuzhou, Najing, and Guangzhou. The company also operates representative offices in Beijing, Xiamen, and Taiwan. In 2003, the group began negotiations to acquire an equity stake in Minsheng Bank, the largest privately held bank in mainland China. Although initial negotiations failed to reach an agreement, a future alliance between the two banks has not been ruled out. HSBC controls just over 62 percent of Hang Seng, which trades on the Hong Kong Stock Exchange and is a member of its Hang Seng Index—created by the bank in the late 1960s. The

group posted an operating profit of HK$10.68 billion ($3.65 billion) in 2002.

Exchange Shop Origins in the 1930s

If Hang Seng emerged as one of Hong Kong's most powerful banks in the late 20th century, its origins could not have been more humble. Founded in 1933, Hang Seng started out as a money changing booth in Hong Kong's Wing Lok Street, in the city's Sheung Wan district. The company, Hang Seng Ngan Ho, was profitable from the start, posting earnings of more than HK$10,000 its first year.

Hang Seng proved true to its name, which means "ever-growing" in Chinese, and soon developed a wider range of banking services, especially after the Chinese Revolution and Hong Kong's separation from the Communist-controlled mainland. By 1952, the company reincorporated, taking on the status of a private limited company (plc), and launching its commercial banking operation. Hong Kong, which became a major destination for China's wealthy expatriates, emerged as one of the Asian region's primary banking centers and banks such as Hang Seng grew quickly servicing the city-state's fast growing economy. By the late 1950s, the bank had come under the control of some of the island's most prominent businessmen.

Hang Seng went public in 1960, although not yet on the Hong Kong Stock Exchange, and ranked among the largest Chinese banks in Hong Kong. In 1965, it caught the attention of the large Hong Kong and Shanghai Banking Corporation. Later known as HSBC, that group had been founded in 1865 by Thomas Sutherland, from Scotland, who launched a banking partnership in order to finance trade between the United Kingdom and Shanghai. Through the first half of the 20th century, HSBC created a banking empire that extended throughout much of mainland China, Southeast Asia, and the Middle East, with offices in London as well. Following the Communist takeover of China, HSBC was forced from the mainland and refocused its operations on its U.K. and Hong Kong branches.

When Hang Seng bank suffered a run on its deposits in 1965, HSBC came to the rescue, buying up a 51 percent share in Hang Seng, the equivalent of £200 million at the time. HSBC later

Company Perspectives:

Our corporate tagline—'Hang Seng Bank. Exceed. Excel.'—highlights the high standards we have set ourselves to exceed your expectations and excel in our operations. We shall continue to grow with you and with Hong Kong in the years ahead, helping you realize your financial aspirations and scaling new heights as the 'ever-growing bank.'

Key Dates:

1933: Founding of Hang Seng Ngan Ho as a small currency exchange office in Hong Kong.
1952: Hang Seng acquires full commercial bank status.
1960: First public offering of Hang Seng.
1965: HSBC acquires a majority interest in Hang Seng.
1972: Hang Seng is listed on the Hong Kong Stock Exchange.
1981: Bank begins opening branches in Mass Transit Railway stations.
1985: The first Hang Seng representative office on the Chinese mainland opens.
1997: A branch office in Shanghai is opened.
2000: E-banking services are introduced.
2003: Company announces plans to invest HK$200 million to open branch office in Beijing.

raised its stake in the company to more than 62 percent. By the beginning of the new century, HSBC's initial investment in the bank had been multiplied by more than 50.

Hang Seng introduced seven-year home mortgages in 1967; by the end of the decade, the bank confirmed its status as a major Hong Kong bank with the launch of the Hang Seng Index, which became the Hong Kong Stock Exchange's primary market indicator, tracking the shares of the colony's top 33 firms—including Hang Seng itself, which joined the Hong Kong Stock Exchange in 1972. The bank's initial public offering valued Hang Seng at HK$2.8 billion.

Hang Seng earned a reputation as a cautious lender, helping it build a solid foundation for itself through the 1980s. The bank also expanded strongly in the consumer retail market, particularly after it was granted the franchise for Hong Kong's Mass Transit Railway system. The company began opening new branches in the city's train stations. By the end of the 1980s, the company boasted some 150 branches in Hong Kong alone.

Mainland Aspirations for the New Century

The 1984 agreement reached between the British and Chinese governments, restoring China's control over Hong Kong, led Hang Seng to make a first, if tentative, approach to establishing operations on the mainland. In 1985, the bank opened its first representative office outside of Hong Kong in the newly created Shenzhen free trade zone. It was not until 1995, however, that Hang Seng opened its first official branch office in mainland China, extending the group's operations into Guangzhou. Two years later, after Hong Kong was reunited with the mainland, Hang Seng opened its second mainland branch, this time in Shanghai.

While Hong Kong was renewing its relationship with the Chinese mainland in the late 1990s, Hang Seng's relationship with HSBC was also strengthened. This was particularly true after the appointment of two officials from Hongkong & Shanghai Banking Corporation, the main HSBC arm in Hong Kong, to corresponding positions with Hang Seng. In 1997, Hongkong Bank's chief executive, David Eldon, was appointed chairman of Hang Seng. The following year, after Hang Seng CEO Alexander Au left the bank to take up a similar position at Standard Chartered, a major HSBC rival in the Asian region, the company named Vincent Cheng, executive director at Hongkong Bank, as the new Hang Seng CEO.

The move raised questions as to Hang Seng's future status amid a difficult economic climate, brought on by the financial crisis that swept through most of Asia in the late 1990s. At the same time, China's fast-growing economy had led to a shifting of the region's financial focus away from Hong Kong and onto the mainland. Analysts questioned Hang Seng's long-term viability, in part because HSBC's own ambitions for growth on the Chinese mainland appeared to limit Hang Seng's maneuverability outside of Hong Kong. For the time being, however, both Hang Seng and HSBC remained committed to maintaining Hang Seng as the independently operating, publicly listed Hong Kong wing of HSBC. Indeed, Hang Seng remained one of HSBC's only publicly listed subsidiaries.

As Hang Seng entered the new century, its role within HSBC's regional ambitions became more clear, as HSBC targeted the growing number of multinational corporations entering the Chinese mainland. Hang Seng, on the other hand, focused its efforts on winning the mainland financial business of the Hong Kong-based business community as it stepped up its own investment on the mainland. Hang Seng's strategy appeared to be paying off, as its net profits soared past HK$10 billion by 2000.

Hang Seng continued to seek new operating sectors, particularly higher margin business. In 2000, the group went online, introducing its own e-banking services. In 2001, Hang Seng introduced a new Prestige Banking department, providing asset management, securities trading, and other services for customers presenting portfolios of at least HK$500,000 (US$64,000). The following year, Hang Seng began offering services based on the Chinese *renminbi* currency, a service originally reserved for foreign passport holders and foreign-invested companies, and for citizens of Hong Kong SAR, Macau, and Taiwan. By the end of the year, however, the group appeared to have come full circle, as it began offering *renminbi* currency services to mainland Chinese customers as well.

A full-fledged entry into the fast-growing Chinese market became Hang Seng's major focus for the new century. In 2003, Hang Seng entered negotiations to buy an equity stake in Minsheng Bank, the largest privately held bank in mainland China. Talks collapsed after the two sides reportedly could not reach agreement on the level of management control Hang Seng was to receive after the acquisition. Thus, Hang Seng was forced to look elsewhere for its mainland entry.

Acquisitions remained a major facet in the bank's mainland expansion strategy. As CEO Cheng explained to *China Daily:* "We have deep pockets and are highly capitalized." Nonetheless, the bank continued to expand into the mainland market through organic growth. In November 2003, Hang Seng announced its intention to open a full branch office in Beijing, investing up to $25 million to do so. With 70 years of success in building one of Hong Kong's leading banks, Hang Seng appeared to have promising prospects in the vast Chinese market in the new century.

Principal Subsidiaries

Bankers Alliance Insurance Company Ltd.; Beautiful Fountain Investment Company Ltd.; Cheer Free Investments Ltd.; Fulcher Enterprises Company Ltd.; Full Wealth Investment Ltd.; Hang Che Lee Company, Ltd.; Hang Seng Asset Management Pte Ltd; Hang Seng Bank (Bahamas) Ltd.; Hang Seng Bank (Trustee) Ltd.; Hang Seng Bank Trustee (Bahamas) Ltd.; Hang Seng Bullion Company Ltd.; Hang Seng Credit Ltd.; Hang Seng Credit (Bahamas) Ltd.; Hang Seng Credit Card Ltd.; Hang Seng Data Services Ltd.; Hang Seng Finance Ltd.; Hang Seng Finance (Bahamas); Hang Shun Lee Company, Ltd.; Haseba International Management Ltd.; Haseba Investment Company Ltd.; Haseba Properties Holdings (USA) Inc.; Haseba Real Estate (USA) Inc.; Hayden Lake Ltd.; High Time Investments Ltd.; HSI International Ltd.; HSI Services Ltd.; Imenson Ltd.; Mightyway Investments Ltd.; Perpetual Publicity Ltd.; Wide Cheer Investment Ltd.; Yan Nin Development Company Ltd.

Principal Competitors

Westpac Banking Corporation; BOC Hong Kong Holdings Ltd.; Bank of Tokyo-Mitsubishi Ltd.; Bank of East Asia Ltd.; Dao Heng Bank Group Ltd.; Nanyang Commercial Bank Ltd.; Schroders Asia Ltd.; CITIC International Financial Holdings Ltd.; Shanghai Commercial Bank Ltd.; Overseas Trust Bank Ltd.; Industrial and Commercial Bank of China Asia Ltd.; Wing Lung Bank Ltd.; Dah Sing Bank Ltd.; Wing Hang Bank Ltd.

Further Reading

"Hang Seng Bank Expands," *People's Daily*, November 11, 2003.
"Hang Seng to Expand in China," *China Daily,* August 6, 2003.
Kynge, James, "Hang Seng Bank Deal Runs Aground," *Financial Times*, April 1, 2003, p. 27.
Leahy, Joe, "Hang Seng Makes a Play for Financial Services to Offset Contracting Margins," *Financial Times*, March 12, 2001, p. 34.
——, "Hang Seng Offsets Fall in Income with New Services," *Financial Times*, March 5, 2002, p. 27.

—M.L. Cohen

Hanson Building Materials America Inc.

1350 Campus Parkway, Suite 302
Neptune, New Jersey 07753
U.S.A.
Telephone: (732) 919-9777
Fax: (732) 919-1149
Web site: http://www.hanson-america.com

Wholly Owned Subsidiary of Hanson plc
Incorporated: 1997 as Cornerstone Construction & Materials, Inc.
Employees: 7,500
Sales: $2.92 billion (2002)
NAIC: 212321 Construction Sand and Gravel Mining; 212111 Bituminous Coal and Lignite Surface Mining; 212319 Other Crushed and Broken Stone Mining and Quarrying; 212319 Other Crushed and Broken Stone Mining or Quarrying; 321918 Other Millwork (Including Flooring); 551112 Offices of Other Holding Companies

Hanson Building Materials America Inc. is the third largest aggregates producer in the United States. Hanson Building's aggregates products—construction materials—include sand, gravel, limestone, asphalt, and ready-mixed concrete. The company also ranks as the largest producer of concrete pipes and precast concrete products in the United States and as the second largest brick manufacturer in the country.

Origins

Hanson Building's contributions were instrumental to the success of its parent company, Hanson plc, during the 1990s. Operating as the U.S.-based subsidiary of its English parent, Hanson Building delivered the greatest financial growth to Hanson plc, whose origins were the origins of Hanson Building.

Hanson plc's corporate roots stretched back to 1964, when James Hanson and Gordon White created Hanson Trust, the predecessor to Hanson plc. Hanson rose to the forefront of the U.K. corporate world during the 1970s and 1980s, when Hanson and White transformed their enterprise into a sprawling conglomerate. During the two-decade span, Hanson and White, both conferred as Lords, invested in an eclectic array of businesses that established their enterprise as multi-national concern. They held interests in chemical factories in the United States, electrical companies in the United Kingdom, and gold mines in Australia. Hanson was involved in making cigarettes, Jacuzzis, toys, and cranes and held interests in the production of cod liver oil capsules, batteries, and golf clubs. Physically and operationally, the conglomerate was spread far afield, its variegated businesses forming an all-encompassing corporate umbrella that was difficult to define as a single entity. To a certain extent, Hanson was all things and operated everywhere.

The need to lend some definition to company arose during the mid-1990s. The need, as perceived in the minds of Hanson executives, stemmed from changes in the minds of investors. Investors' interest in conglomerates was fading, giving way to a preference for investing in companies involved in single business sectors. In response, Hanson officials, still led by Lord Hanson, decided in January 1996 to break the company up into identifiable pieces, leading to the process of de-merging the conglomerate into four separate, publicly traded concerns. The conglomerate began to unravel itself, resulting in the formation of Imperial Tobacco, The Energy Group, and Millennium, the inheritor of Hanson's U.S.-based chemical assets. The remaining interests, comprising heavy building materials businesses, were held by Hanson plc. In the future, the Hanson name would apply only to businesses involved in the worldwide market for construction materials, which was the new, narrowed focus of the former industrial conglomerate.

The de-merger was completed in February 1997, resulting in three companies composing parent company Hanson. The three companies were ARC, Hanson Brick, and Cornerstone. The latter, which was officially named Cornerstone Construction & Materials, Inc., was soon to become Hanson Building. As a part of Hanson, Cornerstone was aptly named because its existence was integral to the health and wealth of Hanson. Cornerstone produced crushed rock, sand, and gravel for highway, residential, commercial, and industrial construction projects. The company made ready-mix concrete, hot-mix asphalt, and cement. As a whole, Cornerstone operated in the construction aggregates industry and represented Hanson in the United States, by far the greatest producer and consumer of aggregates in the world. At the time of the de-merger, the U.S. aggregates market was highly fragmented, populated by more than 5,000 companies. The three largest competitors controlled only 15 percent of the market, which meant there was plenty of opportunity for growth. In contrast, the four largest aggregates companies in the United Kingdom controlled 70 percent of the market. Accordingly, Hanson, with its newly narrowed focus on heavy building materials, attempted to seize the opportunity for expansion by diverting much of its resources to its U.S. representative. By assuming an acquisitive posture in a highly fragmented market, Hanson, through Cornerstone, and later through Hanson Building, bolstered its share of the aggregates market, vying for the number one position in the lucrative U.S. market.

Hanson Building Blossoms in the Late 1990s

During the second half of the 1990s, much of Hanson's financial success was derived from the growth of its U.S.-based operations. The acquisitions completed during this period typically were what the company referred to as ''bolt-on'' acquisitions: the purchase of small- and medium-sized companies involved in businesses and markets where Cornerstone already operated. Rarely did an acquisition usher the company into a new facet of the aggregates market; the company was not diversifying, it was solidifying its existing presence.

In 1997, the streamlined Hanson embarked toward its new tightened vision. Lord Hanson retired during the year, relinquishing his title as chairman to Christopher Collins in December. Cornerstone displayed its strengths from the start. There were several small bolt-on acquisitions completed during the year in California and Kentucky that increased the company's market penetration. The largest acquisition of the year, completed in April, was the purchase of Concrete Pipe and Products, which shored up the company's ranking as the second largest producer of concrete pipe in the country. By the end of the year, the company was operating in more than 20 states, with its operations in California, Georgia, North Carolina, and Texas proving to be particularly important.

During its first full year of operation after the de-merger, Hanson's U.S.-based operations drove the company toward a successful year. In 1998, Cornerstone generated £128.1 million in profits, an increase of 45 percent from the previous year's

total. During the year, the subsidiary produced more than 100 million tons of crushed rock, sand, and gravel for use in highway, residential, commercial, and industrial construction projects. The company also supplied pre-cast floors, roofs, walls, and supporting structural components. By the end of the year, Cornerstone was operating in more than 250 locations in 24 states from coast to coast.

In 1998, Cornerstone was given considerable resources to deepen its presence in the United States. Roughly $300 million was spent on acquisitions during the year, money that was well spent considering the expected surge in business resulting from the passage of an important piece of legislature. Approximately half of Cornerstone's business depended on federal, state, and municipal contracts covering highway infrastructure projects. This significant portion of the company's business received a boost in 1998 when the U.S. Congress passed the Transportation Equity Act for the 21st Century, known as TEA-21. TEA-21 appropriated $215 billion for federal highway spending for a six-year period, a 44 percent increase from the previous highway spending bill. Increased spending meant more business for Cornerstone, which ranked as the second-largest producer of ready-mix concrete in the country. ''TEA-21 gives us lots of confidence for the future,'' Cornerstone's chief executive officer, Alan Murray, remarked in an April 1999 interview with *Pit & Quarry*.

In early 1999, uniformity was given to the entire Hanson organization. Each Hanson plc operating division adopted the Hanson name, giving the global company a single identity and a single brand name. ARC was renamed Hanson Quarry Products Europe, Hanson Brick was renamed Hanson Bricks Europe, and Cornerstone was renamed Hanson Building Materials America. At Hanson Building, the name change was followed by a reorganization of its operations. ''We unified our corporate structure to emphasize that we are a large company and a major player in the building materials industry,'' explained Murray, in his April 1999 interview with *Pit & Quarry*. ''We were operating under a variety of brand names previous to that,'' he added. ''We now operate under two regions: Eastern and Western.''

Hanson Building's spending spree continued in 1999. The company and the two competitors ranking above it, Vulcan Materials and Martin Marietta, drove the consolidation of the industry, which was expected to ''take another decade or two to run its course,'' according to Murray in the May 11, 2000 issue of the *Financial Times*. Hanson Building, like its rivals, focused on the thousands of mom-and-pop businesses, which often operated a single quarry. ''Usually, the deals are $100 million or under,'' a Hanson Building spokeswoman was quoted as saying in the November 24, 2000 issue of the *Dallas Business Journal*. ''Our products don't travel far, so you want a local presence in a metropolitan area—that's where the big buildings, stadiums, arenas, and airports are being built,'' she added.

In return for backing an exhaustive acquisition campaign, Hanson plc gained the workhorse of its organization. There were 12 acquisitions in North American completed in 1999, accounting for three-quarters of Hanson plc's outlay toward acquisitions for the year. The additions, eight of which were based in the United States, strengthened Hanson Building's lead in the concrete pipe and precast products market. The company also acquired two marine-dredging operations in the San Francisco area and extended its presence into Canada by spending £32.8 million on acquisitions. The largest acquisition of the year, the purchase of Jannock's North American brick operations, made Hanson Building the second-largest producer of bricks in North America. By the end of 1999, Hanson Building accounted for 56 percent of its parent company's £1.9 billion in revenue and acted as the chief contributor to its parent company's profit growth.

By the spring of 2000, $900 million had been spent on acquisitions for Hanson Building during the preceding three years. Quarry by quarry, and company by company, Hanson Building had expanded through the addition of bolt-on acquisitions. There was one deal, however, that represented far more than a bolt-on addition to the company's fold. In May 2000, Hanson plc completed the $2.5 billion acquisition of Australia-based Pioneer International Ltd. Although most of Pioneer's assets were located in Europe and Australia, the company held significant interests in the United States. Hanson Building absorbed Pioneer's U.S. operations, which bolstered the company's presence in California and Texas and provided entry into Arizona and Utah, two new markets for the company.

Hanson Building in the 21st Century

The steady bolt-on acquisition campaign continued in the wake of the Pioneer acquisition. In 2000, Hanson Building purchased eight smaller companies that increased its presence in existing markets and led it into new markets. In May 2000, the company announced the purchase of two concrete pipe and products producers for $135.9 million. Joelson Taylor, the larger of the two purchases, established Hanson Building in Florida for the first time. The other acquisition, Cincinnati Pipe, shored up the company's presence in the Midwest market. Smaller acquisitions followed the purchase of Joelson Taylor and Cincinnati Pipe, such as the acquisition of two quarries in Indiana and Texas for a total of $18.5 million, enabling the company to post rousing financial results for the year. For the eighth consecutive year, Hanson Building recorded an increase in profits. Revenues in 2000 increased as well, jumping 55 percent to $1.6 billion.

As Hanson Building entered the 21st century, the economic climate soured, causing reduced demand for heavy building materials. The downturn began in late 2001 and carried on through 2002. For the first time since 1991, volume in the U.S. aggregates industry declined, ending Hanson Building's impressive streak of financial gains. For 2002, profits fell 12.7 percent and revenues shrank 6.2 percent. Acquisitions in that year primarily benefited Hanson Building's concrete pipe and products business.

As Hanson building prepared for the future, the company's leading market positions promised to hold it in good stead when economic conditions improved. The company continued to acquire bolt-on companies while economic conditions remained uncertain. In the first half of 2003, the company purchased quarries in Ohio and Kentucky. Hanson Building also completed the acquisition of Better Materials Corporation, an aggregates producer with strategically important operations in Pennsylvania and New Jersey. Looking ahead, the company promised to be a challenger for the number one position in the U.S. aggregates industry with its commitment to expansion driving the trend toward consolidation.

Principal Subsidiaries

Hanson Aggregates East, Inc.; Hanson Pipe & Products, Inc.

Principal Competitors

Lafarge North America Inc.; Martin Marietta Materials, Inc.; Vulcan Materials Company.

Further Reading

Allen, Margaret, "D-FW Ready-Mix Company Sold to Hanson," *Dallas Business Journal*, November 24, 2000, p. 17.
Bogler, Daniel, "UK: Hanson Changes Body Parts but Holds on to Its Heart," *Financial Times*, May 11, 2000, p. 40
"Good Vibrations," *Pit & Quarry*, July 2001, p. 35.
"Hanson Acquires Operations in Indiana and Texas," *Pit & Quarry*, November 2000, p. 12.
"Hanson Building," *Pit & Quarry*, September 2000, p. 18.

—Jeffrey L. Covell

Highsmith Inc.

W5527 State Road 106
Fort Atkinson, Wisconsin 53538
U.S.A.
Telephone: (920) 563-9571
Toll Free: (800) 558-2110
Fax: (920) 563-7393
Web site: http://www.highsmith.com

Private Company
Incorporated: 1956
Employees: 220
Sales: $60 million (2002 est.)
NAIC: 454113 Mail-Order Houses; 423990 Other
Miscellaneous Durable Goods Merchant Wholesalers

Situated on a rural campus in Fort Atkinson, Wisconsin, Highsmith Inc. is a leading marketer of products for schools, libraries (public, school, and specialty), and businesses. The company's base of more than 350,000 customers spans the globe and includes clients in Africa, Canada, England, Guam, Puerto Rico, the United States, and the Virgin Islands.

Highsmith's offerings are expansive. Its 12 specialty catalogs include more than 25,000 items ranging from furnishings and supplies for classrooms, offices, and libraries to audiovisual equipment and computer software. Highsmith has been recognized nationally for its commitment to employee wellness and promotion of librarianship.

According to the company, in addition to Highsmith Library Supplies and Equipment and Highsmith Contract Sales Group, other core business initiatives include UpstartBooks (library reference and instructional materials), the Upstart line of reading-promotion materials, MindSparks Cartoons and Visuals (history and social studies curriculum materials), and Highsmith Corruboard/Dealer Sales (corrugated display, organizational, and storage products).

Origins

Highsmith is the brainchild of Hugh Highsmith, who grew up in the small town of Johnson, Indiana. As a boy, Highsmith spent a great deal of time reading books at the library in nearby Owensville, where he attended school. Along with a passion for reading, Highsmith gained respect and admiration for libraries and librarians.

At the age of 12, Highsmith joined his brother working on the family farm, where he learned fundamental business and financial skills by selling melons. It was around this time that Highsmith became a student of classified magazine ads and a ''catalog connoisseur,'' according to the company. In the September 1990 issue of the *Highsmith Grapevine*, Hugh Highsmith recalled: ''I learned respect and appreciation for libraries, a customer's view of mail order and that I preferred working for myself—all of which later influenced my life and the development of this company.''

Highsmith eventually attended Indiana University in Bloomington, graduating with a business degree in 1936. After college his career took a varied and mostly unfulfilling path, including stints as an industrial claims adjuster in Chicago; a J.I. Case dealer in Waukesha, Wisconsin; and a department head at the Montgomery Ward store in Woodstock, Illinois. Highsmith then joined the Western Advertising Agency in Racine, Wisconsin, where he ultimately became an account executive.

After leaving Western Advertising, Highsmith pursued his entrepreneurial calling and in 1946 became president of Nasco—a company he bought in partnership. Highsmith sold his interest in the business ten years later to concentrate on a magazine called *Farmer's Digest,* which he had purchased in 1954. He also developed and produced a shelf file for *National Geographic* magazines that his company would keep selling for many years to come.

Incorporation and Steady Expansion: 1956–86

Highsmith incorporated his enterprise on September 19, 1956, under the name United Book Publishers Company. However, when a planned acquisition did not transpire, the name Highsmith Company was adopted three months later. Operations initially took place from a small, three-room suite at 81 North Main Street in Fort Atkinson.

Hugh Highsmith eventually relocated his new company to a 3,000-square-foot farmhouse located on Curtis Mill Road. As

Company Perspectives:

We lead our industry segment by maintaining an unconditional commitment to our customers and by increasing efficiency through an organizational structure that moves decision-making closer to the task. Our commitment to education and information extends to our employees, who are encouraged to choose from an innovative menu of wellness, health risk management, and in-house education programs.

Kathy Brady wrote in the September 1990 *Highsmith Grapevine* article: "Besides working the farm, the company continued to publish *Farmer's Digest,* [sell] magazine files and produce agricultural items. At one time, the company produced 270,000 calf halters for one customer!"

As Brady explains, Highsmith later "had the opportunity to purchase the small book company previously considered from George Knutson, a modest man who had built a business selling overruns of children's books to schools. These books were sold to schools, before the advent of the school library, for students to check out from their teachers. The books were featured in early Highsmith library catalogs, along with book-related products."

Growth soon rendered the Curtis Mill Road location inadequate, prompting Hugh Highsmith to move the company to a newly constructed, 12,000-square-foot facility in 1966. Located east of Fort Atkinson on Highway 106, the new site was situated in a scenic rural area with a spring-fed pond. At this time, the company employed 20 workers, including 13 women.

As Highsmith transitioned into the 1970s, the company continued to grow at an explosive pace. In 1969, Hugh Highsmith sold *Farmer's Digest* and focused solely on marketing supplies. From 1969 to 1973, annual sales—which came exclusively from the company's catalog offerings—grew at a rate of approximately 30 percent. In this short timeframe, Highsmith's employee ranks tripled to 60 workers.

According to the August 8, 1973 issue of the *Daily Jefferson County Union,* during the early 1970s some 85 percent of Highsmith's revenues came from the sale of library equipment and supplies. The rest was attributable to magazine files, as well as agricultural supplies sold mainly to mail order houses, Sears and Roebuck, and the like. Highsmith's catalog had grown to include roughly 7,500 items.

In addition to achieving remarkable growth, Highsmith also was progressive in the area of shipping and logistics. In order to reduce shipping and storage costs, the company shipped certain items directly from manufacturer to customer. In addition, it leveraged information technology to its advantage long before many companies were doing so. The same *Daily Jefferson County Union* article explained: "Invoicing is processed by a computer, which acts as a memory bank for availability of items at a given moment. When an item is low in stock, a printout by the computer at the end of each day makes note of that article."

As the company experienced rapid growth, additional physical expansion was needed. Highsmith nearly doubled the size of its new building after only three years, and further expansion occurred in 1972. By 1973, its headquarters had grown from 12,000 square feet to 30,000 square feet.

As his company prospered, Hugh Highsmith, who had once served as president of his community's local historical society, took the time to share it with others throughout the world. In a report titled the *History of Fort Atkinson Industry,* Bill Starke wrote that in 1973 Highsmith "announced plans to contribute 'seed money' to start free libraries in underdeveloped countries. He was state director of the 'Partners of the Americas' program, had traveled widely in Nicaragua and saw the need for something for their children to read and took action to remedy the problem."

In 1976, Hugh Highsmith's son, Duncan, joined the company as director, design/research. Duncan Highsmith graduated from Antioch College in 1969 and then attended the University of Wisconsin-Milwaukee, where he pursued graduate studies in architecture and urban planning. In the January 1999 issue of *Inc.,* Leigh Buchanan described Duncan as "a fine-arts-student-turned-radical-press-publisher-turned-Japanese-sculptor's-apprentice-turned-architecture-student who vowed never to work for his father's company."

By the early 1980s, Duncan Highsmith had been promoted to executive vice-president and chief operating officer of his family's company, which had sales of approximately $16 million. By 1983, Highsmith offered 20,000 items to its roughly 200,000 customers, 70 percent of which were libraries. The remainder of Highsmith's customers included offices, museums, banks, and individuals. In addition to domestic sales, Highsmith also conducted business with customers in Africa, England, Canada, the Carolinas, Guam, the Marianas, Puerto Rico, and the Virgin Islands.

One innovative development took place in 1984, when the company joined forces with Freeport, Illinois-based Microcomputer Libraries to create what the May 1, 1984 issue of *Library Journal* described as "a non-profit 'national clearinghouse for library management applications of general purpose microcomputer software.'" The clearinghouse involved libraries copying and distributing shareware.

Organizational Evolution: 1987 and Beyond

In 1987, Duncan Highsmith succeeded his father as president and CEO. Sales reached $35 million that year. By August 1988, the company received 3,000 to 5,000 sales calls each week, along with 10,000 pieces of mail and 11,000 customer service inquiries. As CEO, Duncan Highsmith changed the organization's structure by implementing self-directed work teams and enabling workers to have more control over decisions related to their environment and work tasks. In addition, he ensured they had access to outside sources of information, including journal articles, to support their decision-making. In the May 14, 1997 issue of the *Capital Times,* Patrice Wendling cited three goals behind Duncan Highsmith's overall philosophy, known as "the accountable organization": reduce bureaucracy, increase employee motivation, and further continuous improvement.

In Wendling's article, Hugh Highsmith remarked on the impact his son had on the company's evolution, stating: "In the beginning, we were more of a conventional company. I give my

Key Dates:

1954: Hugh Highsmith purchases the magazine *Farmer's Digest*.

1956: Highsmith establishes his company in a three-room suite in Fort Atkinson.

1958: Highsmith relocates to a 3,000-square-foot farmhouse on Curtis Mill Road.

1966: Growth prompts the company's move to a new 12,000-square-foot facility east of Fort Atkinson.

1969: Hugh Highsmith sells *Farmer's Digest* and focuses solely on marketing supplies for various sectors.

1976: Hugh Highsmith's son Duncan joins the company as director, design/research.

1983: Highsmith offers 20,000 items to roughly 200,000 customers, 70 percent of which are libraries.

1987: Duncan Highsmith succeeds his father as president and CEO; sales reach approximately $35 million.

1993: Highsmith is one of only 21 U.S. companies to receive the Wellness Councils of America Gold Award.

1994: Madison School Supply Store is acquired, marking Highsmith's entry into the retail market.

1999: Highsmith renames all of its retail stores Mind-Sparks.

2001: Highsmith exits from the retail market, selling its four MindSparks stores to Moline, Illinois-based Wise Owl Ltd.

2003: Duncan Highsmith succeeds his father as company chairman, with Hugh Highsmith remaining as chairman emeritus.

son, Duncan, a lot of the credit for letting the people feel they are a part of the company. It is wonderful to walk around the building and see people truly interested in what they are doing. In the old days the idea was to control workers, but the new way is to let them blossom on their own. I think the employee does better that way and the company gets that back. We are very fortunate.''

A number of key developments occurred at Highsmith during the 1990s. In 1993, the Upstart brand was acquired from Hagerstown, Maryland-based Freline, Inc. When the company made its Corruboard line of corrugated storage and organization products—an array of colorful, durable storage boxes, portfolios, magazine files, and drawer units—available to the retail market that same year, sales of these products almost tripled. In addition to select ''brick-and-mortar'' retailers, catalog retailer Lillian Vernon was among the retail channels that began offering the Corruboard line to the consumer market. By this time, Corruboard was the only line of products that Highsmith manufactured itself.

Making Corruboard available to the consumer market was only the beginning of Highsmith's foray into the retail market. In January 1994, the company purchased Madison, Wisconsin-based Madison School Supply Store, followed by Pooh Corner Bookstore in the same city the following year. In the January 5, 1995 issue of the *Capital Times*, Duncan Highsmith revealed long-term plans to ''start a national chain of side-by-side stores designed to integrate school and home learning environments.''

While Highsmith closed Madison School Supply in April 1995, it opened a combined Pooh Corner/Highsmith Education Station store in east Madison at the same time and also maintained operations at its first Pooh Corner store. The new combined store included 6,000 square feet of space at Highsmith Education Station and 1,000 square feet at Pooh Corner. Not including books, the retail operation offered 11,000 different items—including software, toys, puzzles, and posters—as well as a classroom area for teacher workshops. This new location was so successful that in February 1996 Highsmith announced plans to close the stand-alone Pooh Corner store it acquired in 1994 and open another combined Highsmith Education Station/Pooh Corner location in west Madison.

In 1999, Highsmith announced it would open a third store in Eau Claire, Wisconsin, and rename all three of its stores as MindSparks. In the July 13, 1999 issue of the *Capital Times*, Highsmith president Paul Moss provided insight into the new name, explaining: ''The name MindSparks accurately captures how our educational toys, books and teacher materials energize lifelong learners. It identifies us as an exciting educational resource and allows us to have an identifiable brand name that we can protect as we expand.''

By 1995, Highsmith's employee base numbered 240, and the company recorded approximately $50 million in annual sales. The following year, Duncan Highsmith established a rather innovative and proactive business practice referred to as ''Life, the Universe, and Everything''—a phrase inspired by Douglas Adams' book *Hitchhiker's Guide to the Galaxy*. As Leigh Buchanan explained in the January 1999 issue of *Inc.*, the practice involved Highsmith and his corporate librarian gathering interesting material from a wide variety of sources, including newspapers, online databases, Web sites, magazines, television, radio, and even conversations with others. Each week, the pair spent two hours sifting through their notes and material, which covered a wide range of subjects. Relevant information was eventually synthesized and stored in a database.

According to Buchanan, ''In this eclectic mix [Duncan Highsmith] is searching for nascent trends, provocative contradictions, and, most important, connections that could eventually reshape his business.'' Ultimately, ''Life, the Universe, and Everything'' enabled Highsmith to look at the long view outside of the organization. This strategy stemmed from an early 1990s sales dip brought on by a decrease in school funding which, according to Duncan Highsmith, possibly could have been avoided by paying better attention to certain conditions.

During the 1990s, Highsmith received national recognition for its commitment to employee wellness. After learning in 1989 that insurance costs were to rise an astronomical 53 percent, the company developed a voluntary program called Wellpower Plus to keep workers healthy and manage rising healthcare costs. It offered financial incentives for employees to stay well and provided opportunities for doing so through a combination of health screening tests, education, and exercise classes. In addition to offering an outdoor track where employees could power walk, Highsmith provided them with access to a variety of exercise classes, including step, aerobics, and circuit training.

In October 1993, Highsmith was one of only 21 U.S. companies to receive the Wellness Councils of America Gold Award. In the May 1995 issue of *Inc.,* Duncan Highsmith spoke of the program's success, revealing that the company's health insurance program was "funded completely by saving in both health insurance and related costs." Furthermore, he said: "Qualitatively, we have much more energetic and self-reliant employees, and that's the best investment."

In time, Highsmith's wellness program evolved along with the company's proactive culture. Measures were implemented to address the emotional needs of employees and help them balance the demands of work and life. These measures included flexible work scheduling, a catalog of work- and non-work-related courses, and even free legal advice.

During the early 2000s, Highsmith continued to reap benefits from proactive wellness initiatives. On June 24, 2001, the *New York Times* reported that Highsmith had reduced workers compensation premiums by 24 percent since 1993. Additionally, turnover dropped 14.5 percent to 7.4 percent in only six years. When compared with other companies in its Health Maintenance Organization (HMO) community pool during 1998 and 1999, Highsmith had 22 percent fewer medical claims.

In addition to benefiting from its wellness initiatives, Highsmith also continued to receive national recognition for them. In 2000, the Wellness Councils of America named the company as one of the nation's healthiest. Then, in 2003, Health and Human Services Secretary Tommy Thompson invited Duncan Highsmith and Bill Herman, vice-president of human resources, to participate in an executive roundtable discussion called "Steps to a Healthier US" in Washington, D.C. The *NBC Nightly News* with Tom Brokaw also featured the company in October 2003 for its leadership status in the corporate wellness arena.

The early 2000s marked Highsmith's exit from the retail market. In 2001, the company sold its four MindSparks stores to Moline, Illinois-based Wise Owl Ltd. In the July 18, 2001 issue of the *Capital Times,* Highsmith executive vice-president Paul Moss explained that it had not been possible to grow the retail division as originally expected and that Highsmith would concentrate on its core market of libraries and schools.

In May 2002, a difficult economic climate, marked by reductions in state budgets, impacted Highsmith's business. The company was forced to reduce its workforce by 15 percent, cutting 30 workers in one day. Despite these challenging times, Highsmith remained committed to its remaining workers. The following year, the company was recognized for its progressive culture when it was nominated to the Wisconsin Honor Roll and given a Corporate Culture Award. According to the *Milwaukee Journal Sentinel* for September 17, 2003, the award "recognizes a company for its focus on employee retention, motivation and involvement in the success of the company." The award was co-sponsored by the *Journal Sentinel* and the Milwaukee office of Deloitte & Touche.

By late 2003, growth had prompted seven major additions to Highsmith's Curtis Mill Road facility. According to the company, these included "the expansion and automation of the warehouse operation, new office areas, a plant-filled atrium and a corporate library." Over the years, the company's culture had truly evolved to role-model status, thanks largely to Duncan Highsmith's enlightened, empowering approach to business.

Duncan Highsmith succeeded his father as company chairman in 2003, with Hugh Highsmith remaining as chairman emeritus. Together, the two men had successfully built their family-owned enterprise into a world library supply leader and established a workforce committed to the company's continued success.

Principal Competitors

Brodart Company; DEMCO, Inc.; Gaylord Bros.

Further Reading

Adams, John S., " 'NBC News' Crew Visits Highsmith," *Daily Jefferson County Union*, October 22, 2003.

Brady, Kathy, "Highsmith: A Company with History," *Highsmith Grapevine*, September 1990.

Buchanan, Leigh, "The Smartest Little Company in America," *Inc.,* January 1999.

Gores, Paul, "5 Companies Get Special Honors," *Milwaukee Journal Sentinel*, September 18, 2003.

Gribble, Roger A., "Profiting from Education," *Wisconsin State Journal*, August 17, 1995.

Hajewski, Doris, "Together, They Catalog. Small Company Puts a Premium on Teamwork and Good Health," *Milwaukee Journal Sentinel*, September 8, 2003.

Hawkins, Lee, Jr., "Highsmith Co. Buys Children's Bookstore," *Wisconsin State Journal*, January 5, 1995.

——, "Wellness Works for Highsmith," *Wisconsin State Journal*, November 17, 1994.

"Highsmith Adds Store, Changes to 'MindSparks'," *Capital Times*, July 13, 1999.

"Highsmith Co. to Receive Chamber Salute Thursday," *Daily Jefferson County Union*, August 8, 1973.

Lunday, Sarah, "A Place Where They Don't Dread Coming to Work," *New York Times*, June 24, 2001.

"Madison Getting Second Education Station Store," *Capital Times*, February 13, 1996.

Masterson, Peg, "Library Suppliers Reading It Right," *Milwaukee Journal Sentinel*, August 25, 1988.

McCann, Carla, " 'This Company Cares'," *Janesville Gazette*, October 6, 2003.

Meyer, Nancy, "Highsmith's Storage Comes to Retail," *HFD—The Weekly Home Furnishings Newspaper*, March 14, 1994.

"Public Domain Software: Another Source Reported," *Library Journal*, May 1, 1984.

Trewyn, Phill, "Wellness Program Draws National Attention," *Business Journal-Milwaukee*, June 29, 2001.

Welch, Lynn, "MindSparks Sold. Illinois Owner Vows Little Change in Kids' Stores," *Capital Times*, July 18, 2001.

Wendling, Patrice, "Highsmith High on Innovation," *Capital Times*, May 14, 1997.

Witte, Sally Salkowski, "Highsmith Meets Needs of Libraries," *Milwaukee Journal Sentinel*, November 5, 1983.

—Paul R. Greenland

Holland & Knight LLP

195 Broadway, 24th floor
New York, New York 10007
U.S.A.
Telephone: (212) 513-3200
Fax: (212) 385-9010
Web site: http://www.hklaw.com

Limited Liability Partnership
Incorporated: 1968
Employees: 2,866
Sales: $514.5 million (2002)
NAIC: 54111 Offices of Lawyers

With 31 domestic and international offices, Holland & Knight LLP is among the 20 largest law firms in the world. The firm's largest offices are in Washington, Chicago, New York, and Boston. Internationally, offices are located in Brazil, Finland, Japan, Mexico, Venezuela, and Israel. Holland & Knight provides legal representation in more than 100 areas of law, divided into five major sections: Business Law; Litigation; Private Wealth Services; Public Law; and Real Estate, Environmental and Land Use.

A Merger Marks a Beginning: 1960s

Holland & Knight was founded in 1968, when the firm of Holland, Bevis Smith, Kibler & Hall merged with Knight, Jones, Whitaker & Germany. Both firms had been long-established Florida practices. Spessard Holland, a former Florida governor (1940–44) and U.S. Senator (1948–1972), opened his Bartow, Florida, practice in 1919; Peter O. Knight, co-founder of Tampa Electric Co. and the Exchange National Bank of Tampa, began his Tampa-based practice in 1889.

In 1968 the managing partner at Holland was Chesterfield Smith, who sought to diversify Holland's then mostly phosphate mining business. A merger with the Knight firm, which represented such companies as Tampa Electric and the Exchange National Bank, was therefore attractive. With Holland's high ambitions for growth, and under the leadership of Smith, Knight also would benefit from the merger. The only real difficulty involved the name, as no lawyer wished to be left out. The

compromise, to keep only the names of each firm's founder, was one on which the firm would remain fiercely protective.

At the time of the merger, Chesterfield Smith emerged as Holland & Knight's managing partner. From the time Smith began working in Holland's office in 1951, he quickly began to build an impressive career. A former chairman of the Florida Constitutional Revision Commission, Smith was completely loyal to the law. Later, he would even have a chapter devoted to him in Tom Brokaw's book, *The Greatest Generation.* In 1969 he was given the Chamber of Commerce's ''Distinguished Floridian of the Year Award.''

Smith, it often has been said, was largely responsible for building Holland & Knight into a powerhouse. He had a vision of a statewide—and nationwide—law firm with no headquarters. By 1983 the firm had opened six new offices. First, Smith looked toward Miami, Florida's most lucrative legal market. The Miami office opened with three lawyers, though a 1980 merger with Glass, Schultz, Weinstein & Moss brought the number to 20, as well as four more in Fort Lauderdale (where the firm had also expanded). Other mergers brought a Holland presence in Fort Myers, Sarasota, and Bradenton. In 1972 Holland & Knight became the first Florida-based law firm to open an office in Tallahassee. The Tallahassee office allowed the firm to lobby on behalf of Florida clients and help them to bid on government contracts. Miami and Tallahassee expansions proved successful for the firm; others, such as Coral Gables and Fort Myers, did not.

As Smith's mergers brought attention to Holland & Knight, so did his associations with political figures. In 1973, as president of the American Bar Association, Smith was very vocal in his criticism of President Nixon for his ''defiant flouting of law and the courts'' during the Watergate scandal. In 1977, when the Miami-Dade State Attorney stepped down, Smith persuaded the governor to appoint his friend, Janet Reno. Other friends of Smith included Senator Bob Graham, as well as former governors Reubin Askew and Lawton Chiles.

Going National: 1980s–90s

While Smith's aggressive growth strategy was making Holland & Knight a name, it was also prompting discussions in the

Company Perspectives:

Holland & Knight has more than 1,250 lawyers serving clients globally in virtually every area of the law. We encourage you to evaluate our firm based on the principles that drive us: strong and supportive relationships with our communities and clients and commitments to diversity and continuing education.

firm regarding strategy. Many partners felt expansion was happening too quickly. This was especially true when, in 1982, Smith opened an office in Washington, D.C., in a merger with Pope, Ballard & Loos. Even as the Washington office increased Holland & Knight's clients' advantage in lobbying and government contracts, some of the firm's attorneys thought the timing was bad. Interest rates were in the double digits; the Reagan administration was deregulating, thereby eliminating legal work; and Holland & Knight's profit margin was lower than in previous years. Regardless, in 1983, the firm expanded further, this time into Orlando. As partners grew more uneasy, Smith did what the law firm least expected: he decided to resign, claiming Holland & Knight needed fresh leadership and that he needed a break.

Internal conflict began when it became unclear who would step in for Smith. Eventually, the firm accepted Smith's suggestion to resolve the conflict: Robert Feagin became the managing partner, while Burke Kibler became chairman of the board. At this point, profits were suffering, having dropped from $10.62 million in 1984 to $10.61 million in 1985. The firm hired a consultant, who gave such suggestions as to bill clients more promptly, reduce overhead, bill clients for copying costs, and to stop providing personal secretaries for every lawyer. The situation did not immediately improve. Groups of lawyers split from Holland & Knight to form their own firms, taking their clients with them. In 1986 more than half of the Miami office and eight attorneys from Fort Lauderdale threatened to defect.

A compromise—involving the use of a three-person, rotating management committee—saved the firm from losing more attorneys (and their clients). The new committee, comprised of Feagin, W. Reeder Glass, and Bill McBride, was able to resolve many past problems in the firm. Pay levels for partners increased; clients were billed more promptly; new committees were formed to attract new clients; and a two-tiered system that made it more difficult to become an equity partner was enacted. Also, for the moment, expansion was halted.

This changed quickly in 1992, when Bill McBride was appointed solo managing partner. Under his direction, Holland & Knight went fully national. The firm established its second out-of-state office in 1994, when it opened an office in Atlanta through a merger with Webb & Daniel, trial litigation specialists. Earlier that year the firm had expanded its existing Washington, D.C., office by merging with the D.C. office of Dunnells & Duvall. From 1995–96, through mergers, Holland expanded its offices in Atlanta and Fort Lauderdale, strengthening the firm's capabilities in the fields of business litigation, health care, real estate, and local government. In 1997, merging with

the 167-year-old firm Haight, Gardner, Poor & Havens, Holland expanded into New York and San Francisco, strengthening its capabilities in aviation, maritime, and international law, as well as confirming its national presence.

In 1998 growth was immense, involving expansion in Jacksonville and Orlando, as well as new offices in Virginia, Rhode Island, and Boston. The firm also established a joint venture office with Gallástagui y Lozano in Mexico City. Combined, the new presences boosted practice in syndication, trusts and estates, construction and intellectual property, banking, financial institutions, education, environmental law, litigation, corporate and securities practices, technology, maritime, and media law.

In 1999 the firm opened an office in Tel Aviv, Israel, through a strategic affiliation with Haim Samet, Steinmetz, Haring & Co. This marked the first time a foreign law firm had entered the Israeli legal marketplace. Also this year there was expansion into Melbourne, Florida.

During this time, Holland & Knight proved a commitment to community service and charity. Its full-time Community Services Team (CST) provided pro bono representation to those who required the resources of a large law firm but could not afford it. The firm was only the second in the country to make a full-time commitment of this nature. Holland & Knight's services to the needy preceded its formation of the CST. Chesterfield Smith, for one, received a number of awards for the free legal services he and the firm provided. Legal Services of Greater Miami named its main office building the "Chesterfield Smith Center for Equal Justice," while the nonprofit Florida History Associates named Smith a "Great Floridian." The firm's other community initiatives included a Holocaust Remembrance Project, run by the Holland & Knight Charitable Foundation, and the Opening Doors for Children charity program.

Increasing Competition after 2000

Holland & Knight's roll-up strategy, which the firm used in most of its expansions, was both imitated and criticized. The strategy involved acquiring, or as those in the firm referred to it, "combining with" an existing firm. The qualities Holland & Knight sought in such firms were: financial strength, a sizeable workforce, desire for growth, a history of community involvement, and a willingness for a new, shared, identity with Holland & Knight. Also, Holland & Knight sought firms that would fill specific areas of law in which they were lacking. The firm has also been known to woo groups of lawyers from other firms in order to fill a legal niche for Holland & Knight.

This type of expansion left some unhappy. Stanley Fineman, president of the Wilkes Artis law firm in Washington, D.C., for one, resented how Holland & Knight—in what the *Washington Post* dubbed a coup—walked away with 17 of its attorneys. While the two firms had spent months discussing a possible merger, Holland & Knight suddenly pulled out. Shortly after, the 17 lawyers migrated, leaving behind eight who specialized in property tax appeals, a practice for which Holland & Knight had no need. Other critics claimed that much of a firm's culture could be lost when expanding externally, though Holland & Knight deliberately sought firms with similar values. Either way, the strategy allowed for an impressive growth rate.

Key Dates:

1968: Holland & Knight is founded.
1972: The company is the first Florida law firm to open an office in Tallahassee.
1973: Chesterfield Smith, the company's managing partner, serves as the American Bar Association's president.
1982: Holland & Knight opens an office in Washington, D.C.
1983: Chesterfield Smith retires; Robert Feagin becomes managing partner; Burke Kibler becomes chairman.
1986: A three-person, rotating management committee is enacted.
1992: Bill McBride is appointed managing partner.
1998: The firm experiences enormous growth, including expansions in Jacksonville, Orlando, Virginia, Boston, and Mexico City.
2001: McBride resigns as managing partner; Feagin takes his place.
2003: Howell Melton is elected the firm's managing partner.

The year 2000 was again big for "combining" activity. In Washington, D.C., six nationally renowned lawyers in the field of diversity counseling and minority business development joined Holland & Knight. In Los Angeles and Seattle, noted Indian law firm Levine & Associates joined Holland. In the same month, the firm expanded to Southern California. Later that year Holland opened a representative office in Caracas, Venezuela, by aligning itself with Tinoco, Travieso, Planchart & Nunez. Then came a move into San Antonio, Texas.

In 2001 Holland & Knight was ranked the fifth largest U.S. law firm. It also scored highly in other categories, including having the largest number of African-American partners and being the first major Florida company to offer spousal benefits to gay employees. The firm also supported a great number of pro bono cases, and it was the only law firm to ever spawn two American Bar Association presidents (Chesterfield Smith and Tallahassee-based Martha Barnett).

Holland & Smith did encounter obstacles in sustaining its status. For instance, the crop of new law graduates was depleted when huge British law firms entered the scene. This so-called "Magic Circle" of London firms—larger and more prestigious than their American counterparts—began recruiting at American law schools. Also, the Big Five accounting firms—with large employee bases and deep pockets—also presented a challenge, as they pressed state bar associations to allow them to provide their own legal services for customers.

Internally, too, some of the issues the firm experienced in the 1980s remained. For one, Holland continued to experience lower than average profits, even as its revenue growth exceeded all but that of one firm in the 1990s. Holland's partners' average salary of $395,000 ranked 81st in 1999; a comparable firm's partners earned an average of $1.6 million. The salary difference, the firm maintained, was due to several factors: regional cost-of-living differences, discount billing rates; public service work; and its acquisition-based growth strategy (which resulted in a large number of partners for the firm).

In 2001 managing partner Bill McBride resigned in order to make a run (ultimately unsuccessful) for governor of Florida. McBride had led the firm for nearly ten years and was largely responsible for its international presence. When Robert Feagin assumed McBride's position, Holland continued to grow, both nationally and internationally. In 2001 it established a formal association with a South American law firm with offices in Rio de Janiero and Sao Paulo. The firm also expanded its offices in Providence, Rhode Island.

In 2002 the firm expanded its practices in Seattle and Chicago. The Chicago merger—with McBride, Baker & Coles—significantly strengthened the firm's real estate/financial services, labor and employment, and corporate and securities practices. Meanwhile, in the same year, Holland & Knight laid off 60 attorneys and 170 staff members nationwide. While the poor economy was cited as a reason for the layoffs, some insiders claimed that rapid expansion had diminished the firm's profitability. The layoffs followed an internal review of the firm, in an attempt to address the company's decreasing profits.

By 2003 the situation was improving for Holland & Knight. Profits were up. Profits per partner had risen to $435,000, 22.5 percent higher than the prior year. Moreover, Holland & Knight was named a top 100 law firm by *American Lawyer* magazine, while *Corporate Board Member* magazine named the firm's Tampa office the number one law firm in Tampa. Holland & Knight was also recognized for the top lawyers it employed. One partner was named one of America's Top Lawyers by *Black Enterprise Magazine*, while 32 other Holland attorneys were recognized as America's Leading Business Lawyers in the *Chambers USA Guide*.

Also in 2003, Howell W. Melton, Jr., was elected the firm's new managing partner. Most of that year's growth involved acquiring new attorneys from other firms. Georgia Senator M. Kasim Reed left the firm of Paul, Hastings, Janofsky & Walker to become a partner at Holland & Knight. The firm's Chicago office, meanwhile, gained Jack Siegel, dubbed "Dean of Illinois Municipal Law," from Altheimer & Gray.

The firm also began plans to significantly expand its Seattle office from 17 to 150 lawyers. The expansion, which would make Holland & Knight the fourth-largest law firm in the city, would enhance Holland & Knight's presence in the West, while also enhancing its capabilities in technology law, admiralty, maritime and aircraft law, and Indian tribal law. Plans for achieving the expansion included hiring lawyers away from other firms and merging with smaller Seattle firms. While the Seattle expansion would certainly increase the size of the law firm, it presumably would not do much to improve Holland & Knight's profitability, which consistently ranked toward the bottom, according to *American Lawyer* magazine.

Principal Competitors

Skadden, Arps, Slate, Meagher & Flom LLP; Cravath, Swaine & Moore; Wachtell, Lipton, Rosen & Katz; Altman Weil Inc.

Further Reading

Barancik, Scott, "Rapidly Expanding Tampa, Fla., Law Firm Faces Several Challenges," *St. Petersburg Times*, May 7, 2001.

Engleman, Eric, "Holland & Knight Plans Exponential Expansion," *Business Journal*, August 4, 2003.

"Holland & Knight Cuts Staff," *Business Journal*, May 1, 2002.

"Holland & Knight Lands Top Spot in Annual Survey," *Business Journal*, June 16, 2003.

Itkoff, Valerie Greenburg, "Florida, Detroit Law Firm Talk Merger," *Miami Review*, July 5, 1991.

Ivice, Paul, "Law Firm Layoffs Hit Region Office Harder, *Business Journal*, May 1, 2002.

Knapp, Becky, "Lawyers Feel Pinch in the Pocketbook," *Business Journal*, February 4, 2002.

Leavy, Pamela Griner, "Economic Times to Bring about 'Firm' Changes," *Business Journal*, April 1, 2002.

Merzer, Martin, and Cindy Krischer Goodman, "Prominent S. Fla. Lawyer Chesterfield Smith Dies at 85," *Miami Herald*, July 17, 2003.

——, "S. Florida's No. 1 Lawyer for Decades Remembered," *Miami Herald*, July 18, 2003.

Qualters, Sher, "Law Firms Boost Profits," *Business Journal*, July 7, 2003.

"Remembering Chesterfield Smith," *Tampa Tribune*, July 18, 2003.

Schmidt, Richard B., "Law Firms' Mergers Create Conflicts," *Wall Street Journal Europe*, June 8, 2001.

Silva, Mark, "Law Firm's Leader Faces Long Odds If He Runs for Governor," *Orlando Sentinel*, June 3, 2001.

Stidham, Jeff, "Floridians Stephen Grimes," *Tampa Tribune*, December 26, 1997.

"Tribute to a Titan of the Law: Chesterfield Smith," *Metropolitan Corporate Counsel*, August 2003.

Wilson, Elizabeth, "Holland & Knight Expand or Expire?," *Florida Trend*, December 1, 1988.

—Candice Mancini

J.H. Findorff and Son, Inc.

300 South Bedford
Madison, Wisconsin 53703-3628
U.S.A.
Telephone: (608) 257-5321
Fax: (608) 257-5306
Web Site: http://www.findorff.com

Private Company
Incorporated: 1946 as J.H. Findorff & Son Inc.
Employees: 550
Sales: $173 million (2002)
NAIC: 236220 Commercial and Institutional Building
 Construction; 236210 Industrial Building Construction

J.H. Findorff and Son, Inc., is a leading general contractor of non-residential buildings serving southern Wisconsin. Based in Madison, where the employee-owned company ranks as the city's oldest general contractor, Findorff also has offices in Milwaukee. Findorff works with clients in different capacities, including that of construction manager, design-builder, and general contractor. The company's unionized workforce is capable of performing a wide variety of construction work, from carpentry, concrete, and drywall to masonry and steel work. In more than 100 years of operation, Findorff has constructed literally thousands of well-known buildings in Wisconsin. These include everything from educational facilities, governmental buildings, and hotels, to offices, parking ramps, and shopping centers.

A Family Affair: 1890–1980

Findorff's roots stretch back to the late 1800s, when a young Middleton, Wisconsin, native named John H. Findorff left his family's farm to work as a carpenter on the Dane County Courthouse, erected in 1885. The son of German immigrants, Findorff went on to work on homes and notable buildings in Madison, including the interior and dome of the state capitol.

Around this time, the city of Madison was experiencing a construction boom. With opportunities abounding, Findorff ac-

quired the Stark Manufacturing Co. and went into business for himself as a carpenter contractor in 1890. According to company literature, "The firm's first contract was building and installing the woodwork and cabinetry for the University of Wisconsin's Armory or 'Red Gym.' This began a long and continuing tradition of Findorff building many of the UW's most notable structures."

Despite an economic depression, Findorff's business prospered. By 1904, he had purchased an old flour mill and constructed an office, lumberyard, and planing mill at South Bedford and West Wilson Streets. A fire destroyed Findorff's base of operations in 1909. However, thanks to generous support from the Madison community, the company was able to be re-established, and operations would continue from the same location for many years. According to Jonathan D. Silver of the *Capital Times*, John H. Findorff was "remembered as a generous man who would occasionally peel a $20 bill from his wallet and hand it to a surprised foreman as a reward for a job well done."

By 1917, the enterprise had evolved into a partnership between Findorff and his son, Milton B. Findorff, who graduated from the University of Wisconsin that year. It was at this time that the company evolved into the city's first general contractor. In its January 16, 1970 issue, the *Capital Times* described Milton Findorff as a "knowledgeable contractor" and "a dynamic businessman," and went on to explain: "In the 1920s, under his guidance, J.H. Findorff and son grew and added many new buildings to its list of completions—the Madison Gas and Electric offices, the University of Wisconsin Engineering Building on University Avenue, and the Wisconsin Power and Light office building among them." In all, Findorff was able to secure some 150 contracts during the 1920s—even though the nation faced dire economic times.

Progress continued during the 1930s. During this decade, Findorff began investing in the newest equipment in order to stay at the forefront of the construction trade. Examples of the company's purchases during this time include a crane in 1936, and a concrete pump the following year. Notable historic buildings constructed by Findorff during the 1930s include East High School and a state office building in 1930, as well as Quisling Apartments in 1937.

Company Perspectives:

Findorff is known for its sophisticated pre-construction capabilities as well as innovative construction methods. We enjoy a high degree of repeat client business due to our clients' knowledge of Findorff as a reliable, financially strong, price conscious, schedule focused, quality contractor.

In 1941, Findorff made history outside of the building realm when it was selected to install the first parking meters in downtown Madison. The company continued to operate as a partnership for approximately 30 years, until incorporating under the name J.H. Findorff & Son Inc. in 1946.

In the wake of material shortages that brought many jobs to a halt, Findorff focused its attention on the war effort during the 1940s, constructing such facilities as Truax Field, the Badger Ordnance, and the Gisholt Machinery Company's Northern Works. At the Badger Ordnance site, Findorff once employed an astonishingly large crew of 900 tradesmen.

By 1948, Milton Findorff had been promoted from vice-president and treasurer to president. He, in turn, received assistance running the company from his son, John R. Findorff, who at the age of 30 had become a company director. Prior to joining his family's company, John R. Findorff served in the Coast Guard during World War II and graduated from Lehigh University in Bethlehem, Pennsylvania, in 1941. He was the third generation of the Findorff family to join the business.

By the time John R. Findorff joined his family's organization, it had evolved considerably since the early years. In addition to functioning as a general contractor, Findorff offered a millwork service, a sizable ready mix concrete operation, and a wholesale and retail lumber business. The company also marketed a variety of building materials. Shortly before his 81st birthday, in the May 2, 1948 issue of the *Capital Times*, John H. Findorff elaborated on his company's growth and success, explaining: "Yes, we have been very fortunate in the type of organization built up. I want first to point out that only because we had loyal and conscientious associates, men who have been with us as long as 45 years, we have succeeded. Recently, we could count something like 30 employees who have been with us a quarter-century. Our construction superintendents are men who know their jobs, and while the general public may not hear very much about them, they are in fact the very core and backbone of the Findorff business."

A construction boom rippled through Madison during the 1960s, and Findorff played a major role. According to the company, major construction projects during this time included the Anchor Savings and Loan Building, Hilldale Shopping Center, the State of Wisconsin Hill Farms Office Complex, and an upper deck addition to Camp Randall Stadium.

In 1961, W. Harold Hastings was named president of Findorff, succeeding Milton Findorff who became chairman. Over the course of many decades, Findorff had witnessed a great deal of change in the area of construction methods and techniques. In the January 20, 1967 issue of the *Capital Times*,

Milton Findorff described the evolution: "First there was the wood era. Then came steel, then concrete, then the reinforced concrete we use today. Now we are also erecting prefabricated metal buildings for certain applications."

During the 1970s, Findorff expanded outside of the Madison area to nearby Milwaukee, where it managed the construction of the Medical College of Wisconsin. Other noteworthy construction jobs during this decade included the Petit National Ice Center and the Henry Reuss Federal Center.

By 1971, *Engineering News Record* recognized Findorff, which then employed approximately 400 workers, as one of the oldest construction companies in the nation. That year, John R. Findorff succeeded W. Harold Hastings as president, with Hastings becoming chairman. Two years later, in a joint venture with Fon du Lac, Wisconsin-based Hutter Construction Co., Findorff received what at the time was reported to be the largest contract ever awarded by the state of Wisconsin. The $23 million contract was for construction of the University of Wisconsin Medical Center's first phase.

As the 1970s progressed, Findorff continued to receive industry recognition for its work. In 1977, the company was ranked 307 in *Engineering News Records'* top 400 construction firms, with more than $37 million in contracts for the year.

Gerd Zoller was named Findorff's president in 1979. Zoller had joined Findorff as a project manager in 1968 after working as a civil engineer in Finland. He had subsequently rose through the company's management ranks, and was named vice-president in 1976.

By 1980, John R. Findorff was serving as Findorff's chairman and CEO. The previous year, Findorff expanded operations outside of Wisconsin when it established a branch in Tampa, Florida. Around this same time, Findorff/Potter, Inc., a separate company, was founded when Findorff teamed with Potter, Lawson & Pawlowsky Architects. The new organization provided design/build services, and also offered pre-engineered metal building systems to customers.

New Ownership: 1980s and Beyond

In 1981, John R. Findorff sold the company his grandfather had founded nearly a century before to three long-time employees: Curt Hastings, Ken Kruska, and President Gerd Zoller. Despite the worst economic conditions within the construction industry since World War II, the company thrived by adapting to change. It also shifted to a more marketing-focused approach instead of waiting to bid on potential projects. Findorff found that customers were relying more on negotiation to choose contractors instead of the bidding process. From 1972 to 1982, the percentage of Findorff's business attributed to negotiation switched from 50 percent to between 60 and 70 percent. Despite a sour economy, Findorff's sales reached $61 million in 1983.

In 1988, Kruska succeeded Zoller as Findorff's president, and Zoller was appointed chairman. Kruska's relationship with Findorff began in 1954, when he joined the company as a carpenter's apprentice. A number of promotions followed over the years, including that of general superintendent. After leaving the company in 1966, Kruska returned in 1971 and made

Key Dates:

1890: John H. Findorff goes into business for himself as a carpenter contractor.

1904: Findorff purchases an old flour mill and constructs an office, lumberyard, and planing mill.

1917: Findorff partners with his son, Milton B. Findorff.

1941: The company is selected to install the first parking meters in downtown Madison.

1946: The company incorporates under the name J.H. Findorff & Son Inc.

1948: Milton Findorff is named president.

1961: Milton Findorff becomes chairman, while W. Harold Hastings is named president.

1971: John R. Findorff succeeds W. Harold Hastings as president, and Hastings becomes chairman.

1977: Findorff is listed among *Engineering News Records'* top 400 construction firms, with more than $37 million in contracts for the year.

1981: John R. Findorff sells the company to three long-time employees.

1983: Company sales reach $61 million.

1990: Findorff celebrates 100 years of operations, and sales reach an unprecedented $92 million.

2002: Findorff reveals its new headquarters overlooking Madison's Lake Monona.

vice-president five years later. In the November 4, 1993, issue of the *Capital Times*, columnist Jonathan D. Silver described Kruska the following way: "A friendly man with a firm handshake, sage eyes that seem to be perpetually half-closed and a mouth that turns down at the corners, Kruska cuts the picture of a rough-and-tumble construction executive. A hard hat looks at home on his head. And the company has left a deep a mark on him as it has on Madison itself."

By the time Kruska was named president, the company's management philosophy had truly evolved. In the December 1989 issue of *In Business*, Kruska said: "I was practically brainwashed into the old style. That meant you were told what to do, and management was always second-guessing everything you did. As a matter of fact, that's one of the reasons I left the company (in 1966), because I felt if I didn't do something exactly as someone wanted me to, I was wrong, no matter what. But now, you look at the ingenuity of some of these people. It's crazy not to use it. They've got good ideas. And it creates a much better morale. You get a lot fewer ulcers this way."

Findorff celebrated 100 years of operations in 1990. The occasion was marked by an anniversary dinner at Madison's Sheraton Inn, where 22 employees were recognized with silver bowls for at least 25 years of service. In all, some 115 employees had received such recognition over the years. By this time, Findorff had grown to be among the state's largest contractors, serving Madison, Milwaukee, and other towns throughout Wisconsin and Illinois.

In Milwaukee, Findorff was recognized as the city's largest minority business in the July 20, 1992, issue of the *Milwaukee Journal Sentinel*. According to the publication, when Milwaukee's Next Door Foundation remodeled its facility, Findorff offered its expertise in the spirit of good corporate citizenship by helping the foundation manage other minority businesses involved in the project.

In 1990, Findorff's sales reached an unprecedented $92 million, a 51 percent increase from 1983 levels. However, an economic recession pushed revenues down to $83 million in 1993. Even so, a great sense of optimism prevailed, and Findorff continued to secure high-profile contracts, including a deal worth more than $60 million to manage the construction of Madison's Monona Terrace convention center, which was based on the design of the legendary Frank Lloyd Wright. By this time, Findorff's employees owned 49 percent of the company. The firm employed many long-time workers, including some whose families had worked there for two or even three generations.

In 1994, Findorff's sales reached $94 million. That year, Ken Kruska succeeded Gerd Zoller as Findorff's chairman, and Curt Hastings was appointed president. With formal training in the field of civil engineering, Hastings had joined Findorff in 1969 as an estimator and was named vice-president in 1977. His father, W. Harold Hastings, had served as Findorff's president and chairman during the 1960s.

Findorff built a permanent office in Milwaukee in 1996. The following year, plans were announced to move the company's building materials and construction yard operations from 601 West Wilson Street to a site at 703 Mayfair Avenue on the city's east side, where Georgia Pacific planned to vacate a distribution center. The new 14-acre site was obtained for $1.35 million. However, Findorff remained committed to the neighborhood in which it had operated since 1890, and opted to keep its headquarters there.

In May 2002, Findorff revealed its new headquarters at 300 South Bedford Street—a 38,000-square-foot, three-story office building overlooking Madison's Lake Monona. Designed by the architectural firm of Potter Lawson, the new $5 million facility contained an employee fitness center, lunchroom, and underground parking. In the June 2, 2002 issue of the *Wisconsin State Journal*, architect Doug Hursh explained how the new building was created with the surrounding neighborhood in mind. "We wanted history to be part of the design," he said. "We looked at the buildings around that neighborhood to relate it specifically to the Bassett Street neighborhood." A foundation of rough-cut Minnesota limestone was used because it was once quarried in the area, and a roof with deep overhangs and large support brackets was inspired by nearby tobacco warehouses.

In addition to its new headquarters, Findorff had much to celebrate in 2002. Topping the list were several high-profile construction projects in Milwaukee. In January, *Midwest Construction Magazine* announced that it had given Findorff an Award of Merit for its work on the $32 million ASQ Center, a historical combination of five buildings that formerly housed Gimbel's department store and Marshall Field's. Serving as general contractor, Findorff renovated the combined structures, which spanned an entire city block and dated back as far as 1890, to create a structure containing offices and a Marriott Residence Inn.

In February, the *Daily Reporter* announced that Findorff had received Excellence in Construction honors from the Wisconsin Department of Administration's Division of Facilities Development. The honors were related to the company's construction of the $62 million Milwaukee Secure Detention Facility—the state's first high-rise detention building. Finally, in July, Wisconsin's governor and lieutenant governor praised Findorff for its work on the 275,000-square-foot Wisconsin State Fair Park Exposition Center. The massive project involved the use of more than 30 different subcontractors.

By 2002, Findorff employed approximately 550 workers in both Madison and Milwaukee, and had sales of $173 million. Each year, the company completed more than $100 million of construction. By this time, Richard M. Lynch was Findorff's president, having succeeded Curt Hastings, who became chairman. A 1974 University of Wisconsin–Madison graduate, Lynch led the company toward a bright future. Beginning with one carpenter's hammer and a dream, Findorff had truly prospered during three centuries of American history.

Principal Operating Units

Preconstruction Services; Construction Phase Services; Post Construction Services.

Principal Competitors

C.G. Schmidt, Inc.; Marshall Erdman and Associates, Inc.

Further Reading

"Award of Merit," *Midwest Construction Magazine*, January 2, 2002.

Balousek, Mary, "Findorff Gets Terrace Job," *Wisconsin State Journal*, October 12, 1993.

Druml, Tom, "Ivory Tusk Comes to Life," *Daily Reporter*, August 31, 2001.

"Excellence in Construction," *Daily Reporter*, February 25, 2002.

"Findorff Elects New Board for 81st Year in Business," *Wisconsin State Journal*, May 30, 1971.

"Findorff Firm, in 77th Year, Has Bridged Several 'Generations' of Building Methods," *Capital Times*, January 20, 1967.

"Findorff Is Part of Madison Story," *Capital Times*, January 16, 1970.

Hickok-Wall, Ellen, "Exposition Center Celebrates Opening," *Daily Reporter*, July 15, 2002.

Ivey, Mike, "Building on Tradition: Contractor Stays Downtown with New Headquarters," *Capital Times*, May 25, 2002.

Kades, Deborah, "The Contractor's New Headquarters Is Next Door to its Former Home," *Wisconsin State Journal*, June 2, 2002.

Martin, Chuck, "Findorff Tradition Builds On," *Wisconsin State Journal*, March 21, 1982.

Molvig, Dianne, "Ken Kruska, CEO & Carpenter," *In Business*, December 1989.

Parkins, Al, "Findorff to Fete 100 Years. Helped Sculpt City Landscape," *Capital Times*, May 18, 1990.

Pitman, Sharon D., "Findorff Adjusts as Construction World Changes," *Capital Times*, May 9, 1980.

Silver, Jonathan D., "Kruska Built His Way to the Top," *Capital Times*, November 4, 1993.

——, "Spanning the Decades. From Old Red Gym to Convention Center, Findorff Leaves its Mark on Madison," *Capital Times*, November 4, 1993.

Sorensen, Sterling, "Findorff Writes American Success Story in Brick and Stone and Steel," *Capital Times*, May 2, 1948.

Vue, Long, "Minority Businesses Get Contracts, Job Training," *Milwaukee Journal Sentinel*, July 20, 1992.

Wendling, Patrice, "Findorff Move Will Open Up 6 Prime Acres in Heart of City," *Capital Times*, January 6, 1997.

—Paul R. Greenland

Simplot

J.R. Simplot Company

999 Main Street
Boise, Idaho 83702
U.S.A.
Telephone: (208) 336-2110
Fax: (208) 389-7515
Web site: http://www.simplot.com

Private Company
Incorporated: 1956
Employees: 12,000
Sales: $3 billion (2002 est.)
NAIC: 311411 Frozen Fruit, Juice, and Vegetable
    Manufacturing; 112111 Beef Cattle Ranching and
    Farming; 325311 Nitrogenous Fertilizer
    Manufacturing; 325312 Phosphatic Fertilizer
    Manufacturing; 325314 Fertilizer (Mixing Only)
    Manufacturing; 325320 Pesticide and Other
    Agricultural Chemical Manufacturing

The J.R. Simplot Company is one of the largest privately-held agribusiness firms in the United States with interests in food, fertilizer, turf and horticulture, and cattle feeding. The company's growth charts the rags-to-riches rise of J.R. Simplot, an Idaho potato farmer who assembled a corporate empire around a small potato growing business to create a remarkable model of vertical integration in the agricultural industry. As one of the largest frozen potato processors in the world, J.R. Simplot produces three billion pounds of french fries each year, supplying the likes of McDonald's, Burger King, and KFC. The company is also one of the largest producers of beef cattle in the United States and the second-largest frozen vegetable producer in the world.

The complexion of Idaho's economy during the early 2000s reflected the fortunes of the state's most prominent citizen. Idaho's chief manufactured good was processed foods; its largest agriculture crop was potatoes; its greatest number of livestock, cattle; its most abundant nonfuel mineral, phosphate; its principal industry, agriculture. Each of these primary segments

of Idaho's economy described part of the diverse empire developed by John Richard (J.R.) Simplot, a self-described "goldurn potato farmer" whose life charted the remarkable progression of an eighth-grade dropout into a multibillionaire. During the course of his meteoric rise in the business world, Simplot became involved in an eclectic array of businesses, assembling a variegated corporate empire that underpinned Idaho's economy and constituted one of the great American fortunes. At the heart of Simplot's wide-ranging business interests was the J.R. Simplot Company, a corporate entity that at first blush appeared to comprise a motley, disconnected collection of businesses, ranging from mining operations to potato fields to livestock feedlots. The J.R. Simplot Company, however, was not the product of J.R. Simplot's compulsion to own everything without regard for the cohesiveness of the whole. Instead, the J.R. Simplot Company's seemingly odd mix of businesses were indicative of J.R. Simplot's intent to control all aspects related to the cultivation and processing of his potatoes. Around the business of growing and processing potatoes, a vertically integrated empire developed, the magnitude of which belied the humble origins of its creator.

Origins

Born in 1909, Simplot began his ascension to the top of the business world in Delco, Idaho, a small frontier town that was home to roughly ten families during Simplot's childhood. There, amid the sprawling plains stretching across the southern reaches of Idaho, Simplot got his working career off to an early start, deciding at age 14 that what lay outside the confines of the community's four-room schoolhouse held more promise than what lay inside. "I had to stop," Simplot later reflected, referring to his decision to drop out of school. "I didn't get along in school. I just didn't like it." Simplot left school and never returned, opting instead for the back-breaking field work that would fill his days for years to come. Those who knew the young Simplot discovered that whatever passion he lacked for formal education was compensated by his remarkable capacity for labor.

Fortune, decisiveness, and a willingness to work would characterize Simplot's resolute march from grade-school dropout to billionaire, beginning with his first job as a potato sorter

Company Perspectives:

Simplot's mission statement, Bringing Earth's Resources to Life, embodies our reason for being in business: we mold many of our planet's raw materials into a wide variety of value-added products which sustain and enhance life. As part of this process, Simplot has made significant investments in environmental quality, and we constantly work to protect the natural resources without which the company could not exist.

for a local firm of potato brokers. During his off-hours, the 15-year-old Simplot moonlighted by shoring up the canals bringing water from the Snake River into irrigation ditches, earning extra money by "riprapping" the canal banks with rocks until he had enough money to rent 40 acres of potato land from his father and purchase several sow hogs. Simplot then constructed hog pens on the banks of a nearby creek, planted potatoes on his rented land, and fattened his hogs by feeding them an unusual hog slop that opened the doors to wealth and provided him with his first break in his fledgling business.

Instead of paying for feed grain as other livestock owners did, Simplot used what was available to him by tracking down the wild horses that still roamed the plains and combining the horse meat with discarded potatoes and a little barley. Once cooked in a huge iron vat, Simplot's hog slop represented a cheaper alternative to feed grain and, as luck would have it, the horse meat-cull potato-barley mash gave the resourceful Simplot an advantage over other pig farmers after a particularly harsh winter cut short the supply of feed grain. The following spring, when pigs were brought to market, Simplot's fat hogs stood in sharp contrast to the skinny hogs deprived of their usual amount of feed grain, enabling Simplot to reap the rewards from his unconventional hog slop.

Buoyed by the profits gleaned from the sale of his portly pigs, Simplot expanded his hog-raising operations, increasing his stock over the years until he owned roughly 500 hogs by the time he sold his spread for $7,500. With the money, Simplot purchased three teams of horses, some farm machinery, and a substantial supply of seed potatoes, then rented land and immersed himself in the business of growing potatoes. Shortly after beginning his new venture, Simplot learned of an electrically driven potato sorter that was invented in a machine shop in eastern Idaho, the first of its kind in the state. Simplot visited the machine shop, took a look at the new piece of time-saving machinery, then convinced the proprietors to make a duplicate, which Simplot and partner Lindsay Maggart purchased in 1928 for $254.

The electrically driven potato sorter proved to be a boon to Simplot's business, enabling him to sort not only his and his partner's crop but also portions of other farmers' crops. Business was growing briskly and running smoothly until a feud developed between Maggart and a potato broker, and Simplot and the electric potato sorter were caught in the middle. Maggart had become angered when he learned that some of the potatoes sorted by the jointly owned machine were being pur-

chased by the broker. Irked that his property was indirectly benefiting his adversary, Maggart ordered Simplot to stop, but Simplot, unwilling to limit his growing business intentionally, reportedly responded, "Let's flip for it." He won the coin toss, gaining full ownership of the electric potato sorter and full control over its future use.

In 1929, Simplot began to lay the groundwork for his potato empire. Winning ownership of the potato sorter was a stroke of luck, but nearly all of Simplot's success to this point was owed to his legendary devotion to hard labor. During his first decade on his own, Simplot had relied on his indefatigable energy to create a burgeoning business, spending all his waking hours constructing hog pens, digging potato cellars, hauling sacks of potatoes, and tilling the soil, among the other endless and sundry duties required to keep his various ventures alive. That Simplot was able to withstand the debilitative effects of the Depression and prosper was a credit to his tireless efforts, but in the midst of the decade-long economic turmoil he began to demonstrate another quality of character that would propel the young farmer toward the billions of dollars his business would later generate.

Federally funded programs aimed at providing relief to the economically devastated nation included the Bureau of Reclamation's prodigious work along the Snake River, which cut a swath of water across the state. To farmers working in an agriculturally intensive state, the work along the Snake River meant much, but Simplot was one of the few farmers to appreciate the ramifications such work would have on agricultural activity in Idaho. A reliable source of water would enable Simplot to diversify within and around the economy of the potato, supporting his entry into several agricultural and nonagricultural businesses that, once established, would strengthen his position considerably as a potato farmer. Though Simplot would continue to be regarded as a hard-working farmer, striving merely "to raise the average potato yield," as he put it, his foresightedness and decisive development of an interdependent collection of businesses powered his transformation from a "gol-durn potato farmer" into Idaho's preeminent industrialist and spawned one of the great American corporate empires.

World War II Diversification

By 1940, Simplot's holdings had grown to include 33 potato warehouses. The development of Simplot's vertically integrated businesses occurred quickly, beginning with his move into onion farming in the late 1930s. From there, forays into other agricultural and nonagricultural areas followed in quick succession. By 1940, Simplot's large scale onion growing operation had expanded to include facilities for dehydrating onions, which drew the attention of a scouting party for the U.S. Army's Quartermaster Corps the following year as the nation prepared to enter the century's second great military struggle.

At the time of the scouting party's inspection of Simplot's onion-drying operations in the spring of 1941, vegetable dehydration was a crude science practiced by only a handful of businesses. There were only five vegetable-dehydrating factories in the country, none of which could dry and squeeze out the water from potatoes without mashing their cell structure. Spurred by the interest shown in his onion-drying facilities by

Key Dates:

1928: John Richard Simplot and Lindsay Maggart purchase an electrically driven potato sorter.
1929: Simplot begins to lay the groundwork for his potato empire.
1940: Simplot now operates 33 potato warehouses.
1942: Simplot begins to supply the U.S. military with dried potatoes.
1956: The J.R. Simplot Company is incorporated.
1999: Simplot teams up with Netherlands-based Farm Frites Beheer BV to create the Simplot-Farm Frites Global Potato Alliance.
2003: The company opens a french fry plant in Manitoba, Canada.

the Quartermaster Corps, Simplot immersed himself and his resources into discovering a way to dehydrate potatoes, developing, after considerable experimentation, a revolutionary method to peel and dry potatoes efficiently and expeditiously. Simplot subsequently began producing dehydrated potatoes for the military on a scale that augured the beginning of the great achievements to come for the grade school dropout. Over a three-year period between 1942 and 1945, Simplot produced an average of 33 million pounds of dried potatoes each year, or roughly one-third of the U.S. military's consumption during the war, catapulting him to the forefront of the potato industry.

As Simplot's business grew during the war, the range of his operations expanded, giving the fiercely independent Simplot the capability to fulfill his need for raw materials. When he ran short of wooden boxes for shipping his products overseas in 1943, Simplot built his own box production plant. When his box production facility was in need of a greater amount of lumber, he purchased his own lumber company. Simplot's supply of the fertilizer needed to grow his potatoes was cut off in 1944, so he decided to develop his own supply of fertilizer and paid a visit to a parcel of land owned by the Fort Hall Indian Reservation. Simplot scratched the surface with a scraper, searching for phosphate rock needed to produce chemical fertilizer, and, as he later related, "Damned if I didn't latch onto the biggest phosphate deposit west of Florida." Simplot leased the land, built a $1 million fertilizer plant with the help of a government loan, and began tapping into the largest phosphate mine in the west.

In a few short years, Simplot had branched out from potato growing and processing to cultivating and dehydrating onions, to mining, to producing fertilizer, and to logging, with each diversifying move bolstering his mainstay potato business. The sheer magnitude of his potato business led Simplot into another business area in 1945, when he built a small feedlot for cattle. The connection between cows and potatoes was the river of potato waste streaming from his processing plants, a mixture of peelings, sprouts, eyes, and other culls that Simplot mixed with alfalfa, barley, and several chemical supplements to make feed for cattle. From the potato, another Simplot business had been created, turning a farmer's modest hope of raising the average potato yield into a well-rounded, self-sufficient enterprise that had begun to take on the trappings of an agricultural conglomerate.

Postwar Growth

The J.R. Simplot Company was incorporated following the diversified growth during the war years, its founding year in 1956 coming midway through the decade in which Simplot's pioneering contributions toward potato processing continued, resulting in an enormously beneficial discovery. During the 1950s, Simplot researchers developed a method to freeze potatoes, engendering frozen french fries and the new engine that would propel the J.R. Simplot Company's growth. During the 1960s, as Simplot's multifaceted agricultural and nonagricultural interests continued to flourish in the postwar era, Simplot developed a business relationship with Ray Kroc, a fast-food operator who became the single most important person in Simplot's business dealings. The fast-food chain Kroc had founded was none other than McDonald's, which had a nearly insatiable need for the frozen french fries first developed by the J.R. Simplot Company a decade earlier. Simplot would go on to become the single largest supplier of frozen french fries to the massive hamburger chain, adding another lucrative trade to the other prosperous enterprises operating under the Simplot name.

By the late 1960s, after two decades of resolute postwar growth, Simplot's various businesses had made their creator a prominent fixture in American industry. Simplot grew more potatoes, owned more cattle, owned more land, and employed more people than any other Idahoan. He ranked as the largest potato processor in the world, the largest dryer and freezer of potatoes in the world, and owned processing plants, fertilizer plants, mining operations, and other enterprises scattered across 36 states, in Canada, and overseas, making him Idaho's foremost industrialist and one of the biggest in the world. In the decades ahead, Simplot continued to demonstrate his resourcefulness and willingness to jump headfirst into new businesses. He began producing ethanol during the 1970s, using his ubiquitous potatoes to manufacture the alcohol-based fuel additive. During the 1980s, he used the waste water from potato processing for irrigation and cattle manure to help fuel methane gas plants. He also entered into various processed food niches.

By the end of the 1980s, Simplot stood atop a $1.2 billion-in-sales, privately held corporate powerhouse. In addition to five potato processing plants, five vegetable freezing plants, a major cattle raising and meat packing operation, and phosphate mines, Simplot was supported by his own construction company, his own finance company, his own transportation company, and his own cogeneration plants. Simplot's corporate reach, to be sure, extended far and wide, rivaling the largest diversified conglomerates in the world and providing a firm foundation for future growth and long-term stability.

The 1990s and Beyond

By the 1990s, Simplot was in his 80s and ready to hand over the reins of command to the next generation of Simplots. In 1994, control over the J.R. Simplot Company was devolved to an office of the chairman comprising three of Simplot's children and one grandchild, keeping management of the privately owned empire within the Simplot family. Over the course of the decade, the company worked to intensify its international operations as well as strengthen its domestic business by trimming costs and streamlining certain functions. In 1995, Simplot and

Nestlé SA teamed up to acquire the Pacific Brands Food division of Australia-based Pacific Dunlop Ltd. The firm also formed a joint venture in China to produce seed potatoes, which in turn would supply the McDonald's restaurants in the region.

In 1999, Simplot partnered with Netherlands-based Farm Frites Beheer BV to create the Simplot-Farm Frites Global Potato Alliance. According to a November 1999 *Frozen and Chilled Foods* report, the alliance was created to "exchange information on the supply of potatoes, the improvement of operational processes and potato processing, product development, environmental management, and other important issues." Supported by the success of its past ventures, Simplot planned for future growth in the new century. In late 2000, the company announced plans to add Nestlé USA's processed potato business to its arsenal.

Demand for frozen potatoes began to falter in 2001—especially after the events of September 11th—and quick service restaurants began to experience a slowdown in frozen potato sales. Simplot, having successfully weathered harsh economic times throughout its history, immediately began making the necessary business adjustments. It continued to diversify its product line, broadened its market reach, and adjusted production levels. In 2002, the company opted to shutter its Heyburn plant, the second plant added to J.R. Simplot's holdings back in its early days and the original manufacturer of McDonald's french fries.

As the company worked to remain profitable during the economic downturn, it was forced to contend with a lawsuit related to a salmonella outbreak in Phoenix in 1998. Eateries Inc. claimed that five of its Phoenix-based restaurants received contaminated chile relleno product manufactured by a Simplot subsidiary in Mexico. The suit dragged on for five years, and in 2003 Simplot was forced to pay $8.2 million in damages.

Despite facing challenges, Simplot continued to forge ahead. The firm began to import nitrogen-based fertilizers, opening ports in California, Portland, and Texas to facilitate the importing process. By this time, revenues from the firm's fertilizer operations were nearly on par with its food division. The company also began to shift some of its manufacturing operations to Canada. In 2003, the firm opened a new state-of-the-art french fry plant in Manitoba in order to capitalize on the economic advantages the region had to offer, including the lucrative exchange rate between the U.S. and Canadian dollar. Led by Chairman Scott Simplot, CEO Larry Hlobik, and a board of directors that included several Simplot family members, the J.R. Simplot Company appeared to be on track to maintain its posi-

tion as one of the largest privately held agribusiness concerns in the United States for years to come.

Principal Divisions

Food Products; AgriBusiness; Land and Livestock.

Principal Competitors

Cargill Inc.; IMC Global Inc.; McCain Foods Ltd.

Further Reading

Anderson, Steven, "J.R. Simplot Adapts to Slump, Taste Trends," *Idaho Business Review*, April 21, 2003.
——, "Spud Processors Eye Taste Trends," *Idaho Business Review*, June 2, 2003.
Brandt, Richard, "J. R. Simplot: Still Hustling, after All These Years," *Business Week*, September 3, 1990, p. 60.
Cohen, Barry, "J.R. Simplot Company," *Wall Street Transcript*," July 8, 1968, p. 13.
Donahue, Christine, "Jacobson's Magic Turns Simplot's Idaho Spuds into Hot Potatoes," *Adweek's Marketing Week*, July 10, 1989, p. 21.
Erickson, Julie Liesse, "Simplot Bites Back in Micro Snack War," *Advertising Age*, February 27, 1989, p. 4.
——, "Simplot Wizardry Zaps Snack Market," *Advertising Age*, May 8, 1989, p. S6.
"Farm Frites and Simplot Aim for Potato Leadership," *Frozen and Chilled Foods*, November 1999, p. 4.
Glick, Daniel, "The Magic of 'Mr. Spud'," *Newsweek*, November 27, 1989, p. 63.
Johnson, Nate, "Changes in Food Industry Prompted Potato Plant's Closure in Heyburn, Idaho," *Knight Ridder/Tribune Business News*, June 2, 2002.
Jones, Steven D., "First Frozen Food Barge Helps Bring French Fries to Orient," *Business Journal—Portland*, November 26, 1990, p. 3.
"J.R. Simplot Co. Acquires a Portion of Frozen Vegetable, Fruit Company," *Nation's Restaurant News*, September 21, 1992, p. 24.
"J.R. Simplot Opens New French Fry Plant," *Nation's Restaurant News*, August 25, 2003, p. 56.
Kiley, David, "Jacobson Sets a New Course for Simplot . . . Again," *Adweek's Marketing Week*, January 1, 1991, p. 7.
Murphy, Charles J.V., "Jack Simplot and His Private Conglomerate," *Fortune*, August 1968, pp. 122–72.
"Simplot to Appeal Court's $8.9M Award to Eateries," *Nation's Restaurant News*, March 4, 2002, p. 60.
Smith, Rod, "Simplot Buys ZX; Becomes Top Five in Cattle Production," *Feedstuffs*, January 10, 1994, p. 5.
Zuckerman, Laurance, "From Mr. Spud to Mr. Chip," *New York Times*, February 8, 1996, p. C1.

—Jeffrey L. Covell
—update: Christina M. Stansell

KENNEDY WILSON

Kennedy-Wilson, Inc.

9601 Wilshire Boulevard, Suite 220
Beverly Hills, California 90210
U.S.A.
Telephone: (310) 887-6400
Fax: (310) 887-3410
Web site: http://www.kennedywilson.com

Public Company
Incorporated: 1979
Employees: 530
Sales: $40.6 million (2002)
Stock Exchanges: NASDAQ
Ticker Symbol: KWIC
NAIC: 531210 Offices of Real Estate Agents and Brokers

Kennedy-Wilson, Inc. is an international real estate services company based in Beverly Hills, California. It maintains a boutique commercial brokerage division; operates a property management division responsible for some 200 office, industrial, and multifamily properties totaling more than 75 million square feet; and invests through joint ventures in both commercial and residential real estate. Internationally, Kennedy-Wilson owns office properties in Japan and maintains operations in five foreign cities. In addition, the company owns eProperty.com, an Internet real estate auction site. It also provides traditional real estate auction services, the company's original business.

Kennedy-Wilson Founded in 1977

Kennedy-Wilson was founded in 1977 in Santa Monica, California, by auctioneers Donald F. Kennedy, John Wilson, and William Stevenson. While Kennedy and Wilson provided the firm's name, Stevenson brought the administrative ability. He had worked as an asset manager for Los Angeles-based Union America, where he oversaw 25 major real estate projects and was involved in the sale of $100 million in properties. This experience convinced him that there was an opportunity, requiring only a modest amount of funding, to build a dominant real estate auctioning company. He also sought to bring legitimacy to real estate auctioning, drawing on the example of what

international auction houses Christie's and Sotheby's did for art (20 years before the reputation of both firms would be sullied by a price-fixing scandal). At the time, real estate auctioning services were in high demand in the company's home market of southern California due to overbuilding in the region, which in turn led to a number of foreclosures. After two years, Stevenson bought out his partners, although Kennedy stayed on to serve as the company's auctioneer.

During the 1980s, Kennedy-Wilson spearheaded the rise in popularity of real estate auctioning across the country. In doing this they had to overcome a prejudice held by many bankers that such a selling method was both sleazy and demeaning, conjuring up images of plants in the audience driving up prices. However, as the real estate industry suffered a major collapse during the decade, many lenders found themselves with an excess of OREO (''other real estate owned'') added to their portfolios because of default, and the advantages of auctioning off these properties gradually outweighed the shame factor. Auctioning offered a quick way to simultaneously unload a large number of unwanted properties, resulting in the lender saving on maintenance, insurance, utilities, property taxes, and other costs. Auctioning also helped banks to bring in new business by allowing them to offer financing to qualified buyers, thus converting a bad loan into a new loan. Kennedy-Wilson, which carefully developed a reputation as an honest broker, was not the only real estate auction house looking to drum up business in a distressed market, but it became the best known, due in large part to some well publicized major sales it conducted using satellite technology. In 1985, it organized a sale of Punta Gorda, Florida, residential lots, attended by 1,000 in Florida and another 500 in an Atlantic City, New Jersey, casino, Caesar's World, where an orchestra played and waitresses attired in tuxedos served cocktails. Several months later, Kennedy-Wilson established a satellite hookup between Hawaii and hotels in Los Angeles and San Francisco to auction off condominiums and home sites on the islands.

William McMorrow Assumes Leadership in 1988

Control of Kennedy-Wilson changed hands in 1988 when William J. McMorrow bought in with an investor group that included Lewis Halpert and Kenneth Stevens. Stevenson retained a significant stake in the business and stayed on as president, with McMorrow becoming chairman and chief executive officer. McMorrow, who held an MBA from the University of Southern California, boasted 17 years of experience in finance and had handled problem real estate matters for insurance companies and various financial institutions. Like Stevenson, he shared the desire to upgrade the image of real estate auctioneers and was determined to bring professionalism to the business. The firm numbered just 30 employees when McMorrow launched a period of aggressive growth. As early as 1989, Kennedy-Wilson became involved in the Japanese market. Nevertheless, the significant revenue was to be found in the United States, where troubled real estate conditions and a subsequent recession led to the firm's greatest opportunities. From 1989 to 1991, Kennedy-Wilson's sales grew from $4.27 million to $19.62 million and net income improved from a loss of $529,000 to a profit of $3.31 million. A major development for the company occurred in 1991 when it signed a one-year contract with the Resolution Trust Corp. (RTC), which was set up in the wake of the Savings and Loan scandal of the 1980s. The three RTC auctions conducted by Kennedy-Wilson included one in Texas that was regarded as the largest real estate auction ever held. Over a seven-day period the firm sold all but four of 1,450 Texas residential and commercial properties as well as raw parcels. Perhaps even more impressive was the fact that the company was given just six weeks to prepare for the sale, half of the lead time normally provided. All told, in 1991 Kennedy-Wilson auctioned off more than $790 million in property.

The poor economy and widespread real estate slump of the 1990s appeared to bode well for the continued prosperity of Kennedy-Wilson, leading its management in 1992 to take the company public. The hope was to raise more than $29 million in order to expand the company's regional and branch office network and to add brokerage operations. When the offering was completed, Kennedy-Wilson raised just $26.3 million, a harbinger of what was to follow, as it soon became apparent that changing economic conditions no longer favored the company's business model. Just as Kennedy-Wilson's stock began to trade on the NASDAQ, the auction business began to slow down. At the same time, the company was facing new competition. Moreover, lenders were rapidly clearing their books of foreclosed properties, RTC was starting to wrap up its work, and, with the economy starting to rebound, sellers were less reluctant to pursue the auction route, which generally resulted in lower prices. Nevertheless, Kennedy-Wilson pressed on with its plans for expansion. The firm, which had just one office when McMorrow took charge in 1988, soon had 20, including operations in New York and Boston, as well as London and Australia. Less than a week after Kennedy-Wilson went public, its stock peaked at $8.50, then slowly lost ground as the

company reported a string of disappointing results. By April 1994, the price dipped below $2.

Management began to adjust to the changing realities as early as 1993, taking steps to transform Kennedy-Wilson from a real estate auction house to a diversified real estate services company. The company did not give up the auction trade, however. In fact, it pioneered a new concept, auction-to-build, in which an auction was held on a property even before construction began. In this way, contractors received loans based on the winning bids. Kennedy-Wilson also purchased buildings itself and auctioned them, an unusual step for an auctioneer. The company even became involved in investment banking in order to offer financing to further stimulate auction sales. It also tried its hand at auctioning off manufacturing equipment. For the most part, however, Kennedy-Wilson cut back on its traditional business, becoming more involved in brokerage services and the operation of a trading business, buying and selling commercial and residential properties. To trim costs, management closed offices, froze some salaries, cut other salaries, reduced some full-time workers to part-time, and eliminated positions. While it closed offices in some markets, Kennedy-Wilson opened a branch in Tokyo in 1995 to take advantage of the company's experience in Japan's real estate market. Overall, however, the fortunes of Kennedy-Wilson touched bottom in 1995, when it posted a net loss of $13 million.

Colony Capital Provides New Funding in 1998

It took several years for Kennedy-Wilson to complete its transformation into an international real estate marketing and investment services company. In 1998, a pivotal year for the company, Colony Capital, a Los Angeles-based private real estate investment firm, provided $26 million in new funding, which allowed Kennedy-Wilson to acquire Heitman Properties for $21 million in cash. Founded in 1969, Heitman Properties, a national property management and leasing operation, was a subsidiary of Heitman Financial, an established firm that originated and serviced commercial real estate mortgage loans for institutional lenders such as pension funds and life insurance companies. Selling its property management and leasing business to Kennedy-Wilson was part of an effort to focus on the firm's core business. Taking over Heitman's national portfolio of 52 million square feet of office, industrial, and residential contracts worth $6.5 billion gave Kennedy-Wilson immediate status as a property management company. Moreover, the new division, called KennedyWilson Properties Ltd., had an alliance with Colony that called for Colony to provide further funding and Kennedy-Wilson to provide brokerage and property management services for Colony's investments. Kennedy-Wilson now looked to sell off its own property portfolio in order to concentrate on property and investment management services. It also planned to take on partners, such as Colony, to invest in real estate assets, which its management arm could then service. Also in 1998, Kennedy-Wilson paid $225,000 in cash and a comparable amount in stock to acquire TechSource Services, Inc., a construction management firm that, among other services, helped owners and managers to customize property services, thus reducing operating expenses and increasing the value of a real estate investment. Overseas, Kennedy-Wilson received further financial help from Colony in the form of a

<table>
<tr><td colspan="2">Key Dates:</td></tr>
<tr><td>1977:</td><td>The company is founded.</td></tr>
<tr><td>1988:</td><td>William J. McMorrow buys in and becomes chair and CEO.</td></tr>
<tr><td>1989:</td><td>Kennedy-Wilson begins doing business in Japan.</td></tr>
<tr><td>1992:</td><td>The company goes public.</td></tr>
<tr><td>1995:</td><td>A Tokyo office is opened.</td></tr>
<tr><td>1998:</td><td>Heitman Properties is acquired.</td></tr>
<tr><td>2000:</td><td>Kennedy-Wilson's first investment fund is launched.</td></tr>
<tr><td>2001:</td><td>Kennedy-Wilson Japan is taken public.</td></tr>
</table>

$100 million joint venture the partners created to invest in Japanese real estate and distressed notes backed by Japanese real estate. Kennedy-Wilson then forged a joint venture with a subsidiary of Cargill, Inc. to trade in Japanese distressed notes. As a result of these developments, Kennedy-Wilson saw its revenues almost double, improving from $26.9 million in 1997 to $50.8 million in 1998. Over this period, net income grew from $4 million to $5.3 million. The price of the company's stock also enjoyed a bump, trading in the $10 range.

In 1999, Kennedy-Wilson added to its property management business. During April of that year, it closed on the acquisition of Los Angeles-based R&B Commercial Real Estate Services, paying an undisclosed amount for more than 6 million square feet in management properties. Later in the year, Kennedy-Wilson acquired San Francisco-based Jones Lang Wooton California Inc., adding another 7 million square feet of office and industrial properties. The company was also active outside of California, increasing its national presence in property management. It picked up 4 million square feet from TRF Management, Inc., a Bellevue, Washington, company. In the Southwest market, Kennedy-Wilson acquired Dallas-based Fults & Associates and its 8 million square feet of properties, as well as SynerMark Companies, an Austin-based firm with 6.4 million square feet of management properties located in Texas, New Mexico, and Oklahoma. Late in 1999, Kennedy-Wilson launched a new initiative, one that hearkened back to the company's early years: the first online real estate auction site, eProperty.com. Although management initially compared eProperty to eBay, rather than becoming an open marketplace for real estate, the venture evolved into an application service provider to build, host, and manage Web applications for the "marketing and disposition of fee owned and leasehold real estate for corporation, institutional owners, and real estate services providers."

Kennedy-Wilson continued its aggressive play in the Japanese market. In 2000, it bought two office buildings, a 27,000-square-foot property in Tokyo and an 86,000-square-foot property in Yokohama, worth a combined $36.7 million. In October 2001, the company announced that it planned to take its Kennedy-Wilson Japan subsidiary public, and in February 2002 it completed an initial public offering that grossed some $23 million. The stock began trading on the Osaka Securities Exchange's NASDAQ Japan stock market. A secondary offering

was then conducted later in the year, resulting in the gross proceeds of an additional $11.7 million. Other developments in 2000 included the formation of Kennedy-Wilson Global Technology Corp. The purpose of the venture was to manage the company's business-to-business venture capital investments with the hope of spurring new investments in both the United States and Asia. Kennedy-Wilson also established a hospitality division that targeted select U.S. markets for acquisition and development as well as management opportunities. The division intended to focus on high-end, full service hotels with 200 to 500 rooms.

Hoping to duplicate its success with investment ventures in Japan, Kennedy-Wilson, in conjunction with Congress Asset Management Company, launched a $25 million fund (KWI Property Fund I, L.P.) to focus on the purchase of suburban office properties located in the South and Southwest. A second fund was formed in 2003, a $600 million, ten-year life, value-added investment fund that would take advantage of difficult economic conditions to target distressed commercial properties located in select West Coast markets as well as such southeastern cities as Atlanta and Miami. The goal was to buy properties, fix problems, and sell the properties at a profit.

In 2003, Kennedy was active on a number of fronts, entering into new markets and opening a regional office in Portland, Oregon. In Japan, its subsidiary was forming a real estate investment trust to buy up distribution facilities. In a matter of ten years, Kennedy-Wilson had undergone an impressive evolution from auctioneer to an international firm providing a myriad of real estate services.

Principal Subsidiaries

Kennedy Wilson International; Kennedy-Wilson Property Services, Inc.; Techsource Services, Inc.

Principal Competitors

CBRE Holdings, Inc.; Grubb & Ellis Company; Lincoln Property Company.

Further Reading

Garbarino, Steve, "Properties for Sale Via Satellite," *St. Petersburg Times*, February 1, 1987, p. 1H.

Hamashige, Hope, "Santa Monica Auction Company Struggles to Adapt," *Los Angeles Business Journal*, April 25, 1994, p. S31.

Hayes, Elizabeth, "Kennedy-Wilson Post Big Returns, On Comeback Trail," *Los Angeles Business Journal*, May 10, 1999, p. 34.

Howard, Bob, "Kennedy-Wilson Bids for New Direction," *Los Angeles Business Journal*, July 24, 1995, p. 12A.

Marshall, Jeffrey, "Going, Going Gone (We Hope)," *United States Banker*, June 1991, p. 32.

Tobenkin, David, "Auction Company Hits Paydirt on real Estate Slump," *Los Angeles Business Journal*, July 22, 1991, p. 32.

Thompson, Terri, "Real Estate Roulette with a New Spin," *Business Week*, April 22, 1965, p. 69.

—Ed Dinger

King Ranch, Inc.

3 River Way, Suite 1600
Houston, Texas 77056
U.S.A.
Telephone: (832) 681-5700
Fax: (832) 681-5759
Web site: http://www.king-ranch.com

Private Company
Incorporated: 1934
Employees: 400
Sales: $300 million (2003 est.)
NAIC: 112111 Beef Cattle Ranching and Farming;
448320 Luggage and Leather Goods Stores; 444210
Outdoor Power Equipment Stores; 11192 Cotton
Farming; 111199 All Other Grain Farming; 111930
Sugarcane Farming; 111310 Orange Groves

King Ranch, Inc. operates one of the largest and most famous cattle ranches in the world. The King Ranch itself covers about 825,000 acres—slightly larger than the state of Rhode Island—on four separate divisions of land in South Texas known as the ''Home Ranches'': Santa Gertrudis, Laureles, Norias, and Encino. The company represents a colorful part of Texas history. From its beginnings in the mid-19th century as a family cattle ranch, the company has evolved into a major multinational operation active in a variety of agricultural and energy-related activities. Although it is perhaps most famous for its agribusiness segment (cattle breeding; horse breeding; farming; citrus groves; commodity marketing and processing; commercial hunting leases), King Ranch also oversees retail operations including luggage and leather goods, farm equipment, commercial printing, and tourism. A private company, King Ranch is owned by 60 or so descendants of company founder Captain Richard King, a legendary figure in the history of cattle ranching in the United States. King Ranch celebrated its 150th anniversary in 2003.

Early History in the 1800s

Captain King started up his ranch in 1853 in an area known at the time as the Wild Horse Desert or the Nueces Strip, bounded by the Nueces River on the north and the Rio Grande on the south. A steamboat pilot by trade, King had arrived in southern Texas about eight years earlier to run a shipping operation on the Rio Grande with partner Mifflin Kenedy. On a trip through the Wild Horse Desert, King noticed a promising piece of land along the Santa Gertrudis Creek. He quickly formed a partnership with another friend, Texas Ranger Captain Legs Lewis. King purchased the land and he and Lewis launched the livestock operation that would eventually grow into the King Ranch.

In order to expand the ranch during its early years, King hired a lawyer to seek out the owners of the old land grants throughout the area. He then bought the parcels and annexed them to the ranch. King also began to buy and sell cattle in huge numbers. His buying trips frequently took him into Mexico. In 1854 King brought north not only all of the cattle from one particular Mexican village suffering through a drought, but all of the village's humans as well. These transplanted villagers went to work on the ranch. Their descendants, who became known as *kinenos* (King's men), have formed the core of the King Ranch workforce ever since.

The ranch managed to survive its early years in spite of a hostile environment created by the presence of bandits, unhappy Indians, and the usual assortment of rustlers, raiders, and ruffians associated with the Wild West. King split his time between his two businesses, steamboating and ranching, during this period. In 1858 King built the first ranch house at the Santa Gertrudis site on a spot suggested by his friend Robert E. Lee, a young lieutenant colonel at the time. During the Civil War, the ranch served as a depot for the export of southern cotton through Mexico, sidestepping the Union naval blockade. King and Kenedy also used their shipping enterprise to supply the Confederate army. By the end of the Civil War, thousands of head of cattle were roaming the ranch, which had grown to nearly 150,000 acres in size. In 1867 King began using the Running W brand to mark his cattle. The Running W eventually became one of the most widely recognized marks in the history of the cattle industry.

By the end of the 1860s, King Ranch longhorns were being sold in northern markets. In order for this to happen, the cattle had to be driven thousands of miles to railroad points as far away as St. Louis, and later, Abilene, Kansas. Between 1869 and 1884, more than 100,000 head of cattle from King Ranch made the trip. Much of the livestock ended up in the Chicago stockyards; other destinations included new ranches springing up in Oklahoma, Nebraska, Colorado, Wyoming, and Montana, as the cattle industry of the West began to mature.

Beginning of the Kleberg Family Reign in the 1880s

In 1884 a young lawyer named Robert Kleberg began handling the legal affairs of King Ranch. Kleberg quickly became an indispensable part of the ranch's operation. When King died in 1885, he left his entire estate to his wife, Henrietta. The ranch covered more than 600,000 acres by this time. Mrs. King, who outlived her husband by 40 years, made Kleberg the full-time manager of the ranch. Kleberg married King's daughter Alice the following year.

Under Kleberg's management, operations at the ranch were streamlined and made more efficient. Kleberg built fences to divide the sprawling ranch into more manageable units. He also began to cross his cowherd with Shorthorn and Hereford bulls, since the expansion of the railroad made the Longhorn's ability to walk long distances irrelevant. One by one, the problems of running a growing ranch were addressed. Annoying wild mustangs and donkeys were captured and shipped elsewhere. Crews were assigned to slow the encroachment of mesquite brush, which was quickly displacing the favorable "climax grasses." During the horrible drought years of the 1890s, Kleberg experimented with various ways of getting water to the land. Finally, in 1899, an artesian well was drilled. This well, originating more than 500 feet below ground, provided enough water to support all of the region's livestock and agriculture. Along the way, the city of Kingsville was incorporated, following the vision of Henrietta King.

During the first 15 years of the 20th century, King Ranch managed once again to thrive in the face of further droughts, wars with Mexican raiders, and Kleberg's failing health. As Kleberg became weaker, he passed on responsibility for running the ranch to his sons, Bob and Dick Kleberg. Along the way, the ranch's selective breeding efforts intensified. They began crossbreeding Brahman bulls native to India with their own Shorthorn stock. The result was a new breed, which they dubbed "Santa Ger-

trudis." The Santa Gertrudis cattle combined the beefiness of the British Shorthorns with the Brahmans' ability to withstand the hot climate of summertime Texas. King Ranch began selling Santa Gertrudis bulls to other ranchers in the 1930s, and in 1940 the U.S. Department of Agriculture recognized Santa Gertrudis as the first ever American-produced beef breed.

Henrietta King died in 1925, at the age of 92. Mrs. King's death brought about a web of complications stemming from the division of her estate, high estate taxes, and various debts. The onset of the Depression, which caused beef prices to drop to the century's lowest levels, made matters even worse. Robert Kleberg died in 1932, signaling a complete generational shift in the ranch's management. By that time, King Ranch had grown to well more than a million acres in size and was home to 94,000 head of cattle and 4,500 horses and mules, the quality of which had become very high through selective breeding.

When Mrs. King's estate was finally untangled, Kleberg's widow, Alice, and her children consolidated as much of the ranch as possible by purchasing the properties of other heirs. In 1935 the Klebergs made King Ranch a corporation so that its future as a single entity would be more secure. Estate taxes had left the ranch with a $3 million debt, however, and for the next few years the company struggled to remain afloat, with Bob Kleberg acting as manager of its day-to-day operations. To get the company back in the black, Kleberg turned to petroleum. He negotiated a long-term lease for oil and gas rights on the entire ranch with Humble Oil and Refining Company, which later became Exxon. Meanwhile, brother Dick served the company from the outside as president of the Texas and Southwestern Cattle Raisers Association and, beginning in 1931, as a seven-term member of the U.S. Congress.

Expansion and Innovation in the 1940s–50s

Beef was not the only thing King Ranch was able to breed successfully. As the company developed its Santa Gertrudis cattle, it also engaged in the King Ranch Quarter Horse program. Bob Kleberg, the driving force behind the program, also became interested in thoroughbred racing horses. In 1938 he bought Kentucky Derby winner Bold Venture as a foundation sire for the ranch's thoroughbred breeding program. He also bought a stake in the Idle Hour Stable in Lexington, Kentucky, in 1946. That year, a King Ranch horse, Assault (a son of Bold Venture), won horse racing's Triple Crown.

During the 1940s and 1950s, a number of innovations improved production and kept King Ranch at the cutting edge of the cattle industry. These innovations included mechanized brush control methods, the identification of new and better grasses, and the development of better corrals for working cattle. Modern game management and preservation systems were also set up. In the 1950s the company went international. By 1952 the company was sending livestock to outposts in Cuba and Australia with the hope of boosting production by introducing Santa Gertrudis genes into the mix. In Australia, one of King's partners was Swift & Co., the biggest buyer of the ranch's U.S. beef output. The company eventually established a presence in Brazil, Argentina, and Venezuela, where the techniques developed to clear mesquite brush in Texas could be

Key Dates:

1853: Captain Richard King starts up his ranch in an area known as the Wild Horse Desert.

1867: King begins using the Running W brand to mark his cattle.

1935: The Klebergs make King Ranch a corporation.

1940: The U.S. Department of Agriculture recognizes the Santa Gertrudis as the first ever American-produced beef brand.

1946: Assault wins horse racing's Triple Crown.

1952: International expansion begins.

1979: The company begins offering commercial hunting licenses on its property.

1993: The company expands its Florida farming operations with the purchase of citrus groves in the southern part of the state.

1999: St. Mary Land & Exploration Co. acquires King Ranch Energy Inc.

2003: King Ranch celebrates its 150th anniversary.

used on South American rain forest. Morocco and Spain soon followed as well.

Dick Kleberg died in 1955. His son, Dick, Jr., had been playing an increasingly important role in company affairs since the 1940s, and in 1969 he was named chairman of the King Ranch board of directors. By the early 1970s, King Ranch controlled about 11.5 million acres of land worldwide. In 1974 Bob Kleberg died after managing the company's operations for more than half a century. The Kleberg family's choice to replace him as president and chief executive officer of the company was James H. Clement, the husband of Ida Larkin, one of Richard King's great-granddaughters (and Robert Kleberg, Sr.'s, granddaughters). In choosing Clement to lead King Ranch into the next generation, the family passed over Robert Shelton, a vice-president and King relative who had been raised by Bob Kleberg. This snub, combined with legal haggling over oil payments to family members, led to Shelton's departure from the company a few years later.

During the 1970s, Clement began to feel that the company had become unwieldy, and he started selling off chunks of King Ranch's overseas real estate. In 1976 Clement hired W.B. Yarborough to take control of King Ranch's oil and gas business. Yarborough, an independent petroleum operator and former Humble Oil geologist—not to mention the husband of Richard Kleberg, Sr.'s, daughter Katherine—decided to take on the task on a part-time basis. Four years later he became the first president of King Ranch Oil and Gas, Inc., a new wholly owned subsidiary formed to handle all of King Ranch's petroleum affairs.

Dick Kleberg, Jr., died in 1979, and soon after that his son, Stephen ''Tio'' Kleberg, took over management of King Ranch South Texas, the company's core ranch operation. Under Tio Kleberg's guidance, the company continued to update its cattle, horse, and farming operations. More and more emphasis was placed on applying modern business principles to these tradition-bound endeavors. Meanwhile, as an outgrowth of the King

Ranch Quarter Horse program, the company became involved in competition cutting—an arena event in which horses try to separate individual heifers from the herd—in the mid-1970s. Within a decade, through a combination of strategic horse purchases and the application of its fabulously successful breeding techniques, King Ranch had established a dynasty of champion cutting horses.

A management upheaval took place in 1987 when, within the span of half a year, Clement retired as president of King Ranch and Yarborough retired as president of the King Ranch Oil & Gas subsidiary. Clement was replaced by Kimberly-Clark CEO Darwin Smith, who became the first chief executive in company history with no familial ties to founder Richard King. Tio Kleberg continued to run the ranch's day-to-day operations. Smith's reign lasted only a year. After his departure, Roger Jarvis, who had been running the company's petroleum operations, was named president and CEO. Leroy Denman, a longtime company affiliate, was elected chairman of the board in 1990.

Diversification: 1990s and Beyond

As the 1990s opened, King Ranch faced a number of questions. As income from both cattle and petroleum operations declined, the company was forced to look for other business areas in which to try its hand. In addition, the number of company shareholders had increased over the years through inheritances, and the very future of the ranch as a single entity was called into question. Although several King heirs wanted to break up and sell the ranch to turn a quick profit, the family decided to keep it intact.

Several new ways to generate revenue were found over the next few years. The company began actively exploring for oil and gas, rather than passively waiting for royalties on the oil and gas found on its property by others. Cotton farming was another area into which the company plunged with a fair amount of success. In 1993, the company formed and acquired a 50 percent interest in Running W Citrus Limited Partnership, a subsidiary created to oversee 16,000 acres of Coca-Cola's Minute Maid Citrus Groves in South Florida. The King Ranch Saddle Shop, once exclusively a supplier of cowboy gear for the kinenos, went into the retail clothing and luggage business. Parts of King Ranch's property were opened not only to hunters—who since 1979 were able to pay nearly $3 million a year to shoot at deer, turkeys, and other animals—but to tourists as well.

Another turnover in management took place in 1995. That year, Jack Hunt, formerly the CEO of California's Tejon Ranch, was named president and CEO of King Ranch. A couple months later, Abraham Zaleznik, a King Ranch director since 1988, replaced the retiring Denman as chairman of the board. By this time, the newer, nonagricultural businesses were accounting for more than half of the company's income, and Tio Kleberg was the only King descendant still actively working the ranch.

Although 60,000 head of cattle continued to graze King Ranch's sprawling acreage and the company remained a major force in the cattle industry, King Ranch evolved into a distinct agribusiness and energy corporation during the 1990s. Both in the cattle business and in its other pursuits, the management and shareholders of King Ranch expressed a commitment to the kind of experimentation and innovation that helped the company to thrive for so many years. Tio Kleberg commented on the company's diversification in a 1995 *U.S. News & World Report:* "We no longer see ourselves in the cattle business, as such. We are in the resource-management business. And we all feel we have a lot of resources to manage."

Indeed, by the late 1990s King Ranch's portfolio was hugely diversified, ranging from oil to citrus to cattle. In 1998, the company merged its Running W Citrus operations with Collier Enterprises to form Consolidated Citrus Limited Partnership. As part of its strategy to build profit in its agriculture business, the newly created firm acquired the Turner Foods groves from Florida Power & Light. The deal catapulted Consolidated Citrus into the upper echelon of citrus producers and secured King Ranch's position as the largest citrus grower in the United States.

King Ranch remained focused on its oil holdings as well and in 1999 spun off its King Ranch Energy Inc. subsidiary just before its merger with St. Mary Land and Exploration Co. The merger—structured as a stock swap worth $53 million between King Ranch and St. Mary shareholders—included properties in the Gulf of Mexico and the onshore Gulf Coast.

The company entered the new millennium preparing to celebrate its 150th anniversary in 2003. Over the course of the previous decade, the company had successfully overcome falling demand for beef by diversifying into new growth areas and selling off its international properties in order to focus on its domestic operations. While King Ranch remained a powerful entity in the business world, a new thorn threatened to shadow its anniversary celebration. A lawsuit was brought against the company by the descendants of Major William W. Chapman, a business partner of Richard King during the formation of the ranch in the 1850s. The descendants claimed that Robert Kleberg had worked for both Richard King and Chapman's widow during a land settlement issue, creating a distinct conflict of interest. The suit claimed that Kleberg deceived Chapman's widow, defrauding her out of control of the Rincon de Santa Gertrudis, a parcel of land equal to approximately 7,500 acres.

Although King Ranch management maintained that the suit had no merit, its legitimacy was upheld in appellate courts and went under review of the Texas Supreme Court. According to a 2003 *New York Times* article, "The ruling could set an important precedent for questioning the legitimacy of land titles secured in Texas in the 19th century, especially for Hispanic families who contend that land grants dating to the Spanish empire were taken over by white settlers through fraudulent methods." In August 2003, however, the Texas Supreme Court ruled against the Chapman descendants, arguing that there was not enough evidence to proceed with a trial. With the controver-

sial lawsuit behind it, King Ranch went ahead with its anniversary festivities, which included a highly publicized cattle and horse charity auction.

King Ranch had made significant changes in its operations since the early 1990s and its business environment would no doubt continue to transform into the years to come as management looked to diversify into new profitable areas. Regardless of its future path, the King Ranch name and its Running W brand would surely continue as one of the most widely recognized identities in the industry.

Principal Competitors

AzTx Cattle Company; Cactus Feeders Inc.; Lykes Bros. Inc.

Further Reading

Barles, Pete, "He Stayed Ahead of the Herd; Be Bold: Richard King, With Grit and Innovation, Built the World's Largest Ranch," *Investor's Business Daily,* April 1, 2003, p. A4.

"Biggest Ranch Jumps Some Oceans," *Business Week,* May 17, 1952, pp. 192–94.

Chapman, Art, "Texas Supreme Court Ruling Adds Appeal to Legendary King Ranch Celebration," *Fort Worth Star-Telegram,* September 21, 2003.

Cypher, John, *Bob Kleberg and the King Ranch: A Worldwide Sea of Grass,* Austin: University of Texas, 1995.

Denhart, Robert Moorman, *The King Ranch Quarter Horses,* Norman, Okla.: University of Oklahoma Press, 1970.

"The Fabulous House of Kleberg: A World of Cattle and Grass," *Fortune,* June 1969.

Godwyn, Frank, *Life on the King Ranch,* New York: Thomas Y. Crowell, 1951.

Gonzalez, John W., "Nostalgia, Prestige Rules Kingsville, Texas, Ranch Auction," *Houston Chronicle,* October 5, 2003.

"King Ranch," *Fortune,* December 1193, pp. 48–61, 89–109.

"The King Ranch: The Last Frontier Empire Confronts the Modern World," *Texas Monthly,* October 1980, pp. 150–73, 234–78.

Lea, Tom, *The King Ranch,* Boston: Little, Brown and Company, 1957.

McGraw, Dan, "A Fistful of Dollars," *U.S. News & World Report,* July 24, 1995, pp. 36–38.

Nixon, Jay, *Stewards of a Vision: A History of King Ranch,* Houston: King Ranch, Inc., 1986.

Pare, Terence, "New Chairman Tenderfoot Takes Over," *Fortune,* August 1, 1988, p. 217.

Romero, Simon, "Betting the Ranch, a Really Big One," *New York Times,* August 17, 2003.

"St. Mary Completes Acquisition," *Oil Daily,* December 21, 1999.

"Today's King Ranch," *Cattleman,* September 1995, pp. 10–32.

"Unbreakable," *BEEF,* December 1, 2002.

—Robert R. Jacobson
—update: Christina M. Stansell

Körber AG

Kurt-A.-Körber-Chaussee 8-32
D-21033 Hamburg
Germany
Telephone: (49) 40 7250-04
Fax: (49) 40 7250-3250
Web site: http://www.koerber.de

Public Company
Incorporated: 1947 as Hauni Maschinenfabrik Körber &
    Co. KG
Employees: 8,083
Sales: EUR 1.37 billion ($1.44 billion) (2002)
NAIC: 333999 All Other Miscellaneous General Purpose
    Machinery Manufacturing; 333291 Paper Industry
    Machinery Manufacturing; 333993 Packaging
    Machinery Manufacturing; 333512 Machine Tool
    (Metal Cutting Types) Manufacturing

Körber AG is the holding company for a diversified machinery manufacturer based in Hamburg, Germany, with 30 production and engineering subsidiaries in Germany, Switzerland, Italy, France, Hungary, the United States, Brazil, and Malaysia and almost 80 sales offices around the globe. Hauni Maschinenbau AG, the Körber group's largest business division, is the world market leader for filter cigarette and tobacco processing machines. The group's machine tool division, led by Körber Schleifring GmbH, delivers every fifth grinding machine purchased worldwide, mainly to the automotive industry, machine tool manufacturers and manufacturers of turbines. Körber PaperLink GmbH is the world's leading manufacturer of systems for sheeting, processing, and packaging fine paper, cardboard, tissue and absorbent hygiene products to the paper making and processing industry with a market share of over 50 percent. Hauni generates roughly half of the Körber group's revenues, the other two divisions add about one-quarter each. About half of Körber's sales are made in Europe, almost one-quarter in Asia and about one-fifth in the United States. In 2002, the group added a new division for pharmaceutical packaging machinery to its portfolio. Körber AG is owned by the German Körber Stiftung, a nonprofit foundation that sponsors programs in the areas of inter-cultural dialogue, civic involvement, education, science, and culture.

Starting with Nothing after World War II

Company founder Kurt A. Körber was born in Berlin in 1909 and learned the electrical technician's trade. For two semesters, he studied at a technical college and then worked for several firms before he started a successful career as an engineer at Universelle Zigarettenmaschinenfabrik J.C. Müller & Co., a cigarette machine manufacturer in Dresden, in 1935. In 1944, at the height of World War II, Körber became the company's Technical Director. With a good portion of luck, he survived the bombing inferno the southeastern German city suffered during the war. After the war ended, Russian occupation forces immediately began dismantling whatever was left intact at the plant. However, they seemed to have no interest in Universelle's cigarette making machines. A friendly Russian officer helped Körber secure a large order of 35 such machines for delivery to Moscow, an action that protected Universelle from further dismantling. The same officer gave Körber a few desperately needed machines the Russians had found at Dresden's Technical University. With more than 500 employees back at work, Universelle was on its way to recovery. However, the future of the Russian-occupied German sector was uncertain. Körber was able to convince the head of Universelle to let him travel to British-occupied Hamburg in order purchase badly needed replacement parts and to set up a subsidiary there, where three major German cigarette manufacturers were located.

As soon as Körber arrived in Hamburg in mid-summer 1946, he contacted friends and business partners of Universelle to find out the best way to go into business. From his contacts with Reemtsma, one of the three large Hamburg-based cigarette manufacturers, he learned about the Hanseatische Lehrenbau-Gesellschaft (HLG) in the Hamburg suburb Bergedorf. HLG was located in the eastern part of Hamburg which, unlike the rest of the city, survived the war almost untouched. Twelve days after he arrived there, Körber rented a small office and basement room on HLG's premises. The new enterprise was named Universelle Dresden, Abteilung Hamburg and legally treated as a department of HLG, which gave Körber access to the host company's resources, including skilled workers.

Starting out with a workforce of eight, Körber helped Hamburg's cigarette makers Reemtsma, British American Tabacco (BAT), and Kyriazi get their production going again by repairing whatever machinery was there. However, this turned out to be a difficult task. At a time when literally everything was scarce, Körber's workers had to supply some of their own tools, and getting the necessary replacement parts for an old machine often meant finding and disassembling other old machines that were partly destroyed. Körber's first financial success came with a hand-operated tobacco cutter that looked much like an old fashioned pencil-sharpener. In the first years after the war, cigarettes had become a valuable good that was widely accepted as a "second currency" and could be exchanged for almost anything on the flourishing black markets. Since cigarettes were scarce at that time, many Germans grew their own tobacco. Körber had successfully tapped into a market niche. The money made from selling tobacco cutters was used to buy materials and parts needed to repair cigarette making machines. Hamburg's cigarette makers in turn supported Körber's small enterprise with even more unfinished goods and machinery (bartering was another hallmark of the time).

Emancipation from Parent Universelle in 1947

Körber's success would not have been possible without the support he received from Universelle and the contacts he had made there. After he got the business up and running, Universelle sent out a memorandum to clients in the industry authorizing the newly established workshop as the preferred repair service provider in the three western German zones. The parent company also helped get the tobacco cutter production going. However, growing differences between Körber's and the parent company's ideas and interests, which were amplified by the political pressure from the Soviet occupation authorities towards separation from the rest of the country, resulted in the official split between Universelle and its Hamburg subsidiary.

The first big order Körber received from Reemtsma in 1946 could be traced back to his visits as a Universelle representative in 1944, when he was trying to interest the cigarette maker in machines that filled cigarettes into the now common "soft packs." Such soft cardboard packages started replacing wooden

boxes or tins in the United States but did not arouse much interest in Germany at a time when packaging material was becoming more and more scarce. Convinced that the new packaging was the way of the future, Körber, in cooperation with other companies in Dresden, developed "A III"—Universelle's prototype of a "soft packaging machine." When Reemtsma ordered several such machines in the fall of 1946, Universelle refused to let Körber have the necessary technical plans. Although it remains unclear how much support Körber ultimately received from the parent company, the development of successor, "A IV," was based on the work Körber had done in Dresden.

In January 1947, Körber explained to Universelle why he thought it would be best if he established the Hamburg subsidiary as a legally independent business. Rising competitive pressures, growing concerns of western German clients about the trend towards expropriation of private businesses in East Germany, and the insecurity about the future of HLG were the reasons Körber gave for wanting to found his own company. A few weeks later, in February 1947, his enterprise was officially registered as Hauni Maschinenfabrik Körber & Co. KG—with "Hauni" an abbreviation for Hanseatische Universelle. In March 1947, an agreement between Universelle and Hauni granted Körber's firm an exclusive license for the manufacture and distribution of Universelle's machines and parts in western Germany at Körber's own risk. Six months later, HLG was liquidated because of the company's involvement in military production during the war. Beginning in 1948, Körber's Hauni leased the whole HLG building and took over 55 employees and the remaining tools, machines, and office furniture and equipment.

Innovation and Internationalization: 1950s–1960s

The license agreement with Universelle initially allowed Körber access to technical documentation from Dresden. However, he and his staff—some of whom Körber had persuaded to leave Universelle and move to Hamburg—soon launched their own innovations. To make sure that he would not run into legal problems down the road, Körber convinced Johanna Schwerin, the daughter of Universelle's former owner (who had moved to western Germany), to become a silent partner in Hauni.

In 1947, the company delivered the first "A IV" soft packaging machines to Reemtsma. In the late 1940s, Hauni focused on the development of cigarette making machines with a high output. The company's "Excelsior-Rapid-KDC" model produced 1,350 cigarettes per minute. Its successor, "Super-Rapid-KDZ," which was introduced in 1951, was able to put out 1,400 cigarettes per minute. In the same year, Hauni exhibited its new tobacco cutting machine, "KT 400," which processed 1,000 kilograms of tobacco in an hour and was equipped with a blade sharpening module that made the usual procedure of taking the blades out of the machine to re-sharpen them much less frequent. Long before the market was ready for his new invention, Körber presented "KFZ," a machine able to produce filtered cigarettes, which began to replace the unfiltered variety during the 1950s, at a rate of 2,500 per minute. The 1956 model "MAX," named after head engineer Max Pollmann and the successor of the "KFZ"-series, became a best-seller during the 1960s. The "GARANT" series was a new generation of cigarette making machines conceived by Körber. The further development of this machine type led to a quantum leap in output, which reached 4,000 cigarettes per minute with the model "GARANT 4." Investment in research and development remained a high priority for Körber. Despite occasional legal disputes, he encouraged his engineers to take risks and to design machines that outperformed those of the competition.

With the German economy getting back on its feet, Hauni expanded rapidly. After only two years, Körber's operation employed more than 200 workers. By 1950, 760 people worked for Hauni. Five years later, there were over 1,200 employees on the company's payroll. In 1955, Körber moved his enterprise to a former food processing plant in Bergedorf. After the war, cigarette smokers began to outnumber cigar smokers. In the early 1950s, however, the public debate about the health risks of smoking moved from the United States to Europe. Instead of giving up their habit, smokers switched to filter cigarettes, which accounted for 20 percent of the market in 1952 but had a share of 90 percent by the end of the decade.

Hauni's growth was greatly supported by the help of the sales affiliates whom Körber and his former colleagues who followed him to Hamburg knew from their days at Universelle. Contacts in cities such as Munich, London, and Rotterdam opened the door for Körber to former Universelle clients. It was through such recommendations that he was invited to participate in the advisory committee the British had established in order to reorganize the German tobacco industry in their zone. These contacts were also instrumental in Hauni's being invited to exhibit their machines at a congress of the international tobacco industry in Amsterdam in 1951, where Körber made further contacts with potential clients from all over the world. One year later, Hauni received an order to fully equip a brand-new cigarette factory in Burma.

Since the domestic market for cigarette making machines was limited, Körber made the development of export markets

one of his foremost concerns. In late 1948, he took his first trip to the United States, where he convinced Eric Warburg, a reputable Jewish banker who had left Hamburg during the Nazi era and settled in New York, to open a Hauni sales office there. On his many other trips to the United States that followed, Körber found a magic formula that gave him access to top executives in the American cigarette industry. All he had to do is mention that he was a friend of Philipp Reemtsma, his loyal German client who also recommended Hauni's "KFZ" filter cigarette machine to his American contacts. In turn, Körber—a master communicator with an intimate knowledge of Hamburg's cultural scene—entertained Reemtsma's American business partners when they visited the German city. With one of Hauni's main international competitors, American Machinery and Foundry Company (AMF), Körber signed an agreement on the mutual use of patents in the early 1950s. In the spring of 1955, Körber acquired property in Richmond, Virginia, the center of the American cigarette industry, where the company's U.S. subsidiary, Hauni Richmond Inc., was established. To better serve his American clients, Körber chartered more than 30 airplanes in the mid-1950s to deliver several hundred cigarette machines across the Atlantic.

During the 1950s and 1960s, Hauni opened a number of sales offices and production plants in other parts of the world. In 1955, a Hauni sales office opened in Rome, followed by a subsidiary in London in 1956. By the middle of the 1960s, the company had established subsidiaries in Argentina, Mexico, and Switzerland and production plants in South Africa and Ireland. Concerned about international political conflicts, given relatively recent historical events such as the Korean War or the Cuban missile crisis, Körber organized all foreign Hauni subsidiaries under the umbrella of a holding company in Switzerland—in case he had to leave Germany for some reason. As early as in the mid-1950s, Hauni machines were shipped to 69 countries around the globe. Ten years later, Körber claimed that most of the world's major cigarette makers used Hauni machines.

Diversification and Reorganization: 1970s–1980s

In the late 1960s, Körber gave in to the pressure from his own top managers as well as from outside advisors to expand into new markets. Despite Hauni's strong market position and despite the fact that the health-damaging effects of smoking did not seem to discourage smokers, they believed that the market for cigarette machines would reach its saturation point and would therefore not be sufficient to secure the company's long-term future. In 1970, Hauni acquired Hamburg-based E.C.H. Will, a manufacturer of paper processing machines with a workforce of roughly 200. The move turned out to be a good one. Notwithstanding two severe crises, in the mid-1970s and again in the early 1980s, the company developed into a profitable activity for Hauni. The takeover of Stuttgart-based Womako Maschinenkonstruktion in 1976 further strengthened the new paper processing arm.

Another move into a new field followed in 1978 when Hauni bought grinding machine maker Blohm. Helmut Schmidt, the Democratic German Chancellor at the time and a good friend of Kurt A. Körber, had asked him to help the struggling firm which was located in Hauni's Hamburg neighborhood. When Körber learned that there was a significant number of highly skilled workers at the firm, he gave green light for the takeover. More than 120 Blohm employees started working for Hauni. The remaining workforce of about 40 kept working for Blohm, which became a Hauni department. The year 1983 saw the acquisition of Stuttgart-based Schaudt Maschinenbau, another machine tool maker.

By the mid-1980s, paper processing machines and machine tool manufacturing had grown to business divisions of a considerable size. In 1987, the company was reorganized to reflect the change. Hauni-Werke & Co. KG was transformed into a privately owned stock corporation with Körber being for all practical purposes its sole shareholder. By that time, the company had grown into a group with almost 6,000 employees who worked in 15 subsidiaries that together grossed over DM1 billion per year.

Foundation Becomes Sole Owner in 1992

Long before Körber AG was created, the company founder had taken steps towards the future that he envisioned for his enterprise. In 1969, Körber founded Hauni Stiftung, a nonprofit foundation that he determined would succeed him as the company's sole owner. Eleven years later, it was merged with A. Körber Stiftung, another nonprofit foundation he had set up in 1959. At the same time, Körber had to find someone who would take over his top management position after he retired. He and his wife had no children, and he decided that neither of his two nephews was suitable for this task. He considered a number of candidates and finally chose Eberhard Reuther, a longtime Hauni employee. Under Körber's tutelage, Reuther took over the management of Blohm and later managed Hauni's production. In 1986, he became the company's CEO. When Körber AG was founded one year later, Körber became president of the new company's board of directors. Although he still reserved the right to make final decisions about key people and major business decisions, Körber retired from the day-to-day business and immersed himself in political, social, and cultural activities through his foundation. Among his main concerns were education and the encouragement of social innovation. Kurt A. Körber died in the summer of 1992, only a few days after he had finished his autobiography. He was 82 years old.

After Körber's death, the nonprofit foundation he set up became the company's sole owner. Three years later, his enterprise was reorganized into three independent business divisions: tobacco machinery, paper and tissue machinery, and machine tools. Körber AG became the group's holding company, with Eberhard Reuther as CEO. In 2000, Reuther became president of Körber AG's advisory board and was succeeded as CEO by the head of the machine tool division, Werner Redeker, an engineer who had joined the Körber group in 1979.

Hauni Maschinenbau AG remained the Körber group's major revenue generator and strengthened its leading position for cigarette machines. In 1989, the company had founded UNIVERSELLE Engineering, a new German subsidiary that reconditioned older Hauni machines. Five years later, a Hungarian cigarette machine manufacturer was taken over, followed by the establishment in 2001 of a subsidiary in Malaysia that offered reconditioning services. With an output of 16,000 cigarettes, Hauni's latest generation of cigarette machines made as many cigarettes in one minute as two average smokers consumed in a year. However, with cigarette consumption stagnating and cigarette manufacturers consolidating and facing the risk of potentially devastating lawsuits, Hauni's future did not look promising. The division was able to profit from the trend towards "light" cigarettes, the production of which required that cigarette manufacturers buy new machinery. On the other hand, Hauni ceased the production of cigarette packaging machines, for which the company had built a new production facility in 1993.

The machine tool division struggled to get out of the red throughout the 1990s. This situation was due to several causes, including high restructuring costs following several acquisitions in Germany and Switzerland, high volatility in the price of raw material, currency exchange rates, and fierce competition that resulted in unsustainable price levels. In 1993, the Schleifring Maschinenbau GmbH was established as the division's managing company. A decade later, to consolidate the division's activities, Schleifring stopped offering special-order machines and complex installations, focusing instead on the serial production of grinding machines. After a severe slump in 2003, when incoming orders plummeted by 50 percent, two production plants in eastern Germany were to be closed down and the division's workforce cut by one fifth.

The group's paper processing division was strengthened by a number of acquisitions in the 1990s, including the purchase in 1994 of majority shares in Italian tissue processing equipment makers Cassoli and Fabio Perini, which had a production facility in Brazil. Renamed Körber PaperLink GmbH, the division saw an increase in demand for tissue processing machines as the worldwide consumption of paper towels, bathroom tissue, and absorbent hygiene products was on the rise. In 2002, Körber AG ventured into a new field when it acquired two Swiss firms—Rondo AG, a producer of a wide variety of packaging solutions for the pharmaceutical industry, and Dividella AG, a manufacturer of machinery for packaging liquid medicines. One year later, Klöckner Medipak, a German maker of packaging machinery for drugs in solid and powder form, joined the group.

Despite the dynamic changes the Körber group of companies was going through in the first years of the 21st century, its new CEO was optimistic about the future. Following the guiding principle of the company's founder, Körber AG's management still made it a priority to be independent from outside investors and to use its own resources for growth. With long-term debt at a minimum, above average investments in research and development, and more than $250 million in liquid assets, CEO Redeker believed that Körber AG was well positioned for the years to come.

Principal Subsidiaries

Hauni Maschinenbau AG; Hauni LNI Electronics S.A. (Switzerland); Hauni Richmond Inc. (United States); Hauni Hungaria Kft. (Hungary); Hauni Malaysia Sdn. Bhd.; Körber Schleifring GmbH; Körber PaperLink GmbH; Schmermund Verpackungstechnik GmbH; Topack Verpackungstechnik; K. Jung GmbH; Blohm Maschinenbau GmbH; Kugler-Womako GmbH; Fabio Perini S.p.A. (Italy); Fabio Perini North America Inc. (United States); Fabio Perini S.A. (Brazil); Baltic Metalltechnik

GmbH; E.C.H. Will GmbH; Schaudt Mikrosa BWF GmbH; UNIVERSELLE Engineering U.N.I. GmbH; Casmatic S.p.A. (Italy); Decouflé S.a.r.l. (France); Ewag AG (Switzerland); Intamag AG (Switzerland); Mägerle AG (Switzerland); Pemco Inc. (United States); United Grinding Technologies Inc. (United States); Diatec S.r.l. (Italy, 76.3%); FinCostruzioni S.p.A. (Italy); Fritz Studer AG (Switzerland); Rondo AG (Switzerland); Dividella AG (Switzerland); Sealand Agency Treasury Company (Ireland); Sofiter S.A. (Luxembourg); Baltic Elektronik GmbH.

Principal Competitors

Barton Tobacco Machinery; Paper Converting Machine Company Ltd.; Erwin Junker Maschinenfabrik GmbH.

Further Reading

Schmid, Josef, and Wegner Dirk, *Kurt A. Körber: Annäherungen an einen Stifter*, Hamburg: Edition Körber-Stiftung, 2002, 240 p.

—Evelyn Hauser

Lam Son Sugar Joint Stock Corporation (Lasuco)

Lam Son Town
Tho Xuan District
Tho Xuan
Vietnam
Telephone: (84) 37 83325784
Fax: (84) 37 83409284
Web site: http://www.lasuco.com.vn

Employee-Owned Company
Incorporated: 1979
Employees: 1,386
Sales: VND 600 billion ($40.6 million)(2002)
NAIC: 311312 Cane Sugar Refining; 311330
Confectionery Manufacturing from Purchased
Chocolate; 312130 Wineries; 312140 Distilleries

Lam Son Sugar Joint Stock Corporation, or Lasuco, is the leading sugar producer in Vietnam, and is also one of the leaders in that country's slow shift toward a market-driven economy. As such, Lasuco is the largest of Vietnam's formerly government-held companies to be privatized. Lasuco operates two sugar refineries, with a total capacity of nearly 6,500 tons per day, or 100,000 tons per year, fed by farmers throughout the mountainous Lam Son region in northern Vietnam. The company has played a primary role in shifting the region from subsistence farming to the profitable planting of sugarcane, and continues to support farmers through: technological services, such as the introduction of new, higher-yield seed types; and financial support, including loans underwriting farmers' preparation, seed, planting, fertilizer, and labor costs. In addition to sugar refining, Lasuco has been branching out in an effort to make full use of sugarcane. In addition to its two sugar refineries, Lasuco operates two alcohol production facilities, the first manufacturing 1.5 million liters of molasses-based alcohol per year, and the second with a capacity of 25 million liters per year for the export market. Moreover, its Dinh Huong confectionery factory produces more than 5,000 tons of candy and cookies each year. The company also produces more than 800,000 liters of draft beer and 600 tons of glucose per year. In

the early 2000s, Lasuco began branching out beyond sugar-based products. The company has encouraged the introduction of dairy cattle herds in the region—using the leftover sugarcane leaves as fodder—and produces more than 30,000 tons of fodder per year in its own production facility. The company also operates a milk processing plant, and has been introducing a new crop, pineapple, to support its fruit juice concentrate plant. Nearly all of the company's production is for the domestic market; nonetheless, Lasuco began exporting for the first time in 2003 and plans to boost exports to 30 percent of sales in the future. Lasuco is led by Le Van Tam; farmers form a large part of the company's shareholder base.

Economic Success Story in the 1970s

Exhausted from nearly two decades of war, the Lam Son region, like much of Vietnam, remained impoverished and underdeveloped at the end of the 1970s. Subsistence farming, chiefly of rice and other crops for personal consumption, had traditionally characterized the highly mountainous region. Lam Son had also seen little development in modern infrastructure, and the vast majority of the population had received no formal education. At the same time, Vietnam as a whole, and the Lam Son region in particular, were faced with severe sugar shortages.

Recognizing that the Lam Son region held great promise as a fertile agricultural center, and especially for the introduction of sugarcane as a cash crop, the Vietnamese government announced its intention to build a sugar refinery in 1979. The facility, to be constructed in Lam Son Town, was to be built in cooperation with the French government, which supplied the equipment, and was to be capable of producing up to 1,500 tons per day of refined sugar. The government began encouraging the conversion of rice paddies to sugarcane plantations.

The project faced long delays, however. The outbreak of war in Cambodia interrupted construction of the refinery, which did not restart until 1982. By 1986, after losing a significant amount of equipment, the French team pulled out of the project. The Vietnamese were forced to take over construction, which ultimately cost the equivalent of $14 million. Production began in 1986, although the Lam Son Sugar Refinery was not completed until

---

Key Dates:

1979: French and Vietnamese government reach a cooperation agreement to build the Lam Son Sugar Refinery in Lam Son Town.

1982: Construction resumes on the refinery after interruption caused by war in Cambodia.

1986: Production begins at the refinery.

1988: The Lam Son refinery is completed.

1992: Lam Son reaches production capacity of 1,500 tons per day.

1994: Company's name is changed to Lam Son Sugar Company (Lasuco), and begins producing alcohol and confectionery products.

1997: Lasuco begins construction of a second sugar refinery.

1999: Still known as Lasuco, the corporate structure is renamed Lam Son Sugar Joint Stock Company.

2000: Privatization begins, with employees and farmers being offered shares in the company.

2003: Company plans a listing on Ho Chi Minh City Stock Exchange.

1988. The operation became a subsidiary of the government-controlled Sugarcane and Sugar Corporation.

The Lam Son Sugar Refinery now ran into a new stumbling block. Despite its capacity for processing 1,500 tons of sugar per day, the site, like other sugar refineries being built in the country, was dependent on locally produced sugarcane as feedstock. Convincing farmers to convert their fields to sugarcane plantations had, however, proven extremely difficult. In its first years, therefore, the refinery ran far below capacity, often at just 10 percent of total capacity. The low level of production in turn made the refinery's sugar expensive to produce, and like much of the Vietnamese sugar industry, Lam Son was forced to produce at a loss.

The naming of Le Van Tam as head of the company marked the beginning of a new era, not only for Lam Son, but for Vietnam's entire sugar industry. Tam correctly recognized that the region's farmers were the key to the sugar company's hopes for success. Tam began a program for winning their trust and worked to implicate the farmers themselves in the company's operations. As Tam explained to *Vietnam Economic Times:* ''We tried to make the farmers the real owners of the factory and not outsiders. Otherwise, they could easily shift to other crops.''

Tam set out to win over the region's farmers in a number of ways. Farmers were promised purchase prices higher than the national average—with price increases each year until 2003. In order to counter farmers' distrust of the company's payment policy, which based payments on measurements of a field's sugar content, the company included farmer representatives on the team measuring crops. At the same time, however, the company enacted a series of initiatives in order to encourage the farmers to plant sugarcane. A major part of that program was the group's willingness to provide financing to farmers, subsidizing the preparation of new sugarcane fields, the purchase of seeds and fertilizers, and the cost of labor in order to plant and harvest.

Despite these initiatives, gaining farmers' trust and converting farmland to sugarcane plantations remained a primary obstacle to the operation's growth until the early 1990s. By 1990, its revenues had reached only VND 6 billion (about $500,000). In 1992, however, the company achieved full capacity at its sugar refinery. The group then began work on expanding the facility, targeting 2,500 tons per day by 1997. During this time the group succeeded in bringing some 30,000 farmers in the region under contract to supply sugarcane to the facility. In 1994, the group formally adopted the name of Lam Son Sugar Company (Lasuco). The following year, it participated in the organization of the Lam Son Sugar Cane Association. Members of the cooperative were then given special benefits from the company.

A major turning point in this effort came with the introduction of automated sugar content measuring systems in 1996. The new system went a long way toward reassuring farmers, who now agreed to be paid at their farms, rather than at the refinery. That same year, the Vietnam government launched a nationwide effort to increase sugarcane output.

Lasuco went still further in its relationship with its suppliers, adding a new series of incentives, not just to individual farmers, but to entire villages. As such, the company promised to build schools and power stations for villages that succeeded in supplying 20 tons of sugar in a single year. Lasuco also offered paid vacations, and began paying university fees for its workers' children. As Lasuco developed into the region's major employer, it also began a number of training initiatives for its work force.

Diversified Leader in the New Century

Lasuco became actively involved in the search for and introduction of new seed varieties, enabling farmers to realize significant increases in sugarcane yield within a short period of time. The increased output allowed Lasuco not only to reach full operating capacity but also to lower production costs, thereby increasing the group's profits. These in turn were reinvested in a variety of corollary operations meant to maximize usage of the sugarcane plant. The byproducts and even the waste products of the refining process presented a number of opportunities for the company. In the mid-1990s, Lasuco opened its first facility for the production of alcohol from molasses

Soon after, Lasuco branched into the production of candy and other confectionery products, including cookies. The company also began supplying glucose to the industrial market. Other facilities built by the company during the 1990s included two bio-fertilizer plants, a draft beer brewery, and, in 1999, a plant for the production of cattle feed using the waste sugarcane leaves. The latter led the company into the dairy market, as it began subsidizing farmers purchases of dairy herds. Lasuco was also becoming increasingly self-sufficient, adding its own power-generation facilities, a mechanical repair workshop, and its own research center.

Refinery operations remained the core of Lasuco's business. With sugarcane production in the region already reaching viable proportions, and with a further rise in production forecasted for the near future, Lasuco began construction of a second refinery in 1997. Completed in 1998, the new refinery boosted the company's total output capacity to nearly 7,000 tons per day. At the same time, the company built a second alcohol production plant, designed to supply the export market with a production level of 15 million liters per year.

The following year, the Vietnamese government began enacting a series of privatization initiatives. As one of the country's largest companies, Lasuco became a prominent part of the government's economic reforms. In 1999, the company's name was changed again, to Lam Son Sugar Joint Stock Company. The following year, Lam Son became Vietnam's largest privatized company.

The Vietnam government retained 37.5 percent of the company. Much of the group's stock, however, was reserved for its employees and farmer producers, who were given the opportunity to acquire shares in the company at discounted rates. While Lasuco's employees took a 32.4 percent stake in the company, its farmer suppliers acquired 22.5 percent, giving the company effective control of a majority of its stock.

By 2000, the total acreage supplying the Lam Son plants topped 16,500 hectares, representing raw sugarcane totals of nearly one million tons. In that year, the group neared 72,000 tons of refined sugar. The rise in the output and the steady decreases in production costs enabled the company to begin eyeing expansion into the export market for the first time.

By 2002, Lasuco's output topped 88,000 tons of refined sugar and sales of VND 600 billion. The company then launched a new series of strategic investments, designed to boost sales past VND 1 trillion by 2005. A major part of this expansion came in the form of a VND 700 billion investment drive funding the construction of a new 25 million-liter alcohol production plant and a new 100,000 ton animal feed plant.

Lasuco continued its diversification as well. In 2003, the company began construction of a new 100,000-liter milk processing plant to support the growing regional dairy herd. It also began promoting the diversification of the region's farmlands, adding products such as mushrooms and pineapples. In support of these products, the group added processing facilities both for fresh and canned mushrooms, and for fruit juice concentrate.

Lasuco's sugar production was expected to pass the 100,000-ton mark by the end of 2003. That year also marked a new milestone for the company, and for the Vietnamese sugar industry as a whole, as Lasuco began its first exports of sugar, to Malaysia. That year, Vietnam expected to export up to 200,000 tons of raw and refined sugar, the first time the country had achieved significant export levels. Meanwhile, the company began plans to list the company on the Ho Chi Minh City Stock Exchange, scheduled for the end of 2003. With plans to step up exports to 30 percent of sales by 2005, Lasuco remained a vital player in Vietnam's future economic development.

Principal Competitors

Bourbon-Tay Ninh; Khanh Hoi Sugar Company; Son Duong Sugar Company; Vietnam-Taiwan Sugar Company Ltd; Lui Li Koung.

Further Reading

"Lam Son Co. Builds Alcohol Plant," *Vietnam News Briefs*, May 24, 2002.

"Lam Son Co. to Become Economic Group," *Vietnam News Briefs*, April 1, 2002.

"Lasuco, Biggest Privatized Company," *Vietnam News Briefs*, May 17, 2000.

"Lam Son Sugarcane Mill Makes Life Sweet for Local Agricultural Industry," *Vietnam News,* May 14, 2002.

"Lasuco to be Listed on Stock Exchange," *Vietnam News*, February 20, 2003.

Mai, Chi, "Sugar Companies Group Together to See Out Storm," *Vietnam Investment Review*, August 15, 1999.

"Sweet Industrialization," *Vietnam Economic News*, August 3, 1998.

"Sweet Success," *Vietnam Economic Times*, March 1, 1999.

—M.L. Cohen

Litehouse Inc.

P.O. Box 1969
Sandpoint, Idaho 83864
U.S.A.
Telephone: (208) 263-7569
Fax: (208) 263-7821
Web site: http://www.litehousefoods.com

Private Company
Incorporated: 1963
Employees: 437
Sales: $85 million (2003)
NAIC: 311225 Fats and Oils Refining and Blending;
311513 Cheese Manufacturing; 42443 Dairy Product
Wholesalers; 31142 Fruit and Vegetable Canning;
42242 Packaged Frozen Food Wholesalers; 311999
All Other Miscellaneous Food Manufacturing

Litehouse Inc. is the second largest supplier of refrigerated salad dressings in the United States. In all, their line of products—also including marinades, dips, salsa, freeze-dried herbs, caramel, and packaged salads—boasts more than 1,300 items from 600 recipes. In 1997, with sales at $31 million, Litehouse merged with another family-owned enterprise, Chadalee Farms, remaining a private company with a new presence in Michigan. In 2003 sales hit $85 million.

Salad Dressing Catches On: 1950s–60s

Litehouse was founded by Ed Hawkins in the small town of Hope, Idaho. In 1958 Hawkins and his wife, Lorena, purchased Herschel's Lighthouse, a restaurant, and renamed it The Litehouse. This was where Hawkins, a chef, created his now-famous bleu cheese dressing. Customers liked the dressing so much, they often brought in empty jars so they could take some home with them. In 1963—in response to slow business during the off-season and to help pay for his children's college tuition—Ed Hawkins started selling the dressing outside his restaurant. Scraping together $1,000 to jar 12 dozen cases of Bleu Cheese and Thousand Island dressing, Hawkins convinced Rogers Thrift in nearby Sandpoint to sell it. The Hawkinses delivered their jars

of dressing in the family's Datsun station wagon. The dressing sold well, but financial success was still years away.

In the early 1970s, several new challenges faced the business. The restaurant in Hope was struggling, and a second Hawkins' restaurant, in nearby Pullman, burned down. Ed Hawkins became ill and was hospitalized, and the family was broke. At this time, Hawkins's sons, Doug and Ed, Jr., each left their teaching jobs to take over the family business, with Ed, Jr., becoming the company's CEO, and Doug stepping in as president. In 1974 the brothers began focusing on the salad dressing business. At the same time, they shared a commitment to the community in which they lived. They supported ball teams, downtown businesses, an art center, and Habitat for Humanity. They also helped with Sandpoint's annual festival and other events that brought people to their town.

Doug and Ed Hawkins promoted the dressing vigorously, traveling to supermarkets in and around Idaho. They quickly landed the dressing on the shelves of grocery stores in Idaho and Montana. In 1974, not including restaurant profits, Litehouse Dressings brought in $100,000. The brothers began approaching supermarkets further out-of-state, eventually selling their dressing to a large grocery chain in Seattle. From that point in 1977, the company moved forward at record speed, gaining more and more accounts with western grocery chains. In response to its continued out-of-state growth, Litehouse purchased three new Class 8 refrigerated tractors in 1979, which allowed the company to move its fresh salad dressing long distances in large quantities.

Explosive Growth in the 1980s and Early 1990s

Operations ran smoothly for a few years, but by 1983, Litehouse experienced a number of maintenance problems with its delivery trucks. Blown engines meant missed deadlines; broken-down tractors meant the product was stuck en route until repairs were finished. In response, Litehouse opened its own repair shop to reduce maintenance bills. Still, delivery time was wasted during repairs. A decision to lease trucks through PacLease for out-of-state deliveries saved Litehouse as much as $22,000 a year.

Company Perspectives:

Integrity isn't just something we talk about. At Litehouse Foods it is part of every decision we make. It comes from three generations of good old-fashioned values. And we take these values seriously, like caring for our customers, vendors and employees. The Litehouse tradition is built on great taste and exceptional products. And we believe that serving our communities by providing good jobs is as important as producing the best-tasting products. Quality you can trust. Service you can depend on. From people who care. From our family to ours, Litehouse is a name you can trust every day.

Shortly after Ed Hawkins, Sr., died in 1984, Litehouse growth skyrocketed. Between 1989 and 1995, sales grew from $6 million to $25 million. Much of this was due to the Hawkins's continued promotional efforts, which included traveling to new supermarkets with their product. Both Doug and Ed, Jr., spent up to 25 weeks a year traveling to new stores. Litehouse's refrigerated dressings filled a niche in the market, as only two other companies—Marie's and T. Marzetti's—offered serious competition.

In 1992 Litehouse spent $500,000 on a 21,000-square-foot addition to the facilities. The addition included new production and cold storage space that allowed the company to double its output of refrigerated salad dressings in just a few years. At the same time, new products were introduced. In 1990 Litehouse began selling two-ounce packages of dressing. In 1993 a salsa product and two dips—Ranch Veggie Dip and Dilly of a Dip—were marketed. Litehouse heavily promoted its dressings' natural ingredients, such as canola oil, while emphasizing that Litehouse products contained neither preservatives nor MSG.

More Growth and a Key Merger in the 1990s

In the period from 1992 to 1997 Litehouse's annual growth averaged over 15 percent. With a workforce of 50 increasing to 240, Litehouse soon became one of Sandpoint's largest employers. In 1994 Litehouse was recognized for its role in the Idaho economy when a group of lawmakers and lobbyists on a bus tour through northern Idaho stopped to tour the business. Those on tour not only saw modest accommodations—Litehouse did not believe in fancy, expensive office space—but also a smooth and profitable operation. The company had recently installed new computer software by Datalogix International, which, after only one year, decreased the number of shorted orders by 66 percent. By the end of the following year, shorted orders were decreased even more. As a result, Litehouse experienced a higher turnover, from five days to two, of fresh ingredients in its inventory.

In 1997 Litehouse sales hit $31 million, while its products lined the shelves of 18 percent of all U.S. grocery store chains. The company ranked third, behind Marie's and T. Marzetti, in the nation's sale of refrigerated salad dressings. In April 1997 Litehouse and its owners were featured in *Entrepreneur* magazine's "75 Entrepreneurial Superstars Tell How They Made Millions." It was also in this year that Litehouse merged with Chadalee Farms, Inc., of Lowell, Michigan.

Merger talks between the two began in 1995, when Litehouse approached Chadalee's president, Wendell Christoff, asking whether Chadalee would be interested in producing Litehouse's product. This would have allowed Litehouse to reduce its shipping costs to the east coast. Christoff did not wish simply to produce known products; he wanted to create a national company. Litehouse seemed an ideal mate: the two companies shared similar values, vision, and history. The Michigan family business had begun in 1951 when Christoff's parents, Clinton and Dorothy Christoff, purchased Chadalee Farms, a company started in 1932. Like Litehouse, Chadalee got its start with a single salad dressing. By the time of the merger, the one dressing had expanded to more than 1,000 products, from salad dressings to sauces, dips, and horseradish products.

Before the merger, Chadalee had 75 employees working in a 77,000-square-foot automated plant. As a result of the merger, Chadalee was able to immediately hire 25 additional employees. As for Litehouse, its projections for east coast-shipping savings were exceeded, as it saved between $200,000 to $300,000.

While the merger went smoothly, Litehouse ran into some trouble in its hometown. In 1998 the city of Sandpoint fined Litehouse $4,000 for violating city waste disposal standards 11 times between 1994 and 1996, as it had exceeded limits in dumping too much oil and fat into the city's sewer system. Earlier that year, Sandpoint itself was fined $27,500 by the Environmental Protection Agency for failure to monitor and enforce industrial wastewater discharge to its sewer plant. Much of the waste cited was Litehouse's. While each violation was minor, according to city authorities, they began to add up.

In response, Litehouse hired a food processing expert to help clean up discharge from the plant. The city credited Litehouse its $4,000 fine for any improvements it made in order to stop future violations. A dilemma loomed, however, as Litehouse faced the challenge of disposing of its daily fat waste of 2,000 gallons. The septic dump it used, the 39-acre Colburn landfill, was nearly full. When the Colburn facility closed in 1999, Litehouse was forced to haul all of its waste to a Montana landfill.

Meanwhile, Litehouse continued to grow. In 1998 it introduced a new seafood condiment line that included Traditional Tartar Sauce, Cocktail Sauce, and Surimi Mustard Dip (for crabmeat). At the same time, they marketed six new "restaurant-quality" seafood marinades, some fat-free sauces and marinades, and four dressings for its new line of classic gourmet dressings: Bleu Cheese Vinaigrette, Balsamic Vinaigrette, Wild Huckleberry Vinaigrette, and Roasted Red Pepper.

In 1999 Litehouse won 12th place in *American Food and Beverage's* American Taste Awards. Two of its marinades also won "best of show" awards. More importantly during this time, however, Litehouse became a known symbol in many grocers' butcher cases. Grocery chains Rosauer's and Albertson's began offering some cuts of meat pre-marinated with Litehouse products, free of charge. This move saved consumers time and was convenient, while allowing Litehouse an easy introduction to a larger audience. By this time Litehouse was selling its products in all 50 states, Canada, and Mexico, and held 17 percent of the refrigerated dressing market.

Key Dates:

1958: Ed and Lorena Hawkins purchase the Litehouse Restaurant.
1963: The Litehouse sells its first jar of salad dressing outside the restaurant.
1974: Founders' sons, Ed, Jr., and Doug Hawkins, take over the business.
1984: Ed Hawkins, Sr., dies.
1992: A building addition allows the company to quickly double its output of salad dressing.
1997: Litehouse merges with Chadalee Farms of Lowell, Michigan.
2001: The company purchases Sandpoint Cheese Factory in order to make its own bleu cheese.
2003: For the company's 40th anniversary celebration, Litehouse markets a new dressing, Big Bleu.

New Products in the New Century

In 2000 growth continued at record speed, as Litehouse promoted a new Veggie Dip line. Five of its new flavors—Sour Cream Ranch, Lite Sour Cream Ranch, Jalapeno Ranch, Lite Sour Cream Dill, and Bleu Cheese—won "best of show" awards at an American Tasting Institute judging.

At the same time, Litehouse continued to struggle with its waste disposal problems. Still hauling the bulk of its waste to Montana, Litehouse had also taken some to the University of Idaho, where researchers were testing a new pretreatment system specific to Litehouse's type of waste. The results of this research eventually allowed Litehouse to propose the construction of a wastewater pretreatment facility to the city of Sandpoint. The proposal, to use city-owned land at the local Airport Business Park, would require Sandpoint to apply to the state department of commerce for a $500,000 grant. In 2001 the city received the grant in full. Litehouse, which helped the city cover the additional $200,000 to $300,000 required to complete the project, would use about half of the plant's total capacity.

In 2001 Litehouse acquired the Sandpoint Cheese Factory so that it could begin making its own bleu cheese. Prior to that, the company had been purchasing 325 tons of bleu cheese a year from various vendors around the country. One problem with this arrangement was that Litehouse used only kosher cheese, which proved a troublesome requirement for some cheese vendors. Thus, the company had long been looking forward to making its own bleu cheese for its famous dressing, and upon purchasing the cheese factory, Litehouse hired six people, including a local cheese making expert, to aid in the task. The Sandpoint Cheese Factory maintained a retail outlet that sold cheese and gift products, and Litehouse decided to keep this popular store running. During this time of rapid growth, Litehouse was recognized as a "Business of the Month" by Idaho's department of labor.

More recognition came in 2002, when Litehouse grabbed the record for the "World's Largest Garden Salad" in the *Guinness Book of World Records* through its sponsorship of the annual Lettuce Days Festival in Yuma, Arizona. The salad, weighing 7,248 pounds, was topped with 750 pounds of Litehouse dressing. Also this year, Litehouse recorded double digit revenue growth, surpassing Marzetti's as second largest producer of refrigerated salad products, and was second only to the Marie's brand made by Dean Foods Company.

Litehouse again introduced a number of new products, including Idaho Bleu (featuring bleu cheese crumbles made in its newly acquired cheese factory), a line of organic salad dressings, and a new freeze-dried herb line. The herbs—Pasta Herb Blend and Salad Herbs—required no washing, sorting, or chopping and, as the label read, were "as close to fresh as you can get." In 2002, Litehouse also began selling its products online.

Having sold its first jar of salad dressing in 1963, Litehouse celebrated its 40th anniversary in 2003. To mark the occasion, Litehouse presented a new dressing, Big Bleu, which it deemed "a bigger, better version of the original that started it all over forty years ago." The company also marketed five new dips and dressings, including Hail!Caesar and Chunky Garlic Caesar. Adding to the celebratory mood was the year's sales, which reached $85 million. In 2003, Litehouse—a company that began with the two owners, Doug and Ed, Jr., lugging boxes of dressing into Roger's Thrift in Sandpoint—employed 367 full-time employees in Sandpoint and 70 in Michigan.

Principal Competitors

Dean Foods Company; T. Marzetti Company.

Further Reading

Berryhill, Mary, "Father's Dream Parlayed into Family Business," *Bonner County Daily Bee*, June 17, 2001, p. 1.

Buley, Bill, "Litehouse Dressing Continues its Rapid Growth," *North Idaho News*, May 16, 1990.

"Caramel Dip Spews Out From Back of Semi-Trailer," *Portland Oregonian*, October 5, 1993.

Carlson, Brad, "Litehouse Sales Hit $41 Million," *Idaho Business Review*, April 28, 1997.

Compton, Sandy, "With Schweitzer Mountain Gone Corporate, the Timber Industry Moving On and Tourism Coming In, Sandpoint, Idaho, is Poised For Change," *Times Mirror Magazines*, December 1, 1999.

DeMasters, Karen, "Salad (Dressing) Days," *Supermarket News*, May 10, 1999.

Drumheller, Susan, "Disposal of Litehouse Dressing in the Fog," *Spokesman Review*, July 20, 1999.

——, "Science Solves Litehouse Woes; Block Grant Will Help Build Pretreatment Plant For Waste," *Spokesman Review*, May 3, 2001.

Gaddy, Angie, "Litehouse in Position to Dress Up its Sales; Merger Has Firm Poised to Make Run for No. 1," *Spokesman Review*, August 4, 1997.

Gunter, David, "Frugal Brothers Guide Growing Corporation," *Bonner County Daily Bee*, November 16, 1989.

——, "Litehouse: Hometown Success Story," *Bonner County Daily Bee*, November 12, 1989.

Keating, Kevin, "Firms Cited For Water Quality Violations," *Spokesman Review*, March 27, 1998.

——, "Legislators Tour Idaho's Other Half," *Spokesman Review*, November 15, 1994.

——, "Sandpoint Hit with EPA Fine," *Spokesman Review*, February 5, 1998.

Kramer, Becky, "Bright Idea Made Litehouse Shine Series: Northwest Originals," *Spokesman Review*, December 26, 1999.

Kulp, Glady, "Horse Creek, Wyoming Has A Touch Of Sandpoint," *Bonner County Daily Bee*, April 21, 1976, p. 76.

"Leasing Allows Companies to 'Keep on Trucking'," *Prepared Foods*, June 1, 1989.

"Litehouse Dressing Updates Operation," *Bonner County Daily Bee*, August 20, 1992.

"Litehouse Starts Freight Trucking Company," *Bonner County Daily Bee*, January 13, 1987.

Longshore, Jan, and Trish Gannon, "Doing Well by Doing Good," *River Journal*, November 1997, p. 1.

Loughran, Siobhan, "Entrepreneur Says a Little Rub'll Do it On Meat, Poultry, Fish," *Portland Oregonian*, June 29, 1999.

Schmeltzer, Michael, "Cooks Turn Specialties into Success," *Spokesman Review*, p. 25.

Sowa, Tom, "Economic Outlook," *Spokesman Review*, February 24, 2003.

Taggert, Cynthia, "Litehouse Is In Its Salad Days," *Spokesman Review*, March 28, 2003.

—Candice Mancini

Little Switzerland, Inc.

161-B Crown Bay
St. Thomas 00802
Virgin Islands
Telephone: (340) 776-2010
Fax: (340) 777-4156
Web site: http://www.littleswitzerland.com

Public Company
Incorporated: 1991
Employees: 447
Sales: $59.6 million (2002)
Stock Exchanges: Over the Counter
Ticker Symbol: LSVI
NAIC: 448310 Jewelry Stores

Little Switzerland, Inc. is a specialty retailer of luxury items that operates 20 retail stores in the Caribbean, Alaska, and Florida. The company's stores, most of which are duty-free units located in the Caribbean, sell jewelry, watches, china and crystal, fragrances, and other accessories. Little Switzerland carries such well-known brand names as Rolex, Baccarat, Lalique, Waterford, and D'Argenta and in some cases controls the exclusive rights to selling a brand in its markets, targeting cruise-ship passengers and hotel guests as its customers. It also carries merchandise from Tiffany & Co., which owns 98 percent of Little Switzerland.

Origins

Although the majority of Little Switzerland's business is conducted overseas, the company's ties to the United States are extremely close. Little Switzerland began as the retail arm of another company, Chelsea, Massachusetts-based Town & Country Corporation. Town & Country was a homespun business that developed into a formidable competitor, a company founded by a teenager who spent four decades building his enterprise into a giant in the U.S. jewelry industry. C. William Carey started Town & Country in 1955 in his basement. Carey was 17 years old at the time and was able to finance the start-up of his enterprise only after his mother offered the Carey family home as collateral for a bank loan. During the ensuing decades, Carey cobbled together numerous jewelry manufacturing concerns, turning his basement workshop into an international conglomerate.

By the mid-1980s, Town & Country was generating roughly $100 million in annual revenue, a total produced by manufacturing plants in the United States, Hong Kong, and Thailand. Town & Country manufactured a wide range of jewelry items. All the merchandise manufactured by the company was sold to retailers, including massive chains such as Sears, Roebuck and Co. and small, independent retail operators. Carey also had started a small retail operation as he aggrandized his manufacturing might. In the Caribbean, he opened several stores whose purpose was to sell jewelry and gift items primarily to U.S. tourists. Travelers arriving in certain parts of the Caribbean could save between 20 percent and 40 percent at Carey's duty-free stores. The company paid no import taxes and enjoyed low tax payments, enabling it to offer a broad selection of merchandise at prices far below those advertised in the United States.

The Little Switzerland stores benefited from other advantages than just low prices. Unlike its parent company, which manufactured private label merchandise, Little Switzerland sold brand name jewelry items and accessories. In some cases, the company was the only retailer authorized to sell certain brands in the markets in which it operated. Little Switzerland sold watches, jewelry, crystal, china, fragrances, gifts, and accessories bearing the most coveted brand names in the world. Brands carried in the company's outlets included Rolex, Tag-Heuer, and Cartier watches; Antonini, DiModolo, and Aaron Basha jewelry; Baccarat, Lalique, and Wedgwood crystal and china; Mont Blanc, Cartier, and Waterman writing instruments; and fragrance lines produced by Yves Saint-Laurent and Christian Dior.

Within the structure of Town & Country, the Little Switzerland organization sprang from a subsidiary named L.S. Holding, Inc., which was incorporated in July 1980. A chain of stores developed from Little Switzerland's flagship store in St. Thomas, U.S. Virgin Islands. By 1987, there were nine Little Switzerland stores in operation on eastern Caribbean islands. The chain by this point had the exclusive Caribbean rights to prestige brands such as Rolex watches and Baccarat crystal. In October 1987, L.S. Wholesale, Inc. was incorporated to pur-

Company Perspectives:

Little Switzerland is a specialty retailer of luxury items. Little Switzerland currently operates 17 distinctively designed retail stores on five Caribbean islands and Alaska. It's not easy to come away from Little Switzerland empty-handed. You'll find the Caribbean's premier duty-free shop overflowing with gold jewelry, precious gemstones, fragrances, crystal, china, and the islands' largest collection of Swiss timepieces. Every purchase is authenticated and guaranteed, so you'll never think twice.

chase inventory for distribution to L.S. Holding's retail stores, the Little Switzerland outlets that dotted nine islands. The following year, a ten-year franchise agreement was signed with Solomon Brothers Limited, a Bahamian company involved in the wholesale and retail distribution of jewelry, gift items, and consumables in the Bahama Islands. Under the terms of this agreement, Solomon Brothers began opening stores under the name Little Switzerland in the Bahamas.

Little Switzerland Gains Independence in 1991

By the end of the 1980s, Carey's collection of jewelry manufacturers represented a more than $400 million-in-sales business. Little Switzerland was benefiting from a 20 percent increase in tourism in its Caribbean markets. The increase in tourism fueled the chain's expansion, and the number of its stores nearly doubled during the late 1980s. By the beginning of the 1990s, Carey had decided to spin-off his retail operations as a separate, publicly traded concern. The entity that emerged on its own was named Little Switzerland, Inc., which was incorporated on May 23, 1991 as a subsidiary of another Town & Country subsidiary named Switzerland Holding, Inc. At the time of Little Switzerland, Inc.'s incorporation, all the assets of L.S. Holding, Inc. and L.S. Wholesale, Inc. were transferred to Little Switzerland, Inc. In July 1991, Town & Country, through Switzerland Holding, Inc., sold 68 percent of Little Switzerland, Inc. to the public. The initial public offering (IPO) of stock, consisting of 5.7 million shares sold at $12 per share, marked the beginning of Little Switzerland's independence, although Town & Country held onto 32 percent of its former subsidiary until divesting its interest in 1994. All the proceeds from the IPO were given to Switzerland Holding, Inc.

When Little Switzerland completed its IPO, the chain comprised 17 stores. In the years immediately following its independence from Town & Country, the company expanded at a measured pace. The success of Little Switzerland was based on the performance of its stores and where it chose to expand rather than a large number of new store openings. Although recessive economic conditions in the United States during the early 1990s delivered a blow to tourism in the Caribbean, Little Switzerland fared well during the downturn. Within a year of its IPO, the company added two new stores, one on St. Thomas and another on St. Kitts, helping it to generate $63 million in sales in 1993.

Little Switzerland made its boldest expansion move of the 1990s in 1994. The company diversified its geographic presence

dramatically by opening a store in Ketchikan, Alaska. Little Switzerland's president at the time, Kenneth Watson, explained the move in an April 25, 1994 interview with *Travel Weekly*. "With the redirection of large numbers of ships to [Alaska] during the summer months," he said, "we are capitalizing on [our] international name recognition in the Pacific Northwest, which has been enjoying steady growth as a tourist destination." With the establishment of a store in Ketchikan, Little Switzerland positioned itself for a substantial amount of new potential business. Ketchikan served as a stopping point for numerous cruise ships traveling to Alaska. An estimated 380,000 passengers arrived in Ketchikan between May and mid-September, brought by more than 450 cruise ships. Aside from introducing the chain into a vast, new market, the establishment of the Ketchikan store gave Little Switzerland business to offset the seasonal cyclicality of its Caribbean business. In Alaska, the peak selling season ran during the spring and the summer. In the Caribbean, the peak selling season ran from late fall through spring.

Little Switzerland performed well during the mid-1990s, aided by a return to more prosperous times in the United States. By 1997, the company operated 27 stores, which generated $88 million in sales. Although the company stocked a wide variety of merchandise, it was reliant on the sale of watches for the bulk of its sales. In 1997, watches accounted for 44 percent of the company's total sales, with Rolex watches accounting for one-quarter of total sales. The watches sold by Little Switzerland ranged in price from $50 to $30,000. The second most significant product line was jewelry, which included rings, earrings, bracelets, necklaces, pendants, and charms. Ranging in price from $30 to $5,000, Little Switzerland's jewelry line accounted for 27 percent of the company's total sales in 1997. The third most important product category was Little Switzerland's selection of crystal, china, gifts, and flatware, which sold for between $20 and $3,000 and accounted for 17 percent of 1997's sales. Fragrances, which sold for between $15 and $150, and accessories such as leather goods, sunglasses, and writing instruments accounted for the remainder of the company's sales in 1997.

Little Switzerland Falters in the Late 1990s

The end of the 1990s represented a time of change at Little Switzerland. Another economic recession in the United States loomed, the onset of which delivered a much more painful blow to the chain than the weak economy of a decade earlier. The company also gained new leadership at this time. Robert L. Baumgardner was appointed president and chief executive officer of the company in August 1999, taking control just as Little Switzerland was set to endure the most difficult years in its history. Before joining Little Switzerland, Baumgardner held senior management positions at Zale Corporation, an operator of a chain of retail jewelry stores, and at Tiffany & Co., the famed New York City-based jewelry store operator. Under Baumgardner's watch, Little Switzerland experienced both highly profitable periods and low periods when it recorded significant losses. It also forged a significant partnership with an esteemed member of the jewelry community.

As Little Switzerland neared the completion of its first ten years as an independent company, it began to suffer profound financial losses. At the end of the company's fiscal year in

---

Key Dates:

1991:   Little Switzerland is spun off from Town & Country Corp.
1994:   Little Switzerland opens a store in Alaska.
2001:   Tiffany & Co. acquires a 45 percent interest in Little Switzerland.
2002:   Tiffany & Co. obtains 98 percent of Little Switzerland.

May 2000, Baumgardner's reign began on a sour note. For the year, Little Switzerland posted a $15 million loss. Sales reflected the chain's diminishing strength as well, with the $55 million generated during the year standing in sharp contrast to the nearly $90 million recorded several years earlier. In December 2000, the company expanded its flagship store in St. Thomas, which helped produce a 40 percent gain in sales at the store to $10.7 million, but the renovation only marginally improved the company's overall financial performance. At the end of May 2001, Little Switzerland posted a loss of $7.6 million on only a slight increase in sales to $56.3 million. By the end of fiscal 2001, however, there was a ray of hope that the company could effect a turnaround. Another company, Baumgardner's former employer, had taken interest in Little Switzerland. The interest translated into cash, giving Little Switzerland's management encouragement as the chain progressed into its second decade of independence.

In the spring of 2001, Tiffany & Co. announced it intended to buy 45 percent of Little Switzerland. As part of the transaction, Tiffany agreed to invest roughly $9 million to purchase newly issued shares of Little Switzerland and promised to provide debt financing of up to $2.5 million. The ties between the two companies grew closer during the ensuing months, as Little Switzerland began stocking merchandise from Tiffany & Co. and Tiffany & Co. steadily increased its stake in Little Switzerland. Little Switzerland opened its first Tiffany Boutique in Barbados in December 2001 and several months later began stocking a small assortment of Tiffany & Co. merchandise in two other stores. In late 2002, Tiffany & Co. greatly increased its investment in Little Switzerland, obtaining 98 percent of the chain.

With the help of Tiffany & Co. and a new merchandising strategy that introduced a bevy of new products, Little Switzerland began to effect a turnaround. The company posted a profit of $165,000 for the three-month period ending in February 2002, the first profitable quarter for Little Switzerland after 15 consecutive quarters without showing a profit. As the company prepared for its second decade of independence, further expansion outside of the Caribbean seemed likely. Little Switzerland opened two new stores in Alaska in May 2001. In 2002, the company opened its third outlet in Key West, Florida.

Principal Subsidiaries

L.S. Holding, Inc.; L.S. Wholesale, Inc.

Principal Competitors

DFS Group Ltd.; SkyMall, Inc.; King Power International Group Co., Ltd.

Further Reading

Andrews, Gregg, "Tiffany to Open Two Boutiques in Little Switzerland Stores," *National Jeweler*, September 16, 2002, p. 10.
"Caribbean-based Specialty Retailer Reports $7.6 Million Loss for Year," *Knight Ridder/Tribune Business News*, September 18, 2001, p. ITEM01261002.
Gelston, Steff, "Town & Country Jewelry Firm Founder Resigns," *The Boston Herald*, January 4, 1997, p. 14.
Gomelsky, Victoria, "Tiffany to Buy 45% Equity in Little Switzerland," *National Jeweler*, May 16, 2001, p. 4.
Jaffe, Thomas, "The Jewel in the Town," *Forbes*, October 5, 1987, p. 246.
"Sales Up at Caribbean-Based Retailer," *Knight Ridder/Tribune Business News*, October 11, 2001, p. ITEM01284005.
Slovak, Julianne, "Town & Country," *Fortune*, April 10, 1989, p. 90.
"The Swiss Are Coming: Island Firm to Open Store in Ketchikan," *Travel Weekly*, April 25, 1994, p. 55.
Teitelbaum, Richard S., "Little Switzerland," *Fortune*, September 7, 1992, p. 75.
"Tiffany Buys Stake in Little Switzerland," *New York Post*, April 11, 2001, p. 31.
Weissenberger, Mark, "Little Switzerland Turns a Third Quarter Profit," *National Jeweler*, May 16, 2002, p. 9.
Young, Vicki M., "Tiffany Closes in on Little Switzerland," *WWD*, October 29, 2002, p. 2.

—Jeffrey L. Covell

Mendocino Brewing Company, Inc.

13351 Highway 101 South
Hopland, California 95449
U.S.A.
Telephone: (707) 744-1015
Toll Free: (800) 733-3871
Fax: (707) 744-1910
Web site: http://www.mendobrew.com

Public Company
Incorporated: 1983
Employees: 94
Sales: $26.10 million (2002)
Stock Exchanges: Over the Counter
Ticker Symbol: MENB
NAIC: 312120 Breweries; 311213 Malt Manufacturing;
   722110 Full-Service Restaurants

Mendocino Brewing Company, Inc. owns three breweries, two in northern California and one in New York, that produce more than a dozen different craft-style beers. MBC operates domestically and internationally, marketing its brands in 36 states and in more than a dozen European countries. The company also is responsible for the U.S. production and sale of Kingfisher Premium Lager, the top-selling brand in India. MBC's brands include Red Tail Ale, Blue Heron Pale Ale, Black Hawk Stout, and Eye of the Hawk Select Ale. The company is controlled and led by Vijay Mallya, who also heads United Breweries Group, an India-based conglomerate with diverse business interests.

Origins

The formation of MBC in March 1983 marked the entry of one of the first competitors in the modern craft brewing industry, a business whose popularity exploded during the 1990s. When the company's brewpub opened in August 1983, it represented the first new brewpub in California and the second such business to open since the repeal of Prohibition. The company's pioneering start, occurring before any substantial numbers of consumers had developed the taste for or the knowledge of handcrafted, traditional-style ales, made its early success that much more remarkable. MBC, however, was founded and oper-

ated with far more zeal than capital, a common characteristic of the craft brewers that would follow in MBC's wake. Craft brewers, particularly during the latter part of the 1990s, were committed to expansion but lacked the financial resources to support the expansion necessary for survival. Despite its financial weakness, MBC enjoyed rousing success during its formative years. The problems occurred later, when the popularity of craft brewing reached unprecedented proportions.

At first, MBC restricted its activities to the confines of Hopland. A signal moment in the company's development occurred in December 1983, when it bottled its first beer at a production facility with a capacity of 400 barrels per year. Red Tail Ale, an amber ale, became the company's flagship brand, contributing substantially to the company's financial health for years to come. MBC quickly exhausted its first supply of bottled Red Tail Ale, enjoying a debut whose success was credited not only to the flavor of the beer but also to the company's innovative packaging. Instead of traditional 12-ounce bottles, Red Tail Ale was packaged in 1.5 liter magnums. The use of over-sized bottles, which would continue for roughly the next 15 years, became a hallmark of MBC, giving the company a distinguishing trait that added to its mystique.

Red Tail Ale, available on tap at the company's brewpub and in 1.5 liter bottles, found a receptive audience in northern California. Hopland became a stopping point for beer enthusiasts, home to the only craft brewing company in existence for thousands of miles. The demand for Red Tail Ale mushroomed, enabling MBC to post record sales for every month in 1984. The increase in demand prompted the company to expand in the spring of 1984, when its production capacity was increased by 67 percent. Despite the expansion, MBC continued to struggle with meeting demand. In 1985, when sales for the year increased by 27 percent, MBC frequently ran out of its signature 1.5 liter bottles of Red Tail Ale, whose popularity further increased after the company introduced another seductive packaging concept. In 1985, the company unveiled carriers designed to hold six 1.5 liter bottles, or 42 pounds of beer.

Growth in the 1980s

As MBC entered the latter half of the 1980s, it found itself leading what industry observers dubbed the American Craft

Company Perspectives:

At Mendocino Brewing Company, we have a certain passion about our beers and are proud that over the years, discerning beer drinkers have shared our passion for quality and class. Although our beers have won many awards, the award we cherish most—is consumer loyalty to our products.

Brewing Renaissance. MBC almost continually expanded between 1985 and 1987, scrambling to match demand with supply. Other brands were developed to complement the company's flagship brand, including Blue Heron Pale Ale, a golden ale, and Black Hawk Stout, a rich-bodied stout. The availability of the company's brands was widening as well, particularly after 1987, when MBC established a wholesale operation. By 1988, the company had developed a network of 300 outlets that greatly expanded distribution. No longer forced to make a pilgrimage to Hopland, fans of MBC's beers found Red Tail Ale, Blue Heron Pale Ale, and Black Hawk Stout in most major restaurants in the San Francisco Bay area, as well as in Napa, Sonoma, and Mendocino counties. Additionally, the company's brands were being distributed to 14 states, giving the company a broad geographic base upon which to rely.

By the end of the 1980s, MBC's management decided the company needed to abandon one of its signature traits. The scope of MBC's distribution network no longer could efficiently accommodate the 1.5 liter bottles that had developed a cult-like following. Accordingly, the company began packaging its brands in conventional 12-ounce bottles. Artists were commissioned to create labels for the company, resulting in a design that centered on illustrations of raptors, a motif that gave MBC a defined identity as it entered the 1990s.

For many craft brewers, the 1990s offered challenges that stemmed from the industry's own success. The idea of making specialty beers had become widely popular to many entrepreneurs, giving MBC a horde of new competition. When it was formed, MBC had existed virtually alone in the industry, but the number of craft brewers later proliferated. By 1997, there were nearly 800 brewpubs in operation throughout the country and more than 1,200 microbreweries. For many of these brewers, access to capital presented the most pressing challenge, as local companies tried to transition to regional concerns and regional companies attempted to make the leap to national contenders. MBC found itself facing its own financial problems during the decade, as its need to expand outstripped its access to new capital and precipitated profound change at the Hopland-based company.

Although MBC suffered from the ills of over-expansion, there were justifiable reasons for the desire to increase production capacity. Financial shortcomings aside, the company was a success. Despite the legions of new, handcrafted beers appearing in the marketplace, MBC's beers stood out among the rest, earning several prestigious awards during the 1990s. In 1990, the company received a gold medal at the Great American Beer Festival, earning the award for its Eye of the Hawk Summer Ale. In competition with domestic and European beers, Red Tail Ale was selected as one of the Top Ten Beers by the magazine *Wine Enthusiast*. The company's flagship brand also drew praise from *Men's Health* magazine, which selected Red Tail Ale as one of the best beers in the United States. In 1997, the *Underground Wine Journal* selected Blue Heron Pale Ale as the recipient of its gold medal. At the World Beer Championship in 1997, MBC won four out of five awards for its entries, with Red Tail Ale capturing the festival's gold medal. MBC's critical acclaim went even beyond its beers: In 1996, the company won a Bay Area ADDY Award for the design of it Blue Heron Pale Ale label and carrier package design. The numerous awards did not bring financial comfort, however. MBC entered the late 1990s forced to confront its weakness, a weakness that was evident to one outside observer in particular.

Midway through the 1990s, MBC sought to cure its financial woes on its own. In 1995, the company completed its initial public offering of stock in a $3.6 million debut as a publicly traded concern. Although the proceeds from the stock offering helped alleviate some of the company's financial pressures, additional capital was soon needed, as the drive to increase capacity continued. In 1996, the company sold 17,000 cases of Red Tail Ale and its complementary brands, generating $3.6 million in sales. MBC's management wanted more, believing that the time was appropriate to expand in an unprecedented fashion. The Hopland brewery, which had undergone a series of additions to increase its production capacity, could no longer sustain the company's demands on its own. A second brewery, located in nearby Ukiah, was constructed, becoming operational in May 1997. The opening of the Ukiah brewery occurred in the same month many of MBC's financial concerns disappeared. Early in May, the company announced it had received a substantial infusion of capital. The source of the funds was an Indian tycoon named Vijay Mallya.

Vijay Mallya Takes Control in 1997

According to numerous press reports, Vijay Mallya was the epitome of a playboy. He owned 26 homes, 260 antique racing cars, a Boeing 727, a Gulfstream jet, and several yachts. He was also in charge of a company, United Brewers Group (UB Group), that included more than 60 companies whose activities were grouped in six main business categories: alcoholic beverages, engineering and technology, agriculture, life sciences, media, and leisure. Mallya inherited the company from his father, Vittal Mallya, who started UB Group by acquiring a controlling interest in India's Kingfisher Beer in 1947. Although Vijay Mallya was renowned for his ostentatious leisure activities, he also embraced the role of businessman with commitment, declaring in an October 26, 2003 interview with the *San Francisco Chronicle*, ''I work seven days a week.'' Evidence of his business abilities was apparent in the growth of UB Group under his stewardship, presenting a record of achievement sufficient to quiet accusations that his wealth was unearned. When Mallya took control of UB Group after his father's death in 1983, the company was generating roughly $100 million in revenue annually. Mallya was in his late twenties at the time he assumed control over a conglomerate with diverse business interests underpinned by Kingfisher, the fourth-leading brand in India's brewing industry. Mallya streamlined the UB Group, divesting interests in processed food, petrochemicals, batteries, pharmaceuticals, and paints, among other businesses. By the time his attention turned to MBC, UB Group represented a $1.4 billion empire. Kingfisher ranked as India's top selling brand, controlling more than 25 percent of the market.

Key Dates:

1983: Mendocino Brewing Co. is founded.
1987: The company establishes a wholesale business.
1995: Mendocino Brewing Co. becomes a publicly traded company.
1997: Vijay Mallya takes control of Mendocino Brewing Co.
1998: Mendocino Brewing Co. acquires Carmel Brewing Co.

Mallya's interest in MBC stemmed from his ambitions as a businessman. "I want to achieve market leadership in this country," he said in reference to the United States in his October 26, 2003 interview with the *San Francisco Chronicle*. When he announced in May 1997 that he had invested $3.5 million in MBC, the investment was part of his plan to create a national microbrewing position by grouping craft brewing concerns under a single corporate umbrella, which would enable him to achieve economies of scale that individual brewing concerns could not attain on their own. One month before pledging his financial commitment to MBC, an announcement that coincided with his $1.75 million acquisition of Arcata, California-based Humboldt Brewing Co., Mallya invested $5.5 million for a 40 percent stake in Portland, Oregon-based Nor'Wester Brewing Co. Together, the small breweries became part of a new U.S. company named United Craft Brewers, a company that was expected to represent a federation of craft brewing companies.

For MBC, the intervention of Mallya proved to be its salvation. Although the company could not be adjudged as close to severe financial difficulties, the influence of Mallya over the company was nonetheless dramatic. Michael Laybourn, one of MBC's founders, credited Mallya with helping to save the company, as reported in the October 26, 2003 issue of the *San Francisco Chronicle*. Aside from Mallya's initial investment, MBC gained control over Kingfisher's U.S. operations, giving the company's annual sales volume a substantial boost. MBC also began operating internationally through a subsidiary named United Breweries International Limited, which distributed beers in more than a dozen European countries. A third production facility, located in Saratoga Springs, New York, joined the company's fold, easing its access to markets in the eastern United States.

After his investment in MBC, Mallya became chairman and chief executive officer of the company. He restructured the company and appointed seasoned executives to oversee MBC's finances, marketing, and advertising. In July 1998, the company completed the acquisition of Carmel Brewing Company. Based in Monterey, California, Carmel Brewing produced 11 ales and lagers, including Carmel Amber Ale and Carmel Hefeweizen.

With Mallya at the helm, MBC matured into a national brewer. Within six years of his leadership, the company's revenue volume swelled from $3.6 million to roughly $25 million. By the time of the company's 20th anniversary in 2003, MBC's brands were available in 36 states and the District of Columbia. As the company planned for the future, it possessed the resources to continue its expansion. MBC had an annual production capacity of 60,000 barrels at its Ukiah plant. The facility was designed with future expansion in mind, giving MBC the ability to increase production to 200,000 barrels annually once new equipment was installed. With Mallya's ambitions to become a market leader in the United States and his vast financial resources at MBC's disposal, the company was expected to figure prominently in the future of the craft brewing industry.

Principal Subsidiaries

United Breweries International, Ltd.

Principal Competitors

Anchor Brewing Company; The Boston Beer Company, Inc.; Redhook Ale Brewery, Inc.

Further Reading

Forder, Tony, "Brew Pub Goes Nationwide," *Record*, October 11, 2000, p. F2.

Fost, Dan, "Vijay Mallya Is Not Your Typical Brewer," *San Francisco*, October 26, 2003, p. I1.

Furfaro, Danielle T., "Saratoga Springs, N.Y., Brewery Gains Exclusive Rights to Popular Brand," *Knight Ridder/Tribune Business News*, August 23, 2001.

Stinton, Peter, "Beer Baron Adds to His Suds Empire," *San Francisco Chronicle*, May 8, 1997, p. B1.

"When Carmel Met Mendocino," *Beverage World*, May 15, 1998, p. 32.

—Jeffrey L. Covell

Montana Coffee Traders, Inc.

5810 Highway 93 South
Whitefish, Montana 59937
U.S.A.
Telephone: (406) 862-7633
Fax: (406) 862-7680
Web site: http://www.coffeetraders.com

Private Company
Incorporated: 1982
Employees: 75
Sales: $25 million (2002 est.)
NAIC: 311920 Coffee and Tea Manufacturing; 722213 Snack and Nonalcoholic Beverage Bars; 445299 All Other Specialty Food Stores; 423990 All Other Durable Goods Merchant Wholesale; 722211 Limited-Service Restaurants.

Montana Coffee Traders, Inc. (MCT), a roaster and seller of high-quality, specialty coffee, is headquartered in a small resort town in the northwest corner of the state not far from Glacier National Park. In addition to great coffee, the company promotes positive working conditions, as well as a concern for the community and the environment. MCT has quietly spread into various markets for its coffee, in the process establishing a coffee-shipping service, three businesses in Montana, one in Texas, and a venture in Russia.

Early Years in Montana

Montana Coffee Traders was founded by R.C. Beall, who came up with the idea of roasting and selling his own beans after drinking a terrible cup of coffee in a late-night café in 1981. For years, Beall—a former logger, back-country guide, and golf course manager from Texas—had been trying to figure out how to make a living in Montana. Perhaps, he thought, coffee could be the answer.

Beall began conducting research on coffee and on Montana. He learned that coffee was the second-most important trading commodity—oil was first—and accounted for a third of all beverages sold in the world. As for Montana, the state had no coffee roasters at the time, meaning no competition. Then again, Montana was a poor state with a small population base. Nevertheless, Beall decided to pursue the idea, teaming up with Whitefish, Montana, artist Scott Brandt to conduct further research. As a result of many hours in the local library and on the phone, they discovered there was a ten-pound coffee roaster, a grinder, and five bags of green coffee beans in a local barn.

Beall sought to purchase the barn, but banks were reluctant to lend him the money. They could not imagine that gourmet coffee would sell in Whitefish. Eventually, First National Bank in Whitefish loaned Beall $4,000, which he used to purchase the barn and its contents. Immediately, Beall began roasting coffee, with some assistance from Michael Sivetz, who owned an airbed roaster business. Using trial and error, Beall attempted to bring out the different characteristics in each bean, recording the results in spiral notebooks. In the process, Beall learned how difficult and exacting it was to roast coffee. For instance, the temperature and time in the roasters had to be precise.

After a lot of practice, Beall became satisfied with the coffee he roasted. In 1982, he opened his coffee-roasting business in a restored old farmhouse in Whitefish, just 25 miles from Glacier National Park. Beall felt confident that he had a great product, but business was slow in starting. A year after opening, Beall sold his Houston golf course to keep the coffee business afloat. It took five years, said Beall, to get the business going. Gourmet coffee, after all, was a hard sell to Montanans, who were used to commercial coffees such as Maxwell House and Folgers. Beall heavily promoted his product in his community, mostly through serving coffee at community events. This, he believed, was the best way to sell people on MCT. He was convinced that once consumers tried one of his freshly roasted and ground coffees, they would agree that the tinned-can brands were under-roasted and stale. Eventually, when consumers did start to agree and MCT moved forward, Beall's motto became: "If you can do it in Whitefish, you can do it anywhere."

MCT Treks to Costa Rica and Russia: Late 1980s and Early 1990s

In 1989, Beall traveled to Costa Rica in search of high-quality coffee beans. He visited a number of cooperatives in the

208

country, hoping to find one that shared MCT's values—community mindedness and concern for the environment—as well as having great beans. When he met with Guillermo Vargas, then the manager of the Santa Elena farm cooperative, Beall saw an opportunity. The coop, located near the renowned Monteverde Cloud Forest Preserve, was at the perfect altitude for growing coffee. In addition, like Whitefish, Santa Elena was being threatened by rapid development. Beall thought if Santa Elena could earn a living growing coffee, its rain forest might be protected.

Ironically, the Santa Elena community—which had never before tasted roasted coffee nor even seen a roaster—did not realize the high quality of their beans. Beall, however, did. Having brought a small roaster with him, Beall allowed them to taste their coffee for the first time. In later negotiations, he agreed to pay a premium price—one of the highest prices given to a Costa Rican coffee grower—in exchange for exclusive North American rights.

Once negotiations were complete, MCT's first "Coffee with a Cause," Café Monteverde, was created. As part of their agreement, MCT committed to donating one dollar per bag sold to special projects for the coop. Such projects included reforestation, educating young Costa Ricans about their environment, and developing organic agricultural practices. Meanwhile, from its new profits, the coop opened a small roasting facility in 1990, finally making it possible to offer home-grown coffee to locals and tourists.

In 1992, Beall set out for another part of the globe: Moscow. Forming a partnership with Russian-born Whitefish residents Aleksandr and Laulette Malchik, MCT-Vostok (meaning MCT-East) was created. The Malchiks had convinced Beall to expand into Russia, claiming that its coffee was terrible. While the market did prove lucrative, and even became self-sustaining within a year, there were problems at the start. It was difficult to find adequate space in the overcrowded city of nine million, the company had no telephone service for months and no supplier for basic office equipment, and they had to bribe local officials at every turn, beginning with their attempt to get the coffee roaster into the country. Fortunately, officials accepted coffee as a bribe. There were also major difficulties with the country's unstable ruble. Because of this, the business largely marketed their product to the city's 100,000 or so foreigners.

By 1993, MCT-Vostok was selling 150 to 200 pounds of coffee a day. At the same time, they began selling grinders, plunge-style pots, and espresso machines. MCT later pulled out of its association with the Russian shop, handing ownership to a Russian resident. No sale was negotiated in the process, as MCT never owned the company. Instead, MCT's role in its "partnership" with the Malchiks was to get the business going. Still, MCT continued to provide assistance to the Russian coffee shop as needed.

MCT Grows Locally in the 1990s

Locally, MCT was growing. In 1992, the coffee roaster opened a shop in nearby Kalispell, Montana. The business, a limited-service restaurant that served specialty foods, snacks, and nonalcoholic beverages (including, of course, coffee), had sales between $500,000 to $1 million within ten years.

By 1993, Montana Coffee Traders had created 150 flavors of coffee, of which they had already sold 175,000 pounds, or fifteen million cups. Beall obtained his green beans through brokers in New Orleans, New York, and San Francisco (as well as Costa Rica), which he would then package and distribute throughout Montana, Idaho, and Washington. One of his most important business strategies simply involved doing the homework—including research and practice—required to achieve a great product.

Beall was also concerned with creating an appealing environment for his customers and set up his Whitefish log cabin/store with this in mind. He placed a covered wagon directly outside the store, while inside the shop was filled with espresso machines, coffee grinders, teapots and kettles, coffee cups, homemade jelly, and chocolate. Upstairs, customers could buy items made by local artists, including hand-woven rugs, baskets, wooden cabinets, and chairs. Pleasant music played in the background. To further enhance a customer's visit to his shop, Beall offered tours of the business. On a typical tour, customers were urged to smell just-roasted coffee beans to distinguish among the different regions from which coffee originated—including Indonesia, Central America, South America, and Africa—and were shown large bags of green beans and coffee roasters that were capable of roasting up to 150 pounds per hour.

To a large extent, Beall depended on his employees to sell his products. Conscious of this fact on both a personal and professional level, he was committed to treating his employees well. MCT paid good wages and provided health insurance for both full-time and part-time workers.

One business tactic Beall did not strongly pursue was advertising. Realizing he could not compete with the advertising campaigns of large companies such as Folgers—which spent millions of dollars a year on advertising—Beall preferred to advertise locally, mostly by providing coffee at community events. Still, convincing both local and out-of-town restaurants to buy MCT coffee—which cost about one or two cents more a cup than commercial coffees—proved challenging. However, when the company discovered that United Parcel Service would ship coffee anywhere in Montana in one day, the business reached a major turning point.

Restaurants and individual consumers were pleased to learn that they could receive MCT's coffee quickly and be billed for it later. The good-faith gesture, as well as the speedy delivery, proved to be effective sales tactics, as did MCT's guarantee of selling only freshly roasted coffee. To do this, MCT used a system of taking orders early in the morning, then roasting no more than the amount needed for the day.

Financial Growth and Community Commitment: Mid-1990s and Beyond

In 1994, Beall traveled to Austin, Texas, to open Texas Coffee Traders. The new location not only returned him to his

Key Dates:

1982: R.C. Beall starts Montana Coffee Traders (MCT).
1989: MCT works out a deal with Santa Elena coffee cooperative in Costa Rica.
1992: MCT helps to jumpstart a coffee shop in Moscow, Russia; the company opens a new coffee shop/restaurant in Kalispell, Montana.
1994: The company starts Texas Coffee Traders, a subsidiary of MCT.
2000: The company opens a new coffee shop in Whitefish, Montana.

home state, but it also provided a good location from which to ship fresh coffee to accounts that were too far from Montana to ensure fresh delivery. It was at that time Beall married; his wife, Beth Beall, became president of Texas Coffee Traders. At TCT, the goals remained the same as in Montana: to sell the best coffee available and to have fun doing it, to treat employees well, and to contribute positively to the community and to the environment.

In its commitment to community and environment, MCT set up programs that contributed part of its sales to various organizations. The company continued its program with Santa Elena, as well as beginning a whole line of Special Project Coffees, all of which donated one dollar for each bag sold. Grizzly Blend provided money for the preservation of grizzly habitat, Four Directions Blend contributed to the Native Families Empowerment program, Abbie Blend furthered the Advocacy for People cause, and Wild Rockies Blend supported wild land protection. MCT has also been committed to fair-trade practices and to buying shade-grown coffee. Growing coffee in the sun, while yielding larger crops, came at a price, including soil degradation, water pollution, worker health risks, and a dependence of the farmer on chemical supplies. Furthermore, cutting down the trees normally associated with coffee plantations has threatened animal habitat.

Other community projects in which MCT has been involved include local land conservation. In 1991, when Beall heard rumors that a substantial piece of land along Whitefish Lake was to be sold, he reacted quickly. With a group of locals, he arranged for a public meeting before the city council, where they convinced council members not to sell the land. Later, the non-profit group convinced Fish, Wildlife, and Parks to lease the land to the group, which created a public park with 400 feet of gravel beach. In another project, Beall organized various fund-raisers (for which he provided the coffee) to bring National Public Radio to the Whitefish listening area.

Meanwhile, in 2000, MCT opened a new store in Whitefish, Montana, bringing its total Montana business to three shops. By 2003, with sales looming between $5 million and $10 million and 75 employees, Montana Coffee Traders had come a long way from its ''beans in a barn'' origins.

Principal Subsidiaries

Texas Coffee Traders.

Principal Competitors

Montana Maid Coffee; Hunterbay Coffee Roasters.

Further Reading

Hensleigh, Christine, ''Coffee Co-op Brews Economic Stability in Costa Rica,'' *Whitefish Pilot*, September 25, 2003.
Jahrig, Shannon H., ''Bad Cup of Coffee Inspires Entrepreneur to Start Business,'' *Montana Business Quarterly*, Autumn 1992, p. 26.
Power, Christine, ''Moscow and Whitefish—united over a Cup of Cappuccino,'' *Fedgazette*, October 1993, p. 10.

—Candice Mancini

National Heritage Academies, Inc.

989 Spaulding Avenue SE
Grand Rapids, Michigan 49546
U.S.A.
Telephone: (616) 222-1700
Toll Free: (800) 699-9235
Fax: (616) 222-1701
Web site: http://www.heritageacademies.com

Private Company
Incorporated: 1995 as Educational Development
    Corporation
Employees: 2,100
Sales: $125 million (2002)
NAIC: 611110 Elementary and Secondary Schools

National Heritage Academies, Inc. (NHA) operates a chain of nearly 40 charter schools—state-regulated, for-profit institutions that serve as a tuition-free alternative to public schools. The company erects the buildings and provides personnel and management services, receiving what local school districts spend per student as compensation. NHA students get a back-to-basics education featuring phonics, math skills, and moral teaching, and follow strict disciplinary and dress codes. To reduce overhead, NHA centralizes many operations, pays its non-union teachers lower salaries, and eschews the use of buses or cafeterias. The Michigan-based company is owned by J.C. Huizenga, a cousin of Blockbuster/Waste Management billionaire Wayne Huizenga.

Beginnings

National Heritage Academies was founded in 1995 by John Charles Huizenga, a wealthy Grand Rapids, Michigan, businessman. Huizenga, whose father had founded the companies that would later become Waste Management, Inc., had grown up attending Christian schools and later earned a master's degree in finance. In his early thirties, he decided to go into business and bought his first company, printing plate manufacturer American Litho. He later became involved with a second firm called JR Automation Technologies, a high-tech machine manufacturer.

When the state of Michigan instituted a law in 1994 allowing the creation of for-profit "charter" schools, which would receive taxpayer funding equivalent to what public schools spent, it created an opportunity for entrepreneurs. Huizenga, who had married a Christian school teacher and had donated to religious schools over the years, was approached by David Koetje, the superintendent of an 11-school Christian system in Grand Rapids. Koetje was now seeking funds for new charter facilities.

Michigan's charter law required that the curriculum adhere to state standards and that the schools, which would be certified by local school districts or state universities, not promote a particular religion. Koetje had second thoughts about the project because of this rule, but Huizenga decided to go forward and found a school of his own. Rather than being explicitly Christian, it would instead have a "moral focus."

Excel Charter Academy Opens in Fall of 1995

Huizenga's new company, Educational Development Corporation (EDC), opened its first school in the fall of 1995. Named Excel Charter Academy, it was located on the southeast side of Grand Rapids in a renovated office suite. It was intended to accommodate more than 150 students from kindergarten through grade five, with another level to be added each year until the eighth grade was reached. A high school, which was more expensive to operate, was not planned. To run his new operation, Huizenga chose Mark DeHaan.

Excel, which received approximately $5,000 per child from the state of Michigan, used Dr. E.D. Hirsch's Core Knowledge Sequence for its curriculum. Classes emphasized the basics of reading, writing and math, and used phonics rather than the newer "whole language" teaching. Each day began with a 20-minute assembly in which students recited the Pledge of Allegiance, sang patriotic songs, and heard a lesson about morals or character. Though religion was kept out of the classroom, Excel teachers gave Bible-based "creationism" equal consideration to Darwin's theory of evolution. The instruction day was seven hours, longer than that of the public schools.

Excel proved a hit with parents in the conservative, highly religious community of Grand Rapids, and initial demand was so high that a second first-grade classroom had to be added, which boosted total enrollment to 174 students. Many more parents wanted their children to attend the second year, forcing Excel to hold a lottery for available spaces.

Three New Schools Open in Mid-1990s

With a total of only 150 charter schools allowed state-wide, Huizenga soon began laying plans for expansion. In the fall of 1996, EDC, which was now using such recruitment methods as billboards and videos, opened three new schools. These were Vanguard Charter Academy and Vista Charter Academy in the Grand Rapids area, and Vanderbilt Charter Academy in nearby Holland.

Though there had been much praise for Excel, the newer academies' first year was not so smooth. In its first months of operation, Vista saw 10 percent of its 279 students leave, with some parents citing problems with discipline. To improve matters, EDC hired additional staff to assist in the classrooms. Ten of the school's original 13 teachers were recent college graduates.

In May 1997, the firm hired Peter Ruppert to serve as president. The 33-year old Harvard MBA had founded Landmark Consulting Group of Chicago, which assisted corporations with strategic and marketing decisions. During 1997 and 1998, more schools were opened near Grand Rapids and around Michigan, which brought the firm to a total of 13 at the start of the 1998–99 school year. Excel Academy had by now outgrown its original location, and it moved into a new building. A K-4th grade school called Ridge Park Academy was opened in its former space.

Huizenga spent his own money to build the company's schools, which were then leased back to each academy's board. The boards in turn gave all but 2 percent of their public funding back to EDC for rent and management services. Company officials openly compared their approach to Wal-Mart, and EDC employed such methods as using the same floor plan for all of its schools. Everything down to the playground equipment and number of books in the library was standardized as well. Teachers received an average of 91 percent of the salary of their public-school counterparts, which worked out to 95 percent given their lack of union dues. The company expected to turn a profit when a school's full K-8 enrollment of about 650 was achieved.

EDC's schools, and those of other charter companies, quickly began having an impact on the education system in

Michigan. Because they were free to attend and were similar in many ways to tuition-charging Christian schools, a number of parents switched their children from such institutions to EDC, causing financial problems and layoffs at some of the former. The public schools in cities like Holland were also affected, with enrollments dropping and staff laid off as public funds were diverted to charters. Critics of EDC charged that it largely enrolled "cheap" students who came from middle-class families and required less special services, leaving the more expensive children to the public system.

Seeking New Investors in the Late 1990s

By the fall of 1998, Huizenga's investment in the firm, which was now going under the name National Heritage Academies, Inc. (NHA), stood at $40 million, with $50 million more borrowed from family and friends. Each new startup cost upwards of $3 million, and Huizenga's plans for further growth were hampered by a limited amount of available capital. Consequently, the company began seeking an outside investor to purchase its school buildings and lease them back to the schools' boards. This would give Huizenga more capital and also save each academy money, as the rental rates would likely be less than what NHA charged. In early 1999, a $100 million deal was nearly reached with a California investment firm, but it fell through at the last minute.

The year 1999 also saw the American Civil Liberties Union of Michigan sue NHA for allegedly promoting religion in its academies. At one school in particular, parents met for weekly prayers, a Baptist church held evening meetings rent-free, and a minister had reportedly given a sermon at a staff training session. A judge later dismissed the case.

In the fall of 1999, NHA opened its biggest crop of schools to date, which raised the total to 22. Half of this number were in the Grand Rapids area, while eight others were scattered around the state of Michigan and two were located in Winston-Salem and Greensboro, North Carolina. With Michigan nearing its legal cap of 150 charters, the firm was now actively seeking other states into which to expand. A total of 8,000 students were enrolled, served by a staff of 700. The company was still not turning a profit, having lost $1.5 million in its most recent fiscal year.

At the beginning of 2000, NHA secured $50 million in financing from a consortium of lenders and $35 million in new equity funding from an investor. The firm was now the second-largest charter management company in the United States after the New York-based Edison Project, which had 51 schools. In the fall of 2000, six new academies were opened in North Carolina, Michigan, and Rochester, New York. NHA's revenues totaled $49.1 million for the year, and its staff topped 1,000.

A new school that was opened in Detroit at the start of the 2001–02 school year added 455 children, which helped boost total enrollment to 13,300 students system-wide. Of these, 68.7 percent were white, 23.3 percent were African-American, and 5.8 percent were Hispanic. More than two-thirds had transferred from a public school, with about 18 percent coming from a private school, 9 percent from another charter, and 4.5 percent from a home-schooling environment. The company reported a waiting list of 2,600 for spots in its schools. NHA was now

Key Dates:

1995: J.C. Huizenga opens Excel Charter Academy in Grand Rapids, Michigan.
1996: Huizenga's firm, Educational Development Corporation, adds three new schools.
1998: The company changes its name to National Heritage Academies, Inc. (NHA).
1999: The first two out-of-state schools open in North Carolina, giving the company a total of 22 schools.
2000: A lawsuit involving religious issues in NHA schools is dismissed; the first New York school opens.
2001: The company records its first profitable year.
2002: A new academy in Dayton, Ohio, increases the number of states in which the company has a presence to four.
2003: Seven new openings, including the first one in Indiana, bring the company's total number of schools to 39.

ranked 19th on the *Inc.* magazine list of the 500 fastest-growing companies in the United States.

In the summer of 2002, the firm secured another $25 million in credit as it prepared to open four new schools in Detroit; Dayton, Ohio; Charlotte, North Carolina; and Syracuse, New York. NHA, as it had done every year, also added grades to existing schools, while two other academies relocated from rented quarters to new buildings. Annual revenues topped $100 million for the fiscal year ended in June, bringing the firm its second profitable year in a row.

In the fall of 2003, NHA opened seven more academies. They were located in Hamtramck and Belleville, Michigan; Dayton and Cincinnati, Ohio; Buffalo and Brooklyn, New York; and Indianapolis, Indiana, the latter of which expanded the company's reach to five states. Enrollment now topped 20,000. NHA officials announced that expansion would continue until there were a total of more than 200 schools in operation.

In less than a decade, National Heritage Academies, Inc. had grown into one of the top private school management companies in the United States. Its combination of back-to-basics academics and moral teaching appealed to many parents as an alternative to public schooling, while its standardization of buildings and other cost-containment measures helped the company make a profit. NHA had staked out a solid claim in the still-evolving field of for-profit K-8 education.

Principal Competitors

Edison Schools, Inc.; Nobel Learning Communities, Inc.; Chancellor Beacon Academies, Inc.

Further Reading

"Excel Charter School Gets Approval For Building," *Grand Rapids Press*, August 11, 1995, p. A12.

Franklin, Amy, "Federal Court Dismisses Lawsuit Against Charter School," *Associated Press Newswires*, September 27, 2000.

Golden, Daniel, "Common Prayer: Old-Time Religion Gets a Boost at a Chain of Charter Schools," *Wall Street Journal*, September 15, 1999, p. A1.

Kirkbride, Ron, "Banking Syndicate Raises $25 Million to Expand National Heritage Schools," *Grand Rapids Press*, July 12, 2002, p. A6.

Knape, Chris, "National Heritage Remains in Class of Its Own," *Grand Rapids Press*, August 13, 2003, p. A10.

Molinari, Deanne, "Peter Ruppert: Inside Track," *Grand Rapids Business Journal*, June 30, 1997, p. 5.

"National Heritage Makes Money Running Charter Schools," *Associated Press Newswires*, December 2, 2001.

Rent, Katy, "Going to the Head of the Class," *Grand Rapids Business Journal*, November 19, 2001, p. 3.

Riede, Paul, "State Oks Southside Charter School," *Post-Standard* (Syracuse), December 21, 2001, p. A1.

Schuetz, Kym, and Roland Wilkerson, "Charter School Sale Would Fund Expansion," *Grand Rapids Press*, October 9, 1998, p. A1.

Singhania, Lisa, "Companies See Profit in Charter Schools," *Associated Press Newswires*, April 28, 2000.

Weiker, Jim, "Charter Group Says It Has Funds To Grow," *Grand Rapids Press*, January 18, 2000, p. B1.

——, "Will Charter Schools Make the Grade?," *Grand Rapids Press*, January 23, 2000, p. F1.

Wilkerson, Roland, "Charter Captain–J.C. Huizenga Runs Four Schools," *Grand Rapids Press*, April 6, 1997, p. E1.

——, "Charter Operator Seeks $100 Million Deal," *Grand Rapids Press*, January 19, 1999, p. A1.

——, "Charter Schools Deal Falls Through," *Grand Rapids Press*, March 4, 1999, p. A1.

Williamson, Lisa Ann, "Charter School Looking to Build," *Grand Rapids Press*, April 22, 1996, p. B1.

——, "Charting a Course: Some Parents Opt Out as New School Weathers Some First-Year Woes," *Grand Rapids Press*, December 15, 1996, p. B1.

Wyatt, Edward, "Charter School to Raise Topic of Creationism," *New York Times*, February 18, 2000, p. 1.

Ziegenbalg, Dawn, "Pairing Profit and Education; Traditionalists Remain Wary of Company Running Charter Schools," *Winston-Salem Journal*, December 18, 2000, p. 1.

—Frank Uhle

New York City Health and Hospitals Corporation

125 Worth Street
New York, New York 10013
U.S.A.
Telephone: (212) 788-3339
Fax: (212) 788-3348
Web site: http://www.nyc.gov/hhc

Government-Owned Corporation
Incorporated: 1969
Employees: 35,000
Revenues: $4.18 billion (2003)
NAIC: 622110 General Medical and Surgical Hospitals;
    622310 Specialty General Medical and Surgical
    Hospitals; 623110 Nursing Care Facilities

The New York City Health and Hospitals Corporation (HHC), a public-benefit corporation, is the largest urban healthcare agency in the United States. It consists of acute-care hospitals, long-term-care facilities, diagnostic and treatment centers, community health clinics, certified home healthcare agencies, and its own managed-care health-maintenance plan. The HHC, frequently financially beleaguered and often the focus of political contention and pressures, is a behemoth whose facilities serve over 1.3 million people a year—one in six New Yorkers—and account for more than one-third of all emergency-room and hospital-based clinic visits in the city.

Origins in the 18th Century

Bellevue Hospital Center, the oldest public hospital in the United States, is also New York City's largest municipal hospital and largest unit within the HHC. Bellevue serves as the medical facility for dignitaries visiting New York City, including presidents of the United States and United Nations diplomats, inmates of its detention and correctional facilities, and injured city police and firefighters. Its emergency department is considered one of the nation's best, and its psychiatric services are world renowned. Bellevue also is a regional center for brain and spinal-cord injuries and a leading center for trauma, microsurgery, and comprehensive pediatric services. It is the princi-

pal teaching hospital for its affiliate, the New York University School of Medicine. Once the hospital of sole resort for the city's poor and unwanted, Bellevue was where composer Stephen Foster died in 1864, alone and unrecognized, a half-written lyric scrawled on a piece of envelope at his side.

Bellevue's origins can be traced to a six-bed infirmary for contagious disease on the top floor of a public workhouse and jail erected in 1736. The chief scourge at this time in what was now New York was smallpox, and inoculation was sometimes as dangerous as the disease. The impending threat of yellow fever in 1794 inspired the municipal government to purchase Belle Vue, a five-acre country estate bordering on the East River well beyond the city limits, with a two-story building convertible to a hospital. The adjacent 150-acre farm was subsequently purchased, with possession taken in 1811. On this tract, stretching between the East River and Second Avenue and East 23rd and 28th streets, the city built two six-room brick hospitals along with an almshouse, insane asylum, and jail. Part of the site was later sold at auction despite protests from physicians who wanted to build a medical school there.

Bellevue Hospital, its name adopted in 1825, was sorely tested in this period by typhus and cholera epidemics plus the continuing problems of smallpox and yellow fever. A study found filthy conditions, egregious neglect of patients, and positions filled by political patronage. After a second cholera epidemic in 1847, the hospital was put under the control of the College of Physicians and Surgeons. A medical college opened on the site in 1861 and a school of nursing in 1873. By 1870, Bellevue had 1,200 beds. Among its achievements were the following "firsts" in the United States: the first hospital Caesarian section (1867), the first hospital-based ambulance service (1869), the first children's clinic (1874), the first emergency pavilion (1876), the first pathology and bacteriological laboratory (1884), the first in-hospital appendectomy (1887), and the first ambulatory cardiac clinic (1911).

About 1900, the medical college housed at Bellevue merged with New York Medical College to form what became the New York University College of Medicine, Bellevue's primary source of medical staff. Bellevue's first female doctors were admitted in 1914. A pathology building was completed in 1910, a psychopathic building with 500 beds in 1933, and an administration building in 1938. The Children's Psychiatric Service, founded in 1920, developed into the first center in the nation to study autistic children and to train child psychiatrists. The hospital's psychiatric division was turned over to New York University's medical college in 1942. A department of rehabilitation and physical medicine, under New York University auspices, was established after World War II.

By the mid-1950s, Bellevue Hospital was a complex of 14 or 15 buildings with 2,670 beds and an average daily population of about 9,700. Its grounds included its own post office, a state court for commitment proceedings of psychiatric patients, two public schools—including the first public school for emotionally disturbed children located in a public hospital—a prison, several libraries, three chapels, and a mortuary. It was, however, a complex in a state of decay. A master plan drafted in 1957 called for every existing building to be replaced. A 25-story structure, built at a cost of $160 million, was completed in 1973 on the eastern part of the grounds adjoining the administration building. One improvement resulting from the new structure was the replacement of 26-bed wards with rooms that accommodated one, two, or four patients.

Other Municipal Hospitals Before 1970

As New York spread northward, Metropolitan and Harlem hospitals were established in the 1870s in upper Manhattan as extensions of Bellevue. (Metropolitan was originally a homeopathic municipal institution on Wards Island). Brooklyn was in the process of becoming a city when Kings County Hospital was founded in 1831 as its first municipal hospital. A Manhattan home for elderly African-Americans developed into the Bronx's first city hospital, now Lincoln Medical and Mental Health Center, in 1902. Queens's biggest municipal hospital, Elmhurst Hospital Center, opened in 1832 on Blackwell's Island (later Welfare Island and now Roosevelt Island) as a facility for prisoners. It later became City Hospital, moved to Queens in 1957, and took its present name in 1988.

The municipal hospital system experienced many organizational changes before being united in a new Department of Hospitals in 1929. The system was extensively refurbished in the 1930s with the aid of federal funds, and its budget more than doubled between 1934 and 1946. Queens General Hospital opened in 1935. A new hospital for chronic disease was com-

pleted in 1939 on Welfare Island; it later became Coler-Goldwater Memorial Hospital, the largest of the HHC's five facilities for long-term care. Physicians in city-hospital outpatient departments earned salaries for the first time, new laboratory facilities were constructed, a blood bank was organized, and maternity services and equipment were upgraded. At the end of this period, the 20,500 beds (compared to 12,000 in 1934) in the 20 municipal hospitals were fully occupied.

During the 1950s, the city opened four new hospital facilities but existing ones deteriorated as available funds lagged behind new technology, which made hospital care more expensive. Group hospital insurance plans became widespread, providing many workers with an alternative to the municipal hospitals, which also faced a shortage of physicians as younger and better-trained doctors gravitated to the suburbs. This problem was met in the early 1960s by affiliations with private hospitals and medical schools.

The creation of Medicare and Medicaid in 1965 accounted, within a year, for 86 percent of the income received by the municipal hospital system, but many of the elderly migrated for the first time to now-affordable private hospitals. The public system was left to serve the Medicaid and uninsured indigent, and limits on Medicaid eligibility soon raised the proportion of uninsured. As a result, even while experiencing a drop in the number of patients, city hospitals suffered from shortages of funds and understaffing. A 1967 commission concluded that conditions in the hospitals were deplorable and recommended that the city turn over management to private institutions.

The HHC: 1970–2002

The New York City Health and Hospitals Corporation, a new public corporation, was created in 1969 to replace the city's Department of Hospitals as the agency responsible for operating the municipal hospitals and whatever other healthcare facilities the city might assign it. This liberated the new corporation from direct control by the city's budget agency and freed it to make its own purchasing arrangements. Ownership of the facilities as well as responsibility for capital improvements remained with the city, but HHC was responsible for collecting all third-party revenues. The corporation was supposed to be in existence only until each public hospital was placed under private management. The city would then pay the private hospitals a management fee and monitor their performance.

In practice, the HHC became a continuing agency under which administrators hired by the city managed the municipal hospitals in partnership with doctors from private institutions. Critics charged that the medical schools and voluntary (private) hospitals failed to provide first-class medical care or provide the HHC with full value for its money; the medical schools and voluntary hospitals in turn felt they were inadequately appreciated and recompensed. HHC presidents regularly fell victim to the corporation's board, which was dominated by city officials and joint appointees of the mayor and council. Five consecutive presidents resigned during the 1970s, unable to dispel repeated charges that the agency had exacerbated the very mismanagement and waste it was created to eliminate.

There was more stability in the 1980s as the HHC fell under the close control of Mayor Edward Koch. Expenditures more

Key Dates:

1736: A six-bed infirmary is the predecessor of Bellevue, oldest public hospital in the United States.

1811: New York City takes possession of what becomes the grounds of Bellevue Hospital.

1831: Kings County becomes Brooklyn's first public hospital.

1946: The 20,500 beds in the 20 municipal hospitals are fully occupied.

1970: The New York City Health and Hospitals Corporation comes into operation.

1973: Completion of a 25-story building transforms Bellevue's physical plant.

1993: The HHC records a record deficit of $289 million for the fiscal year.

1995: Dr. Bruce Siegel is the 15th HHC president in 25 years.

2000: The HHC finishes in the black for the fifth consecutive fiscal year.

than doubled during the decade but increased reimbursements by Medicare, Medicaid, and Blue Cross allowed the city to reduce the share of the corporation's expenses that it subsidized. However, the fiscal situation worsened in the late 1980s as the system faced increased costs from the AIDS epidemic while city and state spending on healthcare stagnated. In fiscal 1993 (the year ended June 30, 1993), the HHC recorded a net loss of $289 million on revenues of $1.47 billion. To try and make ends meet, the corporation cut 300 beds and 3,500 of its almost 50,000 employees in 1994 and created a health-maintenance organization, MetroPlus Health Plan, offering members a network of hospitals, the ability to choose a family doctor, and a 24-hour emergency number. It also suspended its largest capital project, a reconstruction of Kings County.

Bellevue, always the focus of media attention, had its own problems as the hospital of last resort in the southern half of Manhattan. In 1990, Bellevue doctors estimated that as many as 80 percent of the patients operated on there had AIDS. Homeless patients were estimated to fill at least half of the beds in Bellevue's adult psychiatric wards. Of the 2,100 patients admitted to Bellevue on average in 1995, nearly one-third, including homeless people and undocumented immigrants, were uninsured patients. About 80 percent of its in-patients were entering via the emergency room, which the following year became the second-largest in the nation. The bill for uncompensated care came to $43 million fiscal 1995. In the face of Bellevue's growing deficit, the hospital's executive director outlined a plan to reduce spending that called for 26 services to be restructured or eliminated and a 40 percent staff cut.

A 1995 *New York Times* article painted an ugly picture of the state of the municipal hospitals. Its authors, Dean Baquet and Jane Fritsch, wrote that the HHC had become "a permanent bureaucracy hampered by political meddling" and that its 11 acute-care hospitals barely met the minimum standards of the national agency that evaluated them. Two of the 11 had even lost their accreditations because of poor care and unsafe

conditions. Dr. Bruce Siegel, who became the HHC head in 1994, accused the "barons of American medicine" who ran the city's prestigious private hospitals of using public funds to finance arcane specialties for the teaching programs of their young doctors while ignoring the needs of the communities they were supposed to be serving. He conceded that the HHC had done little to monitor the care being provided in the hospitals. The authors noted in this regard that the HHC had had 14 presidents during its 25 years, many of whom had fallen victim to political pressures before being able to master the "byzantine" system.

One former deputy mayor called the HHC "the last great bastion of patronage in the city." This evaluation came a week after Mayor Rudolph Giuliani offered to sell three of the 11 hospitals—a proposal dismissed by the courts as illegal.

By the following year, the public hospitals were facing another problem in the form of competition from the city's private hospitals. Compensation had once seemed too low to make Medicaid patients desirable, but HMOs (managed-care companies) had reduced their own payments to the point that Medicaid fees were attractive to hospitals in some areas, notably obstetrics. The HHC began a major effort to retain these payments by remodeling its hospitals' maternity wards, even installing private showers and bathrooms. Bellevue built a natural-childbirth center.

Its plan to get the city out of the hospital business thwarted, the Giuliani administration began pressing the HHC to survive on its own, slashing its subsidy to the corporation from $329 million in fiscal 1994 to $123 million in fiscal 1997. The corporation reduced the average time of patient stay by about one third, a considerable savings because its hospitals were paid by the case, not by length of stay. It also shifted many patients from hospitals to community clinics and cut employment by at least 9,000. The HHC earned a $143-million surplus in fiscal 1996 and remained in the black for the next four years. Nevertheless, it continued to lose Medicaid patients to private hospitals and felt so strapped for cash that in 2001 it began charging a fee for prescription drugs at the pharmacies of all its public hospitals and community clinics. In 2001, public-hospital officials unsuccessfully sought the state's permission to shut 27 school and neighborhood health clinics, most of them serving uninsured people in poor immigrant neighborhoods.

The HHC ended fiscal 2001 with a $72-million deficit and was expected to end fiscal 2002 some $200 million in the red. The corporation had found that it did not pay to shift patients from hospitals to clinics, both because Medicaid payments were lower and because the clinics attracted a much higher proportion of uninsured visitors. In the wake of the 2001 twin-towers tragedy, the city was threatening to reduce its subsidy even further. Nevertheless, the corporation could point to some successes. By making a concerted effort to enroll more eligible patients into Medicaid, the number of uninsured patients served by the system fell from 560,000 to 490,000 in fiscal 2000. A new program, Family Health Plus, was intended to insure many families earning too much to qualify for Medicaid. Based on the HHC's favorable financial record in recent years, the corporation's bond ratings were raised in 2001. Dr. Benjamin Chu succeeded Siegel as president of the corporation in that year.

The HHC's facilities remained essential for public health in New York City. The emergency rooms of its hospitals handled nearly a million health emergencies in fiscal 2002. Patients made about five million walk-in visits to the corporation's outpatient and community-based clinics, including nearly two million primary-care visits. The hospitals provided inpatient care for about 200,000 people during the year. The HHC was the single largest provider of psychiatric services in New York City. It provided health services to more than 120,000 prisoners. Mothers gave birth to nearly 23,000 babies in its hospitals. Besides the 11 acute-care hospitals (and their outpatient services), six diagnostic and treatment centers, four long-term-care facilities, and certified home healthcare agency, there were more than 100 community health clinics. Bellevue boasted the largest array of behavioral-health programs in the United States, and its geriatric ambulatory-care program was the largest in the nation. Latinos accounted for about 45 percent of the people served, African-Americans for about 40 percent, and Asians for some 10 percent.

Principal Divisions

Community Health and Intergovernmental Relations; Corporate Planning; Finance and Capital; Medical and Professional Affairs.

Principal Competitors

North Shore-Long Island Jewish Health System; Catholic Healthcare System.

Further Reading

Baquet, Dean, and Jane Fritsch, "In Chaotic City Hospital, a Bureaucracy to Match," *New York Times*, March 7, 1995, pp. A1, B2–B3.

Benson, Barbara, "Bellevue Seeks Independence from the City," *Crain's New York Business*, September 24, 1995, pp. 1, 35.

Brecher, Charles, and Sheila Spiezio, *Privatization and Public Hospitals: Evolution of the Health and Hospitals Corporation*, New York: Twentieth Century Fund, 1995.

Carmody, Deirdre, "Ancient Bellevue Is About to Open New Building," *New York Times*, October 3, 1973, p. 47.

Cooper, Page, *The Bellevue Story*, New York: Crowell, 1948.

Fein, Esther B., "At Bellevue, Luring Back New Mothers with Luxury," *New York Times*, February 8, 1998, pp. 33, 36.

Finkelstein, Katherine Eban, "Bellevue's Emergency," *New York Times Magazine*, February 11, 1996, pp. 45–49, 50, 52, 60, 65.

Flynn, Don, "Ben Chu Molds New public Hospital Image," *Medical Herald*, October 1, 2003.

Gelb, Arthur, and Barbara Gelb, "Plus Side of the Bellevue Story," *New York Times Magazine*, June 2, 1957, pp. 12, 56, 58, 60.

Opdycke, Sandra, and David Rosner, "Hospitals," In Kenneth T. Jackson, ed., *The Encyclopedia of New York City*, New Haven: Yale University Press, 1995.

Rosenthal, Elisabeth, "Hospital Agency Is Striving to Adapt in Competitive Era," *New York Times*, February 27, 1995, pp. A1, B2.

Schwartz, Harry, "A Focus for Urban Pressures," *New York Times*, April 29, 1973, Sec. 4, p. 7.

Shipp, E.R., "For the Sickest Patients, an Ailing Hospital," *New York Times*, April 7, 1991, pp. 1, 29.

Steinhauer, Jennifer, "After 5 Years of Fiscal Success, City Public Hospitals Face Deficit," *New York Times*, May 23, 2001, pp. A1, B2.

——, "Hospitals Agency Girds Itself for Challenges of Medicare," *New York Times*, December 8, 1998, pp. B1, B6.

——, "Putting City Hospitals on Firmer Footing," *New York Times*, March 11, 2002, p. B3.

Sullivan, Ronald, "Hospitals New Regimen," *New York Times*, April 30, 1977, p. 35.

—Robert Halasz

Nippon Life Insurance Company

3-5-12, Imabashi, Chuo-ku
Osaka 541-8501
Japan
Telephone: (06) 6209-5525
Fax: (03) 5510-7340
Web site: http://www.nissay.co.jp

Mutual Company
Incorporated: 1889
Employees: 72,784
Total Assets: ¥43.9 trillion ($365.3 billion, 2003)
NAIC: 524113 Direct Life Insurance Carriers

Nippon Life Insurance Company operates as the largest life insurance provider in Japan and one of the world's largest companies based on total assets and policies in force. The firm offers individual and group life and annuity products, medical care and long-term insurance products, other non-life products, and asset management services. Nippon Life is also involved in reinsurance through alliances with Swiss Reinsurance Company and Munich Reinsurance Company. Nippon Life has a strong network of overseas subsidiaries and stands as the only Japanese insurer to underwrite group insurance products in the United States. The company and its domestic counterparts have struggled since the mid-1990s due to competition brought on by deregulation, low interest rates, a faltering stock market, and a sluggish domestic economy.

As Japan's largest insurer, Nippon Life has a remarkable number of firsts to its credit, beginning in 1889, when the company originated the policies that helped make it the first major life insurance company in Japan. In 1947, Nippon Life also became the first of Japan's life insurance companies to reorganize itself as a mutual life insurance company. In 1959, the company originated made-to-order insurance, combining payment on maturity and payment on the death of the policyholder—a product innovation that dominated the market for more than a decade. The 1970s saw a flurry of Nippon Life product innovations. The company had pursued a vigorous program of overseas investment since about 1915, and in 1981

it achieved another first when it established the industry's first overseas real estate subsidiary. That same year, Nippon Life became the first Japanese life insurance company to acquire real estate in the United States—a 50 percent interest in a New York City office building.

Long since an industry front-runner, Nippon Life has traditionally placed a high priority on its close relationships with other companies, both in Japan and overseas. As an underwriter and purveyor of financial services as well as an investor, Nippon Life is committed to globalization. Despite some necessary retrenchment of foreign investment to cope with market conditions, Chairman Josei Itoh continues to emphasize globalization in the 21st century.

Origins in the Late 1800s

Close relationships among influential financial institutions in the busy mercantile center of Osaka in the late 1880s created the opportunity for Sukesaburo Hirose to found Nippon Life. In the three decades that had passed since Japan's dramatic opening to Western commerce and culture, the centers of trade had begun to reflect a new receptivity on the part of consumers to concepts that were well established overseas. The idea of providing personal financial protection for future exigencies was not entirely foreign, but for centuries it had taken the form of mutual-aid societies centered within religious communities.

Hirose, a banker from Shiga Prefecture, sensed that a secular form of financial protection would be readily accepted in a busy urban center such as the Kansai region. He consulted bank executives in Osaka about starting a company. The ten biggest banks there had formed a powerful bankers' association, which, with the new Meiji government's help and encouragement, eventually controlled the supply of money in Osaka. These bankers helped Hirose cope with such problems as opposition from rival business factions, and on July 4, 1889, Nippon Life began operations in Osaka as a limited company.

Public acceptance came quickly. As residents of an island nation with limited resources, the Japanese felt personally vulnerable, and opportunities to gain protection from future adversities have generally been welcomed. For example, Japan has

Postwar Growth

<table>
<tr><td>

Company Perspectives:

We aim to be the company that customers trust the most in any operating environment, no matter how challenging. To this end, we are working to build an even stronger management foundation for our operations. All of us, the management and staff of Nippon Life, will continue to exert our utmost efforts to fulfill our responsibility as an insurance underwriter and will strive to offer the best, most comprehensive insurance services in both life and non-life insurance sectors.

</td></tr>
</table>

traditionally had one of the highest ratios of savings to income. This factor—along with a need to trust one another as members of close-knit, interdependent communities—has conditioned Japanese consumers to buy a large amount of insurance.

By April 1890, Hirose opened Nippon Life's first branch office—a storefront in Tokyo. Three years later, visitors to the World Columbian Exposition in Chicago could witness Hirose's rapid outreach to the overseas market: Nippon Life's collection of annual reports and bilingual versions of its prospectus. The company was neither tapping overseas markets nor investing in them yet, but it did gain visibility as a basis for future outreach to foreign markets.

The next branch office to be opened—in Kyushu in 1895— reflected the company's growing prosperity. It was a spacious, free-standing building. Before the turn of the century, Nippon Life was Japan's top purveyor of life insurance based on insurance-in-force figures. The company became an important lender to local merchants. Rapid growth continued through the first decade of the 20th century and accelerated as Japan entered the world political arena as a World War I Allied power. By 1916, Nippon Life was investing in British, French, and Russian bond issues.

In the early 1920s, growth slowed with the pace of the post-World War I economy and as a result of the widespread destruction of the Great Kanto Earthquake in 1923. The following year, the company established the Nippon Life Lifesaving Society, described in the company's literature as "a major step forward" because it directly supported healthcare services.

Intensive direct marketing helped turn Nippon Life's growth curve upward by the end of the decade, and the company regained its leadership position in contracts issued. Team spirit among personnel was cultivated formally through sales training and informally through company-sponsored athletics. At one such session in 1933, management made the prophetic announcement: "Nippon Life aims to be number one in the world."

As preparations for war went forward in the 1930s, Nippon Life developed one of its innovations—a new type of insurance based on the contribution method (an allocation of profits that has since become the basis of most Japanese-issued insurance). The new insurance went on the market in 1940, and Nippon Life insurance-in-force contract values soared to approximately 20 percent of the nation's total.

Postwar Growth

Destruction and defeat in World War II brought Nippon Life's progress to a standstill. In 1947, under General Douglas MacArthur's forces, Nippon Life took its first steps toward recovery when the company reorganized itself as a mutual life insurance company. Again under strict control by a government encouraging its growth, the company began to cope with problems such as forfeiture of overseas holdings and inflation that not only devalued insurance contracts but also slowed development of new business. By 1949, however, Nippon Life had recovered sufficiently to start a new community service: a "mobile angels clinic" in the form of a van carrying medical services to underserved areas. By 1950, some businesses were already beginning to prosper and income was on the rise.

The company introduced another product in the 1950s that immediately became popular: monthly-installment-based insurance. At the same time, women began to figure prominently among the company's representatives, who fanned out on door-to-door sales sweeps each morning after a brief pep rally. In 1953, female sales representatives numbered 2,000. By 1990, there were more than 80,000, constituting some 95 percent of Nippon Life's workforce.

Nippon Life introduced the first made-to-order insurance with a term rider, combining payment on maturity and payment on the policyholder's death, in 1959. It became a leading product throughout the following decade and well into the 1970s. The company introduced a large-scale IBM computer system in 1962 to automate its burgeoning sales and investment records.

The 1960s were marked by further expansion into many areas of business and community service—corporate welfare and pension plans, for example. With the increased variety of company activity came increased emphasis on training, and in 1961 the company built a special training facility at Nakanoshima. In 1963, Nippon Life opened its Nissay Musical Theatre in Tokyo. As the nation's economy boomed, raising profits and personal incomes, the traditions of saving and investing in insurance and other financial products remained strong, supporting further company growth.

In the 1970s, some government restrictions were lifted, which made it possible for Nippon Life to develop and introduce a new range of insurance-related products. Individual term insurance and annuity plans and life insurance related to asset formation were products that continued to be popular. The company also diversified its investment portfolio, adding consumer loans, real estate, bonds, and other equities. As deregulation spread from the Western economies, Nippon Life had new opportunities for risk-taking.

With the first purchase of real estate interests in the United States in 1981, Nippon Life acquired more of the type of investment the company has traditionally favored: long-term income properties. Not all these investments have been successful from the start, however. For example, among the large office towers the company purchased in major U.S. cities was a $200 million building in Dallas, Texas, that was slow to lease.

The stock market crash in the late 1980s provided some sobering experiences. Nippon Life's strong asset base, how-

Key Dates:

1889: Sukesaburo Hirose establishes Nippon Life in Osaka.
1947: The company reorganizes itself as a mutual life insurance company.
1959: Nippon Life originates made-to-order insurance, an industry first.
1981: The company establishes the industry's first overseas real estate subsidiary.
1990: By now, women constitute nearly 95 percent of Nippon Life's workforce.
1996: Deregulation in Japan's insurance industry begins.
2001: Subsidiary Nissay General Insurance Company and Dowa Fire and Marine Insurance Company merge to form Nissay Dowa General Insurance Company.

ever, made such events affordable as learning experiences. For example, seven months after paying $508 million for a 13 percent share in Shearson Lehman Brothers in 1987, the value of Nippon Life's stake in the company had dwindled to about $225 million. Shearson's majority owner, American Express, began to offer American Express cards through Nippon Life's salespeople. Knowing how to benefit from close ties with other businesses continued to be a key factor in Nippon Life's success throughout history.

Despite some liberalization, the life insurance business in Japan was still under strict, but favorable, government control in the late 1980s. Nippon Life dwarfed its competitors in sheer asset size at this time, as well as in the number and value of contracts. Among the company's greatest assets was its good sense of timing and the patience to get to know a market thoroughly before entering it. Because Nippon Life did not rush into a market without thorough research, the company did not plan to compete for life insurance sales in the United States. Although the company's investment capital overflowed domestic opportunities as the 1990s began, market reverses triggered a quick hold on investment in the United States, Europe, and Southeast Asia during the late 1980s, a policy that stayed in effect until signals of a stable recovery were detected. Nippon Life's management made it clear that prompt expansion—notably into the European Economic Community and Southeast Asia—would come when the conditions were right.

Overcoming Obstacles in the 1990s and Beyond

By the early 1990s, Japan's banking sector, along with the insurance industry, was experiencing difficulties brought on by a plethora of bad or non-performing loans and a faltering stock market. During the prosperous years of the 1980s, many banks and insurance companies, including Nippon Life, invested significantly in both real estate and stocks. This investment strategy, however, came back to haunt many companies when the Japanese property market collapsed in the early 1990s. In fact, a 1992 *Wall Street Journal* article reported that Nippon Life had invested approximately one trillion yen during the bubble years of the 1980s. By 1992, those investments had dwindled in value and were worth just 600 billion yen. According to *Barron's,* Nippon

Life and its domestic counterparts lost 11 trillion yen—$82.1 billion—in unrealized profits from their stock portfolios in 1992.

While better off than many of its domestic peers in the mid-1990s, Nippon Life was not isolated from industry problems. Japan's economy continued to weaken, its banks were in financial disarray, interest rates were reaching record lows, and, for the first time since World War II, individual life insurance and pension policies were on the decline. In order to revitalize its financial markets, Japan began to lay the groundwork for deregulation in its finance and insurance sectors, believing that looser regulations and new competition would remedy the problems facing these industries. In 1996, life insurance companies were given the nod to enter competitor's markets.

In order to succeed in a liberalized environment, Nippon Life continued to make key investments and forge partnerships. In 1996, the company formed Nissay General Insurance Company, which signaled its commitment to securing a stronger foothold in the non-life insurance sectors. This subsidiary merged with Dowa Fire and Marine Insurance Company in 2001 to form Nissay Dowa General Insurance Company. In 1997, Nippon Life teamed up with U.S.-based Putnam Investments in order to gain experience in asset management. The company also looked to develop new products to shore up its bottom line. In 2001, Nippon Life began offering a cancer insurance line and Ikiru Chikara, a medical whole life insurance product.

During the early years of the new century, Japan's insurance industry continued to be plagued with problems and deregulation had yet to prove that it would bring about positive change. In 2000, four life insurance companies in Japan were declared insolvent, which cast doubt on the overall health of Japan's life insurance companies. By now, policy cancellations, low interest rates, and Japan's faltering stock market had forced many insurance providers to report dwindling profits. As such, Nippon Life set forth a new strategy designed to build consumer confidence. The firm pledged to strengthen its management platform, to continue to develop new products and services, and to expand its service network. Nippon Life also eyed deliberate diversification and expansion as crucial for future success. While an immediate turnaround in Japan's insurance industry was unexpected, Nippon Life stood well positioned to overcome the obstacles it would no doubt face in the years to come.

Principal Subsidiaries

Nissay Dowa General Insurance Company Ltd.; Nissay Asset Management Corporation; Nissay Information Technology Company Ltd.; Nippon Life Insurance Company of America; NLI Insurance Agency Inc. (United States); Nippon Life Insurance Company of the Philippines Inc.; NLI International Inc.; NLI International PLC (United Kingdom); NLI Properties East Inc. (United States); NLI Properties Central Inc. (United States); NLI Properties West Inc. (United States); NLI Properties UK Ltd.; PanAgora Asset Management Inc. (United States); DG PanAgora Asset Management GmbH (Germany).

Principal Competitors

Asahi Mutual Life Insurance Company; The Dia-Ichi Mutual Life Insurance Company; Sumitomo Life Insurance Company.

Further Reading

Du Bois, Peter C., "Stock Woes Hobble Japanese Insurers," *Barron's*, April 20, 1992, p. 56.

Dvorak, Phred, "Results at Japanese Life Insurers Fuel Worries about the Industry," *Wall Street Journal*, November 28, 2000, p. A23.

Inoue, Hiroshi, "Japanese Insurers See Profits Fall Amid Weak Stocks, Low Rates," *Wall Street Journal*, June 2, 2003, p. C15.

"Insurance Sectors Crossing Barriers," *Nikkei Weekly*, September 3, 2001.

"Japanese Life Insurers Are Still Feeling Pain," *National Underwriter Property & Casualty-Risk and Benefits Management*, December 18, 2000, p. 38.

"A Losing Roll," *Economist*, May 26, 2001.

Prindl, Andreas R., *Japanese Finance: A Guide to Banking in Japan*, New York: John Wiley & Sons, 1981.

Reischauer, Edwin O., *Japan: the Story of a Nation*, Tokyo: Charles E. Tuttle Co., Inc., 1971.

Quentin, Hardy, "Japan Insurers Face Problems on Holdings," *Wall Street Journal*, September 28, 1992, p. C1.

Yamamoto, Yuri, "Insurer Performance Mixed in Deregulation," *Nikkei Weekly*, June 16, 1997, p. 13.

——, "Top Life Insurer Seeks Alliances, but No Mergers," Nikkei Weekly, August 10, 1998, p. 12.

—Betty T. Moore
—update: Christina M. Stansell

Norcal Waste Systems, Inc.

160 Pacific Avenue, Suite 200
San Francisco, California 94111
U.S.A.
Telephone: (415) 875-1000
Fax: (415) 875-1124
Web site: http://www.norcalwaste.com

Private Company
Incorporated: 1983 as Norcal Solid Waste System
Employees: 2,100
Sales: $351 million (2002)
NAIC: 562111 Solid Waste Collection

Norcal Waste Systems, Inc. is an employee-owned company based in San Francisco that through some two dozen subsidiaries provides garbage collection to both residential and commercial customers, runs various recycling programs (including material recovery, composting of food and organic wastes, and construction and demolition debris recycling), and owns or manages numerous landfills. In addition to a monopoly on garbage collection in San Francisco, Norcal operates in more than 50 California communities, serving over 570,000 residential and 55,000 commercial accounts.

Company Origins Trace back to 1906 San Francisco Earthquake

Before the concept of waste management came into being, and even before the advent of organized municipal trash collection, the practice of scavenging provided a livelihood for many immigrants in America. According to a 1985 *Forbe's* article, "The Garbage Game," "As the various waves of immigration broke over the U.S., the newcomers invariably moved into the least desirable jobs, and garbage pickup was a natural point of entry. In the New York area, garbage collection came to be dominated by people of Italian descent—Calabrians and Sicilians in New York and Long Island, immigrants from a town near Naples in much of New Jersey. But the business is by no means an Italian specialty. Elsewhere other ethnic groups have predominated—Armenians in Southern California, Dutch in Chicago,

Scandinavians in Minnesota." In many cases immigrants did not provide trash pickup but simply resorted to scavenging, looking for anything of value in the garbage of the well-off—in essence, an early form of recycling. In San Francisco, it was Italians from Genoa that dominated the scavenging trade. Many of them arrived shortly before the devastating 1906 earthquake that leveled the city. The damage caused by the quake and resulting fires provided a great deal of opportunity for scavengers. However, an endeavor that was disorganized to start with became even more so following the earthquake. After the cleanup was complete, many scavengers remained in the business, but there was much less need for their services. Ten years after the earthquake, there were more than 150 trash collectors in the city. According to Stewart Perry in his book *San Francisco Scavengers*, competition was fierce: "Several wagons and their owners might be picking up refuse from the same city block, each coveting the other's customers on that block—or any other block."

To get a grip on the scavenging business, which was threatening to spiral out of control, San Francisco City officials in 1921 set rates for garbage collection, established collection districts, and ultimately required permits. Because of these new regulations, individual collectors began to merge their efforts and eventually formed two cooperative companies: Scavenger's Protective Association and Sunset Scavenger Company. Every employee of these companies was a shareholder, with retired members selling their shares to newcomers. The price of shares rose steadily over the years. The two groups, both of which were comprised of Italians from Genoa, divided up the city's business. Scavenger's Protective Association took care of the city's financial district and surrounding neighborhoods, and Sunset Scavenger Company handled the outlying residential areas. Because of this division, Scavenger's Protective Association came to concentrate on commercial trash pickup as well as servicing densely populated neighborhoods. Sunset Scavenger Company, on the other hand, became more of a residential trash collector. Despite their delineated roles, however, the two companies often worked in concert. In 1935, for instance, they established Sanitary Fill Company, a landfill venture and the first of a number of subsidiaries the two companies would create together.

Both San Francisco collection companies were early recyclers, or, more accurately, modern day scavengers. Until the introduction of today's back-loading, compacting garbage trucks in the 1960s, one person was delegated to ride in the back of the open truck to set aside valuable refuse. Among their recycling efforts, the companies washed bottles to sell back to area wineries, bailed paper to be made into pulp, and repacked rags and sold them to Standard Oil.

Golden Gate Disposal Company Formed in 1965

Both of San Francisco's waste companies expanded over the years in keeping with the city's own growth. In 1965, Scavenger's Protective Association changed its name to Golden Gate Disposal Company. Sunset Scavenger Company changed its name in 1973 to Envirocal Inc., reflecting the company's diversification into a number of waste management areas and the growing importance of caring for the environment. Furthermore, the population of San Francisco was declining, leading to a reduced need for collection services. Over the next decade, both Golden Gate Disposal Company and Envirocal borrowed money and bought up garbage companies throughout northern California. Envirocal moved into such communities as Cupertino, Los Altos, Los Altos Hills, Morgan Hill, Mountain View, Portola, and Woodside. For its part, Golden Gate acquired collection companies serving Auburn, Eureka, Garberville, Oroville, Vacaville, and Vallejo. In 1983, Golden Gate was reorganized to accommodate its slate of subsidiaries, becoming Norcal Solid Waste Systems.

As had been the case for more than 50 years, both companies continued to be governed by a board of directors, comprised of 11 members, who met each week. All officers and directors owned a share of stock in their respective companies, but by the mid-1980s the price of each share had ballooned to the point that younger workers simply could not afford to buy into the business. As a result, the requirement that all employees be shareholders was dropped. In the 1940s, these shares could be bought for about $8,500, but now Envirocal's 281 shares were worth $103,000 each and Golden Gate's 156 shares were worth $100,000. What made the situation even more untenable was that because there was a lack of buyers, retirees were unable to sell their stock and had to make do with the modest dividend the companies paid. One option, of course, was to simply sell the companies as a way to allow shareholders to cash in. There were even press reports that an unnamed Los Angeles investor offered $75 million for the companies. Industry consolidators Browning-Ferris Industries and Waste Management Inc. were also suitors, but the companies wanted to stay independent and retain something of their heritage. (The employees were still predominantly Italian, although they became more inclusive following litigation in 1975 charging discriminatory hiring practices against Blacks and Hispanics. The litigants were vic-

torious and were awarded cash and shares in the companies. Moreover, Envirocal and Golden Gate were forced to change the way in which they hired and promoted minorities.) The ability of both companies to support growth was also hampered. San Francisco law allowed them a 5 percent profit margin and forbade their revenues to be used for operations outside of the city. Finding sufficient funds for necessary capital expenditures was also a difficulty. A new garbage truck, for instance, cost as much as $120,000.

In 1986, Norcal's president, Leo Conte, read about the employee stock ownership plan (ESOP) concept, presented the idea to the board, and with its approval hired lawyers and retained investment bankers to convert Norcal to an ESOP. The ownership arrangement was advantageous on a number of levels: shareholders gained liquidity, the company's 570 employees gained a stake in the business without having to raise $100,000 each, and that year Norcal saved more than $2 million on corporate taxes, gaining funds that could be used to pay the fees of lawyers and bankers to complete the transaction.

Norcal Becomes Employee Owned in 1987

Norcal became employee owned officially on January 1, 1987. Envirocal now began to look into creating an ESOP itself, but late in 1987 elected to accomplish this goal by combining with Norcal, which bought the company for $83.6 million, or $305,000 a share. Norcal subsequently changed its name to Norcal Waste Systems, Inc. To help pay off some of the debt incurred in establishing the ESOP, Norcal sold approximately $30 million in developed property the company owned in northern California, including apartments, shopping malls, grocery stores, and warehouses. It also took on a considerable amount of debt: $48.8 million to finance the ESOP from a consortium of banks led by Chase Manhattan Bank and Bank of America, plus another $25 million for working capital and real estate financing. All told, the cost of converting both Norcal and Envirocal to ESOP status burdened the combined entity with over $138 million in debt.

Now America's fourth-largest garbage company, Norcal looked to aggressively pursue greater growth in the years following the merger of San Francisco's long-time trash collectors. Many expected the 1990s to be the decade of the environment and a boon time for garbage handlers and specialized cleanup companies. Over the course of 1989 and 1990, the company spent over $40 million on acquisitions, becoming involved in such areas as asbestos abatement. Revenues for this period increased from $187 million in fiscal 1989 to more than $250 million in fiscal 1990. During this time, the company also became embroiled in controversy. To help pay off the debt incurred in establishing an ESOP, Norcal petitioned San Francisco's Public Utilities Commission in the spring of 1990 for a 15 percent rate increase, a request that was not well received in all quarters and was ultimately denied. The company also came under fire when the news media reported that Norcal had come under investigation by the FBI, which was looking into charges that the company tried to use campaign contributions to influence legislation before the California State Assembly. In particular, the probe focused on Norcal's relationship with Assembly Speaker Willie Brown, who was a lawyer for Norcal even as the assembly debated bills that impacted the company. In the end,

---

Key Dates:

1906: San Francisco earthquake leads to large number of scavenging operations.
1921: San Francisco begins to regulate trash collecting, resulting in the formation of Scavenger's Protective Association and Sunset Scavenger Company.
1965: Scavenger's Protective Association becomes Golden Gate Disposal Company.
1973: Sunset Scavenger Company becomes Envirocal Inc.
1983: Golden Gate changes its name to Norcal Solid Waste Systems.
1986: Norcal becomes employee owned.
1987: Norcal acquires Envirocal, becoming Norcal Waste Systems, Inc.

---

no charges were filed. Norcal also faced opposition from groups in Kansas City, where it was attempting to receive permission to operate a landfill. In another effort to raise the money to pay off its heavy debt, Norcal attempted to make a public offering of stock in 1990, but a week after word leaked about the FBI investigation, the IPO was shelved. Management insisted, however, that the decision to forego the offering was made earlier and was based on difficult economic conditions and the resulting poor climate for IPOs.

Economic conditions were so poor, in fact, that by the spring of 1991 Norcal found it difficult to meet its financial obligations. Payments amounting to $1.7 million to 430 former shareholders were delayed, and the company was also unable to meet certain financial tests required by lenders of its approximate $150 million debt burden. Norcal was forced to lay off personnel and unload some of its niche operations, such as Excel Environmental, a Bay Area asbestos abatement company that experienced a dramatic drop off in business with the advent of the recession. Again, Norcal appealed to the Public Utilities Commission for an increase on the basic rates for trash pickups. Although opponents sought to actually cut rates by 15 percent, arguing that San Francisco residents should not have to foot the bill for Norcal's merger and acquisition costs, the company in the end received a 9.8 percent increase.

Norcal was able to successfully retrench in the early 1990s and return to growth mode during the balance of the decade. In 1999, the company suffered another public relations setback, however, when one of its executives, Vice-President Kenneth James Walsh, was one of seven individuals indicted on federal bribery charges. He had already been terminated by Norcal several weeks earlier after he refused to speak with company lawyers regarding the case. The matter concerned the bribing of a San Bernardino County administrative officer named James J. Hlawek. Walsh was accused of making at least 28 payments to Hlawek in amounts ranging from $650 to $5,400. During the

time Hlawek held his post, from 1994 to 1998, Norcal received approximately $20 million in county contracts. In addition, a former county administrative officer, Harry M. Mays, was paid $4.2 million by Norcal to lobby his ex-colleagues regarding a county landfill contract. According to *Waste News,* government officials said that Hlawek received payments in two ways: "In the first, Harry M. Mays, a Norcal consultant, paid bribes to Hlawek and paid kickbacks to Walsh, who oversaw Mays' consulting work for Norcal. In the second scheme, Walsh received kickbacks from Hernandez Trucking, a dirt-hauling company that did business with Norcal; then Walsh split the money with Hlawek and Harry M. Mays." Both Mays and Walsh pleaded guilt to conspiracy to make and accept bribes. Walsh was sentenced in October 2000 to 18 months in federal prison and ordered to pay $277,000 in restitution to San Bernardino County. In the meantime, Norcal faced a civil suit initiated by the county and ultimately agreed to pay $6.6 million to settle the matter. Furthermore, it agreed to pay half of any money it recovered from Walsh or Mays as a result of the civil lawsuits the company filed against the two men. The terms of the settlement also prevented Norcal from seeking business with the county for five years.

In the midst of this untoward publicity, Norcal was about to launch an ambitious recycling effort. In 2003, the company opened a new state-of-the art recycling center capable of sorting and baling single-stream and co-mingled materials. Although a high-tech operation, the center was very much in keeping with the company's scavenger roots.

Principal Subsidiaries

SF Recycling & Disposal, Inc.; Golden Gates Disposal & Recycling Co.; Norcal Waste Services, Inc.

Principal Competitors

Kaiser Ventures LLC; Waste Connections, Inc.; Waste Management, Inc.

Further Reading

Calbreath, Dean, "Faced with Debt, Norcal Digging in During the '90s," *San Francisco Business Times*, October 25, 1991, p. S1.
Cook, James, "The Garbage Game," *Forbes*, October 21, 1985, p. 120.
Pelline, Jeff, "Immigrants Started Trash Industry," *San Francisco Chronicle*, February 18, 1986, p. 31.
——, "Trash Firm Returns to Roots," *San Francisco Chronicle,* December 24, 1986, p. 41.
Perry, Stewart E., *San Francisco Scavengers*, Berkeley: University of California Press, 1978, 236 p.
Rauber, Chris, "Norcal Waste Hits Garbage Big-Time," *San Francisco Business Times*, September 17, 1990, p. 1.
Wiley, Walt, "Former Norcal Exec to Land in Prison," *Waste News*, October 2, 2000, p. 5.

—Ed Dinger

DAIRY
The natural goodness of Maine®

Oakhurst Dairy

364 Forest Avenue
Portland, Maine 04101
U.S.A.
Telephone: (207) 772-7468
Fax: (207) 874-0714
Web site: http://www.oakhurstdairy.com

Private Company
Incorporated: 1921
Employees: 240
Sales: $85 million (2003 est.)
NAIC: 311511 Fluid Milk Manufacturing; 311513 Cheese
    Manufacturing

Oakhurst Dairy, the largest dairy in Maine and the largest independent dairy in northern New England, was founded in 1921 and has been managed by the same family for three generations. Oakhurst sells branded and private label milk, cottage cheese, dairy creams, buttermilk, juices, and flavored specialty milks to retail and food service customers in Maine, New Hampshire, Vermont, Massachusetts, and upstate New York. Between 2000 and 2001 Oakhurst grew between 20 percent and 30 percent, helping the family-run business remain competitive with larger operations. In July 2003, Monsanto Corporation, the manufacturer of the only bovine artificial growth hormone available in the United States, sued Oakhurst for deceptive business practices for the dairy's labeling, which states on their milk products: "Our Farmers' Pledge: No Artificial Growth Hormones." The lawsuit became a touchstone of debate on both the use of artificial growth hormones and the right of commercial free speech.

Origins as a Family Business

Oakhurst Dairy traces its roots to a dairy business begun by Arthur Leadbetter in Portland, Maine, in 1902. By 1918 Leadbetter had changed the name of his dairy to Oakhurst, and two years later, Oakhurst employed Stanley T. Bennett to manage the dairy. Bennett had started his career in 1913 as a driver and salesman for the Portland business Cushman Bakery. Bennett's success in sales helped him gain the attention of Cushman

Bakery president, Nathan Cushman. In 1921, Cushman financed the purchase of Oakhurst for Bennett; Oakhurst Dairy was incorporated under the Cushman family and Bennett was named manager of the business. A year later, Bennett moved the dairy, which had been located near a grove of oak trees on Woodford Street, to a new location on Forest Avenue. At that time, there were 80 dairies in Portland licensed to sell milk.

When Stan Bennett began shaping the direction of Oakhurst, milk was transported by two horse-drawn milk wagons along two delivery routes, and sales were centralized. At that time, during the early 1920s, dairy products had a short shelf life, so milk had to be delivered to the customer the same day that it was bottled. Oakhurst carved its niche in the Portland area by producing high-quality milk. Oakhurst maintained its standards of quality through frequent farm inspections and hygienic plant conditions. Two years after Bennett took over operation of Oakhurst, the company had increased its number of routes to 12.

By 1929 Oakhurst had expanded its operations by adding a branch plant in Bath, Maine, and the company maintained 26 retail routes as well as two wholesale routes. Oakhurst invested in machinery to maintain a high-level of efficiency and sanitation in its plants. In 1933 the company employed 14 people in its plants and had 33 deliverymen who, through Bennett's initiation, drove trucks with their own names painted on the sides. Beginning in 1933, Oakhurst was the first dairy in the United States to require that all milk they purchased be tested for tuberculin.

During the 1940s Oakhurst grew its wholesale business, selling to such grocers as IGA and A&P, as well as to Maine General Hospital and the area's public schools. At this point, Oakhurst was the largest dairy in Portland and its environs. Since 1921, Stan Bennett had been buying control of Oakhurst from the Cushman family, which still maintained an ownership interest in the company. By 1941 the Bennett family had bought all stock interest in Oakhurst.

Stanley Bennett's son, Donald Bennett, graduated from the Rensselaer Polytechnic Institute with an architectural engineering degree in 1935. Don entered the family business in 1940, working every position at the dairy until he joined the Navy during World War II and served in the Pacific. Following his return after the war's end, Don once again joined his father and began assuming management responsibilities. After his father died in 1953, Don Bennett was named president of Oakhurst.

1950s–60s: New Leadership in a New Era

In 1954 Oakhurst completed a major plant expansion and renovation, designed in part by Donald Bennett. At the time, the plant was recognized for its state-of-the-art facilities and was featured in national publications. Following the expansion, Oakhurst tripled the plant's original size and increased production capacity to 40,000 quarts of milk per day.

Oakhurst has been active in the Maine dairy industry for decades. Stan Bennett had been a founding member of the Maine Milk Commission. At the onset, the Maine Milk Commission proposed minimum pricing for milk as a way to protect the Maine dairy industry. In 1954, 17 states carried milk control laws as a means to help small farmers stay in business.

Donald Bennett continued his father's interest in the Maine dairy industry, serving on the Maine Milk Commission, the Maine Milk Dealers Association as president, and the Maine Milk Dairy Council as a founding director. Additionally, Don Bennett was a founding member of the National Dairy Council, and he also served as director of the Milk Industry Foundation from 1961–67.

The make-up of Maine's dairy industry changed in the 1970s, and, as with other dairy processors, Oakhurst was forced to make changes to remain competitive. One major change was eliminating home delivery of milk to small customers in January 1976. The company maintained they could no longer make a profit delivering to residential customers with the increased price of gasoline and operating costs. Two years earlier, Oakhurst had added other products, such as bread, eggs, and cheese, to their home delivery line to increase route sales, but the profit margin remained low. By mid-1976, Oakhurst conceded it would eliminate all home delivery service after July 28. In addition to the high gasoline prices, the elimination of glass containers had also endangered home delivery.

In 1975 the Maine legislature revamped its Maine Milk Commission so that it no longer had any members who were directly involved in the dairy industry. New mandates from the Commission, which required processors to pay dairy farmers two cents more per quart yet lowered the minimum retail price two cents on the gallon, hurt dairy processors across Maine and

caused many dairies to close. Through the direction of Don Bennett, Oakhurst continued to grow and emerged as the leading dairy processor in Maine by the late 1970s.

1970s–90s: Acquisitions, Quality Standards, and Marketing

Donald Bennett's sons, Stanley T. Bennett II and William P. Bennett, began working at Oakhurst in 1973 and 1975, respectively. Daughter Althea Bennett Allen entered the family business in 1981. Don Bennett retired as president in 1983 but would remain chairman of the board until his death in 1999. Meanwhile, Stanley T. Bennett II became Oakhurst's president, continuing the company's focus on quality and integrity.

During the 1970s and 1980s Oakhurst increased its geographic range by acquiring many small, independent dairy processors throughout Maine, including Sanford Dairy in 1977, Smiley's Dairy in 1983, and Gifford's Dairy in 1983, among others. One independent operation, Fitzpatrick Dairy, forced Oakhurst to court in an antitrust lawsuit filed in 1988. Judging in favor of Fitzpatrick Dairy, James Fitzpatrick, the dairy's former owner, was awarded $1.9 million in 1990.

From the company's beginnings in 1921, the Bennett family members who guided the business maintained exceptional standards for quality, standards that helped distinguish Oakhurst Dairy from its competitors. The founder's grandson, Stan Bennett, explained in *Oakhurst Dairy: The Natural Goodness of Maine*, ''Our family has always been fanatical about the level of quality of our products. We buy from the highest caliber farms, and we keep our plant cooler and cleaner than others. Our standards for bacteria-counts and butterfat level, along with all other objective criteria, are always higher than government standards and higher than competitive standards.''

Oakhurst management insisted that the quality of the product was only as good as the quality of the farms from which they purchased their milk. Oakhurst carried out regular, thorough inspections of all supply farms and began giving out Oakhurst Annual Quality Awards to those dairy farmers who produced the best quality milk. Oakhurst also rewarded its farmers by paying more than the farm-to-dairy price. Dating back to 1953 Oakhurst was the first dairy in Maine to install an on-site laboratory for quality testing. Over the years Oakhurst consistently scored high marks from the U.S. Food and Drug Administration (FDA) for compliance ratings, with consecutive perfect ratings from 1995 to 2001. In 2002 Oakhurst became one of the first dairies in the United States to voluntarily use a new FDA food-safety program called Hazard Analysis of Critical Control Points (HACCP). Bennett claimed in the *Portland Press Herald,* ''HACCP provides a daily window into the food-safety process. It's just a better system for ensuring product quality and freshness.''

Oakhurst built its reputation on high-quality products and leveraged this reputation through print, radio, and television advertising, spending close to two percent of sales on advertising, public relations, and community involvement. The emphasis for its ad campaigns, which often featured members of the Bennett family, always stressed a premium image that helped Oakhurst establish control of 75 percent of branded milk sales in its core market area in 2000.

Key Dates:

1902: Arthur Leadbetter establishes a dairy business in Portland, Maine.

1918: Leadbetter's dairy name changes to Oakhurst.

1920: Stanley T. Bennett is made manager of Oakhurst.

1921: Nathan Cushman buys Oakhurst and incorporates company as Oakhurst Dairy; Bennett begins buying shares, becoming president and achieving full ownership by 1940s.

1922: Oakhurst moves plant to new building on Forest Avenue in Portland.

1929: Oakhurst opens a branch plant in Bath, Maine.

1953: Stanley's son, Donald H. Bennett, assumes role of company president.

1954: Company expands plant to more than triple the original size.

1970: Oakhurst's first television advertisements air.

1974: The Bath plant closes.

1976: Oakhurst discontinues its home delivery service.

1977: Oakhurst purchases assets of Sanford Dairy in Sanford, Maine.

1983: Stanley T. Bennett II succeeds his father as president; William P. Bennett assumes role of vice-president of operations and Althea Bennett Allen is made customer service manager.

1992: Oakhurst converts all trucks and trailers in fleet to use environmentally friendly non-CFC refrigerants.

1994: Bennett publicly states Oakhurst's opposition to the use of artificial growth hormones.

1999: Environmental Protection Agency gives Oakhurst an Environmental Merit Award.

2000: Oakhurst extends retail sales to New York state.

2001: Oakhurst celebrates its 80th year of operation.

In addition to advertising efforts, Oakhurst built its brand presence through active community involvement and contributions to non-profit organizations that benefitted child welfare, education, and the environment. Stan Bennett asserted in *Dairy Field* in 2000 that "We have tried to position ourselves as not only the quality leader in the industry, but also as the environmental leader of the dairy companies in the region with the greatest corporate conscience." In the *Casco Bay Weekly,* Bennett attributed the company's interest in the environment to good business, noting that "Improving the environment here in Maine has a direct effect on maintaining the quality of life that we all enjoy so much in this state. Anything that affects the environment affects the cows that produce our milk, so we're vitally interested in doing everything we can to keep the quality level very high." Oakhurst received numerous community and industry awards, including the Eagle Feather Award in 1998 from the Maine Businesses for Social Responsibility, the Environmental Protection Agency's Environmental Merit Award in 1999, and the Vendor of the Year in 2001 from the Maine State Grocers Association.

In March 1994 in a letter to the editor of the *Portland Press Herald,* Stan Bennett publicly announced that Oakhurst Dairy was opposed to the use of artificial growth hormones in dairy cows. Bennett asserted that the company received written agreements from all 70 of its dairy farmers that they would not use artificial growth hormones. Farmers continued to provide notarized affidavits every six months verifying they have not used growth hormones on their cows.

In 2000, in response to consumer concerns over the use of artificial growth hormones, Oakhurst began labeling its milk products with the statement: "Our Farmers' Pledge: No Artificial Growth Hormones." The label distinguished Oakhurst products from others on the market, and sales rose 10 percent each year between 2000 and 2003.

In July 2003 Monsanto Corporation, a biotechnology giant headquartered in St. Louis, Missouri, sued Oakhurst Dairy over the company's labeling. Previously, in 1994, Monsanto had settled lawsuits out of court with a Texas dairy and an Illinois dairy on similar grounds after the dairies agreed to change their labels. Monsanto, which produced Posilac, the only bovine growth hormone (BGH) in the United States, claimed that Oakhurst's label misled consumers in suggesting that Oakhurst's products are safer than products that contained Posilac. Although the FDA approved BGH use in 1993 in the United States, both Canada and the European Union banned its use. There was no scientific evidence to suggest that products with BGH were any different from those without. Still, Bennett maintained in the *New York Times* that "We don't feel we need to remove that label. We ought to have the right to let people know what is and is not in our milk." Similar claims on other hormone-free products were allowed when they also included a qualifying statement that there was no difference between milk from BGH-treated and untreated cows. Oakhurst acknowledged in a statement on the Monsanto lawsuit, "While we make no claims regarding the science of artificial growth hormones, we feel strongly that keeping our customers fully informed is the right thing to do."

The lawsuit not only raised questions over the widespread use of genetically altered food, it also elicited concerns over commercial free-speech. Ralph Nader, consumer advocate and Green Party presidential candidate in 2000, joined the debate when he announced he would provide free legal assistance through his foundation that supported freedom of speech. Oakhurst also gained strong support worldwide through e-mails, letters, and phone calls, with some people even sending checks, which Oakhurst returned, to help pay legal costs.

Many observers suggested that the lawsuit represented a David versus Goliath battle, pitting Oakhurst with $85 million in sales against Monsanto with $4.7 billion in sales. Bennett stated in the *Portland Press Herald,* "When a company [Monsanto's] size brings a lawsuit against a little company like ours, sure I'm concerned, because who knows how much it will cost to litigate. But we feel strongly that we're doing the right thing." The trial date was originally scheduled for January 2004, but the two companies entered into settlement agreements just prior, so whether David and Goliath would ever actually do battle remained to be seen.

Principal Competitors

H.P. Hood Inc.; Dean Foods Company.

Further Reading

Anderson, Alice Hellstrom, ''Oakhurst Dairy History and Local Facts,'' *Casco Bay Weekly,* August 14, 2003 pp. 16–23.

——, *Oakhurst Dairy: The Natural Goodness of Maine,* Portland: Penmor Lithographers, 2002, 77 p.

Barboza, David, ''Monsanto Sues Dairy in Maine over Label's Remarks on Hormones,'' *New York Times,* July 12, 2003, p. C1.

Bystrynski, Craig, ''Oakhurst Dairy Buys Main Division of Gifford's'' *Portland Press Herald,* December 30, 1983, p. 22.

''Close-Up: Stanley T. Bennett II,'' *Portland Press Herald,* March 15, 1988, p. 11.

''Dairy Owner Testifies in Lawsuit,'' *Portland Press Herald,* July 12, 1990, p. 35.

''Emphasis on Quality Serves Three Generations,'' *Maine Sunday Telegram,* March 3, 1985, p. 39G.

Lawrence, J.M., ''Monsanto Sour on Milk Marketers' Hormones Claim,'' *Boston Herald,* July 4, 2003, p. 10.

Livingtone, Paul, and Matt Wickenheiser, ''Nader Enters Ring in Oakhurst Corner,'' *Portland Press Herald,* August 14, 2003, p. 1A.

Mack, Sharon Kiley, ''Oakhurst, Monsanto Gird for Federal Court Battle,'' *Bangor Daily News,* October 31, 2003, p. 9.

Mohl, Bruce, ''Got Growth Hormone? Dairies Play on Fear in Marketing Milk without the Additive,'' *Boston Globe,* September 28, 2003, p. J1.

Murphy, Edward D., ''Lawsuit Reflects Fight over Altered Food,'' *Portland Press Herald,* July 9, 2003, p. 7C.

——, ''Oakhurst Adopts New FDA Program for Quality Control,'' *Portland Press Herald,* October 16, 2002, p. 7C.

——, ''Oakhurst Lawsuit: David vs. Goliath,'' *Portland Press Herald,* July 13, 2003, p. 1A.

''Oakhurst Dairy Loses Lawsuit,'' *Portland Press Herald,* July 25, 1990, p. 21.

''Oakhurst Halts Deliveries,'' *Portland Press Herald,* January 12, 1976, p. 18.

''Oakhurst Merges with Winslow Dairy,'' *Portland Evening Express,* March 22, 1983, p. 6.

''Plant Expansion Opens New Chapter in 67-Year History of Maine's Foremost Dairy,'' *Portland Press Herald,* March 21, 1989, p. 5.

Sleeper, Frank, ''Oakhurst Dairy Purchases Most Sanford Dairy Assets,'' *Portland Press Herald,* November 16, 1977, p. 28.

——, ''Oakhurst Milkmen: A Species Awaiting Extinction,'' *Portland Evening Express,* June 23, 1976, pp. 1, 8.

Talerico, Shonda, ''The Main(e) Ingredient,'' *Dairy Field,* April 2000, pp. 1–5.

——, ''Growing Pains,'' *Dairy Field,* April 2000, pp. 22–27.

Weir, George, ''Oakhurst Dairy Expanding for 'Year 2000','' *Portland Evening Express,* October 11, 1988, p. 17.

Wickenheiser, Matt, ''Oakhurst Sued by Monsanto over Milk Advertising,'' *Portland Press Herald,* July 8, 2003, p. 1A.

—Elizabeth Henry

O'Charley's Inc.

3038 Sidco Drive
Nashville, Tennessee 37204
U.S.A.
Telephone: (615) 256-8500
Fax: (615) 256-5043
Web site: http://www.ocharleys.com

Public Company
Incorporated: 1984
Employees: 15,700
Sales: $499.9 million (2002)
Stock Exchanges: NASDAQ
Ticker Symbol: CHUX
NAIC: 72211 Full-Service Restaurants

O'Charley's Inc. operates a chain of casual dining restaurants that feature aged prime rib, chicken, seafood, pasta, and home-made rolls and salad dressings. The restaurant was developed by David K. Wachtel, who purchased one existing O'Charley's unit in 1984 and quickly built it into a regional chain. During the early years of the new millennium, O'Charley's added the Ninety Nine Restaurant & Pub and Stoney River Legendary Steaks chains to its arsenal. The O'Charley's family includes more than 260 restaurants clustered in New England, the Southeast, and Midwest.

Origins

Two distinct eras described O'Charley's first three decades of existence. One was a period of little change and the other was a period of constant change and ambitious growth that transformed a solitary restaurant into a chain of restaurants generating nearly $200 million a year in sales. Not surprisingly, the two contrasting eras were led by different individuals pursuing different objectives. First came Charlie Watkins, the founder of O'Charley's, who opened the company's first restaurant in 1969. Watkins ran his lone O'Charley's for the next 15 years. Watkins sold his restaurant in 1984, marking the beginning of O'Charley's era of steady expansion and the arrival of the company's second leader.

Watkins sold his restaurant to David K. Wachtel, whose professional life had been spent in the restaurant business. For 23 years Wachtel had worked for Shoney's, a Nashville, Tennessee-based family dinner house chain. Wachtel eventually became president and chief executive officer of the restaurant company, resigning his twin posts in 1982. Two years later, he struck the deal with Watkins and gained control of the solitary O'Charley's restaurant; he had in mind, however, plans different from operating a single restaurant. Wachtel was intent on developing O'Charley's into a restaurant chain and, in less than three years, he accomplished much toward expanding the dining concept that he had acquired. In mid-1987, the 12th O'Charley's opened in Lexington, Kentucky, occupying a site formerly used by the Bennigan's chain of restaurants. While the Lexington grand opening was under way, Wachtel was working on plans to convert two more Bennigan's units into O'Charley's by the end of the year—one in Huntsville, Alabama and the other in the company's headquarters city of Nashville.

Quickly, Wachtel had developed one restaurant into a small regional chain that operated as a casual-theme dining concept featuring fresh fish, cut and aged meats, hamburgers, and fresh baked products. Although expansion had been rapid, it had not been wide-ranging. Of the 12, 180-seat O'Charley's units in operation during the summer of 1987, all were located within 200 miles of each other. It was a strategy Wachtel planned to follow in future expansion. "We'll concentrate on our current O'Charley's cities in the Southeast," he informed a reporter from *Nation's Restaurant News,* "which should keep us busy for three years but will interfere with my golf game." Wachtel's hours away from the restaurant business were a precious few, indeed, leaving little time for recreational pursuits. In addition to opening his 12th O'Charley's and planning the establishment of two others, he opened his first Trapper's restaurant in Nashville in 1987, a "red-meat-and-alcohol" concept that he planned to expand in the southeastern United States. Wachtel's involvement with business ventures aside from O'Charley's would eventually lure him away from leading the company, but during the immediate years ahead he spearheaded the expansion of his flowering O'Charley's chain.

Company Perspectives:

The commitment to quality drives everything we do at O'Charley's, Ninety Nine, and Stoney River. It is evident in the smiling faces of our servers; the fresh and specialty items for which we are famous; and the broad appeal of our appetizers, entrees, and desserts. Most of all, it is expressed by the trust our customers place in us and the satisfaction they get from high quality and attentive customer service.

1990 Public Offering

From the end of 1987 to the beginning of the 1990s, 13 new O'Charley's restaurants were opened, with expansion expected to pick up pace following the company's July 1990 initial public offering (IPO) of shares. The conversion to public ownership represented the second tool used by Wachtel to speed expansion. The first had been establishing a franchising program, which had engendered eight franchised restaurants by the time of the July public offering, but the timing of the stock sale reduced its effectiveness as a means for expansion. The timing could not have been worse. O'Charley's made its debut in the public spotlight just before tensions in the Persian Gulf flared and the United States implemented Operation Desert Storm. Many of the company's 27 restaurants at the time were situated near military bases with populations drained by the transfer of troops to the Middle East, and patronage at the company's restaurants declined as a result. Further, a national economic recession was under way, exacerbating the effects of O'Charley's ill-timed IPO.

In the wake of O'Charley's July 1990 offering, per restaurant sales and profits plunged, falling to among the lowest in the restaurant industry nationwide. At the same time, investors decided to risk their dollars elsewhere, and O'Charley's stock price fell to roughly two-thirds of its initial value. Changes were clearly needed, as the company took faltering steps under the eye of public scrutiny and into the new decade. Wachtel and other company executives assessed their position, looking at O'Charley's operations and the demands of its customers. In early 1991, management made the moves it hoped would restore vitality to the ailing chain.

What management found were problems associated with the restaurants' menus, which, as one industry observer noted, were beginning to resemble tomes the size of *War and Peace.* O'Charley's was not alone in this practice—it was an industry-wide phenomenon—but the company's commonality with its competition did not lessen the effects of its burdensome menus. As part of the effort to find a solution to O'Charley's difficulties in late 1990, Wachtel hired Charles F. McWhorter, Jr., as senior vice-president and chief operating officer to help improve service and bolster customer traffic. A longtime employee of the Ryan's and Quincy's steakhouse chains, McWhorter noted that O'Charley's lengthy menu "was hard to execute 100 percent all the time; we were trying to be all things to all people." The solution was a smaller menu, which the company began testing in February 1991 in Knoxville, Tennessee and in Biloxi, Mississippi. The scaled-down menu was then refined and tested at a restaurant in Atlanta in preparation for chainwide distribution, which occurred in mid-1991.

The smaller menus offered roughly half of the entrees listed in the larger menus. "We looked at what was selling and what wasn't," McWhorter explained, "and dropped all the marginal items." Dropped from the old menu were four appetizers, five hamburger and sandwich selections, four steak and rib entrees, and items from the soup and salad listings, leaving O'Charley's with a pared-down menu that enabled quicker service and heightened food quality because kitchen staff had fewer menu selections with which to contend. "With the smaller menu we can do more things from scratch, and it frees up more time to do different things," McWhorter explained, declaring the switch to a more concise menu a success. Further adjustments were made in 1991, including a reduction in prices for dinner entrees to lunchtime prices and the addition of an Express lunch menu featuring 13 entrees priced under $6 that were guaranteed to be on the diner's table in less than 10 minutes.

While these changes were being made and company officials waited to gauge their success in sparking customer traffic, sales, and profits, expansion of the O'Charley's concept continued. Five new restaurants were opened in 1990 and another five debuted in 1991, entrenching the company's presence in Atlanta; Jackson and Memphis, Tennessee; and Brandon, Florida. By mid-1992, O'Charley's was a 37-unit chain with restaurants clustered in eight states, having blanketed the southeastern United States in less than a decade. Three more restaurants were slated for openings by the end of 1992 and another five units were scheduled to be developed in 1993, as Wachtel steadily added more links to his fast-growing chain. Part of the renewed optimism regarding the company's expansion plans was attributable to the first financial results recorded after the menu and pricing changes were made in 1991. For the first fiscal quarter of 1992, O'Charley's reported a 30 percent jump in sales and a more encouraging 37 percent gain in profits, convincing management that the switch to a smaller menu had been the right move.

On the heels of the welcomed financial news, Wachtel led O'Charley's in a new direction that promised to strengthen the company's financial clout. In June 1992, O'Charley's signed a letter of intent to form a partnership to purchase Logan's Roadhouse restaurant, a casual steakhouse restaurant with a grill in public view, concrete floors, muraled walls, and buckets of peanuts in a "honky-tonk" atmosphere. Under the terms of the deal, the partnership called for the establishment of a minimum of five additional Logan's Roadhouse restaurants during the ensuing five years, with the second unit targeted for its grand opening in Nashville in August 1992. O'Charley's became a 20 percent owner in the partnership with the remaining 80 percent belonging to a small group of investors that included Wachtel and McWhorter.

Slightly less than a year after Wachtel signed the Logan's Roadhouse agreement, he began to fade from the foreground at O'Charley's. In May 1993, Wachtel relinquished day-to-day control as president and chief executive officer to devote more time to other business projects, but continued to serve as chairman of O'Charley's. In his place, Gregory L. Burns was named president and selected to the additional post of chief financial officer, while McWhorter climbed the corporate rungs to the chief executive position. Although the orchestrator of O'Charley's resolute expansion for the previous nine years had stepped aside, the pace of expansion did not slacken in his

Key Dates:

1969: Charlie Watkins opens the company's first restaurant.
1984: Watkins sells his restaurant to David K. Wachtel.
1990: O'Charley's goes public.
1994: Wachtel resigns; former employees file a federal lawsuit charging the restaurant chain with racial discrimination against African Americans.
1996: O'Charley's agrees to settle the racial discrimination lawsuit.
2000: The Stoney River Legendary Steaks chain is acquired.
2003: The company completes its purchase of the Ninety Nine Restaurant & Pub chain.

absence. Five new O'Charley's were opened in 1993, giving O'Charley's a total of 45 restaurants. By the end of the year, future expansion seemed destined to be brisk.

In December 1993, Burns and McWhorter announced the formulation of a growth strategy designed to carry the 45-unit chain into the ranks of the country's largest regional dinner-house chains. "Over the past two years, we strengthened many of our internal programs and execution," Burns explained before vowing, "We plan to aggressively grow this company." According to the projections of the five-year plan, the company would lift its restaurant count to 100 units by 1998, a goal that would require it to exceed the expansion rate of the previous years. The company also announced plans to open a minimum of two Logan's Roadhouse units to add to the three restaurants already in operation.

Mid-1990s Lawsuit

Heading into 1994, the company planned to open at least eight new O'Charley's restaurants, situating the new units primarily in southeastern markets such as Cookeville, Tennessee; Louisville and Paducah, Kentucky; and Palm Harbor, Florida. It was a year expected to be filled with news of new restaurant openings, but as the calendar flipped to 1994 other headlines grabbed the attention of both those inside and outside the company. In February 1994, Wachtel resigned as chairman of O'Charley's, citing his "pressing commitments" with other business interests, the most notable of which was the 300-unit Western Sizzlin' budget steakhouse chain he had acquired in 1993. Wachtel's full departure from O'Charley's made room for advancement for Burns and McWhorter. Burns was named chief executive and co-chairman and McWhorter was tapped as president and co-chairman. One month after Wachtel's resignation, the company received devastating news when it was announced that four former O'Charley's employees had filed a federal lawsuit charging the restaurant chain with racial discrimination practices against African Americans in the company's hiring, assignment, and promotion procedures. Burns flatly denied the charges, saying the lawsuit was "without merit and the company intends to defend it vigorously."

Brighter news for O'Charley's management arrived in 1995 when the company's involvement in the Logan's Roadhouse partnership turned into a source of cash to fund expansion during the year. The partnership completed an IPO in July 1995, netting O'Charley's $11 million, or more than half of the money needed to open the 11 new restaurants scheduled for grand openings in 1995. Meanwhile, to Burns's and McWhorter's consternation, the attorneys for the plaintiffs in the racial discrimination lawsuit were seeking to win class-action status, which threatened to broaden the scope and deepen the damage of the lawsuit. The attorneys were successful in winning class-action status.

With the specter of the lawsuit casting a dark cloud over corporate headquarters in Nashville, senior executives moved forward with their expansion plans, striving to open between 12 and 14 new O'Charley's restaurants in 1996. By July 1996, there were 60 O'Charley's restaurants in operation and a new concept as well. The company opened a more upscale restaurant called Rhea Station Grille in historic downtown Nashville that featured herb-encrusted salmon, lemon artichoke chicken, and pasta and fresh fish in a setting decidedly unlike O'Charley's. Inside, piano entertainment was offered, as well as a room for private parties able to accommodate as many as 100 people. The Rhea Station Grille restaurant basked in the limelight for barely more than a month, its debut occurring weeks before O'Charley's agreed to settle the racial discrimination lawsuit it had been facing since 1994. In agreeing to settle the suit, and pay what eventually would amount to $6.2 million, Burns was adamant in his denial that there was any truth supporting the charges, declaring, "We agreed to this settlement because of the significant distraction the lawsuit has had on management and the uncertainty it has caused in the marketplace." One month after the settlement was announced, another management shakeup occurred when McWhorter resigned as president after his six-year tenure at the company. His departure left Burns in full power, occupying the posts of chief executive officer, president, and chairman of the board.

The settlement of the lawsuit struck a decisive blow to O'Charley's profit total for 1996. After recording $10.6 million in profits for 1995, which had been inflated by the money gained through the sale of its stake in Logan's Roadhouse, O'Charley's registered a $1.15 million loss for 1996 on an 11 percent gain in sales to $164.5 million. The lawsuit was behind it, however, as it entered 1997, freeing the company to concentrate on expansion. A total of 12 new O'Charley's were added during the disruptive 1996 year, and in the first two months of 1997 four more restaurants were added to the chain. With 72 restaurants in operation in early 1997, Burns was anticipating adding between 12 and 14 more restaurants by the end of the year. Sales for 1997 surpassed $200 million, a sure sign that the company's efforts were paying off.

Continuing Growth: Late 1990s and Beyond

With its problems in the past, O'Charley's looked to significantly expand in the following years. By 1999 store count had surpassed 106 units. Led by Burns, the company began to entertain the idea of a growth-through-acquisition strategy. The firm made a play for the J. Alexander's chain in 1999 but its attempts were rebuffed by the J. Alexander's board of directors. At the same time, O'Charley's itself opted to turn down a buyout offer made by Wachtel, who believed the chain's shareholders would best be served by taking the chain private through a management-led leveraged buyout.

Undeterred by the failed acquisition attempt in 1999, O'Charley's forged ahead with its growth plans and made several key moves in the early years of the new millennium. The company added the upscale Georgia-based Stoney River Legendary Steaks chain to its arsenal in 2000, planning to open three new locations each year until 2005. O'Charley's then took its strategy one step further with the purchase of the casual-dining Ninety Nine Restaurant & Pub, an 80-unit chain with locations in Massachusetts, New Hampshire, Rhode Island, Maine, Vermont, and Connecticut. Announced in late 2002 and completed in early 2003, the deal bolstered the company's holdings by nearly 40 percent and gave it a solid foothold in the northeastern U.S. market. Burns commented on the deal in a January 2003 company press release stating, "The remarkably similar operating philosophies and strategies of O'Charley's and Ninety Nine as well as the wealth of new locations available in Ninety Nine's core market create a unique opportunity to sustain the historic growth of the Ninety Nine concept and diversify the growth of O'Charley's Inc."

During 2002, O'Charley's opened 24 new restaurants, bringing its total store count to more than 180 locations. The company was named to *Forbes*'s "200 Best Small Companies in America" list for the third consecutive year in 2002, a testament to its successful expansion efforts during a considerable downturn in the U.S. economy. With sales and profits climbing steadily, management remained focused on strengthening its position as a multi-concept operator. The company also was looking into franchise options as a vehicle for future growth.

Principal Operating Units

Stoney River Legendary Steaks; Ninety Nine Restaurant & Pub.

Principal Competitors

Applebee's International Inc.; Brinker International Inc.; Darden Restaurants Inc.

Further Reading

Carlino, Bill, "O'Charley's Charts Growth Plan," *Nation's Restaurant News,* December 13, 1993, p. 3.

"Former O'Charley's Employees Claim Race Discrimination," *Nation's Restaurant News,* March 7, 1994, p. 2.

Frydman, Ken, "Wachtel Rolls 12th O'Charley's," *Nation's Restaurant News,* July 13, 1987, p. 2.

Hayes, Jack, "O'Charley's Plans to Develop Stoney River Legendary Steak Concept," *Nation's Restaurant News,* June 12, 2000, p. 8.

——, "O'Charley's Rises from Rocky Past As Bigger Contender," *Nation's Restaurant News,* April 27, 1998, p. 3.

Howard, Theresa, "O'Charley's Reaps Pay-Off from Service, Value Focus," *Nation's Restaurant News,* June 8, 1992, p. 14.

Keegan, Peter O., "O'Charley's Trims Menu, Cuts Prices, Adds Express Lunch," *Nation's Restaurant News,* June 10, 1991, p. 4.

"Lawsuit, Writedowns Result in Year-End Loss at O'Charley's," *Nation's Restaurant News,* March 3, 1997, p. 12.

"O'Charley's Beats Bad Weather," *Nation's Restaurant News,* May 24, 1993, p. 27.

"O'Charley's Debuts Rhea Station Grille," *Nation's Restaurant News,* July 29, 1996, p. 66.

"O'Charley's Inc. Agrees To Settle Class-Action Suit," *Nation's Restaurant News,* August 5, 1996, p. 156.

"O'Charley's Inks Deal with Logan's," *Nation's Restaurant News,* June 15, 1992, p. 14.

"O'Charley's Names Burns Prexy, Chairman," *Nation's Restaurant News,* September 23, 1996, p. 132.

"O'Charley's Prexy McWhorter Exits After 6-Year Stint," *Nation's Restaurant News,* September 16, 1996, p. 68.

"O'Charley's To Develop Logan's Roadhouse," *Nation's Restaurant News,* July 20, 1992, p. 18.

Papiernik, Richard L., "O'Charley's to Acquire Upscale Steak Concept," *Nation's Restaurant News,* May 15, 2000, p. 12.

——, "Partnership Payout Finances O'Charley's Unit Expansion," *Nation's Restaurant News,* September 11, 1995, p. 3.

Peters, James, "Casual Shopper: O'Charley's Latest to Buy a Dinner Chain," *Nation's Restaurant News,* November 11, 2002, p. 1.

Pollack, Neal, "Chains Promote Diverse Menus and Family Dining," *Restaurants & Institutions,* July 24, 1991, p. 99.

Prewitt, Milford, "O'Charley's Regroups in Quest for J. Alexander's," *Nation's Restaurant News,* May 3, 1999, p. 1.

"Wachtel Resigns As O'Charley's Chair," *Nation's Restaurant News,* February 21, 1994, p. 2.

—Jeffrey L. Covell
—update: Christina M. Stansell

Osaka Gas Co., Ltd.

Osaka Gas Company, Ltd.

4-1-2 Hiranomachi
Chuo-ku
Osaka 541-0046
Japan
Telephone: (06) 6202-2221
Fax: (06) 6227-0745
Web site: http://www.osakagas.co.jp

Public Company
Incorporated: 1897
Employees: 15,020
Sales: ¥947.9 billion ($7.88 billion, 2003)
Stock Exchanges: Tokyo Osaka Nagoya
Ticker Symbol: 9532
NAIC: 221210 Natural Gas Distribution; 486210 Pipeline
    Transportation of Natural Gas

Osaka Gas Company, Ltd. (Osaka Gas) is Japan's second largest supplier of gas, after Tokyo Gas. The company supplies over 6.56 million customers in the Kansai region with liquefied natural gas (LNG). Through a network of 56 subsidiaries, Osaka Gas is involved in the manufacture, supply, and sale of gas, gas appliances, and liquified petroleum gas (LPG) and natural gas, as well as house pipe installation, real estate leasing, and a host of other activities including engineering and information processing. The company's service area includes 69 cities and 41 towns in six prefectures. Deregulation of Japan's gas industry began in the late 1990s, forcing Osaka Gas to cut costs, restructure, and diversify into such areas as the independent power producer and retail electricity markets.

Osaka's Gas Industry Gets Its Start in 1871

Osaka's gas industry originated in 1871 when Japan's first gas-powered lamp was unveiled, providing lighting for the city mint. This came just 18 years after the United States Navy, under Admiral Perry, had forced Japan to open up her doors to the Western world and restore the power of the emperor for the first time since the 17th century. What followed was a remark-able and rapid period of industrial development that originated from the major cities of Tokyo and Osaka.

The introduction of gas lighting to Osaka was soon repeated in Japan's other major cities. At the same time, kerosene lamps were also imported from the West. For a time, the latter became more popular than gas, being easy to use, but widespread fires caused by these lamps convinced authorities that gas was the best source of city lighting. Consequently, Osaka Gas was formed in 1897 with capital provided by the municipal authorities and also by overseas investors. Osaka Gas's foreign patron was the Edison Power Company in the United States. An Osaka businessman, Taro Asano, had met the president of Edison, Anthony Brady, while in New York, and the two became friends. Brady was impressed with Asano and sent an Edison representative, Alexander Chizon, to Osaka to arrange financing and aid the fledgling operation in technical matters. Along with Asano, in 1902 the Edison Company became a large shareholder in Osaka Gas, with a 50 percent stake that it later sold to Japanese investors. Asano and other Japanese investors held the remaining 50 percent.

Masagi Kataoka was chosen as the company's first president, and his first task was to prepare the infrastructure for the production and distribution of gas in Osaka. In the 19th century, all city gas was produced using coal as the raw material; the technology required to tap and transport natural gas had yet to be developed. In the Iwazaki area of Osaka, a factory was constructed consisting of eight gas-producing retorts imported from the United States. Using coal, this factory could produce 4,000 cubic meters of gas per day. Underground piping was installed to transport this gas to various parts of the city. In the relatively short space of two years, from 1902 to 1904, 80 kilometers of piping were laid by manual laborers and animal power. A steel gas storage tank was constructed with a capacity of 10,000 cubic meters of gas. At the time, it was hailed as the largest gas tank east of the Suez canal. In 1905, after Kataoka had traveled to New York to finalize arrangements for financing from the United States, gas supplies finally commenced. Initially, 3,350 homes were connected and supplied with gas, which was monitored with installed meters. The price was ¥0.08 per square meter, which meant that only the affluent could afford this new source of lighting.

Company Perspectives:

Aiming to become a one-stop energy solution provider, Osaka Gas strives to achieve superior competitiveness in all facets of its business, from cost and efficiency to environmental preservation and customer services. In all of our activities we aim to become the corporate group that is the preferred choice of our customers.

Early Growth: 1900–30s

Byproducts of the gas production process included coke, tar, and benzene and were sold to industry. An agreement was signed with Sakamitsu Industries, a local metal-casting firm, to supply coke for Sakamitsu's metal reduction needs. Osaka Gas also began refining and selling coal tar that was, among other things, used to pave roads. By 1908, the success and expansion of the company seemed assured, with four branch offices opening throughout the city. The factory was now operating at full capacity. Due to the comparatively high price and unreliability of electricity, the alternative source of power to city gas, demand for gas was high. In the rapidly expanding Japanese economy, gas-powered engines became popular. This trend began to change during the early 1900s, however, with the advent of hydroelectric power and the tungsten lamp replacing gas as a source of lighting energy. From this time onward, gas would be used for the more high-power function of heat production. For consumers, this meant the use of gas for heating and cooking and for industry in furnaces and engines.

Japan's victory in the Sino-Japanese War of 1897 and the Russo-Japanese War of 1904 made the country a major world power in both industrial and military terms, and the following 20 years were a period of intense economic growth. Although this growth brought rapid inflation, the price of gas rose by only 50 percent between 1905 and 1925. This compared with a rise of 250 percent in coal and rice prices and showed how heavily the industry was subsidized and regulated by the government. After World War I and the ensuing depression in Japan, Osaka Gas was allowed to regulate its prices. The management of the company under Kataoka set the long-term strategy of dropping gas prices. This had the twofold effect of preventing customers from being forced to give up their gas supply and winning the company new customers, as firewood became scarcer and more expensive as a source of heating. The results were dramatic. In 1927, the number of households supplied by Osaka Gas doubled to 110,000 and rose to 300,000 by 1933.

During the late 1920s and early 1930s, the company conducted market research, sending employees out on door-to-door surveys of households in Osaka. A campaign was initiated to promote gas use in Osaka, utilizing billboards and exhibitions. In 1928, Kataoka and 20 of his executives traveled to the United States and Europe to witness the applications of city gas in the West. At an exhibition of gas appliances in Europe they saw gas-powered refrigerators manufactured by Electrolux of Sweden. The result of the visit was the promotion in Osaka of an array of gas-powered appliances, including refrigerators, irons, and rice cookers. The ensuing demand for gas prompted the construction of a second factory unit at the Iwazaki site in 1928, followed by a third in 1935.

In the 1930s, the use of gas for home cooking spread throughout the major cities in Japan, including Osaka. In 1937, Osaka Gas decided to invest heavily in a major new project—the construction of a huge gas works on Yujima Island in Osaka Bay. The facility, completed in 1940, was capable of producing 35,000 tons of gas per day and also manufactured tar, pitch, naphthalene, and benzene as byproducts for industrial use. A second coke burner was added in 1942. During this time, the Japanese government was steering the economy toward war-related production, and Osaka Gas, as a key industry, was in close contact with the military government regarding its production plans. The Japanese invasion of Manchuria and China in 1931 gave Japan a plentiful and virtually free source of coal that greatly aided the war machine. Consumer and industrial demand for gas soared during the war years.

During 1944, however, the tide turned against Japan, and its cities were increasingly the targets of bomber attacks by the B-29s of the United States Air Force. Although less publicized than the atomic bomb attacks, these raids resulted in far greater damage and casualties. Indeed, on August 14, 1945, the day Nagasaki was destroyed by an atomic bomb, Osaka was attacked by 180 B-29s resulting in widespread fires in the city, the destruction of 40,000 homes, and more than 80,000 casualties. This and similar raids caused severe damage to Osaka Gas's production and pipeline distribution facilities. All the major city gas companies in the region were similarly affected, and in December 1944 they merged to help ensure their survival. The main companies in this merger were Osaka Gas Company, Ltd.; Kobe Gas Company, Ltd.; and Kyoto Gas Company, Ltd. Following Japan's surrender, the Allied powers—led by the United States—took temporary control of the country. Gas supply in Osaka was sporadic at best and explosions, due to damaged pipelines, were frequent. The years 1945 through 1950 were spent identifying and repairing pipeline and reconnecting as many households as possible. Like most essential items in Japan immediately after the war, gas was rationed; its use by the public was limited to two hours a day.

Postwar Expansion

In 1949, under the Law for the Elimination of Excessive Concentration of Economic Power, implemented by the Allies to break up the big Japanese industrial groups, the merged gas companies were split up, and Osaka Gas became a separate entity again. The year 1949 also saw the death of Kataoka, who had led the company since its founding. He was replaced by Jiro Iiguchi, a former vice-president of the company. During the years 1950 to 1955, Japan underwent a remarkable period of reconstruction that involved the united efforts of the entire Japanese population. Using manual labor when necessary, Osaka Gas began a full-scale rebuilding of its Yujima facility, which had returned to its prewar production level by 1952. A gas appliance research center was opened in the same year, and in 1953 the Yujima factory produced its first oil-based gas. Using German technology, high-pressure storage and gas transport mechanisms were added. A combination of U.S. aid and cheap educated labor fueled Japan's growth during the 1950s, and toward the end of the decade the Japanese began to see the fruits of their hard work in the form of consumer goods such as televisions and cookers. The government promoted the use of gas in all areas of Japan as an alternative to firewood for cooking and heating. Osaka Gas stepped up its own promotional campaign, hailing gas as being four times as cheap and twice as quick as electricity for heating and cooking purposes. Customer service was made a priority, with a fleet of three-wheeled motorized bicycles providing emergency cover and a Univac computer introduced at the company's Osaka headquarters.

In 1960, the capacity of the Yujima factory was increased. In 1962, the production capacity at Iwazaki was closed, the site being demoted to a storage facility. Osaka Gas's high-pressure storage and supply network was expanded in 1961 into what became known as the 370-kilometer network, in reference to the length of high-pressure gas piping installed throughout the city. In 1964, the company announced a "calorie-up" program in which the energy content of its city gas was upgraded from 3,600 kilocalories per cubic meter to 4,500. This necessitated the inspection of 6.5 million appliances in 1.7 million homes being supplied by Osaka Gas. The company also began to sell gas in the form of liquid propane gas steel canisters to customers who were not connected by the pipe network. Company representatives delivered filled canisters to customers and took away the empty ones for refilling.

By 1965, Osaka Gas was a major corporation with several thousand employees and staff training facilities. A five-day, 40-hour working week was introduced. In 1966, a research and development center with 160 employees was opened adjacent to the production site on Yujima. By 1968, the Japanese economy ranked second only to the United States in terms of gross national product (GNP), which continued to grow uninterrupted between 1966 and 1973. This period, known as the Izanagi Boom, ended abruptly with the oil shock of 1973. Japan had come to rely on cheap, plentiful Middle Eastern oil for more than 70 percent of its energy needs, and when OPEC trebled its oil prices overnight the effects on the economy were profound. In 1974, for the first time since World War II, the Japanese economy registered a negative year-on-year growth figure of −0.5 percent, and the Japanese government set about reducing its dependency on oil. There were

three major alternatives: nuclear power, coal, and natural gas. At that stage, Osaka Gas produced all of its gas from relatively cheap oil and coal, the import of natural gas being uneconomical. Technological advances in the storing and transport of natural gas as a liquid, coupled with the sharp increase in the price of oil, now made the import of natural gas feasible. Osaka Gas began to amass a supply of gas in 1980, with huge refrigeration ships transporting the liquefied natural gas (LNG) at −160 degrees centigrade from fields throughout Southeast Asia and Australia. This achievement required the rapid development of refrigeration technology by the company, which it undertook with other Japanese users, notably Tokyo Gas. Beginning in 1980, Osaka Gas relied increasingly on LNG for the bulk of its gas supply, and by 1990 it used LNG exclusively.

During the 1980s, Osaka Gas used its considerable engineering expertise to diversify into other areas. This process began with the sale of coal-related byproducts such as coke, benzene, and coal-tar products, which had been supplied by the company since its founding. In 1987, a subsidiary, Donac Company, was formed to produce the Donacarbo carbon fibers used in a range of products, including golf clubs, that were sold throughout the world. Another subsidiary, Harman Company, developed and manufactured gas-run appliances and relied heavily on Osaka Gas's research and development facilities. Osaka Gas imported three million tons of LNG at this time, about 10 percent of Japan's total. It used the low temperature of the gas while being shipped to collaborate with the food industry, forming Kinki Cryogenics as a supplier of frozen foods. This subsidiary also became the first company in the world to utilize LNG to produce liquid carbon dioxide.

In 1978, Osaka Gas Engineering was formed, providing technological assistance to outside clients. Offices were established in the United States and England in the late 1980s to market this expertise. Like many Japanese utility and transportation companies, Osaka Gas took advantage of rapidly rising city land prices between 1984 and 1990. As a major land owner in Osaka, it formed Urbanex Company in 1989 to develop surplus company land for commercial and private use. Other diversified businesses included retail and restaurant operations and business consulting services.

Deregulation Leads to Changes in the 1990s and Beyond

During the early 1990s, the supply of gas remained the core business of the Osaka Gas Group, accounting for almost 75 percent of revenue. The group was organized into five main business divisions: gas-related, refrigeration, engineering services, computer services, and consumer services. The last division, which included real estate, was the fastest-growing. The group launched a major restructuring effort in 1993 in order to bolster operating efficiency. Masafumi Ohnishi, president since 1981, stated his desire to increase the international activities of Osaka Gas in many of the group's business areas. This policy, along with ongoing diversification and investment in new technology, continued into the latter half of the 1990s as the company faced changes related to market liberalization.

Just before deregulation hit Japan's market, however, Osaka Gas was dealt a major blow. On January 17, 1995, a devastating earthquake shook Western Japan that caused over $1.9 billion in damages to the firm's gas network. Throughout most of 1995, the company worked diligently to restore gas supply to its customers and had to rebuild its damaged facilities.

At the same time, Osaka Gas continued to strengthen its business holdings as deregulation started. Beginning in 1995, the Japanese government partially liberalized the electric utility industry, allowing independent power producers (IPPs) to sell electric power to the regional companies. Then, in March 2000, these IPPs were allowed to market directly to customers, enabling both foreign and domestic competition in the retail electricity market. The gas industry was in the process of deregulating as well, which gave Osaka Gas the impetus to expand further. The company was the first gas concern to enter the IPP market. In April 2000, the firm began construction on a 150-megawatt power generation facility in Torishima, Osaka. In April 2002, the plant went online and provided wholesale electricity to Kansai Electric Power.

While deregulation brought with it increased opportunities for expansion, it also set the stage for intense competition. In response to the changing business environment, Osaka Gas launched a new management plan in 1999 entitled Vision 2010. Two specific strategies were the cornerstone of the plan—diversification into multi-faceted energy activities and branching out into new business areas. The initiative also focused on "value creation management," a corporate mission based on generating value for shareholders, customers, and society.

Japan's deregulation moves started to significantly change the industry during the early years of the new century. An April 2002 *World Gas Intelligence* article claimed that LNG businesses were "slashing prices, buying fuel more efficiently, tying up with foreign oil companies, and using new pricing methods." In addition, Osaka Gas and its competitors pursued new opportunities made available by industry deregulation. During 2001, the company moved into the electricity retailing sector when it partnered with NTT Facilities Inc. and Tokyo Gas Company Ltd. to launch ENNET Corporation. Osaka Gas also began supplying LPG to its customers by teaming up with Nissho Iwai Petroleum Gas Corp.

While natural gas remained a core business in Osaka Gas's portfolio, the company continued to strengthen its electric power business with the intent of making it a significant portion of its business. According to the company, it planned to market electricity to specific customers, propose multiple energies to these customers, and then expand into a larger geographical area.

By 2003, Osaka Gas's management was confident that deregulation would continue to bring positive changes to the company and the customers it served. The firm's Energy Business unit included natural gas, electricity, LPG, and energy solutions divisions. Its Non-energy Business unit was comprised of real estate, restaurant and food, information, materials, and service holdings. While competition would remain intense in the years to come, Osaka Gas was intent on securing its position as a multi-faceted energy services group. With a solid strategy in place, the company appeared to be on track for future growth.

Principal Subsidiaries

Nabari Kintetsu Gas Company Ltd. (85%); Kinki Piping Company Ltd.; Harman Company Ltd. (60%); Ehime Nissho Propane Company Ltd. (66.7%); Gasnet Company Ltd. (55%); CYRO-AIR Company Ltd. (55%); Cold Air Products Company Ltd. (55%); Liquid Gas Company Ltd.; Liquid Gas Kyoto Company Ltd.; Kinki Ekitan Company Ltd. (51%); Kochi Nissho Propane Company Ltd.; Shanshin Engineering Company Ltd.; Nissho Iwai Gas Company Ltd.; Nissho Iwai Gas Energy Company Ltd.; Nissho Iwai Petroleum Gas Company Ltd. (70%); Nissho Gas Supply Company Ltd.; Nissho Propane Sekiyu Company Ltd.; Hokuriku Nissho Propane Company Ltd. (70%); Mie Nissho Gas Company Ltd.; Urbanex Company Ltd.; OG Capital Company Ltd.; Harman Planning Company Ltd.; Kyoto Research Park Company Ltd.

Principal Competitors

Tokyo Gas Company Ltd.; The Kansai Electric Power Company Ltd.

Further Reading

"Another Supply Deal Underpins NW Shelf Expansion," *Oil and Gas Journal*, March 25, 2002, p. 39.
"Asia-Pacific Focus of Coming LNG Trade Boom," *Oil and Gas Journal*, November 16, 1992, p. 26.
"Japanese Gas, Power Utilities Join Forces," *World Gas Intelligence*, August 5, 2003.
"Japan's Deregulation Delivers a Punch," *World Gas Intelligence*, April 16, 2002.
Livingstone, J., J. Moore, and F. Oldfather, *Postwar Japan: 1945 to Present*, London: Random House, 1973.
"Osaka Gas Details Obstacles," *FT Energy Newsletters—International Gas Report*, March 17, 1995.
"Osaka Gas Sets Spending," *International Oil Daily*, January 22, 2003.
"Osaka Gas to Break Even Despite Quake-Inflicted Damage," *Japan Economic Newswire*, July 25, 1995.
"Osaka Gas to Post Loss for Year," *Wall Street Journal*, February 2, 1996.

—Dylan Tanner
—update: Christina M. Stansell

Polar Air Cargo Inc.

2000 Westchester Avenue
Purchase, New York 10577
U.S.A.
Telephone: (914) 701-8000
Fax: (914) 701-8001
Web site: http://www.polaraircargo.com

*Wholly Owned Subsidiary of Atlas Air Worldwide
  Holdings, Inc.*
Incorporated: January 1993
Employees: 660
Sales: $300 million (2001)
NAIC: 481112 Scheduled Freight Air Transportation

Polar Air Cargo Inc. is one of the world's leading all-cargo airlines. A subsidiary of Atlas Air, Inc., Polar operates a fleet of 15 Boeing 747s. Its operations have always been strongest in the Pacific, though the company operates scheduled routes to all inhabited continents. Polar markets its services mostly to freight forwarders.

A Niche in 1993

Air cargo was a growing business in the early 1990s in spite of the generally depressed state of the world economy. The founders of Polar Air Cargo saw their niche in the Pacific region served on a scheduled basis by Flying Tigers before its 1989 takeover by Federal Express.

Polar Air Cargo, L.P. was formed in January 1993 as a partnership between Polaris Holding Company, Southern Air Transport, Inc., and NedMark Transportation Services Inc. Southern Air, a major unscheduled cargo airline based in Miami, operated the planes, which were owned by Polaris Holding of San Francisco, a subsidiary of General Electric Capital Services; the three Boeing 747 freighters had formerly carried passengers for Pan American. NedMark, based in Long Beach, California, was formed to market the business mainly to freight forwarders.

Southern Transport began operating scheduled flights under the Polar Air Cargo name with a charter flight from New York to Vienna in April 1994. Scheduled operations began in May 1993 with a New York-Shannon, Ireland-Moscow route. This route was extended to Hong Kong and the United States for Polar's first transpacific service. Another connected New York to Hong Kong with stops in Los Angeles, Honolulu, and Sydney while returning via Taipei, Anchorage, and the major cargo hub of Columbus, Ohio.

Ned Wallace, head of NedMark, was named CEO of the partnership, supported by president Mark West. Wallace had been an executive with the Flying Tiger Line and was formerly chairman of Evergreen International. West had also been at both airlines. Though the market was competitive, Polar Air's planners sought to exploit low lease rates for aircraft and low rates for contract maintenance.

In March 1994, the whole arrangement was restructured due to Polar Air's rapid growth (the company would end the year with a fleet of nine planes). Southern Air Transport withdrew from the partnership entirely. NedMark Transportation Services changed its name to Polar Air Cargo Inc. on March 9, 1994. It was certified as an air carrier on July 4, 1994 and took over responsibility for flight operations. Polaris had formed a subsidiary called PALC II to lease the aircraft. Polaris was soon renamed GE Capital Aviation Services and relocated to Stamford, Connecticut.

Polar Air Cargo had 175 employees, 45 of them pilots, and operated a fleet of four Boeing 747s. Sales were about $168 million in 1994 and $234 million in 1995. Polar had become profitable in its first couple of months in business. The fleet numbered a dozen aircraft by July 1995. London, Amsterdam, and three stops in Brazil were added to the scheduled route network in 1996. Sales rose to $258 million, making Polar the largest all-cargo airline in the United States, according to *Air Transport World*.

Japan Added in 1997

The company launched scheduled service between the United States and Japan in April 1997, becoming only the third U.S.-based all-cargo airline in the market. During the year, Polar had also expanded its network to Bangkok, New Delhi, Manila, and Dubai.

Company Perspectives:

Polar Air Cargo's mission is to work in partnership with international air freight forwarders and agents by providing them high quality, efficient services at competitive prices and with the highest safety standards of any airline in the world. International air freight forwarders and agents are assured that they and their customers will be served by Polar's experienced and proven air freight professionals in sales, customer service, flight operations, maintenance, freight handling, and accounting. We strive to be the "cargo airline of choice."

Key Dates:

1993: Polar Air Cargo begins operations in a booming international freight market.

1997: Service from the United States to the lucrative Japanese market launched.

2001: Atlas Air acquires Polar.

2003: The company's headquarters are relocated from Long Beach, California to Purchase, New York.

Polar had 550 employees at the end of 1997. It posted a net profit of $4.3 million on sales of $335.3 million for the year, after losing $4.4 million on revenues of $256.2 million in 1996. The company's operations in the Pacific, its only profitable region in 1997, accounted for about three-quarters of revenues.

By 1998, Polar was the world's fourth largest all-cargo airline. It flew to 19 countries on five continents. Polar typically flew for freight forwarders, not passenger airlines. A marketing arrangement with Air New Zealand announced in August 1999 gave Polar a new stream of westbound cargo on its Pacific crossings. Polar's eastbound business had been much stronger.

The Asian financial crisis of 1997–98 greatly affected Polar's Pacific business, reducing the region's cargo traffic by one-third. Fortunately, U.S. and European markets remained strong, and there were good prospects for growth in other parts of the world.

In April 1998, Polar became the first all-cargo airline in the United States to equip its fleet with the Traffic Alert and Collision Avoidance System II (TCAS II). However, this was not designed to prevent mishaps such as one of the company's 747s being damaged at Anchorage International Airport in 2000 after 100 mph winds pushed it into a cargo loader.

Revenues were $300 million a year in the late 1990s. The shipping market contracted in 2001 as the world economy slumped. Polar laid off more than 50 workers, including two dozen pilots, or about 10 percent of staff.

Polar Bought by Atlas Air Holdings in 2001

Atlas Air Worldwide Holdings, Inc. announced the acquisition of Polar Air Cargo for $84 million in July 2001, and the deal was closed four months later. Atlas had been formed in Colorado around the same time as Polar Air and carried freight under contract for other airlines. It had long sought to enter the Japanese air cargo market, the world's fourth largest, where Polar had a presence with 16 weekly flights.

Polar had also been awarded coveted rights to fly between Hong Kong and Seoul. Polar began flying from the United States to Korea, via Hong Kong or Tokyo, in October 2001. Taipei and Manila were also connected to this service. Inchon, South Korea, became Polar's Asian hub, with more than two dozen flights a week starting in 2003. Polar planned to connect

Hong Kong to its service from the United States to India via Europe in 2003. Polar operated 17 Boeing 747s at the time it was acquired by Atlas. The company employed 660 people, about a third of them at its Long Beach headquarters.

Polar announced a code share agreement with Qantas in April 2002. Under the deal, the two carriers would market cargo space on each other's planes in the South Pacific. The company was also expanding its operations between the United States and Europe, increasing services to the United Kingdom, Ireland, Sweden, and continental Europe.

In March 2003, Polar's head offices were moved to Purchase, New York, next door to those of Atlas Air. Polar's sales and marketing functions remained in Long Beach. Parent company Atlas Air Worldwide Holdings was entering a "prepackaged" Chapter 11 bankruptcy filing in December 2003.

Principal Competitors

Evergreen International Airlines; FedEx Corporation; Northwest Airlines.

Further Reading

Armbruster, William, "Air Cargo's Young Guns," *Journal of Commerce*, January 9, 1995, p. 9.

Barling, Russell, "Atlas Launches Global Hub Network; Acquisition of Polar Air Boosts Cargo Capabilities," *South China Morning Post* (Hong Kong), November 21, 2001, p. 1.

——, "Picking Inchon as Its Asian Hub, the Carrier Has Boosted Its Flights to South Korea and the Philippines," *South China Morning Post* (Hong Kong), December 13, 2002, p. 5.

——, "Polar Air Plans Global Freighter Link with HK Approval," *South China Morning Post* (Hong Kong), March 7, 2003, p. 6.

Hall, Kevin G., "Southern Air, Ex-Tigers to Link US, Australia; All-Freight Service Seeks Asia Inroads," *Journal of Commerce*, March 23, 1993, p. 1A.

Hanigan, Ian, "New York Air Cargo Company Plans to Buy Long Beach Rival," *Press-Telegram*, July 13, 2001.

Iritani, Evelyn, "High Flier; Look Out, FedEx and UPS," *Los Angeles Times*, April 18, 1997, p. D2.

Kaye, Ken, "Freight Line Going to Asia, Australia," *Sun Sentinel* (Fort Lauderdale), April 12, 1993, p. 12.

Mongelluzzo, Bill, "All-Cargo 'Rookies' Show Off Their Wares," *Journal of Commerce*, April 25, 1994, p. 6.

Nelms, Douglas W., "When Niche Means Most," *Air Transport World*, July 1995, pp. 56ff.

"New International Cargo Service to Begin in May," *Aviation Daily*, March 19, 1993, p. 440.

Page, Paul, "Polar Air Cargo to Start Up in May as Aircraft Lessor," *Traffic World*, March 29, 1993, p. 23.

''Polar Air Cargo Enters Strong Freight Market,'' *Aviation Week & Space Technology*, March 29, 1993, p. 33.

''Polar Air Cargo Restructures to Operate International Freighter Service,'' *Aviation Daily*, March 31, 1994, p. 516.

''Polar Air Cargo Surges in 4Q Earnings,'' *Airline Financial News*, March 23, 1998.

''Polar Buy Sees Atlas' Freight and Charter Revenues Surge,'' *South China Morning Post* (Hong Kong), November 19, 2002, p. 6.

''Polar Challenge: A Young Cargo Airline Still Prospers Despite the Asian Downturn,'' *Flight International*, April 29, 1998, p. 44.

Putzger, Ian, ''By Polar,'' *Air Cargo World*, December 1999, p. 24.

Ragsdale, Rose, ''Polar Air to Consolidate Operations, Relocate Into Expanded Space,'' *Alaska Journal of Commerce*, September 1, 1997, p. 6.

Stapleton, Rob, ''Damaged Polar Air Jet Likely to Sit Until Boeing Strike Ends,'' *Alaska Journal of Commerce*, March 5, 2000, p. 24.

——, ''Polar Air Cargo, Atlas Air Inc. to Lay Off Pilots, Other Staff as U.S. Economy Slows,'' *Alaska Journal of Commerce*, May 27, 2001, p. 8.

—Frederick C. Ingram

PT Bank Buana Indonesia Tbk

Jl. Asemka Nos. 32-36
Jakarta Barat 11110
Indonesia
Telephone: (21) 6922901
Fax: (21) 6912005
Web site: http://www.bankbuana.com

Public Company
Incorporated: 1956
Employees: 4,473
Total Assets: IDR 13.28 billion ($1.49 billion)(2002)
Stock Exchanges: Jakarta
Ticker Symbol: BBIA
NAIC: 522110 Commercial Banking

PT Bank Buana Indonesia Tbk has come through the Asian economic crisis of the late 1990s in fine form. With a rising assets base and stable financial base, Bank Buana has achieved Class A certification from the Bank of Indonesia and has successfully converted into a publicly listed bank. One of Indonesia's top 20 banks, Bank Buana has traditionally focused on the trade finance segment, targeting especially small and mid-sized businesses. The retail distribution market is also a primary target of the group. Bank Buana offers a full range of retail and commercial banking services, including a range of savings products and e-banking services. The company's loans include working capital loans, export-import loans, bank guarantees, and investment loans. Bank Buana serves its market through nearly 150 locations throughout Indonesia, as well as through its eMobile Mbank online service. In 2002, the bank posted total assets of more than IDR 13.2 billion (approximately $1.5 billion).

Origins and Development: 1950s to Early 1990s

PT Bank Buana Indonesia was founded in 1956 as a private bank in Jakarta. The bank remained small, and by the early 1960s found it difficult to keep afloat. In 1965, the bank was bought up by a group of five Indonesian industrial companies, which each took an approximately equal share in Bank Buana. Among the bank's new owners were a producer of glass and a textile manufacture. Owning a bank for these modestly sized businesses was not merely for the prestige but was also a way of cutting back on their own banking charges. Yet the equal shareholder status of the five owners made it difficult to reach agreement over the bank's management policies and long-term strategy. This situation led the bank to adopt a highly conservative approach to growth and to focus its customer portfolio on the trade finance market, rather than on the consumer market.

Nonetheless, Bank Buana grew strongly in the 1970s. Mergers and acquisitions marked the group's expansion during this period, beginning with the 1972 merger with PT Bank Pembinaan Nasional, in Bandung. In 1974, Bank Buana expanded its operations again by absorbing PT Bank Kesejahteraan Masyaraka, in Semarang, and then again, in 1975, by merging with PT Bank Aman Makmur, based in Jakarta.

A turning point for Bank Buana came in 1976, when it was awarded a foreign exchange license—only about 20 percent of Indonesia's many banks were to achieve this status. As such, Bank Buana was able to develop into one of the country's leading foreign currency and trade finance specialists. The bank stepped up its growth through the 1980s, opening more than 100 branch offices throughout the country. By 1990, Bank Buana had become Indonesia's twelfth largest bank.

By the late 1980s, however, Bank Buana's five-way ownership structure, and the inability to reach consensus, had left the bank vulnerable in the buoyant Indonesian banking market. Starting in about 1989, the bank went into a period of relative stagnation; by 1994, it had slipped back to 35th place among the country's top 50 banks. As both its loan portfolio and assets base slipped back, the bank continued to lose ground in the booming Indonesian banking sector.

Fuelled by increasingly liberal government banking policies, the Indonesian economy, and its banking sector, grew quickly in the late 1980s and early 1990s. Bank Buana appeared to sit on the sidelines, while its competitors increasingly gained ground. By the early 1990s, Bank Buana seemed at a standstill in what

<table>
<tr><td>

Company Perspectives:

From the very beginning, we have always concentrated our business on catering to the needs of our retail customers, distributors as well as small to medium sized enterprises. These sectors have been proven to endure, even during the most difficult economic periods. Our full commitment to these sectors has paid off as it has allowed us to weather the economic crisis in 1997 and enabled us to achieve a sustainable growth. We will continue to expand our network of offices, human resources, and information technology to reach our mission: to be the most reliable, trusted, and sound bank in the nation in serving small to medium scale businesses.

</td><td>

Key Dates:

1956: PT Bank Buana Indonesia is established in Jakarta.
1965: Bank Buana is acquired by a partnership formed by five industrial companies.
1972: The bank merges with PT Bank Pembinaan Nasional, in Bandung.
1974: PT Bank Kesejahteraan Masyaraka, in Semarang, is acquired.
1975: The bank merges with PT Bank Aman Makmur, based in Jakarta.
1976: Bank Buana is granted a foreign currency license.
1989: The bank forms a joint-venture with Japan's Mitsubishi Bank, PT Mitsubishi Buana Bank (later PT DBS Buana Bank).
1990: A joint-venture is formed with DBS and TatLee, PT DBS TatLee Buana Bank.
1994: A new holding company is created, PT Sari Dasa Karsa, which acquires nearly 90 percent of Bank Buana's shares and installs new management.
1999: The bank receives class A certification from Bank of Indonesia and sells out its share of DBS Buana Bank.
2000: Bank Buana goes public with a listing on the Jakarta Stock Exchange.
2002: The banks lists on the New York Stock Exchange as ADRs.
2003: International Finance Corporation, a subsidiary of the World Bank, acquries seven percent stake in Bank Buana.

</td></tr>
</table>

some observers described as an "overbanked" Indonesian financial market.

Instead of growing its own business, Bank Buana concentrated on forming joint-ventures, partnering with foreign banks seeking entry into the fast-growing Indonesian market. As such, the group formed a joint-venture with Japan's Mitsubishi Bank, named PT Mitsubishi Buana Bank, in 1989. The following year, Bank Buana partnered with DBS Bank and TatLee Bank of Singapore to create DBS Buana TatLee Bank. DBS later took over Mitsubishi's stake in the former bank, which changed its name to DBS Buana Bank, then sold out its stake in the Buana-TatLee partnership, which became Keppel TatLee Buana Bank.

Restructured for Growth in the New Century

The year 1994 marked a significant change for Bank Buana. In that year, the company changed its shareholder structure, placing more than 89 percent of its shares into a newly created holding company, PT Sari Dasa Karsa. At the same time, the bank installed a new management team, which began a more aggressive growth policy. The bank's new management specifically targeted expansion of the bank's loan policy, which grew by some 40 percent into the middle of the decade.

In the second half of the 1990s, Bank Buana's new growth drive had returned it to Indonesia's top 20 banks. However, concerns that the bank was now expanding too fast led management to scale back its growth. Although analysts consistently referred to the group's management strategy as conservative, Bank Buana itself favored "prudent" as a more descriptive term for its strategy. Nonetheless, Bank Buana began preparing for an initial public offering, initially slated for 1997.

The crash of Indonesia's financial community—amid the economic crisis that swept through Asian markets in the late 1990s—put a temporary halt to the group's plans for a stock listing. As the Indonesian banking sector reeled from the sudden collapse of the country's economy, and as many of Bank Buana's competitors slipped into bankruptcy, Bank Buana's more conservative approach enabled it to emerge relatively unscathed from the crisis. Indeed, when the Bank of Indonesia reviewed Bank Buana, it became one of few to receive certification as a Class A financial institution.

Bank Buana once again began preparations for its public listing at the end of the 1990s. As part of that process, the bank sold off its share of the DBS Buana joint-venture. Bank Buana went public in July 2000, listing on the Jakarta and Surubaya Stock Exchanges in a successful offering that was several times over-subscribed. The bank continued expanding its shareholder base, adding two new major shareholders in the early 2000s, including PT Makindo Tbk, which boosted its stake in the bank to 6.92 percent in 2002.

Bank Buana split its stock for the first time, in a 2-for-1 split, near the end of 2002. Soon after, Bank Buana was admitted to the New York Stock Exchange as well, where its shares began trading as American Depositary Receipts (ADRs). In April 2003, the International Finance Corporation, a subsidiary of the World Bank, acquired nearly 7 percent of the bank, underscoring Bank Buana's status as one of the country's most stable smaller banks. That purchase reduced PT Sari Dasa Karsa's stake in the bank to just over 55 percent.

Despite its commitment to a conservative management strategy, Bank Buana continued to display strong growth at the beginning of the 2000s. By the end of 2003, the bank was able to forecast growth of some 10 percent over the previous year, when its total assets topped IDR 13 billion ($1.5 billion). Although tiny by international standards, Bank Buana, through its commitment to its core trade finance business, could claim a place as one of Indonesia's most respected small banks.

Principal Competitors

Bank Negara Indonesia Tbk; Bank Central Asia Tbk, PT; Bank Rakyat Indonesia, PT; Unibank, PT; Prima Express Bank; Bank Pacific, PT; Bank Danamon Indonesia Tbk; Bank Artha Grahai.

Further Reading

''Bank Buana Indonesia to List on NYSE,'' *Asia Pulse*, December 27, 2002.

''Bank Buana to Go Public,'' *Jakarta Post*, June 16, 2000.

''Bank Buana to Issue New Shares,'' *Jakarta Post*, August 25, 2003.

''Indonesia's Bank Buana Posts 5.58% Decline in Net Profit,'' *Asia Pulse*, October 31, 2003.

—M.L. Cohen

Puig Beauty and Fashion Group S.L.

Travessera de Gracia 9
08021 Barcelona
Spain
Telephone: (34) 93-400-70-00
Fax: (34) 93-400-70-10
Web site: http://www.puig.com

Private Company
Incorporated: 1914 as Antonio Puig S.A.
Employees: 5,000
Sales: $1.04 billion (2002)
NAIC: 325620 Toilet Preparations Manufacturing;
424210 Drugs and Druggists' Sundries Merchant
Wholesalers; 423940 Jewelry, Watch, Precious
Stones, and Precious Metal Merchant Wholesalers

Puig Beauty and Fashion Group S.L. is one of the world's leading cosmetics and perfume companies and the largest such company in Spain. The firm manufactures fine perfumes, cosmetics and toiletries as well as mass-market brands. It runs ten manufacturing centers, with locations in Spain, France, and Mexico, and operates three fashion design centers, with locations in Spain, France, and the United States. Puig distributes its lines in more than 150 countries worldwide. Almost 70 percent of the company's sales come from Europe, with another 20 percent originating in the United States. Some of Puig's well-known brands are Lavanda Puig, Agua Brava, Azur de Puig, and Quorum. Puig also owns the established French perfume company Nina Ricci. Some of the firm's leading scents are associated with renowned fashion designers, including the Venezuelan designer Carolina Herrera and French designer Paco Rabanne. Puig also has a marketing agreement with the Italian fashion house Prada. The firm began as a distributor of French perfumes in Spain and became the foremost Spanish toiletries firm. Puig expanded into Europe and North America in the 1980s and 1990s and has continued to grow quickly through acquisitions. Puig owns two of its former major Spanish competitors, Myrurgia and Perfumeria Gal. Puig Beauty and Fashion Group is owned by members of the founding Puig family,

though in the 2000s the chief executive position passed for the first time to a non-family member.

Modest Beginnings in the 1920s

Puig Beauty and Fashion Group was originally named for its founder, Antonio Puig, a Barcelona native and son of a wealthy businessman. Puig traveled to France and England as a young man, and on his return to Spain he decided to become a distributor for foreign cosmetics and perfumes. Spain had very little native toiletries industry at the time, and several companies that became Puig's major competitors also set up around this time, just before World War I. Antonio Puig, S.A. was established in 1914, and the company imported perfumes such as the French brands D'Orsay and Ricci. Spain remained neutral during World War I, and its markets flourished. In 1922, Puig began making his own cosmetics in addition to importing. The company launched Milady that year, which was the first lipstick ever manufactured in Spain.

Puig remained a small firm through the 1920s, but the perfume industry began to take hold in Spain. In 1931, Antonio Puig became the first president of the newly formed Spanish association of perfume manufacturers, which was headquartered in Barcelona. Puig established firm business relations with perfumers and essential oil suppliers in France, Germany, and Switzerland. The Spanish Civil War (1936–39) brought chaos to Spain, and the ensuing years under the dictator Francisco Franco saw very different economic conditions than in the prewar years. Franco insisted that Spain's economy be self-sufficient and isolated from international markets. This gave local businesses the opportunity to grow without international competition, but it also put extreme strictures on companies like Puig, which depended on imports. Puig managed to negotiate the new economic reality fairly well, however. In 1939, the company launched Lavanda Puig, an eau de cologne that became one of its best-selling brands. Lavanda Puig was made with Spanish-grown lavender. It was a local product designed for the domestic market, and it became a household name in Spain.

Puig remained a purely Spanish company through the 1940s. Antonio Puig continued to chair the perfume industry associa-

---

Company Perspectives:

One aspect of our activity is reflected in art, in glamour, intuition, passion, taste, and the perception of our society's changing values. The other facet is the most rigorous research, the most advanced design, the continual search for new solutions to the new demands of our customers and the never-ending quest for excellence in everything we do. From fashion and accessories to fragrances, advanced cosmetics, and personal care; we are working, designing, and innovating for you. This is our raison d'etre.

---

tion, which had become a compulsory organization under government control. Nevertheless, while Puig manufactured and sold perfumes in Spain, the company was able to maintain its connections to the European perfume industry. Puig had close ties to the German manufacturer Muhlens, known for its No. 4711 brand of toilet water. Muhlens represented Puig's products in Germany in the 1940s. In the 1950s, some of the strictures on the Spanish economy began to relax, and Puig began to explore more international marketing.

Growth Outside Spain in the 1950s and 1960s

By the mid-1950s, Antonio Puig had been joined in the business by his four sons—Antonio, Mariano, Jose Maria, and Enrique. The Puig sons were all educated at a Spanish business college called IESE, which was modeled after Harvard's business school. Puig and his sons began traveling, meeting with Spanish contacts in France, the United States, and elsewhere. These exploratory meetings set up export routes for Puig products, though it was years before the company could adequately expand beyond Spain. In the early 1960s, Puig began creating a more international image for its products, hoping to woo markets abroad. Puig worked with the foremost designers in Barcelona, Andre Ricart and Yves Zimmerman. Barcelona soon became a magnet for modern industrial design. The company's new packaging for Lavanda Puig in 1963 won many design awards. The packaging combined traditional Spanish elements, particularly a wooden cap and raffia ties, with a very modern, industrial-looking flask. This became a signature look for Puig products, described by an analyst of the Spanish perfume industry for *Business History* (July 2003) as "Mediterranean urban modernity." The Puig look was Spanish but not old-fashioned, and the company began to make inroads into European and North American markets. Spanish consumers also evidently liked the Puig image, which seemed fresh and urban. Puig launched two successful new products in the 1960s. It brought out Agua Brava in 1968 and Azur de Puig in 1969. These remained best-sellers for the company for decades.

In 1968, Puig began a marketing venture with the French designer Paco Rabanne. Rabanne grew up in France, the son of Spanish immigrants, and was one of the most flamboyant designers of the 1960s. Rabanne's designs were thought too cutting-edge for Spain at the time, but Rabanne helped market Puig's perfumes in France. The company was doing well and invested in 1968 in a new manufacturing facility in Barcelona. Puig also established a base in New York around this time, founding a

subsidiary, Puig International. Then, in the early 1970s, Puig formed a joint venture, named Isdin, with a Barcelona firm called Laboratorios Dr. Esteve, to develop dermatological products. This led to several new skincare brands.

After Franco: Mid-1970s through the 1980s

When Francisco Franco died in 1975, Spain made a remarkably painless transition to a constitutional monarchy under King Juan Carlos. Spain rapidly turned towards Europe, ending its decades of isolation, and the country experienced a wave of modernization and urbanization. Other European countries had dealt with industrial growth and population shifts toward urban centers in the wake of World War II. Spain was in many ways decades behind. Puig seemed to do well in this era. Its innovative packaging gave its brands a strong association with modernity, a good sell in Spain. Yet there was more to Puig than packaging. The company worked with top fragrance designers, and its laboratory was up-to-date and sophisticated. Puig brought out several popular new fragrance lines in the 1970s. These were Moana Bouquet, Estivalia, and Vetiver de Puig.

Antonio Puig died in 1979, and leadership of the company passed to the second generation. The Puig sons had long been active in the company and were ready to continue the firm's gradual expansion into European and North American markets. In 1981, Puig launched one of its most successful products ever—a men's scent called Quorum. Quorum was a hot seller in the 1980s and was eventually one of the best-selling scents in England. It also had strong sales in the United States, where it became one of the top European fragrances on the market. Quorum won a packaging award in the United States in 1982. Puig continued to present an image of Spanish modernity and also linked its brands with the popular Spanish royal family. The company sponsored international sailing races, building the brand's sporty image and spreading the name of Puig products, particularly Agua Brava and Azur de Puig.

Puig had strong marketing in the United States in the 1980s. In men's toiletry, it was known for its Paco Rabanne line as well as for Quorum. In the 1980s, Puig began a relationship with the Venezuelan clothing designer Carolina Herrera. Herrera was thinking about marketing a fragrance when she met a Puig executive in 1984 at a fragrance industry group award ceremony where she was a presenter. She agreed to license her name to Puig. The scent the company produced was a copy of what Herrera herself wore, a fragrance she mixed on her own out of jasmine and tuberose oils. The packaging, in white with black polka dots, reflected a pattern Herrera often used in her clothing. The Herrera scent debuted in 1988 in top-tier U.S. department stores. It also sold in Canada, Puerto Rico, Spain, and the United Kingdom, and later went into other European markets.

Expansion in the 1990s and Beyond

In the 1990s, Antonio Puig, S.A. consolidated its position in Spain and made further inroads into international markets. In the early years of the decade, the company began making more mass-market personal care goods. It introduced a skin care line called Vitesse in 1990 and then developed a bath and shower line called Avena Kinesia and a line of children's colognes and lotions. In 1995, the company acquired another mass-market

Key Dates:

1914:	Antonio Puig founds a company in Barcelona.
1922:	Puig debuts the first Spanish lipstick, Milady.
1939:	The company launches a wholly Spanish eau de cologne, Lavanda Puig.
1968:	Agua Brava brand debuts.
1981:	The company launches a men's scent, Quorum.
1988:	The first Carolina Herrerra perfume is introduced.
1995:	The company acquires a majority of Spanish rival Perfumeria Gal.
2000:	Puig acquires another domestic rival, Myrurgia.

Spanish bath and shower line, Genesse. Puig also began distributing the personal care products line of U.S. company Bristol-Myers Squibb in Spain in the early 1990s. Puig also sold over-the-counter dermatological preparations and sun screens through Isdin, its joint venture with Laboratorios Dr. Esteve. By the mid-1990s, Isdin was the market leader, with a share of almost 40 percent of the Spanish sun screen market and over 50 percent of the acne preparations market.

The company put out new scents in both men's and women's lines. Carolina Herrerra brought out a men's fragrance in 1991. This became a top-seller in Spain and also did well in the United States. Paco Rabanne had a strong line of men's scents with Paco Rabanne pour Homme and then XS, which debuted in 1993. XS won awards both for its packaging and for the fragrance itself, which sold very well in France and the United Kingdom. Puig continued its association with designers by signing up an Italian duo in 1992, Victorio and Lucchino.

Puig began a joint-marketing agreement with one of its Spanish competitors, the Madrid-based Perfumeria Gal, in 1995. The two companies set up a joint subsidiary to distribute mass-market personal care lines in Latin America. The subsidiary also distributed Puig's fine perfumes in Argentina. Later that year, Puig bought an 85 percent interest in Perfumeria Gal. Gal was, like Puig, an old family company. It was established in 1901, and since 1905 it had marketed one of Spain's best-known brands, the soap Heno de Pravia. Gal had had strong marketing in Mexico and Latin America in the 1920s, though this decayed in the Franco years. Gal's Heno de Pravia brand had as much as a 70 percent share of the Spanish toilet soap market, and this remained the company's top seller into the 1990s. Puig's acquisition of Gal gave it a much stronger position in the domestic mass market. It also gave Puig inroads into Gal's Latin American distribution. Worldwide sales for Puig rose to $500 million by 1997.

The Perfumeria Gal acquisition was followed by several others. In 1998, Puig bought the French fashion firm the Ricci Group. The Ricci Group comprised Nina Ricci Perfumes and Nina Ricci Couture. Puig had been associated with Nina Ricci since its earliest years, when Antonio Puig had imported Ricci scents from Paris. Ricci's most famous scents included Deci Dela and L'Air du Temps. Shortly after the Ricci acquisition, Puig announced a change in management. The four Puig brothers stepped down in 1998, and the company was then run by a team of three of their sons and Javier Cano. Cano was the first chief executive to come from outside Puig family ranks. After this, Puig moved quickly, hoping to double its sales by the middle of the next decade. In 2000, the company bought another long-time Spanish competitor, Myrurgia. Founded in 1916, Myrurgia was also a Barcelona perfumery. It had been in family hands, like Puig and Perfumeria Gal, through three generations. It made fine perfumes and had a strong export business, particularly in Latin America. Some of its classic perfumes were Maja and Joya. With this acquisition, Puig gained a leading share in the Spanish perfume market and rivaled the giant French firm L'Oreal in other cosmetics and body care market niches.

L'Oreal, which was the largest player in the Spanish market, was a truly global company. Puig began to take on a similar scale in the 2000s as it pressed into more export markets. By 2000, more of its sales came from abroad than from Spain. France and the United States were the firm's best markets. Puig gained in Germany, too, after its purchase of Myrurgia, which had a German perfume division, Etienne Aigner. Worldwide sales in 2001 were estimated at $783 million. Puig continued its association with Carolina Herrerra in the 2000s. Her scents were big sellers worldwide. In 2002, Puig signed licensing agreements with three more leading designers. The company first snagged Hussein Chalayan, a young Turkish designer who worked in London. Chalayan was a rising star who had never done a fragrance before. Later that year, Puig negotiated a joint venture with the Italian design firm Prada to distribute both perfumes and skin care products under the Prada name. Prada was one of the most prestigious European design houses of the 1990s. Next, Puig signed an exclusive licensing agreement with Comme des Garcons Parfums. Comme des Garcons was a cutting-edge Parisian design firm with a dedicated following in Japan, France, and the United States. Comme des Garcons already had an established perfume line, and in 2000 it had opened its first freestanding perfume shop. The arrangement with Puig called for opening more Comme des Garcons perfumeries worldwide. Puig would also give wider distribution to Comme des Garcons' fragrance lines. Puig's long-term business plan called for strengthening its position in prestige perfumes. These three new arrangements with designers gave Puig a much larger stable of names and talent.

Also in 2002, the company reorganized in order to focus more on coming growth. Puig planned to double sales by 2006. The firm divided into three main divisions, Puig Prestige Beauty Brands, Puig Fragrance & Personal Care, and Fashion. The company name changed to Puig Beauty and Fashion Group S.L. Fashion was by far the smallest division, accounting for some 3 percent of sales, and included the Ricci couture house and the non-fragrance lines of Carolina Herrerra and Paco Rabanne. The Prestige Beauty Brands division accounted for about 47 percent of overall sales. Puig hoped to increase its sales in North America. The Fragrance & Personal Care division, which comprised Puig's mass-market brands, grew rapidly with the addition of Myrurgia and Perfumeria Gal. Puig bought the remaining outstanding shares of Gal in 2002, making the firm a wholly owned subsidiary. About 70 percent of mass-market sales were made in Spain, but Puig believed its products had strong export potential, particularly in Latin America. Puig planned to speed its international growth and also looked to make more acquisitions over the next several years.

Principal Subsidiaries

Puig USA; Puig Codina S.A.; Myrurgia S.A.; Perfumeria Gal, S.A.; Sucesora de Jose Puig y Cia C.A. (Venezuela); Isdin; Creaciones Victorio & Lucchino; Genesse Hispania; Veritas; Accesoria Selecta S.A.

Principal Divisions

Puig Prestige Beauty Brands; Puig Fragrance & Personal Care; Puig Fashion.

Principal Competitors

L'Oreal S.A.; Chanel S.A.; LVMH Moet Hennessy Louis Vuitton S.A.

Further Reading

"Antonio Puig: At the Leading Edge of Spanish C&T," *European Cosmetic Markets*, June 1994, p. 233.

Born, Pete, "Puig to Test U.S. Waters with Sybaris," *WWD*, July 27, 1990, p. 11.

Corson, Alice, "Antonio Puig, Family Roots Meet Global Vision," *European Cosmetic Markets*, December 2000, p. 497.

"Deci Dela? Sanofi Sells Ricci to Puig," *Cosmetics International*, January 10, 1998, p. 1.

"Puig Extends Its Reign in Spain," *Soap Perfumery & Cosmetics*, August 2000, p. 5.

Puig, Nuria, "The Search for Identity: Spanish Perfume in the International Market," *Business History*, July 2003, p. 90.

Raper, Sarah, "A Younger Generation Takes Over at Puig," *WWD*, June 19, 1998, p. 1.

Weil, Jennifer, "Chalayan Signs Scent Deal," *WWD*, January 11, 2002, p. 14.

——, "Puig, Comme des Garcons in Deal," *WWD*, September 13, 2002, p. 6.

——, "Puig's 5-Year Plan on Track," *WWD*, January 18, 2002, p. 10.

——, "New Scents Top Puig Growth Plans for 2003," *WWD*, January 31, 2003, p. 6.

Wiest, Robin, "Carolina Herrerra Sets Scent's Debut," *WWD*, February 19, 1988, p. 6.

Zargani, Lisa, and Amanda Kaiser, "Prada in Beauty Joint Venture," *WWD*, June 17, 2002, p. 2.

—A. Woodward

RAG AG

Rellinghauserstrasse 1-11
Postfach 103262
45128 Essen
Germany
Telephone: (0201) 177 01
Fax: (0201) 177 34 75
Web site: http://www.rag.de

Private Company
Incorporated: 1968
Employees: 87,500
Sales: EUR 13 billion ($13.62 billion) (2002)
NAIC: 212111 Bituminous Coal and Lignite Surface
   Mining; 212112 Bituminous Coal Underground
   Mining; 213113 Support Activities for Coal Mining

RAG AG, formerly known as Ruhrkohle AG, is the largest coal-producing company in Germany. The conglomerate has a plethora of holdings focused mainly on domestic and international coal mining, chemicals, and real estate. Its largest subsidiaries include Deutsche Steinkohle AG, which oversees its domestic coal and coking mining activities; RAG Coal International AG, its international mining arm; Rütgers AG, which is responsible for its chemicals and plastics operations; and RAG Immobilien, the company's real estate and construction concern. Prompted by deterioration and changes in Germany's coal mining and energy sectors, RAG was forced to implement significant restructuring efforts during the 1990s and into the new century. During 2003, the company was in the process of acquiring a majority stake in Degussa AG, the world's largest specialty chemicals manufacturer.

Origins

Ruhrkohle's foundation came about in several stages. It was brought into being on November 27, 1968, by 19 companies in the Ruhr area, which held the largest coal resources in Germany. This foundation was provisional; since the Grundvertrag (Articles of Association) had not yet been signed. This contract was concluded on July 18, 1969; the parties to it were the Federal Republic of Germany, that is, the federal government; 23 mining companies, which had declared their willingness to enter into the treaty; and the company Ruhrkohle AG itself.

The foundation of the company had come about mainly as a result of political pressure but on a private basis. Not all of the 26 independently operating, privately structured companies in the Ruhr coal field were willing to submit to this massive exertion of political influence. Ruhrkohle's commercial structure was without parallel in Germany. Although the company was run according to the principles of private enterprise, it was dependent on support from the state from its beginnings. This support was given mainly in the form of subsidies but also through laws protecting German coal interests in some sectors.

The evolution of Ruhrkohle AG should be understood in the context of the development of West Germany's energy policy after the end of World War II. In the years immediately after the war, German coal was a highly sought-after commodity. In the years of hunger before the currency reform in 1948, miners—or Kumpel, as they were known—received special grocery rations to enable them to carry out their heavy work. They were also given special advantages in looking for accommodation in the towns of the Ruhr area, which had suffered great destruction during the war. The largest of these towns were Essen, Duisburg, Bochum, and Dortmund. The byword of those years was coal production at any price.

The market economy of the 1950s and early 1960s, with liberalized external trade, was introduced by Professor Ludwig Erhard against strong opposition, and formed the basis of the German "economic miracle." At this time an idea was aired which had prevailed in many economic circles in the years immediately after 1945, particularly among the unions and the Social Democratic Party—that the basic industries of coal and steel should be nationalized.

Disaster Strikes in the 1950s

In 1956, disaster struck more or less overnight for the German coal mining industry, which, in the mid-1950s, produced 150 million tons of coal and employed over 600,000 miners. The steady rise in oil consumption, especially in the form of

Company Perspectives:

In pursing a three-pronged strategy of focusing on coal mining, real estate, and chemicals, the RAG Group is laying the groundwork for a secure and prosperous future.

light fuel oil on the heating market and of heavy oil for industrial use, had gone almost unnoticed. As a result, within a relatively short period, coal stockpiles had grown so big that short-time work had to be introduced extensively for the miners in 1958 in order to prevent these stockpiles, suddenly unsaleable, from reaching the sky. Coal, so long in demand, which had been particularly sought after in the early postwar years, could now find no buyers. As late as 1957, when 133 million tons of coal were produced in the federal republic, the high commission of the European Coal and Steel Community—later to become the European Community—was still demanding a rise in production in Germany of 40 million tons within 20 years.

At first it was believed that the fall in demand at the end of the 1950s was merely a transient economic phenomenon. Yet stockpiles grew to over 15 million tons, and for the first time pit closures had to be considered. At this point, it became clear that this was no short-term economic crisis. It was, rather, a structural crisis based on long-term shifts in demand. Imported oil was, in the long term, much cheaper than German coal and ousted coal from the heating market. Cheaply produced imported coal, especially from the United States, forced its way into the growing German industrial and heating markets.

Confronted with the prospect of multiple pit closures in the German coal fields—the Ruhr accounted for around 70 to 75 percent of coal production in the Federal Republic—as well as by protest demonstrations by miners, public demand for a coal and energy plan grew. Increasing weight was given to the suggestion that the mining industry of the Ruhr area, which at the beginning of the 1960s still consisted of around 30 independent private companies, should be brought together in a single company or group.

More than a dozen plans were proposed in those years to rehabilitate the coal industry. Yet all these plans had a common focus in the assertion that the sharp reduction in work force numbers, which would have to be faced, must take place in a socially acceptable manner.

From 1958 to the end of 1990, during which time the number of employees in the German coal mining industry declined from 607,000 to around 130,000, not a single miner was dismissed via the unemployment office. All the affected miners received special state support payments, whether these took the form of compensation, pension supplements, or some other type of payment. Support was given not only to the miners affected by pit closures but also to the companies, which received millions of marks worth of finance from the state. These payments were given in the form of closure premiums; that is, the companies received a certain sum of money when they closed pits with the aim of adjusting the overcapacity to the sharply reduced overall demand.

Federal governments attempted to get a grip on the retreat of the coal industry; since its disordered beginnings, it had already swallowed billions of marks. Too many attempts had been made to cure the symptoms with restrictions on coal imports, agreements of voluntary restrictions with the oil industry, the promotion of coal-fired power stations, and taxes on fuel oil. Finally, in 1967–68, the measures which had been taken to reconcile coal production and demand were standardized and new targets were formulated.

The Coal Adjustment Law of 1968

In May 1968, the Kohleanpassungsgesetz—"coal adjustment law"—was passed. The basis of the law was that optimal cost effectiveness was only possible in a single company; in this way, the pits which were least profitable would be closed. Individual closures in over 30 separate companies might prevent the continued functioning of relatively profitable pits while allowing unprofitable pits to survive. Measures to concentrate the coal businesses therefore formed the core of the Kohleanpassungsgesetz. As the government's most important instrument in achieving this aim, the law laid the foundations for the removal of a series of privileges which had hitherto been granted, especially the high premiums for pit closures and the subsidies for coke production. It was this legal threat above all—that subsidies would be withdrawn from companies below the optimal size after January 1, 1969—which hastened the process of concentration and thus the foundation of Ruhrkohle AG. Without subsidies, practically any mining company operating at this time was condemned to a swift demise, which continued to be the case into the 1990s.

During the foundation phase of Ruhrkohle AG, the concept of optimal size became a magic formula. The fact that no one defined it exactly, not even the government, made it seem all the more ominous for the independent survival of most small and medium-sized companies. The law defined it simply as "such size as is necessary to achieve the greatest possible economic efficiency."

In the public sphere, this abstract threat was received exactly as it was meant by the politicians, who were tired of throwing good money after bad, namely as a means of exerting pressure, to drive the hesitant pits to join a common company in the Ruhr. There were to be no subsidies without "optimal size," that is, the merger of the coal companies—all of them if possible—to form a single company.

The two largest coal mining companies on the Ruhr, the Gelsenkirchener Bergwerks AG (Gelsenberg) and the Bergswerksgesellschaft Hibernia, part of the Veba group, made renewed efforts to achieve concentration in the form of a conventional merger of the two businesses. Investigations as to the viability of a merger had already taken place earlier. The miners' union IG Bergbau und Energie had demanded that such a company be created—with as strong a state influence as possible—for a long time.

After lengthy negotiations, the Grundvertrag was, as stated, signed in July 1969; this formed the basis of the existence and business activities of Ruhrkohle AG. The parent companies undertook to provide Ruhrkohle AG with a share capital of DM

Key Dates:

1968: The coal adjustment law is passed; nineteen companies in the Ruhr area combine to form Ruhrkohle AG.

1969: The Grundvertrag—the articles of association for Ruhrkohle—are signed.

1989: The company acquires a majority stake in coal mining firm Eschweiler Bergwerks-Verein (EBV).

1997: The company changes its name to RAG AG.

1998: RAG takes control of Saarbergwerke AG and renames it Deutsche Steinkohle AG (DSK).

1999: Preussag Anthrazit GmbH is added to DSK's holdings in a move that consolidates all of Germany's mining activities under one corporate umbrella.

2002: The European Union Council of Energy Ministers sets forth new regulations for state aid for the German coal industry through 2010; plans are set in motion to acquire a majority interest in Degussa AG.

600 million. Ruhrkohle AG and the parent companies made Einbringungsverträge, or contribution agreements. The members of the work force had to be kept on. A provision of the Grundvertrag stated that ''profit is not the principal aim of Ruhrkohle AG.''

Thus the parent companies made various financial commitments. Although they could not, according to the company's Articles of Association, expect a profit from the capital they had invested, they were to be paid interest on their contributions at a rate of 6 percent. The government also took on extensive commitments, initially giving guarantees of up to DM 2.2 billion, two-thirds from the federation and one-third from the state of Nordrhein-Westphalen.

These founding arrangements were accompanied by two treaties which were vital to the company's existence: the Hüttenvertrag, regulating the agreement between Ruhrkohle and the seven steel-producing Ruhr groups which had brought their pits into the joint company, and the power-station treaties, or agreements with the electricity supply businesses. Both were essentially concerned with competitive prices: Ruhrkohle had to supply the steel companies with coal at world market prices, and public money would be paid to compensate for any difference.

For sales of coal to power stations, the electricity consumers would pay the difference between the price of the expensive Ruhr coal and cheaper imported coal—or oil—in the form of the Kohlepfennig, or ''coal penny.'' This amount would be added to the bill of each individual consumer.

Complaints were made from the beginning by all parties, and especially by the managers of Ruhrkohle themselves, that this company, which was eventually joined by 26 of the 28 mining companies on the Ruhr, had been brought to life in ''skeletonized'' form, stripped of its assets, without the large, productive, and thoroughly profitable power stations and above all without the valuable land holdings which the companies, some of them well over a century old, had accumulated over time. Apart from the land needed for operational purposes, none

of this extensive property had remained under the ownership of Ruhrkohle AG.

Upon its creation, Ruhrkohle was structured as a private enterprise but was unable to exist without the support of the state, unless energy prices were extremely high, around $35 for a barrel of oil. It had to operate as efficiently as it could, and it could not, according to its constitution, make any profit. It was forced to manage itself alone as far as possible, yet it was not allowed to undertake all that it wished. The state—the Federal Ministry of Economics—ensured that nothing was undertaken outside the company's main area of operation, the production of coal, and which could involve any risk. This restriction was meant to prevent the need for additional subsidy requirements. The former owners, the Altgesellschafter, paid close attention to ensuring that Ruhrkohle did not become a competitor in sectors in which they were active—for example, in certain trading and service sectors, such as waste management. The principal companies concerned here were Veba AG, with a shareholding of 39.2 percent; the electricity supply company Vereinigte Elektrizitätswerke Westfalen AG, with 30.2 percent; Thyssen Stahl AG, with 12.7 percent; and Hoesch AG, with 7.2 percent.

From its inception, Ruhrkohle AG has been a company unlike others of its kind, and continues to be so. The company had a bad start. In 1969, its first year of operation, it had to overcome a loss of DM 330 million, which used up more than half of its share capital. According to the laws governing shares, this loss should have been reported and an extraordinary shareholders' meeting should have been called. However, Heinz P. Kemper, the first chairman of the supervisory board and formerly chairman of Veba's management board, together with the first chairman of the management board Hans-Helmut Kuhnke, was able to reduce the loss to DM 199 million and thereby to gain time. This was achieved through what Kemper called ''accounting policy measures.'' When a steel crisis developed in 1971, leading to a dramatic reduction in sales to the steel industry—which, along with the electricity industry, was the largest purchaser of Ruhr coal—it became essential to strengthen the company's weak capital base. Otherwise bankruptcy would have been inevitable, with incalculable consequences for the 170,000 employees. Again a joint action resulted: the shareholders decided to forego, in part, the interest income owed to them, amounting to approximately DM 700 million. Also, the government conceded a debt register claim, which the company was to pay back if it made profits, of DM 1 billion.

Although the company's financing and balance-sheet arrangements were stabilized, it became clear that Ruhrkohle AG could not become competitive in the long term, even with the most modern mining technology and the continual adaptation of its production to demand, because of difficulties presented by the nature of German coal deposits. Kuhnke, his successor Karlheinz Bund, and Heinz Horn, chairman of the management board of Ruhrkohle AG since 1985, emphasized the company's function in ensuring the coal supply, embodied in the three energy programs produced by the federal government after 1973. The theory of a necessary safe base provided by German coal in the face of Germany's very high dependence on imported oil and gas for its energy requirements, has for many years been an important, and controversial, component of Germany's energy policy.

In the late 1980s and early 1990s, the European Commission made repeated interventions. The commission underlined the incompatibility of German coal subsidies with policies within the European Community—subsidies without which Ruhrkohle could not survive. In reaction, the German government produced another program to adapt production to demand and thus to reduce the need for subsidy payments, which at the time amounted to DM 8 billion to DM 10 billion per year as a result of low world energy prices and the low U.S. dollar rate. Ruhrkohle AG was hopeful that the union of East and West Germany would result in additional markets for coal in the five new federal states, although energy experts warned that such expectations should not be too high.

During this time, Ruhrkohle continued to strengthen its coal-related holdings. The Eschweiler Bergwerks-Verein (EBV) become one of the firm's newest subsidiaries. Ruhrkohle took a majority stake (97 percent) in the long-established coal-mining company on the Aachen coal field in 1988–89. In 1989, EBV produced approximately 4.2 million tons of coal and achieved a turnover of DM 1.9 billion. A second investment in the coal sector followed, also within the framework of Ruhrkohle's goals in coal politics, when the group took over 99.72 percent of Sophia Jacoba GmbH at Hückelhoven, from the Robeco Group of the Netherlands, on January 1, 1990. Sophia Jacoba was essentially an anthracite mine, with production of around 1.7 million tons in 1989 and a turnover of DM 570 million.

The long-term survival of Ruhrkohle appeared certain in the early 1990s, even with the prospect of a reduction in coal production in the federal republic in the years to come, following the recommendations of a state commission that production should stand at between 45 and 55 million tons annually, rather than 70 million tons. Despite the high, economically controversial subsidies needed by Ruhrkohle AG, a halt to coal production in Germany did not appear imminent, as was the case in some neighboring western countries in past years.

Changes in the 1990s and Beyond

Germany's coal problems continued to remain a political hot topic well into the 1990s. By 1993, German crude steel production was faltering, which in turn led to diminished demand for Ruhrkohle's coal. The following year, the company reduced its output capacity by three million tones. At the same time, Germany as a whole was determining where its future energy sources should come from—coal, nuclear resources, or imported coal and gas. At the end of 1993, the European Commission drafted new grant legislation for the hard coal mining industry that was effective through July 23, 2002. The German government also created a new "Articles Act" which allowed for the use of German hard coal for electricity generation from 1996 through 2005. At the same time, however, German utilities were deregulating, which allowed those companies to seek out alternative sources of energy.

In order to keep pace with changing times, Ruhrkohle began to diversify its holdings in the mid-1990s by branching out into non-mining-related fields. By 1996, the company reported that for the first time in its history, its non-coal businesses secured a higher turnover than its coal mining operations. Overall, Ruhrkohle began to morph into a diversified conglomerate. The company marked this transition by changing its name to RAG AG in 1997.

By 1998, RAG had taken control of Saarbergwerke AG and renamed it Deutsche Steinkohle AG (DSK). Preussag Anthrazit GmbH was added to DSK's holdings the following year in a move that consolidated all of Germany's mining activities under one corporate umbrella. By this time, German coal production had fallen to 46 million tons and was expected to drop to 30 million tones in the next few years, while the number of active coal mines was anticipated to drop to just ten or eleven.

As German's coal market faltered, RAG looked to the international scene for growth. In 1999, the company—through its RAG Coal International subsidiary—acquired Colorado-based Cyprus Amax Coal Co. It also purchased a 95 percent stake in the Burton Coal Joint Venture, a coking coal mine based in Australia. The company continued to fight against cutbacks in subsidies that under current laws were ensured until 2005. These subsidies were to be reduced from DM 10.4 billion per year to DM 5.3 billion by 2005. RAG management as well as industry employees felt that the subsidies needed to stay at current levels to ensure RAG's future. According to a 2000 *Handelsblatt* article, "RAG's existence, including its non-mining activities trade, power generation, process technology, chemicals, plastics, and the environment would come under threat if no compromise on subsidies to Germany's coal industry was reached." Karl Starzacher, RAG's chairman at the time, commented that unless a compromise was met, "it would mean the end of hard-coal mining in Germany." In December of 2000, the European Commission authorized state aid for the industry for 2000 and 2001.

During the early 2000s, RAG operated in a dramatically different fashion than it had in its past. The company continued to make strategic moves to ensure its future viability. In 2002, the company acquired the shares of Steag AG that had been previously owned by RWE AG and E.ON AG. The deal allowed RAG to assume full control over Germany's second-largest coal-fired power plant operator. More importantly, the company made a play for specialty chemicals group Degussa AG as part of its strategy to move into high growth areas. The deal was expected to be completed in 2004.

In June 2002, the European Union Council of Energy Ministers set forth new regulations for state aid for the German coal industry through 2010. This new regulation was adopted just as the treaty that originally established the European Coal and Steel Community, which allowed for the granting of state aid to the coal industry, expired.

Conditions in the German coal mining industry continued to weigh heavily on RAG's operations. As such, the company set a strategy in place to focus on three main business areas: mining, real estate, and chemicals. As part of its focus, it planned to sell off its interests in power generation and gas and its plastics holdings. While the future of German coal mining remained uncertain, RAG appeared to be on track for growth in the years to come as a diversified conglomerate.

Principal Subsidiaries

Deutsche Steinkohle AG; RAG Coal International AG; RAG Immobilien AG; Rütgers AG; Steag AG; RAG Saarberg AG; RAG Bildung Gmbh; RAG Informatik GmbH; RAG Versicherungs-Dienst GmbH.

Principal Competitors

BHP Billiton Ltd.; CONSOL Energy Inc.; Peabody Energy Corporation.

Further Reading

"Coal Mines Close, Domestic Mining Industry Fades," *Coal Week International*, March 5, 2001, p. 5.

"German Coal Plan Will Boost Imports," *Coal Week International*, March 18, 1997, p. 1.

"Germany's Ruhrkohle Confident for Subsidy-Free Future," *European Energy Report*, July 5, 1996, p. 19.

"Labor Unrest Faces Ruhrkohle," *The Mining Journal*, September 24, 1993, p. 217.

Payne, Mark, "German Coal," *Mining Magazine*, June 1999, p. 293.

Peel, Quentin, "Future of German Energy Industry in Doubt," *Financial Times*, October 29, 1993, p. 2.

"RAG Sees Existence under Threat Without Subsidies Coal Mining," *Handelsblatt*, October 23, 2000.

"RAG to Get Control of Degussa in Complex Deal with E.ON," *Chemical Market Reporter*, May 27, 2002, p. 2.

"Ruhrkohle Adapts to Changes; Sees Big Gain in Imports," *Coal Week International*, July 4, 1995, p. 1.

"Ruhrkohle Reconfigures Itself for Life After Subsidies," *Coal Week International*, March 3, 1998, p. 2.

Spiegelberg, Friedrich, *Ein Geschäft im Wandel, 10 Jahre Kohlenkrise*, Baden-Baden: Nomors, 1970.

Stein, George, "Germany Reassures Hard-Coal Industry," *Journal of Commerce*, June 16, 1993, p. 5C.

Wiel, Paul, *Wirtschaftsgeschichte des Ruhrgebiets, Siedlungsverband Ruhrkohlenbezirk*, 1970.

—Heiner Radzio
—update: Christina M. Stansell

Red Bull GmbH

Brunn 115
A-5330 Fuschl am See
Austria
Telephone: (+43) 662 65 82-0
Fax: (+43) 662 65 82-31
Web site: http://www.redbull.at

Private Company
Incorporated: 1984 as Red Bull GmbH
Employees: 1500
Sales: EUR 1.15 billion ($1.32 billion) (2002)
NAIC: 312111 Soft Drink Manufacturing

Red Bull GmbH produces the world's leading energy drink. More than a billion cans a year are sold in nearly 100 countries. Red Bull holds a 70 percent share of the world market for energy drinks, or functional beverages, a category it was largely responsible for building. Its dominant position in the fastest-growing segment of the soft drink market in a number of countries has drawn a number of imitators. Red Bull has become a case study in successful guerilla marketing in the United States and United Kingdom. Marketing is aimed at hip young people with active lifestyles, though the formula began as a popular tonic for blue collar workers in Thailand.

Globetrotting Origins

Dietrich Mateschitz was born in 1946, a native of the Styria (Steiermark) region of Austria. As a student in Vienna, he studied world trade and commerce. After graduating, he worked for Unilever, then Blendax, a German manufacturer of toothpaste. This position involved much global travel.

In 1982, Mateschitz visited Thailand and brought home with him a number of energy drinks he sampled there. According to *The Economist,* Mateschitz was sold on a product called Krating Daeng after it took away his jet lag. He later claimed to consume up to eight of the drinks a day.

Krating Daeng, which is Thai for "Red Bull," was a drink popular among cab drivers and other blue collar workers. It had been produced since the early 1970s by the T.C. Pharmaceutical Co., founded in Thailand in 1962 by Chaleo Yoovidhya, a Blendax licensee. (T.C. Pharmaceutical eventually formed the subsidiary Red Bull Beverage Co. Ltd.)

Mateschitz founded Red Bull GmbH in Austria in 1984 as a 49 percent partner with Chaleo Yoovidhya and his son. The company began marketing its namesake drink in Austria in 1987; a million cans were sold in the year.

The original formula was altered for Western palates. Some ingredients were dropped and carbonation was added. Components of the legendary elixir included B vitamins, glucuronolactone, sodium, and caffeine. One ingredient, the amino acid taurine, was derived synthetically, not from bull testicles, as rumor had it. Red Bull's selling proposition was that it increased stamina and mental concentration, making it a natural for one of the original target users, long-distance drivers. The taste of the thick yellow beverage, said to be akin to liquid gummi bears, lent added distinction to the brand.

International Expansion in the 1990s

Red Bull's distribution expanded into neighboring countries Hungary and Slovenia in 1992. Red Bull was introduced in Germany in March 1994. By June, it was claiming a quarter of the sports drink market there, reported the Associated Press, putting it ahead of Gatorade. It was priced about three times as much as a can of Coca-Cola. Red Bull was introduced in the United Kingdom in 1994 and marketed there as Red Bull Stimulation after 1996.

Red Bull entered the United States in 1997, focusing at first on four western states: California, Oregon, Texas, and Colorado. It was marketed to Americans as a non-corporate alternative to Coke and Pepsi, and both packaging and pricing helped set it apart. The drink was sold in unique, narrow 8.3-ounce cans for $2 a pop.

Red Bull associated itself with the nascent extreme sports movement. The company sponsored snowboarding and freeskiing contests and Flugtag, a homemade flying machine challenge (Mateschitz was an enthusiastic collector of vintage aircraft).

Company Perspectives:

Red Bull is much more than a soft drink—it is an energy drink. It was made for moments of increased physical and mental stress and improves endurance, alertness, concentration, and reaction speed. In short: it vitalizes body and mind. The effectiveness of Red Bull Energy Drink has been proven by a large number of scientific studies and is appreciated by many of the world's top athletes and drivers, opinion-leaders and hard-working people with active lifestyles.

Key Dates:

1982: Dietrich Mateschitz samples Krating Daeng, a Thai energy drink.
1984: Beverage producer Red Bull GmbH is founded in Austria.
1987: Red Bull's product begins sales in Austria.
1992: Red Bull GmbH expands to its first foreign markets.
1997: Red Bull enters the U.S. market via California.
2003: Red Bull Sugarfree is introduced.

While Red Bull had appealed to athletes and, in the United States, tired white collar workers, the real story of Red Bull's growth lay in the promise of further endurance at clubbing, giving it a special appeal for young people exhausted from working hard all week. The *Los Angeles Times* reported that the beverage appeared to glow green under the fluorescent light of nightclubs. The drink became a very popular mixer, especially with vodka. Red Bull deepened its involvement with the club scene by sponsoring a month-long school for deejays in New York City called the Red Bull Music Academy.

Worldwide sales were logged at 300 million cans in 1998 by *Beverage World.* By the end of 1999, Red Bull was sold in more than 50 countries, and sales estimates varied between 600 million and one billion cans worldwide. Red Bull led the energy drink category in the United States and the United Kingdom, where it displaced the venerable Lucozade brand owned by pharmaceutical company SmithKline Beecham (later Glaxo-SmithKline).

The company promoted the lift the beverage offered with the slogan "Red Bull gives you wings." Traditional advertising was limited, as the company focused heavily on getting product samples into the right hands. The company sometimes put up edgy, graffiti-style billboards. In the late 1990s, Red Bull produced animated TV ads for mature markets.

By this time, Red Bull GmbH was the most highly valued company in Austria, worth about $11 billion according to one estimate. This made Mateschitz, with his 49 percent holding, the country's richest individual.

Continued Success in the 2000s

Mammoth beverage marketers such as Coca-Cola Co. and Anheuser-Busch were pouring out new drinks designed to capture a share of the success of "cult" energy drinks, a $300 million market. PepsiCo acquired South Beach Beverages, maker of the SoBe brand, in 2000, and Quaker Oats, owner of Gatorade, the next year. Liquor distributors were also eyeing Red Bull's share of the mixer market, introducing pre-mixed premium drinks such as Smirnoff Ice. Former Red Bull employees launched a competitor, Roaring Lion, in 2001, its marketing and distribution tailored for the nightclub market.

Red Bull sued a number of bars for surreptitiously substituting knock-offs when customers ordered mixed drinks specifying Red Bull. Red Bull's Australian distributor rolled out its own competing beverage called LiveWire. A court later found Sydneywide Distributors copied Red Bull's packaging too

closely. The *Bangkok Post* reported that more than a hundred other brands had tried to copy Red Bull's formula in Europe.

Red Bull made its first forays into the southern hemisphere, via South Africa and Brazil, in 2001. In October 2002, Red Bull opened a regional headquarters in Dubai and was planning to build a plant there as well. Red Bull's worldwide sales were estimated at EUR 1.4 billion ($1.32 billion) in 2002.

Much of Red Bull's success in the United States can be attributed to the dedicated, one-brand distribution network operated by the company. Mateschitz set up a separate company to develop and market other drinks, including LunAqua, a New Age brand of water bottled during full moons. A sugar-free version of Red Bull was rolled out in January 2003.

Principal Subsidiaries

Luftfahrzeug-Betriebs GmbH; Red Bull North America Inc.; Red Bull UK.

Principal Competitors

Britvic Soft Drinks Ltd.; Coca-Cola Co.; Hansen Beverage Co.; GlaxoSmithKline; Snapple Beverage Group; South Beach Beverage.

Further Reading

Allen, Arthur, "German Kids Are Bullish on a Wonder Drink," Associated Press, Bus. News, August 19, 1994.
Baca, Ricardo, "Red Bull vs. Lion in Bar-Mixer Duel; Energy Drinks Taking Off the Gloves," *Denver Post*, September 22, 2003, p. F1.
Behar, Hank, "Running of the Bull," *Beverage World*, December 15, 2001, p. 18.
Cassy, John, "Enragingly Ubiquitous: The High Energy Fizz Drink Has Taken a Lead in Trendy Bars as a Vodka Mixer But Can It Stay the Pace in the Full Light of Day?" *Guardian* (Manchester, United Kingdom), City Sec., June 26, 2001, p. 21.
Chura, Hillary, "Grabbing Bull by Tail," *Advertising Age*, June 11, 2001, pp. 4f.
"Energy Pumps up Soft Drinks Trade," *Sunday Business Post* (Ireland), December 5, 1999.
"Entrepreneur Took the Bull by Its Horns," *Des Moines Business Record*, December 17, 2001, p. 4.
"Exec Welcomes the Bull," *Houston Chronicle*, Bus. Sec., July 30, 2000, p. 1.
Goodman, Matthew, "Fast-Consolidating Food, Drinks Industry Targets British Energy Drinks," *Sunday Business* (London), October 1, 2000.
Hall, Alan, and Steve Bird, "Magical Formula Found in Bangkok," *Times* (London), Overseas News, July 12, 2001, p. 3.

Hein, Kenneth, "A Bull's Market," *Brandweek*, May 28, 2001, p. 21.

——, "Red Bull Charging Ahead," *Brandweek*, October 15, 2001, p. M38.

Huffstutter, P.J., "Red Bull's Buzz Rides Tech Bust; The Energy Drink, Hyped as a Powerful Stimulant, Is a Favorite Among Dot-Commers Struggling to Survive," *Los Angeles Times*, July 2001, p. A1.

Intarakomalyasut, Nondhanada, "Trendy Brits Get Kicks Out of Red Bull: Energy Drink Takes Market by the Horns," *Bangkok Post*, November 22, 2000, p. 10.

——, "Red Bull Extra Repositions Itself as Mixer to Lure Youth," *Bangkok Post*, May 22, 2003.

Johnson, Branwell, "Has the Energy Drinks Market Lost Its Fizz?" *Marketing Week*, August 29, 2002, p. 18.

Kositchotethana, Boonsong, "Red Bull Charging," *Bangkok Post*, August 29, 2003.

Lawton, Christopher, "Marketer Battles Bars Serving Phony Red Bull," *Wall Street Journal*, September 24, 2003, p. B1.

McCarthy, Michael, "Big Players to Offer Own Energy Drinks; Companies Look to Copy Success of Cult Beverages," *USA Today*, August 28, 2000, p. 5B.

Monaghan, Gabrielle, "Red Bull's Bad Image Makes It a Hot Pop; Austrian Power Drink Thrives on Rumors," *Plain Dealer* (Cleveland), July 30, 2000, p. 1H.

Oram, Roderick, "The Kick Inside," *Financial Times* (London), October 10, 1996, p. 19.

Ortiz, Vikki, "Energy Drink Is All the Buzz," *Milwaukee Journal Sentinel*, January 7, 2001, p. 1A.

Potterton, Louise, "Red Bull Gives Its Creator Financial Wings," *Scotland on Sunday*, July 30, 2000, p. 23.

Rahman, Saifur, "Red Bull Plans to Set Up Dubai Plant," *Gulf News*, April 6, 2003.

"Red Bull CEO Takes Foot off Gas," *Nation* (Thailand), November 26, 2001.

"Red Bull Sets Sights Up-Market," *Bangkok Post*, July 12, 2001.

"Red Bull Swaps Wings for Wheels in Bid for F1 Team," *Marketing*, June 27, 2002, p. 1.

"Red Bull Takes Extreme Sports by the Horns," *Brandweek*, January 22, 2001, p. 18.

"Red Bull's Roar Heard in America," *Bangkok Post*, March 14, 2002, p. 1.

Rohwedder, Cacilie, "Teens at the Center of a New Red Scare Sweeping Germany," *Wall Street Journal*, August 15, 1994, p. A7G.

"Sales of Red Bull Beverage in the United States Grow to 10.5 Million Cases," *Bangkok Post*, March 14, 2002.

Schmidt, Lucinda, "Copycats Trip Over Spitting Images: Big Brands, after a Landmark Court Win, Have a New Weapon Against Imitators," *Business Review Weekly*, November 7, 2002, pp. 74ff.

"Selling Energy; Face Value," *Economist* (United States), May 11, 2002.

"The Supply Structure," *Market Intelligence*, July 2001, pp. 13ff.

"Thai Businessman Chaleo Yoovidhya Joins Billionaires' Ranks," *Bangkok Post*, March 1, 2003.

Walker, Rob, "Bull Marketing," *Australian Financial Review*, August 31, 2002, p. 41.

—Frederick C. Ingram

Rose Acre Farms, Inc.

Rural Route 5
Seymour, Indiana 47274
U.S.A.
Telephone: (812) 497-2557
Fax: (812) 497-3311
Web site: http://www.roseacrefarms.com

Private Company
Incorporated: 1939
Employees: 800
Sales: $280 million (2001 est.)
NAIC: 112310 Chicken Egg Production; 311999 All
      Other Miscellaneous Food Manufacturing

Rose Acre Farms, Inc. is the second largest egg producer in the United States. Operating from a string of large chicken farms in the Midwest, the firm supplies grocers around the country with fresh eggs, and also makes dried and liquid egg products for foodservice use. Lois Rust, the ex-wife of company patriarch David Rust, owns a 49 percent stake in the firm and runs it with their seven children.

Origins

The beginnings of Rose Acre Farms date to 1939, when the Rust family began operating a farm near Seymour, Indiana. In addition to growing vegetables like sweet corn, they soon built three hen houses that could hold 900 chickens. In 1943 son David Rust graduated from high school and began selling the family's eggs and corn at a farmer's market 70 miles north in Indianapolis. Over the next few years the Rusts' egg-laying operations were expanded, until 3,000 dozen eggs per week were being produced for sale to grocery stores. In 1955 they added a new, larger chicken house, and by 1965 Rose Acre Farms had 100,000 hens, which were known in the industry as layers. This number continued to grow, topping the one million mark in 1975. By this time David Rust had taken full control of the business.

Rust, who had married in the late 1950s and with his wife Lois had seven children, found himself in a mid-life crisis in the early 1980s. In 1984, at the age of 58, he decided he wanted "more children and more chickens," as he later told *Crain's Chicago Business*. Leaving his wife, he took up with a one-time Polish exchange student, and also announced plans to add one new egg farm every year for the next ten years. Each facility, which would cost $10 million to build, was to house more than 1.6 million hens. Funding for the expansion came from a combination of bank loans, an industrial development bond issue, and Rust himself.

Rust was well known for his eccentric behavior, which extended to the way he ran his organization. He paid employees a $100 bonus if they attended monthly quality control meetings or drove a car that was painted eggshell white, and each week gave out a free vacation trip to Florida to his most productive worker. Rose Acre also printed Bible verses on its egg cartons and displayed huge American flags at all of its farms, while Rust himself had a tree house 70 feet above the ground from which he could view the company's main production facility, as well as his childhood home.

By 1987 Rust had built four new farms, three in Indiana and one near Winterset, Iowa, and had also fathered four new children. Rose Acre Farms now had more than eight million layers and was the number two egg producer in the United States. It shipped five million eggs per day and took in revenues of $70 million per year. Two more farms were planned for Iowa, the largest of which would employ 80 and house more than two million hens. The state had courted the firm, eager to bring in new jobs as well as to sell Rose Acre some five million bushels of corn per year for feed.

Rust's success was due in large part to his farms' efficiency, which allowed him to sell eggs for as much as five cents less per dozen than his competitors. The firm reduced costs by vertically integrating production—breeding chicks, milling feed, harvesting, cleaning, sorting, and packing eggs all at the same location and then shipping them in semi-trailers directly to retailers' warehouses. Rose Acre also did not box eggs in packages with grocers' names on them, which interrupted production, and did not have a full-time USDA inspector on site, which would cost extra money but allow packages to be labeled "USDA Grade A." Some grocers, such as leading Chicago chains Jewel Food

Stores and Dominick's Finer Foods, balked at using Rose Acre eggs because of these restrictions, but the firm found many other customers who were not so choosy.

In addition to its stronghold of the Midwest, Rose Acre was now distributing its eggs to much of the rest of the United States. The company's aggressive growth was ruffling the feathers of its competitors, however, and some banded together to fight back. In California a group of egg producers launched a $2.5 million ad campaign that urged consumers to "Buy California," while a group of six midwestern companies sued Rust for alleged violations of federal antitrust laws. In the fall of 1987 a jury agreed with their claim that Rose Acre had used different price structures in different markets, and awarded them $9.3 million, which the law required be tripled to $28 million. A judge later overturned the verdict, however, citing errors in instructions to the jury.

1989: Lois Rust Takes Control

Meanwhile, David Rust's wife Lois, the corporate secretary of Rose Acre Farms, had filed for divorce. In the bitter fight that followed, she aligned with their seven children to wrest control of the company away from its patriarch. Although he would remain a shareholder, in 1989 David Rust was forced out of management, leaving Lois Rust, with a 49 percent ownership stake, to take the company's helm.

Under her leadership, and with the help of her children, Rose Acre soon became a more focused and less eccentric organization. One of her first tasks was overseeing the construction of a new egg-breaker plant at the firm's Cort Acres farm in southern Indiana, which could process eggs into liquid egg product. It was a first step toward what would eventually become a major revenue source for the firm.

In the fall of 1990 eggs produced in six of Rose Acre's Indiana hen houses were linked to an outbreak of salmonella poisoning among 1,000 convention-goers in Chicago, which led the U.S. Agriculture Department to order Rose Acre to stop selling fresh eggs from those facilities. The company was allowed to use them for fertilizer or pasteurize them, but this resulted in its taking a loss on some 700 million eggs. Federal regulators also insisted on a thorough wet-cleaning of the suspect hen houses, which resulted in damage to their electrical wiring. Rose Acre later filed suit against the government for its actions and over strict new regulations that it had imposed for egg production. Several incidents like this one, along with Americans' growing worries about the high level of cholesterol found in eggs, helped drive per-capita egg consumption to a low of 233 in 1990. It had been in decline for years from the 400 recorded when David Rust first started selling eggs.

In spite of these problems, Rose Acre's expansion continued in the early 1990s, with several new facilities added in the northwestern corner of Illinois, including a plant that made dried egg products. In 1992 Rose Acre Farms was ranked the 25th largest firm run by a woman in the United States by *Working Woman* magazine. The company boasted $127 million in annual sales and employed 800.

In early 1993 Rose Acre made a deal to license a patented method of processing liquid eggs with microwaves to extend their shelf life. By this time the company's output of processed eggs had increased dramatically, growing from 5 percent of total sales in 1990 to an estimated 30 percent in 1993. Dried and liquid egg products were favored by institutional customers like schools and hospitals, which preferred them for convenience as well as their reduced potential for salmonella.

Expansion Continuing in the Mid-1990s

In 1994 Rose Acre built a third egg-laying facility in Iowa, which would house 1.5 million hens. The following year the company bought Agri-Foods, Inc. of Hawk Point, Missouri, an egg-laying operation owned by Schnuck Markets, Inc. Agri-Foods had 450,000 layers, which produced ten million eggs annually, and it continued to supply Schnuck with eggs after the sale. Rose Acre would later expand the operation. It was the firm's second facility in Missouri, the other being an egg-breaking and processing plant in Marshall. In addition to fresh, dried, and liquid eggs, Rose Acre was now also marketing brown eggs, organic fertilizer, and processed soybean products. The firm's fresh eggs were sold in 30 states around the United States.

The summer of 1995 brought a heat wave that killed more than 750,000 of Rose Acre's 13 million chickens. In addition to destroying more than 5 percent of the firm's hens, the heat reduced productivity in those that survived, with many of their eggs smaller or rough-shelled. In the heat wave's immediate aftermath, egg prices increased by as much as 50 percent in some areas.

In early 1998 Rose Acre introduced a new egg called Golden Premium that contained seven times the vitamin E of regular eggs and enhanced levels of omega-3 fatty acids. The eggs, which were produced by changing the nutritional content of a chicken's diet, cost a third more than standard ones. A total of 80,000 chickens were initially dedicated to their production. By now, the company's annual revenues stood at $280 million.

In the spring of 1999 Rose Acre began using laser technology to print dates on eggs to indicate when they were laid. The move came in the wake of a story that had aired on NBC that showed unsold eggs being repackaged by an Ohio egg producer in cartons that had new "sell-by" dates. Rose Acre initially indicated the date an egg was laid, but confusion among the public led to it being changed to a "use-by" date. The firm, which was the first in the country to do so, used a special inkjet printer that could mark 2,400 eggs per minute with food-grade red ink. In addition to the date, the eggs showed a Rose Acre Internet address, www.goodegg.com.

In July of 2001 70,000 Rose Acre chickens were killed in an arson fire that destroyed a hen house at one of the firm's Indiana

Key Dates:

1939: The Rust family farm is founded in Seymour, Indiana.

1943: David Rust begins selling eggs and corn at a farmer's market in Indianapolis.

1955: A new, larger hen house is constructed.

1965: The number of chickens tops 100,000.

1975: The hen population reaches one million.

1984: David Rust begins an expansion program of adding one new farm per year.

1989: Lois Rust takes control of the company after divorce from David Rust.

1990: A salmonella outbreak linked to the firm's eggs leads to losses, new federal rules; Rose Acre builds its first egg breaking and processing plant.

1999: The company begins printing "laid on" dates on eggs.

2002: The firm is awarded $6 million plus interest in a lawsuit over the 1990 salmonella outbreak.

farms. The total loss was estimated at $900,000. Two men were later arrested and charged with setting the blaze.

The year 2002 saw the firm introduce an improved milk replacement product for dry animal feed that used the inedible portion of eggs as a protein substitute. The patented product was one of a number of new ways of using eggs under development by Rose Acre researchers. The firm now had more than 16 million layers and had eclipsed rival Michael Foods to again become the number two egg producer in the United States, after Cal-Maine Foods, Inc. Egg consumption was now on the rise, with each American eating an average of 253.5 per year.

Winning the Salmonella Case in 2002

In the late summer of 2002 Rose Acre Farms was awarded $6 million plus 12 years' interest by a federal judge in compensation for the losses the firm had suffered during and after the salmonella outbreak of 1990. The judge found that the government's new regulations "were misguided because they relied on ineffective testing methods." The regulations had not been enforced since the mid-1990s.

The year 2002 also saw the United Egg Producers organization adopt a new set of animal welfare standards under pressure from animal rights activists. The guidelines recommended giving each hen 40 percent more room. Most chickens on factory farms spent their lives in cages that gave them a space the size of a half-sheet of typing paper, with no room to even raise their wings. Their beaks were clipped so they could not peck their cage-mates to death, and they were alternately fed and denied food to yield increased egg production. The voluntary standards would reduce the number of chickens each hen house could

hold by 16 percent, though the number of eggs laid per bird was expected to increase slightly. Rose Acre adopted the new standards, while also offering some eggs from uncaged "free-range" chickens for consumers who desired them.

In the summer of 2003 Rose Acre entered the early stages of planning for a massive new production facility in North Carolina that would house three to four million chickens. The farm was expected to cost $55 million and employ 125. While conservationists were concerned about the operation's possible negative impact on a neighboring wildlife refuge, many citizens of the rural county it was proposed for welcomed the prospect of new jobs.

More than 60 years after its founding, Rose Acre Farms, Inc. had grown from a small family farm into a network of giant egg-production facilities. The firm's 16 million chickens supplied fresh eggs to customers in most parts of the United States, as well as dried and liquid egg products for use by the foodservice industry. Plans for further expansion were on the drawing board.

Principal Competitors

Cal-Maine Foods, Inc.; Michael Foods Egg Products Company; DeCoster Egg Farms; Buckeye Egg Farm.

Further Reading

Allegood, Jerry, "Proponents Say Egg Farm in Hyde County, N.C., Would Bolster Economy," *News & Observer* (Raleigh, N.C.), August 19, 2003.

Bamford, Janet, and Jennifer Pendleton, "The Top 50 Women-Owned Businesses," *Working Woman*, October 1, 1997, p. 34.

Bauer, Julia, "Down on the Farm, Even Eggs Are Now High-Tech," *Grand Rapids Press*, September 25, 2003, p. A16.

Dobie, Maureen, "Judge Noland Overturns $9.3 Million Verdict in Rose Acre Discrimination Case," *Indianapolis Business Journal*, January 4, 1988, p. 9.

Drell, Adrienne, "Ind. Farm Tied to Salmonella Told to Curb Fresh Egg Sales," *Chicago Sun-Times*, December 6, 1990, p. 21.

Kaelble, Steve, "Designer Eggs," *Indiana Business Magazine*, March 1, 1998, p. 7.

Snyder, David, "Eggcentric: Farmer-Mogul Ruffles Feathers," *Crain's Chicago Business*, July 27, 1987, p. 1.

Stroud, Jerri, "Schnucks Sells Egg Business—Indiana Firm to Buy Agri-Foods Inc.," *St. Louis Post-Dispatch*, June 28, 1995, p. 7C.

Sutherly, Ben, "Activists Say Animals Endure Silent Suffering—Activists Label Megafarm Methods Cruel," *Dayton Daily News*, December 2, 2002, p. 8A.

——, "Egg Producers Face Harsh Reality: Grow or Go Out of Business," *Dayton Daily News*, December 3, 2002, p. 8A.

——, "Processed Food Becoming the Norm," *Dayton Daily News*, December 1, 2002, p. 14A.

Thorsen, Eric, "Egg Freshness Date 'Laid On' Chicago Retailers," *Supermarket News*, April 19, 1999.

Willoughby, Jack, "Eggshells Everywhere," *Forbes*, May 29, 1989, p. 254.

—Frank Uhle

Sally Beauty Company, Inc.

3900 Morse Street
Denton, Texas 76208
U.S.A.
Telephone: (940) 898-7500
Toll Free: (800) 275-7255
Fax: (940) 898-7501
Web site: http://www.sallybeauty.com

Division of Alberto-Culver Company
Incorporated: 1964
Employees: 14,000
Sales: $1.67 billion (2002)
NAIC: 423850 Service Establishment Equipment and
Supplies Merchant Wholesalers; 453998 All Other
Miscellaneous Store Retailers (Except Tobacco Stores)

Sally Beauty Company, Inc., is the world's leading retail distributor of professional beauty supplies. Sally Beauty occupies a unique niche, operating a chain of stores that sell primarily to beauty salons and cosmetologists. Sally owns and operates over 2,000 retail outlets. These are found across the United States and in Mexico, Puerto Rico, the United Kingdom, Japan, and Germany. Sally Beauty stores stock some 5,000 different items, from hair, skin, and nail products to professional cosmetology equipment. The company serves its stores through distribution centers in the United States in Jacksonville, Florida; Reno, Nevada; and Columbus, Ohio. The firm started with a single store and began rapid expansion in the 1980s. Sally has been owned by the Alberto-Culver Company since 1969.

Modest Beginnings in the 1960s

The Sally Beauty chain, now worldwide, began as a single store in New Orleans, Louisiana, in 1964. The shop, located on Magazine Street, sold beauty supplies and equipment to registered beauticians. The original owner franchised the idea, and within five years there were 12 Sally Beauty stores in the New Orleans area. The chain might have stayed a modest regional phenomenon if it had not been discovered by Leonard Lavin, chief executive of the Alberto-Culver Company. Alberto-

Culver began as a Los Angeles beauty supply company, Blame Culver, which made hundreds of shampoos and beauty products, including Alberto VO5 Conditioning Hairdressing. In 1955, Leonard and Berenice Lavin bought the Los Angeles company and moved its headquarters to Chicago. The Lavins revamped the company, discontinuing most of its product lines to focus on Alberto VO5, which had been developed by a chemist at Culver specifically for Hollywood movie stars. Lavin was traveling in New Orleans in 1969 when he was intrigued by Sally Beauty. It offered a new way to distribute hair care products. At the time, most large hair salons were serviced by traveling salespeople. Some of the best-known names in the U.S. beauty business started out door-to-door, including Charles Revlon and Vidal Sassoon. Nevertheless, the salon sector was and remains extremely fragmented, and so this kind of distribution was patchy at best. In New Orleans, salon owners could go to a Sally Beauty store and buy directly the shampoos, dyes, and lotions they needed. Leonard Lavin thought the Sally Beauty chain was a great way to sell hair care products, so Alberto-Culver bought the company for around $1 million.

Sally Beauty was not an immediate success for its new owners. In 1972, Alberto-Culver gave management of the division to Michael Renzulli, a trained pharmacist. Renzulli described his early years with Sally to the *Dallas-Fort Worth Business Journal:* ''I served as a Jack-of-all-trades, traveling from store to store with beauty products in a station wagon.'' The chain did not make money, and Renzulli decided to discontinue the franchise arrangement. The company bought out the franchisees and ran the retail outlets itself. Still, another Alberto-Culver executive described the early Sally in *Institutional Investor* (January 2002) as ''very problematic for most of the 1970s.'' Despite some discouragement, the chain did grow, and by 1980 it had evolved into a company-owned chain of almost 40 stores. Revenue increased, and Sally began to make a profit. At that point, the chain began to grow through acquisitions.

National Growth in the 1980s

Sally Beauty first focused on buying beauty supply operations in the South, giving it regional strength. It bought four Southern beauty chains in the early 1980s, including a Tennessee business with 20 stores and a Houston chain that had 26

Company Perspectives:

As the largest purveyor of professional beauty supplies in the world, Sally Beauty has more than 2,200 stores that offer the salon professional and the consumer, between salon visits, more than 5,000 salon-quality products for hair, nail, and skin care.

stores and a warehouse operation. In 1982, Sally purchased Gibson Beauty Supply, based in Denton, Texas. That year, Sally moved its corporate headquarters to Denton. Alberto-Culver headquarters remained in suburban Chicago. In 1985, Sally bought two beauty supply chains near its parent's headquarters in Illinois. This moved Sally into the Midwest and brought the chain 50 more retail outlets. The Illinois chains also gave Sally two new distribution centers. In addition to acquiring competitors, Sally built new stores on its own. By the mid-1980s, it was opening six or seven stores a month.

By 1986, chainwide sales had reached $135 million. This was roughly a third of Alberto-Culver's total sales. Sally brought in about a third of Alberto-Culver's net income as well. By 1987, Sally Beauty had 440 stores spread across 24 states. The chain had grown very quickly, but it was still going strong. On the brink of becoming a nationwide chain, Sally had no national competitor. Its retail formula seemed to work well and to answer a real need. The Sally chain was able to buy in bulk from major suppliers, so it could offer attractive discounts to the professional beauty operators who made up the majority of its customers. It did not manufacture its own products, but some manufacturers produced special lines exclusively for Sally. The stores were generally located in strip malls, where customers could conveniently drive up and load their cars with boxes of goods. Though at first the stores focused on hair care items, by 1987 Sally was selling cosmetics and skin care products as well. Managers at the Denton headquarters assisted the stores with marketing, sending flyers to thousands of licensed beauty professionals within a new store's area. Sally's warehouse system was quite up-to-date and efficient, so the chain seemed able to absorb its rapid growth smoothly. By the mid-1980s, the chain used four warehouses, each of which was automated and computerized for quick fulfillment of orders.

Sally was handling its expansion so well that its president, Michael Renzulli, compared it to fast-food hamburger chain McDonald's. In 24 states by 1987, Renzulli planned to move into all 50 states by 1990. Coast-to-coast coverage took a little longer than that—Sally stores were found in 46 states by 1990. Nonetheless, it was clear that Sally had a winning formula, and there was plenty of room left in the market. In 1987, Sally began to test the waters overseas, again expanding through strategic acquisitions.

International Growth in the 1980s and 1990s

Sally Beauty's first international acquisition was a chain of beauty supply stores in Scotland, Ogee Hair & Beauty Supply, which had about 40 outlets and was the largest U.K. retailer of its type. The United Kingdom seemed a good place for Sally to start its international growth, since its parent's hair care brands, Alberto VO5 and Tresemme, were already well-known there.

Sally's international expansion proceeded more slowly than its domestic growth. In 1994, the company made its second foray abroad, forming a joint operating agreement with a small beauty supply chain in Japan. Sally chose C&C Cash & Carry Beauty Supply, though it had only four stores. Over the next decade, Sally gradually expanded its presence in Japan. By 1997, the firm operated 12 outlets in that country. That year Sally made another acquisition in the United Kingdom, buying the 30-store chain Embassy Ltd. By this time, Sally had added new stores beyond what it had bought from Ogee, and with the Embassy purchase it now had close to 100 U.K. outlets. The Embassy stores were expected to add some $20 million in revenue. Sally also ventured into Germany in the mid-1990s. In 1996, it purchased a chain of six stores called Friseurland-Kosmetik Gmbh. Sally planned to focus its growth on these three countries— Japan, Germany, and the United Kingdom—for the time being. The firm hoped to have 400 stores in both Japan and Germany eventually. By 2003, it had 150 stores in the United Kingdom, 35 in Germany, and 23 in Japan.

Meanwhile, Sally Beauty continued to expand rapidly at home. By 1997, chainwide sales had reached $880 million, which was half of parent Alberto-Culver's revenue. About 10 percent of this came from Sally's international operations. Domestically, Sally was opening a new store every three days on average in the mid-1990s. It continued to buy up small regional chains. In 1992, the company bought most of the assets of its only large competitor, the 174-store chain Milo Beauty & Barber Supply. Milo, based in Akron, Ohio, was in the midst of bankruptcy proceedings, and its stores went for only $1.3 million. Milo had followed a trajectory similar to Sally's, beginning with Ohio stores in the early 1950s and then snapping up regional chains after 1967. In 1984, it bought an 88-store chain, Beauty Fair USA, which turned out to be a real money-loser. Milo had problems of its own when its founder was murdered, and his brother was convicted of hiring a hit man to do the crime. Milo, with less than 200 stores, was a distant second to Sally in size. By 1993, Sally had over 1,000 stores. That year, it bought Beauty Biz Inc., an Oklahoma chain of 35 retail beauty supply stores. Through acquisition and opening new stores, Sally Beauty had more than 1,800 retail outlets by 1997.

Changes in the Late 1990s and After

Sally Beauty grew in new ways in the late 1990s and into the 2000s. The company kept abreast of its expanding empire by investing in its distribution network. In the mid-1990s, the retail outlets were served through four distribution centers, and the company was now looking for a new way to serve its southeastern market. In 1995, Sally made an investment of more than $15 million to build a huge new warehouse and distribution center in Jacksonville, Florida. It then made plans to close its older facility in Atlanta, Georgia. The 13-acre Jacksonville site housed a 225,000-square-foot building. Sally left room to expand the plant by an additional 100,000 square feet in the future. The company also invested more in advertising in the late 1990s. Sally had previously handled much of its marketing and advertising internally. In 1995, it spent over $1 million on advertising. In 1998, Sally hired a Texas-based advertising firm, BJK&E, to come up with a new store image campaign. At the same time, Sally hired another Texas agency to come up with television and radio advertising aimed at Latino customers.

Key Dates:

1964: Sally store is established in New Orleans.
1969: Alberto-Culver buys the Sally chain.
1972: Michael Renzulli becomes president of Sally division.
1981: The chain begins national growth.
1987: The company begins international expansion with the acquisition of Ogee in Scotland.
1994: Sally moves into the Japanese market.
1996: The company buys a German beauty supply chain.
2000: Company sales top $1 billion.

Sally began to court a slightly different group of customers beginning in the mid-1990s, when it developed a new subsidiary, its Beauty Systems Group. Sally stores were open to the public, though most of its customers were beauty business professionals, who received a special rate. Beginning in 1996, Sally bought three midwestern chains which sold only to salon owners. These were Barnum Beauty Supply, of Cleveland, Ohio; Victory Beauty Supply, a Chicago chain; and Locklear Beauty Supply, based in Rochester, New York. Because these stores, and others that became part of the Beauty Systems Group, sold only to store owners, they were able to stock some products that had previously been kept out of other Sally outlets. Some well-known hair care lines, including Redken, Nexxus, and Matrix, sold only through beauty salons. These lines had not been sold through Sally stores. The Beauty Systems Group stores, which were known as full-service stores or "professional business" units, were able to sell Redken and other salon-only product lines. Alberto-Culver's president Howard Bernick, the son-in-law of founder Lavin, told *WWD* (October 24, 1997) that he believed Sally's professional business division alone could one day bring in $500 million. This was at a time when Sally's worldwide sales were $880 million. Bernick also told *WWD* that he believed Sally "can and will be a $2 billion to $3 billion entity in the next five to ten years."

This may have seemed an extravagant aim, yet nothing seemed to get in the way of Sally's continued growth and prosperity. By 2001, the Sally Beauty chain had grown to 1,900 stores in the United States. The Beauty Systems Group was a fast-growing subsidiary, with 265 professional-only stores. As the market slowed down for regular Sally Beauty outlets, the professional business group found more locations. Its stores were concentrated in the East, Southeast, and Midwest, meaning there were still many possible markets in other regions. Sales chain-wide passed the billion-dollar mark in 2000, and the company invested $5 million to renovate and expand its corporate headquarters in Denton. More and more, Sally Beauty was recognized as the engine behind its parent's success. Alberto-Culver, a public company that was still run by members of the founding Lavin family, had had ten straight years of record sales and earnings growth by 2002. In that year, Sally contributed 60 percent of Alberto-Culver's sales and some 70 percent of the parent's profits. Though Alberto-Culver's consumer goods division, which consisted of hair care brands and several other niche products, saw its sales go up and down, Sally was a consistent earner. Even as the economy in the United States went into recession after 2000, Sally showed its solidity. As the economy dipped, women's visits to beauty salons also dropped off. Nevertheless, Sally's Beauty Systems Group did well despite poor conditions. "We've never been as large in that business during a recession as we are this year," Alberto-Culver's CEO Bernick told *Institutional Investor* in January 2002. For Alberto-Culver, the recession meant "a fantastic pickup in the Sally business." So the two Sally business groups balanced themselves out.

With worldwide sales approaching $2 billion in the early 2000s, the Sally chain planned continued growth. In 2001, the Beauty Systems Group bought a competitor called Armstrong-McCall. Sally's parent limited its acquisitions in 2002, investing less than $20 million in purchases that year compared to almost $145 million in 2000. However, the parent realized that strategic acquisitions had worked extremely well for it in the past. By 2003, Sally had more than 2,750 retail outlets in total. The company's presence in Europe and Japan was still relatively small, though Sally had at one point planned to have hundreds of stores in its foreign markets. Perhaps in the coming decades international growth would rival Sally's domestic growth in the 1980s and 1990s. The Beauty Systems Group also seemed to be a growing market, one that harbored the potential to make Sally Beauty into an even larger worldwide presence.

Principal Subsidiaries

Beauty Systems Group, Inc.

Principal Competitors

Walgreens Company; CVS Corporation; Wal-Mart Stores, Inc.

Further Reading

"Alberto's Sally Buys Barnum," *WWD*, January 5, 1996, p. 2.

Brookman, Faye, "RX Chains, Discounters Discover Manhattan," *WWD*, December 23, 1994, p. 7.

"Creditors Get Nothing from Bankrupt Akron, Ohio Beauty Company," *Knight Ridder/Tribune Business News*, December 30, 1993.

Curry, Kerry, "Sally Beauty Expanding in Denton," *Dallas Business Journal*, June 8, 2001, p. 3.

Feldman, Amy, "When Lenny Met Sally," *Forbes*, February 13, 1995, p. 62.

Fest, Glen, "BJK&E to Give Sally Beauty Retail Face-Lift," *Adweek Southwest*, October 12, 1998, p. 8.

"Helen of Troy Sells Retail Beauty Unit," *HFD*, October 4, 1993, p. 163.

"Howard Bernick of Alberto-Culver Co: Clean Streak," *Institutional Investor*, January 2002, p. 24.

"In Great Condition," *European Cosmetic Markets*, March 2003, p. 83.

Mathis, Karen Brune, "Incentives Help Jacksonville, Fla., Land a Beauty," *Knight Ridder/Tribune Business News*, June 23, 1995.

Narum, Beverly, "Sally Beauty Seeks Status as Worldwide Retailer," *Dallas-Fort Worth Business Journal*, June 1, 1987, p. 1.

"Sally Side Up," *SalonNews*, September 2000, p. 1S4.

Tanner, Lisa, "CEO Staffs Company Stores Looking for Tips," *Dallas Business Journal*, February 2, 2001, p. 19.

Tode, Chantal, "Alberto-Culver: Doing It Quietly," *WWD*, October 24, 1997, p. 8.

Waters, Jennifer, "Alberto-Culver's Beauty Supply Chain Sallying Abroad," *Crain's Chicago Business*, July 28, 1997, p. 14.

—A. Woodward

Sealaska Corporation

1 Sealaska Plaza, #400
Juneau, Alaska 99801-1276
U.S.A.
Telephone: (907) 586-1512
Fax: (907) 586-1826
Web site: http://www.sealaska.com

Private Company
Incorporated: 1971
Employees: 290
Sales: $102 million (2002)
NAIC: 113110 Timber Tract Operations; 114111 Finfish
   Fishing; 212311 Dimension Stone Mining and
   Quarrying; 311711 Seafood Canning; 327331
   Concrete Block and Brick Manufacturing; 327320
   Ready-Mix Concrete Manufacturing; 336111
   Automobile Manufacturing; 424460 Fish and Seafood
   Merchant Wholesales; 531120 Lessors of
   Nonresidential Buildings; 55111201 Offices of Other
   Holding Companies; 813910 Business Associations;
   113310 Logging; 813910 Business Associations;
   423310 Lumber and Wood Merchant Wholesales;
   541613 Marketing Consulting

A Native-owned corporation with more than 16,500 share-holders, Sealaska Corporation is the largest private landholder in southeast Alaska. The company's principal investments include forest products, financial markets, telecommunications, entertainment, plastics, and minerals development. Its primary assets include 290,000 acres of land containing 3.5 billion board feet of merchantable timber, as well as 600,000 acres of subsurface land. The company is also invested in telecommunications, with ownership interest in more than forty markets. Since its start, Sealaska has become involved in a variety of businesses, becoming a leader in exports and an economic and political force for Alaska.

Birth of Sealaska in 1971

Sealaska Corp. was one of 13 for-profit corporations formed in 1971 under the Alaska Native Claims Act (ANCSA).

ANCSA was formed in order to resolve century-old land-claims disputes between Alaska Natives and the state and federal governments. Dubbed the "Billion Dollar Deal," ANCSA offered Alaska Natives $967 million in cash and 44 million acres of land, but instead of handing over the money and land, Congress created corporations, such as Sealaska, to manage the assets. In dividing the assets, each Alaska Native born on or before December 18, 1971 received 100 shares of stock. In return, Natives had to forgo all other land claims. They were also required to contribute 70 percent of their natural resource earnings to a common fund, which would later be divided on a pro rata basis among the corporations.

On the Brink of Bankruptcy: Early 1980s

Of the 13 corporations formed under ANCSA, most, including Sealaska, sustained major setbacks. In 1982, when Byron Mallott was named CEO, Sealaska suffered a staggering $28 million loss, largely due to a botulism scare. The threat began when a Belgian man died from botulism poisoning after eating salmon that had been packed at a plant operated jointly by Whitney Fidalgo Co. and Ocean Beauty. Ocean Beauty was a Sealaska subsidiary. FDA officials recalled all cans that had been packed in 1980 and 1981. Other factors contributing to the company's 1982 losses were a faltering timber industry and sky-high interest rates. By the end of the year, Sealaska considered declaring bankruptcy.

Having escaped bankruptcy, Sealaska looked ahead. In 1984, the company formed an export trade group with seven other southeast Alaska native corporations. The export trading association, named the Southeast Alaska Native Log Export Association, would promote export sales of logs. The group had been able to form because of the Webb-Pomerane Act, a federal statute permitting limited exemption from federal antitrust law for export trading associations.

In 1985, Sealaska recovered a fraction of its 1982 losses, reporting a $1.8 million profit for the fiscal year. Nevertheless, in forming new businesses, such as the Southeast Alaska Native Log Export, Sealaska could not cash in on most of its sales for the year, which amounted to $215 million. At the same time, Sealaska was having difficulties with one of its subsidiaries,

---

Company Perspectives:

Sealaska's philosophy is to protect and grow our corporate assets to provide economic, cultural, and social benefits to current and future generations of our shareholders.

Pacific Western Lines. In 1985, the Seattle-based barge service went defunct. Excess shipping capacity, depressed freight rates, an oversupply of ships and an undersupply of cargo—all of which led to price wars—were to blame for the failed company. Pacific Western, whose revenue dropped from $24 million to $16 million bewteen 1983 and 1984, sold its equipment to another carrier, Lynden Inc. Sealaska used the money from the sale to invest in other businesses.

Another possible factor contributing to the company's enormous profit losses of the early 1980s came to light in 1986, when financier R. Michael Crowson was accused of defrauding Sealaska of millions of dollars. Prosecutors claimed that Crowson paid out more than a million dollars in kickbacks and bribes between 1980 and 1983 in return for leasing purchase contracts with two subsidiaries of Sealaska. Crowson was convicted of 19 counts of racketeering, mail and wire fraud, and tax evasion.

Meanwhile, Sealaska's future began looking brighter. While the Alaskan economy had been sluggish for years—mostly due to oil prices—Sealaska's expansion into fish and timber left them exempt from many of their former problems. Fishing had recently made a strong comeback, and timber proved especially lucrative. In 1985, Sealaska exported 150 million board feet of round logs to Asia, helping it to become the biggest timber exporter in Alaska. In 1986, Sealaska officially recovered from its financial mess of 1982, touting total revenues of $237 million and profits at $23.9 million.

Continued Growth amid Environmental Controversy: Late 1980s

In 1987, Sealaska celebrated its then best-ever year for profits, $30 million, with total revenues of $260 million. Meanwhile, its Seattle-based subsidiary, Ocean Beauty, earned sales of $187 million ($10 million more than the previous year), and Sealaska Timber Corp. earned a profit of $24 million on sales of $57 million. At the same time, Sealaska's long-term debt dropped under $25 million, from $37 million in 1986 (and far below the $106 million debt from 1982); its capital base rose to $120 million; and its assets grew to $216 million. Still, even while moving forward, Sealaska remained dedicated to the Tlingit, Tsimshian, and Haida Native people it represented; they confirmed their dedication through education programs, scholarships, and the Sealaska Heritage Foundation, which honored the Natives' traditions in an annual celebration event.

In 1988, environmentalists began speaking out against the Native corporations' logging practices, which cut down approximately 15,000 acres of trees in that year alone. The excessive logging began in 1980, when Native corporations began to receive the 470,000 acres of land they had been promised in the 1971 Alaska Native Claims Settlement Act. Because the land was privately owned by the Natives, it was difficult for environ-

mentalists to fight the logging practices. Furthermore, corporations such as Sealaska lauded the boost in the economy resulting from the logging. The company also felt its responsibility to shareholders to maximize profits trumped other concerns. However, some restrictions were enforced: when Sealaska wanted to cut down 700 acres above Hydaburg's reservoir, the project was terminated after only 100 acres had been cut.

Sealaska received the Governor's Alaskan Exporter of the Year Award in 1989, mainly for the exports of two of its subsidiaries, Sealaska Timber Corp. and Ocean Beauty Seafoods. The timber business exported 219.6 million board feet of products to Japan, Korea, and China in 1988, with total sales of $118.1 million; Ocean Beauty's export sales reached $58 million, up from $50 million the year before. The seafood company owned twelve processing facilities in Alaska, Washington, and Oregon and had eight regional distribution centers in five western states. With 800 full-time employees (and up to 2,000 at peak times), Ocean Beauty marketed more than 100 million pounds of seafood in the United States and abroad, with combined annual sales of $200 million. These figures notwithstanding, Sealaska placed Ocean Beauty up for sale later that year, earning $14.6 million on the deal.

Ongoing Prosperity in the Early to Mid-1990s

In 1991, Native corporation Klukwan Inc. offered to purchase Sealaska for $201 million. Sealaska, which had 15,750 shareholders at the time, rejected the offer. Klukwan was the most prosperous Native corporation, with a $30 million fund that paid its 270 shareholders large annual dividends. Sealaska asserted that it was not for sale. In 1991, Sealaska's net earnings were $21.3 million on revenue of $127.3 million. Meanwhile, the company paid out dividends to shareholders totaling $7.9 million and deposited $6.7 million into the Elders' Settlement Trust fund, which had been created in 1991. The shareholder permanent fund, created in 1986, increased to $68 million. At this point, after eight consecutive profitable years, Byron Mallot stepped down as Sealaska's president and CEO. Leo H. Barlow, a key Sealaska Timber Corp. executive, took his place.

Sealaska continued its success, claiming its ninth consecutive year of profitability in 1992. In 1993, the company's net income was $19 million on revenue of $167 million. This represented a 30 percent increase from the previous year's revenue, at $128.4 million. The substantial increase was made possible by Sealaska Timber Corp., which accounted for $155 million of the year's revenue. The timber operation sold 231 million board feet of timber.

In 1994, Sealaska earned a net income of $22.7 million, 36 percent over the previous year. Again, success was owed to the corporation's timber industry. Total revenues for the year, at $227 million, exceeded the previous year's by $60 million. In 1994, Sealaska Timber Corp. had its most profitable year to date. Furthermore, while other corporations had been suffering from an erratic investment climate, Sealaska's investment portfolio closed at $238 million, up $7 million from the previous year.

Environmentalists were once again questioning Native logging practices by 1995. While public logging companies were being shut out of public lands, Native logging on private land

Key Dates:

1971: Sealaska forms under the Alaska Native Claims Settlement Act (ANCSA).

1982: The company is on the brink of bankruptcy; Byron Mallott is named CEO.

1984: Sealaska joins seven other Alaska Native corporations to start the Southeast Alaska Native Log Export Association.

1985: The company's subsidiary, Pacific Western Lines, goes out of business.

1986: Financier R. Michael Crowson is accused and convicted of defrauding Sealaska of millions of dollars.

1989: Sealaska receives the Governor's Alaskan Exporter of the Year Award.

1991: Byron Mallot steps down as Sealaska's president and CEO; Leo H. Barlow takes his place.

1996: Sealaska purchases a calcium carbonate mine.

1997: The company purchases a 90 percent interest in TriQuest Precision Plastics for $65 million.

2001: Chris McNeil is named the new president and CEO of the company.

continued. Sealaska, for one, planned to go ahead with its intense logging practices, claiming it had enough timber to log for another ten to twenty years.

In 1996, Sealaska's net profits rose to an astounding $43.4 million on $237 million in revenues, while its Permanent Fund (an investment fund that has ensured shareholders dividends) reached $100 million. However, because of a provision of the Alaska Native Claims Settlement Act, the company was required to pay about $21 million to other Native corporations. Also in 1996, Sealaska's board of directors approved the investment of $13 million in capital expenses to open a calcium carbonate mine at Calder on Prince of Wales Island. An open quarry was constructed from which Sealaska began extracting ore to make limestone. Nonetheless, it was timber, which provided $210 million in revenues, that remained central to Sealaska.

Financial Struggles and Recovery in the New Century

In 1997, Sealaska expanded into a new market, plastics, when it purchased a 90 percent interest in TriQuest Precision Plastics for $65 million. TriQuest, an injection-molded plastics manufacturer for high-tech industries, had $90 million in sales in 1996. TriQuest teamed with Sealaska because it needed the capital to fund an aggressive expansion campaign, with the goal of becoming a $200 million company. TriQuest began its campaign in 1998 with the opening of its second Mexico factory.

Sealaska requested that the U.S. Forest Service stop exporting unprocessed timber from Alaska's Tongass National Forest in 1998, claiming that the timber should be processed in Alaska. Sealaska, the largest private harvester of timber in southeastern Alaska, felt that the exported timber reduced its returns in the market. In the same year, Sealaska and another Native corporation participated in an acre-for-acre land ex-

change with the federal government. The government received 2,400 acres of watershed lands, while the Native corporations received an equal number of acres of national forest land, with rights to log on them.

In 1999, Sealaska Timber Corp. adopted new techniques to remain competitive in the face of a changing Japanese market. Japan represented Alaska's largest export source. Strategies included reducing overall volume and adhering to a policy of ''just-in-time'' production, shipping, and sales. At the same time, due to recent costly ventures, as well as large dividend payments to shareholders, Sealaska's yearly profits dropped to $10 million on $176 million in revenues.

Sealaska subsidiary TriQuest announced it would merge with another plastic manufacturer, Arctic Slope Regional Corporation, in 2000. The new company was named TriQuest-Puget Plastics. Sealaska supported the merger, hoping it would bring further expansion. Later that year, Sealaska invested in a 40,000-square-foot casino in Escondido, California, with the San Pasquel Indian tribe. While Sealaska would neither own nor manage the casino, they invested $14.7 million in the $180 million project. In another venture that year, Sealaska joined Arctic Slope Regional Corp. and Doyon Limited, with an agreement with AT&T, to form Alaska Native Wireless. The cost of the new company, which the corporations won in a U.S. government auction bid, was $459.6 million (of which Sealaska provided $40 million).

Sealaska ended the 2000 fiscal year in a state of disaster, with the company recording an astounding $122 million loss on $72 million in revenues. Largely to blame were the failings of two of its four recent investments ventures, TriQuest and SeaCal. Other contributing factors included steep competition and a bear market on Wall Street. Poor timber prices were also blamed for the losses, even as timber remained Sealaska's most lucrative market (contributing $80 million in gross revenues that year).

The company's timber market, in the face of such disaster, seemed to be its only real hope. Trees they had begun replanting in 1982 were up to fifty feet tall and eight inches thick, and about 150,000 seedlings would be planted on 1,000 acres in the following year. Such replanting figures would allow the company to maintain its harvesting rate indefinitely, creating something like a ''permanent fund'' for the company. Nonetheless, timber alone could not save Sealaska from its 2000 financial woes.

In 2001, Chris McNeil was named the new president and CEO of Sealaska as part of its rebuilding process. Among his top priorities was to sell Sealaska's precision plastics and limestone mining businesses. Combined, the two businesses had cost Sealaska a total of $73 million in losses. In 2000, Sealaska's permanent fund investment had fallen $24 million in value. In 2001, the company laid off 12 workers to reduce overhead, bringing its total employee count to 100.

In 2002, Sealaska sold a minority interest of TriQuest to Massachusetts-based Nypro Inc. A few months later, TriQuest closed its injection molding plant, laying off 155 employees. In addition, Sealaska's new venture, Alaska Native Wireless LLC, was put on hold, since the licenses had belonged to recently bankrupted Next Wave. Later in the year, Sealaska and its partners in the venture received 85 percent of their investments back, while the U.S. Supreme Court dealt with a dispute in the transaction.

In an attempt to regain footing, Sealaska decided to stay in the plastics business, believing its new status as a minority-owned company might eventually be profitable. TriQuest Nypro's financial situation did improve in 2002, when the company broke even. TriQuest-Puget Plastics, meanwhile, was closed and assets were sold off; at the same time, mining in SeaCal ceased. Also in 2002, the San Pasquel casino repaid Sealaska its original $14.7 million investment, as well as an extra $8.7 million in interest and management fees.

Sealaska's cost-cutting formula for 2002, which included closing down failing operations, contributed to a significant recovery for the company. By the end of the fiscal year, Sealaska recorded earnings of $40.5 million on $170 million in revenues. Also contributing to the recovery was Alaska Native Wireless, which earned the company $33 million in profits. Meanwhile, Sealaska Timber earned more than $8 million. In 2003, the timber operation won the Governor's Exporter of the Year Award and timber export sales continued to bring in strong profits. Sealaska's revenues and profits in 2003 were on a similar course to those in 2002.

Principal Subsidiaries

Sealaska Timber Corporation (STC); Alaska Native Wireless LLC; TriQuest-Nypro Plastics.

Principal Competitors

Silver Bay Logging; Titan Plastics Group; Western Wireless Corp.

Further Reading

"Across the USA: News from Every State," *USA Today*, November 18, 1996.

"Alaska Corporations Buy Licenses for Wireless Operation," *Anchorage Daily News*, January 27, 2001.

"Alaska Group Offers to Buy Sealaska," *Seattle Times*, September 10, 1991.

"Alaska Native Regional Corporations," *Business Publishing Company, Inc.*, September 1, 2001.

Bauman, Margaret, "Sealaska Management Digs In," *Alaska Journal of Commerce*, January 14, 1991.

——, "Sealaska's Mallot Will Resign This Summer," *Alaska Journal of Commerce*, April 27, 1992.

——, "Barlow Named Sealaska CEO," *Alaska Journal of Commerce*, August 10, 1992.

Bella, Rick, "TriQuest Precision Plastics Is Sold," *Portland Oregonian*, December 25, 1997.

——, "TriQuest Precision Plastics Is Staying Put in Vancouver after All," *Portland Oregonian*, October 4, 2000.

Bonham, Nicole A., "Just-in-time Production, Shipping Help Sealaska Compete," *Alaska Journal of Commerce*, March 22, 1999.

Bradner, Tim, "Timber: Where's the Rebound," *Alaska Journal of Commerce*, September 9, 1991.

——, "Timber Industry Shakeout May Have Bottomed Out," *Alaska Journal of Commerce*, July 31, 1995.

——, "Sealaska Corp.: Looking for a Major Acquisition to Diversify, Strengthen Holdings," *Alaska Journal of Commerce*, February 17, 1997.

——, "Sealaska, Aleut Corporations Building Shareholders' Future on Timber, Fishing Developments," *Alaska Journal of Commerce*, February 20, 2000.

——, "Sealaska Works to Keep Timber Its Bright Spot," *Alaska Journal of Commerce*, February 25, 2001.

——, "Sealaska Hopes to Regain Profitability in 2002," *Alaska Journal of Commerce*, May 26, 2002.

Cook, John, "TriQuest to Close Plastic Plant, Lay off 155," *Seattle Post-Intelligencer*, February 23, 2002.

Dirks, Jennifer and Craig Brown, "TriQuest to Launch 2nd Mexico Plant," *Columbian*, May 8, 1998.

Dobbyn, Paula, "Anchorage, Alaska-Based Wireless Start-Up Makes Bids for Telecom Territory," *Anchorage Daily News*, December 15, 2000.

——, "Bad Investments Help Put Alaska Native Corporation $122 Million in the Hole," *Anchorage Daily News*, April 29, 2001.

——, "Juneau, Alaska-Based Company Lays Off Twelve Workers to Reduce Overhead," *Anchorage Daily News*, May 4, 2001.

——, "Juneau, Alaska-Based Regional Corporation Reports $21 Million Loss," *Anchorage Daily News*, May 7, 2002.

Enders, John, "Alaska Natives Fear Losing Their Land," *Seattle Times*, January 5, 1992.

Michelson, Mike, "Sealaska Corp. Takes a High Tech Approach to Land Management with Global Information," *Alaska Journal of Commerce*, September 14, 1992.

Nogaki, Sylvia, "Low Rates Take Toll on Cargo Business," *Seattle Times*, October 8, 1985.

Rogoway, Mike, "Vancouver, Wash., Plastics Firm Receives Bad News from Parent," *Columbian*, January 5, 2001.

Stricker, Julie, "Sealaska Corp.: Hard Times Have Fallen on This Native Corporation, but There Is Hope for a Brighter Future," *Business Publishing Company, Inc.*, March 1, 2002.

—Candice Mancini

Seneca Foods Corporation

3736 South Main Street
Marion, New York 14505
U.S.A.
Telephone: (315) 926-8100
Fax: (315) 926-8300
Web site: http://www.senecafoods.com

Public Company
Incorporated: 1949 as the Seneca Grape Juice Company
Employees: 2,299
Sales: $644.4 million (2003)
Stock Exchanges: NASDAQ
Ticker Symbol: SENEA
NAIC: 311421 Fruit and Vegetable Canning; 311411
   Frozen Fruit, Juice, and Vegetable Manufacturing;
   481211 Nonscheduled Chartered Passenger Air
   Transportation

A familiar name to consumers throughout the United States, Seneca Foods Corporation processes vegetables and fruits, marketing its canned, frozen, and packaged products under the ''Seneca'' brand name, as well as under several other brands, including ''Libby's,'' ''Blue Boy,'' ''Lohmann,'' and ''Aunt Nellie's Farm Kitchen.'' Seneca also operates a small nonfoods division which oversees an air charter service. During the early years of the new century, Seneca operated out of 29 manufacturing plants and warehouses, stretching from the eastern United States to the northwestern part of the country, where vegetables and fruits were processed and packaged and then sold to wholesale and retail grocery companies. A large portion of the company's sales stems from its alliance with Pillsbury to supply products under the ''Green Giant'' label.

Origins

Seneca Foods Corporation got its start when Cornell University business student Art Wolcott attended the bankruptcy auction of Dundee Grape Juice Company in 1949. Wolcott had set his sights on a typewriter; however, he believed that the failed com-

pany still held promise. Acting on this conviction, Wolcott acquired the firm and renamed it Seneca Grape Juice Company. During the following decade, Seneca grew steadily through strategic acquisitions and product development. The company also forged key partnerships such as its venture with Minute Maid to package the first frozen grape juice sold in the United States.

The firm changed its name to Seneca Foods Corporations during the 1960s. In order to facilitate growth, it added new plant facilities and continued to launch new products, including the first Vitamin C enriched apple juice. As Seneca entered the 1970s, much of what constituted the company had recently been added to its operations. Though Seneca had been established in 1949, it would be two decades before the company began to take on the look of a diversified food processor, with many of the characteristics that described the company from the 1970s forward being adopted after the 20th anniversary year of the Seneca business. Beginning in the 1970s, Seneca added significantly to its business scope through a series of acquisitions that bolstered its revenue and paved the way for the growth to come during the ensuing decades.

At the outset of the 1970s, The company's largest business unit was its Seneca division, which represented the original part of the company founded during the late 1940s. Producing more than three million cases of consumer products and generating more than $10 million in sales each year by the beginning of the decade, the Seneca division comprised two manufacturing plants—one in Dundee, New York, and another in Westfield, New York—and two warehousing operations, one in Penn Yan, New York, and another in Geneva, New York. At the Dundee manufacturing plant, the company formulated, packaged, and distributed an extensive line of frozen concentrated fruit juices and fruit drinks, bottled and canned juices, and a frozen nondairy coffee creamer. All of the bulk grape juice and grape concentrates that were formulated into finished products at the Dundee plant were produced at Westfield, where Seneca operated a grape processing plant. Also included within the range of operations at Westfield was another use for the grapes processed by the company, a relatively new business area for Seneca, yet one that was expected to increase in importance as the decade unfolded. At Westfield, Seneca had entered the wine business,

Company Perspectives:

Seneca is committed to remaining an independent, publicly traded company and to meet the quality, service, and cost expectations of our customers across America and around the world. With modern plants and a strong balance sheet, Seneca is well positioned to pursue strategic business opportunities and to continue our tradition of surviving and succeeding in a rapidly consolidating industry.

marketing a line of dry, high-quality table wines sold under the Boordy Vineyards label.

The second-largest business unit after the Seneca division was the company's Marion division, one of the new additions to the company as the 1970s began. A contributor of nearly $10 million in annual sales to Seneca's revenue volume, the Marion division was the result of an acquisition completed in May 1970, when the company purchased the Marion Canning Company. With the acquisition of Marion Canning, Seneca gained two manufacturing plants, both of which were located in the company's home state of New York. Together, the plants in Marion and Williamson processed two million bushels of apples and 5,000 tons of string beans, as well as lesser quantities of rhubarb, plums, seckel pears, and crab apples. Among this roster of various fruits and vegetables, apples were by far the most important product in the Marion division's business, specifically apples that were used to make apple sauce. Through the Marion division, Seneca ranked as the third-largest producer of apple sauce in the United States, all of which was packed under the "Seneca" label, selling enough of the fruit compote to control 8 percent of the national market. Though the division represented a new facet to Seneca's operations at the beginning of the decade, considerable resources were devoted to its development immediately following the acquisition of Marion Canning, when an expansion program was initiated that was expected to increase the division's volume 50 percent by 1973.

The third and smallest food processing division operating under the Seneca corporate umbrella was the Prosser division, which produced most of the same consumer products packed by the Seneca and Marion divisions but, unlike the two larger divisions, was located across the country in Prosser, Washington. The Prosser plant, which produced 13,000 tons of grapes and 500,000 bushels of apples annually, had been constructed in 1964, then expanded in 1968 and 1970. The division drew its strength from its location in the heart of the Yakima Valley, the epicenter of grape and apple production in the United States. On average, Concord grape and apple yields per acre were three times greater per acre than those recorded in other major producing areas in the country. Despite its prime location, the Prosser division had recorded several years of serious financial losses following the establishment of its processing plant in 1964. However, by 1968 the division had begun to prove successful, demonstrating consistent profitability in the early 1970s, when it collected more than $4 million in sales annually.

Combined, Seneca's three food processing divisions— Seneca, Marion, and Prosser—generated $24 million in annual sales at the beginning of the 1970s, $10 million of which was derived from the sale of products marketed under the "Seneca" label. Of the $24 million in total volume, more than half—$13 million—was collected from sales to retail consumers, while the balance was derived from sales to institutional and industrial customers. This aspect of Seneca's business told only part of the story, however, because the company relied on another important business segment to fuel its growth: Seneca's non-food companies.

1970 Acquisition of Rochester Group, Inc.

Of Seneca's non-food businesses, the smallest was the company's transportation division, a captive trucking firm that operated 15 tractor-trailer combinations to service Seneca's food divisions on the East Coast. Seneca's transportation division was its lone non-food business—an enterprise that allowed the company "to get another squeal out of the pig," as one Seneca executive noted—until the company completed another acquisition six months after purchasing Marion Canning Company. In November 1970, Seneca acquired Rochester Group, Inc., giving the company its first genuine non-food processing businesses, since the company's trucking fleet was directly involved with the production of fruit and vegetable consumer products.

With the acquisition of Rochester Group, Inc., Seneca greatly increased its presence outside the food industry, gaining control of Tapetex Products and Lehman Brothers Corporation. The larger of the two new companies, Tapetex Products operated as a textile converting company specializing in the production and sale of materials used as linings in men's apparel and used as exterior fabrics for men's and women's outerwear garments. Each year, the company handled between 30 and 35 million yards of material, enough to generate between $12 and $15 million annually and eclipse the revenue volume of Seneca's largest food processing division.

The other company obtained through the acquisition of Rochester Group, Inc. was Lehman Brothers Corporation, which generated $4 million in sales annually—a total roughly equal with the sales collected by the Prosser division—but earned a higher percentage of profit than any other Seneca division. From its manufacturing plant in Jersey City, New Jersey, Lehman Brothers Corporation produced a full line of interior and exterior paints, enamels, and varnishes, selling its products to more than 500 independent wholesale and retail outlets primarily under the Ox-Line label.

Such was the composition of Seneca's operations as the 1970s began, its scope expanded and diversified significantly through the May 1970 acquisition of Marion Canning Company, which spawned its second-largest business unit, the Marion division, and the November 1970 acquisition of Rochester Group, Inc., which marked the arrival of Tapetex Products, Lehman Brothers Corporation, and nearly $20 million in annual sales into the company fold. Though sweeping and definitive changes had occurred during a six-month period in 1970, no respite from the comprehensive additions executed during the first year of the decade was taken by Seneca's management. In 1971, Seneca entered into a joint venture project known as Snake River Vineyards, investing enough money to become a one-third participant in the wine production venture. Under the terms of the deal, 1,700 acres of grapes, projected to start producing in 1973, were all under contract to Seneca, complementing the 200,000 gallon winery constructed in 1971 at Penn Yan, where the bottling and distribution of Boordy Vineyards wine were being conducted.

1973 Acquisition of S.S. Pierce

On the heels of this joint venture agreement, Seneca completed an acquisition that at least equaled the importance of its Marion Canning and Rochester Group acquisitions. In March 1973, Seneca acquired Boston, Massachusetts-based S.S. Pierce Company, a food and beverage producer with $50 million in annual sales. The acquisition immediately doubled Seneca's revenue volume, increasing the company's sales to $110 million, and gave it ownership over several sizeable and profitable companies. Included within the S.S. Pierce acquisition was the company's Institutional Food Service division, which by itself generated $20 million in annual sales from the production of a broad line of dry grocery and frozen food products for restaurants, schools, hospitals, and caterers in New England. Another $10 million in annual sales were added to Seneca's volume through another S.S. Pierce business unit—its Wine and Spirits division—which bottled and distributed a complete line of hard liquors and low-priced domestic wines under the ''S.S. Pierce'' label.

Rounding out the collection of companies gained by Seneca through its acquisition of S.S. Pierce were State Line Potato Chip Company, Kennett Canning Company, and Lincoln Food, Inc. The smallest of these three companies was Kennett Canning Company, a $4.5 million-in-sales firm that grew and canned more than five million pounds of mushrooms annually under the ''S.S. Pierce'' label. Second-largest was S.S. Pierce's State Line Chip Company, which manufactured and sold retail size packages of potato chips, popcorn, corn chips, and other snack products. This company added another $5 million in annual sales to Seneca's revenue volume, contributing half of the $10 million generated by Lincoln Foods, Inc., a processor and distributor of a full line of ''hot packed'' bottled and canned fruit juices and fruit drinks sold under the ''Lincoln'' and ''Bessey'' labels.

The acquisition of S.S. Pierce marked a singular achievement in Seneca's history, enabling the company to broaden and entrench its market presence with the swipe of a pen. The significance of the acquisition had a pervasive effect on the then 24-year-old company, making its arrival known on all levels of Seneca's operations, including the name under which it operated. Four years after the acquisition, Seneca adopted the corporate title of its most integral acquisition, changing its name from Seneca Foods Corporation to S.S. Pierce Company, Inc. in December 1977.

Three days after the name change, the company sold its 33.3 percent interest in Snake River Vineyards, letting go of its involvement in the joint venture on the first day of 1978. Another important divestiture was completed in 1983, when S.S. Pierce sold Lehman Brothers Corporation, the paint business acquired in the 1970 acquisition of Rochester Group. The company continued to operate as S.S. Pierce until resurrecting its original name of Seneca in November 1986, when S.S. Pierce Company, Inc. once again conducted business as Seneca Foods Corporation.

The 1990s and Beyond

During the 1990s, Seneca continued to add to its juice processing capabilities through acquisitions, but the early years of the decade were also notable for the departure of one of the company's long-held, non-food businesses. In August 1993, ten years after Lehman Brothers Corporation had been sold, Seneca divested the other company obtained through the purchase of Rochester Group, Inc. in 1970, Tapetex Products. A contributor of 13 percent of Seneca's $257 million in total sales during its last year with the company, the Tapetex division was sold for $8.4 million, which facilitated a series of acquisitions that were completed during the ensuing months. In November 1993, the company purchased the Wapato, Washington, juice processing business belonging to Sanofi Bio-Industries for $3.3 million. Then, in December 1993, Seneca acquired certain assets, including manufacturing facilities located in Eau Claire, Wisconsin, owned by ERLY Juice, Inc. and WorldMark, Inc., producers of products marketed under the ''TreeSweet'' brand.

Less than a year after obtaining the trademarks, inventory, and accounts receivable belonging to ERLY Juice and WorldMark, Seneca completed another acquisition, purchasing M.C. Snack, Inc., a snack food maker of apple chips, based in Yakima, Washington. Four months later, in February 1995, Seneca made a pivotal move that represented the highlight of the year for the company and ranked as perhaps its single most important development during the first half of the 1990s. On February 10th, the company formed an alliance with Pillsbury and, for $86.1 million, obtained six vegetable processing plants and a 20-year agreement that named Seneca as the primary supplier of ''Green Giant'' canned and frozen vegetables. Under the terms of the agreement, Pillsbury would continue to be responsible for the sales, marketing, and customer services functions associated with the ''Green Giant'' brand, but Seneca would take over the vegetable processing and canning operations previously conducted by Pillsbury.

In a year that saw Seneca widen its lead as the number one marketer of frozen concentrated apple juice, the alliance with

Pillsbury represented a definitive move, elevating the importance of vegetable processing in Seneca's business. In the years ahead, vegetables would play a substantial role in the company's future, providing a promising area of growth to complement Seneca's strong position in the fruit processing industry. The company moved toward the late 1990s and its 50th anniversary year as a leading market competitor, strengthened by the integral acquisitions it had completed during its first four decades of existence.

As the decade came to a close, Seneca made another significant change in its operations when it sold its applesauce and juice holdings in order to focus on what was now its core business—vegetables. The firm broadened its brand portfolio as well, acquiring the marketing rights to the "Libby" brand of canned vegetables, fruits, pastas, and baked bean products. Seneca also remained actively involved in its smaller, nonfoods division, which included a flight operations unit. The company landed a position as a fixed based operator at Yates County Airport, added new aircraft to its fleet, and constructed a state-of-the-art hanger facility. By the time Seneca entered the new century, it was poised as a financially solid major produce processing concern.

With 50 years of history under its belt, Seneca was confident that it was on the path for continued success in the years to come. The company bolstered its holdings in 2000 with the purchase of Agrilink Foods' Midwest private label canned vegetable business, which included a plant in Minnesota. In 2003, Seneca acquired competitor Chiquita Processed Foods L.L.C. in a deal that secured Seneca's position as the largest supplier of private label canned vegetables to the retail, export, and food service markets in the United States.

Seneca had indeed come a long way from its roots as a grape juice processor. In 2003, 98 percent of the company's sales stemmed from its food processing operations. Its canned vegetables unit secured nearly 85 percent of company sales, while frozen vegetables accounted for 12 percent. Fruit products shored up the remaining 3 percent. Its lucrative deal with Pillsbury remained a cornerstone in its operating structure and was responsible for over 40 percent of Seneca's product sales. As the company looked to the future, its customer pledge remained constant—"We are committed to delivering high-quality products that you can trust and depend on."

Principal Subsidiaries

SSP Seneca Foods, L.L.C.; Marion Foods, Inc.; Seneca Foods International, Ltd.; Seneca Snack Company.

Principal Competitors

Chiquita Brands International Inc.; Del Monte Foods Company; Pro-fac Cooperative Inc.

Further Reading

"Chiquita Taking Major Step to Trim Operations," *The Food Institute Report*, March 10, 2003, p. 1.

Halversen, Kirsten, "Seneca Joins Chiquita Frupac in Marketing Branded Apples," *Supermarket News*, September 13, 1993, p. 40.

"Northland Cranberries Inc. to Purchase Juice Division of Seneca Foods Corp.," *The Food Institute Report*, August 24, 1998.

Potts, Mary Lou, "Seneca Foods Plant Gets Busy, Boosts Buhl, Idaho-Area Economy," *Times-News*, June 3, 2003.

——, "New Leaders at Frozen-Vegetables Plant in Buhl, Idaho, Discuss Industry Changes," *Times-News*, June 15, 2003.

"Seneca Foods Corporation," *Wall Street Transcript*, April 5, 1971, pp. 23, 730.

"Seneca Foods Corporation," *Wall Street Transcript*, June 18, 1973, pp. 33, 448.

"Seneca Foods to Purchase Agrilink Foods' Midwest Private Label Canned Vegetable Business," *PR Newswire*, September 16, 1999.

—Jeffrey L. Covell
—update: Christina M. Stansell

Shikoku Electric Power Company, Inc.

2-5, Marunouchi
Takamatsu 760-8573
Kagawa
Japan
Telephone: (+87) 821-5061
Fax: (+87) 826-1250
Web site: http://www.yonden.co.jp

Public Company
Incorporated: 1951
Employees: 5,274
Sales: ¥584.7 billion ($4.87 billion) (2003)
Stock Exchanges: Tokyo
Ticker Symbol: 9507
NAIC: 22111 Hydroelectric Power Generation; 221112
    Fossil Fuel Electric Power Generation; 221113
    Nuclear Electric Power Generation; 221119 Other
    Electric Power Generation; 221122 Electric Power
    Distribution

Shikoku Electric Power Company, Inc. is one of the ten major regional power companies that generate, transmit, and distribute electricity throughout Japan. The company supplies electricity to all four of Shikoku's prefectures—Tokushima, Kochi, Ehime, and Kagawa—and serves over four million customers. As of March 2003, its generating capacity was 6,894 megawatts, stemming mostly from its thermal and nuclear generating operations. Japan partially deregulated its retail electric power sector in March 2000, leaving Shikoku's market open to competition. As such, the company is focused on strengthening its core operations while branching out into new business areas.

Shikoku Electric was formed as a company on May 1, 1951, when the General Headquarters of the Allied Powers (GHQ) under General MacArthur approved a plan submitted by the Japanese government to reorganize and rationalize the electrical power industry. Under the scheme, which was developed in 1948, the nation was divided into nine blocks, each with its own privately owned electric power company (EPC). In 1972, the Okinawa EPC was added as a tenth company.

At the time of inauguration, the nine companies served 16 million customers with a combined capacity of 8,500 megawatts (MW). Of this, Shikoku Electric's portion was a relatively small 290MW, or just over 3 percent. Shikoku was the smallest and least developed of Japan's four main islands but since ancient times maintained close ties with the old capital cities in Honshu such as nearby Kyoto, Nara, and more recently Tokyo. It has played an important role as a transit island in shipping between Japan and its trading partners through ports such as Kochi on the south Pacific Coast. Although the chief industries in the region have traditionally been low-technology, such as forestry and handicrafts, there was a boom in the Ehime and Kagawa prefectures in the high-technology sector in the 1980s, prompted in part by the government's "Technopolis" scheme to promote high-technology industry in Shikoku. There was also an increase in tourism on the island, peaking in 1989. Thus the history of electric power on a large scale in Shikoku starts fairly recently.

Early History of Japan's Electric Power

The history of electric power in Japan as a whole, however, goes back to 1878 when Professor W.E. Aryton of the Institute of Technology in Tokyo unveiled an arc lamp to celebrate the opening of the Central Telegraph Office. Japan's first electric utility company was established in 1886, seven years after Thomas Edison invented the incandescent lamp in the United States. The company was Tokyo Electric Lighting Company, and its first electric power plant—which was also the first in Japan—was completed in 1887 as a 25 kilowatt (kW) facility in Nihonbashi, Tokyo.

Throughout its history, Japan had been able to assimilate and improve upon outside technology and ideas, and electric power was no exception. After the opening of the Tokyo Electric Lighting plant, many electric utilities started up in main cities. Although demand had increased rapidly—electricity was a great improvement over the troublesome oil lamps then in use—service was generally limited to government and commercial offices and factories. Most of the first plants in Japan were thermal, powered by coal, but in 1891 the first hydroelectric power station was completed in Kyoto. A large part of the demand for electricity came from the electric railways that were

---

Company Perspectives:

Making effective use of its human, technological, and other corporate resources, Shikoku Electric Power, as a leading enterprise in the locality, carries on positive business operations in various sectors in cooperation with Shikoku Electric Group companies under its three-point basic corporate philosophy: "Living together with the local community, advancing with the local community, and prospering with the local community."

---

springing up all over the country. Spurred on by these developments, electricity in the form of electric lighting was first introduced to Shikoku in 1896 by the Tokushima Electric Lighting Company in Tokushima City. The next seven years saw the spread of electric lighting into Shikoku's four prefectures by Takamatsu Lighting, Tosa Lighting, and Iyo Hydroelectric Power, which pioneered hydroelectricity in Shikoku by building the first plant in Ehime prefecture in 1903. The years 1896 to 1912 saw the rapid development of these four power companies. The turnover of Tokushima Electric, for example, increased a thousandfold between 1900 and 1912. The most common initial usage of electricity was in the lighting of streets and public areas, but increasingly the upper-class town dwellers had electric lights installed in their homes.

In 1911, the government enacted the Electric Utility Industry Law. The law necessitated government permission for the production and distribution of electric power. By 1920, there were 3,000 power companies in Japan, riding on Japan's economic boom, and the number operating in the towns of Shikoku numbered about 50. The depression of the 1920s in Japan, following its defeat in World War I, was exacerbated by the Great Kanto Earthquake in 1923 and the worldwide market crash in 1929. While the Great Depression did not have an excessive effect on the economy of Shikoku, it did prevent growth during this period. The period between 1926 and 1937 can be characterized as the era of the "Big Five" in the history of electric power in Japan. It was dominated by Tokyo Electric Lighting and Daido Power in particular. The government regulated the industry by passing four laws in 1938 which ensured state control over prices, plant development, transmission, and all other aspects of the industry. In effect, it had formed one of the largest electric companies in the world with the establishment of JEGTCO (Japan Electric Generation and Transmission Company). The Allied bombing of Japan from 1943 to 1945 seriously damaged 44 percent of Japan's power stations and devastated Japanese industry. Shikoku, however, not being a strategic target, was largely untouched. The GHQ, which was effectively in charge of Japan from 1945 to 1952, made sweeping changes in Japan's electric power industry.

Postwar Changes

The Council for Reorganization of Electric Utility Industry was formed in 1949 and chaired by Yasuzaemon Matsunaga, former president of Toho Electric Power Company. After much negotiation, a plan was produced that divided the country into nine areas, each with its own privately owned electric power

company. Thus the Shikoku Electric Power Company was formed, with initial capitalization of ¥400 million ($1.1 million).

The first chairman was Yoichi Takeoka, who was formally in charge of Takamatsu Electric Light Company. Takeoka began a consolidation of Shikoku Electric's facilities and the company embarked on an immediate expansion program. Just two months after the company's establishment, work began on a hydroelectric facility on the Kuro River. Like the rest of Japan, much of the center of Shikoku is mountainous and thus a good source of hydroelectric power, on which most of Shikoku's power facilities at this time operated. The company began to promote the use of electric power in the more rural areas that had previously been uneconomical markets for the smaller utilities in Shikoku. The central headquarters were rationalized and divisions between the regional offices abolished. Pensions, healthcare, and insurance were offered on an equal basis to all company employees. Some of the less modern generating facilities were closed and replaced with more efficient plants, with more thermal facilities being built. A listing on the Osaka Stock Exchange in October 1952 was followed by a Tokyo listing in May 1953. By the end of 1953, customer service branches were established in all the major towns of Shikoku, and the capitalization of the company had trebled to ¥1.19 billion. Also in this year, a pioneering automatic combustion control system was installed on all Shikoku Electric's transmission and generating equipment to regulate the amount of fuel burnt and hence save energy. This was followed in the 1950s and early 1960s with a series of technological upgrades. Emphasis was also placed on the training of staff and customers in the safe use of electrical equipment. As a result, Shikoku had the lowest electricity-related accident rate in the country.

In 1956, company president Chikuma Miyagawa initiated research into the use of nuclear power by the company. Shikoku Electric was at this time the most advanced of Japan's nine regional electric utility companies with regards to nuclear power. By 1985, nuclear energy had become the dominant source of power in Shikoku, accounting for 39 percent of the total, and was expected to rise to 50 percent by the year 2000. Realizing that the potential of hydroelectric power in the region was ultimately limited, a section was created within the company in 1956 devoted to the development of coal, gas, and oil-fired power. In order to keep abreast of the latest technology in electric power generation, Shikoku Electric sent its chief engineers and planning officers to Europe and the United States on conferences, training courses, and exchange programs. This was typical of Japanese industry at the time, which was desperate for the technological knowledge which it saw as the key to success.

During this period, the company began in earnest the process of closing down redundant transformer substations and replacing them with a smaller number of higher voltage, more efficient units. Also in 1956, by boosting the existing capacity of Hirayama Power Station by 470kW to 2900kW, Shikoku Electric came to own the largest hydroelectric facility in the country and in 1959 began operating the country's first reverse wheel hydroelectric plant, the 11,800kW facility on Omori River. The year 1958 saw changes in the organization of the company, with increasing centralization of planning, engineering, and sales operations. In 1960, Miyazawa took over as chairman of the company, which by this time was the largest company in Shikoku

Key Dates:

1911: Japan enacts the Electric Utility Industry Law.
1920: By now, there are 3,000 power companies in Japan.
1948: The General Headquarters of the Allied Powers creates nine regionally based electricity generation and distribution companies.
1951: Shikoku Electric is incorporated to provide power to the island of Shikoku.
1978: The Ikata Nuclear Plant goes online.
1995: Japan partially liberalizes its electricity market.
2000: Deregulation begins in the retail sector of Japan's electric power industry.

with a capitalization of $19 million. For the next decade, like the other EPCs in Japan, Shikoku Electric concentrated on the building of oil-fired generating stations such as the 125MW plant completed in Tokushima in 1963. Cheap and plentiful Middle Eastern oil and lax environmental controls at the time made this form of generation the most economically attractive.

Ikata Nuclear Plant Goes Online in 1978

The oil shocks of 1973 and 1978 and increasing emission control quotas changed all this, however, and Shikoku Electric's main priority following these events was the development and construction of a nuclear power station. With technological help from and cooperation with France's nuclear power program, as well as the other domestic companies, Ikata Nuclear Plant was completed in 1978 with two initial pressurized water reactors and a combined output of almost 1,200MW, with an additional 890MW planned for 1995. Japan's nuclear program was a sensitive public issue and therefore extremely stringent safety controls were laid down. Japan's nuclear energy safety record was one of the world's best at the time, and Shikoku Electric had the additional distinction of operating the world's most efficient reactor.

During the 1970s, Shikoku Electric's sales trebled, and although the company's work force remained fairly steady at about 5,000, its revenues and profits increased dramatically. These profits were spent almost entirely on capital investment and research. In the early 1980s, plans for the largest bridge in the world, to link Shikoku with the main island of Honshu, were drawn up. The impressive Seto bridge was completed in 1988 at a cost of about ¥1.13 trillion and had the important effect of creating a tourist boom and urban renewal in the area. For Shikoku Electric, not only did the Seto bridge bring in more business, it could also be used to carry a major trunkline connecting the company with Kansai Electric Power's grid.

The late 1980s saw a slowdown in growth as Shikoku Electric's market matured. To some extent, the company diversified into new areas such as telecommunications with the formation of Shikoku Information & Telecommunication Network and the production of electric power equipment with Techno-Success Company. At the time, it was unlikely that these ventures would contribute significantly to profits and the firm's main emphasis remained on the continued development of the electric power

market. Some examples of the company's efforts in this area were the all-electric house, increased customer service, and the application of the hourly rate fluctuation system. On the international scene, the company continued to exchange information with similar companies worldwide and was a founding member of the World Association of Nuclear Operators formed in 1989. As most of the company's crucial raw materials came from abroad, a tight check was kept on commodity prices, and long-term purchase agreements such as those for uranium from France and Australia were entered into. Financially, the company was in an excellent position, holding a AAA rating with regard to raising money on the domestic bond market. Overseas, the company conducted two bond issues in Europe in 1989.

To mark the 40th year of business as Shikoku Electric, the company in 1991 launched a new corporate profile based on the environmentally safe and efficient generation of power along with increased provision for the development of customer services related to the core business of power generation.

Deregulation in the Mid-1990s and Beyond

In the years leading up to the new century, Shikoku Electric faced a host of challenges brought on by liberalization in Japan's energy sectors. By the mid-1990s, the electricity industry in Japan was undergoing major changes. In 1995, adjustments to the Electricity Utilities Industry Law allowed competition to enter into the electricity generation and supply market. Then, in 1996, a wholesale electric power bidding system enabled non-electric power companies to sell electricity to electric power companies. Finally, in March 2000, the retail sale of electricity was partially deregulated, allowing large-lot customers—those demanding large amounts of electricity—to choose their power supplier.

The intent of deregulation was to foster competition, which in turn would lower the electricity costs in the country. The deregulation was slow to change the Japanese industry, however, and during 2001 Shikoku Electric and the nine other regional companies still controlled 99 percent of the market. In fact, only six Japanese-based companies—other than the original ten—supplied power to large customers such as retail stores and office buildings. This accounted for a .2 percent share of the overall market.

Nevertheless, Shikoku Electric and its domestic peers were forced to deal with the changes brought on by deregulation. The electric companies were also pushed to seek out and develop environmentally friendly power sources. According to a March 2000 *Business Week* article, nuclear power accounted for nearly 35 percent of Japan's electricity. For much of the 1990s, Japan's industry had aggressively focused on shifting from expensive and polluting coal-fired plants to nuclear power. Due to rising concerns over the safety of these nuclear facilities, Japan's government was forced to rethink its expansion efforts, cut back on its nuclear development plans, and find alternative sources of power.

As such, Shikoku Electric worked not only to diversify its holdings in response to the changing business environment but also looked for new alternative methods for generating power. Believing that competition could eventually wreak havoc on its bottom line, the company moved into new business areas, including Internet access, cable television, real estate, engineering, aviation, and energy equipment manufacturing. Cable Media Shikoku Company Inc., a cable television broadcasting and telecommunications subsidiary, was established in 1995. The following year, Netwave Shikoku Company Inc. was created to oversee Internet provider services. The firm also set up subsidiaries related to video production, nursing facilities, and forestation.

While Shikoku Electric set new strategies in place, it faced yet another challenge. During the early years of the new century, Japan's economy was faltering. Demand from steel and manufacturing sectors fell, and in fiscal 2002 electricity sales were lackluster at best. The company's operating revenue fell in 2002 and again in 2003. In order to shore up profits, Shikoku Electric focused on several key initiatives: providing enhanced customer service and consulting services, continual diversification in the energy and telecommunication fields, streamlining costs, and restructuring its businesses into a divisional system. Japan's electric industry would no doubt continue to institute deregulating measures in the upcoming years, forcing Shikoku Electric to adapt its business polices as necessary. As one of Japan's original regional electric utilities, the company stood well positioned to face future obstacles head on.

Principal Subsidiaries

Shikoku Research Institute Inc.; Eco-Tech Company Inc.; Yondenko Corporation; Yonden Engineering Company Inc.; Yonden Consultants Company Inc.; Shihen Technical Corporation; Shikoku Instrumentation Company Ltd.; Techno-Success Company Inc.; STNet Inc.; Netwave Shikoku Company Inc.; Cable Media Shikoku Company Inc.; Shikoku Air Service Company Ltd.; Yonden Business Company Inc.; Yonden Energy Services Company Inc.; Ikata Service Company Inc.; Tachibana Thermal Power Port Service Company Inc.; Yonden Media Works Company Inc.; Yonden Life Care Company Inc.; Yonden Afforestation Australia Pty. Ltd.; Tokushima Automobile Service Company Inc.

Principal Competitors

The Kansai Electric Power Company Inc.; Nippon Telegraph and Telephone Corporation; The Tokyo Electric Power Company Inc.

Further Reading

Bogler, Daniel, ''Profits Tumble at Japanese Electricity Groups,'' *Financial Times*, November 21, 1996, p. 38.

Bremner, Brian, ''Tokyo's Nuclear Dilemma,'' *Business Week*, March 15, 2000.

''Ehime Residents Lose Lawsuit over Nuke-Plant Red Tape,'' *Japan Economic Newswire*, February 9, 2001.

Goto, Yasuhiro, ''No Single Recipe for Deregulation of Utilities,'' *Nikkei Weekly*, March 5, 2001.

History of the Electric Power Industry in Japan, Tokyo: Japan Electric Power Information Center, 1989.

''Nuclear Industry Seeks to Regain Public Trust,'' *Yomiuri Shimbun/ Daily Yomiuri*, November 1, 2003.

''Shikoku Elec. Profit, Sales Drop in FY '96,'' *Jiji Press Ticker Service*, May 23, 1997.

''Shikoku Electric Sets up Tree-Planting Firm in Australia,'' *Jiji Press Ticker Service*, April 7, 2000.

—Dylan Tanner
—update: Christina M. Stansell

Shure Inc.

5800 West Touhy Avenue
Niles, Illinois 60714
U.S.A.
Telephone: (847) 600-2000
Fax: (847)600-1212
Web site: http://www.shure.com

Private Company
Founded: 1925
Employees: 1,400
Sales: $245 million (2001 est.)
NAIC: 334419 Other Electronic Component Manufacturing;
 334310 Audio and Video Equipment Manufacturing

Shure Inc. is one of the world's largest, most respected manufacturers of microphones. Shure's microphones have been used by the world's leading performers and public speakers for over seventy years. The company makes a broad range of sound equipment, including mixers, conferencing systems, phonograph cartridges, signal processors, and personal monitor systems. Shure products are endorsed by over 240 of the world's best-known performers in the entertainment industry. The company markets its products outside the United States through a network of subsidiaries and distributors. Shure Incorporated has been owned by the Shure family since its founding.

Founded at the Dawn of the Radio Age

Shure Incorporated was founded in Chicago in 1925 by Sidney N. Shure. Shure became interested in amateur radio as a child and, like every other radio buff at the time, built his own radio sets. After his graduation from the University of Chicago, he set up a company to distribute radio parts. Radio's popularity was growing by leaps and bounds in 1925, but ready-made radios were still not available for purchase. If a consumer wanted a radio, he had to build it himself. The firm took off. After Shure's brother, Samuel J. Shure, joined the company in 1928, the name of the firm was changed to Shure Brothers Company. At the time, with over 75 employees and a bustling site in downtown Chicago, the business seemed to be on solid footing.

Microphones for War and Peace in the 1930s

Serious challenges lay ahead for the young firm. The Great Depression struck in 1929; however, more important for the Shure Brothers was a critical shift in the radio market. By 1930, the National Broadcasting Corporation was operating two networks in the United States, and 13.5 million finished radio sets were sold that year. Suddenly, radio was no longer a hobby market—it was a consumer market. The demand for parts plunged. Sidney Shure cannily saw new opportunities in the collapse of his market. The dawn of the radio age was also the dawn of the microphone age. Microphones were needed for broadcasting, for police radio, for aviation. There were, however, few major microphone manufacturers in the United States. Many of the best microphones came from overseas and were quite expensive. Shure dove into the microphone business, licensing microphone patents and hiring engineers to develop new products.

The Shure Brothers released their first microphone, the Shure Two-Button Carbon Microphone, in 1932. The new product had everything going for it. It was compact, durable, lightweight, versatile, and dependable. It won immediate popularity for live sound and two-way radio applications. Both professional and amateur broadcasters bought it. Its most alluring characteristic was undoubtedly its price. The Two-Button Carbon Microphone sold for about $30 at a time when other microphones—primarily imports from Germany—cost several hundred dollars. Shure established a network of sales representatives to market the new microphone through electronic parts distributors. The businesses that less than five years earlier had been the Shure Brothers' competitors now became their outlets.

Microphone development was still in its infancy in the 1930s, and Shure experimented with various types throughout the decade to find out what types worked best and what the public wanted. The firm introduced its first high-end condenser microphone, the Model 40D, in 1933. It put a crystal microphone into production in 1935 and two years later brought out the world's first noise-canceling mic. In 1939, Shure researchers, under the direction of engineer Ben Bauer, hit pay dirt with the groundbreaking development of the Model 55 Unidyne microphone, the world's first single-element unidirectional microphone. The development of unidirectional mics was significant because they greatly reduced extraneous noise and limited feedback.

Unidirectional microphones existed before the Unidyne, but they were constructed from two elements that had to be combined electronically. Bauer found a way to make a unidirectional microphone from a single element, greatly simplifying production and reducing costs. The Unidyne also had a striking Art Deco design based in part on the front grill of a 1937 Cadillac.

The Unidyne established Shure's name as an important manufacturer of microphones. Politicians addressing large crowds of the time were almost certain to speak into a Unidyne. The new product also launched a change in popular music. Singers of the big band era no longer had to rely on their own volume. Smooth-voiced, intimate crooners, like Bing Crosby and Frank Sinatra, came into vogue. The start of World War II in Europe helped the Unidyne as well. Once German microphones were no longer available, the Unidyne mic became the dominant microphone in the United States. Its reasonable $45 piece tag also helped sales.

The war brought Shure a major new market. Microphones were needed in ships, tanks, planes, and the infantry. Beginning in 1941, when the War Department contracted with Shure to produce microphones, Shure developed a range of models for the military. Shure's best-known war mic was undoubtedly the T-30 Throat microphone, which was fastened near the collar of a bomber pilot's jacket and operated by throat vibrations. With metal at a premium, Shure also developed mics made of plastic, an early manufacturing application of the new material.

Becoming a Consumer Company in the 1950s

With the end of World War II in 1945, the annual demand for tens of thousands of mics for the military dried up. Nevertheless, the late 1940s and 1950s witnessed another successful period in the company's history. Once again, Shure shifted focus, this time to a consumer market that was on the verge of

explosive growth: home hi-fis. Shure had launched a line of phonograph cartridges in 1937. It was a natural extension of its product line. Phono cartridges and microphones work on precisely the same principle: a magnet or coil of wire generates an electric signal from an acoustic or mechanical signal. Almost from the start Shure's phono cartridges were supplied to the country's leading phonograph manufacturers, including RCA, Emerson, and Magnavox. Although for a time the firm also produced playback and recording heads for tape recorders, the bulk of its efforts went into developing better cartridges. By the 1950s, Shure was the leading manufacturer of phonograph cartridges in the world.

It continued to work on new microphone technologies as well. In 1953, it developed the Vagabond, the world's first wireless microphone for performing, a product that utilized walkie-talkie and hearing-aid technologies. The microphone sent a signal to a perimeter of wire that encircled the stage. A performer had to stay within that perimeter for the microphone to operate. It was used for a short time in Las Vegas, with Frank Sinatra its most noteworthy tester. Unfortunately, the Vagabond was fragile and undependable. In addition to its technical shortcomings, it was also extremely expensive, selling for about $800 in 1953. The Vagabond was phased out in the mid-1950s. Another thirty years would pass before wireless microphone technology came into its own. A Shure component was also part of another product that was ahead of its time. In the mid-1950s, the company manufactured a phono cartridge for Chrysler's short-lived in-car phonograph, the Highway Hi-Fi.

Shure introduced a number of other products that were more enduring during the 1950s. In 1958, it brought out the world's first stereo phonograph cartridge, the M3D. A year later, it changed the way microphones would look forever with the Unidyne III. Previously, microphones were designed to detect sound from the side. The Unidyne was wand-shaped and picked up sound from its end. Within a few years, it would be the most common microphone design in the world. In 1956, Shure gave up its production and office facilities just outside Chicago's Loop and moved into spacious new headquarters in suburban Evanston. It set up a new microphone factory in the same complex.

A major impulse for the development of new microphones in the 1950s was the rise of rock and roll. With electric guitars more and more the instrument of choice, volumes were climbing ever higher, and vocalists could not perform without a microphone. As concert venues grew larger over the next two decades, other instruments began to be miked as well, in particular drum kits. Shure continued to refine its mics during the 1960s to meet musicians' increasingly demanding standards for sound fidelity as well as to better cope with the high sound levels on stage. In 1965, Shure released the SM57. Extremely versatile, the SM57 could be used to amplify speech, singing, or musical instruments. It has been on the podium of every American president since Lyndon Johnson.

A year later, Shure set a new standard for the industry with the introduction of the SM58. ("SM" stands for "studio model.") Accurate and rugged, the SM58 has become the standard microphone for vocalists in every genre of popular music, especially rock. It is the best-selling microphone in Shure's history. Ironically, while the SM57 and SM58 have

Key Dates:

1925: Shure Radio Company is founded in Chicago by Sidney N. Shure.

1928: Shure's brother Samuel J. Shure the joins firm, which is renamed Shure Brothers Company.

1932: The company introduces its first microphone, the Shure Two-Button Carbon Microphone.

1933: Production of the Model 40D, the company's first high-end microphone.

1937: The company's first phonograph cartridge is introduced.

1939: The Model 55 Unidyne microphone is launched.

1941: The company begins production of microphones for the War Department during World War II.

1946: The company is renamed Shure Brothers Inc.

1953: The Vagabond, the world's first wireless microphone system, is introduced.

1966: The SM58, the most popular microphone in Shure's history, is introduced.

1968: The M67 battery-powered mixer makes live remote news coverage possible for broadcasters.

1989: Beta microphone line is launched with the introduction of the Beta 58 microphone.

1990: Shure re-enters the wireless microphone market.

1995: Founder and chairman of the board Sidney Shure dies at the age of 93.

1999: The company is renamed Shure Inc.

2000: Shure celebrates it 75th anniversary.

2003: Company headquarters are moved to Niles, Illinois.

major played a role in the growth of rock music, they were originally designed by an engineer who disliked rock and roll. However, sound engineers for touring rock bands soon discovered the SM58's rugged construction and reliable sound and made it the microphone of choice for leading rock groups, including the Beatles, Rolling Stones, and the Who.

At the same time it was bringing out the SM57 and SM58, Shure broadened its product offerings for musicians with the VocalMaster, a portable public address system that appealed to weekend performers as much as it did to seasoned professionals.

Shure made a major contribution to television news in 1968 with the development of the M67, a battery-powered mixer that could be used outside a studio. For the first time, TV camera crews and reporters were able to cover news stories live on location with battery operated equipment. Shure portable mixers were eventually used to cover many of the major stories of the late 1960s, including the space shots and the Woodstock Festival.

Technologies Shift in the 1970s and 1980s

Shure continued to expand and develop its phono cartridge line during the 1960s, introducing the first of its V15 Cartridges in 1964. By the 1970s, the company had evolved into a manufacturer of expensive, high-end, audiophile stereo components,

and the V15 was the showpiece of the line. Shure continued to supply its phono cartridges to most leading makers of stereo equipment. By the 1970s, with Baby Boomers reaching adulthood, phonograph sales were hitting all-time highs. At their peak, the company produced a line of approximately forty different cartridge models ranging in price from $20 to $150. So profitable was the line in the 1970s that Shure focused most of its energies on phono cartridges during the decade. It even constructed a plant in Phoenix, Arizona, specifically for their manufacture.

In the 1980s, however, disaster struck the phonograph industry. The CD player was introduced, and phonograph sales plummeted. Shure's cartridge segment which, according to the *Journal of Commerce*, had grown 700 percent in the 1970s until it comprised 67 percent of the firm's business, had dwindled to 16 percent by the mid-1990s. The market shrank so rapidly that for a while the company may have been in danger of going out of business. In response to the crisis, Shure made the fourth radical shift of its history, largely abandoning its old consumer base and reinventing itself again as a company that made tools for sound professionals. It expanded its selection of products for broadcasters, introducing the Field Production line of sound mixers for the burgeoning Electronic News Gathering (ENG) markets, perhaps most popularly represented by cable station CNN, which at the time was an upstart news organization. It also began aggressively marketing its microphone line to music stores once again. Music and broadcasting were not the only fields to appreciate the quality of Shure microphones. Since the National Aeronautics and Space Administration could not use electrical connections between the space shuttle and the rockets that powered it—the rockets break away once their fuel is spent—Shure mics were used to monitor performance acoustically.

Growth into New Markets in the 1990s

As the 1990s got underway, Shure was making inroads into teleconferencing systems, a market in which it had first become involved in the mid-1980s. Teleconferencing was a natural extension of the firm's expertise in microphones and sound mixers. This market gave birth to a completely new division of Shure, one that specialized in selling teleconferencing systems which, unlike microphones and cartridges, sold for thousands of dollars. Furthermore, teleconferencing was still relatively unfamiliar outside the United States at the time. To publicize the usefulness of the technology, Shure set up the first global interactive teleconference between 21 cities in the United States, Canada, Europe, Japan, Australia, South Korea, and South Africa. The first transatlantic trial, held between Milwaukee, Wisconsin, and London, England, also used Shure equipment.

By the mid-1990s, according to the *Journal of Commerce*, exports comprised 35 percent of Shure's total teleconferencing systems sales. Foreign markets had long been important to Shure. For years it had been active in England, Western Europe, and Japan. In the early 1990s, soon after the fall of communism in Eastern Europe, Shure began distributing its products in Poland, Hungary, and the Czech Republic. Later in the decade, it expanded into Ecuador, Paraguay, Guatemala, and Vietnam. By 1995, China was Shure's main export market, accounting for 22 percent of its total foreign sales. At this time, the company began moving some of its production out of the

United States. In an effort to keep its labor costs as low as possible, Shure built plants for the assembly of microphones and phono cartridges in Agua Prieta and Juarez, Mexico.

Shure's microphone line was refined and expanded in the 1990s. It finally entered the burgeoning wireless market it had given up in the 1950s when it abandoned the Vagabond. Shure had nevertheless been active in the wireless market, albeit indirectly, through much of the previous decade, during which it had produced microphone heads for other manufacturers' wireless systems. The company's leaders eventually realized that the huge numbers of heads they were producing represented an equally vast market they could be selling to directly. Its "L" series of modern wireless mics was introduced in 1990. Shure also actively promoted its line of high-performance Beta microphones first developed in 1989. Because of their improved design, these microphones reproduced vocals with even greater fidelity than the old "SM" series. In addition, the new mics possessed hardened grills and sturdier shock mounts.

A third new market that Shure aggressively courted in the 1990s was sound contractors. Shure products had always been favorites of these businesses which specialized in the design and installation of sound systems in churches, auditoriums, and similar buildings. Shure developed a new line of products specifically for the needs of sound contractors.

In 1995, at the age of 93, after leading the company for seventy years, Sidney Shure passed away. He had given up running the day-to-day operations of the company in 1981, when a new president was named. He remained as chairman of the Shure board of directors until his death, when his widow, Rose Shure, succeeded him. Mr. Shure had been an individual of broad and continuing interests. He was a renowned collector of stamps who eventually donated much of his collection to the Smithsonian Institution. He trained himself to be an accomplished photographer. He had a longstanding interest in languages and began learning Hebrew when he was in his eighties. His modest, unassuming nature helped create a family-like atmosphere for workers at Shure.

A Long History Continues into the 2000s

When Shure Incorporated celebrated its 75th anniversary in 2000, the difficulties of the 1980s were forgotten. Microphones, wired and wireless, were once again the central focus of the company's business. The line that had included about 50 various mics in the 1950s had grown to some 300 items in 2000. The introduction of inexpensive digital recording gear—especially for home recording—led to the growing popularity of Shure's KSM line of mics, which were designed especially for recording. By 2003, Shure had lines of microphones for broadcasters, sound contractors, recording studios, live sound, two-way communication, and paging. Other new products were also beginning to gain in popularity, including a selection of in-ear monitors for live performance situations. In the spring of 2003, Shure left its longtime headquarters in Evanston for a futuristic building designed by architect Helmut Jahn in Niles, Illinois.

Principal Subsidiaries

Shure UK; Shure Europe; Shure Asia.

Principal Competitors

Sennheiser; Audio Technica; Telex Communications Inc.

Further Reading

Gilpin, Kenneth N. "Stanley Shure, 93, an Industry Leader in Audio Electronics," *New York Times*, October 21, 1995, p. A27.

Kouri, Charles J. *Shure: Sound People, Products, and Values*, Evanston, Ill.: Shure, 2001.

"Manufacturing Operations In Wheeling, Ill., Are Bought," *Wall Street Journal*, September 7, 1999, p. A11

"Shure Brothers Inc," *Journal of Commerce*, May 12, 1995, p. 5A.

"Sidney N. Shure; Owned Microphone Company," *Chicago Sun-Times*, October 22, 1995, p. 61.

—Gerald E. Brennan

The Singing Machine Company, Inc.

6601 Lyons Road
Building A-7
Coconut Creek, Florida 33073
U.S.A.
Telephone: (954) 596-1000
Fax: (954) 596-2000
Web site: http://www.singingmachine.com

Public Company
Incorporated: 1982
Employees: 54
Sale: $95.6 million (2002)
Stock Exchanges: American
Ticker Symbol: SMD
NAIC: 334310 Audio and Video Equipment
Manufacturing; 512240 Audio and Video Equipment
Manufacturing

The Singing Machine Company, Inc. develops and distributes karaoke machines and music for home use. Its karaoke machines are manufactured under contract in China and are sold in North America, Europe, and Asia. Most of the nearly 3,000 songs the company uses with its machines are mixed and produced at its Florida studios. Singing Machine was one of the first in the industry to target consumers rather than businesses for its products. Its success has partly stemmed from effective cross-marketing deals, which allow it to distribute its karaoke machines under the MTV, Nickelodeon, Hard Rock Academy, and Motown brand names, as well as under its own label. Singing Machine does the bulk of its sales in the United States during the holiday season at mass retailers, including Wal-Mart, Toys ''R'' Us, Best Buy, and Sears. After a string of phenomenal years in which the company annually achieved record sales and profits, Singing Machine fell on harder times. After the company was forced in 2003 to restate earnings for the fiscal years of 2001, 2002, and 2003, shareholders filed suit, alleging that the company had materially misrepresented its financial bona fides.

Early Years: 1982–87

Legend has it that karaoke—a Japanese word meaning ''empty orchestra''—was invented in the Japanese city of Kobe in the early 1970s when a band failed to show up for its nightclub act. In an attempt to keep the crowd occupied, the club's owner played tapes of music without vocals and handed around a microphone that members of the audience used to sing along. The impromptu entertainment was a hit, and a cultural phenomenon was born. By the mid-1970s, several Japanese audio companies had begun producing karaoke machines and the musical tapes to go along with them.

Karaoke found its way to the United States in the early 1980s, as karaoke bars sprang up in major cities. While karaoke gained adherents among some Americans, the activity was nowhere near as popular as it was in Japan, where it had become ''a way of life,'' according to *Transpacific*. However, karaoke did catch the eye of some state-side investors who saw in it a business opportunity. One such pioneer was Earl Glick, the head of Hal Roach Studios Inc. in Hollywood, who had become enchanted with the concept of karaoke while he was vacationing on a cruise ship. Roach Studios, the producers of the *Laurel and Hardy* and *Li'l Rascals* movies, was a venerable Hollywood institution.

Glick launched The Singing Machine as a Roach Studios subsidiary in 1982. Soon thereafter, he met with Ahihiko Kurobe, an executive with Nikkodo, one of the leading karaoke machine companies in Japan. Glick and Kurobe agreed to team up, with Nikkodo manufacturing karaoke devices for Singing Machine, which would become the first American company striving to reach the American karaoke market. (Singing Machine would later terminate this production contract with Nikkodo and instead directly contract out the manufacture of its karaoke machines to Asian factories.) Like other karaoke equipment producers, Singing Machine pitched its products not to individual karaoke users but to the karaoke bars and nightclubs that were beginning to gain popularity. The machines were technically sophisticated and quite expensive, with Singing Machine's early models typically costing over $2,000. The company also began to produce the taped background music that the machines played, which involved acquiring licenses from record labels and artists, and then hiring musicians to re-record the original songs without vocals.

Although the market for Singing Machine's products was relatively small, the company performed well in its early years. By 1987, Singing Machine had sold 30,000 machines and expanded its line to include five types, ranging in price from $250 to $2,300, and a library of 1,500 different background tracks on both tape and compact disc. However, Singing Machine's parent company was stretched too thin. Roach Studios had aggressively entered new markets in the 1980s but had overextended itself. In 1987, Roach Studios sold Singing Machine to a group of entertainment and toy industry investors for $1.75 million.

New Challenges: 1988–97

A pivotal moment for the young company took place in 1988, when Edward Steele joined Singing Machine. Steele, a veteran executive from the toy industry, had become fascinated with karaoke machines after seeing their popularity in Asian bars. In 1989, Steele acquired a significant stake in the company and began to chart its course for future growth. Steele believed that karaoke had broad appeal in the United States but that Singing Machine had been misguided when it sought to follow a Japanese marketing model and rely almost exclusively on sales to bars and nightclubs. Rather, Steele believed, karaoke must be brought directly to American consumers. "You can sell a lot more machines to the population than to karaoke clubs," a company executive would later tell the *Miami Herald*.

To implement Steele's vision of marketing directly to consumers, the company aggressively expanded its product line to include cheaper and less sophisticated machines that individuals could afford to buy and use at home. An early iteration of this idea was Singing Machine's $49 dual cassette recorder, which could tape a singer on one side using pre-recorded music on the other. Nevertheless, the company did not abandon its original market of bars and nightclubs but continued to oversee the manufacture and marketing of high-end machines designed for those venues.

The early 1990s proved the viability of Steele's foresight. Domestic karaoke machine sales exploded from $75 million in 1990 to $590 million by 1992, and consumer awareness of karaoke had risen to 80 percent by the latter year. However, with the karaoke market expanding, more competitors entered the field. By 1992, sixty-five different American companies

were engaged in the manufacture of karaoke hardware (machines), software (tapes and CDs), and accessories. Fortunately for Singing Machine, the company had a solid foothold since it had entered the sector early.

Singing Machine's two-pronged strategy of targeting both institutional customers and individual consumers did not yield immediate results. The company's earnings were erratic. In an attempt to raise capital, fund expansion, and smooth operations, Singing Machine opted to become a public company in 1994. An initial stock offering of 1.2 million shares netted the company $4.7 million. Steele, who had assumed the post of chief executive officer, retained a 9.5 percent stake in the company.

Singing Machine's position looked secure after its stock offering. The company significantly expanded the array of products available to consumers to include eighteen different models of karaoke machines marketed under four trademarks—The Singing Machine, Karaoke Kassette, Karaoke Compact Disc, and Karaoke Video Kassette. In 1995, the company also launched its own version of the latest karaoke technology—compact discs with graphics (CD+G). When played in a karaoke machine, this compact disc scrolled the lyrics of the song in time with the music, making it easier for singers to follow along.

Despite these positive developments, Singing Machine faced significant obstacles in the wake of its stock offering. The karaoke equipment sector had become even more crowded as a range of companies recognized karaoke's growth potential. "Every major multimedia, electronics, and software company in the United States is involved with this newest entertainment medium," an industry analyst told the *Orlando Sentinel* in 1994.

Singing Machine responded to these new threats on different fronts. In an attempt to boost its sales by making its machines stand out from the competition's on store shelves, the company reached an agreement with Memcorp, Inc., which allowed Singing Machine to use the Memorex trademark on its electronic karaoke equipment. Singing Machine also sought to drive sales with greater retail penetration. In 1995, the company reached key agreements with Camelot Music Stores and Radio Shack that allowed Singing Machine to test products in Camelot stores and display its latest catalogue in over 6,000 Radio Shack outlets. Singing Machine also looked to its own operational efficiencies to improve its bottom line. In 1995, the company formed a wholly owned, Hong Kong-based subsidiary, International SMC (Hong Kong) Ltd. With this new unit, Singing Machine anticipated that it could book 100 percent of its Far East merchandise sales, which would increase its revenues by an estimated $2.5 million. (With its existing arrangement, Singing Machine could only attribute a percentage of its Asian sales as commission revenue from direct sales.)

However, Singing Machine's situation did not improve. After renegotiating the terms of its financing agreement with Banker's Capital, the company reported a net loss of $152,000 on sales of about $5.9 million in fiscal year 1995. The following year did not bring better results, as revenue dropped and losses widened. The company pledged to reduce expenditures, cut employees, and initiate new programs to drive sales. Singing Machine abruptly fired its president, Eugene Settler, in 1996,

Key Dates:

1982: Singing Machine is incorporated as a subsidiary of Hal Roach Studios Inc.
1987: An investor group acquires Singing Machine.
1990: The company moves its headquarters from California to Boca Raton, Florida.
1994: Singing Machine becomes a public company.
1995: The company forms International SMC (Hong Kong) Ltd.
1997: Singing Machine seeks Chapter 11 protection.
2000: Singing Machine signs a merchandise licensing agreement with cable television channel MTV.
2001: Singing Machine enters into a distribution agreement with Arbiter Group plc.
2002: Singing Machine signs a licensing agreement with Viacom International Inc. to create a line of Nickelodeon branded karaoke machines and software.
2003: Singing Machine restates its earnings for the previous three fiscal years; a class action shareholder suit is filed against the company.

and Steele took over Settler's administrative functions in addition to his own as CEO. Nevertheless, these steps could not halt Singing Machine's downward spiral. In 1997, the company filed for protection from its creditors under the provisions of Chapter 11. Steele remained optimistic about Singing Machine's prospects, though. "The pressure is now off," he said in an April 18, 1997 press release. "Chapter 11 will give us the opportunity to put into place a comprehensive restructuring plan." Singing Machine emerged from Chapter 11 in 1998.

Restructuring and Growth: 1998–2002

The cornerstone of Singing Machine's post-Chapter 11 restructuring plan was to improve retail penetration. In the early 1990s the company had made some headway in pitching its machines to individual consumers, but it had struggled to gain access to the types of stores that could generate the volume of sales it required. Its main retail customers were PACE Membership Warehouse and Handelman, not the retail giants that could make or break a brand. In 1997, Steele brought in John Klechna as Singing Machine's chief operating officer, and Klechna immediately turned his attention to this problem. "We basically had to beg, borrow, and steal to get retail programs in at the ground level and convince retail buyers that it's a dynamic category," Klecha told the *Miami Herald* in 2000.

By 1999, Singing Machine had distribution agreements with Best Buy, Sears, and JC Penney, and in the following year the company reached crucial agreements to bring its products to Toys "R" Us and Wal-Mart.

Once it had secured these retail agreements, Singing Machine focused on building its customer base. Despite its growing popularity in the United States—by 2000 the domestic karaoke market was estimated at more than $200 million— karaoke still retained associations from its past as a nightlife activity for adults. Singing Machine saw the future of karaoke

in younger consumers and cast about for ways to draw them to its products, as well as convince their parents that karaoke was family-oriented fun.

To fulfill this strategy, Singing Machine reached an agreement with MTV—"that perennial arbiter of all things youthful," as *Cable World* dubbed the network—in 2001. In exchange for royalties of $650,000 over three years, Singing Machine received the right to market a line of MTV-branded karaoke machines and to get input from MTV's creative staff in designing the two initial models and creating the song lists that were sold with the karaoke machines. The deal was an unequivocal triumph for Singing Machine. "Since their introduction . . . our MTV-branded karaoke systems have grown to become the most successful products in our history," Klechna (who had assumed the post of president in 2001) said in a January 8, 2002 company press release.

Hoping to build on the success of its MTV deal, Singing Machine signed a multi-year domestic merchandise licensing agreement with Nickelodeon, a unit of Viacom International Inc. Under the terms of the deal, Singing Machine would produce a line of Nickelodeon-branded karaoke machines and software featuring music for the television network's core audience. While its relationship with MTV was intended to draw teenage and young adult consumers, with the Nickelodeon product line, Singing Machine sought to appeal to an even younger demographic—pre-schoolers and pre-teens, whom the company believed represented tremendous growth potential.

Singing Machine did not want to overlook its original consumers either, and used its cross-branding strategy to shore up its position with older karaoke fans. In 2002, the company signed a three-year agreement with Hard Rock Academy, a division of the trendy Hard Rock Café, to produce a line of Hard Rock branded machines and music software. Later that year, the company entered a similar agreement with Universal Music Group to produce Motown Originals software and karaoke machines, which Singing Machine directed at baby boomer consumers who wanted to reconnect with the Motown music of their youth.

However, Singing Machine's growth strategy involved more than licensing agreements. In 2001, the company hired the advertising and public relations firm DK 13 & Partners to step up its marketing efforts. Recognizing that karaoke's potential outside the United States and Asia was virtually untapped, the company entered a distribution agreement with London-based Arbiter Group PLC, a leading distributor of consumer electronics products to major retailers in the United Kingdom and throughout Europe. "We believe that our opportunity in Europe rivals our opportunity on this side of the Atlantic," Klechna said in a company press release on November 28, 2001.

The company's post-bankruptcy efforts were successful. Singing Machine's revenue shot up from $6 million in fiscal year 1997 to $9.5 million in fiscal year 1999 and to $19 million the following year. The company's sales grew at an annual average rate of 83 percent between 1999 and 2001, when revenue reached $59 million. In 2002, the company's revenue grew another 80 percent to exceed $61 million. Equally impressive was the jump in earnings, which rose an average of 136 percent a year to top $9 million in 2001. *Business Week* named Singing Machine its top "Hot Growth" company in 2002. "We're really on the tip of the iceberg of where this can go," an ebullient Klechna told the *Miami Herald* on April 14, 2003.

Rebuilding: 2003 and Beyond

However, Singing Machine's fortunes changed dramatically in 2003, when the company was forced by its auditors to restate its earnings for fiscal years 2001, 2002, and 2003 because of a tax issue with its Hong Kong subsidiary. The subsidiary generated most of the company's profit, yet Singing Machine had not paid any foreign income tax because it assumed it would get an exemption from the Hong Kong tax authority, since all of its profits were generated from exporting to customers outside Hong Kong. Within one day of the announcement, Singing Machine's share price fell 38 percent.

On the heels of this bad news came reports that Singing Machine's prospects were not quite as rosy as they once appeared. In 2002, Klechna had overseen an agreement in which Singing Machine agreed to sell to a major retail customer on consignment (and thus not get paid until the karaoke machines were sold). The customer pulled out of the deal at the last minute, leaving Singing Machine with a backlog of inventory worth $2.6 million. To compound this problem, the company performed poorly that holiday season—the period that typically accounted for nearly 80 percent of its annual sales. This in turn caused Singing Machine's inventory to balloon even more. Saddled with so much unsold merchandise, Singing Machine's debt climbed. By the end of 2002, the company owed some of its creditors $8.5 million, and its net worth had fallen to $26 million, which violated a covenant of a loan agreement with La Salle National Bank that required the company to maintain a minimum net worth of $30 million. This stream of bad news prompted shareholders to file a class action lawsuit against Singing Machine for making material misrepresentations to the market between 2001 and 2003. The company's auditors expressed substantial doubt about its ability to continue as a going concern.

Singing Machine took steps to allay doubts about its future. After the consignment debacle came to light, Klechna stepped down as president and COO and was replaced as COO by Y.P. Chan. In July 2003, Steele resigned as CEO. Robert Weinberg was named CEO and president, and Howard Moore assumed Steele's position as chairman of the board of directors. The company remained optimistic that it could get itself back on track. "We made a couple of mistakes last year; we're paying for it," Chan told the *Miami Herald* on July 1, 2003. "The company has grown substantially the last five years. Along with the growth, we have had growing pains."

Principal Subsidiaries

International SMC (Hong Kong) Ltd.

Principal Competitors

Casio Computer Company, Ltd.; Pioneer Corporation; Victor Company of Japan, Ltd.

Further Reading

Buckley, Cara, "Singing Machine Racks up Revenue," *Miami Herald*, November 15, 2000.

Danner, Patrick, "Singing All the Way to the Bank," *Miami Herald*, April 14, 2003.

——, "Behind Singing's New Take," *Miami Herald*, July 1, 2003.

——, "Inventory Spike Causes Worry," *Miami Herald*, July 16, 2003.

——, "Singing Machine's CEO to Resign," *Miami Herald*, July 24, 2003.

Lorek, L., "Public Offering Sells Shares in Karaoke Company for a Song," *Fort Lauderdale Sun-Sentinel*, November 18, 1994.

"Karaoke = Kurobe," *Transpacific,* October 1, 1994.

Kopetman, Roxana, "Japanese-Style Karaoke Bars Put Singing Patrons in Spotlight," *Los Angeles Times*, August 1, 1989.

McGowan, Chris, "Though Not Yet a Boom, Karaoke Has Made Significant Gains in the U.S. Market," *Billboard*, May 30, 1992.

Pascual, Aixa, "Thanks to Partnerships and Clever Marketing Moves, Singing Machine Is Making Happy Music," *Business Week*, June 10, 2002, p. 98.

Schultz, Christopher, "Say What? MTV Sings Duet With Karaoke Maker," *Cable World*, July 2001.

"The Singing Machine Company Establishes European Distribution," *Business Wire*, November 28, 2001.

"The Singing Machine Company Files Chapter 22," *PR Newswire*, April 18, 1997.

"The Singing Machine Company Signs License Agreement with Nickelodeon," *Business Wire*, January 8, 2002.

—Rebecca Stanfel

LE FIGARO

Société du Figaro S.A.

37 rue du Louvre
Paris F-75002
France
Telephone: (+33) 1 42 21 62 00
Fax: (+33)1 42 21 29 38
Web site: http://groupe.lefigaro.fr

Private Company
Incorporated: 1826
Employees: 1,200
Sales: EUR 500 million ($480 million)(2002 est.)
NAIC: 511140 Database and Directory Publishers;
511110 Newspaper Publishers; 511120 Periodical
Publishers; 511130 Book Publishers; 518111 Internet
Service Providers

One of France's oldest newspaper groups, Société du Figaro S.A. reigns as one of the country's major media players. The company is focused on its daily newspaper, *Le Figaro,* the country's leading daily with an average circulation of around two million. The success of its newspaper has led Société du Figaro to build up a stable of related titles, including *Le Figaro Magazine,* a leading weekly news and information magazine; the newspaper supplement *Le Figaro Enterprises,* formerly *Le Figaro Economique*; the highly popular *Madame Figaro,* which, in addition to its success in France is also published in Japan, Taiwan, China, and Korea; and the more specialized titles *Le Figaro Patrimoine, Le Figaro Etudiant, L'indicateur Bertrand,* and *Le Figaroscope.* Société du Figaro is itself wholly owned by media group Socpresse, which in turn is controlled by the Hersant family. The highly secretive Socpresse controls a larger list of French regional and media newspaper titles, as well as newspapers in the French Antilles, and is said to control as much as 30 percent of the French news media market. Socpresse also acquired two widely read French news and information magazines, *L'Expansion* and *L'Express* in 2002. At the end of 2003, Société du Figaro sparked controversy in the French media market when it announced its intention to pull out of the Paris Press Trade Union. Société du Figaro has never officially re-

leased sales figures, although sales have been estimated to top EUR 500 million ($480 million) in 2002.

Making Newspaper History in 19th Century France

The origins of Société du Figaro reach back to the early years of the Parisian press. An early version of the newspaper appeared in 1826 under the leadership of Maurice Alhoy and Auguste Lepoitevin Saint-Alme. The daily, which comprised four pages, remained in publication until 1833. A number of attempts were made to revive the paper over the next three decades, with a total of nine different newspapers using the name *Figaro* or *Le Figaro* appearing between the years 1835 and 1847 alone.

In 1854, Hippolyte de Villemessant launched a rendition of *Figaro* that met with more lasting success. The new *Figaro* initially appeared as a weekly paper that distinguished itself by its opinionated editorial stance. Villemessant proved an innovator in the French newspaper world, introducing the concept of regularly published features and sections and adding news briefs that forced journalists to adopt a more clear, concise style. *Figaro* enjoyed early success, and by 1856 the paper began publishing as a bi-weekly.

In the early 1860s, *Figaro* was faced with the emergence of a rival paper, *Le Petit Journal.* Although targeting a market that was more populist than that of *Figaro,* the new paper's fast growth nevertheless threatened *Figaro*'s own growing subscriber base. In 1865, Villemessant quickly launched a second newspaper, the daily *L'Evenement,* as a direct competitor to *Le Petit Journal.* However, Villemessant's new publication failed to catch up to its rival; worse, in 1866, after publishing on article on "the rights of the poor," *L'Evenement* was banned by the French government.

In response, Villemessant converted *Figaro* into a daily newspaper, and, on its second day of publication, the newspaper took on the name *Le Figaro.* The newly expanded newspaper displayed an avowedly apolitical stance and began catering to a less exclusive class of readers. At the end of 1866, the newspaper commissioned a certified circulation count—the first French newspaper to do so—and *Le Figaro*'s official circulation was placed at 56,000, including 15,000 subscribers.

The liberalization of the press in the late 1860s encouraged *Le Figaro* to adopt a more political tone. The paper also began to attract leading names in the French press and literary scene, such as the controversial Henri Rochefort, Emile Zola, Alexandre Dumas, and Alphonse Daudet.

The Commune of Paris of 1871 formed a turning point for *Le Figaro*. Suppressed by the Communards soon after the revolt, *Le Figaro* resumed publication only after the victory of Versailles several weeks later. *Le Figaro* now adopted an editorial policy favoring the conservative political viewpoint and quickly became the newspaper of reference for Paris's bourgeois and aristocratic classes. The newspaper's right-of-center political affiliation became its hallmark and enabled the company to build a solid and consistent readership base.

Villemessant continued to lead the newspaper until his death in 1879. In 1874, *Le Figaro* expanded its format to eight pages. The newspaper then became the first in France to feature weather information in its pages in 1876. Villemessant had by then begun to prepare his successors, taking on Francis Magnard as editor-in-chief in 1875. Magnard then became one of three co-directors of the newspaper after Villemessant's death.

Le Figaro served as the launching point for Emile Zola's campaign during the Dreyfus affaire at the turn of the century, a campaign which culminated in the famous ''J'accuse'' published in rival paper *L'Aurore* in 1898. The newspaper continued to innovate into the new century, adding a new weekly literary supplement in 1906. That year also saw the publication of the first photograph, one illustrating an advertisement, in the newspaper's pages. *Le Figaro* did not use photographs to illustrate news items until 1934.

Interwar and Postwar Changes

By then, the newspaper had undergone a change of ownership after François Coty, the perfumer, acquired a majority of *Le Figaro* in 1922 as part of his expanding media empire. Under Coty's ownership, the newspaper temporarily changed its name back to *Figaro* in 1929 and expanded its readership through the acquisition of *Le Gaullois*. At the same time, the paper expanded to ten pages. The new format provided space for added features, such as the newspaper's first crossword puzzles. However, Coty's open admiration for fascism and avowed anti-Semitism (Coty also published a number of rabidly anti-Semitic titles) compromised the newspaper, leading to its decline in the 1930s.

After Coty died in 1934, ownership of the newspaper was taken over by Coty's widow, who brought in Pierre Brisson as editor. Brisson now worked to resurrect the paper's reputation, changing its name back to *Le Figaro* and re-orienting it with an emphasis on literature. *Le Figaro* now became the home for many of the interwar period's top literary figures, including François Mauriac, Jean Giraudoux, and André Maurois. At the same time, *Le Figaro* became noted for its coverage of international events, such as its reporting of the Spanish Civil War, and sent reporters on assignment around the world.

During World War II, Brisson's editorial line led the newspaper into conflict with the Nazi occupiers and the Vichy government. The newspaper moved its offices to Tours in 1939, and from there to Bordeaux, then Clermont-Ferrand, and finally Lyon in 1940. *Le Figaro* was finally forced to suspend publication in 1942.

Le Figaro reappeared on newsstands soon after the liberation of Paris in 1944 and began the steady growth that was to mark the paper's fortunes in the second half of the century. By 1945, the newspaper had already reached printing runs of 213,000, and even this was not enough to meet demand. Restrictions on individual publications due to paper shortages during the postwar period led the company to separate its literary supplement from the main newspaper, forming the self-standing paper *Le Littéraire* in 1946. Renamed *Le Figaro Littéraire* in 1947, the new paper featured many noted literary names of the period, including Colette, Julien Green, and Paul Claudel.

In 1950, Coty's widow sold half of *Le Figaro* to media magnate Jean Prouvost, whose stable of titles included *Paris Match, France Soir,* and *Marie Claire.* At the same time, *Le Figaro* itself was incorporated as Société Fermière d'Edition du Figaro et du Figaro Littéraire. Pierre Brisson was named CEO of the new company, a position he held until his death in 1964.

Le Figaro enjoyed great success in the postwar period, seeing its subscription base rise to 90,000 and its total circulation top 500,000 by the 1950s. In 1960, the paper expanded to a 24-page format. By then, the company had also established press offices in New York, Washington, Rome, Brussels, Bonn, Moscow, London, and Tokyo, as well as correspondents in Greece, Brazil, Israel, and Algeria.

Media Group for the New Century

Coty's widow sold her remaining shares in the company to Prouvost and partner Ferdinand Beghin in 1965. Prouvost then acquired complete control of *Le Figaro* in 1970. In 1975, however, Prouvost announced his intention to sell a majority of *Le Figaro* to one of France's most controversial media figures, Robert Hersant. The announcement met with a great deal of outcry, and a large number of *Le Figaro*'s editorial staff resigned from the paper in protest.

Hersant had build a French media empire since the 1950s, starting with the launch of *L'Auto Journal* in 1949. Through his company, Socpresse, Hersant then began gathering a collection of primarily smaller provincial newspapers. Yet Hersant's past proved a source of continual embarrassment for the media magnate. His pro-Nazi and pro-Vichy activities during the war had led to his being condemned in 1946 to a ten-year sentence of ''national indignity.'' Although the sentence was dropped as part of the national amnesty in 1952, Hersant—whose penchant for buying up newspapers earned him the nickname ''papivore''—continued to inspire distrust throughout his life.

Key Dates:

1826: *Figaro,* a daily newspaper, is launched in Paris.
1833: The original *Figaro* ceases publication.
1854: Hippolyte de Villemessant relaunches *Figaro* as a weekly newspaper.
1866: *Le Figaro* becomes a daily newspaper.
1906: Launch of a literary supplement.
1922: Perfumer Francois Coty acquires majority control of *Le Figaro.*
1934: After Coty's death, Pierre Brisson is named head of *Le Figaro* and revives it as a literary newspaper.
1942: *Le Figaro* is forced to cease publication.
1944: *Le Figaro* is relaunched.
1946: Paper shortages lead *Le Figaro* to launch its literary supplement as a separate publication, *Le Littéraire,* which becomes *Le Figaro Littéraire* the following year.
1950: Coty's widow sells half of the company to Jean Prouvost.
1965: Prouvost-Beghin partnership takes full control of *Le Figaro.*
1970: Prouvost buys out Beghin.
1975: Prouvost sells majority control of *Figaro* to Robert Hersant.
1976: Hersant acquires *L'Aurore,* which is merged into *Le Figaro.*
1978: *Le Figaro Littéraire* become *Le Figaro Magazine.*
1980: *Madame Figaro* begins publication.
1985: *Le Figaro Economie* supplement is launched.
1990: A Japanese edition of *Madame Figaro* begins publication.
1996: Robert Hersant dies; *Le Figaro Multimedia* and *Maison Madame Figaro* are launched.
1999: Carlyle Group and partners acquire the rights to 40 percent of *Le Figaro.*
2002: Carlyle Group sells back its stake in *Le Figaro*; the publication's parent company Socpresse sells a 30 percent interest in *Le Figaro* to Serge Dassault.
2003: *Le Figaro* announces its plan to withdraw from Paris Press Trade Union.

Nonetheless, Hersant considered himself first and foremost a newspaperman. Under Hersant, *Le Figaro* blossomed into a full-fledged media group. One of Hersant's first moves was the acquisition of two other newspapers, *L'Aurore* and the popular right-leaning evening daily *France Soir.* These purchases led the socialist government to enact a new law in an attempt to limit consolidation in the media sector. That law became known as Hersant's Law, in that it clearly targeted Hersant's control of some 40 percent of France's newspaper market. Hersant emerged the victor, however, when the courts declared that the law could not be applied retroactively.

Hersant then merged *L'Aurore* into *Le Figaro,* which became the clear leader in France's daily newspaper market. Hersant next began developing the *Le Figaro* name as a brand—a rare and innovative move in the French media market. In 1978, *Le Figaro* repackaged *Le Figaro Littéraire* as a weekly

news magazine, called *Le Figaro Magazine.* Two years later, the group added a second offshoot of its core newspaper, *Madame Figaro.* Launched as a monthly at first, the popularity of the women's format encouraged the company to move to a bimonthly publishing schedule in 1983, and then to a weekly schedule the following year.

Le Figaro next targeted the financial market, launching a weekly supplement to the newspaper, *Le Figaro Economie,* in 1985. Two years later, the company added a weekly cultural supplement as well, *Le Figaroscope.* The company also launched a weekend supplement magazine in emulation of the British newspaper market. In the late 1980s, Hersant, seconded by his son Phillip Hersant and right-hand man Yves de Chaisemartin, began to steer *Le Figaro*'s editorial style closer to the more concise, fact-oriented British reporting style as well. In another break with French newspaper tradition, Hersant moved to take control of *Le Figaro*'s—along with his other publications'—printing processes, opening a printing plant, Roissy Print, in 1989. The following year, the company rolled out a Japanese edition of *Madame Figaro.*

In the meantime, Hersant, through Socpresse, had continued expanding his larger media empire, even venturing into television, along with Italy's Silvio Berlusconi, in the ill-fated Tele 5 venture. Hersant began running up huge debt loads in order to support his purchases. While many of Hersant's publications remained money-losers, their losses were covered by the healthy profits enjoyed by *Le Figaro* into the early 1990s.

Yet Hersant's empire began to unravel as *Le Figaro,* hit hard by a crisis affecting the French newspaper market in general in the 1990s, slipped into losses as well. Hersant was forced to trim a number of titles, including the sale of some 20 magazine titles to Britain's Emap in 1995. When Hersant died the following year, many observers expected Socpresse, and *Le Figaro* with it, to collapse.

Le Figaro quickly named de Chaisemartin as head of Socpresse, as well as president of *Le Figaro.* Socpresse promptly sold off money-losing *France Soir* and de Chaisemartin was then able to turn his attention to getting *Le Figaro* back on track. The company's new strategy involved the launch of two new titles, *Le Figaro Multimedia* and *Maison Madame Figaro,* the latter title being a companion to the company's highly popular women's magazine. In the meantime, as the company's financial position weakened into the second half of the 1990s—with its debt levels rising to more than one-third of its revenues—*Le Figaro* was forced to begin considering the addition of new investors.

After rejecting approaches by media group Havas and aviation tycoon Serge Dassault—which would have forced the Hersant family to give up much of their control of the group—Socpresse agreed to sell a 4.9 percent stake in *Le Figaro,* as well as a series of convertible bonds worth up to 40 percent of the group, to the American concern the Carlyle Group. The purchase, described as a leveraged buyout of *Le Figaro,* enabled the group to pay down much of its debt and restructure its financial situation.

As part of its restructuring effort, *Le Figaro* underwent a facelift in 2000, marking the first time in some 20 years that the newspaper had changed its format. The new style was meant to present a more modern and dynamic image to the paper's readers, who now numbered more than 1.5 million, a figure signifying *Le Figaro*'s continued leadership position in the French market. That year, the company also launched its Web site, which boasted its own editorial team.

Another part of the newspaper's restructuring involved the transition of the *Le Figaro Economie* supplement into the newly styled *Le Figaro Entreprises*. *Madame Figaro* remained the group's most successful international title after the launch of a Chinese edition in 1999. The company then added a Korean edition in 2000 before expanding the magazine to Taiwan in 2001.

Although the Carlyle Group had originally hoped to recoup its investment in *Le Figaro* through a public offering of its shares, in 2002 the group agreed to sell back its stake in the paper to Socpresse, giving that company 100 percent control of its flagship newspaper group once again. In addition, the years in partnership with the Carlyle Group had enabled *Le Figaro* to rebuild its financial situation. Soon after the Carlyle Group sale, the Hersant family agreed to allow Serge Dassault to buy a 30 percent stake in Socpresse, enabling the family to maintain a 70 percent stake in the company and continued control over *Le Figaro*.

The addition of Dassault, and his money, enabled Socpresse to expand its position in the French media market, notably through the acquisition of *L'Expansion, L'Express,* and a number of other prominent titles in 2003. Yet these purchases once again saddled Socpresse with a heavy debt—this time a short-term load of some EUR 230 million to Dassault himself. Rather than allow Dassault to increase his shareholding in the group to as high as 45 percent, Socpresse sought means of cutting costs, leading *Le Figaro* to announce, at the end of 2003, its decision to pull out of the Paris Press Trade Union.

Principal Competitors

Lagadere SA; Hachette Filipacchi Medias; Havas Media SA; Le Monde S.A.; Spir Communication S.A.; Liberation.

Further Reading

Baudry, Claude, "Une nouvelle phase de la restructuration presse," *L'Humanité*, September 4, 2002.

Besse, Elise, "Hersant: L'empire renaît de ses cendres," *Actudes Medias*, November 29, 2002.

James, Barry, "Hersant's Legacy," *International Herald Tribune*, April 23, 1996, p. 11.

Kosman, Josh, "Carlyle Group Invests in French Newspaper," *Buyouts*, July 19, 1999.

Mortished, Carl, "Dassault Grip on *Le Figaro* Is Extended," *Times* (London), March 28, 2002, p. 33.

Santi, Pascale, "*Le Figaro* Decision to Leave Press Union Roils French Press Congress," *World New Connection*, November 22, 2003.

Tille, Albert, "Qui a peur du groupe Hersant?," *Domaine Public*, March 15, 2002.

—M.L. Cohen

The Stephan Company

1850 West McNab Road
Fort Lauderdale, Florida 33309
U.S.A.
Telephone: (954) 971-0600
Fax: (954) 971-2633
Web site: http://www.thestephanco.com

Private Company
Incorporated: 1952
Employees: 125
Sales: $25.1 million (2002)
NAIC: 325620 Toilet Preparation Manufacturing

The Stephan Company, operating out of Fort Lauerdale, Florida, is a small manufacturer and distributor of haircare and personal products for both the retail and wholesale markets. The public company is comprised of three operating segments: Professional Hair Care Products and Distribution, Retail Personal Care Products, and Manufacturing. Business is conducted through eight subsidiaries. Foxy Products, Inc. offers the Magic Wave line of hair care products for African-Americans. Morris Flamingo-Stephan, Inc. serves the barber and beauty salon markets through catalogs under the Morris Flamingo and Major Advance labels. Old 97 Company sells more than 100 hair and skin care products, fragrances, and personal grooming aids under the Old 97, Knights, and Tammy labels. Scientific Research Products, Inc. of Delaware manufactures and distributes products primarily aimed at African-Americans. Formerly known as Heads or Nails, Inc., Stephan & Co. distributes personal care products to cruise ships. Stephan Distributing, Inc. markets professional hair care products and a retail hair care line acquired from New Image Laboratories, Inc. Trevor Sorbie of America, Inc. manufactures and distributes beauty salon products. The last of Stephan's subsidiaries is Williamsport Barber and Beauty Corp, a mail order beauty salon and barbershop supply company. Stephan also operates five manufacturing facilities.

History Dates Back to 1897

The Stephan Company was founded in Worcester, Massachusetts, in 1897 by German immigrant Karl H. Stephan., who started out producing barber equipment and surgical tools. He added barber and beauty supplies, becoming the first professional men's hair care company in America as well as the first to sell products only through barber shops. It was through the barber shop trade that the company gained a reputation for the quality of its products. Stephan's bestselling product was a dandruff remover, which relied on a 19th-century formula. Under the ownership of its founder, the company thrived and even branched out to sporting goods. By 1920, the business was generating annual revenues of $5 million. In the 1930s, however, the Depression hit the company hard. One of Karl Stephan's 11 children, Richard Stephan, took charge of the business in 1938 and concentrated on the dandruff remover product to nurse the company back to health.

In 1952, Richard Stephan moved the company's headquarters from Worcester to Fort Lauderdale and incorporated Stephan in Florida. By now, Stephan, which had manufacturing facilities located in Worcester, St. Louis, and Fresno, California, had regained enough sales in barber shop hair tonics and shampoos to reach the $2.5 million mark in annual revenues. In 1960, the company went public, and by the middle of the decade its dandruff-removal product was a market leader. However, because of the cultural upheaval of the 1960s, when long hair became popular with men and a younger generation began to eschew the barbershop experience, Stephan saw its business adversely impacted. Richard Stephan attempted to find outlets for the company's products outside of the barber shop channel and even launched a national advertising campaign. This effort succeeded only in alienating its base of barber shop customers. The price of Stephan stock plummeted to 12 cents a share, leading the American Stock Exchange to delist the company. Over the next decade, Stephan passed out of family hands, annual sales fell to the $300,000 level, and its workforce was reduced to just three people.

In 1981, new ownership arrived in the form of Frank F. Ferola, an Avon executive of 16 years who had been involved

---

Company Perspectives:

With over 100 years of experience, The Stephan Company continues to keep one step ahead of the ever-changing hair and personal grooming products industry.

---

in product packaging development. For some time, he and his wife Vera had wanted to run their own business and were attracted to the Ft. Lauderdale weather, but more importantly they recognized that Stephan possessed a great deal of underutilized manufacturing capacity at its 32,000-square-foot office and factory. As Ferola told the *South Florida Business Journal* in a 1993 profile, "The Stephan Family had purchased so much equipment over the years that they never did catch up." Along with a group of small investors, Ferola raised $200,000 to purchase Stephan's stock. With his wife serving as office manager, Ferola took over a company that he told *The Miami Herald* had just one product out of 29 that was selling. Moreover, Stephan had just $13,000 in the bank and was burdened with some $250,000 in debt. To generate much needed income and make greater use of his factory, Ferola looked to manufacture private-label products. He developed product concepts and approached prospective customers about applying their labels to the items. He also managed to snare larger players like K-Mart Corp. The best known of these custom-manufactured products were Easy Net Gel and Gold Bond talcum powder. All of Stephan's customers paid cash in advance. As a result of the push into custom manufacturing, revenues improved by an average of 36 percent over the next three years, and the company was able to pay off all its debt. Now, only one-quarter of the products produced by Stephan Company carried its labels.

Foxy Products Acquired in 1986

Stephan became so liquid, in fact, that Ferola eventually concluded it was advantageous to grow by acquisition, targeting profitable brands that were small enough to escape the attention of major companies and either had a niche in the marketplace or were once high-selling brands that had lost their luster. The first of these acquisitions occurred in 1986 when Stephan acquired Foxy Products, Inc. and its line of Magic Wave products aimed at the African-American market. Two years later, Stephan bought Old 97 Company, a Tampa, Florida-based company founded in 1930. Old 97 manufactured a wide range of cosmetics, toiletries, and household products sold door-to-door in smaller markets in the South. In addition, Old 97 engaged in some private label manufacturing, producing hair and skin care products for a limited number of customers.

The price of Stephan's stock, which traded over the counter, remained a sore point for Ferola. In 1989, he decided to pay for a Standard & Poor's credit report. After receiving a favorable B+ rating, Stephan garnered more positive attention when *Investor's Daily* assigned a 99 percent rating for the company's earnings-per-share growth. As a result, Stephan, despite its size and scarcity of outstanding shares (more than a third were held by insiders), caught Wall Street's attention as the company continued to string together strong results. In 1989, Stephan

recorded $4.66 million in revenues and a $375,000 profit, followed by sales of $5.5 million in 1990 and more than $10 million in 1991. Net income increased from $589,000 in 1990 to $1.6 million in 1991. The future looked even more promising in light of a 1991 deal with the Phar-Mor Inc. chain of 300 drugstores, which gave the company national distribution. All these positive developments combined to boost the price of Stephan's stock, which in the first ten months of 1991 grew from $4.40 to $24, adjusted for splits, or a 440 percent increase. Moreover, according to a company spokesman, a share of Stephan stock purchased ten years earlier at $1.12 had grown by more than 5000 percent.

Ferola continued to take a conservative approach to running Stephan. The company either made do with the equipment it already owned or in some cases built its own. One notable example was the $275 the company spent to construct its own cooling tunnel for molten products. A commercially bought tunnel to perform the same function would have cost as much as $50,000. Stephan also maintained a clean balance sheet by mostly paying cash for acquisitions and taking on virtually no debt. Rather than spend money on advertising and marketing, the company cut the price on its products to gain a competitive edge. In 1992, Stephan once again added new businesses, closing in January on the purchase of Williamsport Beauty & Barber Supply. The company paid $250,000 in cash, as well as a note payable over 7 years for $350,000 and 45,000 shares of restricted stock. Founded in 1939, Williamsport Beauty served its customers primarily through a mail order catalog (later augmented with a Web site), generating annual sales in the $2.3 million range. In February 1992, Stephan bought from Dow Brands the Massimo Faust line of upscale beauty salon products sold in drug stores and supermarkets. The deal called for Stephan to pay $15,000 a year for five years and a royalty of 3 percent of product sales during that same period. Both acquisitions helped Stephan maintain its impressive growth rate, as sales improved to $14.7 million in 1992 and net income to nearly $2.4 million. In 1993, *Forbes* magazine ranked Stephan No. 17 on its list of America's best small-growth companies, and *Business Week* designated the company No. 23 on its comparable list.

Continuing to scour for opportunities, Stephan made two acquisitions in 1993. In August, it completed the purchase of Penny's Heads or Nails, Inc., a cruise ship salon concessionaire, paying $357,116 in cash and 23,007 shares of stock. Next, in December 1993, Stephan paid an undisclosed amount of cash and stock to Muelhens Inc. to acquire the Frances Denney line of cosmetics, skin care products, and fragrances, sold nationwide by such major retailers as Sears, Roebuck and JC Penney. Although it was not able to duplicate a 100 percent growth rate in revenues, Stephan continued to post strong results. In 1993, net sales increased to $16.7 million and net income totaled $2.78 million. The following year would prove to be even brighter, fueled to a great degree by the April 1994 acquisition of Scientific Research Products, Inc. for 500,000 shares of stock. The Pompano Beach, Florida-based company, founded in 1950, manufactured and distributed hair and skin care products for African-Americans, Asians, and Hispanics. Its best known brands were LeKair, New Era, and T.C Naturals. As a distributor, Scientific Research had been Stephan's largest customer. Ferola explained his reasoning for buying the company to *Busi-*

<table>
<tr><td colspan="2">Key Dates:</td></tr>
<tr><td>1897:</td><td>The Stephan Company is founded in Worcester, Massachusetts.</td></tr>
<tr><td>1952:</td><td>The company moves to Florida.</td></tr>
<tr><td>1960:</td><td>The company goes public.</td></tr>
<tr><td>1981:</td><td>Frank Ferola acquires control of the company.</td></tr>
<tr><td>1992:</td><td>Williamsport Beauty & Barber Supply is acquired.</td></tr>
<tr><td>2003:</td><td>The company is taken private.</td></tr>
</table>

ness in Broward in a 1995 story: "Scientific was growing on the sales side and we were growing on the manufacturing side over the years. So ... the joint development of new products between The Stephan Company and Scientific really fueled the growth of the company." The proof would be reflected in the bottom line. In 1994, revenues improved by 50 percent over the previous year, totaling more than $24.3 million. Net income also exhibited strong growth, topping the $4 million mark. Also of note, Stephan's stock once again began trading on the American Stock Exchange.

Several Orphan Products Acquired in 1995

In 1995, revenues grew at a more modest rate to $26.2 million, while profits increased to more than $4.3 million. That same year, Stephan acquired several orphan products, brands that were past their prime but retained a certain level of customer loyalty. Stephan paid Colgate-Palmolive $12 million for Cashmere Bouquet Talc, Wildroot Cream Oil, Balm Barr Cocoa Butter Lotions and Creams, Protein 29 Hair Groom, Quinsana Powders, and Stretch Mark Crème. The best-known of the group was Wildroot, a popular 1950s hair cream. During their last year with Colgate, these products totaled $7.6 million in combined sales. Stephan did not, however, succeed as well as Colgate, and sales fell off.

Stephan completed one major acquisition in 1996, paying stock worth $518,000 and assuming some $3 million in debt for Trevor Sorbie of America, maker of professional hair care salon products sold to more than 100,000 salons in the United States. Stephan's salon business would be complemented by the 1997 acquisition of two product lines from New Image Laboratories at a cost of $5 million in stock. The Image line of professional hair care products sold in 125,000 salons located in the United States and abroad, including such countries as Australia, Brazil, Denmark, France, Germany, Italy, Sweden, and Thailand. In addition, Stephan picked up the Modern line of retail products, sold under the "Stiff Stuff" trademark.

Revenues topped $27 million and net income $5 million in 1997, which proved to be a high water mark for the company. Although sales climbed to nearly $35 million in 1998, the company essentially broke even, and Stephan began to trend downward. Stephan completed one more significant acquisition, paying $3.7 million in stock and assuming $1.9 million in debt for Morris-Flamingo, L.P., a distributor of hair care and beauty supplies by way of catalogs, using both the Morris Flamingo and Major Advance brand names. It would be the addition of Morris Flamingo, according to Stephan officials,

that led the company to overstate earnings in the second and third quarters of 1998. A "change in the overall product mix" caused some confusion, the company claimed, resulting in its mistaken use of historical gross profit percentages. Although such an event was out of keeping with Stephan's reputation for conservative management, the firm's stock took a hit because of the revelation. The error was little more than an embarrassment, especially in light of more significant factors affecting the company's business. As early as January 1998, *Florida Trend* commented, "For 100 years, The Stephan Co. has been making products to deal with problems like tired, limp hair. But after a recent buying spree in which it added both companies and individual brands, it may have ended up with too many tired, limp products." The Colgate products, in particular, failed to live up to expectations, but Stephan also faced a challenging new retail environment that threatened to have a lasting impact. As the drug store industry consolidated, the surviving mega-chains began to demand large discounts and promotional allowances, which bled profits from suppliers like Stephan. Furthermore, consolidation took place in the distribution network for professional products, resulting in declining revenues for Stephan's professional and manufacturing business segments. After peaking in 1998, revenues began to fall steadily, to $34.4 million in 1999, $31.1 million in 2000, and $28.3 million in 2001. After recording a net profit of $1.8 million in 1999, Stephan saw its income drop to $622,000 in 2000 and $608,000 in 2001.

With its stock falling to the $3 range, Stephan decided in 2001 to hire investment banker Robinson-Humphrey Co. to assess its options, including a management-led group to take the business private. In April 2002, these investors offered $4 per share for Stephan, or $17.6 million. That amount would be increased to $4.50 per share, or $19.3 million, in August 2002. The deal was postponed for several months because of a class action suit filed by a shareholder who claimed she wanted to bid on the company. Finally, in July 2003, the suit was dismissed and the transaction to take the company private was approved by the board. Although Stephan was now free of the pressures associated with being a public company, it still faced a challenging future. In 2002, a year in which sales continued to fall, totaling $25 million, Stephan posted a loss of $6.3 million. Stephan would have actually earned $500,000 for the year, but management elected instead to write-down goodwill and other intangible assets, a move that reduced income by some $6.8 million. At the very least, Stephan, once again a privately held company, entered the next phase of its history with a clean balance sheet.

Principal Divisions

Hair Care Products and Distribution; Retail Personal Care Products; Manufacturing.

Principal Subsidiaries

Foxy Products, Inc.; Old 97 Company; Williamsport Barber and Beauty Corp.; Stephan & Co.; Scientific Research Products, Inc. of Delaware; Trevor Sorbie of America, Inc.; Stephan Distributing, Inc.; Morris Flamingo-Stephan, Inc.

Principal Competitors

The Procter & Gamble Company; Revlon, Inc.; Unilever plc.

Further Reading

Clary, Mike, "An 1890's Formula Is Working Wonders," *Florida Trend*, December 1991, p. 65.

Kane, Cheryl, "The Stephan Co.'s 3 Cs: Caution, Cost-cutting, Conservatism," *South Florida Business Journal*, July 2, 1993, p. 9B.

Shillington, Patty, "Fort Lauderdale, Fla., Firm's Only Splash Is in Profits," *Miami Herald*, January 8, 1996.

Taylor, Germaine, "Just A Little Off The Sides . . . ," *Business in Broward*, September 1, 1995, p 16.

—Ed Dinger

Strombecker Corporation

600 North Pulaski Road
Chicago, Illinois 60624
U.S.A.
Telephone: (773) 638-1000
Toll Free: (800) 944-8697
Fax: (773) 638-3679
Web site: www.tootsietoy.com

Private Company
Incorporated: 1876 as The National Laundry Journal
Employees: 350
Sales: $72.7 million (2001 est.)
NAIC: 339932 Game, Toy, and Children's Vehicle
Manufacturing

Strombecker Corporation is the leading maker of bubble blowing toys and cap guns in the world, controlling about half of each market, and also makes other basic toys like die-cast metal cars, wood blocks, and dish sets. The company's best-known brands are Tootsietoy, Mr. Bubbles, Hearts 'n Home, and Hard Body Die-Cast, and it also makes items using characters or designs licensed from Disney, Looney Tunes, Pfaltzgraff, General Motors, and Ford, among others. Strombecker is owned by the Shure family, which has run the company for four generations.

Origins

The roots of the present-day Strombecker date to 1876, when a trade paper called the *National Laundry Journal* was started on the West Side of Chicago. Its publishers, brothers Charles O. and Samuel Dowst, later began to make small laundry accessories like die-cast collar buttons and cufflinks. In 1893 Samuel Dowst saw a Mergenthaler Linotype machine at the Chicago World's Columbian Exposition, which made metal type for printing by injecting hot lead into molds. Realizing it could also effectively produce metal buttons, he convinced the company to purchase one.

Dowst soon began producing more metal items, including die-cast promotional trinkets for clients like the Flat Iron Laundry Company, which bought them to give away to its customers' children. These items, which included a flatiron, a top hat, a Scottie dog, and a candlestick, would much later be adopted for use as tokens in the board games Monopoly and Clue. In 1906 Dowst introduced the world's first die-cast toy car, and several years later began making one patterned after the Model T Ford, which went on to sell more than 50 million copies. The firm's toy vehicles were known as "Tootsietoys," after company founder Charles O. Dowst's granddaughter "Toots." Their popularity was such that automobile manufacturers paid for creation of the molds so they could be included in the company's line.

One of the firm's competitors was the Cosmo Manufacturing Company, which had been founded in Chicago in 1892 by Nathan Shure. Cosmo's niche was making small prizes for inclusion in boxes of Cracker Jack, which was made by another Chicago-area firm. In 1926 Cosmo bought Dowst, and the merged companies took the name Dowst Manufacturing Co. Together they would make a variety of die-cast toys like train sets, doll furniture, airplanes, cars, and trucks, as well as Cracker Jack prizes and game tokens. By this time the firm had abandoned its publishing operations.

Dowst's business continued to grow despite the hardships of the Great Depression and World War II, during which the company turned to producing detonators for grenades and mines, as well as belt and parachute buckles. Because of severe restrictions on the use of metal, Dowst Manufacturing's only wartime toys were made of paper.

After the cessation of hostilities, the company returned to full-time toy production. Dowst soon added new items like western-style cap gun sets, which would prove popular in the late 1950s. By that time control of the firm had passed to Nathan Shure's grandsons Myron, Richard, and Alan.

Slot Car Boom, and Bust, in the 1960s

The 1950s had seen the emergence of a number of new electronic toys, including slot cars, motorized $\frac{1}{32}$ size plastic vehicles that could be raced against each other on an electrified track. The cars, which were replicas of actual models made by the likes of Jaguar and Ferrari, quickly became popular with youngsters, especially boys. To cash in on the trend, in 1961 Dowst acquired the hobby division of manufacturer Strombeck-Becker, hired 14 designers, and retooled its factory to facilitate production of the car-and-track sets. Sales of the toys, which were marketed under the name Strombecker, jumped from 20,000 to 500,000 sets by 1963, making the company one of the industry's leaders in this category. With the cars now comprising the firm's main source of revenue, Dowst Manufacturing changed its name to Strombecker Corporation.

For several years the company rode high on the slot car fad, but then sales plunged in the latter half of the decade. When the firm's largest customer, Sears, Roebuck & Co., canceled orders and tried to return all of its inventory, Strombecker faced financial ruin. The firm, which had recorded profits of $3 million at the peak of the boom, suddenly found itself facing annual losses of more than $6 million. As a consequence, Myron, Alan, and Richard Shure were forced to personally guarantee the company's loans, and to avoid bankruptcy they decided to return to the more traditional toys with which the firm had earlier found success. At this time Alan Shure left to run a business that made small electric motors, leaving Myron and Richard to run the company.

Strombecker bounced back with the introduction of the ''Jam-Pac,'' a set of ten die-cast cars that sold for a dollar. Placed by the counter at supermarkets throughout the country, it became ''the world's best shutter-upper,'' according to Myron Shure's son Daniel, as parents in the checkout line could buy it for a child in order to keep them quiet. The Jam-Pac sold ten million sets in its first year, and continued to do well thereafter.

During this same period Strombecker acquired exclusive rights to manufacture Kewpie Dolls, which had been created in the early 1900s by Rose O'Neill. The firm hired Jean Cantwell, secretary-treasurer of the Rose O'Neill Club, to act as spokesperson. The venture was not a major success, however. By the mid-1970s Strombecker's annual sales were a relatively modest $6 million.

1979: Bringing Mr. Bubbles to the Firm

In 1979 the company bought Chem-Toy, which made soap bubble toys under the Mr. Bubbles name in a variety of formats and sizes. Helped by the new acquisition, as well as by an increase in sales of toy guns as the antiwar sentiment of the 1960s and early 1970s faded, Strombecker's revenues grew to approximately $30 million by 1983.

When Richard Shure died in 1988, Myron Shure began seeking a partner to help buy out his and Alan's shares. Al-

though Myron's three daughters were not interested, his youngest son Daniel was, and the latter moved back to Chicago from Hong Kong to become the firm's president. This period also saw the company redesign its packaging, putting the Tootsietoy name on its entire line of more than 100 products.

Under Daniel Shure, who had earned his M.B.A. at Cornell and later worked for Proctor & Gamble, Strombecker began a round of strategic acquisitions. In 1989 the firm bought Sandberg Manufacturing Co., a producer of wooden toys for preschoolers under license from Sesame Street. Later, a company that made paper roll caps was acquired, as well as another that produced small plastic action figures.

By 1993 Strombecker had 450 employees and was operating showrooms in Dallas, New York, and Hong Kong. Manufacturing was done at two plants in the Chicago area, as well as at others in Amsterdam, New York, in Durant, Oklahoma, and in Canada. Starting in the 1980s the company had begun contracting out production of most of its toy cars to manufacturing firms in China, and this outsourcing grew to account for 40 percent of the firm's total output. The Shures had taken this step reluctantly, as they were strongly committed to their employees, who were, in large part, residents of the impoverished West Side of Chicago. Many had worked for Strombecker for decades, and in some cases for generations.

A key to the firm's success was its image as a low-overhead, no-frills operation. The company's basic toys were not advertised, but generated steady sales year after year due to their classic nature. They were popular with major retailers like Toys 'R' Us and Wal-Mart because of their high profit margins, typically 45 to 50 percent as compared with the 17 to 20 percent for heavily advertised toys. Most of Strombecker's items retailed for less than $5, with the most expensive priced at $30. The company offered hundreds of different items, and each year introduced new ones like a 12-inch plastic crossbow that emitted bubbles when fired, or plastic baseball bats and tennis racquets that created hundreds of bubbles when waved through the air. The firm was now producing some 70 percent of the bubble solution sold in the United States.

Realistic Toy Gun Issues in 1994

In 1994 Strombecker suffered a setback when news reports about children who had been shot by police while brandishing toy guns led several retail chains, including Toys 'R' Us and Kay-Bee, to pull authentic-looking toy weapons from their shelves. Strombecker had control of 60 percent of U.S. sales in this category, and 30 percent of the firm's revenues were derived from it. Although deals were quickly made to offset the cutbacks by boosting orders of the firm's other products, and some guns were redesigned to make them less realistic, the company announced that it would lay off 20 in the fall. Strombecker was able to keep most of its U.S. workforce of 500 on the job, however, with the most drastic cuts made to orders from China. Sales of handgun and assault weapon toys were affected the most, while demand for western-style pistols and rifles fell off less sharply, though they too were banned by at least one retailer.

The company was able to recover from this setback, however, and by 1996 revenues had rebounded to a record level of

Key Dates:

1876: Charles O. and Samuel Dowst start *The National Laundry Journal.*

1892: Nathan Shure founds Cosmo Manufacturing to make toys.

1893: Dowst Bros. buys a linotype machine to make die-cast buttons and trinkets.

1906: Dowst introduces the first die-cast Tootsietoy automobile.

1926: Dowst and Cosmo merge to become Dowst Manufacturing Co.

1930s: Dowst toys are used as tokens in the newly created Monopoly game.

1940s: Dowst makes detonators, buckles for the U.S. war effort.

1950s: Nathan Shure's grandsons take control of the firm; toy guns become strong sellers.

1961: The Strombeck-Becker hobby division is purchased; Dowst later is renamed Strombecker.

1960s: Sales of slot cars boom, then bust; Strombecker returns to making basic toys.

1979: The acquisition of Chem-Toy adds the popular Mr. Bubbles line.

1980s: The firm moves most toy car manufacturing to China.

1989: The firm purchases Sandberg Manufacturing, maker of Sesame Street wooden toys.

1994: Major chains remove toy guns from shelves; Strombecker lays off 20.

1996: The company rebounds, posting record sales of $50 million.

2002: Board chairman Myron Shure dies.

approximately $50 million. That year saw Strombecker make two acquisitions and form a joint venture with Daisy Manufacturing Co. to license and distribute Daisy's line of toy guns. The firm also introduced its first toys aimed solely at girls, which included tea sets and play cosmetics.

The late 1990s saw Strombecker's bubble toy market share drop below 50 percent, but this climbed back to 54 percent during 2001. Sales of toy guns also went up late in the year following the September 11 terrorist attacks on the United States. The company was still the market leader in this category in the United States, with sales of its guns, bubbles, and other toys also strong around the world.

In December of 2002 board chairman Myron Shure passed away. In addition to his many years in the toy business, Shure had amassed a collection of so-called "Outsider Art" and served as director of Intuit: The Center for Intuitive and Outsider Art near Chicago.

After more than 125 years Strombecker Corporation had found its niche as a leading maker of basic toys like bubbles, guns, wooden blocks, tea sets, and cars. The Shure family, which continued to own and manage the firm, kept it on track for further growth through strategic acquisitions and new licensing deals.

Principal Subsidiaries

Strombecker Canada Ltd.; Strombecker UK Ltd.; Strombecker Hong Kong Ltd.

Principal Competitors

Mattel, Inc.; Hasbro, Inc.; The Toysmith Group; Panline USA.

Further Reading

Burns, Greg, "When It's Basic Toys You Want, This Firm Has Them," *Chicago Sun-Times,* February 21, 1988, p. 4.

Cleaver, Joanne, "Toy Firm's Growth Plan Built on Blocks," *Crain's Chicago Business,* May 1, 1989, p. 1.

Jervis, Laverne, "Miniature Car Racing Zooms in Popularity; Spurs Sales of Models," *Wall Street Journal,* May 16, 1963, p. 1.

Johnson, Robert, "Keeping It Simple," *Wall Street Journal,* February 22, 1983, p. 1.

"Jump Ropes, Soap Bubbles: 'Old-Fashioned' Fun by the Truckload," *Chicago Sun-Times,* May 19, 1991, p. 48.

Klemesrud, Judy, "And Now, Maybe Son of Kewpie Doll," *New York Times,* September 17, 1971, p. 48.

Levinsohn, Florence Hamlish, "Where Smiles Roll Off the Assembly Line," *Chicago Enterprise,* July 1, 1993, p. 24.

Mathews, Jay, "Toy Gun Maker Reduces 'Realistic' Weapon Output," *Washington Post,* February 14, 1995, p. A4.

Pereira, Joseph, "Toyland Sounds a Call to Arms," *Wall Street Journal,* November 7, 2001, p. B1.

Podmolik, Mary Ellen, "Toy Soldiering—Strombecker Wields Tootsietoys in Battle to Stay on Store Shelves," *Chicago Sun-Times,* November 4, 1994, p. 53.

Steinberg, Neil, "In Toyland, It's Not All Games," *Chicago Sun-Times,* December 25, 1997, p. 18.

Stewart, Janet Kidd, "Toymaker's Tally—Strombecker Posts Best Sales Year Ever," *Chicago Sun-Times,* December 25, 1996, p. 55.

Strom, Stephanie, "It's High Noon for a Big Maker of Toy Guns," *New York Times,* October 23, 1994, p. F4.

Sweeney, Annie, "Myron Shure; Ran Toy Business," *Chicago Sun-Times,* December 29, 2002, p. 54.

Weiskott, Maria, "The Type For Success: Linotype Machine Launches Button-Popping Company Hit," *Playthings,* June 1, 2002, p. 6.

—Frank Uhle

◆ SUMITOMO LIFE

Sumitomo Life Insurance Company

1-4-35, Shiromi, Chuo-ku
Osaka 540-8512
Japan
Telephone: (06) 6937-1435
Fax: (03) 5550-1160
Web site: http://www.sumitomolife.co.jp

Mutual Company
Incorporated: 1907 as The Hinode Life Insurance
  Company, Ltd.
Employees: 57,466
Total Assets: ¥21.9 trillion ($182.9 billion, 2003)
NAIC: 524113 Direct Life Insurance Carriers

Sumitomo Life Insurance Company operates as one of Japan's largest life insurance concerns along with competitors Nippon Life Insurance Company and Dai-Ichi Mutual Life Insurance Company. Through its subsidiaries, the company offers individual, group life, and long-term care policies, as well as pension plans, asset management, and accident, fire, and auto insurance. Sumitomo Life and its peers in the insurance industry have struggled since the mid-1990s as a result of bad loans, competition brought on by deregulation, low interest rates, and a sluggish domestic economy. The company is part of the Sumitomo *keiretsu*, or business group, which can trace its history to the early 17th century.

Early History

The Hinode Life Insurance Company was founded in 1907 and, from the start, established close business ties with the Sumitomo *zaibatsu*, or conglomerate. By 1925, these ties had become such that the Sumitomo *zaibatsu* took over the management of Hinode. Because Hinode was a mutual company, however, it was not owned outright by the Sumitomo *zaibatsu* but rather by its policyholders. Hinode was certainly a member of the conglomerate, and since much of its business involved other branches of the *zaibatsu*, those branches, in effect, owned a large part of Hinode.

In 1926, to signify this close relationship, Hinode became The Sumitomo Life Insurance Company. Sumitomo Life continued to expand its business until after World War II, when the Supreme Commander for the Allied Powers ordered Sumitomo and all other *zaibatsu* to disband.

Like other former *zaibatsu*, however, the Sumitomo companies—each operating independently—began to come together again, even before the end of the occupation of Japan in 1952. Japanese law prohibited the huge *zaibatsu*, and the postwar *keiretsu* were held together by a looser arrangement than were the *zaibatsu*.

The companies were connected partly by relationships between executives who grew up in the *zaibatsu* tradition, but financial links between the companies and cross-ownership of stocks were often more important and became stronger as time went on. The Sumitomo Corporation, which operated as the leader of the *keiretsu*, "has fostered trade among companies within the group, expanded the financial interrelationships, and strengthened formal management ties among companies at the core of the group," stated *Business Week* (March 31, 1990).

Beginning in the 1950s, the life insurance business in Japan grew and expanded along with both the Japanese economy and the increase in assets of individuals. As the Japanese economy underwent a tremendous expansion in the 1970s and 1980s, the country's life insurance business also went through a transformation of products and markets in the same period. Sumitomo Life's portfolio was continuously adjusted to take advantage of opportunities, such as those presented by changing regulations, which determined what type of products could be offered.

In the 1980s, most life insurance companies fundamentally changed their investment strategies, which meant a decrease in loans to large corporations and an increase in stock purchases. Prior to the 1980s, 20 percent of asset increases were invested in securities and real estate, with the remaining new money used for long-term loans. In the 1980s, the loan market changed and Sumitomo Life had favorable results making loans to small and medium-sized companies. The market had then become more competitive, and with changes in laws regulating the Japanese insurance industry, the majority of funds were reallocated to overseas investments.

Changes Lead to Diversification

The factors affecting the Japanese life insurance business in the late 1980s that in turn guided its operations for the 1990s were the deregulation of Japan's financial industry, which created competition from banks and securities firms; an aging Japanese society in which 13.8 million people in 1990 were 65 or older, with the number increasing steadily; globalization of markets in which Sumitomo Life could offer a variety of services worldwide; unification of the European Economic Community in 1992; the strength of the yen; rising interest rates; fluctuations in the stock market; and the changing lifestyles and values of the Japanese.

Sumitomo Life had responded by providing timely new products and services, by strengthening its internal operations to improve sales and efficiency, and by strengthening its presence and visibility in communities in which it did business. A three-year "New Challenge" plan, instituted in 1989, was aimed at increasing profitability, competitiveness, and efficiency.

A subsidiary, Sumitomo Life Insurance Agency America, was established in 1986 with offices in New York and Los Angeles to provide employee benefit assistance and to act as an insurance advisor concerning overseas employee benefit schemes for Japanese companies around the world. Reinsurance agreements were signed with 17 major life insurance companies in 13 countries. One example was a 1989 agreement with a Mutual of Omaha affiliate, United of Omaha, to market group life, health, dental, and long-term disability contracts to Japanese-owned businesses in the United States and to share in the profit and losses of such a venture. While still new, the program was expected to be highly profitable.

One of Sumitomo's goals during this time period was to be a total life insurance planner and financial advisor to individuals at various stages of their lives. The new products developed in response to a changing society were directed toward two broad categories of the life insurance market: death-benefit policies and survivor-benefit policies. Japan's aging society and large rise in personal assets called for increased single-premium endowment policies, savings policies, and individual pension policies. Sumitomo Life saw a growing need for medical insurance and group pensions for the aging population to supplement the public pension system. In 1990, individual pension policies made up one of the fastest growing areas in the Japanese life insurance industry. Other trends included variable insurance (first introduced in 1986), group life insurance for small companies through their unions and cooperatives, and welfare plans and supplementary packages for medium-sized companies. Since 1988, life insurance companies were allowed to sell government bonds over the counter, and Sumitomo Life

was offering new products that combined life insurance with government bonds.

One of the most important ways for a life insurance company to invest its assets was through loans to corporations, government agencies, homeowners, and consumers. In addition, assets could be allocated to capital market activities such as investments in securities and real estate. Sumitomo Life had been strengthening its foreign operations and global investments, as well as diversifying its assets, to remain profitable and competitive in the 1990s. It had learned about employee benefit and social security systems in other countries and had formed relationships with insurance organizations around the world. Sumitomo Life had 13 subsidiaries licensed to invest in securities. Ties with international financial institutions were strengthened with a 1990 agreement forming a new investment advisory firm with Security Pacific Corporation, a California bank, called Sumisei Secpac Investment Advisors. The company also established ties with the Sedgewick Group PLC, the third largest insurance broker in the world, according to which Sumitomo Life would introduce Japanese firms to the Sedgwick Group, which would then advise on insurance matters. In 1982, Sumitomo Life Realty in New York was established to invest in real estate in major U.S. cities. It bolstered its overseas real estate efforts with offices in London and Australia. In 1990, the realty operations had assets of $1.5 billion in office buildings, hotels, and shopping centers. The company also focused on real estate investments in public works and urban development projects.

Sumitomo Life contributed to corporate good-citizenship in 1990 by financing, along with Yamaha Corporation, a musical center in Poland in memory of Polish composer Frederic Chopin, and Izumi Hall, a concert hall at Osaka Business Park, designed for classical concerts, among other such efforts.

A significant move during the early 1990s to increase profitability and reduce risk in rapidly changing financial markets was the development of a computer system to set forth the difference in the fund management techniques used by life insurance companies compared to those of other financial ventures. Users were able to evaluate Sumitomo Life's overall risk level, giving the company a new level of expertise in the industry.

Overcoming Hardships in the 1990s and Beyond

By the early 1990s, Japan's banking sector, along with the insurance industry, was experiencing difficulties brought on by a plethora of bad or non-performing loans and a faltering stock market. During the prosperous years of the 1980s, many banks and insurance companies, including Sumitomo, invested significantly in both real estate and stocks. This investment strategy, however, came back to haunt many companies when the Japanese property market collapsed in the early 1990s.

While better off than many of its counterparts, Sumitomo still felt the pains of its exposure to poor investments. In 1996, the company wrote off $4.58 billion in bad loans—the largest write-off by a life insurer in a single year. To make matters worse, Japan's economy was weakening, its banks were in financial disarray, interest rates were reaching record lows, and, for the first time since World War II, individual life insurance and pension policies were on the decline.

Key Dates:

1907: The Hinode Life Insurance Company is founded.
1925: The Sumitomo zaibatsu takes over the management of Hinode.
1926: Hinode changes its name to the Sumitomo Life Insurance Company.
1986: Sumitomo Life Insurance Agency America is established with offices in New York and Los Angeles.
1996: Deregulation begins; Sumitomo writes off $4.58 billion in bad loans.
1999: The company becomes the first Japanese insurance company to offer long-term care insurance.
2001: Sumitomo launches its Live One insurance product.

In order to boost its financial market, Japan began laying the groundwork for deregulation in its finance and insurance sectors, believing that looser regulations and new competition would remedy the problems facing these industries. In 1996, Sumitomo was given the nod to enter its competitor's markets. The company worked diligently to develop new products and services that would give it an edge during the liberalization process, which continued into the new century. In 1999, it launched a long-term care insurance package called Kaigo no Sumisei, becoming the first insurance firm in Japan to offer long-term care insurance options. It also acquired a stake in Taiheiyo Securities and Taiheiyo Investment Trust Management in order to gain a stronger foothold in the financial services market. In 2001, the firm developed Live One, a cutting-edge insurance product that allowed customers access to both life insurance and a variety of financial services.

Meanwhile, Japan's insurance industry continued to be bogged down with problems, and deregulation had yet to prove that it would bring about positive change. In 2000, four life insurance companies in Japan ceased operations, which left many analysts and industry watchdogs expressing doubts with respect to the health of Japan's life insurance companies. Sumitomo forged ahead while low interest rates, and lackluster stock prices wreaked havoc on the firm's bottom line.

Troubles continued in 2003, forcing Sumitomo to restructure in an attempt to shore up earnings. The company also sought out ways to reduce its exposure to risk; these included reducing its equity holdings and lessening the percentage of its high-risk equities to just 6.4 percent of total assets. Sumitomo also set forth a strategy designed to strengthen its position in both the long-term care and medical care insurance fields. As the company worked to restore consumer confidence within the insurance industry as a whole, its fate rested on a turnaround of the Japanese economy. While Sumitomo's longstanding history played in its favor, it faced distinct challenges in the years to come.

Principal Subsidiaries

Sumitomo Life Reality Inc. (United States); Sumitomo Life Investment Singapore Ltd.; Sumitomo Life Insurance Agency America Inc.

Principal Competitors

Dai-Ichi Mutual Life Insurance Company; Nippon Life Insurance Company; Meiji Life Insurance Company.

Further Reading

Dvorak, Phred, ''Results at Japanese Life Insurers Fuel Worries about the Industry,'' *Wall Street Journal*, November 28, 2000, p. A23.

Hardy, Quentin, ''Japan Insurers Face Problems on Holdings,'' *Wall Street Journal*, September 28, 1992, p. C1.

''Insurers Race for New Channels, Products,'' *Nikkei Weekly*, September 6, 1999, p. 10.

''Life Insurers Hit by Decline in Policies,'' *Nikkei Weekly*, December 1, 1997. p. 1.

''No Return: Life Insurers Need to Make Some Tough Decisions,'' *Asahi Shimbun*, July 9, 2002.

''Sumitomo Life Buys into Taiheiyo,'' *Japan Times*, October 5, 1998, p. 14.

''Sumitomo Life to Write Off $4.58 Billion in Bad Loans,'' *Wall Street Journal*, June 11, 1996, p. A10.

Uemura, Nobuyasu, ''Insurance Sectors Crossing Barriers,'' *Nikkei Weekly*, September 3, 2001.

Yokota, Kazunari, ''Year of Financial Turmoil Sets the Stage,'' *Nikkei Weekly*, December 29, 1997, p. 1.

—Paula Cohen
—update: Christina M. Stansell

Sweet Candy Company

3780 West Directors Row
Salt Lake City, Utah 84104
U.S.A.
Telephone: (801) 886-1444
Toll Free: (800) 669-8669
Fax: (801) 886-1404
Web site: http://www.sweetcandy.com

Private Company
Incorporated: May 7, 1900
Employees: 100
Sales: $25 million (2002 est.)
NAIC: 311330 Confectionary Manufacturing from
Purchased Chocolate; 311340 Nonchocolate
Confectionery Manufacturing

Sweet Candy Company is the world's largest manufacturer of saltwater taffy. It also manufactures jellybeans and other candies and confections, 250 varieties in all. Sweet Candy ships 15 million pounds of product a year. Among its best-loved sweets are chocolate-covered orange and raspberry sticks. Other products include caramel and peanut brittle. While the company once produced chocolate bars and boxed chocolates, these offerings were eventually discontinued. Sweet Candy has remained in the hands of the founding family for more than a hundred years, quite an achievement in a very competitive industry.

Sweet Origins

The Sweet Candy Company was formed in Portland, Oregon, in 1892 by Leon Sweet and his business partner, T.H. Broderick. According to *Candy Industry,* the creator of the Pacific Coast's first steam-operated candy factory, Louis Saroni, funded Sweet's venture with $1,500 and became the company's president. Among the original products were jawbreakers, lollipops, and licorice candies.

Leon Sweet and his brother Arthur relocated to Salt Lake City, where the business was incorporated as a Utah company on May 7, 1900. Sugar beets from nearby farms supplied an important input; Utah Sugar Company had been refining and exporting sugar for nine years. In addition, Utahns have traditionally been known to be enthusiastic consumers of candy. The Sweet business soon merged with several other small confectioners as distribution expanded across eleven western states and even as far as Australia.

The company's product line-up was extended to include hand-dipped chocolates and other confections after the move to Salt Lake City. Arthur Sweet began delivering the goodies in a horse-drawn wagon. The Sweets took on another partner, William "Cass" Cassidy, as Saroni was no longer involved in the company's daily operations.

Sweet Building Built in 1910

Ten years after moving to Utah, Sweet Candy built a four-story brick building in downtown Salt Lake City (224 South 200 West) a few blocks away from the original location (15 East 100 South); the company would remain there for ninety years. Employees told the *Deseret News* that a pair of friendly ghosts roamed the building. The building underwent a $500,000 expansion in 1920.

By the 1920s, the company had become one of the first to package its candies in cellophane, according to *Candy Industry.* (Candy had previously been packaged in wooden boxes and metal tins.) Leon Sweet bought Saroni's share of the business in 1925, becoming president and general manager.

Leon Jack Sweet, son of the founder, joined the company in 1931 after graduating from the Wharton School of Finance at the University of Pennsylvania. He was credited with introducing several important innovations. In 1936, he developed a new method for producing saltwater taffy that involved adding egg whites. This became the company's best-selling product.

Tony Sweet told the *Salt Lake Tribune* of his grandfather's passion for making candy bars, a line of business later discontinued. The Brown Bomber was named in honor of 1937 heavyweight boxing champion Joe Louis. Other confections sported names such as Rodeo Bars, Razzle Dazzle, and Pink Lady Chocolates.

Tony Sweet also told the *Deseret News* that his grandfather had begun making the company's signature saltwater taffy as a non-melting substitute for chocolate in the days before air conditioning. Proximity to the Great Salt Lake had nothing to do with it, since there is actually no saltwater among the ingredients.

Arthur Sweet, brother of the founder, was named president in 1941. He had previously been in charge of sales. Jack Sweet, who had served in the Navy during World War II, took over the business in 1950. The building underwent another expansion that year. A cardboard sailboat merchandising display created by Jack Sweet in the 1950s was so popular it remained in use 40 years later. Jack Sweet is also credited with helping create the company's perennially popular Chocolate Orange Sticks with jellied candy centers, which were introduced in 1948. Jack Sweet became company president in 1962, two years after the death of company founder Leon Sweet.

In the mid-1960s, Sweet Candy began producing Cinnamon Bears. A dark red variety was marketed for a time at Yellowstone National Park gift shops as "Smoky Bears," reported the *Deseret News.*

Jack Sweet's son Tony, a graduate of Stanford University, was named president and CEO in 1971. After the arrival of financial vice-president Bob Thomas in 1976, the company began to computerize its operations. The building underwent yet another expansion in 1982.

Moving Candy in the 1990s

Sweet candy sold 15 million pounds of confections in 1995 as annual sales approached $20 million, reported *Candy Industry.* Forty percent was marketed under the Sweet brand, the rest sold wholesale.

As reported the *Deseret News,* the company replaced its slowest sellers every year with new products. A chocolate-covered version of the perennially popular Cinnamon Bears came out in the mid-1990s. In 2000, Sweet added its line of tart, fruit flavored "Totally Taffy" aimed at younger generations. The next year, Sweet Candy entered the fruit snack segment with its Yummy Nummy Bears.

In 1995, Sweet's built a 35,000-square-foot distribution center near the Salt Lake City International Airport. Four years later, the company relocated manufacturing operations from its historic building in downtown Salt Lake City to a new $12 million, 185,000-square-foot facility in the Sorenson Technology Park near the airport. The plant opened in April 1999; it was said to be able to handle a three- or four-fold increase in tonnage. Unlike the original Salt Lake building, the new plant had all operations on the same floor.

Chairman and president R. Anthony "Tony" Sweet spent the next few years upgrading technology in order to keep the company viable in an increasingly competitive business. This eventually resulted in Tony Sweet being named Business Executive of the Year by the Utah Manufacturers Association in November 2003.

The company logo was updated in the late 1990s. At this time, Sweet Candy was producing 15 million pounds of candy and confections a year. It employed 140 people. Leon Jack Sweet died on May 15, 2000. By now, a fourth generation of the family represented by granddaughter Rachel was involved in the company's management.

Alpine Confections contracted Sweet Candy to produce a saltwater taffy line in commemoration of the 2002 Olympic Winter Games held in Salt Lake City. The company added four flavors to its six best-selling ones to create a boxed set of ten.

It was natural for Sweet Candy to celebrate the international theme of the Olympics. The company often employed immigrants in its factory; in 2000, it began awarding U.S. flags to those who became naturalized citizens. It also encouraged its managers to learn foreign languages, particularly Spanish. Most of Sweet's employees were not native speakers of English; in 1996 the company began offering English classes on-site.

The company was known for its loyal workforce. For their part, the Sweets counted convenience to the employees as one of the main reasons for staying in the Salt Lake area instead of seeking incentives to relocate elsewhere.

Principal Competitors

Hershey Foods Corporation; Jelly Belly Candy Company; Kencraft Inc.; Mars, Inc.; Nestlé S.A.

Further Reading

Bringard, Lara, "Success Is Sweet for Salt Lake's Sweet Candy Co., Celebrating One Hundred Years of Business in a Highly Competitive Industry," *Enterprise* (Salt Lake), May 11, 1992, p. B3.

"Candy Firm Building Distribution Center," *Enterprise* (Salt Lake), June 5, 1995, p. 7.

Edwards, Jane, "Open Mind, Open Heart; Corinne Sweet Had Equal Embrace for All Humankind," *Salt Lake Tribune*, March 24, 1996, p. J1.

Ennen, Steve, "A Taste for the Future," *Food Processing*, March 1, 2000, p. 90.

Fulmer, Brad, "Candy Maker Excited to Move into 'Sweet' New Manufacturing Facility," *Intermountain Construction*, May 1, 1999, p. 34.

"Funeral Services Held for Leon Jack Sweet," *Deseret News*, May 19, 2000, p. B4.

Hobbs, Nancy, "Makers Hoping Tree Sweetens Fund-Raiser," *Salt Lake Tribune*, November 24, 1999, p. C1.

Jones, Lara, "Candy Maker to Build New 12-Acre Production Plant," *Enterprise* (Salt Lake), December 1, 1997, p. 1.

Lopez, Jesus, "Sweet Candy Goes Beyond Job Training," *Salt Lake Tribune*, June 16, 2000, p. D1.

Mathur, Shruti, "Sweet Candy's Thomas, 79, Dies of Heart Attack," *Salt Lake Tribune*, June 7, 2002, p. C7.

Mitchell, Lesley, "Workers Compensation Fund Honors Safety Efforts; A Dozen Utah Businesses Praised for Preventing Accidents and Keeping Insurance Premiums Down," *Salt Lake Tribune*, June 11, 1998, p. B4.

"New 'Piggyback' Marketing Channel Leads to Sweet Success," *Food & Drug Packaging*, June 1, 1999, p. F3.

Nii, Jenifer K., "Helping Workers Become Citizens Is Sweet Job," *Deseret News*, July 4, 2001, p. C1.

Oberbeck, Steven, "Liquor Quicker? Utah Firms Find Sweet Niche in Candy," *Salt Lake Tribune*, August 15, 1993, p. F1.

——, "Sweet on the Grinch," *Salt Lake Tribune*, December 1, 2000, p. D1.

Sahm, Phil, "The Future Looks Sweet for Utah Candy Maker," *Salt Lake Tribune*, July 16, 1999, p. C1.

——, "Utah Adjusts to Changes, Too," *Salt Lake Tribune*, May 14, 2001, p. D1.

——, "Work's Sweet for S.L. Candy Kin," *Salt Lake Tribune*, February 23, 1992, p. D13.

O'Neill, Marina, "Merchants Tasting Sweet Success," *Deseret News*, January 29, 2002, p. B5.

Sneddon, Sharon, "Flexibility Drives Sweet's Competitive Edge," *Candy Industry*, June 1996, pp. 24ff.

Stephenson, Kathy, "Spill the Beans," *Salt Lake Tribune*, March 27, 2002, p. D1.

"Sweet Reaps 100 Years of Sweet Success," *Candy Industry*, August 1, 1994, p. 94.

Wadley, Carma, "Candy Biz Sweet for Sweets," *Deseret News*, February 14, 2001, p. C1.

Wallace, Brice, "Candy Building Still Sweet," *Deseret News*, April 2, 2001, p. D6.

Williams, Jean, "Candy Factory," *Deseret News*, June 22, 1999, p. C1.

——, "How Sweet It Is . . ." *Deseret News*, June 22, 1999, p. C1.

—Frederick C. Ingram

☰ TAIHEIYO CEMENT

Taiheiyo Cement Corporation

St. Luke's Tower, 8-1
Akashi-cho, Chuo-ku
Tokyo 104-8518
Japan
Telephone: (3) 6226-9018
Fax: (3) 6226-9154
Web site: http://www.taiheiyo-cement.co.jp

Public Company
Incorporated: 1881
Employees: 18,770
Sales: ¥927.9 billion ($7.72 billion) (2003)
Stock Exchanges: Tokyo
Ticker Symbol: 5233
NAIC: 327310 Cement Manufacturing

Taiheiyo Cement Corporation operates as Japan's largest cement manufacturer. The company has over 570 subsidiaries in its arsenal, all of which are involved in the construction, construction materials, and real estate sectors. Taiheiyo's core business segments include cement and minerals and aggregates, along with its zero-emissions division, an environmentally friendly unit that focuses on turning waste materials into resources. Chichibu Onoda Cement Corp. and Nihon Cement Co. Ltd. merged in 1998 to form Taiheiyo, the fifth-largest cement concern in the world.

Origins in the Late 1800s

The history of the Onoda Cement Company—a major predecessor in the Taiheiyo group—begins during Japan's Meiji era, from 1867 to 1912. During this era, the Japanese social structure changed from feudal to Western forms through government-sponsored industrial expansion. One of the first steps taken by the Meiji government to modernize was the construction of port and harbor facilities. The first cement in Japan, imported from France in 1870, was used in the construction of piers in the port of Yokosuka. As the demand for infrastructure increased, so did the demand for cement and other imported goods. In an effort to reduce the outflow of gold and silver due to increased imports, the Meiji government began a domestic industrial development program.

Except in military industries and strategic communications systems, private concerns carried out this industrial development program. In certain industries, however, the Meiji government sponsored and constructed pilot plants. One of these industries was cement. The construction bureau of the Ministry of Finance built Japan's first cement plant at Fukagawa, Tokyo, in 1873. Portland cement was manufactured there two years later, in 1875, the same year cement production began in the United States.

One of the crucial features of the Meiji era, the disbanding of the samurai warrior class in 1869, helped provide the financial basis for Onoda Cement Company. After their dismissal from government service, the samurai received pensions from the government that amounted to a percentage of their original salary and varied in value. After about seven years, the pensions became too expensive and were replaced with interest-bearing, nonconvertible bonds. The samurais' incomes fell to a fraction of their original levels, and only a few of them had enough commercial experience to go to work to replace their lost incomes. At the same time, inflation due to weakened paper currency and increased government expenditures reduced the real value of their fixed holdings. Inflation later became a principal reason for the government's decision to sell its various pilot plants.

In May 1881, at Onoda-Mura, Yamaguchi Prefecture, Junpachi Kasai founded Onoda Cement, the first privately owned cement company in Japan. A year later, Onoda Cement purchased the government's pilot plant at Onoda. Kasai, himself an ex-samurai warrior, led a group of samurai who pooled their pensions to capitalize the company. Kasai became one of Japan's leading industrialists and part of a group of business leaders who helped reinforce Japan's national integrity. Through their industrial successes, these businesspeople resisted the expansion of Western interests into Japan during a period of global colonization. During the presidency of Kasai's son, Shinzo Kasai, between 1900 and 1930, Onoda became the largest cement firm in Japan.

Transportation was crucial to profitability in the cement industry because cement was traditionally a high-bulk, low-value good. Manufacturers maximized revenues by placing plants near either the final market or a water transportation facility, since water transport was the cheapest mode of bulk carriage. Prior to World War II, Onoda solely produced cement; it did not have its own sales and distribution network. Mitsui Bussan, a large zaibatsu, or conglomerate, was Onoda's sales and distribution agent in both foreign and domestic markets. The relationship did not compromise Onoda's independence. Onoda was not a subsidiary of Mitsui Bussan but rather a client of its trading services. From its founding Onoda had been proud of maintaining its corporate independence.

The firm expanded extensively before World War II, especially into China and the Japanese colony of Korea, the closest areas for increasing market size. By the beginning of the war, over 60 percent of the firm's assets, roughly 19 plants, were in Korea and China.

Overcoming Problems in the 1920s and 1930s

In 1924, the cement federation, Rengokai, a cartel organization, was formed to control output. The cartel set uniform curtailment rates that required cement manufacturers to limit production to 60 percent of capacity. Uniform production curtailment rates favored established firms over newer firms. Established firms retained older equipment, normally scrapped in a competitive environment, simply for the purpose of counting it as production capacity. Older firms could curtail production to 60 percent of capacity by using 100 percent of their new equipment and none of their older equipment. Newer firms with a higher percentage of newer equipment found that the 60 percent cap cut into the machinery they could use in a competitive market, putting them at a disadvantage.

The cement federation agreements covered Japan proper, the colonies, Manchukuo, and the South Seas Mandatory territories. Tensions within the cartel, intensified by the Great Depression, prompted the formation of sales associations to fix exclusive sales territories with sales quotas and standard prices. In 1932, Onoda's Dairen factory seceded from the cartel over a dispute about Manchurian quotas. In December 1933, the cartel responded to this challenge by setting up a mechanism by which to divide markets, the Cement Exporters Association.

In 1934, Onoda and the Oita Company withdrew from the cartel on the grounds that the industry's leader, the Asano Group, gained an unfair advantage from the uniform curtailment rates because it had predominantly older equipment. When the cartel lost its control, it appealed to the government for intervention. In December 1934, the Minister of Commerce and Industry enforced Article 2 of Japan's Major Industries Control Law, for the first time ever, on the cement industry. The government's intervention forced the "outsiders" to comply with the cartel's cur-

tailment rates but actually did very little to control competition since the law applied only to production in Japan proper.

To get around this constraint, Onoda built plants in Korea, Kwantung, and Manchukuo and supplied the home market from these sources. This move was easy to accomplish because Onoda and the other "outsiders" operated mainly in western Honshu, Kyushu, and Korea. The national and municipal governments became some of Onoda's biggest customers, since the company now could undercut cartel prices. The cartel responded to these Onoda successes by having the Asano, Mitsubishi, and Yasuda zaibatsu set up their own colonial companies. It also secured the 1936 revision of the Major Industries Control Law, which extended the government's control into the colonies as well. The government's solution to the conflict was to have agents of the Rengokai and Onoda meet every three months to set prices and production limits. This arrangement lasted until the eve of World War II, at which time Onoda operated 27 plants with an annual production of 3.5 million tons.

Postwar Growth

As a result of World War II, Onoda lost 60 percent of its assets, or a total of 19 plants, including its foreign holdings in China and all of its then domestic holdings in Korea. The plants left to Onoda after World War II included Ofunato, Fujiwara, Tahara, Hikone, Atetsu, Onoda, Yahata, Tsunemi, and Oita. Together with the loss of plants, Onoda lost its distribution arrangement with Mitsui Bussan when that zaibatsu was broken up by the occupation government. The new arrangement called for Onoda to operate its own domestic sales and distribution network while employing Mitsui as its foreign sales and distribution agent.

After the war, Onoda president Toyoroku Ando rebuilt the business to re-emerge as the industry's leader in Japan. Ando was a 1921 graduate of Tokyo University and a lifelong employee of Onoda. He spent his first 25 years with the company in Korea, where he rose to manage the Pyongyang factory in 1944. Ando became president in 1945 and improved the efficiency of Onoda's production, distribution, and transportation systems. Under his direction, the company began extensive diversification plans. Onoda produces or conducts research into specialized types of Portland cement, ceramics, electronics, ionics, biotechnologies, fluorochemicals, and computer systems.

Onoda began to expand outside Japan in the 1960s with a joint venture with two partners, Mitsui Bussan and Hong Leong Corporation. This joint venture, Singapore Cement, was a bulk importer of Onoda's "Dragon Brand" cement. In 1974, Onoda set up P.T. Semen Nusantara in Indonesia to operate a cement plant at Cilacap, in central Java. Later, Onoda expanded into several markets, including Hong Kong, Australia, Hawaii, Malaysia, and regions of the Pacific Rim. In the late 1980s, Onoda began to expand into both the Chinese and U.S. markets.

Onoda's entry into the United States began with a joint venture with Lone Star Industries of Greenwich, Connecticut, in 1988. The $60 million operation, Lone Star Northwest, conducts business in three states: Washington, Oregon, and Alaska. The venture imports cement and manufactures concrete and aggregates—crushed stones used in making cement and in highway construction.

<table>
<tr><td colspan="2">Key Dates:</td></tr>
<tr><td>1881:</td><td>Junpachi Kasai establishes Onoda Cement.</td></tr>
<tr><td>1924:</td><td>Rengokai, a cement federation, is formed to control output.</td></tr>
<tr><td>1945:</td><td>By now, Onoda has lost 60 percent of its assets as a result of the war.</td></tr>
<tr><td>1974:</td><td>P.T. Semen Nusantara is set up in Indonesia to operate a cement plant.</td></tr>
<tr><td>1988:</td><td>The company enters the U.S. market.</td></tr>
<tr><td>1994:</td><td>Onoda merges with Chichibu Cement Co. Ltd.</td></tr>
<tr><td>1998:</td><td>Chichibu Onoda joins forces with Nihon Cement Co. Ltd. to form Taiheiyo Cement Corp.</td></tr>
<tr><td>2000:</td><td>Taiheiyo acquires a 28 percent stake in South Korea-based Ssangyong Cement Co. Ltd. and a majority interest in Grand Cement Co. of the Philippines.</td></tr>
</table>

Onoda's second entry into the U.S. market that year was the purchase of the CalMat Company's cement division, California Portland Cement Company, for $310 million. CalMat was a Los Angeles-area firm dealing in sand, gravel, asphalt, concrete, and land development. The purchase included 13 ready-mix concrete plants, three cement plants, and a cement-importing terminal, and it made Onoda the largest cement producer in California. In 1989, Onoda invested in China in a joint venture with Mitsui Bussan and two Chinese firms, Huaneng Raw Material Corporation and Dalian Cement Factory. This venture, Dalian Huaneng-Onoda Cement Company, planned to construct a $150 million plant at the port of Dalian, Liaoning Province. The plant would be capable of producing 1.4 million tons of high-quality cement for export.

By now, the company's principal innovations included the reinforced suspension preheater (RSP), an advanced cement-manufacturing process developed in 1964 that substantially reduced the amount of energy used in the manufacture of cement. The RSP system was used in more than 20 countries and was recognized as an industry standard. The O-sepa separator was an air separation system sold worldwide. The system, developed in the late 1970s, saved electric energy and improved particle-size distribution. A third product, Bristar, was an efficient, nonexplosive demolition agent used in urban areas to minimize the traditional side effects of explosives: flying debris, noise, vibration, gas, and dust. Another innovation was Chemicolime, developed in the late 1960s. This quicklime technology, which stabilized wet soils, was used by the U.S. military in Vietnam to strengthen jungle and marshland roads. Its contemporary uses involved construction projects near coastal regions.

During the late 1980s, Onoda operated Japanese plants in Ofunato, Fujiwara, and Tsukumi and had 104 subsidiaries, all in Japan, except Onoda U.S.A., Inc. and Onoda California, Inc. The company had five product divisions. The cement-products division was the largest and accounted for about one-third of net sales. The building-materials division produced materials that complement concrete construction. The limestone and related-products division produced limestone, gypsum, slag, and specialized sands. The civil and architectural engineering division helped to construct cement plants in other nations and devel-

oped applications of soil stabilizers and concrete reconditioners. The final division, the "others" division, dealt in chemicals, electronics, and land management.

Changes in the 1990s and Beyond

By the early 1990s, Japan's cement industry was plagued with problems. Onoda faced intense competition while struggling against a downturn in government works projects and overcapacity. To top it off, the country's economy was faltering. Many of Japan's leading companies were forced into merger activity, an uncommon occurrence in the Japanese business world. Sure enough, Onoda, positioned as one of Japan's largest cement manufacturers, and Chichibu Cement Co. Ltd., Japan's sixth-largest cement concern, joined forces in October 1994. The merger created Chichibu Onoda Cement Corp., Japan's largest cement manufacturer with a 24 percent share of the market.

Changes continued into the late 1990s as the company once again found itself in the midst of a major deal. Chichibu Onoda solidified its leading position in the industry by teaming up with Nihon Cement Co. Ltd. in 1998. Taiheiyo Cement Corp. was born out of the union and controlled over 40 percent of the domestic cement market. Even with its enviable position, Taiheiyo faced tough times due to continued weak demand. As part of a restructuring effort, the firm initiated a round of job cuts, reduced production capacity, and took other cost-cutting measures with a plan of saving ¥37 billion per year through 2001.

As Taiheiyo entered the new century, the company looked to international expansion as a means of shoring up profits. The firm acquired a 28 percent stake in South Korea-based Ssangyong Cement Co. Ltd. and a majority interest in Grand Cement Co. of the Philippines in 2000, making it the fifth-largest cement concern in the world based on output capacity. Despite these positive steps, Taiheiyo and its domestic counterparts continued to deal with falling demand, among other obstacles. In April 2000, The *Nikkei Weekly* reported that "Japan's cement industry seems immune to economic recovery. The problem can be traced to the sector's distribution structure, which negates the benefits of manufacturer cost-cutting by fostering intense competition among suppliers of ready-mix concrete. Complex conflicts of interest have made it extremely difficult for cement manufacturers to address the issue."

Nevertheless, Taiheiyo began to reform its distribution and logistics practices during this time period. It raised cement prices, stopped paying sales commissions, and began utilizing a uniform pricing structure in hopes of bolstering its financial position. In 2002, the company launched a new three-year program aimed at reducing debt. It sold off various real estate and securities assets and slashed capital spending.

During 2003, the operating environment in the cement industry remained challenging, especially for Taiheiyo. Demand in the government sector—which had accounted for nearly 60 percent of domestic cement demand in the past—continued to dwindle, forcing the company to look down different avenues for growth. One such area was recycling waste, which the company participated in through its zero-emission promotion business. The company secured a profit in fiscal 2003 and remained optimistic about its future. Despite a lackluster outlook for Japan's cement industry, Taiheiyo appeared to be on track for future growth through diversification.

Principal Subsidiaries

Bay Frontier Onoda Co. Ltd.; Chichibu Taiheiyo Cement Corp.; Daiichi Cement Co. Ltd.; Kawara Taiheiyo Cement Corp.; Kokusai Kigyo Co. Ltd.; Myojo Cement Co. Ltd.; Sanyo White Cement Co. Ltd.; Tsuruga Cement Co. Ltd.; DPS Bridge Works Co. Ltd.; Onoda Chemico Co. Ltd.; A&A Material Corp.; Chichibu Concrete Industry Co. Ltd.; Clion Co. Ltd.; ILB Co. Ltd.; Material Technology Laboratory Co. Ltd.; Taiheiyo Materials Corp.; Taiheiyo Precast Concrete Industry Co. Ltd.; Abekawa Kaihatsu Co. Ltd.; Buko Mining Co. Ltd.; Chichibu Mining Co. Ltd.; Chuoh Shoji Co. Ltd.; Ishizaki Co. Ltd.; Kansai Matech Co. Ltd.; Kosyu Saiseki Co. Ltd.; Okutama Mining Co. Ltd.; Ryushin Mining Co. Ltd.; Shin Kansai Asano Mining Co. Ltd.; Tsukumi Mining Co. Ltd.; Yuko Mining Co. Ltd.; Nihon Ceratec Co. Ltd.; Sanshin Electric Co. Ltd.; Ichihara Ecocement Corp.; NACODE Corp.; Taiheiyo Soil Corporation.

Principal Competitors

Lafarge S.A.; Mitsubishi Materials Corporation; Ube Industries Ltd.

Further Reading

Baker, Michael, "Taiheiyo Cement Finds Bargains Next Door," *Daily Deal*, September 25, 2000.

"The Cement Industry of Japan," *Far Eastern Economic Review*, August 8, 1957.

"Cement Makers Seek Concrete Gains," *Nikkei Weekly*, April 24, 2000, p. 16.

"Consolidating Mergers in Japan," *Mergers and Acquisitions*, January/February 1994, p. 16.

Fushimi, Kazuko, "Merger Fails to Yield Concrete Gains," *The Nikkei Weekly*, January 27, 2003.

Masson, R.H.P., *A History of Japan*, New York: Free Press, 1972.

Sapsford, Jathon, "Mergers' Growing Acceptance in Japan is Fortified by Fair Trade Panel's Move," *Wall Street Journal*, January 12, 1994, p. A7.

Schumpeter, E.B., *The Industrialization of Japan and Manchukuo*, New York: Macmillan, 1940.

"Taiheiyo Cement Fails to Build Strong Performance," *Nikkei Weekly*, October 23, 2000.

"Taiheiyo Cement Mounts Drive into Asian Markets," *Nikkei Weekly*, October 16, 2000.

"Two Cement Firms in Japan Announce Plans for a Merger," *Wall Street Journal*, November 12, 1993, p. A7.

—John C. Bishop
—update: Christina M. Stansell

Topco Associates LLC

7711 Gross Point Road
Skokie, Illinois 60077
U.S.A.
Telephone: (847) 676-3030
Fax: (847) 676-4949
Web site: http://www.topco.com

Cooperative
Incorporated: 1944 as Food Cooperatives, Inc.
Employees: 284
Sales: $3.5 billion (2001 est.)
NAIC: 422410 General Line Grocery Wholesalers

Topco Associates LLC is a leading procurer and distributor of private label grocery products to retail, wholesale, and food-service accounts. The firm also offers national brand buying, equipment purchasing, and other services. Topco is a cooperative that is owned by more than 50 member companies, including Associated Grocers, Inc., Meijer, Schnuck Markets, Fresh Brands, Big Y Foods, and Giant Eagle. The company distributes more than 7,000 products such as canned and frozen foods, produce, flowers, paper goods, pet food, and health and beauty care items. In addition to providing in-store brands exclusive to some members, Topco distributes a dozen lines of private label products under such names as Top Crest, Food Club, Full Circle, World Classics, Dining In, Shurfresh and Shurfine. The latter two were added in 2001 when Topco Associates, Inc. and Shurfine International merged to form the present organization. Topco's members are located around the United States as well as in Canada, Israel, and Japan.

Beginnings

The roots of Topco date to World War II, when a group of Wisconsin grocers founded a small buying cooperative to help them procure dairy products and paper goods, which were scarce due to wartime shortages. The company, called Food Cooperatives, Inc., began operations on September 29, 1944. After the war it also began distributing a line of grocery products for members under the Food Club label, and in December 1950 the organization merged with another co-op called Top

Frost Foods, with which it shared some members. The combined firms took the name Topco, using part of each company's name. Members at this time included Alpha Beta, Fred Meyer, Hinky Dinky, Penn Fruit Company, Big Bear Stores, Brockton Public Market, Furr's, and Star Markets.

Topco's offerings now included products manufactured for it by outside firms under the Food Club, Top Frost, and budget Elna brand names, which were sold in members' stores as so-called "private label" goods. The products in these lines, which included canned and frozen foods and other basic items, sold for less than their nationally advertised counterparts. In addition to giving consumers a price break, they also provided grocers with exclusive products that had higher profit margins.

During the 1950s, Topco added new categories such as fresh produce, which it began distributing in 1958. In 1960, general merchandise, store equipment, and some health and beauty care products were introduced as well. By this time, the firm had a total of 27 members, each of whom paid one percent of the cost of their private label goods back to the cooperative to cover its operating expenses. Membership was open to retailers with a minimum of $10 million in annual sales, and each member was required to pay $5,000 for common stock and buy an amount of preferred stock that was based on a percentage of annual sales. The advantages to members included lower prices on private label products due to group buying, as well as higher quality achieved through the cooperative's quality assurance program. Topco now had a staff of 70 deployed at its headquarters as well as in several growing regions to oversee purchasing and quality control. The organization was selling about $60 million worth of products annually.

During the 1960s, Topco's offices were moved to new quarters in the Chicago suburb of Skokie, Illinois, and a number of other retailers joined the cooperative, including Tom Thumb, King Soopers, Giant Eagle, and McCarty-Holman. By the middle of the decade, the firm was distributing more than 1,000 food and non-food items to stores in 33 states.

Supreme Court Rules against Topco in 1972

In 1968, the U.S. Justice Department filed suit against the company for its practice of giving members exclusive rights to sell the firm's brands in specific territories. Though a lower court found in the company's favor, the case was appealed to the U.S. Supreme Court, which ruled against Topco in 1972. Afterwards, the organization began to place a greater emphasis on developing its members' individual private labels.

The 1970s saw the introduction of unbranded, starkly-packaged, ''generic'' low-cost products across the United States, and Topco responded with a new line called Valu Time. This was the first nationally marketed generic brand to include such items as cigarettes and paper products. Its success helped Topco's sales exceed $1 billion in 1979.

In the 1980s, the firm's membership ranks grew with such new additions as Riser Foods, Randall's, Pueblo International, Smith's Food & Drug Centers, and Schnuck Markets. In 1988, Topco added a new line called World Classics, which featured nearly 100 higher-priced, ''gourmet'' products that were promoted in the style of national brands and offered retailers higher profit margins. Included were such items as white asparagus, raspberry vinegar, and cappuccino wafers. That year also saw a new line of health and beauty care items debut under the name Top Care. One hundred different products were offered, and the brand rapidly became a strong seller for the company.

In 1989, Topco named Robert Seelert president and CEO to replace Marcel Lussier, who had run the organization for a decade. Seelert had previously headed General Foods' World-wide Coffee and International Foods unit. In 1990, the company introduced GreenMark, an environmentally friendly ''green'' product line. The 20 items initially offered included paper towels and napkins made from recycled paper, biodegradable compost bags, and coffee filters made from unbleached paper. GreenMark caught on quickly with consumers, and other items were soon added.

Daymon Associates Named Broker in 1991

In March 1991, Topco named New York-based Daymon Associates to handle private label merchandising at member stores. Daymon was to deploy 150 staffers at retail locations around the United States to assist in positioning and displaying items, doing in-store advertising, and handling coupon give-aways and product demonstrations. Daymon would also provide input about packaging, quality, and other issues. Though the arrangement had already been successfully tested at Giant Foods, and Topco's board had unanimously voted in favor of the move, there was some controversy about the decision among vendors. A short time after the Daymon agreement was reached, CEO Seelert resigned to take a new position, though he denied leaving over the Daymon issue. He was replaced in November by Lyman ''John'' Beggs, former president of Norelco Consumer Products Company.

The U.S. economy was now in a recession, and the economic downturn served to boost sales of less expensive, private-label goods. Their share of overall supermarket sales increased from 16.4 percent in 1987 to 17.5 percent in 1991. For the latter year, Topco's gross sales hit $2.9 billion, a 21 percent increase over 1990. The organization had grown to 36 members.

In 1992, Topco reintroduced its stagnant World Classics line with new packaging and a greater promotional push. It was revised to focus on twelve popular categories, including pasta, carbonated drinks, and cookies. In September, the company named its third CEO in as many years, Steven Rubow. He had been with Topco since 1987, most recently serving as executive vice-president.

Topco's membership was now growing and reached a total of 45 by 1994. Member firms had some 3,000 stores around the country, which accounted for 14 percent of supermarket sales in the United States. New companies included the Pennsylvania-based, 30-store Insalaco Markets, the 19-unit Kings Super Markets chain of New Jersey, and Carr Gottstein Foods of Alaska, which had 23 stores and supplied a number of other independent grocers. In 1995, Topco became an international supplier with the membership of Canada's Oshawa Group and the Japanese SEIYU. Companies in Israel and Puerto Rico would later join as well. The company's annual sales now approached $3.9 billion.

In 1998, Topco added a new service for its members in association with Illinova Energy Partners. Illinova would perform utility accounting services to help cut costs and consumption, as well as check for billing errors, contest rate changes, and supply some Topco members with natural gas. That same year also saw Topco redesign its Top Care and Top Crest packaging to help boost sales. Logos were repositioned, the product guarantee was given a more prominent position, and label colors were refined to better mimic those of national brands. Among the firm's best sellers at this time were internal analgesics and cold and cough remedies, as well as batteries and camera film. Private label goods now accounted for 20.1 percent of total sales in supermarkets.

The mid-1990s saw the grocery industry experience a wave of consolidation, which caused membership in Topco to decline as member firms were bought up by larger companies. The loss of such chains as Dominick's Finer Foods of Northlake, Illinois, and Buttrey Food & Drug Stores Company of Great Falls, Montana, left the firm with 30 members by early 1999. Some were joining, however, including the 115-store Piggly Wiggly Carolina, which switched its private label health and beauty care line to Top Crest. Despite such gains, membership would later bottom out at 25.

In 2000, Topco began marketing a line of organic foods known as Full Circle, which included frozen vegetables, soy milk, and cereal. The firm also boosted its gourmet food offerings, adding Deli meats and cheeses and fancy chocolate bars. Another new product line, dubbed Skillet Dinners, featured meals that could be heated quickly at home.

Merger with Shurfine in 2001

In September 2001, the company announced it would merge with Illinois-based Shurfine International, a private label manufacturing and distribution cooperative which primarily serviced

Key Dates:

1944: Food Cooperatives, Inc. is founded.
1950: Food Cooperatives merges with Top Frost Foods to create Topco.
1958: Topco begins marketing fresh produce.
1960: General merchandise, store supplies, and health and beauty products are added.
1972: The U.S. Supreme Court bars Topco from granting exclusive sales territories.
1979: Revenues top $1 billion with help from new Valu Time generics.
1988: World Classics premium foods and Top Care health and beauty aids are introduced.
1990: GreenMark "environmentally friendly" products debut.
1991: Daymon Associates is hired as a food broker to boost private-label sales.
1995: Canadian and Japanese retailers join Topco.
2000: Full Circle organics are introduced.
2001: A merger with Shurfine International creates Topco Associates, LLC.

wholesale and foodservice accounts. Shurfine, which had been founded in 1948, moved its operations to Skokie, and the expanded company became known as Topco Associates, LLC. The members of Topco would own 85.7 percent and those of Shurfine 14.3 percent. Topco president and CEO Steven Lauer, who had headed the firm since 1999, retained the top posts. Shurfine's experience in wholesaling and foodservice, and Topco's recent efforts to move into the latter category, were expected to help stimulate growth for the firm.

After the agreement was finalized, Topco would have 54 members. It was restructured into Retail, Foodservice, and Wholesale divisions, with Shurfine CEO John Stanhaus given charge of the latter. The three units were set up to allow "cross-channel" procurement of products and services. Topco was now distributing 7,000 different products.

To obtain goods for its members, the company utilized a staff of 150 buyers who negotiated prices and sought cost savings from suppliers. A group of 20 quality assurance experts tested 130,000 samples annually to insure that they met or exceeded the quality of similar national brands. Topco also negotiated with 30 major vendors to earn discounts for its members on nationally-advertised products.

In 2003, Topco expanded the Full Circle natural and organic line with new rice, bean, popcorn, cookie and soy milk products, bringing its offerings to more than 125 items in 24 categories. The company also began using online auctions to speed the procurement process for canned foods and other goods. A new line of 50 prepared food products, dubbed Dining In, was introduced as well. It included microwaveable entrees like beef pot roast au jus and Cajun-seasoned chicken breasts, as well as other meat, seafood, and pasta dishes. Topco teamed up with Sweet Baby Ray's Gourmet Sauces and Certified Angus Beef

for the project, which had taken a year to develop. The year 2003 also saw the company gain a new member, Stater Bros., which operated 157 grocery stores.

After nearly 60 years, Topco had grown into one of the leading procurers and distributors of private-label goods in the United States. The addition of Shurfine International had given it an entrance into the wholesale market, as well as a greater presence in foodservice sales. It continued to produce a wide range of items that gave consumers a lower-cost alternative to national brands.

Principal Divisions

Retail; Wholesale; Foodservice.

Principal Competitors

Wal-Mart Stores Inc.; Kroger Company; Wakefern Food Corporation; Associated Wholesale Grocers; Unified Western Grocers; Roundy's, Inc.

Further Reading

Andreoli, Tom, "The Thriving Private (Label) Side of the Food Business," *Crain's Chicago Business*, May 4, 1992, p. 4.

Coia, Anthony, "Topco Cuts Costs With E-Auctions," *Supermarket News*, April 21, 2003, p. 78.

Crown, Judith, "Local Private-Label Firm Blazes 'Green' Trail," *Crain's Chicago Business*, April 22, 1991, p. 16.

Elson, Joel, "Updated Packaging Brightens Topco's Day," *Supermarket News*, April 16, 1999.

Fagnanai, Stephanie, "Topco to Add to Its Full Circle Line," *Supermarket News*, March 3, 2003, p. 47.

Gibson, Richard, "Marketing: Grocers' Private Labels Go from Low to Lofty," *Wall Street Journal*, February 14, 1990, p. B1.

"High Court to Weigh Antitrust Implication of Firms' Geographic Division of Markets," *Wall Street Journal*, April 20, 1971.

Karolefski, John, "Bob Seelert Plans to Resign as Topco's President, CEO," *Supermarket News*, April 15, 1991, p. 6.

——, "Topco Adds In-House Broker," *Supermarket News*, March 25, 1991, p. 1.

Littman, Larry, "Genuardi's, Piggly Wiggly Makeover to Topco HBC," *Supermarket News*, March 20, 2000, p. 49.

Margulis, Ronald A., "Door Is Open for Private Labels," *U.S. Distribution Journal*, November 15, 1991, p. 38.

Miller, Lynne, "Topco Rolls out Prepared Foods," *Supermarket News*, May 5, 2003, p. 96.

Murray, Barbara, "Cooperative Introducing Many New Products," *Supermarket News*, February 5, 2001, p. 43.

Nagle, James J., "Co-op Found Boon by Small Chains," *New York Times*, February 14, 1957, p. 43.

Pierce, John, and Peter Berlinski, "Organic Food Lines Gain Momentum," *Private Label*, May/June 2002.

Schneider, Martin, "Shurfine-Topco Merger Would Create $3.45B Company," *Supermarket News*, September 24, 2001, p. 1.

Simmons, Tim, "Private Arrangements," *Supermarket News*, April 15, 1991, p. 2.

"Topco Loses Decision," *New York Times*, March 29, 1972, p. 55.

Turcsik, Richard, "A Run For the Money (Private Label)," *Progressive Grocer*, November 1, 2001, p. 85.

"What's New at Topco?," *Private Label*, March/April, 2002.

—Frank Uhle

Tops Markets LLC

6363 Main Street
Williamsville, New York 14221-5855
U.S.A.
Telephone: (716) 635-5000
Toll Free: (800) 522-2522
Fax: (716) 633-0898
Web site: http://www.topsmarkets.com

Wholly Owned Subsidiary of Ahold USA
Incorporated: 1977 as SB Investors Inc.
NAIC: 445110 Supermarkets and Other Grocery (Except
    Convenience) Stores

Tops Markets LLC is a subsidiary of the U.S. operations of Dutch supermarket giant Royal Ahold N.V. In addition to the Tops chain, Ahold also owns Stop & Shop, Giant Food, BI-LO, and Bruno's Supermarkets. With its headquarters located in Williamsville, New York, Tops is comprised of some 160 Tops Friendly Markets, more than 200 Wilson Farms and Sugar Creek convenience stores, and B-Kwik Food Markets superettes. Tops' units are located in central New York and neighboring parts of Pennsylvania and Ohio.

Company Origins in the 1920s

The Castellani family has been the driving force in the development of Tops throughout its history. The roots of the company can be traced to the 1920s, when Ferrante Castellani opened a small neighborhood grocery store in Niagara Falls at a time when orders were still being filled by clerks and before the self-service concept was pioneered by Clarence Saunders and his Piggly Wiggly stores. In the years following World War II, the modern supermarket took shape. Ferrante's son, Armand, would take the family business into this new era. He learned the business from an early age, serving as manager of his father's store when he was only 16. After a stint in the military, he struck out on his own, establishing the Great Bear Market in Niagara Falls in 1951. He then forged a partnership with Thomas A. Buscaglia, a grocery equipment salesmen, to create the T.A. Buscaglia Equipment Company in 1953, a business that equipped grocery stores.

Later in the decade, the company became involved in the retail food business, offering support services for an alliance of small company-owned and third-party grocery stores in Upstate New York, primarily in the Buffalo area, which would evolve into the Tops chain. In 1960, the business was renamed Niagara Frontier Services, and in the same year the company opened its first modern supermarket, a 25,000-square-foot store located in Niagara Falls. The Tops Friendly Markets chain was launched in 1962 as a franchise system for supermarkets and the B-Kwik banner was coined for smaller stores.

Thomas Buscaglia died in 1967. Armand Castellani succeeded him as Niagara's chief executive officer and continued the company's growth. A year after his partner's death, Castellani took the company public. In 1969, Niagara opened its first convenience store under the Wilson Farms Neighborhood Food name. As the company became a regional leader, it ceased franchising and began to expand beyond the Buffalo area, by the mid-1970s moving into the Rochester market and northern Pennsylvania. Whenever possible, the company bought out its franchised stores. For the most part, however, Niagara flew under the radar screen. Armand's son, Larry Castellani, told the *Rochester Business Journal* in 1993, ''We were virtually ignored through the '60s and '70s, and I think one of the reasons we were able to grow through our infancy was probably because a lot of the national chains many, many times our size ignored us.'' Larry Castellani, representing the third generation of his family to be involved in the grocery business, started out at the age of five sorting bottles and sweeping up at his father's Great Bear Market. In 1962, as a teenager, he went to work as a Tops stock boy. He studied business administration at Niagara University but never earned his degree, opting instead for a practical education with the family business. He graduated to director of operations in 1975 and became president of Top's retail division in 1980.

Going Private in the Early 1980s

The 1980s saw changes in ownership for the company. In May 1983, Niagara was taken private in an $82.6 million leveraged buyout by SB Investors Inc., a subsidiary of New York City Investment firm AEA Investors Inc. AEA negotiated terms for the acquisition and arranged for the financing. Of that $82.6

305

Company Perspectives:

What started as a small association of franchised stores grew into a regional leader and would eventually become part of one of the world's leading retailers, while remaining an integral part of the fabric of the community in which it all began.

---

million, $58.6 million came from bank loans and through the issuance of $24.5 million in stock and notes. Armand Castellani, who remained chairman of Niagara, earned more than $11 million in stock and stock options, then turned around and paid $2.1 million to SB Investors for a 14.3 percent interest in Niagara.

Over the next three years, Niagara spent more than $75 million on its largest capital program in company history. Tops moved into the profitable superstore concept, which featured more high margin products and specialty departments. Eight Tops Friendly Markets were converted to superstores and another seven superstores were built during this period. In addition, Tops introduced a number of initiatives, including direct debit service, Instabank ATMS, and the first CarryOut Café service. During this period, Niagara acquired four supermarkets from franchisees and greatly expanded the number of Wilson Farms stores, which increased from 39 in 1982 to 60 by 1986. At this stage, the company also owned and operated 53 Tops Friendly Markets and two B-Kwik superettes. In addition, it franchised another 11 Tops markets, 11 BiKwiks, and six Wilson Farms, along with owning a 10 percent stake in Supermarket Operators of America Inc., a Minneapolis-based company involved in the franchising of Cub super warehouse food stores. For the fiscal year ending June 1984, Niagara generated sales of $705.6 million and posted a profit of $6.15 million. A year later, revenues improved to $742.9 million but net income fell off, totaling $5.42 million.

As was the case with many companies, Niagara was taken private, then spruced up to be once again taken public in an offering that would prove highly profitable to investors. In preparation for a new offering, SB Investors changed its name to Tops Markets Inc. in January 1986. An offering was then completed on March 12, 1986, with 2.12 million shares sold at $19.50 a share. The company netted $18.6 million, which was then used to pay off outstanding debt. However, Tops would be publicly owned for little more than a year. After recording revenues of $790 million and net profits of $6.6 million for the year that ended June 28, 1987, Tops was again taken private. Management hired New York investment banker Goldman Sachs, which then found a buyer: the Los Angeles-based merchant banking firm of Riordan, Freeman & Spogli, which paid about $280 million, including debt, for the company. RFS already owned other supermarket concerns, including Bayless Southwest Cocompany in Phoenix, P&C Foods in Syracuse, Boys Markets in Los Angeles, and Piggly Wiggly Southern in Vidalia, Georgia.

Ahold Parentage in 1991

Tops would be owned by RFS for less than four years. During this transitional phase, Larry Castellani was named pres-

ident of the company. Tops continued its expansion efforts, although the balance did not reflect its overall health. The company lost $13.3 million in 1988, $12.1 million in 1989, and $2.8 million in 1990, but according to management these results were essentially "paper losses" connected to the 1987 buyout. Annual revenues reached $812 million by this point. Moreover, the chain experienced a significant increase in operating income, and cash flow improved by 50 percent. An objective reflection of the company's state was provided in 1991 when the Dutch conglomerate Ahold N.V., through its U.S. subsidiary, Ahold USA, decided to buy the chain. Ahold, which generated more than $10 billion in annual revenues, split equally between the United States and the Netherlands, was interested only in acquiring quality properties. According to a statement issued by Ahold USA president Rob Zwartendijk, "Top Markets represents a remarkably good fit with Ahold's existing U.S. operations in terms of its retailing formats, market approach and geographic location." The acquisition also elevated Ahold to the status of a top ten food retailer in the Unites States. According to a Tops management statement, becoming a part of the Ahold family was also a positive development for the supermarket chains: "Backed by the extensive financial and technical resources of a highly successful international retailing group, Tops Markets is about to enter a bright new growth phase in its development." With the financial backing of its new corporate parent, Tops hoped to accelerate the conversion of existing stores to the superstore format and open new units, as well as to extend its geographic reach.

Over the course of the 1990s, with Larry Castellani now serving as CEO, Tops expanded into central New York state and Northeast Ohio. In 1994, it opened a new headquarters in Williamsville, New York, then in 1996 opened a major state-of-the-art distribution center in western New York. Tops also launched a number of marketing initiatives. Allying itself with M&T Bank, the company co-branded a popular Visa credit card that offered stores credits. Tops also opened Fantastic ticket outlets in some of its stores to sell tickets for the Buffalo Bisons minor league baseball team and Buffalo Sabres National Hockey League team, as well as to events held at the venues where the teams played. Tops added significantly to its portfolio in 1996 when Ahold merged its Ohio-based Finast supermarket chain into the operation, adding 43 stores, mainly located in northeast Ohio. Although they adopted the Tops colors and added the Friendly Markets tag, the supermarkets retained the Finast name until 1999, when all the northeastern Ohio stores were rechristened Tops Friendly Markets. In another development in 1996, Ahold announced that it was going to use the Tops banner on supermarkets it planned to open in Thailand as part of a joint venture with Bangkok-based Central Group. For the parent corporation, this alliance was part of a larger effort to expand its supermarket operations into Malaysia, Indonesia, and Singapore.

In October 1997, Larry Castellani resigned as Tops president and CEO in order to take a corporate position with Ahold. Stop & Shop's CEO, Bob Tobin, filled in on a temporary basis. In January 1998, a replacement was named, 39-year-old Steve Odland, who took over as president and CEO of Tops in February, despite having no retail experience other than working at the store level while attending college. After earning an undergraduate degree in business administration from the University

Key Dates:

1951: Armand Ferrante opens Great Bear Market in Niagara Falls.
1953: Ferrante co-founds T.A. Buscaglia Equipment Company.
1960: Buscaglia is renamed Niagara Frontier Services.
1968: The company goes public.
1983: Niagara is taken private in a leveraged buyout.
1986: Niagara's parent company is renamed Tops Markets and taken public.
1991: Ahold USA acquires Tops.
2003: Tops CEO quits in the wake of accounting scandal.

of Norte Dame, followed by an MBA from Northwestern University, he gained many years of executive experience at Quaker Oats, where he served as vice-president of Quaker Oatmeal Cereals U.S Business Unit, Vice President-Strategic Development for international foods, and Vice President Marketing of Golden Grain Division. He also worked for Sara Lee Bakery as president of the foodservice division before joining Tops. The first non-Castellani family member to head the company, he took over the management of 238 stores: 73 Tops Friendly Markets, 43 Finast Friendly Markets, 102 Wilson Farms Convenience Stores, 12 Vix Deep Discount drug stores, and eight B-kwik superettes.

According to the *Buffalo News,* Odland "hit the ground running with a number of initiatives that have given the company a new look, both at its headquarters and in its aisles. Internally, Odland totally revamped the management team, adding many newcomers, including a number of high-ranking women executives and several non-supermarket managers." In addition, he consolidated some administrative functions with other Ahold chains and outsourced other functions, thereby reducing headcount by 160. He sold off Vix to Drug Emporium, and in 2000 bolstered the Wilson Farms division by acquiring the 87-unit Sugar Creek chain of convenience stores, located across New York state. A large portion of the stores were renamed Wilson Farms, thereby giving the Wilson Farms banner an immediate presence in markets that Tops' management deemed desirable. Odland was also instrumental in Tops reversing course on its commitment to the superstore concept. The chain now introduced smaller format, easier-to-shop stores ranging in size from 45,000 to 55,000 square feet. This was part of an effort to promote Tops as a "fast, fun, family" place to shop. The smaller format of the new Tops stores, which featured wider and shorter aisles, was intended to permit quicker access to checkout lines. In addition, freezer cases were designed with more shelving in order to allow for as much variety as Tops superstores were able to offer. The chain also continued its

interest in offering non-grocery services, such as in-store banks and full-service pharmacies. In 2000, Tops opened its first fueling stations at its supermarkets, again adding to the chain's emphasis on customer convenience. Another decision as part of an effort to improve service was to close stores from midnight to six a.m. rather than operate them 24 hours a day.

In June 2000, Odland took over as chief operating officer of Ahold USA. He was replaced as Tops' CEO by Frank Curci, who was brought in from Ahold's BI-Lo chain. He oversaw a number of developments in the next two years. In February 2001, Ahold acquired 56 Grand Union stores, 22 of which were converted into Tops Friendly Markets. In April of that year, the company introduced its Tops Xpress convenience store format. Tops sold its warehouse operations to C&S Wholesale Grocers in 2002. That same year, the company celebrated its 40th anniversary, and founder Armand Castellani died at the age of 84.

Tops endured months of turmoil in 2003. There were rumors that Ahold might switch Tops to another of its brand names or even consider selling the chain, although that appeared highly unlikely. In the end, as part of the implementation of a long-term shared services strategy, Ahold decided to consolidate the management of Tops and Giant Food Stores (Carlisle, Pennsylvania). After three years of heading Tops, Curci was slated to become chief operating officer at another Ahold chain, Giant Food of Landover, Maryland, but an accounting scandal enveloped Tops in May 2002 when Royal Ahold discovered millions of dollars in overstated profits in its U.S. operations. Curci promptly resigned, as did several other Tops executives. Tony Schiano, president and CEO of Giant Food Stores, in keeping with the earlier reorganization plan, now took on the additional role of Tops' president and CEO. In charge of running day-to-day affairs as Tops' general manager was Max Henderson, who previously served as Vice President of Operations and Merchandising at Giant-Carlisle.

Principal Competitors

The Penn Traffic Company; Wegmans Food Markets, Inc.

Further Reading

Glynn, Matt, "Departure of Tops Markets' CEO Aids Ahold Image, Analysts Say," *Buffalo News,* June 26, 2003, p. 1.

Hagerty, Bob, "Dutch Concern Agrees to Buy Tops Markets," *Wall Street Journal,* February 28, 1991, p. A4.

Hyland, Bruce, "Tops Markets Plans Return to Public Status," *Business First–Buffalo,* February 10, 1986, p. 1.

Janoff, Barry, "Thinking Smaller," *Progressive Grocer,* December 1999, p. 57.

Zwiebach, Elliot, "Tops Execs in LBO Bid for Chain's 145 Stores," *Supermarket News,* June 15, 1987, p. 1.

—Ed Dinger

Until Every One Comes Home.

United Service Organizations

USO World Headquarters
Washington Navy Yard, Building 220
1008 Eberle Place S.E., Suite 301
Washington, D.C. 20374
U.S.A.
Telephone: (202) 610-5700
Toll Free: (800) 876-7469
Web site: http://www.uso.org

Nonprofit Corporation
Incorporated: 1941 as United Service Organizations for
    National Defense, Inc.
Employees: 800 (est.)
Sales: $37 million (2001 est.)
NAIC: 813410 Civic and Social Organizations

The United Service Organizations (USO) is a nonprofit corporation that operates various support services for people enlisted in the United States armed forces. The group began in World War II, and it was widely known for providing entertainment to the troops. Some of Hollywood's biggest stars and the country's leading musicians donated their time to entertain U.S. soldiers at home and abroad. The USO continues to arrange entertainment for the armed forces, setting up tours at domestic military camps and at installations across the globe. The group supports the military in many other ways as well. The USO provides childcare for the families of military personnel; it runs deployment centers, providing snacks and rest areas for personnel in transit; it operates a contingency travel fund to help military families in need, and it runs Operation Phone Home, providing donated prepaid phone cards to servicemen and women. The USO also runs mobile canteens, which are four-wheel drive vehicles that can go out in the field to provide troops with rest facilities and access to phones and e-mail. The USO also runs cyber-canteens, which provide Internet access to military personnel. The group operates family and community centers domestically and abroad. Besides serving currently enlisted military personnel, the group provides services to veterans and to the families of people in the military. The USO is not funded by the government, though the President of the United States serves as its honorary chairman. It is backed by individual and corporate donations and has an endowment of around $25 million. The group is run by an estimated 12,000 volunteers worldwide. The USO operates more than 120 centers, split almost evenly between domestic and international operations. The USO serves roughly five million people each year.

Roots in World War II

The United Service Organizations was founded in 1941 as a response to the rapid mobilization of U.S. forces as the country entered World War II. Some charitable groups had worked with American soldiers in France during World War I, providing them with recreation and food and helping them maintain contact with their families. In 1940, several of these groups met in New York under the auspices of the National Jewish Welfare Board to consider similar action in the current conflict. At the same time, President Roosevelt was worried about the morale of troops waiting to deploy overseas. He wanted a centralized organization that could set up near bases all over the country. Six nonprofit groups formed the United Service Organizations for National Defense: the National Jewish Welfare Board, the Traveler's Aid Association, the Salvation Army, the National Catholic Community Service, the Young Women's Christian Association (YWCA), and the Young Men's Christian Association (YMCA). The leaders of the new USO met with Roosevelt and basically agreed to run the organization along lines he proposed. The government would be responsible for putting up buildings for the USO, and the USO would organize recreation in them. The USO incorporated in 1941 and quickly raised $16 million under the leadership of Thomas Dewey. Dewey resigned to become governor of New York, and the chairmanship of the USO passed to Prescott Bush in 1942. Bush was later elected senator from Connecticut and was the father of President George H.W. Bush and grandfather of President George W. Bush. Over the World War II years, the USO raised $33 million.

The money the group raised was quickly spent on installations across the United States and behind the front lines in Europe. The foremost function of the USO clubs was to keep

Company Perspectives:

The great intangible of America's wars beyond logistics, beyond strategy, beyond wonder weapons and generals, is the spiritual force of its fighting men and women—and that is the force that the USO so magnificently serves. The USO is a private nonprofit, charitable organization, which serves as a link between military personnel and the American people. The USO's mission is to enhance the quality of life of the men and women of the armed forces and their families worldwide.

soldiers and sailors occupied before they shipped out. The United States had a relatively small military before World War II. The country instituted a draft in 1940, and by the end of the war the United States had 12 million people in uniform. Many soldiers were young and had never been away from home before. Rural army bases often had no entertainment facilities beyond perhaps one small movie theater. Conversely, big cities offered a wealth of diversions that could be overwhelming for small-town enlistees. USO centers and clubs opened near bases and in areas where large numbers of military personnel passed through. The clubs provided free coffee and snacks, and civilians, mainly women, could volunteer to work at the USO centers, doing whatever was needed. This could be cooking, cleaning, chatting, or serving as a dance partner.

Soon after the USO's own incorporation, it incorporated a subsidiary company called Camp Shows, Inc. Camp Shows was fully funded by the USO, but its executives were people from the entertainment industry like Abe Lastfogel, head of the William Morris Agency. Camp Shows quickly organized four main tour circuits, bringing full-cast Broadway shows to some venues and arranging for smaller vaudeville acts, singers, and entertainers to perform for troops at far-flung bases. Camp Shows, Inc. brought some 7,000 performers on tour during World War II. Entertainments were held in Burma, China, Brazil, Bermuda, Alaska, the South Pacific, and the Soviet Union, as well as in many other spots in countries in Europe and across the globe. Camp Shows drew the biggest stars of the day, including Humphrey Bogart, Clark Gable, Gary Cooper, Ann Sheridan, Dinah Shore, the Andrews Sisters, and Bob Hope, who became more than any other performer the face of the USO. The stars donated their time and often put themselves in danger to bring their acts to troops in combat zones.

Adapting to New Roles after World War II

The USO was a huge popular success during World War II. It involved thousands of volunteers and by the end of the war brought hundreds of shows daily to military personnel scattered across the world. Immediately after the war, the USO focused its efforts less on entertainment and more on giving practical aid to soldiers returning home. Then, in January 1948, the USO's president announced that the group had fulfilled its mission and was now disbanded. USO canteens were taken down or restored to other uses. Only six months later, Secretary of Defense James Forrestal, worried about the growing Cold War with the Soviet Union, inquired about reinstating the USO. Members of the six

founding organizations met again, and in January 1949 the USO was reconstructed. The organization got a new president, Harvey S. Firestone, Jr. of the Firestone Tire and Rubber Co., and a new mission. The USO was to support the military whether in peace or war and to help both veterans and enlisted personnel negotiate between civilian and military life.

The new USO was to be supported by community charity groups such as the Community Chest. However, such charities often had other priorities, and funding for the peacetime USO fell far short of expenditures. After only a year, the new USO was out of money. The group officially suspended operations, only to be brought back with the outbreak of war in Korea. The USO was given a renewed mandate by the Department of Defense. The USO then raised some $13 million to support the troops in Korea. From 1950 to 1953, the USO again sent scores of big-name entertainers to perform for service personnel. The group also poured resources into service centers located near large rural military bases. By the end of the Korean War in 1953, the USO ran almost 300 service centers domestically and overseas.

The USO continued as a peacetime organization through the 1950s. However, financial support for the group fell, and by 1962 the USO was again near folding. At that time, the group reorganized, making some of the larger domestic USO centers responsible for their own fundraising. U.S. military involvement in Vietnam began to escalate in the early 1960s, and the USO opened its first club in Saigon in 1963. More and more troops entered Vietnam in 1964, and the USO soon ran more than a dozen clubs in Vietnam and Thailand. Entertainers such as Bob Hope, John Wayne, and Raymond Burr dedicated themselves to USO tours during the Vietnam War. The USO also began providing other services for military personnel, such as opening free phone lines so troops could call their families back home. The USO also ran a chartered flight service between 1970 and 1972, taking soldiers on leave home to the United States inexpensively.

The Vietnam War engendered massive public resentment to the military. After the United States withdrew from Vietnam in 1973, the USO found itself again lacking funding. The military itself changed after Vietnam, converting to an all-volunteer force. The USO had to adapt to these new conditions. The Department of Defense and the charitable organization United Way commissioned a study in the early 1970s to determine if the USO was still essential. The study concluded that the USO had an important role to play, particularly in bridging the gap between the military and civilians. As the group closed clubs and service centers in Vietnam, it opened or enlarged facilities elsewhere abroad, such as in Japan and Germany. The USO also began focusing on the different needs of the all-volunteer force in the 1970s. After the Vietnam era, more military enlistees had families. The USO set up family centers to provide education, daycare, and social support to military wives and children. Women also began to enlist in greater numbers in the 1970s, and the USO set up women's resource centers to help them.

The USO underwent several organizational changes at the end of the 1970s. In 1977, the group moved its world headquarters from New York to Washington, D.C. This brought it closer to the heads of the armed forces. Until the late 1970s, the six groups that had founded the USO had continued to play a role in

---

Key Dates:

1941: USO incorporates.
1947: USO disbands.
1951: USO is reactivated to serve troops in Korea.
1977: USO's world headquarters is moved from New York to Washington, D.C.
1979: The organization is granted a congressional charter.

---

its management. In 1979, the YMCA, the YWCA, the Salvation Army, and the other groups severed their ties with the USO. The USO was given a federal charter by act of Congress that year. This stimulated fundraising and also gave the USO a bigger slice of funds generated by the umbrella charitable organization the United Way.

New Challenges in the 1980s–90s

The USO continued to run hundreds of service centers and clubs near military bases at home and abroad in the early 1980s. During peacetime, however, the organization had a low profile. Fewer celebrities were interested in touring for the USO. In the mid-1980s, the USO suffered a blow when it was evicted from its quarters in New York's Times Square. The USO had had a presence on or near Times Square since its inception in 1941. The area was the center of huge victory celebrations at the close of World War II, and the USO continued to serve tens of thousands of military personnel annually out of its Times Square building into the 1980s. In 1986, the building the USO rented was sold and slated for demolition. The New York USO moved twice, for a time operating out of a hotel room.

In 1987, an American sailor died in a grenade attack on a USO club in Barcelona, Spain. In 1988, the USO club in Naples, Italy, was struck by a car bomb. Five people died and more than a dozen were wounded. Even in peacetime, the American military presence abroad was often resented, and the USO, as a gathering place for soldiers, was targeted.

In the Philippines in 1989, threats against the American military forced commanders to confine all personnel to their bases. The USO then took on the job of entertaining the soldiers and sailors who were confined without leave. Though the USO's celebrity entertainment wing had become much smaller, the group still attracted some big stars in the 1980s, such as Billy Joel, who performed in the Philippines in 1989. The USO was also successful in bringing aboard country music stars in the 1980s, including Loretta Lynn and the mother-daughter duo the Judds.

USO in the Gulf Wars

The USO went back into high gear in 1990 with the build-up of troops in the Persian Gulf. Many corporations made large contributions to the USO at the start of the first Persian Gulf War. Four corporations, the Coca-Cola Co., beer manufacturer Anheuser-Busch Cos., the communications company AT&T, and the American International Group each donated $500,000 to the USO. The money was used to pay for celebrity entertainment for the troops in the Persian Gulf. (Though entertainers donated their talent, travel and other costs could run quite high.)

The USO operated some 150 centers in the United States and overseas by 1990. The group saw a swell in its donations and number of volunteers as troops shipped out for the Middle East.

After the short-lived Persian Gulf War, the USO slipped again into peacetime mode. It continued to send entertainers on tours of military facilities around the world. The USO made a new effort to bring in black artists in the mid-1990s. Over half the U.S. military at that time was African-American. The group began a series of rhythm-and-blues tours in the mid-1990s. Some of the tours had direct corporate sponsorship, such as an AT&T-sponsored tour of popular singers to bases in the Caribbean in 1994. The USO also focused on efforts to ease family life for military personnel. At bases abroad, the USO sponsored language classes, cooking clubs, and local tours. Near military bases in the United States, the USO set up computer terminals with free Internet access, allowing families left at home to e-mail relatives deployed abroad or on ships at sea. By 2000, the USO was bringing in just over $8 million in annual funds.

In 2001, the USO of Metropolitan New York assisted firefighters and wreckage crews after the destruction of the World Trade Center on September 11. The USO organized volunteer chefs, many from prestigious Manhattan restaurants, to cook food for rescue workers aboard a donated commercial ship. In 2002, the USO got a new president and chief executive, Edward A. Powell, Jr. Powell had worked in the Department of Veterans Affairs after leaving the Navy. The USO increased its fundraising and added to its endowment in the early 2000s. The terrorist attacks in 2001 initiated a flood of donations to the USO. The group, which had always lost visibility in peacetime, had worked hard in the late 1990s to find more donors. By 2002, the USO had a host of new corporate backers. These included the Walt Disney Company, the cable network ESPN, Northwest Airlines, Nissan, General Dynamics, and Wal-Mart. The organization also continued to be supported by the United Way, private foundations, and the Combined Federal Campaign.

With troops again deployed to the Persian Gulf in 2003, the USO was at the forefront, coordinating various efforts to support the military. The USO held fundraisers in conjunction with several large grocery chains, allowing supermarket shoppers a convenient way to donate money and supplies. The USO coordinated a campaign to donate prepaid phone cards to personnel deployed in Iraq. In addition, the group found volunteers to staff overburdened transit centers. The USO center at the Los Angeles airport, for example, saw triple the amount of people pass through weekly as troops were sent to the Middle East. To cope with the sudden influx of soldiers, the USO went from a volunteer staff of four to a staff of almost 40. In June 2003, the USO launched its first entertainment tour in Iraq since the official end of hostilities. The USO sent not only singers like Wayne Newton and long-time USO entertainers the Dallas Cowboys Cheerleaders, but also sent professional basketball players to run basketball clinics for soldiers. The USO had been officially disbanded once in its history and was close to closing its doors several other times. Nevertheless, over 60 years the group had shown that it was always ready in a crisis and never idle for long.

Further Reading

Brady, James, ''Pitching in at Ground Zero,'' *Crain's New York Business*, October 1, 2001, p. 9.

Chawkins, Steve, ''Airport USO Offers Troops a Bit of Home,'' *Los Angeles Times*, March 23, 2003, pp. B1, B10.

Coffey, Frank, *Always Home: 50 Years of the USO: The Official Photographic History*, New York: Brassey's, 1991.

Curreri, Joe, ''USO Brought Touch of Home to Troops,'' *Grit*, October 27, 2002, p. 16.

Dunlap, David W., ''Times Sq. Still Home for U.S.O.,'' *New York Times*, August 26, 1987, p. B3.

Griffin, Anna, ''Day-to-Day Scenes of Today's USO More Practical Than Glamorous,'' *Knight-Ridder/Tribune News Service*, October 26, 2001, p. K5433.

Kilday, Gregg, ''Grant Fete to Recall USO Heyday,'' *Hollywood Reporter*, April 23, 2003, p. 15.

Nathan, David, ''USO Provides Live Outlet for Acts,'' *Billboard*, January 15, 1994, p. 15.

Pope, Tom, ''USO Is Out to Make Some New Memories,'' *Non-Profit Times*, March 15, 2002, p. 1.

''PR Offensive Hits Persian Gulf,'' *Advertising Age*, September 3, 1990, p. 53.

Ravo, Nick, ''U.S.O. Center Facing Eviction After Decades as Beacon to Soldiers,'' *New York Times*, December 20, 1986, pp. 29–30.

''Supermarkets Continue Support for Troops,'' *Supermarket News*, April 21, 2003, p. 18.

Suro, Roberto, ''5 Die in Explosion Outside Naples U.S.O.,'' *New York Times*, April 15, 1988, p. A3.

Tierney, John, ''At 50, U.S.O., in a New War, Battles Fears,'' *New York Times*, October 8, 1990, pp. B1, B4.

—A. Woodward

Uwajimaya, Inc.

<table>
<tr><td>
4601 6th Avenue South
Seattle, Washington 98108
U.S.A.
Telephone: (206) 624-3215
Toll Free: (800) 889-1928
Fax: (206) 624-3001
Web site: http://www.uwajimaya.com

Private Company
Incorporated: 1962
Employees: 650
Sales: $100 million (2002 est.)
NAIC: 445110 Supermarkets and Other Grocery (Except Convenience) Stores
</td></tr>
</table>

Uwajimaya, Inc. operates as a specialty Asian food and gift retailer and wholesaler. Uwajimaya's three retail supermarkets offer food and non-food items imported from Japan, China, India, the Philippines, Thailand, Vietnam, Korea, Mexico, and Indonesia. The company's retail outlets, which enjoy recognition as tourist attractions, are located in Seattle, Washington, a suburb of Seattle called Bellevue, Washington, and in Beaverton, Oregon, a community outside Portland. Each of the company's stores is patterned after the flagship store in Seattle's International District: a massive, 60,000-square-foot emporium outfitted with authentic Japanese architectural features. Inside the stores, there are several specialty departments complementing the grocery department, which stocks numerous types of noodles, soy sauces, rice, sushi ingredients, Asian beers and sake, as well as a host of other products ranging from staple foods to exotic fare. The stores also include a seafood department with live fish and shellfish tanks, a meat department, a produce department, a delicatessen department, and a gift department. In addition, Uwajimaya operates as a wholesaler through a division called Seasia, which imports thousands of items used by the company's three stores and other retailers, restaurants, and supermarkets. Uwajimaya is owned and operated by the Moriguchi family.

Origins

Uwajimaya's distinct and impressive place in the retail industry began humbly, starting from the back of a pick-up truck. The owner of the truck was Fujimatsu Moriguchi, a native of Yawatahama, Japan, whose entrepreneurial career began in Tacoma, Washington, 30 miles south of Seattle. Before immigrating to the United States, Moriguchi had learned to make fish cakes and other Japanese delicacies on the Japanese island of Shikoku in a village named Uwajima. It was from this village that Moriguchi drew the name for his modest enterprise, naming it Uwajima-ya, which roughly translates as "Uwajima-store." Moriguchi began selling his fresh fish cakes and other items in 1928, building a customer base from the Japanese laborers working in the logging and fishing camps dotting the Puget Sound area.

Moriguchi, with the assistance of his wife, Sadako Tsutakawa, fared well with his itinerant business until an ignoble chapter in U.S. history peremptorily stripped him of his livelihood. After the Japanese bombed Pearl Harbor on December 7, 1941, the response by the U.S. government had one regrettable manifestation: the establishment of internment camps for Japanese-American citizens and Japanese persons living in the United States. An entire ethnic group was imprisoned in a fervor of suspicion and paranoia. Among the interned were Moriguchi, Sadako, and their children. The family was sent to Thule Lake Internment Camp, located in California. There, where three of their seven children were born, the Moriguchis spent the war years, awaiting release and a return to normal life in the Pacific Northwest.

Following World War II, the Moriguchis moved to Seattle and made their first foray into the retail industry. They opened a retail store and fish cake manufacturing company on South Main Street, in the heart of Seattle's Chinatown (later renamed the International District). Not long after opening his store, Moriguchi began importing food and gifts from Japan, giving the family-run enterprise the broad and eclectic merchandise selection that would later characterize Uwajimaya. Sadako Moriguchi assumed responsibility for running the gift operation, beginning a direct involvement in running Uwajimaya that would span roughly four decades. The store became a fixture within the Nikkei community, building a sturdy customer base among Japanese and Japanese-American residents of Seattle that provided the springboard for the Uwajimaya's penetration into the non-Asian community.

Business Thrives After the 1962 World's Fair

A turning point in Uwajimaya's development occurred during the same year the company lost its patriarch. In 1962, Fujimatsu Moriguchi passed away, leaving behind him a thriving retail operation primed for expansion. Successive generations of Moriguchis embraced the concept of expanding Uwajimaya and expanding upon the merchandising ideas of Fujimatsu Moriguchi, which found their greatest expression just before he died. The World's Fair was hosted by Seattle in 1962, and Moriguchi decided to operate a small kiosk at the event—a moment in the company's history often erroneously cited as its starting date. Although Moriguchi passed away during the summer of 1962, his preparatory work was on display at the fair. The kiosk enabled the company to reach out to the non-Asian community, offering a look at the gifts, kitchenware, and delicacies produced and imported by Moriguchi. Uwajimaya's presence at the 1962 World's Fair was deemed an unmitigated success, introducing the company to a wealth of new market opportunities.

Building on the pivotal success of the kiosk at the World's Fair, the next generation of Moriguchi stewardship concentrated on cultivating Uwajimaya's appeal to non-Asian customers. The company offered Asian cooking classes and began importing foods and gifts from Korea, China, the Philippines, and a host of other countries. As Uwajimaya's merchandise mix became more diverse, so too did its customer base, prompting Fujimatsu Moriguchi's heirs to adopt an ambitious approach to Uwajimaya's growth. The second generation of the family incorporated the business and pursued expansion, forming its first entity in 1966, when Uwajimaya entered the wholesale business. Seasia was formed as the company's wholesale division, and began importing and distributing Japanese and other Asian products to other Asian retailers, restaurants, and supermarkets. Soon, the rapidly growing company found itself in need of a new store, one that could house the breadth and depth of Uwajimaya's retail vision.

In 1970, Uwajimaya opened its signature store, a pioneering food and gift emporium that expressed a retail concept years ahead of its time. Built two blocks south of the original store, the new store spanned 20,000 square feet, which made it the largest Japanese supermarket in the Pacific Northwest. The store, which incorporated authentic Japanese architectural features such as blue roof tiles, was expanded in 1978 by 16,000 square feet, space sorely needed for the company's broad and progressive vision of what a supermarket could become. Inside, the store contained a delicatessen, live fish tanks filled with an extensive selection of sea life, and a gift department offering artwork, books, records, cosmetics, fabrics, and kimonos.

The same year the company expanded its store in Seattle's International District, a second store was opened. Located in Bellevue, Washington—an affluent suburb just east of Seattle—the second Uwajimaya emulated the company's flagship store, offering a broad selection of food, gift items, and specialty departments.

With two stores and its wholesale operation supporting it, Uwajimaya began to hit its stride financially during the 1980s. Along with the robust growth came the emergence of the Moriguchi family as a force in Seattle's social and political scene. The company demonstrated a strong commitment to giving to the community, particularly to the residents of the International District. By the 1980s, the company enjoyed a loyal following among International District residents, some of whom had been shopping at Uwajimaya for three or four generations. The existence of this stable customer base provided reliable financial support for Uwajimaya. Augmenting the consistency of the International District clientele was the growing demand for Uwajimaya's hard-to-find merchandise among the non-Asian community. The addition of the Bellevue store helped fuel the extension of Uwajimaya's audience, as did the increasingly more diverse culinary tastes of the American population at large. The combined affect propelled Uwajimaya into a nationally recognized name in the supermarket industry, despite the fact that the company maintained a presence restricted to the Pacific Northwest.

Expansion in the 1990s and Beyond

By the mid-1990s, Uwajimaya was an enterprise whose multifaceted vibrancy belied its origins as a business run from the back of a pick-up truck. The company ranked as the largest Asian food retailer in the United States, producing annual sales hovering around $50 million. The company employed 200 full-time workers and 100 part-time workers, many of whom were fluent in several languages. Although the company's retail operations grabbed most of the public's attention, Uwajimaya's wholesale operations served as an indispensable contributor to the company's success. Seasia, which accounted for roughly half of the company's sales, imported more than 3,500 food items and 1,200 non-food items, dealing with goods from Japan, Thailand, Hong Kong, South Korea, Taiwan, and the Philippines.

During the latter half of the 1990s, Uwajimaya busied itself with expansion, taking on the biggest projects in its history. After a three-year search for a suitable location in the Portland, Oregon, area, the company completed construction of its first out-of-state store at the end of 1997. In December, Uwajimaya celebrated the opening of its store in Beaverton, a suburb of Portland. At roughly the same time of the Beaverton opening, preparations were underway for the grandest project to bear the Uwajimaya name.

On November 22, 2000, residents in the Puget Sound region were treated to the grand opening of the signature Uwajimaya property: Uwajimaya Village. The new development included a new store located across the street from the site originally occupied in 1970. The new flagship store measured 60,000

Key Dates:

1928: Fujimatsu Moriguchi begins selling fish cakes from the back of his pick-up truck.
1962: The company operates a kiosk at the World's Fair hosted by Seattle; Fujimatsu Moriguchi dies and his heirs and wife Sadako continue to operate the family business.
1966: Seasia, Uwajimaya's wholesale division, is formed.
1970: A new flagship store is opened in Seattle's International District.
1978: Uwajimaya's second store, located in Bellevue, Washington, is opened.
1997: Uwajimaya's first out-of-state store, located in Beaverton, Oregon, is opened.
2000: Uwajimaya Village, featuring a new store and a housing complex, opens in November.
2002: Sadako Moriguchi dies.

square feet, 56 percent larger than its predecessor. Inside, the haphazard layout of the previous store—a maze engendered by 30 years of remodeling projects—was replaced by an efficient and attractive floor design that impressed supermarket industry observers. Outside, among numerous other features, stood a 58,000-pound granite lantern imported from China. The store was one part of the $35-million Uwajimaya Village project. The company also constructed retail space for complementary businesses and constructed a residential development that included 176 apartment units, with monthly rents ranging from $880 for a studio apartment to $2,600 for a two-bedroom, two-bath unit.

In 2002, as Uwajimaya's 75th anniversary approached, the company marked the passing of an era. In the summer, Sadako Tsutakawa Moriguchi died of Alzheimer's complications at the age of 94. Although the loss of the Moriguchi matriarch was profound, the future resilience of the company was ensured by the strength of the legacy she left behind. Tomio Moriguchi, who served as chief executive officer of Uwajimaya, was one of six of her children who held executive positions within the company. Together, the Moriguchi family held fast to business principles displayed by their parents, the company's founders. Looking ahead, the company declared its intent to add to its three-store retail operation, although no specific time or location was revealed. Once the company did expand, however, there was every expectation that the new addition would be as successful as its predecessors, adding further to the luster that described Uwajimaya's operations.

Principal Subsidiaries

Uwajimaya Real Properties L.L.C.

Principal Divisions

Seasia; Kustom Foods.

Principal Competitors

Larry's Markets, Inc.; Safeway Inc.; The Kroger Co.

Further Reading

Liebman, Larry, "Uwajimaya Fans Out," *Puget Sound Business Journal*, November 21, 1997, p. 26.
Lightbourne, Lesa, "Good Works Plays Big Part in Grocer's Success," *Puget Sound Business Journal*, April 15, 1994, p. S19.
"Matriarch Who Co-Founded Uwajimaya Dies," *Seattle Post-Intelligencer*, July 29, 2002, p. B6.
Moriwaki, Lee, "The Flavor Is Asian; New Uwajimaya Store Is Open," *Seattle Times*, December 9, 2000, p. C5.
Mulady, Kathy, "Uwajimaya's Treasures; Historic Store Anchors Area," *Seattle Post-Intelligencer*, July 9, 2001, p. E1.
"Uwajimaya Chairman Considering Bid for Schell's Port Seat," *Seattle Times*, November 11, 1997, p. F2.
"Uwajimaya Hoping to Start Work Soon on Plaza Project," *Seattle Post-Intelligencer*, April 20, 1998, p. C1.
"Uwajimaya Plans Beaverton, Ore., Store," *Seattle Times*, November 21, 1997, p. D1.
"Uwajimaya Sketches Out Expansion in International District Asian Store," *Seattle Times*, April 15, 1998, p. C1.

—Jeffrey L. Covell

Vita Plus Corporation

1508 West Badger Road
Madison, Wisconsin 53704
U.S.A.
Telephone: (608) 256-1988
Web site: http://www.vitaplus.com

Private Company
Incorporated: 1948
Employees: 130
Sales: $87.6 million (2002 est.)
NAIC: 311119 Other Animal Food Manufacturing;
    325411 Medicinal and Botanical Manufacturing

Based in Madison, Wisconsin, Vita Plus Corporation is an employee-owned manufacturer of animal and livestock feed, supplements, and base mixes. According to the company, it mainly serves livestock producers in the midwestern United States—including its home state of Wisconsin, as well as Illinois, Indiana, Iowa, Michigan, Minnesota, Ohio, and South Dakota—through more than 200 dealers and "on-farm feed manufacturers."

Along with supplying feed products to farmers, Vita Plus considers itself to be a "technology interpreter" by conferring with a wide variety of agricultural experts in the development of its products. These experts include industry leaders, production managers, as well as private and university-based researchers and scientists.

Finding the Right Mix: 1948–59

Vita Plus got its start in 1948 when Lyle H. Hill and Walter J. Henderson formed the company in the back of a rented barn in Fitchburg, Wisconsin, using a feed mixer they bought for $25. The two men had met years earlier during the Depression years of the 1930s while attending the University of Wisconsin's College of Agriculture. Early on, Hill and Henderson demonstrated that they were a problem-solving team. While working for *Wisconsin Country Magazine,* they helped get the publication out of difficult financial straits.

After college, Hill and Henderson entered the feed industry. Before long they developed the idea of providing livestock producers with an alternative to so-called "complete" feeds. As Doug Moe explained in the February 1983 issue of *In Business,* the two men "felt the future of the livestock feeding business would be away from complete feeds toward a vitamin and mineral 'base mix,' which the farmers or feed dealers would then mix with the proteins (usually soybean meal) and carbohydrates (usually corn). Hill and Henderson felt this to be the future mainly because it was cheaper."

Several things inspired the name that Hill and Henderson chose for their new enterprise. According to Robert C. Bjorklund in the November 16, 1969 issue of the *Wisconsin State Journal,* Hill once explained that Vita Plus was so named based on the fact that it involved vitamins, because the word "vita" meant "life" in Latin, and due to a concept that Hill's boyhood scoutmaster used to talk about—the "plus factor."

In 1951, Vita Plus moved to 1508 West Badger Road in Madison, Wisconsin, a location that would serve the company into the 21st century. The concrete structure measured a mere 2,500 square feet, but that figure doubled the following year when strong growth fueled expansion. Around this time, some 134,000 animals were fed base feed mixes from Vita Plus.

Science Drives Success: 1960–79

In 1960, Vita Plus added a market research department in response to an expanding product line and a growing distribution area. That year, the company erected the fourth addition to its Madison plant. By the decade's end, the plant would receive yet another addition, bringing its value to approximately $500,000. In the November 16, 1969 issue of the *Wisconsin State Journal,* Robert C. Bjorklund dubbed the facility an "engineering system marvel," explaining: "One man, with an ear tuned toward the right sounds of mechanical and electronic devises, can get 80 tons of feed supplement material out of a giant rail car and mixed into prescribed portions. Then, with two other men, it is all bagged and moved to the warehouse, where it is readied for shipment."

Vita Plus introduced a more scientific focus to its operations in 1961, when it established a 60-acre research center in Verona, Wisconsin, to study feeding methods. According to the

Company Perspectives:

In today's fast moving agri-business world, your success depends on every piece fitting together perfectly. At Vita Plus, we are dedicated to maximizing each livestock producer's results. Through innovative feed products and comprehensive services, Vita Plus gives you the edge. No matter what challenges you face, depend on Vita Plus for the solutions.

February 1983 issue of *In Business,* Vita Plus "worked closely with the University of Wisconsin Meat and Animal Science Department in projects relating to animal diseases, new farm products, artificial insemination, and milk replacers."

In 1965, Vita Plus's sales reached $795,000, supported by a sales force of 13 men who served customers in Wisconsin, Illinois, Minnesota, and Iowa. The following year, sales exceeded the $1 million mark for the first time. New products played a key role in the company's rapid growth; approximately 42 percent of sales were attributable to products Vita Plus did not offer seven years before.

As of 1966, Lyle Henderson remained president and chairman of Vita Plus, and Walter Henderson continued to serve as vice-president. During that year, the company bought an additional 80 acres of land next to its hog research center in Verona, Wisconsin, in order to expand the center's scope to include dairy and beef cattle. The acquisition increased the facility's total size to 160 acres. As evidence of its growing sophistication, Vita Plus added a number of new departments in 1967. These included a marketing department to handle advertising, market research, and sales, as well as an educational and public relations department.

By 1968, Vita Plus had expanded into Indiana. That year, the company added a "gestation house" to its research center in order to study feeding requirements of sows and gilts. It also opened the research center up to other companies, including those in the pharmaceutical industry, that were interested in performing studies involving large animals under farm conditions. Vita Plus also introduced the Vita-Plus N-Richer Feed Manufacturing Franchise. This enabled the company's base mixes to be combined with ingredients grown locally and then marketed under the Vita Plus brand name.

During the late 1960s, Vita Plus made two acquisitions in Iowa. The first involved the Trend Feeds division of Iowa-based Corn King Company. Then, in 1969, Vita Plus acquired Spencer, Iowa-based Welco Feed Manufacturing Company, giving it increased production capacity for supplements and concentrates, as well as complete feeds for both poultry and livestock.

In 1969, sales reached almost $1.6 million, and Vita Plus produced enough feed each month to support 130,000 hogs from birth to market. The company also began offering retail feed franchises, the first of which was opened in Dodgeville, Wisconsin. New products during the late 1960s included Vita Plus Foot Rot Guard and Vita Plus Foot Rot Treatment, both of which were developed at the company's research center in Verona.

An important development took place in 1971, when Vita Plus moved its corporate offices to nearby Fitchburg, Wisconsin, a mile away from the plant on West Badger Road. In addition to accommodating the company's growing employee base, the new facility included a new computer center used "for standard office procedures, market research, and new product analysis," and to "program data to aid Vita Plus dealers in their individual businesses," according to the July 7, 1971 *Wisconsin State Journal.* That year, approximately 1.54 million animals were fed Vita Plus's base mixes, up from 134,000 animals 20 years before. It was in 1971 that the company bought the Columbus Mills feed dealerships in Fall River and Columbus Mills, Wisconsin. Columbus Mills was a long-established operation that had been in business for more than 100 years, serving first as a flour and grist mill before venturing into feed manufacturing.

Vita Plus expanded internationally in October of 1972, when it formed Vita Plus of Canada, Inc. The new firm, headed by Canadian native Don Pestell, was based in New Hamburg, Ontario, and operated a warehouse facility in Mitchell, Ontario. Commenting on the move, Lyle Hill told the news media that Vita Plus based its expansion decision partially on the similarities between Wisconsin and Ontario agriculture.

There was much to celebrate at Vita Plus in 1974. In the course of only five years, the company's sales volume had more than doubled. Expansion and a host of new products—including milk replacement formulas for calves and baby pigs—fueled this accomplishment. In 1973 alone, sales had increased 28.5 percent. It also was in 1974 that Vita Plus worked with the University of Wisconsin to convert the barn in Fitchburg, where the company was founded, into what *In Business* described as "an aquaculture center" devoted to the study of commercial pike and perch production. By 1976, the number of animals receiving Vita Plus's base mixes had surpassed the 2 million mark. Accomplishments such as these allowed the company to prosper throughout the remainder of the decade.

Exponential Growth: 1980 and Beyond

Vita Plus ushered in the 1980s with the acquisition of the Sunnyside Feedmill in Portage, Wisconsin. The company continued to manufacture base mixes for farmers, who combined its products with their own protein sources. Vita Plus offered base mixes for a diverse array of animals, including beef and dairy cows, deer, dogs, horses, and pigs. The company even honored special requests to provide special mixes for certain birds.

The strong growth achieved in previous years continued during the early 1980s. By 1982, sales had more than tripled during the previous five years, and Vita Plus shipped 65 tons of base mix per day, which eventually became 2,400 tons of feed upon mixing. By this time, the company employed 61 people, 25 of whom were based in Madison.

By 1982, Vita Plus was still owned by the family of Lyle Hill, as well as four employees: President Ed Gustafson, Production Vice-President Larry Elhorn, Research Director Art Palmer, and Treasurer Robert Tramburg. In 1986, an employee stock ownership plan was established. Sales had increased approximately 400 percent in only ten years.

<table>
<tr><td colspan="2" align="center">**Key Dates:**</td></tr>
<tr><td>**1948:**</td><td>Founders Hill and Henderson start Vita Plus in a rented barn in Fitchburg, Wisconsin.</td></tr>
<tr><td>**1951:**</td><td>Vita Plus moves to facilities in Madison.</td></tr>
<tr><td>**1961:**</td><td>A 60-acre research center is established in Verona, to study feeding methods.</td></tr>
<tr><td>**1966:**</td><td>Sales surpass $1 million, driven by new product offerings.</td></tr>
<tr><td>**1972:**</td><td>International expansion occurs with the establishment of Vita Plus of Canada, Inc.</td></tr>
<tr><td>**1986:**</td><td>An employee stock ownership plan is established; sales increase approximately 400 percent over 1976 levels.</td></tr>
<tr><td>**1992:**</td><td>Sales reach $45 million.</td></tr>
<tr><td>**2003:**</td><td>Vita Plus purchases a 27,000-square-foot facility located at 2514 Fish Hatchery Road in Madison.</td></tr>
</table>

Computerized formulas, which Vita Plus provided to individual farmers, continued to play a central role in the company's success during the 1980s. These formulas enabled farmers to get the most meat or milk from their animals. President Ed Gustafson commented on the company's success with this approach in the January 12, 1986 issue of the *Wisconsin State Journal,* explaining: ''What we're really doing is providing a more economical way of producing feeds to produce livestock. That's why we're experiencing growth whereas agriculture in general is in such difficult times.''

In October 1987, Treasurer Robert Tramburg was named president of Vita Plus, which then recorded annual sales of $13 million. Tramburg had joined the company in 1972, when he served as general manager of Vita Plus's grain operation in Fall River, as well as its Columbus feed plant. Ed Gustafson remained with the company as a consultant, and founder Lyle Hill, at age 77, remained chairman of the board.

As Vita Plus entered the 1990s, the company continued its pattern of remarkable performance. Sales increased from $4 million in the early 1970s to $45 million in 1992. In addition to its headquarters in Madison, operations had grown to include five centers devoted to distribution and production. Vita Plus's staff, which included nutritionists and scientists, continued to assist farmers with specialized software applications that helped them to plan more effectively. Employees numbered 130 in 1993, including 80 in Madison.

During the 1990s, Vita Plus continued to provide its customers with individualized attention and personalized service. Indeed, some 70 percent of the feed mixes sold by Vita Plus went to individual farms or farm groups. As Dairy Feed Specialist Sharon Brantmeier remarked in the July 1, 1993 *Wisconsin State Journal:* ''We've been doing all along what Fortune 500 companies are trying so hard to do now. We've got a team approach to everything we do. Our office technical staff probably spends 25 to 30 percent of its time out in the field [with customers].''

By 1997–98, Vita Plus's sales had reached the $70 million mark, reflective of a growth rate of 113 percent in only five years. Such growth had led to cramped quarters for staff as early as the 1990s. By May 2003, relief came in the form of a 27,000-square-foot facility located at 2514 Fish Hatchery Road in Madison, which the company purchased. Formerly owned by Newell Rubbermaid, the building contained 21,000 square feet of office space, as well as a warehouse area spanning 6,000 square feet.

During the early 2000s, Vita Plus had its sights set on the $100 million mark. As an employee-owned operation, the company's staff members were ever cognizant of their importance in reaching that goal. This awareness was evident in comments President and CEO Robert Tramburg made to Julie Orchard in the August 1999 issue of *Feed & Grain,* in which he stated: ''We're at higher risk than a big conglomerate. The impact that every single employee has on this company is much greater than the big companies. Whether it's somebody in production or trucking, customer service, technical sales or office support, the difference is significant in how they treat our customers.''

Principal Competitors

ConAgra, Inc.; ContiGroup Companies, Inc.

Further Reading

About Us, Madison, Wisconsin: Vita Plus Corp., 2003.

Bjorklund, Robert C., ''Plus in 'Vita Plus' Adds Up to $2 Million,'' *Wisconsin State Journal,* November 16, 1969.

''Expansion Move,'' *Capital Times,* July 7, 1971.

Flaherty, Mike, ''Feed Company 'Bursting At Seams,' '' *Wisconsin State Journal,* July 1, 1993.

Moe, Doug, ''The Spirit of Growth at Vita Plus—Feeding Barnyard Animals Is Big Business,'' *In Business,* February 1983.

Orchard, Julie, ''True Teamwork,'' *Feed & Grain,* August 1999.

Parkins, Al, ''Vita Plus Going Strong,'' *Capital Times,* April 5, 1982.

Riddle, Jennifer, ''Tramburg to Head Vita Plus,'' *Wisconsin State Journal,* October 23, 1987.

——, ''Vita Plus Helps Feed Livestock Economically,'' *Wisconsin State Journal,* January 12, 1986.

''Vita Plus Buys Welco Feed Co. Effective July 1,'' *Wisconsin State Journal,* June 8, 1969.

''Vita Plus Corp. Buys All Assets of Columbus Mills,'' *Wisconsin State Journal,* February 11, 1971.

''Vita Plus Develops Marketing in Canada,'' *Wisconsin State Journal,* January 28, 1973.

''Vita Plus Expands,'' *Capital Times,* November 8, 1967.

''Vita-Plus Offers Research Facilities,'' *Wisconsin State Journal,* July 28, 1968.

''Vita Plus Opens Canadian Branch,'' *Wisconsin State Journal,* November 26, 1972.

''Vita Plus Purchases Feedmill,'' *Wisconsin State Journal,* May 11, 1980.

''Vita Plus Sales Reach Million-Dollar Figure,'' *Capital Times,* January 20, 1967.

—Paul R. Greenland

Vitamin Shoppe Industries, Inc.

4700 Westside Avenue
North Bergen, New Jersey 07047
U.S.A.
Telephone: (201) 866-7711
Toll Free: (800) 223-1216
Fax: (800) 852-7153
Web site: http://www.vitaminshoppe.com

Private Company
Incorporated: 1977
Employees: 2,000
Sales: $263 million (2002 est.)
NAIC: 446191 Food (Health) Supplement Stores; 454110
   Electronic Shopping and Mail-Order Houses

Vitamin Shoppe Industries, Inc. operates a chain of more than 160 stores that sell vitamins, nutritional supplements, herbal products, and related goods. The company also offers its wares through a monthly direct-mail catalog and via the Internet. Vitamin Shoppe stores, which are located in nearly 20 states and the District of Columbia, offer discount prices on more than 8,000 items from over 350 brand names, including the company's own private label, with a wider selection available through mail order. The stores also feature informational computer kiosks and a free lending library of books on vitamins and alternative medicines. In 2002 Vitamin Shoppe Industries was acquired by an equity capital unit of Bear Stearns Cos.

1970s Beginnings

The Vitamin Shoppe was founded in 1977 by Jeffrey Horowitz (then going by the name of Howard) as a retail shop on the corner of 57th Street and Lexington Avenue in Manhattan. The initial outlet's success led Horowitz to open several other locations in New York City, and in 1981 he began publishing a monthly catalog from which consumers could purchase vitamins by mail. By 1987 the chain had grown to nine New York locations, and over the next several years reached 15 stores in the area. Looking for new places to expand, Horowitz subsequently opened stores on Long Island and in Westchester County, New

York, and then in Connecticut and New Jersey, where the company established its headquarters in the town of North Bergen.

Much of The Vitamin Shoppe's success was due to Horowitz's strategy of discounting prices by 20 percent or more on each item. The company had also developed its own line of private label goods, which were more profitable because they were not advertised. In addition to vitamins, the firm had by now added herbal products and nutritional bodybuilding supplements, which accounted for up to a quarter of sales. More than 400 different brand names were offered, with as many as 17,000 different products available through the mail. To help customers decide what to buy, the company's stores featured a free lending library of books on vitamins and other health topics. The Vitamin Shoppe also distributed 12 million copies of its direct mail catalog each year, and mail orders accounted for as much as a third of the company's estimated $65 million in annual revenues for 1997. By this time, the chain had grown to 18 stores.

Seeking to increase the rate of expansion, in 1997 Horowitz sought outside financing and sold 70 percent of the company to investment firms J.P. Morgan Partners and FdG Associates. With the new backing, the pace of store openings was ramped up, bringing the firm to a total of 39 locations in 1998.

In April of that year the company launched a Web site from which consumers could order vitamins and supplements by mail. To promote it, The Vitamin Shoppe purchased all of the online advertising space on Time, Inc. New Media's "Ask Dr. Weil" Web site for a year. The cost of blanketing the site, which featured the advice of Dr. Andrew Weil, a well-known alternative medicine exponent, was reportedly more than a million dollars. Viewers of the Dr. Weil "Vitamin Adviser" feature who got a personalized vitamin regime prepared for them would see an on-screen button that linked them directly to VitaminShoppe.com. Similar sponsorship deals were later cut with other Web sites. For 1998, The Vitamin Shoppe's annual sales leapt to $132 million.

1999 Spin Off

In the summer of 1999, as the Vitamin Shoppe chain neared a total of 60 stores, the company decided to spin off its Vitamin-

Company Perspectives:

Since 1977, The Vitamin Shoppe has grown into one of America's leading discount retailers of quality vitamins and nutritional supplements. What began as a single store in New York City has evolved into over 160 stores in 18 states with new grand openings planned every month during 2003. And the addition of our popular monthly catalog plus comprehensive website and online learning center allows The Vitamin Shoppe to reach thousands of visitors daily who are interested in the best products for their healthy lifestyle.

Key Dates:

1977: Jeffrey Horowitz founds first Vitamin Shoppe store in New York City.
1981: Company begins publishing catalog for mail order sales.
1987: The Vitamin Shoppe has nine stores in New York City.
1997: Horowitz sells 70 percent of firm to J.P. Morgan Partners, FdG Associates.
1998: Web site launched; chain grows to 38 stores.
1999: VitaminShoppe.com spun off on NASDAQ exchange.
2001: Vitamin Shoppe Industries absorbs failing Internet unit.
2002: 100th store opened; Bear Stearns Capital Partners II L.P. buys firm.

Shoppe.com operation as a separate entity. Former Hearst Corporation HomeArts Network founder Kathryn Creech was named the unit's president and CEO, and in October an initial public offering (IPO) was made on the NASDAQ exchange. Some 4.5 million shares were sold at $11 each, which brought the new company nearly $50 million in funding to advertise the Web site and make improvements to it. More than 80 percent of the shares were held by its parent company, which was officially known as Vitamin Shoppe Industries, Inc., or VSI. In December a second Web site called vitaminbuzz.com was also launched which offered information about vitamins and nutritional supplements. Its content was largely licensed from the firm Healthnotes Online.

During the fall and into early 2000, VitaminShoppe.com spent heavily on Internet advertising as it sought to bring in new customers. In January CEO Creech departed, leaving Horowitz in charge. Though he had predicted profitability for its first full year as a public company, VitaminShoppe.com's revenues lagged far behind expenditures, and by December 2000 it had incurred net losses of $61.3 million. With its stock now selling for less than fifty cents and close to delisting by the NASDAQ, VSI offered to buy back the outstanding shares for $1 each to reacquire the unit. Earlier, attempts had been made to sell the company alone or in combination with VSI, but there had been no serious offers. While the buy-back was being completed the Web unit's offices were moved from New York City to VSI headquarters in New Jersey, and its staff was cut by more than half, to 37.

In June of 2001 VSI named former Barnes & Noble retail division president Thomas Tolworthy to the posts of president and chief operating officer, with Horowitz retaining the jobs of CEO and chairman. In August the company opened its 95th and 96th stores near Atlanta, Georgia, reflecting its strategy of locating outlets in densely populated areas which had above-average income and education levels. The company was now firmly entrenched on the East Coast of the United States, where it had stores in eleven states plus the District of Columbia. The chain's reach extended all the way south to Florida, where 13 stores had been opened over the previous year. VSI's skills in site selection were exceptional, with no store having ever been closed. One key indicator the firm looked at when adding new locations was the high level of catalog sales found in a particular area. The large number of retirees in Florida, for example, generated significant mail order business, and the new stores that were opened there did well.

Another part of the firm's strategy was saturation of the metropolitan markets it entered, which it had done in New York and had repeated in such cities as Washington, D.C., where there were now 15 locations. VSI stores were typically opened in freestanding locations, rather than the malls favored by industry leader GNC, whose stores were about one-third the size of a typical Vitamin Shoppe. The firm's stores now averaged between 3,000 and 4,000 square feet, more than triple the space of its original locations in Manhattan. VSI's goal was to be ''the Home Depot of the vitamin industry,'' according to a company spokesperson, and each store continued to offer an extensive selection of goods at discount prices. Products were displayed in wide aisles, and employees were deployed on the floor to offer customers suggestions or refer them to the in-house lending library for additional information. The company's stores cost an estimated $405,000 to open and became profitable within a year.

100th Store Opened in 2002

In January 2002 the 100th Vitamin Shoppe was opened, in Princeton, New Jersey, and the same year saw VSI moving westward, with new stores opened in major Midwestern markets like Chicago. The company had by now outgrown its administrative and distribution facilities in North Bergen and Secaucus, New Jersey, which occupied a total of 100,000 square feet of space in four buildings. In May a lease was signed on a vacant 230,000 square foot building in North Bergen where these operations would be combined in early 2003. The company was also considering adding a second regional distribution center to serve the growing number of stores it was opening in the Midwest and West.

In August 2002 VSI announced it was expanding its use of the Healthnotes informational database, which would be made available both online and in stores via new touch-screen kiosks. November saw the debut of The Vitamin Shoppe Radio Health Series, hosted by natural health and alternative medicine guru Gary Null. The weekly show, which would cover health and nutrition topics, was initially aired on KLSX in Los Angeles, where the firm was preparing to open several stores. By now

VSI's revenues had reached $263 million, as estimated by Moody's Investor Service. One-third of this figure continued to be generated by mail-order and Internet sales.

In the late fall of 2002 a deal was reached to sell VSI to Bear Stearns Capital Partners II, L.P., a unit of Bear Stearns Cos., for approximately $300 million. FdG Associates, CEO Horowitz, and President Tolworthy would retain small stakes in the firm. FdG had triggered the sale, seeking to get its investment back in the near term rather than waiting for the company to go public, which was under consideration as a way to fund VSI's ongoing national expansion. The company was now growing more rapidly than ever, with a total of 160 stores open by fall, including 17 in California and eight in Texas. A total of 500 stores were planned by 2007.

VSI had grown over the past 25 years from a single location in New York to a national presence with more than 160 "category killer" stores and a thriving mail-order business. As the American population aged and increasing media attention was given to the benefits of vitamins and nutritional supplements, the firm's growth looked assured for some time to come.

Principal Competitors

General Nutrition Companies, Inc.; NBTY, Inc.; Whole Foods Market, Inc.; Wal-Mart Stores, Inc.

Further Reading

Christinat, Joe, "Bear Stearns Acquires Vitamin Shoppe From FdG," *Buyouts*, December 16, 2002.

Clarke, Roger, "For an Instant Pick-Me-Up, Trip Along to the Vitamin Shoppe," *Independent—London*, November 4, 1995, p. 12.

Coleman-Lochner, Lauren, "Fortifying Moves; The Vitamin Shoppe Is Expanding Westward," *Record* (New Jersey), April 3, 2002, p. B1.

Holman, Kelly, "Bear Stearns Swallows Vitamin Shoppe," *Daily Deal*, December 3, 2002.

Robbins, Connie, "Fun-Sized to Super-Sized," *Chain Store Age*, February 1, 2002, p. 58.

Ruth, Joao-Pierre S., "Vitamins Build Muscles and Market Presence," *Business News New Jersey*, March 25, 2002, p. 14.

Scannell, Kara, "Bear Stearns Unit Agrees to Acquire Vitamin Shoppe," *Wall Street Journal*, December 2, 2002, p. B4.

Snyder, Beth, "Vitamin Seller Makes Big Web Buy," *Advertising Age*, April 6, 1998, p. 12.

"Vitamin Shoppe Faces Healthy Store Growth Challenge," *Loan Market Week*, November 25, 2002, p. 7.

"VitaminShoppe.com Completes IPO," *Record* (New Jersey), October 9, 1999, p. A17.

Weissman, Dan, "Vitamin Shoppe Sees Strong Business," *Star-Ledger* (Newark, N.J.), September 1, 2002, p. 3.

—Frank Uhle

W.L. Gore & Associates, Inc.

551 Paper Mill Road
Newark, Delaware 19711
U.S.A.
Telephone: (302) 738-4880
Fax: (302) 738-7710
Web site: http://www.gore.com

Private Company
Founded: 1958
Employees: 6,000
Sales: $1.2 billion (2003)
NAIC: 325211 Plastics Material and Resin
Manufacturing; 325212 Synthetic Rubber
Manufacturing; 331222 Steel Wire Drawing; 334412
Printed Circuit Board Manufacturing; 334417
Electronic Connector Manufacturing; 334511 Search,
Detection, Navigation, Guidance, Aeronautical, and
Nautical System and Instrument Manufacturing

W.L. Gore & Associates Inc. is a high-technology company that develops and manufactures fluoropolymer products used in aerospace, clothing, medical, automotive, chemical, electronic, and other applications. With operations spanning the globe, Gore's most notable product is Gore-Tex, a high-performance fabric developed in the late 1960s. All in all, the company has over 650 U.S. patents to its name. Known for its unique lattice system of management, W.L. Gore repeatedly has been cited as one of the best 100 companies to work for in the United States.

Origins

W.L. Gore & Associates is the progeny of renowned American entrepreneur, scientist, and inventor Wilbert L. (Bill) Gore. Gore began working for DuPont in 1941 when he was 29 years old. He helped to advance that company's research into polymers, resins, and plastics. On the advice of his wife, Vieve, Gore left his research job in 1958 to start his own company. Before his departure, Gore had been working on new DuPont-developed synthetic material called polytetrafluoroethylene (PTFE, or tef-

lon). He hoped to build a company that developed and marketed new uses for the material. Gore and Vieve started the enterprise on a shoestring budget in the basement of their home.

Gore's first commercially viable products were wire and cable products insulated with teflon. Bill's son, Bob, was integral to those innovations. Bob, who was a chemical engineering student at the time, is credited with coming up with the concept that resulted in Gore's first patent for teflon-insulated wire and cable. For ten years, in fact, such products were the core of the Gore enterprise. The high-tech cables were respected in their industry niche and were even used in the Apollo space program for the first moon landing.

A Unique Management Philosophy

From their basement office, the Gores expanded into a separate production facility in their hometown of Newark, Delaware. Sales were brisk after initial product introductions. By 1965, just seven years after the business had started, Gore & Associates was employing about 200 people. It was about that time that Gore began to develop and implement the unique management system and philosophy for which his company would become recognized. Gore noticed that as his company had grown, efficiency and productivity had started to decline. He needed a new management structure, but he feared that the popular pyramid management structure that was in vogue at the time suppressed the creativity and innovation that he valued so greatly. Instead of adopting the pyramid structure, Gore decided to create his own system.

During World War II, while on a task force at DuPont, Gore had learned of another type of organizational structure called the lattice system, which was developed to enhance the ingenuity and overall performance of a group working toward a goal. It emphasized communication and cooperation rather than hierarchy of authority. Under the system that Gore developed, any person was allowed to make a decision as long as it was fair, encouraged others, and made a commitment to the company. Consultation was required only for decisions that could potentially cause serious damage to the enterprise. Furthermore, new associates joined the company on the same effective authority

Company Perspectives:

W.L. Gore & Associates is a provider of unique, innovative, best-in-class, high value, high quality products that consistently do what we say they do. Gore was established for the purpose of developing and utilizing technology in the field of fluorocarbon polymers, especially polytetrafluoroethylene.

level as all the other workers, including Bill and Vieve. There were no titles or bosses, with only a few exceptions, and commands were replaced by personal commitments.

New employees started out working in an area best suited to their talents, under the guidance of a sponsor. As the employee progressed there came more responsibility, and workers were paid according to their individual contribution. "Team members know who is producing," Bill explained in a February 1986 issue of the *Phoenix Business Journal*. "They won't put up with poor performance. There is tremendous peer pressure. You promote yourself by gaining knowledge and working hard, everyday. There is no competition, except with yourself." The effect of the system was to encourage workers to be creative, take risks, and perform at their highest level. One of the key people to help the company succeed in the Apollo moon landing project, for example, came to Gore with only a sixth-grade education.

Gore reasoned that even under his management system organizations would begin to decline in effectiveness after reaching about 200 members. That was partly because too many people in a group caused a reduction in trust and cooperation. For that reason, he and Vieve decided to build a second manufacturing facility. In 1967, the company opened a new plant in Flagstaff, Arizona. The selection of Flagstaff reflected Gore's love of the outdoors, particularly in the western regions of the United States. The new plant helped the company to regain its productivity and creativity, and from that point forward Gore built a new facility each time the magic number of 200 was breached. Gore's unique and successful management system and philosophies proved valuable over time and became lauded as a model for management during the 1980s and 1990s.

Gore-Tex Leads to Explosive Growth: Late 1960s–1980s

The immense success of Gore's teflon-insulated wire and cable products, combined with savvy management during the middle and late 1960s, resulted in explosive growth at Gore. Indeed, during the late 1960s, Gore established manufacturing and sales operations in Arizona, Scotland, and Germany and even launched a venture partnership in Japan. The company continued to post big gains during the 1970s as well. Perhaps more important to Gore's success during the 1970s and 1980s than the company's management system, however, was a pivotal product innovation that would help to make Gore one of the most successful private companies in the United States. That innovation came in 1969, about the time that Bill's son Bob became president of the company (Bob and his mother, the secretary and treasurer of the company, were the only two employees in the company with job titles).

Bob, who had gone to work at Gore after receiving his Ph.D. in chemistry, discovered that teflon could be quickly stretched to produce a material with many of the properties that scientists had been trying for years to create. Under the right conditions, the product could be stretched to form a material that was as strong as the original teflon and laced with microscopic holes, the size of which could be adjusted in the manufacturing process. The breakthrough was momentous because of the numerous properties exhibited by the material. For example, it shed water droplets like other synthetic materials but was also breathable and would allow small airborne moisture particles and body heat to move through the fabric. The obvious advantage: stretched teflon could be used to make waterproof clothing that was also breathable.

W.L. Gore & Associates applied for a patent for their invention in May 1970. The Gores dubbed the new material Gore-Tex. The patent was granted in 1976, by which time Gore was already marketing a number of products made with Gore-Tex. Among other advantages, Gore-Tex was chemically inert and resistant to infection. That made it an excellent material for dozens of medical applications—artificial arteries made with Gore-Tex, for example, eventually accounted for about 85 percent of this market segment throughout the world. It was also beneficial for various uses ranging from household items to defense-industry goods. Gore-Tex was used to manufacture space suits and sporting apparel, as well as dental floss and telecommunications gear. By the late 1980s, filters made with Gore-Tex were being used in virtually every intravenous bag in the world. In fact, Gore-Tex became the fabric of choice in most applications that necessitated a high flow-rate along with maximum particle retention in both air and liquid filtration.

Gore experienced explosive growth during the 1970s and early 1980s, mostly as a result of the breakthrough success of Gore-Tex. The still-private company remained tight-lipped as always about its financial performance. Its success, though, was clearly evidenced by the rapid expansion of production facilities and sales and marketing offices. Gore was soon peddling its products throughout the world. Besides pushing Gore-Tex, the company continued to expand its other product lines and to develop new ideas. For example, Gore was called in to custom-manufacture teflon-insulated cable to help in the aftermath of the Three Mile Island nuclear accident. It also broadened its teflon-coated cable products to meet new needs in computer, telecommunications, aerospace, and medical industries. Still, Gore-Tex became the company's cash cow and eventually grew to represent more than 80 percent of the organization's revenues.

By the mid-1980s, Gore was churning out an estimated $200 million to $300 million in annual revenues and supporting a whopping 29 plants throughout the world; its workforce ballooned to 4,200 worldwide. In addition to his inventions, Bill Gore was being lauded as a leading contributor to the art and science of management. Bill Gore died on July 26, 1986, at the age of 74, of a heart attack suffered while hiking in the Wind River Range of Wyoming. Gore had been known for taking extended treks in the outdoors. On this particular occasion, he had been hiking with his wife and several grandchildren. "If a man could flow with the stream, grow with the way of nature, he'd accomplish more and he'd be happier doing it than bucking the flow of the water,'' Vieve Gore recalled of her husband's business philosophy.

Overcoming Patent Disputes

W.L. Gore & Associates continued to thrive following the death of its founder, despite ongoing disputes over its patent to Gore-Tex. Indeed, the company had been battling claims against its rights to the invention since the early 1970s. In 1982, in fact, a federal lawsuit in Cleveland resulted in the removal of Gore's patent rights, but the decision was soon overturned and the rights were restored. In 1984, Gore filed suit against a Tempe, Arizona, company called IMPRA Inc., claiming that IMPRA had violated Gore's patent in the manufacture of its artificial arteries. The judge's research showed that a Japanese company had tried to patent a material identical to Gore-Tex in 1963 and had gotten the patent in 1967. After several years of weighing the evidence, the judge decided in 1990 to terminate Gore's patent rights. Gore managed to keep patents for individual Gore-Tex products and manufacturing processes, however. At the time the decision was handed down, Gore was capturing an estimated $700 million annually from sales of Gore-Tex-related products.

The loss of the Gore-Tex patent predated the scheduled termination of patent rights by about three years. Thus, it opened the door for other companies to begin manufacturing Gore-Tex products earlier than they might have otherwise. Gore's product-development arm was healthy, though, and the company sustained its growth. In 1991, Gore announced plans to build two new 60,000-square-foot manufacturing facilities in Arizona at a cost of about $10 million. By the end of 1993, Gore was operating more than 40 facilities and employing about 6,000 workers. Interestingly, the plants were all located in non-metropolitan areas because the Gores believed that such locations offered a higher quality of life for their employees. Evidencing the success of Gore's overall management philosophy, the company was named as one of the 100 best companies to work for two years in a row—a feat accomplished by only nine other companies at the time.

Going into the mid-1990s, W.L. Gore & Associates was operating 45 manufacturing and sales offices throughout the United States and in Germany, Scotland, and Japan. Gore-Tex products still accounted for the bulk of its sales. New Gore-Tex products being developed and introduced in 1994 and 1995 included Intervent, an allergen exclusion technology used, for example, in bedding; various surgical sutures used in vascular, cardiac, and general surgical procedures; and protective gear designed to reduce the spread of diseases like AIDS. The company was also developing and manufacturing various teflon-related electronics goods for industrial, defense, computer, telecommunication, and medical industries. Its four operating divisions at this time were Electronic Products, Fabric Products, Industrial Products, and Medical Products. The still-private company did not release financial information but claimed to have achieved compound sales and profit growth rates exceeding 20 percent annually between 1975 and 1995.

Innovation in the 1990s and Beyond

Gore's success continued into the late 1990s and beyond due mostly to the company's consistent drive to add innovative new products to its arsenal. In 1996 alone, the company was issued a record 89 U.S. patents. The company launched its Elixir line of guitar strings in 1997, and the brand quickly became the leader in the U.S. market. A new group of Gore-Tex fabrics made their debut the following year. Along with new product introductions in its medical division, Gore also became well known for its contributions in the development of fuel cell technology. In the mid-1990s, the company began developing Membrane Electrode Assemblies (MEAs), which were used in the polymer electrolyte, or proton exchange, membrane (PEM) fuel cell industry. The firm's first MEA was offered in 1995, followed by a second-generation launch two years later. Gore became the first commercial supplier in 2002 with the release of the Series 56 MEAs, which were used in stationary PEM fuel cells.

Gore entered the new century on solid ground. A March 2000 *Industry Week* article summed up the company's success with the statement that "few companies can claim that their products have orbited the earth, been on top of Mt. Everest, appeared on Seinfeld, and even helped mend some broken hearts." Indeed, with over 650 U.S. patents to its name and thousands across the globe, Gore's ability to cross over into cutting-edge technologies within the electronics and medical industries helped to secure its position as a leading privately held company. By this time, the company's medical products line, which included synthetic vascular grafts, interventional devices, surgical meshes used in hernia repair, and surgical sutures, had been used in over 7.5 million procedures.

While the company continued to develop new products, it also focused on cost-cutting measures and streamlining in order to maintain its remarkable financial track record. *Fortune* magazine reported in 2003 that Gore had posted a profit every year since its founding. In August 2002, the firm announced that it planned to sell off its fiber optic business. Gore sold its Glide Dental Floss unit to Proctor & Gamble the following year but continued to manufacture the product under the terms of the agreement.

W.L. Gore & Associates attributed many of its achievements throughout its history to the unique management structure that empowered company associates worldwide. Although the business environment surrounding the firm had shifted dramatically since its founding in 1958, Gore's basic guiding ideology set forth by the founder himself remained unchanged. The firm continued to adhere to its values—fairness, encouragement, holding steadfast to commitments, and open communication among associates—and with many years of success behind it, W.L. Gore appeared to be on track for good fortune in the years to come.

Principal Operating Units

Medical Products; Electronic Products; Industrial Products; Fabric Products.

Principal Competitors

Belden Inc.; Burlington Industries Inc.; Malden Mills Inc.

Further Reading

Barron, Kelly, "Stormy Weather," *Forbes*, February 19, 2001, p. 66.

Day, Kathleen, "A Clothes Call with Danger: Microbe, Chemical Phobias Drive up Demand for Protective Gear," *Washington Post*, March 11, 1995, p. 1C.

Fiscus, Chris, "Flagstaff Approves Gore Plan," *Arizona Business Gazette*, March 22, 1991, p. 1.

Harrington, Ann, "Who's Afraid of a New Product?," *Fortune*, November 10, 2003, p. 189.

Hasek, Glenn, "The Right Chemistry," *Industry Week*, March 6, 2000, p. 36.

Jaffe, Susan Biddle, "Employee Freedom Is Gore Family Tradition," *Philadelphia Business Journal*, May 1, 1989, section 2, p. 6B.

Morrell, Lisa, "Tempe Medical-Products Firm Wins Round in Patent Lawsuit," *Arizona Republic*, May 15, 1990, p. 13C.

Nelton, Sharon, "In Appreciation of Innovators," *Nation's Business*, December 1986, p. 64.

Norris, Scott, "PDL&C Markets Gore-Tex Fabric to Military for Soldiers' Outerwear," *Rochester Business Journal*, September 24, 1990, p. 4.

Rhodes, Lucien, "William Gore 1912–1986," *Inc.*, November 1986, p. 22.

Sommer, Anthony, "Gore-Tex Patent Held as Invalid," *Phoenix Gazette*, May 15, 1990, p. 1C.

Stern, Jonathan, "Workers Manage Themselves under Inventive Philosophy," *Phoenix Business Journal*, February 3, 1986, p. 11.

Weinreb, Michael, "Power to the People," *Sales & Marketing Management*, April 2003, p. 30.

Wilke, Paul W., "Newark Root of W.L. Gore's Success," *Delaware Business Review*, January 31, 1994, p. 13.

—Dave Mote
—update: Christina M. Stansell

Waffle House Inc.

5986 Financial Drive
Norcross, Georgia 30071
U.S.A.
Telephone: (770) 729-5700
Fax: (770) 729-5999
Web site: http://www.wafflehouse.com

Private Company
Incorporated: 1955
Employees: 16,500
Sales: $410 million (2003)
NAIC: 722110 Full-Service Restaurants

Waffle House Inc. operates a chain of about 1,400 Waffle House Restaurants located in 25 states. The restaurants, which are either company-owned or franchised, pride themselves on serving good food fast, at a reasonable price, in a diner atmosphere 24 hours a day, 365 days a year. The menu includes everything from waffles and eggs to steaks and salads. Family-owned, Waffle House Inc. is known for being an extremely private company. In recent years, however, the company has found itself in the public spotlight, due to lawsuits filed against the company relating to civil rights violations and sexual harassment.

Company Origins

Waffle House, according to information released in 1995 for the company's 40th anniversary, began as the dream of two neighbors, Joe Rogers, Sr., and Tom Forkner, who envisioned a company dedicated to both its customers and employees. The partners wanted to create a place where friends and neighbors could get together to enjoy good food served with a friendly smile. On Labor Day in 1955 they opened the first Waffle House restaurant in Avondale Estates, Georgia, a suburb of Atlanta. The first Waffle House restaurant was a smash, and the owners soon opened other Waffle House eateries throughout Georgia.

The "Good Food Fast" Concept Paying Off: 1950s–70s

Waffle House made a name for itself during the late 1950s and 1960s by living up to its promise of "Good Food Fast," which became one of the company's mottos. Waffle House located many of its restaurants along interstates, and truckers and travelers came to know that the Waffle House sign meant good food and friendly service. The company eventually spread outside of Georgia's borders and into neighboring states including Alabama, Louisiana, North Carolina, South Carolina, and Florida. As the U.S. interstate system expanded throughout the Southeast during the 1950s and 1960s, new Waffle House outlets were added along major arteries like Interstate 75, which trails from the southern tip of Florida through Tennessee to northern Michigan, and Interstate 85, which traverses Virginia and extends southwest into Alabama. Waffle House eventually built up a network of several hundred restaurants throughout the Southeast.

Waffle House also began franchising its name and concept to individual operators, which allowed the company to expand without assuming heavy debt and without having to sell shares to the public. Keeping Waffle House private was very important to its owners, because taking the company public would have required them to release financial and operating information. "There are three types of companies," explained Bryan Elliott, analyst at Robinson-Humphrey, in the September 19, 1988 *Atlanta Business Chronicle.* "There are public companies that trade stock and have to share information. Then there are private companies that don't trade stock but are somewhat open about their operations and numbers. And then there are the companies that won't even acknowledge that they exist. And that is Waffle House. They are a very, very private and tight-lipped company." For that reason, details about the growth and expansion of Waffle House and about the lives of its founders and executives are scant.

During the 1970s and into the 1980s, the roadside restaurant market became dominated primarily by two styles of eateries: fast-food chains like McDonald's and Burger King, and large sit-down restaurants like Shoney's and Cracker Barrel. The traditional diner-style eatery, in contrast, declined in popularity, with the chief exception of Waffle House. Indeed, Waffle House restaurants in the new millennium looked much the same as they did 50 years before. An exposed grill was located behind a long counter, at which customers could sit on stools. Other guests were seated in the booths that lined the restaurant. Waffle House continued to advertise solely through word-of-mouth, relying on its loyal clientele instead of promotion to reach new customers.

Even the Waffle House menu of southern fare had changed little since the 1950s. The restaurants still emphasized their famous T-bone steak, waffle, and egg meals, and claimed to have "America's Best" coffee. Meals that became a tradition at Waffle House included the "King Size T-bone & Eggs" dinner, which included a ten-ounce steak, hashbrowns, and two eggs or a salad—for just $8.99 in 1995. Other signature menu items included pecan waffles, Bert's chili, raisin toast, and cheese 'n eggs. Waffle House took particular pride in its hashbrowns, which it served six different ways: "scattered" (on the grill); "smothered" with onions; "covered" with cheese; "chunked" with hickory-smoked ham; "topped" with chili; and "diced" with fresh tomatoes.

In addition to its proven menu items, Waffle House prided itself on cooking all of its meals to order, and on using only the best ingredients in its food. Waffle Houses used only Kraft cheese, Minute Maid orange juice, and Heinz sauces, for example. The company also distinguished itself by staying open 24 hours a day and 365 days each year, which let highway travelers know that they were always welcome. In addition to proclaiming itself "America's Best Place to Eat"—a slogan that supplanted "Good Food Fast"—Waffle House touted its organization as "America's Best Place to Work." Workers were referred to as associates, rather than employees, and the company sought to provide good jobs and careers for them.

Expansion Continuing in the 1980s–90s

Although Waffle House's operating strategy had changed little by the 1980s, the size of the chain had. In 1987 Dun & Bradstreet reported that Waffle House had 351 franchisees in addition to its network of company-owned stores. It also was reported that Waffle House employed a workforce of 4,500 people, had a financial worth of roughly $60 million, and had total assets of about $81.2 million. *Nation's Restaurant News* estimated that in 1987 Waffle House had generated about $210 million in sales, up from about $175 million a year earlier, including receipts from franchise units. Excluding franchise sales, company revenues were about $87.5 million, which was up only slightly from a 1976 estimate of $84.6 million.

Waffle House remained a closely held company, with virtually all of the ten million shares of stock owned by company employees and the company still being run by the Rogers family. Joe W. Rogers, Jr., served as president. (His father, Joe W., Sr., had cofounded the company and presided over its expansion during the 1950s, 1960s, and 1970s.) M. Michael McCarthy, who joined the company in 1973, served as secretary-treasurer. J. Michael Upton, a former general manager of Old Hickory House, was a vice-president, as was Robert Bowman, who had worked with Arthur Andersen & Co. before joining Waffle House in 1976.

Going into the late 1980s Waffle House was operating in ten states; Alabama, Arizona, Louisiana, Florida, Georgia, Mississippi, Oklahoma, North Carolina, South Carolina, and Texas. It also was operating two subsidiary companies; WHI Inc., a real estate holding company that had its own vending machine subsidiary called Metro Distributors Inc.; and LaVista Equipment Supply Co., a designer and retailer of restaurant equipment. The real estate company reflected Waffle House's hefty property holdings: unlike many other chains, Waffle House owned much of the property on which its restaurants were built. According to Dun & Bradstreet in 1987, retained earnings had increased and the company's total debt was in line with its net worth. McCarthy confirmed in 1988 only that company sales were up in 1987 as a result of new restaurant openings, higher menu prices, and increased sales per store.

Waffle House grew rapidly as a result, in part, of its franchising. Announcements in 1988 made by Waffle House management, however, cast doubt on the financial success of the franchising strategy. Nancy Wilson, an employee in the franchising division, told the *Atlanta Business Chronicle* that the company planned to cease all new franchising efforts, making the statement as part of an effort to exclude Waffle House from the newspaper's list of top Georgia franchises. Joe Rogers, Jr., refused to confirm the report, stating, "It's our policy never to share information with the press."

Some industry insiders at the time cited the rumor that Waffle House had stopped franchising as evidence that the chain was stagnating in a rapidly changing restaurant industry and that it needed to update its image and menu. Waffle House did not change much during the next few years, however, nor did executives squelch the franchising program. In fact, Waffle House expanded at a rapid clip during the late 1980s and early 1990s, opening restaurants in existing markets and branching out into Arkansas, Colorado, Illinois, Indiana, Kentucky, Missouri, New Mexico, Ohio, Tennessee, and Virginia. Interestingly, the stores in Indiana were named "Waffle and Steak" because the Waffle House name was already being used when Waffle House Inc. entered that state. Waffle House celebrated its 40th anniversary in 1995 by opening Unit #1000, the chain's 1,000th store. The shop was located just a few blocks from the site of the original Waffle House #1 that had opened its doors in 1955.

Surviving in the Late 1990s and Beyond

The company often found itself in the public spotlight in the late 1990s and into the new millennium. The news was unrelated, however, to the launch of new menu items or the opening of additional restaurants. Instead it focused on the increasing number of lawsuits filed against the company. The *Atlanta Journal and Constitution* reported that from 1995 to 2000, more than 90 claims had been filed against the firm, mostly related to civil rights infractions against employees and customers. The aforementioned April 2000 article reported that "some customers and employees say the image of a down-home, friendly restaurant company is more illusion than reality. In interviews and court documents they describe a company with its head

Key Dates:

1955: Joe Rogers, Sr., and Tom Forkner open the first Waffle House restaurant in Avondale Estates, Georgia.

1987: The company operates 351 franchisees in addition to its network of company-owned stores.

1995: Waffle House opens its 1,000th location.

2000: By now, more than 90 lawsuits related to civil rights infractions and sexual harassment have been filed against the company.

buried in the sand, where racial discrimination and sexual harassment complaints go virtually ignored.''

According to a 2000 *Nation's Restaurant News* article, Joe Rogers, Jr., claimed that Waffle House had ''successfully addressed growth, diversity, and many challenges throughout our 44-year history.'' Nevertheless, its critics argued that Waffle House was turning its back on its corporate responsibility to provide a restaurant free of racial and gender discrimination. The company's policy of remaining extremely tight-lipped also came under fire, as many began to question the company's intentions.

Despite its litigation woes, Waffle House remained dedicated to maintaining its position as one of the leaders in the family-style restaurant sector. Determined to continue its tradition of serving ''good food fast,'' the firm pushed forward with expansion plans. By 2002, there were more than 1,375 restaurants in 25 states. In fiscal 2003, that number climbed to more than 1,400 units, with sales topping out at $410 million.

Touting itself as ''America's Place to Work. America's Place to Eat,'' Waffle House appeared to be on the track for continued growth well into the future. Regardless of the claims made against the company, its management team remained focused on solidifying its market strength in the southern region of the United States. With nearly 419 million waffles served since its beginnings in 1955 and more than 80 million cups of coffee handed out each year, Waffle House was poised to remain a favorite among its customers in the years to come.

Principal Competitors

Denny's Corporation; Huddle House Inc.; Shoney's Restaurants Inc.

Further Reading

''Blacks Allege Race Bias in Waffle House Lawsuits,'' *Nation's Restaurant News,* September 29, 2003, p. 64.

Boldt, Ethan, ''Southern Heat,'' *Restaurant Business,* July 15, 1999, p. 21.

Cooper, Ron, ''More Waffle Houses Making Themselves at Home in Area,'' *Business First-Louisville,* December 6, 1993, p. 1.

Fullam, Peter, ''SunQuest Systems Reveals Plans,'' *Indianapolis Business Journal,* October 20, 1986, p. 1.

Hayes, Jack, ''Waffle House Discounts Stacks of Bias Lawsuits,'' *Nation's Restaurant News,* May 8, 2000, p. 5.

Poole, Sheila M., ''Raft of Lawsuits Casts a Cloud Over Waffle House Management,'' *Atlanta Journal and Constitution,* April 23, 2000, p. 1F.

Porretto, John, ''Waffle House Plans 15th Restaurant in Coastal Mississippi,'' *Sun Herald,* August 25, 1996.

''Toledo, Ohio, Breakfast Eaters Gain Choices As Restaurants Wage Waffle Wars,'' *Knight Ridder/Tribune Business News,* February 18, 2003.

Welch, Mary, ''Is Waffle House Cooking Up Changes? Restaurant Halts Franchise Growth,'' *Atlanta Business Chronicle,* September 19, 1988, p. 3A.

—Dave Mote
—update: Christina M. Stansell

Wausau-Mosinee Paper Corporation

1244 Kronenwetter Drive
Mosinee, Wisconsin 54455-9099
U.S.A.
Telephone: (715) 693-4470
Fax: (715) 692-2082
Web site: http://www.wausaumosinee.com

Public Company
Incorporated: 1910 as Wausau Sulphate Fibre Company
Employees: 3,200
Sales: $948.7 million (2002)
Stock Exchanges: New York
Ticker Symbol: WMO
NAIC: 322121 Paper (Except Newsprint) Mills

Wausau-Mosinee Paper Corporation is a leading producer of specialty, fine printing and writing, and towel and tissue papers. Through its ten production facilities, the company manufacturers a broad range of products including labels for consumer products; specialty papers used in food, medical, and industrial applications; laser-printable copy paper; stationary; and towel, tissue, soap products, and dispensing systems. Wausau-Mosinee Paper was formed after the 1997 merger of two Wisconsin-based firms—Mosinee Paper Corporation and Wausau Paper Mills Company.

Early History

The mill that eventually became Mosinee Paper Corporation was built in 1910, 64 years after the first commercial production of wood pulp in America. First called Wausau Sulphate Fibre Company, the mill was built toward the end of a period that saw the formation of dozens of paper companies along Wisconsin's largest rivers. Located on the Wisconsin River, the Mosinee mill was the first in the state—and one of the first in the country—built specifically to produce sulphate, or kraft, pulp and paper. Among the company's founders were Olai Bache-Wiig, Louis Dessert, Karl Mathie, B.F. McMillan, and F.P. Stone, all of whom were from Wausau, Wisconsin, a well-known center of paper-manufacturing activity.

The Mosinee mill began operating in 1911, employing about 150 workers. From the start, Wausau Sulphate's core product was kraft wrapping paper. For its first several years of existence, in fact, that was its only product. In 1914 the company first began to guarantee the quality of its wrapping and packaging papers. As new uses of specialty papers began to evolve, the company found a niche as a maker of custom papers to order. With new industries appearing every year, Wausau Sulphate was able to position itself as a supplier of papers to meet the precise specifications of these emerging industries.

Two major changes took place at Mosinee in 1928. First the company changed its name to Mosinee Paper Mills Company, allowing its name to match its location for the first time. Later that year, the company purchased the Bay West Paper Company, a paper towel and tissue manufacturer based in Green Bay, Wisconsin. Bay West remained a major part of the Mosinee operation since that time and focused on essentially the same products throughout its history as a subsidiary of Mosinee—namely "away-from-home" paper towels and tissue paper for restaurants, hospitals, factories, and other institutions. Other early Bay West products included windshield wipe for use at gas stations—a product pioneered by Bay West—and the dispensers to go with a number of its paper goods.

Advances in Technology Fuel Postwar Growth

Over the next several decades, Mosinee's growth ran parallel to the overall advance of technology. As industries became more automated, their paper needs became more exacting. Mosinee continued to find a growing market for its made-to-order sulphate papers in these increasingly high-tech industries. By the middle of the 1960s, the company was producing about 40 grades of industrial papers to meet roughly 5,000 different specifications. Every order required something different, and Mosinee was equipped to make the necessary adjustments. Among the multitude of papers the company was putting out by that time were flameproof papers, moldproof papers, and creped papers. In 1964 Mosinee completed a new executive headquarters building. A new warehouse, a new water treatment plant, and at least one new machine for customizing specialty papers were also put into operation at about that time.

In 1971 the company changed its name to Mosinee Paper Corporation. After turning back an attempt that year by one of its stockholders—cheese merchant Francis Rondeau—to seize control of the company, Mosinee continued to expand its operations. Work was begun in 1972 on a $1.25 million water treatment facility for its Pulp and Paper Division. In 1974 Mosinee purchased J.U. Dickson Sawmill Inc., in Sturgis, South Dakota, a mill that employed about 50 people. Renamed Dickson Forest Products, Inc., the $1.5 million purchase was integrated into the company as a subsidiary. Mosinee also launched a $325,000 expansion program at its Converted Products Division in Columbus, Wisconsin, that year.

By 1976 Mosinee had 900 employees and annual sales of more than $60 million. With the help of over $2 million in tax credits for making large capital investments, the company turned a profit of $5.3 million that year. In 1981 James Kemerling, a 20-year Mosinee employee, was named company president. The company added another major division in 1983, when it purchased Sorg Paper Company of Middletown, Ohio, for $18 million. Initially a producer of printing and writing papers and specialty papers like deep-color tissue, Sorg's operations were restructured after a few years to produce tissue and towels for Mosinee's Bay West division. The idea was that Bay West could be made more profitable if less of its raw material had to be purchased from outside companies.

Overcoming Problems: 1980s–Early 1990s

Kemerling was given the additional title of chief executive officer in 1984. The following year Mosinee set up a new wholly owned subsidiary, Mosinee Paper International, Inc., based in the Virgin Islands. The Dickson Forest Products unit was sold off in 1986. Meanwhile, the integration of Sorg into the Mosinee process was not going as smoothly as company officials had hoped. Part of the problem was the 400-mile distance between Sorg and Bay West, resulting in higher than ideal transportation costs. While the rest of Mosinee's operating units remained profitable, Sorg lost money from 1986 to 1988.

When Kemerling resigned abruptly in May 1988, Mosinee was able to lure Richard Radt, the former head of Wausau Paper Mills, out of early retirement as his replacement. As CEO of Wausau from 1977 to 1987, Radt had overseen several successive years of record earnings. Even more impressive was the fact that those gains in income were made on fairly modest increases in sales. Radt's strategy at Wausau was to find profitable niche markets that were too small to interest the bigger companies. Shareholders at Mosinee hoped that he would be able to duplicate that plan with his new company and to yield similar results.

One of Radt's first moves as president and CEO of Mosinee was to shut down two of Sorg's paper machines and lay off 128 of its employees. Those and other cost-cutting measures enabled him to return Sorg to the break-even point by the fourth quarter of his first year at Mosinee. Radt also examined each product made by the other divisions as well, eliminating the unprofitable ones and seeking new outlets for the profitable ones. By 1989 Mosinee controlled about 20 percent of the market for roll-wrap, a wax-laminated product used by manufacturers to protect paper rolls against moisture and other kinds of damage. Another important product was the creped paper used as backing on masking tape, a big seller to such customers as 3M Corporation. By exploiting niche markets overlooked by other companies, Mosinee reached number 14 on Consolidated Paper's annual financial ranking of paper companies in 1989.

For 1989 Mosinee reported sales of $233 million. Under Radt, the company continued to cut costs wherever possible, while at the same time investing lavishly in keeping its facilities up to date. Although company sales dipped to $202 million for 1990, company officials insisted that Radt's restructuring measures would pay off soon. In 1991 alone, the company sank $100 million into capital expenditures. By that time, the Sorg subsidiary was focusing on such specialty products as vacuum cleaner bag filter paper and decorative laminate papers, and the unit was no longer losing money.

The Bay West operation was moved to Harrodsburg, Kentucky, at about the same time. That move put Bay West closer to both its customers and to its new source of raw materials—100 percent recycled tissue and toweling—in Middletown, Ohio, where it had taken over and refurbished part of the facility abandoned by Sorg during its downsizing process. Part of the new arrangement at the Middletown site involved an agreement by Bay West to hire some of the employees that Sorg had previously laid off. In addition, a new wholly owned subsidiary, Mosinee Holdings, Inc., was formed as a mechanism by which Bay West and Sorg could receive electricity and steam from a single shared coal-fired powerhouse at Middletown.

By the end of 1991, Mosinee had 1,200 employees, and although sales dropped slightly again (to $197 million for the year), the company's Radt-engineered overhaul was still considered promising by many investment analysts. In 1992, however, Mosinee experienced a handful of setbacks that saw its stock price plummet by 50 percent between March and October of that year. During the summer, the company lost about $2 million when a supply of waste paper it had purchased was found to be contaminated by bits of glass. To make matters worse, the paper had already been de-inked and recycled into raw material for paper towels by the time the contamination was discovered.

Another nagging problem was a steep drop in prices. The U.S. economy was so weak during 1992 that Mosinee was unable to sell some of its products at profitable prices. This problem was compounded by the actions of Fort Howard Corporation, a competitor based in Green Bay, Wisconsin. As Fort Howard cut prices on its tissue and towel products in order to keep control of its share of the market, Mosinee was forced to adjust its own prices accordingly. When the economy began to improve in 1993, Mosinee's profits began to stage a comeback as well. That year, the company reported net income of $9.6 million on sales of $244 million.

Citing health reasons, Richard Radt stepped down as president and chief executive officer of Mosinee in 1993. His succes-

Key Dates:

1899: Wausau Paper Mills is established.
1910: Wausau Sulphate Fibre Company is established.
1928: Wausau Sulphate changes its name to Mosinee Paper Mills Company; Bay West Paper Company is acquired.
1971: The Mosinee Paper Corporation name is adopted.
1983: Sorg Paper Company is acquired.
1997: Mosinee merges with Wausau Paper Mills to become Wausau-Mosinee Paper Corporation.
2000: The company launches a $46 million upgrade campaign at its Rhineland facility to manufacture a new release liner paper.

sor was Daniel Olvey, formerly the company's executive vice-president and chief operating officer. Under Olvey's leadership additional gains were recorded by Mosinee in 1994, when the company earned a record $12.3 million on sales of $267 million.

Demand for Mosinee's products remained strong during the mid-1990s. Even sharp increases in raw materials, which would have been disastrous just a few years earlier, did not hurt the company, since most of this additional cost could be passed on to customers. Officials at Mosinee were confident that demand for the company's products—particularly the tissue and towels that made up 40 percent of its business—would remain strong during the near future.

Late 1990s and Beyond: Wausau-Mosinee

During the latter half of the 1990s, the paper industry as a whole experienced a wave a consolidation as many companies opted to join forces as a means of controlling costs. Sure enough, Mosinee announced in August 1997 that it would partner with neighboring company Wausau Paper Mills Company in deal that was expected to save over $20 million in costs per year. Established in 1899 by Norman H. Brokaw and brothers W.L. and E.A. Edwards, Wausau Paper had beefed up its holdings in recent years through the acquisitions of Rhinelander Paper Company, the Grovetown Mill, and Otis Specialty Papers. It soon set its sights on Mosinee, which by now was operating as one of the most profitable companies in the industry.

Both companies looked at the deal as a merger of equals; however Wausau Paper actually acquired Mosinee in a $477 million stock transaction. While the two companies had headquarters just 15 miles apart from each other and shared San W. Orr, Jr., as chairman, they were not considered competitors since there was little market overlap in each firm's product divisions.

After the deal was completed in December, the company operated as Wausau-Mosinee Paper Corporation. The newly merged entity faced a series of challenges as the paper industry began to suffer from low selling prices, overcapacity, and higher costs related to raw materials. In 2000, the company announced that it planned to shutter its Sorg Paper Company mill in Ohio. The 150-year-old facility had been losing nearly $750,000 per month due to the aforementioned problems.

To make matters worse, CEO Olvey resigned suddenly in 2000 forcing Wausau-Mosinee to find a successor. Thomas J. Howatt was named to the post later that year and implemented a series of cost cutting strategies to shore up the company's bottom line. At the same time, the firm embarked on a mission to develop new, cutting-edge products. A $46 million upgrade project was launched at its Rhineland facility to enable the plant to utilize a new process for manufacturing release liner paper. The new product proved to be a success, exceeding first-year expectations by nearly 50 percent.

The tough times continued into the early years of the new millennium. Howatt was quoted in an April 2002 *Milwaukee Journal Sentinel* article as claiming, "2001 will be remembered as perhaps the most difficult year in decades for the paper industry. Recessionary business conditions existed throughout the year, with most segments of the paper industry recording major declines in demand." Wausau-Mosinee forged ahead, determined to prevail over the hardships. Its strategy paid off and in 2002 the company reported a significant increase in earnings—over double what it had reported in the previous year.

Under Howatt's direction, Wausau-Mosinee continued to focus on increasing productivity, reducing capital spending, cutting expenses, and new product development. Against the backdrop of a weak economy, the company did not expect an upturn in the industry in the near future. Nevertheless, management remained optimistic that the firm would overcome the challenges it faced. With a long-standing history of success behind it, Wausau-Mosinee would no doubt remain Wisconsin's leading paper maker in the years to come.

Principal Subsidiaries

Bay West Paper Company.

Principal Divisions

Specialty Paper Group; Printing & Writing Group; Towel & Tissue Group.

Principal Competitors

Georgia-Pacific Corporation; International Paper Company; Kimberly-Clark Corporation.

Further Reading

Barrett, Amy, "Mosinee Paper: If You Missed the Ride at Wausau Paper," *Financial World*, December 10, 1991, pp. 18–19.

Bowman, Francis F., Jr., *Ninety-Two Years of Industrial Progress*, Mosinee, Wis.: Francis F. Bowman, Jr., 1940, p. 13.

Byrne, Harlan, "Riding a Boom," *Barron's*, March 20, 1995, p. 17.

Dresang, Joel, "CEO of Wisconsin-Based Specialty Paper Maker Resigns," *Milwaukee Journal Sentinel*, February 25, 2000.

——, "Mosinee, Wis.-Based Paper Company Commands Roll-Wrap Market," *Milwaukee Journal Sentinel*, May 4, 2003.

——, "Wausau-Mosinee Paper in Mosinee, Wis., Announces Need to Cut Costs," *Milwaukee Journal Sentinel*, February 1, 2002.

——, "Wisconsin-Based Paper Company Doubles Earnings Last Year," *Milwaukee Journal Sentinel*, January 31, 2003.

——, "Wisconsin's Wausau-Mosinee Paper Improved Performance in 2001, CEO Says," *Milwaukee Journal Sentinel*, April 19, 2002.

Harrison, Andy, "Bay West Adds Papermaking Facility to Bolster Its Converting Operation," *Pulp and Paper*, July 1992, pp. 73–76.

Johnson, Jim, "Wis Paper Firms to Merge," *Waste News*, September 1, 1997, p. 16.

Keane, Stephen, "Mosinee Targets Market," *Wisconsin Business*, February 1986.

Loeffelholz, Suzanne, "Encore, Encore," *Financial World*, August 22, 1989, pp. 62–65.

Martin, Chuck, "Frustrations Add Up for Mosinee Paper," *Milwaukee Journal*, October 11, 1992.

Miller, James P., "Wausau Paper to Acquire Mosinee for Stock Valued at $42 Million," *Wall Street Journal*, August 25, 1997, p. B4.

The Story of Paper at Mosinee, Mosinee, Wis.: Mosinee Paper Mills Co., 1965.

"Wausau, Mosinee in $477 Million Deal," *Pulp & Paper*, October 1997, p. 21.

—Robert R. Jacobson
—update: Christina M. Stansell

Westerbeke Corporation

Myles Standish Industrial Park
150 John Hancock Road
Taunton, Massachusetts 02780
U.S.A.
Telephone: (508) 823-7677
Fax: (508) 884-9688
Web Site: http://www.westerbeke.com

Public Company
Incorporated: 1937 as J.H. Westerbeke Corporation
Employees: 79
Sales: $25.5 million (2002)
Stock Exchanges: NASDAQ
Ticker Symbol: WTBK
NAIC: 335312 Motor and Generator Manufacturing

Based in Taunton, Massachusetts, Westerbeke Corporation designs, manufactures, and markets diesel and gasoline marine engines and generators, as well as marine air conditioners and industrial diesel generators. The company's business is organized under two segments: Marine Products and Industrial Products. On the marine side, Westerbeke is a well-respected brand, supplying propulsion engines and generators to high-end boat builders—including Hinckley Yachts, Little Harbor, and Grand Banks—and production boat builders such as Bayliner, Beneteau, Chris-Craft, Catalina Yachts, and Sea Ray. The company's generators are also used by houseboat manufacturers such as Lakeview, Sharpe, Somerset, and Stardust. In addition, Westerbeke supplies the engines and generators used in the United States and other countries for harbor pilot boats, police boats, fire boats, and high speed drug patrol boats. The company also provides an extensive line of spare parts and accessories for its 22 models of propulsion engines and 26 models of electrical generators, plus discontinued models. To market its marine products around the world, Westerbeke maintains a distribution network that includes more than 65 master distributors and their dealers, as well as warehousing in Europe. All told, the company supplies marine products to some 65 countries around the world, plus the 12 islands of the Caribbean and certain islands in Europe

and the Far East. A more recent product offering, marine air conditioning, accounts for a negligible amount of business. Westerbeke Industrial Products segment converts the company's marine generators for land use, resulting in nine models of electrical generators used as a secondary power source at a fixed site or installed on fire trucks, rescue vehicles, motor coaches, refrigerated trucks, and other specialty vehicles. The Westerbeke family owns nearly 60 percent of the public company and in 2003 launched an effort to take the business private once again.

Founder Born in 1909

The man behind the company's name was John Henry Westerbeke. He was born in Fairhaven, Vermont, in 1909, and four years later moved with his family to Meredith, New York, where his father bought a farm. In 1918, his father became a victim of the great flu epidemic that affected one out of every four Americans, killing 675,000 in the United States and 20 million worldwide. Westerbeke then went to live with his grandparents in Opelika, Alabama, until he went off to college in 1927. With limited funds, he was forced to borrow money to attend St. Lawrence University in Canton, New York. After his freshman year, he turned to his "Uncle Bill," William Westerbeke, for a summer job in Boston. The summer job turned into full-time employment, and John Westerbeke never returned to college.

William Westerbeke owned a number of fishing gear stores in the Boston area, as well as a fishing trawler named the Vagabond. John Westerbeke signed on as a deckhand on the Vagabond and gained a practical education about fishing, the sea, and—by necessity—marine engines. During his time on the Vagabond, Westerbeke displayed a penchant for prescient thinking that would mark later achievements with his marine engine business. For example, in the autumn of 1930 the Vagabond encountered large schools of undersized haddock. He recognized the danger of catching these fingerlings and allowed them to reach their market weight of five to eight pounds each. Not only were current catches reduced, but future fishing would also be affected. Westerbeke wrote and published an article on the subject in the April 1931 issue of *Fishing* magazine, titled "The Fisherman Speaks—A Warning." In it, he presented his concern about overfishing—an issue that would gain greater currency decades later. Around 1933, when he was still only 24 years old, Westerbeke became the captain of the Vagabond. While that may have been the height of ambition for a man raised in the fishing trade, Westerbeke decided to pursue his future on land. With his uncle's backing, he bought the United Welding Company, a Boston business that made trawlboards, which were used to weigh down fishing nets and prevent them from floating to the surface.

In 1936, Westerbeke learned about a revolutionary new diesel engine, the GM 71 Series (also known as the Detroit Diesel 6-71), capable of delivering much greater power for its weight than other engines of the day. From his time spent on a fishing trawler, hampered by heavy, low-powered diesel engines, Westerbeke knew the difference the GM 71 could make if it were converted to marine use. In 1937, he discovered that the Gray Aldridge Marine Corporation owned the distribution rights to the engine. Westerbeke sold United Welding and bought Gray Alridge, which was folded into a corporation he formed, J.H. Westerbeke Corp. He was now in the engine business.

Although he was not trained as an engineer, Westerbeke was able to adapt the GM 71 for marine use, installing his first engine after being in business only a year. He enjoyed success in growing the company, but World War II intervened. The government commandeered all GM 71 engines for wartime use, forcing Westerbeke to scramble to find something to sell during this period. For a time, he distributed Hendy, Gray Marine, and Continental diesel engines.

Postwar Prosperity

It was during the postwar years, when he once again had access to the GM 71, that Westerbeke's company began to prosper. He expanded beyond propulsion engines, turning to generators for both land and marine use. In 1951, he bought a Boston company called Smallcraft, picking up an outboard motor line and two lines of boats, one of which was a sailboat line that became Westerbeke's passion for the next several years. He championed the sailboat, branded the Thistle, in the Boston area until 1957, after which he abandoned this market. In the meantime, his company fitted lighthouses all along the East Coast with new generators.

The company reached another turning point in 1959 when Westerbeke read about the latest development from England-based Perkins Engine Company: a small block, 4-cylinder, water-cooled diesel engine known as the Perkins 4-99. It was an engine intended for general industrial purposes and was especially suited for power tractors. However, Westerbeke immediately recognized the potential for the 4-99 to provide auxiliary power to sailboats. For some time, there had been a clamoring among sailboat makers and enthusiasts for a suitable diesel engine that could replace the gasoline engines that were in common use. Gasoline fumes, if not properly vented, would pool below the deck of a sailboat, and all too often an unsuspecting owner would start the engine and cause an explosion. An engine using diesel fuel avoided this serious danger. Westerbeke immediately flew to England to secure the import rights to the Perkins 4-99. In addition to converting the engine for use on sailboats, he also built marine generators from the 4-99. For several years, Westerbeke had a clear field for exploiting the marine uses of the 4-99 in America. Of note was the solid contract business he developed supplying engines for the 26-foot whaleboats used by the U.S. Navy and lifeboat engines specified by the Coast Guard. By the mid-1960s, however, his supplier, Perkins, became his competitor, offering 4-99 engines designed for marine use under the Perkins name.

In 1966, Westerbeke's son, John Henry Westerbeke, Jr., joined the company. Over the next ten years, he held a number of managerial positions as he was groomed to succeed his father in running the business. During this period, the company sought new sources of engines in an effort to wean itself off the Perkins 4-99. It purchased ''long block'' engines and added systems and components of the company's own design and manufacture. In 1976, John Westerbeke, Jr., at the age of 36, replaced his father as president of the company. Westerbeke, Sr., although of retirement age, retained the chairmanship and remained highly active in the company's day-to-day affairs.

John Westerbeke, Jr. Continues Tradition of Growth

By this stage in the company's history, three-quarters of Westerbeke's revenues were derived from propulsion engines and the balance from generators. There was a great deal of potential in the generator market, but the company was restricted to producing engines in the ten to 45 kilowatt range, which were suitable only for the high end of the market. In the late 1970s, Westerbeke became one of the first Western companies to turn to Japan as a source for engines appropriate to serve the major part of the marine generator market (requiring less than ten kilowatts). Moreover, this new line of generators was a major advance for the marine market. They were the smallest available—lightweight, quiet, and dependable. As a result, the generator portion of the company's revenues began to increase steadily. Westerbeke moved into a larger facility in Avon, Massachusetts, roughly 34,000 square feet in size, providing greater production capacity. The company also eased away from distribution, thus freeing up additional space. Westerbeke was developing such a strong name in the marine generator business that customers asked the company to develop a line of gasoline marine generators. With this additional product launched in 1983, the company enjoyed annual growth in revenues in the 20 percent range over the next few years. By the end of 1986, generators accounted for two-third's of Westerbeke's sales and propulsion engines just one-third, a major change in the company's sales mix accomplished in just six years.

In 1986, John Westerbeke, Sr. stepped down as chairman, replaced by John Westerbeke, Jr. The elder Westerbeke stayed on as a board member, holding the title of chairman emeritus, and continued to come into the office several days a week. Also in that year, the company was approached by Carolina Securities

---

Key Dates:

1937: The company is formed by John Westerbeke, Sr.
1959: The company offers new sailboat propulsion engines.
1966: John Westerbeke, Jr. joins the company.
1976: Westerbeke, Sr. turns over the company's presidency to his son.
1986: The company is taken public.
2000: John Westerbeke, Sr., dies at the age of 90.
2003: Steps are taken to return the company to private ownership.

Corp, a North Carolina-based regional brokerage firm, about taking Westerbeke public. The board agreed, and in preparation J.H. Westerbeke Corp. was reincorporated in Delaware as Westerbeke Corporation. An initial public offering was then conducted, led by Carolina Securities and First Albany Corp., and the company's stock began trading on the NASDAQ. With the proceeds from the offering, Westerbeke retired some debt and laid away working capital, but it made no use of its stock as a way to pay for acquisitions. External growth was never a major part of the company's strategy. In 1990, Westerbeke completed two acquisitions. In January of that year, the company paid $195,000 in cash, plus the issuance of a $115,000 subordinated note and assumption of $220,000 of liabilities, to acquire Rotary Marine, Inc. As a result, Westerbeke entered the marine air-conditioning market. However, the company's success with the product never approached what it achieved with marine generators and propulsion engines. Later in 1990, Westerbeke bought the Universal Motors product line from Medalist Industries, Inc., paying $1.13 million in cash and assuming another $150,000 in warranty liabilities. This transaction gave Westerbeke the rights to an engine it had formerly distributed.

For the most part, Westerbeke continued to focus on internal growth in the 1990s, as it had throughout its history. During the economic boom years in the second half of the decade, one of the company's greatest worries was simply keeping major customers happy by meeting the high demand for Westerbeke products. Net sales grew from $26.2 million in 1998 to more than $34.5 million in 2000. Business was so strong that the company made plans to move into a larger facility. At first, the intention was to develop a greenfield site, but an ideal existing structure was found at the Myles Standish Industrial Park in Taunton, Massachusetts. At 110,000 square feet, the plant was nearly three times the size of Westerbeke's longtime location in Avon. According to John Westerbeke, Jr., when he first showed his father the company's new home in 2000, they stood in one corner and looked across at the opposite corner of the massive

structure. The elder Westerbeke simply muttered, "Oh, Johnny," which his son interpreted as concern that he might have taken too ambitious a step.

John Westerbeke, Sr. was now 90 years old. He had launched his business during the Great Depression and nursed it through a number of changes in the marine industry before turning over the reins to a second generation. Only in recent months had he given up his driver's license, but he continued to come into the office a day or two each week, a limousine providing his transportation. Some weeks after visiting the company's new facility, on May 8, 2000, he died in a hospital in Milton, Massachusetts.

When the economy slipped into recession in 2001, Westerbeke, like many companies, felt the effect on its balance sheet. In addition, the company lost a major customer in Brunswick Corporation. Revenues dropped to $28.7 million in 2001 and $25.5 million in 2002. Nevertheless, Westerbeke remained profitable. At this point, there was little reason to remain a public company, especially in light of the expense corporations now faced in complying with the new reporting requirements following a spate of corporate scandals such as that which led to the collapse of Enron. Thus, in 2003, John Westerbeke, Jr. began the process of taking the company private, forming an entity named Westerbeke Acquisition Corporation which then offered $3 a share. Although he controlled nearly 60 percent of the company, completing the transaction proved troublesome. Suitors emerged, attempting to buy the company, only to be rebuffed. One shareholder initiated a lawsuit. As of December 2003, the plan to merge Westerbeke Corporation with Westerbeke Acquisition Corporation had yet to be finalized, but John Westerbeke was confident that the company his father founded would once again return to private status.

Principal Subsidiaries

Westerbeke International, Inc.

Principal Competitors

Suzuki Motor Corporation; AB Volvo; Yamaha MotorCo., Ltd.

Further Reading

"John Westerbeke," *Patriot Ledger* (Quincy, Massachustess), May 11, 2000, p. 28.
"John Westerbeke, at 90, Pioneer in Marine Industry," *Boston Herald,* May 13, 2000, p. 51.
"John H. Westerbeke, 90, Was Designer of Marine Engines," *Boston Globe,* May 12, 2000, p. B13.

—Ed Dinger

The WesterN SizzliN Corporation

317 Kimball Avenue Northeast
Roanoke, Virginia 24016
U.S.A.
Telephone: (540) 345-3195
Toll Free: (800) 24-STEAK
Fax: (540) 345-0831
Web site: http://www.western-sizzlin.com

Public Company
Incorporated: 1992 as Austins Steaks & Saloon, Inc.
Employees: 450
Sales: $28.5 million (2002)
Stock Exchanges: Over the Counter
Ticker Symbol: WSZZV
NAIC: 722110 Full-Service Restaurants

The WesterN SizzliN Corporation, based in Roanoke, Virginia, operates and franchises several restaurant concepts: Austin Steaks & Saloon, WesterN SizzliN Steak & More, WesterN SizzliN Wood Grill, Great American Steak & Buffet, Quincy Steakhouses, and Market Street Buffet and Baker. The flagship chain is 173-unit WesterN SizzliN Steak & More, known for its signature "Flamekist" steaks.

WesterN SizzliN Chain Founded in 1962

WesterN SizzliN was founded in Augusta, Georgia, in 1962 by Nick Pascarella, a native of Pennsylvania whose choice of a place to start up his business was strictly fortuitous. According to company lore, he was traveling around the country in search of cheap land on which to build a steakhouse, and he stopped in Augusta because of a flat tire. It was the tire store employees who convinced him to locate his restaurant in Augusta. What made Pascarella's steakhouse stand out was his unique way of grilling. According to company literature, "If searing the bottom of the steak made it juicy [Pascarella] reasoned that adding flames to the top would make them twice as good. He was right and the world famous Flamekist steak was born! This unique process locks in the flavor as the steak is seared to a savory perfection." Pascarella would eventually build a second restau-

rant in Augusta, across the street from the first, which would also house the company's headquarters. In 1966, he began to sell franchises of his WesterN SizzliN concept. Over the next 20 years, the restaurant operation grew to become the second-largest steakhouse chain in the country, with 600 units generating some $500 million in annual revenues. Pascarella was hardly a micromanager and took a hands-off approach that allowed franchisees to operate as they saw fit. There was also very little advertising that emanated from the top of the chain. Nevertheless, WesterN SizzliN was a successful chain until Pascarella's death in March 1988. *Restaurants & Institutions* magazine named it the top steakhouse chain in America in 1984, 1985, and 1987. Near the end of Pascarella's reign, however, same-store and systemwide sales grew stagnant and a number of units closed. In addition, the chain lagged well behind the competition in sales per unit. While Ryan's Family Steak House averaged $2.3 million per restaurant, Sizzler $1.5 million, and Bonanza $1 million, WesterN SizzliN generated just $800,000. Moreover, a large number of stores, perhaps as many as 100, were doing less than $500,000 in annual sales.

Following Pascarella's death, his wife Nora and son Edward chose to sell WesterN SizzliN. Although the chain was struggling, with the right management team it was, in the opinion of many, capable of becoming a category powerhouse. There was no lack of suitors, and interested buyers included the Marriott Corporation. In the end, it was an investment group head by Pizza Hut co-founder, Frank Carney, who prevailed with a bid of $95 million in a leveraged buyout.

Carney, along with former Pizza Hut executive Michael Stack and five unnamed food-service executives, teamed up to acquire a 49-percent stake, while enlisting La Jolla-based Triton Group Ltd. and its holding company, Intermark Inc., to pick up the balance. Back in 1958, Carney and his brother Dan had scraped together $3,000 to launch the Pizza Hut chain in Kansas City, converting a bar located next to their father's grocery store. They built Pizza Hut into a 4,000-unit chain before selling it to Pepsico in 1977. After leaving Pepsico in 1980, Carney sought a new restaurant concept but had no success with China Rose, a Chinese restaurant; Pasta Ficio, a pasta restaurant; or a restaurant chain called Flakey Jake's.

Company Perspectives:

Our primary goal has always been to exceed our guest's expectations for both quality and service. Our restaurants strive to provide a relaxing, enjoyable dining experience in a friendly, family oriented atmosphere.

Carney took over as chairman and Stack became chief executive officer at WesterN SizzliN and promptly moved the company's headquarters from Augusta to more strategically located Dallas. Carney expressed high hopes for the chain, which he hoped to transform into the price-value leader in the family steakhouse segment. His five-year plan was to grow the chain to 1,000 units and increase the per-unit sales volume to $1.1 million. To achieve this lofty goal, Carney and his management team quickly moved on a number of fronts. WesterN SizzliN introduced a new logo, replacing one that had served the chain for 27 years. It also tried to emulate the competition by downplaying steak and broadening its offerings, in particular a new 12-item lunch menu that included chicken, fish, and sandwich plates. At the same time, the chain moved away from the food bar concept, opting instead to focus on salads and soups. WesterN SizzliN also launched its first national television advertising campaign in 1989 and became much more involved with franchisees than the company ever had been under Pascarella. The franchisee agreement was rewritten and a restaurant evaluation program was instituted. According to one franchisee quoted in *Nation's Restaurant News,* ''We've had more corporate visits in one month than we did in several years.'' Management also got the franchisees involved in the advertising by forming a 12-member board, eight of whom were voted on by the franchisees. Furthermore, WesterN SizzliN developed prototype restaurants and introduced them into new territories. It expanded into Canada, followed in 1990 with a deal to build WesterN SizzliN restaurants in Japan. There was even talk about entering Saudi Arabia.

WesterN SizzliN Files Chapter 11 in 1992

Carney and his management team enjoyed some success, boosting per-store sales volume above $900,000, but instead of growing to 1,000 units within five years, the WesterN SizzliN chain shrank to 350 within four years. Stiff competition in the segment from such chains as Ryan's Family Steak House and Golden Corral curtailed WesterN SizzliN's growth, forcing many franchisees to change concepts or simply close their doors. Carney's group was also hobbled from the moment it took control, because $95 million was simply to high a price to pay for the chain in light of the royalties collected from franchisees. The corporation that owned the business, WSI Holdings Corp, was so burdened with debt that it and its six subsidiaries had assets of just $5.4 million and liabilities of $51.2 million by November 1992. At that time, WSI filed for Chapter 11 bankruptcy, which required the company to present a reorganization plan to the U.S. Bankruptcy Court. Carney put a positive spin on the move, telling *Nation's Restaurant News,* ''This is our chance to clean up the balance sheet. Our operations are sound, and we feel comfortable with the company. Over the past year we felt we've turned the corner somewhat.''

Carney never got another chance to realize his dreams with WesterN SizzliN, which operated under Chapter 11 bankruptcy protection for nearly a year. In October 1993, a group of 28 franchisees led by veteran restaurateur Dave Wachtel bought the chain, now reduced to 320 units, for a modest $10 million. Wachtel's association with restaurants dated back to 1959 when as a teenager he washed dishes and bussed tables for 65 cents an hour at Ray Danner's first Shoney's restaurant. He worked at another Danner restaurant while attending the University of Tennessee-Knoxville but left school to take a management position with Danner in 1968. Wachtel launched the Mr. D's seafood concept, now known as Captain D's, and ultimately succeeded Danner as CEO of Shoney's. However, he soon fell out with the autocratic Danner and left Shoney's in 1982. Wachtel became a WesterN SizzliN franchisee in 1984, operating as many as nine units before selling them back to the chain in 1990. Issued a note for $1.3 million, Wachtel grew concerned that he might never be repaid, prompting him to lead a group of franchisees to buy out WesterN SizzliN.

Like Carney, Wachtel believed that WesterN SizzliN held great potential. He attributed most of Carney's difficulties in growing the chain to the high price his group paid for the business. ''There was never anything wrong with the brand name,'' Wachtel told *Nation's Restaurant News.* Once in charge of WesterN SizzliN as president and chief executive officer, he moved the headquarters to his native Nashville, created a purchasing program, and developed a centralized marketing plan. As a result, in 1994 the company posted its first operating profit since the chain was sold by Pascarella's heirs. Nevertheless, Wachtel's tenure at the top would prove to brief. He fell out with his board over the direction to take WesterN SizzliN and attempted to acquire the chain, offering about $13 million. His bid was rejected, and in March 1995 the board terminated his management contract and replaced him with Victor Foti, a franchisee operating in Roanoke, Virginia, where the company's headquarters subsequently moved. Wachtel filed a lawsuit against the directors, claiming he had been wrongfully terminated, but the case was dismissed by a judge in February 1997. In the press, he blamed Foti and another board member for his ouster.

Over the next three years, the WesterN SizzliN chain continued to decrease in size and by 1999 it consisted of 21 company-owned units and 230 franchised units. The next major development in the company's history came in March 1999, when it became a publicly traded company in a reverse merger with Lincoln, Nebraska-based Austins Steaks & Saloon Inc. As a result, WesterN SizzliN Corporation was subsumed by Austins Steaks & Saloon, Inc., which now became the corporate home of the WesterN SizzliN restaurant chain. Austins Steaks was an eight-unit casual upscale steakhouse chain launched in Omaha in 1989 with the opening of a single restaurant. Two other Omaha units opened in 1992, followed by a fourth in 1996. Austins Steaks opened a restaurant in Sante Fe, New Mexico, and one in Lincoln, Nebraska, in 1994. Restaurants in Scottsdale, Arizona, and Albuquerque, New Mexico, were established in 1995, the same year that Austins Steaks went public, netting $4 million. The hope was to open another eight to 12 restaurants by the end of 1996. Instead, the company struggled for the next three years, and due to intense competition in the restaurant industry it failed to launch any new units. Austin Steaks posted three consecutive years of losses: $568,000 in 1996, $1.6 million in 1996, and $1.5 million in 1997. By 1999, Austins' management concluded that it needed to combine with a larger operation in order to survive, leading to the merger with WesterN SizzliN.

Quincy Family Steakhouses Picked up in 2000

Foti stayed on as CEO of the combined company, which received a major financial boost in June 2000 when it reached a temporary agreement with Scottsdale, Arizona-based Franchise Finance Corporation of America to operate 97 Quincy's Family Steakhouse restaurants after Quincy's owner, Atlanta-based Buckley Acquisition Corporation, was unable to meet its credit obligations. Ultimately, the arrangement became a lease agreement. Quincy's was founded in Spartanburg, South Carolina, in the early 1970s. A major Hardee's franchisee, Spartan Food Systems, acquired the nine-unit chain in 1977. Spartan was acquired two years later by TransWorld Corporation, which built Quincy's into a chain of more than 200 restaurants. Business peaked in 1990 when Quincy's generated revenues of $282 million from 212 restaurants. Serial changes in ownership took its toll, however, and by 1998 Quincy's had dipped below 100 units in size. Austin Steaks soon discovered that the damage done to the Quincy's brand was severe, and in March 2001 management decided to close some 50 Quincy's and convert another 43 into WesterN SizzliN grill-buffet restaurants, leaving only three Quincy's operating in markets where a WesterN SizzliN was already located.

The sale of 43 Quincy's to franchisees provided much needed relief to Austins Steaks, which was able to post a profit of $226,000 in 2001 after losing more than $1.4 million the year before. This development notwithstanding, the company was clearly experiencing financial difficulties. In November 2001, management announced that it was "actively looking at other ways to enhance shareholder value," including a merger and even sale of the company. Then, in July 2002, Austins Steaks hired investment banking firm J.H. Chapman Group as a financial adviser. Four shareholders, controlling about a quarter of the company and dissatisfied with the state of Austins Steaks, took steps to oust Foti and most of the board of directors

through a proxy war. Over the next few months, the dissidents and board haggled in the press and SEC filings, maneuvered in the board room, and filed lawsuits and countersuits. Finally, in September 2002, the two sides met to attempt to strike a deal. The company offered to buy out the dissidents for $2.2 million, and Foti and chairman J. Carson Quarles offered not to stand for re-election at the next shareholder's meeting. However, both offers were rejected. In the end, Foti agreed to leave the board immediately but would remain as CEO until the June 2003 annual meeting. Quarles agreed to give up the chairmanship but stayed on as a director. Foti left much sooner, however, departing the company in December 2002, at which time he stated to the press, "I did not voluntarily resign." His only association with the company was now as a franchisee. The proxy war as well as the closing of ten stores had an adverse impact on the balance sheet in 2002, as the company reported a $1.1 million loss for the year.

Following Foti's departure, Austin Steaks immediately launched a search for a new CEO. In July 2003, the board settled on James Verney, who had 28 years of experience in the food industry. He came to Austins from North Carolina-based Claremont Restaurant Group, where he served as president and CEO of 85 restaurants operating under three brands: Sagebrush Steakhouses, Western Steer, and Prime Sirloin. A plan to revitalize the business was already in place, calling for the closure of underperforming restaurants and a focus on the core units that were prospering. Upon accepting the top post at Austins, Verney announced, "My first objective is to listen to existing franchisees to learn how we can provide better support. Then, we'll assist our existing operators to open new units, and later we'll invite others to join our family." Several weeks later the company announced positive results for the quarter ending June 30, 2003, prompting hopes that the corner had been turned. In October 2003, in recognition of the prominent position of the WesterN SizzliN chain at Austins Steaks, the company changed its name to WesterN SizzliN Corporation.

Principal Subsidiaries

Austins Omaha, Inc.

Principal Competitors

Investors Management Corporation (Golden Corral); Metromedia Restaurant Group; Ryan's Family Steak Houses, Inc.

Further Reading

Bernstein, Charles, "Carney Plots Western Sizzlin' Growth," *Nation's Restaurant News*, February 13, 1989, p. 3.
Bruno, Karen, "Carney Corrals Western Sizzlin," *Nation's Restaurant News*, August 15, 1988, p. 1.
Carlino, Bill, "Western Sizzlin': Back to Basics under Wachtel," *Nation's Restaurant News*, January 24, 1994, p. 7.
——, "Western Sizzlin' Files For Ch. 11 Protection," *Nation's Restaurant News*, November 9, 1992, p. 3.
Sturgeon, Jeff, "Western Sizzlin Merger Is Announced," *Roanoke Times*, March 6, 1999, p. A5.

—Ed Dinger

Wheaton Science Products

1501 North Tenth Street
Millville, New Jersey 08332
U.S.A.
Telephone: (856) 825-1400
Toll Free: (800) 225-1437
Fax: (856) 825-1368
Web site: http://www.wheatonsci.com

Wholly Owned Subsidiary of Alcan Inc.
Incorporated: 1888 as T.C. Wheaton and Company
Sales: $3.5 billion (2003)
NAIC: 327213 Glass Container Manufacturing; 32616
   Plastics Bottle Manufacturing; 326199 All Other
   Plastics Product Manufacturing

With origins in glass production dating back to 1888, Wheaton Science Products is a wholly owned subsidiary of and operates as a key component in the packaging division of its parent company. Wheaton manufactures and markets over 4,500 laboratory products, including instruments and equipment, liquid handling equipment, and specialty glass apparatus. It also produces a wide variety of glass and plastic containers used by the laboratory and diagnostic packaging industries. For most of its history, Wheaton operated as a family-run private company. The firm was bought by Zurich-based Alusuisse-Lonza Holding Ltd. in 1996. Alusuisse, in turn, was acquired by Alcan Inc. in 2001. As a result, Wheaton became an integral unit in Alcan Packaging, one of the world's largest packaging concerns.

Early History

Wheaton Industries survived a stormy beginning. Construction of a new glass factory in Millville, New Jersey, under the ownership of two entrepreneurs, Mr. Shull and Mr. Goodwin, was delayed by the devastating East Coast blizzard of 1888. When operations finally got underway, the partners fell behind schedule in production of the glass tubing needed to supply their lamp room. In addition, they were losing market share to Western glass companies prospering under more advantageous fuel costs, easier access to raw materials, and a superior transportation network. To raise much-needed capital, the fledgling company borrowed

$3,000 from a local pharmacist and physician, Dr. Theodore C. Wheaton. In an effort to protect his investment, Dr. Wheaton participated in company planning. His involvement rapidly increased, and on October 24, 1888 he purchased a controlling interest in the firm, thereby founding T.C. Wheaton and Company.

The new company's subsequent growth reflected the medical interests of its founder as it came to specialize in homeopathic and screw-cap vials used by scientific laboratories, chemists, perfumers, pharmacists, and physicians. Within a year, a new lamp room had been constructed alongside the factory. It accommodated 13 glass workers, as well as room for sorting, cutting, inspecting, and packing the tubing. In addition, a new shop was constructed for the manufacture of prescription bottles. Presses were designed to supply matching stoppers and other solid ware. Nursing bottles, breast pump glasses, and other druggist supplies were added to the Wheaton line.

In addition to the usual risks of starting a new company, Dr. Wheaton had to contend with fire hazards typical of the glass industry. On November 24, 1889, six of the original factory buildings were lost to the first of numerous fires with which the business had to contend over the years. Other major fires occurred in 1908, 1912, and 1925.

By June 1890, Dr. Wheaton had abandoned his private medical practice in order to focus all his energies on developing the glass business. In the summer of 1890, the doctor traveled to the West Coast to establish new contacts. In 1891, his younger brother, Walter Scott Wheaton, opened a sales office in Denver, Colorado. Further contacts were made during Dr. Wheaton's periodic trips to Philadelphia, Boston, and New York, where he opened a sales office in 1892.

The same year, Dr. Wheaton gambled on substantial growth by investing $10,000 in a plot of land surrounding the existing factory. By 1894, the number two furnace was operational, and, in 1896, $14,000 was invested in 12 pot furnaces and a new building constituting the number three factory. These additions were designed to employ approximately 250 new workers and to double production capacity.

Expanding business required new staff, for which Dr. Wheaton had cultivated two outstanding candidates: his two

Company Perspectives:

Through continuous quality improvement, we are dedicated to being incredibly easy to do business with. In meeting the requirements of our customers, we will service them through accurate and timely deliveries as well as strong technical and after-sales support. Wheaton Science Products will pursue these commitments to achieve our goal of providing positive growth and greater profitability for our customers, our employees, and our company.

sons. In 1899, Frank H. Wheaton joined the company at a starting salary of $5 per week. Frank's career and education were closely allied with the company. After graduating from Millville High School in the spring of 1898, he studied general business subjects at the Eastman Business College in Poughkeepsie, New York, and took a summer course in chemistry at the Philadelphia College of Pharmacy and Science. These skills were put to immediate use in the family business. By 1903, he was elected to the company board and shortly thereafter assumed the post of secretary and treasurer.

His younger brother, Theodore C. Wheaton, Jr., also joined the family enterprise, concentrating more on public relations and marketing than on production. Theodore was born on September 30, 1888, the year T.C. Wheaton Company was founded. After finishing his studies at the Worcester Polytechnic Institute in Massachusetts, he served on the domestic front of World War I, primarily in Washington, D.C. He eventually became vice-president of the New York sales office of T.C. Wheaton Company and established valuable business ties over the course of his career.

In the pre-World War I years, the company grew quickly, trying new ventures with varying success. In 1903, Wheaton entered the window glass market, or window lights as they were called at the time. Profits were extremely low for this segment of the business, and the company had to allocate profits from other operations to finance the loans on the window glass division. By 1908, the window plant ceased to be used. In 1903, the company also had to contend with the unexpected resignation of two top executives, who started their own glass factory, Millville Bottle Works, working in direct competition with T.C. Wheaton in the areas of medicine bottles and laboratory ware. Wheaton would eventually acquire the firm, thus acquiring a competitive edge in this market sector.

The glass industry, and particularly T.C. Wheaton, prospered in the early years of the 20th century. When Carl Sandburg visited Millville in 1905, he described the setting in unforgettable terms: "Down in Southern New Jersey they make glass. By day and night, the fires burn on in Millville and bid the sand let in the light. . . . Big, black flumes, shooting out smoke and sparks . . . and bottles, bottles, bottles of every tint and hue from a brilliant crimson to the dull green that marks the death of sand and the birth of glass."

Growth During the War Years

With the onset of World War I, the "fires burning in Millville" redoubled their heat as the United States became a chief supplier of war materials. Discontinued importation of German glassware, which had dominated the world market, gave American producers the impetus to prove that their products were at least as competitive. Among the many glassware needs of the war effort, the Chemical Warfare Service of the U.S. Army required specially designed canisters known as L.E.C. bottles. According to a company report, T.C. Wheaton Company produced the only L.E.C. bottles that met the exacting standards of military engineers at the Lakehurst Proving Grounds in New Jersey. After the United States' declaration of war in 1917, Dr. Wheaton offered President Wilson the company's services in the production of "a diversified line of scientific glassware, as glass stopcocks, tube funnels, test tubes, pipettes, ampules, etc., as well as blown bottles for prescriptions and supply bottles for hospital use." The offer helped establish valuable new business opportunities and won a personalized note from the president thanking Dr. Wheaton for his "generous and patriotic offer."

The post-World War I era marked substantial expansion. Additions to the plant included a new etching facility for perfumery ware, a metal and concrete warehouse for storing chemicals, a new mold room and batch house, sheds for grinding, and other improvements. Even after a devastating fire in June 1925 and the death of Dr. Wheaton's brother, Walter Scott Wheaton, company growth continued unhindered. The company acquired Millville Bottle Works in 1926, gaining its competitor's proprietary line of prescription and medicine bottles and laboratory ware, thus establishing T.C. Wheaton Company as a major player in the laboratory glassware business.

With the advent of the Great Depression, T.C. Wheaton withstood turbulent markets as well as unforeseen changes in personnel. On September 7, 1931, Dr. T.C. Wheaton died, leaving the post of president and chair of the board to Frank H. Wheaton, Sr. That same year, Frank Wheaton, Jr. departed for the Boston University School of Business, where he spent a short time before returning to the family business to work his way up the company ladder from batch mixing assistant to truck driver's helper and, before too long, to manager and ultimately president.

Frank Wheaton, Jr.'s reputation as "new idea man" was reinforced by his introduction of automated glass production in the late 1930s. Earlier in that decade, he helped introduce handmade borosilicate glass tubes for select pharmaceuticals (borosilicate glass could be molded into long, narrow tubes without collapsing like standard soda-lime glass). For a short time, the company successfully sold handmade serum containers to Eli Lilly, Parke-Davis, and other pharmaceutical companies. However, competing companies had developed automated production facilities, and Wheaton had to either follow suit or lose business. In 1937, Frank Wheaton, Jr. negotiated with the Hartford-Empire Company to lease a single section semi-automatic machine for the production of perfume bottles. That machine's success prompted further negotiations toward the lease of a four-section I.S. Machine, which would increase the company's productivity to eight times its former level. Though the terms of the lease were restrictive, the machine was installed. By 1938, the factory itself had been automated, and its first bottles were produced wholly by mechanical means.

World War II brought a flood of needs that, paired with shortages in iron and steel, prompted innovation and diversification of Wheaton products. On the medical and laboratory front, the company supplied products for the blood serum

Key Dates:

1888: Dr. Wheaton purchases a controlling interest in a glass manufacturer and establishes T.C. Wheaton and Company.

1892: Wheaton invests $10,000 on a plot of land surrounding the existing factory.

1926: Millville Bottle Works is acquired.

1937: Automatic production begins when the company leases a four-section I.S. machine.

1946: The Wheaton Glass Company is established.

1954: The firm acquires the rights to a Swiss manufacturing process called Novoplast.

1971: Wheaton Industries is created to act as a parent company.

1996: The company is acquired by Alusuisse-Lonza Holding Ltd.

2001: Alusuisse is acquired by Alcan Inc.; Wheaton Scientific Products becomes part of Alcan's packaging division.

program, serum containers, Halazone containers (used to purify water on the battlefield), and a wide variety of scientific glassware. Experimentation in material substitutes showed that glass could be used in the place of metal, sometimes with unexpected advantages. Wheaton No-Sol-Vit glass was ground to machinery tolerances and fashioned into three types of glass gages: ring gages, tri-lock gages, and taper lock plug blanks. Glass also replaced metal in many electronic applications, for which Wheaton developed water-resistant glass-to-metal seals sold under the Tronex trademark. The seals were especially useful in radio equipment vulnerable in water-prone combat situations. Wheaton prided itself, among other things, on never missing a single shipment during the war. In February 1943, the company was awarded the Army-Navy "E" Award for its provision of war equipment. As new techniques and new machines were designed to meet diverse war needs, Wheaton gained expertise in industrial machine design and construction, one of its new specialties after the war.

At the close of the war, the glass industry saw a tremendous surge in demand for new molds and new glass containers on the domestic front. In 1946, under the driving influence of Frank Wheaton, Jr., the Wheaton third generation established a new company, Wheaton Glass Company, designed to function separately but in tandem with the older company. For its initial year and a half, Wheaton Glass manufactured only type I (borosilicate) glass due to extremely high demand in the market. Afterwards, the new company shifted to long-run soda-lime items.

Diversification: 1950s–80s

The 1950s saw the rise of industrial plastic, which was quickly exploited by Wheaton and other companies as a powerful packaging medium. In September 1950, the company acquired in Mays Landing the closed grounds of a plant belonging to the Millville Manufacturing Company, comprising 240,000 square feet of floor space. In 1953, Frank Wheaton, Jr. designed a new container for those aerosol products that were chemically

incompatible with metal canisters. His solution involved a glass container coated with a polymer product, polyvinyl chloride, manufactured by the Goodrich Company. The result was a nonvolatile, break-resistant container that launched a new company line, Wheaton Plasti-Cote. The company also developed a small injection molding machine to make plastic snap caps, which, along with Plasti-Cote items, marked the first products of the Wheaton Plastics Company.

Wheaton Plastics worked quickly to develop automatic machinery that could manufacture plastic containers with the same injection blow mold system used for glass. In 1954, the company acquired the rights to a Swiss manufacturing process called Novoplast. The company's General Machinery division, with the combined expertise of Ted Wheaton and the engineering group, developed the VB65-1 machine, the first in a series of bigger and faster injection blow molding machines.

By 1950, the T.C. Wheaton office force had outgrown its old site, and plans were drawn up for new facilities that would include expanded central offices as well as new research and visitors centers. The complex, completed in September 1951, was referred to as "the Pentagon," a reference to its rambling and impressive size.

The 1960s and 1970s marked ever-increasing diversification and the formation of new affiliate companies with various specializations. In 1960, General Mod and Machinery was established, and in 1966 Wheaton Scientific was formed. In the mid-1960s, the company entered the consumer products market. In 1964, Central Research and Development was established to service all Wheaton companies, especially the rapidly growing Wheaton Plastics. In February 1974, Decora was formed to specialize in decorating and labeling operations for glass and plastic containers. In 1975, the Wheaton Cartage Company was established, growing from an in-house carrier to a full-service, national trucking company. In 1977, part of Wheaton's glass operations were transferred to Flat River, Missouri, where fuel costs and transportation facilities were more favorable than those in New Jersey. The Flat River Glass Company was thus founded. In January 1977, American International Container, Inc. was established to distribute Wheaton and other name brands in Florida, Central and South America, the Caribbean, Europe, Asia, Australia, and Africa. Topping the whirlwind expansion of the 1970s, a new Wheaton research and development center was appended to the so-called Pentagon in 1979. The massive facility would be a driving engine for continued research and product expansion in the 1980s and beyond.

Despite rapid changes in the 1970s, two developments helped define Wheaton as a unified organization with a distinct place in history. The first development was the 1971 formation of Wheaton Industries, which was thereafter considered the parent company of its numerous divisions. The second development was the 1976 dedication of Wheaton Village, a period rendition of the original 1888 glassworks, complete with one of the finest glass museums in the United States. The historical park was the result of careful planning and funding on the part of Frank H. Wheaton, Jr. and associates. In 1968, Frank Wheaton had helped found the Wheaton Historical Association as the first step in researching the town's past and organizing historical resources. In 1984, the Creative Glass Center of

America, an organization working in concert with Wheaton Village, started a fellowship program to select and fund contemporary artists who would produce works using the company's vintage glass making facilities. The primary objective was to mix old traditions with new art forms and to expand the costly facilities beyond the scope of traditional, and less experimental, paperweight making.

Rapid diversification and expansion continued in the 1980s, a time when foreign competition forced many American businesses to run leaner operations. In mid-1980, Wheaton Fine Glass was created to produce high-quality glassware products for the American market. Due to the rising value of the dollar and lower wages in foreign industries, the division yielded no profit and discontinued operations in 1984, followed by the closing of all consumer operations in 1986. Another venture launched in 1983, Carolina Glass Works, also folded under the weight of heavy competition. The operation produced state-of-the-art borosilicate flint glass, and was fully computerized and environmentally controlled to produce what the company called "the world's most precise glass containers." The plant closed in 1985. Nevertheless, Wheaton adapted to the changing market, opening Wheaton Science Plastics in 1987 to manufacture injection-molded and blow-molded plastic products for the laboratory. Additionally, the Wheaton Glass Company completely renovated its Plant I in 1987, installing all the capabilities for advanced glass production that had been lost in the Carolina Glass Works.

The 1980s also marked various milestones in Wheaton's long history. On March 16, 1981, the company celebrated the 100th birthday of Frank Wheaton, Sr. Then, in September 1988, the company celebrated its own centennial, attended by former president Gerald R. Ford and New Jersey Governor Thomas H. Kean, among roughly 7,000 others.

Changes in Ownership in the 1990s and Beyond

By the 1990s, Wheaton Industries constituted over 30 subsidiaries with worldwide distribution. In September 1992, Beijing-Wheaton Glass Company, Ltd. realized the first Sino-foreign joint venture to produce glass containers for cosmetics, foodstuffs, and other products. That same month, Wheaton Science Products, Inc. signed a marketing and distribution agreement with Endotronics, Inc., a Minneapolis-based company providing cell processing products and healthcare and biotechnology services. Endotronics agreed to market Wheaton's Integral Bioreactor System along with its BioPro software throughout the United States and Canada. In December, Wheaton contracted with Sandretto Industrie, an Italian firm, to assemble a limited number of machines for U.S. distribution. The venture was discontinued due to recession and aggressive competition from the Far East, according to the managing director of the operation in a December 1992 *Modern Plastics* article. It nevertheless marked an increasing trend of international cooperation in the 1990s. By this time, Wheaton had grown from a family business to a family of businesses held together by an increasingly cosmopolitan parent.

Indeed, as one of the top producers of specialty glass and plastic packaging for the pharmaceutical and personal care industries, Wheaton stood well positioned to benefit from increased international exposure. In fact, the company's diverse holdings began to catch the eye of possible suitors oversees. In 1996, Wheaton ended its long run as a private company when it agreed to be acquired by Zurich-based Alusuisse-Lonza Holding Ltd. in a deal worth over $400 million.

Founded in 1888 as an aluminum company, Alusuisse had been on the hunt to add to its packaging holdings. In 1994, the company purchased Canadian packaging firm Lawson Mardon. By adding Wheaton to its arsenal, Alusuisse not only strengthened its hold over the industry but secured a position as a leading pharmaceutical packaging concern. "This acquisition represents a significant step in our long-term strategy to expand our packaging activities in the pharmaceutical and personal care markets," claimed Alusuisse CEO T.M. Tschopp in a company press release. "Wheaton's impressive reputation in and share of these markets, which have been built up over the last 108 years, will make us the world's leading packaging supplier to the pharmaceutical industry with the widest range of product offerings."

Under new ownership, Wheaton continued to thrive in the late 1990s and into the new century. Ownership of the company once again changed hands in 2001, when Alcan Inc. acquired Alusuisse in a multi-billion dollar transaction. Canada-based Alcan, a major player in the aluminum industry, approached Pechiney SA of France and Alusuisse in 1999, suggesting the trio merge to form a company worth over $20 billion. When regulators began putting conditions on the deal, Alcan backed down from its original plans and instead pursued Alusuisse by itself. Along with bolstering its aluminum holdings, the acquisition significantly increased Alcan's packaging business. By taking Alusuisse under its wing, Alcan's packaging revenues increased from 9 percent to 22 percent of total sales.

Upon completion of the merger, Wheaton Science Products functioned as an Alcan Packaging Company. Together, the companies that comprised the Alcan division provided packaging products for the food, pharmaceuticals, healthcare, cosmetics, personal care, tobacco, and scientific applications industries. The division had 85 locations in 14 countries and secured over $3 billion in sales by 2003. Wheaton itself produced over 4,500 items, making it a key component in Alcan's packaging unit.

With a strong parent company overseeing its operations, the future for Wheaton Science Products looked promising. While its business structure had changed dramatically from its days as a family-run private entity, its focus on providing high quality products to its customers had remained unchanged throughout its history. As a member of one of the world's largest packaging divisions, Wheaton appeared to be on track for success in the years to come.

Principal Competitors

Anchor Glass Container Company; Compagnie de Saint-Gobain S.A.

Further Reading

"Alusuisse-Lonza Holding Ltd. Acquisition of Wheaton Inc. Complete," *PR Newswire*, May 22, 1996.
"Alusuisse-Lonza Seeking Wheaton," *New York Times*, May 3, 1996, p. D5.

''Alusuisse-Lonza to Acquire U.S.-Based Wheaton Inc.,'' *Canada NewsWire*, May 3, 1996.

''Endotronics, Inc. and Wheaton Science Products, Inc. Announce Marketing and Distribution Agreement,'' *PR Newswire*, September 1, 1992.

''F. H. Wheaton Jr., 85; Headed Glass Works,'' *New York Times*, August 3, 1998, p. B8.

''Frank Wheaton Sr., 102, Dies; Major Manufacturer of Glass,'' *New York Times*, April 17, 1983, Section 1, Part 1, p. 36.

Gibbens, Robert, ''Alcan CEO Engen Looks to Packaging: Key Growth Area,'' *National Post*, May 7, 2001, p. C1.

''How To Manufacture a Menagerie of Glass from Grains of Sand,'' *Los Angeles Times*, March 17, 1991, p. E5.

Jacobs, Muriel, ''Antiques; The Fires Burn on in Millville, Where Glass Lets in Light,'' *New York Times*, June 22, 1986, p. 21.

Malarcher, Patricia, ''Crafts: A Wedding of Art and Industry,'' *New York Times*, February 12, 1984, Section 11NJ, p. 18.

Ozanian, Michael, and Tina Russo, ''Private Enterprise,'' *Forbes*, December 14, 1987, p. 150.

Ravensbergen, Jan, ''Alcan Is on a Roll,'' *Gazette*, October 17, 2000, p. D3.

Rogers, Jack K., ''Sandretto Is Reviewing U.S. Assembly Venture,'' *Modern Plastics*, December, 1992, vol. 69, No. 13, p. 13.

''Wheaton Glass Works Operational,'' *Xinhua General News Service*, September 24, 1992.

''Wheaton Shuts Glass Plant: Cites Import Competition for Losses,'' *Weekly Home Furnishings Newspaper*, April 30, 1984, p. 41.

—Kerstan Cohen
—update: Christina M. Stansell

Wheelabrator Technologies, Inc.

---

4 Liberty Lane West
Hampton, New Hampshire 03842
U.S.A.
Telephone: (603) 929-3000
Fax: (603) 929-3139
Web site: http://www.wheelabratortechnologies.com

Wholly Owned Subsidiary of Waste Management Inc.
Incorporated: 1985
Employees: 850
Sales: $798 million (2002)
NAIC: 562213 Solid Waste Combustors and Incinerators

Wheelabrator Technologies, Inc. develops, owns, and operates commercial waste-to-energy facilities that convert over 23,000 tons of solid waste into clean electricity each day. The company—a subsidiary of Waste Management Inc.—operates 16 plants in Connecticut, Florida, Maryland, Massachusetts, New Hampshire, New Jersey, New York, Pennsylvania, and Washington. It also has eight independent power producers in its arsenal that burn solid waste, transferring it into steam to be used by electric utilities. Overall, the company's plants provide enough electricity to power over 800,000 homes. By 2001, Wheelabrator had converted over 100 million tons of municipal waste into 50 billion kilowatt-hours of clean energy.

Origins

The American Foundry Equipment Company, Wheelabrator's predecessor, was established in 1911. The name Wheelabrator originated in Mishawaka, Indiana, in 1932. The company manufactured a "wheelabrador," a rotating three-sided wheel that sprayed shot onto a surface to abrade away paint, plaster, rust, and other substances. The wheelabrador collected dust and other particulate matter resulting from the process in a baghouse enclosure which kept the air clean. When the company took its name, it was not permitted to copyright a generic term and therefore altered the spelling to Wheelabrator for use as a company moniker. (The company's current logo is a representation of the triangular device.)

Expanding into Environmental Products in the 1960s and 1970s

Wheelabrator remained a small manufacturer of these and other devices well into the 1960s. In anticipation of Clean Air Act legislation, the company expanded interest in environmental products by acquiring a license for electrostatic air cleansing technologies from the German company Lurgei. This led to the establishment of the Wheelabrator Clean Air Company in Pittsburgh, which manufactured systems that electronically removed dust, soot, and other particles from flue gas.

Wheelabrator was then acquired by a small conglomerate called the Equity Corporation. The company was paired with another subsidiary, Frye Copy Systems, a manufacturer of printing inks and carbon paper. Equity encountered severe financial problems in the mid-1960s. The company was taken over and reorganized by a New York investor group led by Michael Dingman of the Burnham securities firm. Dingman eliminated the Equity company and merged the Wheelabrator and Frye units.

In 1968, the company, now called Wheelabrator Frye, procured Rust International from Litton Industries. Rust was a construction engineering firm that held an exclusive license to the technologies of von Roll, a Swiss engineering company. The von Roll technologies included highly efficient mechanical processes which Rust applied to incinerator designs.

With the engineering expertise of Rust, and with exclusive access to the Lurgei and von Roll technologies, Wheelabrator built its first waste-fueled energy plant at Saugus, Massachusetts. The plant came on line in 1972, at the height of the first environmental movement in the United States. A second plant was not built until 1983, when more efficient plant designs made incineration cheaper.

Changes in Ownership in the 1980s

Wheelabrator Frye was acquired by The Signal Companies Inc. in 1983, for $1.5 billion. Dingman, chairman of Wheelabrator Frye, was subsequently named president of the new parent company. Wheelabrator, its name changed to Signal Environ-

Company Perspectives:

As a leader in renewable energy, Wheelabrator is committed to customer satisfaction and long-term relationships while protecting the environment.

mental Systems, continued to develop new resource recovery systems in areas where landfills were nearing capacity and garbage dumping fees were rising. As a result of the Signal merger, the unit took on numerous engineering operations of the parent company, including engineering services for the petroleum, paper, metals, and chemical industries.

In August 1985, Edward Hennessy, chairman of the chemical giant Allied Corporation, engineered a merger with Signal— then an aerospace, electronics, and engineering company. Three months later, Allied-Signal resolved to spin off all operations not related to the core businesses. The company identified 35 units to sell, including Frye and the Wheelabrator environmental systems unit. Rather than dispose of the companies individually, a process that would take more than two years, Allied-Signal created a holding company under Michael Dingman. Dingman, a rowing enthusiast, named the new corporation after the English rowing mecca, Henley. One of the largest subsidiaries of the new Henley Group was the environmental systems unit, which took the name Wheelabrator Technologies.

As an independent organization, Henley was run more as an investment company than an operating company. In 1987, as Henley's Wheelabrator, Fisher Scientific, and other manufacturing groups prospered, Dingman engineered a series of creative schemes to maximize shareholder value. He took each of the units public, selling non-controlling interests to shareholders and simultaneously raising cash for other investments while gaining independent stock valuation. Shareholders paid a premium for the opportunity to directly share the risk of operating single-industry divisions with the parent company.

After dabbling with substantial investments in the Santa Fe South Pacific Corporation during 1988, Dingman turned Henley's focus back to revaluation schemes. In a so-called "reverse spin-off," he created two independent companies, Wheelabrator Group and a new Henley Group, which divided the assets of the old Henley company. Over the next three years, Henley's investment in Wheelabrator dwindled to less than 10 percent of the company's shares. Phillip Rooney took over as head of Wheelabrator.

While Dingman was ringing up his successes with share value maximization, he oversaw a significant series of events in the structural development of Wheelabrator. Shortly after being spun off from Allied-Signal, Wheelabrator exchanged 22 percent of its shares for the underperforming waste incineration assets of rival Waste Management, Inc. The agreement was more of a business arrangement than the result of a competitive battle. Waste Management had established an incineration business purely as a defensive measure against competitors such as Wheelabrator and the Ogden Corporation, but lack of engineering know-how and pressure from various forms of public opposition hindered Waste Management's ability to enter the business on a significant and profitable basis. The deal with Wheelabrator included exclusive rights to dispose of incinerator fly ash at Waste Management facilities and other transferred properties, which was essential for Wheelabrator's growth as new incineration plants could not be built without guaranteed ash disposal resources.

Meanwhile licensing for disposal sites had become nearly impossible to gain due to strong public opposition. Wheelabrator responded by conducting excellent public education campaigns and proposing to work with any public advocacy group that opposed Wheelabrator incinerators. The company sponsored several series of public hearings, offering to answer any questions, and taking every opportunity to demonstrate the environmental advantages of incineration over landfills. In addition, as landfill charges rose to more than $50 per ton and incineration costs fell to $30, Wheelabrator could demonstrate growing economic advantages to its methods of disposal. Once public approval was gained for construction of an incinerator, Wheelabrator would conduct regular tours of the site, inviting the public to inspect the operation personally and ask questions. By maintaining an honest and open relationship with the public, Wheelabrator managed to neutralize the NIMBY, or "not-in-my-backyard" syndrome.

Wheelabrator plants were placed strategically near landfills that were nearing capacity and where power cogeneration would yield profitable electricity sales. Those in the north were equipped to provide electricity in the summer and industrial heating steam in the winter. Plants were built near large metropolitan areas in Washington, Florida, Maine, New Hampshire, Massachusetts, and Maryland.

While more economical and environmentally friendly than landfills, incinerators still had their problems. Highly toxic materials, such as car batteries, were frequently put into the furnaces. To guard against further environmental harm from acid gas and dioxins, Wheelabrator fitted its plants with calcium sprayers and fabric filters that "scrubbed" harmful emissions from the exhaust.

Operating as a Waste Management Subsidiary in the 1990s and Beyond

Wheelabrator once shared offices with the Henley Group in Hampton, New Hampshire, but relocated to suburban Chicago in 1992 and eventually made its home in New Hampshire. Its association with Dingman's Henley Group continued, but Wheelabrator's business relationship with Waste Management grew. In 1990, Wheelabrator became a majority-owned subsidiary of Waste Management. Through a merger, Waste Management secured control of 55 percent of Wheelabrator's common stock.

With its experience in operating 14 incinerators and designing pollution control systems, Wheelabrator was established as a leader in building water and air purification systems by the early 1990s. The company's Rust International subsidiary was the sixth largest engineering and construction contractor in the United States in 1992. In addition to engineering strengths, Wheelabrator differed from its main competitor, Ogden, in its offering of fully integrated plants based on exclusively licensed technologies built by Rust International. This standardized ap-

Key Dates:

1911: American Foundry Equipment Company is established.
1932: The firm changes its name to The Wheelabrator Corporation.
1968: The company—now operating as Wheelabrator-Frye Inc.—acquires Rust International.
1983: The Signal Companies Inc. acquires Wheelabrator in a $1.5 billion deal.
1987: Wheelabrator goes public.
1990: The company becomes a subsidiary of Waste Management Inc.
1998: Waste Management purchases the remaining shares of Wheelabrator that it did not previously own.
2001: Wheelabrator reaches the milestone of converting 100 million tons of municipal solid waste into energy.

proach enabled the company to maintain consistently high performance from its plants.

By this time, Wheelabrator Technologies was poised for further growth and was often cited by analysts as a promising company. Virtually no other company had as much experience in gaining public support for waste disposal systems or as much expertise in designing them as Wheelabrator did. With virtually no alternative to landfills, a growing number of cities were likely to seek large-scale waste disposal solutions from Wheelabrator, putting it in an enviable position among its competitors.

In the mid-1990s, Wheelabrator was operating waste-to-energy plants in Connecticut, Florida, Maine, Maryland, Massachusetts, New Hampshire, New Jersey, Pennsylvania, and Washington. Having entered the independent power production (IPP) market in the late 1980s, the company remained heavily focused on constructing and operating small power facilities that utilized waste fuels. Wheelabrator was soon overseeing eight of these plants that were located in California, Florida, Maine, and Pennsylvania.

Meanwhile, Waste Management began to experience financial difficulties which eventually led to faltering profits. While many of its shareholders called for a major restructuring that included the sale of its Wheelabrator unit, Waste Management instead took a different route. In 1997, it made a play for the remaining shares of Wheelabrator. The company's original $15 per share offer was rebuffed by Wheelabrator shareholders who felt the bid undervalued the firm. The dispute was resolved, and in 1998 Waste Management purchased nearly 53 million shares of Wheelabrator—at $16.50 per share.

Wheelabrator entered the new century on solid ground. In 2001, the company reached a significant industry milestone—the conversion of 100 million tons of municipal solid waste into

energy by its 16 waste-to-energy facilities. According to a June 2001 *Waste Treatment Technology News* article, the company's accomplishment stemmed from its "success in developing progressive public/private partnerships; integrating source reduction, recycling, and landfill options; pioneering new energy and environmental technologies; and demonstrating operating procedures that have set high industry standards for efficiency and regulatory compliance."

The company bolstered its holdings in 2003 when it agreed to partner with The Counties of Warren and Washington Industrial Development Agency (IDA) to purchase a waste-to-energy plant in Hudson Falls, New York. The plant, previously run by Foster Wheeler Ltd., had been a cash drain for years and both Wheelabrator and the IDA were optimistic that it would start running at capacity—burning 126,000 tons of trash a year—after the takeover was complete.

With the leading provider of waste management services in North America as its parent, Wheelabrator was well positioned for future growth during this time period. The demand for environmentally friendly and alternative methods to managing solid waste would no doubt continue to increase in the future—and along with it, growth opportunities for the company in the years to come.

Principal Competitors

Allied Waste Industries Inc.; Republic Services Inc.; Waste Industries USA Inc.

Further Reading

"After Years of Losses, Trash-to-Energy Plant in Hudson Falls, N.Y., Is Sold," *Knight Ridder/Tribune Business News*, October 3, 2003.
Cook, James, "Not in Anybody's Backyard," *Forbes*, November 25, 1988.
——, "Garbage into Gold," *Forbes*, January 22, 1990.
Hepp, Mark P., and John M. O'Sullivan, "Improving Efficiency of Energy Production from Wastes," *Solid Waste & Power*, January/February 1992.
Jantzef, Monica F., "Bresco, Three Years Later," *Waste Age*, October 1988.
Luoma, Jon R., "Using New Incinerators, Cities Convert Garbage into Energy," *New York Times*, August 2, 1988.
"A Sweetened Bid for Wheelabrator," *New York Times*, December 9, 1997, p. D4.
Tritschler, Don, "Public Schools, Private Interests," *Worcester Business Journal*, January 6–19, 1992.
"Waste Management Turns on the Compactor," *Business Week*, November 24, 1997.
"Waste Management/Wheelabrator Merger Terms," *Haznews*, January 1, 1998.
"Wheelabrator Marks Milestone," *Waste Treatment Technology News*, June 2001.
Zemba, Stephen G., and Laura C. Green, "Perspectives on Mercury," *Solid Waste & Power*, May/June 1992.

—John Simley
—update: Christina M. Stansell

The White House, Inc.

6711 Baymeadow Drive
Glen Burnie, Maryland 21060
U.S.A.
Telephone: (410) 487-7747
Fax: (410) 487-4688
Web site: http://www.whiteandblack.com

Wholly Owned Subsidiary of Chico's FAS, Inc.
Founded: 1985
Employees: 693
Sales: $67 million (2003)
NAIC: 448120 Women's Clothing Stores

The White House, Inc. is a women's apparel retailer that operates more than 100 stores under the ''White House/Black Market'' banner. The company's stores carry only white-colored and black-colored merchandise. Product selection at the stores, which average 1,800 square feet, includes day and evening wear, lingerie, handbags, jewelry, and other accessories. The company's stores are located in 30 states, Puerto Rico, and the Virgin Islands.

A Single Store Opens in 1985

Richard D. Sarmiento spent most of his adult life working in a hotel before his entrepreneurial desires found expression. For 15 years, Sarmiento worked for Hyatt Hotels, serving the last five years of his career with the hotel giant as the general manager of Hyatt Regency Inner Harbor in Baltimore, Maryland. Sarmiento decided to start his own business while he was acting as the Hyatt Regency's general manager, an arrangement that would give him the security of stable employment while he navigated the precarious waters of entrepreneurship. Sarmiento enjoyed immediate success with his new business primarily because of its unique concept, but this concept alone was not the impetus for its creation. Sarmiento was motivated by a location rather than a concept, convinced that a business situated in Baltimore's Harborplace would fare well. At first, he wanted to open a lingerie store in the Gallery, a mall located at Harborplace, but the slated debut of a Victoria's Secret in the mall forced Sarmiento to search

for another business idea. For help, he turned to the mall's developer and owner, The Rouse Corporation.

The format underpinning The White House's success was conceived at a meeting between Sarmiento and executives at Rouse. During the meeting, the idea of a women's clothing boutique selling only white apparel was proposed, an idea that Sarmiento viewed with some skepticism. ''At first,'' he said in a July 5, 1991 interview with the *Baltimore Business Journal*, ''I wondered what's going to happen once Labor Day comes? Will everyone stop wearing white?'' Sarmiento's initial trepidation was not enough to keep him from moving forward, however. With a $35,000 loan from Sovran Bank, he opened his store in 1985, a 286-square-foot boutique named The White House. On the store's racks and shelves, the only items available were white or in shades of white. Although the store featured modestly priced merchandise, the store catered to an upscale clientele, with sweaters and leather items priced as high as $700.

Sarmiento's store performed extremely well from the start, finding a receptive audience among women in their 30s and 40s. Although the first, small store was successful, Sarmiento had a difficult time convincing others that the store's success was attributable to more than mere novelty. ''People were still telling me it wouldn't work,'' he remarked in a September 2002 interview with *Chain Store Age*, ''but I felt sure I had stumbled across what could be a national chain.'' Sarmiento's conviction led him to make what he described as one of the most difficult decisions of his life. In 1986, a year after starting out, he decided to give The White House his full attention. He resigned from the Hyatt Regency and funneled his retirement savings and assets into his burgeoning business. By the following year, there were three stores under his control. Together, the stores generated $700,000 in sales for the year.

Sarmiento's financial commitment to his company paid dividends. By 1989, his stores generated nearly $2 million in sales. By the following year, there were stores in Maryland, Washington, D.C., New Jersey, South Carolina, and Florida. Combined, the stores generated $3.1 million in sales. By this point Sarmiento was thoroughly convinced The White House was ready to take a major step forward, the strength of its format having proven to be more than a passing fad. As Sarmiento would later explain, the novelty of the chain was its strength. "We occupy a narrow niche to be sure," he said in his September 2002 interview with *Chain Store Age*. "But that niche makes us memorable and unique. It gives us a positioning advantage. And in today's competitive climate, any advantage you have is very powerful. People remember our store."

Expansion and Merchandise Diversification in the 1990s

At the beginning of the 1990s, Sarmiento began his bid to transform his company into a national chain. In 1991, he signed a contract with National Retail Group, a North Carolina-based consulting firm specializing in helping retailers expand. As part of its services, National Retail helped retailers select markets for expansion, pinpoint sites, and negotiate with developers. When Sarmiento hired National Retail, he had ten stores in operation. Disparately sized, the stores ranged from a 372-square-foot store in the Georgetown neighborhood of Washington, D.C. to a 1,450-square-foot store in Cherry Hill, New Jersey. On average, Sarmiento's stores generated $600 in sales per square foot. As Sarmiento and National Retail plotted The White House's expansion, new stores were expected to measure between 1,000 square feet and 1,200 square feet. In a departure from the chain's original stores, the new stores would focus on selling merchandise that retailed for between $60 and $100, eschewing the expensive $700 sweaters found in the company's stores during the 1980s.

Sarmiento's plans for national expansion were ambitious. To the ten stores in operation in mid-1991, he planned to add seven new locations. By 1996, he anticipated presiding over a chain of 60 stores located in California, Arizona, and Texas, among other new markets. For the first wave of expansion, new store locations were slated for Orlando and Boca Raton, Florida; Charleston, South Carolina; Charlotte and Durham, North Carolina; Menlo Park, New Jersey; and Bethesda, Maryland. "There is always a risk in expanding, but there also are opportunities," Sarmiento said in his July 5, 1991 interview with the *Baltimore Business Journal*. "We have the opportunity to make some good real estate deals now and get some construction allowances. We are not going to bring in a lot of new capital and you can't get financing. We are taking whatever profits and cash flow we have and putting it back into the company."

Sarmiento followed through with his plans to expand nationally. As he did so, the blossoming chain registered rousing

success, attracting customers who were intrigued by the all-white day and evening apparel, lingerie, jewelry, handbags, and other accessories. In 1995, after a decade of selling merchandise exclusively in shades of white, Sarmiento launched a new retail format, dubbing the concept "Black Market." As its name suggested, Black Market dealt exclusively in black-colored merchandise, representing an exact contrast to The White House chain. The same year Sarmiento introduced the new concept, he experimented with housing the two concepts under one roof. Not long after seeing that the experiment worked, the company began converting its existing stores to the White House/Black Market combination concept.

Sarmiento failed to meet his projected goal of 60 units by 1996, but the shortfall did not reflect the chain's waning strength. By the end of the 1990s, there were 50 stores comprising the chain, which generated an estimated $33 million in annual revenue. The company had stores operating in 14 states, with plans calling for a foray into San Juan, Puerto Rico. The entry into Puerto Rico represented one aspect of the company's expansion plans at the end of the decade. For 15 years, Sarmiento had managed to finance expansion without converting to public ownership. Capital had been secured through private investments and by investing profits back into the company, enabling Sarmiento to direct the company as he wished, free from having to please shareholders and analysts. He planned to keep the company private as he looked ahead to the 21st century, but his desire to stay out of the public spotlight did not seem to dilute his ambitions for growth. In mid-1999, aided by a $5.6 million venture capital investment from Invesco and the Philips Smith Specialty Retail Group, Sarmiento announced he intended to double the number of his stores within the ensuing 30 months.

As the 20th century turned to the 21st century, and a weak economic climate shackled commercial growth, Sarmiento's chain expanded robustly. New stores opened in numerous markets, enjoying encouraging success. The chain's format, which by this point constituted primarily the combined White House and Black Market concept, was embraced by legions of customers. The stores offered new merchandise three times a week, opting for variety rather than depth in their inventories. The parade of white and black items appealed to many women, enabling Sarmiento to expand his chain to 100 stores by mid-2002, only slightly behind his projected schedule. Sarmiento achieved his goal without straining the company's resources, but by 2003 he wanted more. The desire to expand persisted, prompting Sarmiento to consider new ways to finance the expansion of his company.

New Ownership in the 21st Century

Sarmiento wanted more stores and a bigger distribution center. To fulfill his desire, Sarmiento decided the best option was to convert to public ownership. By May 2003, the company had announced it intended to complete an initial public offering (IPO) of stock, hoping to raise as much as $50 million to fuel its growth. With the anticipated proceeds from the stock offering, Sarmiento planned to open 22 stores in 2003 and between 25 and 30 stores in 2004. The proposed public offering excited the retail sector, which had not seen an IPO completed by a retailer in more than a year. As onlookers waited and watched, pegging the health of retail, to a certain extent, on investors' reaction to

The White House's IPO, their vigilance turned out to be in vain. Sarmiento did not complete his company's IPO, but he did cede ultimate control of his firm to others.

The White House came close to completing its IPO in July 2003 when an interested suitor made its proposal. Fort Myers, Florida-based Chico's FAS Inc., an apparel retailer with 415 stores, had considered acquiring The White House several times before Sarmiento filed with the Securities and Exchange Commission (SEC) for an IPO. Chico's board of directors shied from acquiring Sarmiento's business because it felt the timing was bad, but when The White House filed for its IPO, Chico's board realized that time was running out. Furthermore, the details revealed in The White House's regulatory papers filed with the SEC gave Chico's management a clear look at Sarmiento's operations. "The IPO filing really led to increased exposure for The White House within the potential buyer stratosphere that included Chico's," an industry observer noted in the September 15, 2003 issue of *Investment Dealers' Digest.*

In the late summer of 2003, Chico's made Sarmiento a tantalizing offer. The $531 million-in-sales Florida company offered $90 million for Sarmiento's $67 million-in-sales chain. In the August 1, 2003 issue of *Knight Ridder/Tribune Business News,* Scott Edmonds, Chico's president and chief operating officer, remarked, "It is clear to us The White House has a proven store model and we are convinced that there should be a tremendous fit with our organization from a strategic, financial, cultural, and operational viewpoint." Sarmiento was enthused as well, declaring in the August 1, 2003 issue of the *Daily Record,* "This is just a great marriage of two companies. The merger will help The White House on the marketing side and get us where we want to go faster." The transaction was concluded in September 2003.

As the White House plotted its future course, its merger with Chico's promised a continuation of the chain's expansion. For Chico's, the corporate marriage helped it broaden its customer base because its typical customer was 15 years older than the typical customer at Sarmiento's chain. For The White House, the union promised a spate of new store openings. Initial plans called for the opening of eight White House/Black Market stores by the end of 2003 and 25 to 30 new stores in 2004. Edmonds saw the potential for between 400 and 500 stores. As The White House prepared for its 20th anniversary and the years beyond, further expansion promised to extend the company's unique merchandising mix to a bevy of new markets. Sarmiento remained in charge after the merger, managing the company as a separate division of Chico's. Although The White House was a distinct entity, the presence of its parent company provided the marketing sophistication and the financial resources to transform Sarmiento's entrepreneurial creation into one of the nation's largest apparel retailers.

Principal Competitors

Ann Taylor Stores Corporation; Donna Karan International Inc.; Liz Claiborne, Inc.

Further Reading

"Are IPOs Still a No-Go?," *Investment Dealers' Digest*, September 15, 2003.

Butler, Stacey, "Sarmiento Hoping White Is the Hot Color of the 1990s," *Baltimore Business Journal*, July 5, 1991, p. 5.

De Marco, Donna, "Retailer to Buy Glen Burnie, Md.-Based Black-and-White Clothing Firm," *Knight Ridder/Tribune Business News,* August 1, 2003.

——, "The Washington Times Retail and Hospitality Column," *Knight Ridder/Tribune Business News*, May 26, 2003.

Dickens, Patrice, "The White House Inc. Merges with Chico's FAS Inc.," *Daily Record*, August 1, 2003, p. 5.

Hancock, Jay, "The Baltimore Sun Jay Hancock Column," *Knight Ridder/Tribune Business News*, June 15, 2003.

Jarboe, Kathleen Johnston, "Women's Apparel Chain, The White House, Files for Public Offering," *Daily Record*, June 25, 2003, p. 3.

Mirabella, Lorraine, "The White House Chain Plans Initial Public Offering," *Knight Ridder/Tribune Business News*, May 24, 2003.

Much, Marilyn, "Chico's FAS Inc. Fort Myers, Florida; Retailer Eyes Younger Crowd with Purchase," *Investor's Business Daily*, September 17, 2003, p. A08.

Skokna, Christopher, "Retailer Speeds Growth," *Baltimore Business Journal*, May 21, 1999, p. 1.

Weitzman, Jennifer, "The White House Inc. Files with SEC for $50M IPO," *WWD*, May 27, 2003, p. 12.

Wilson, Marianne, "No Gray Areas," *Chain Store Age*, September 2002, p. 57.

—Jeffrey L. Covell

Wilkinson Sword Ltd.

Sword House
Totteridge Road, High Wycombe
Bucks HP13 6EJ
United Kingdom
Telephone: +44 (0) 1494 533 300
Web site: http://www.shaving.com

Wholly Owned Subsidiary of Energizer Holdings Inc.
Incorporated: 1772
Employees: 3,500
Sales: $650 million (2002)
NAIC: 332211 Cutlery and Flatware (Except Precious)
Manufacturing; 325620 Toilet Preparation
Manufacturing

Wilkinson Sword Ltd., formerly known as Schick-Wilkinson Sword in the United States, is the world's second-largest maker of razor blades and shaving accessories and other personal care products, a market that has dominated the brand's focus since the company's invention of the stainless steel blade in the 1950s. However, the company is one of the world's most distinguished names in sword-making history, and that operation continues to manufacture ceremonial and commemorative swords in its United Kingdom workshop. Wilkinson Sword was also long associated with high-quality gardening shears and scissors, which are manufactured under license by Finland's Fiskars. The Wilkinson Sword brand has undergone a number of ownership changes, including its purchase by battery maker Energizer Holdings in 2003. With new owner, Wilkinson Sword has prepared a new thrust at its arch rival, Gillette, which also owns rival battery maker Duracell. In May 2003, Wilkinson Sword debuted its newest razor innovation, the four-bladed Quattro.

From Guns to Swords in the 19th Century

Wilkinson Sword's origins lay in the late 18th century, when Henry Nock founded a gun manufacturing company in London, in 1772. Having learned the gun maker's trade in Birmingham, Nock quickly established himself as a noted innovator of the day. Among Nock's achievements were the "screwless" lock, and a number of so-called volley weapons capable of firing several rounds at the same time. One of these featured a seven-barrel charge and won Nock an order for 600 rifles from the British navy.

Nock was joined by his son-in-law, James Wilkinson, in the 1890s and by the turn of the century the company had begun producing its own rifle bayonets as well. Nock, in the meantime, worked closely with the British military to develop new gun and rifle designs. A turning point in the company's fortunes came before the end of the century, when Nock was commissioned to produce an order of 10,000 flintlocks for the British army. The order, at the time the largest ever placed by the British government, allowed Nock to adopt the slogan as "the Supreme Gun Maker of the Age."

In 1804, Nock's company received a new honor when it was appointed as the official gum maker to King George III. Although Nock himself died that year, James Wilkinson took over the business and the royal appointment. Over the next decades, the company remained a chief supplier to the British military, as well as the exclusive gun maker for Great Britain's noble classes.

James Wilkinson passed along the company to his son, Henry Wilkinson, in 1824. The younger Wilkinson appeared to have inherited his grandfather's spirit of innovation, as well as a strong business sense. One of Henry Wilkinson's most important moves was to relocate the business to Pall Mall—next door to its major customer, the Board of Ordnance. Wilkinson also continued Nock's policy of working closely with that board's Master General to develop new weapons designs.

Yet Henry Wilkinson also turned his inventive interest to sword-making. Because swords of the period had become prone to breaking, Wilkinson began investigating methods not only for strengthening the blades but also for making them more resilient. By the 1840s, Wilkinson had succeeded in improving the company's sword and bayonet designs.

Aiming for the assurance of high quality, Wilkinson then invented a testing machine, called the Eprouvette, in 1844. Using this machine, Wilkinson, by then joined by general manager and son-in-law John Latham, was able to test each of the company's swords against conditions surpassing even those

Key Dates:

1772: Henry Nock sets up gun maker's workshop in London.
1804: Nock becomes royal gun maker to King George III; James Wilkinson, Nock's son-in-law, takes over business after Nock's death; begins production of bayonets.
1824: Henry Wilkinson, James' son, takes over business and begins developing stronger blade production techniques.
1844: The Eprouvette sword-testing machine debuts.
1858: John Latham takes over business after Wilkinson retires.
1889: Company formally incorporates as Wilkinson Sword.
1890: Company begins production of razors.
1896: The first safety razor design, the Pall Mall, is introduced.
1920: Garden shear production commences.
1956: First stainless steel razor blade is introduced.
1961: The Teflon-coated stainless steel blade is launched.
1964: Wilkinson Sword goes public on London Stock Exchange.
1973: Acquires Scripto in diversification move; British Match acquires Wilkinson Sword, forming Wilkinson Match.
1978: Allegheny International acquires Wilkinson Match and breaks company up into its components.
1986: Wilkinson Sword sold to Swedish Match.
1988: Swedish Match is sold to Stora Kopparberg.
1989: Stora Kopparberg sells off consumer products division, including Swedish Match and Wilkinson Sword, to Eemland Holdings consortium.
1992: Eemland sells off Wilkinson Sword to Warner Lambert, which forms Schick-Wilkinson Sword.
2003: Schick-Wilkinson Sword is sold to Energizer Holdings.

found on the field of battle. Blades that passed the Eprouvette were then marked, certified, and numbered.

Wilkinson's commitment to quality was recognized when the company was named the official Sword and Gun Maker to Queen Victoria. The company began picking up a number of other illustrious customers, including the Prince of Wales, the King of Naples, and other members of the British and European noble classes.

Sword-making was to provide the company's lifeline after the middle of the century, when, in 1857, the British government took over the entirety of its firearm production needs. The following year, after Wilkinson retired, Latham—who was not only a sword maker, but also a fencing enthusiast—led the company to focus exclusively on sword-making.

Growth and Diversification in the 20th Century

Wilkinson's production remained relatively modest until the 1880s. The high bending and breakage rates of the British Army's bayonets during fighting in the Sudan in 1885 were blamed for a large number of deaths there, leading to public outcry. In order to replace the blades, the Ordnance Board turned toward Wilkinson, contracting for an order of 150,000 bayonets. The order encouraged the company to expand its production facilities, and by 1899, Wilkinson had opened a second production plant, in Chelsea.

By then, Latham had added a new partner, introducing the Randolph family as a major force in the company's future growth. In 1889, the company formally incorporated, becoming Wilkinson Sword. Soon after, the company began diversifying its business. In 1890, Wilkinson Sword started to produce cut-throat, or straight-edge, razors. The company also began to develop other cutting edges, and particularly, one of the first safety razor designs. By 1896, the company had hit upon a new design featuring a hollow, rounded singe-edged blade. That razor became known as the Pall Mall, launched in 1898. Its success enabled the company to expand its production again, with the opening of a plant in Acton.

While cutting edges seemed a natural outgrowth of the company's long experience in sword-making, Wilkinson Sword's diversified interests ranged widely in the decades leading to World War II. In the early years of the 20th century, Wilkinson Sword added a number of new products, including bicycles, typewriters, motorcycles, and automobiles. By the 1930s, the company had parlayed this production expertise into a new product category, that of fire and safety systems for aircraft, under a licensing agreement made in 1934 with Graviner Manufacturing Company. In support of that activity, the company built a new manufacturing plant in Coinbrook in 1939.

Cutting edges remained a company staple, however. During World War I, the company's production became vital to the British war effort, with a contract for two million bayonets. Following the war, the company turned its production of cutting edges to a new area, that of pruning sheers and gardening equipment. Wilkinson Sword soon grew into the United Kingdom's leading manufacturer in this market.

Meanwhile, sword production had become a fading sector. By the outbreak of World War II, the bayonet had become more and more outmoded, and Wilkinson Sword's orders for that conflict amounted to just 10,000 bayonets. Steel shortages throughout the conflict also limited the company's razor blade production. Yet Wilkinson Sword remained a highly respected name in sword-making. The company crafted, among others, the sword presented to Josef Stalin by Winston Churchill after Russia's defeat of the German army at Stalingrad in 1943.

Postwar Stainless Steel Pioneer

Carbon steel shortages continued to slow Wilkinson Sword's production in the years immediately following World War II. In the 1950s, however, the company began developing a new generation of shaving blades using stainless steel. For this effort, the company formed a joint-venture with Germany's Osberghaus KG, based in Solingen. By 1955, the partners had begun full-scale manufacturing of the world's first stainless steel blade, which was launched onto the consumer market the following year.

Wilkinson Sword, which until then had largely limited itself to the United Kingdom, now began to attract attention from the international market as well. This trend picked up strongly in the early 1960s, with the launch of a new and revolutionary Wilkinson Sword blade in 1961. This blade featured a thin Teflon coating that vastly improved its comfort and safety, and thrust Wilkinson into the top ranks of the world's shaving accessories makers.

By the middle of the 1960s, Wilkinson Sword blades were being sold in more than 50 countries, and exports had risen to a more than 40 percent share of the company's sales. Razor blades had by then come to represent the largest share of the group's revenues, and Wilkinson Sword now began the process of redefining itself as a personal care accessories manufacturer.

In order to meet the rising demand for its blades, Wilkinson Sword acquired a factory outside of Newcastle-upon-Tyne. The company, which had remained under the control of the Latham and Randolph families, also prepared a public offering, made in June 1964. By the following year, the company's exports had already swelled to some 60 percent of its annual sales, supported by subsidiaries in Germany, the United States, Canada, and elsewhere. By then, shaving products alone represented 75 percent of the company's revenues. This growth also enabled Wilkinson Sword to merge its aircraft fire and safety systems division, which had continued to produce under the Graviner name, with Graviner Manufacturing in July 1964.

Despite being the first in the coated blade category, Wilkinson was soon overtaken by its far-larger U.S. competitors, which then included Schick, Persona, and Gillette. The company found itself dwarfed in the race for market leadership; indeed, Gillette's advertising budget alone was larger than Wilkinson Sword's total revenues.

New Owners in the 1970s and 1980s

Wilkinson Sword attempted to fight back in two different directions. On the one hand, the company continued its research and development effort, which resulted in the launch of the first bonded blades—razor blades encased in a plastic housing—in 1970. This development briefly gave Wilkinson a new boost in the international shaving market. Yet once again the company was caught by its rivals, which released similar products.

On the other hand, the company attempted to diversify. At the beginning of 1973, Wilkinson Sword took over the U.S. manufacturer Scripto, which had been a leading name in disposable pens. Wilkinson Sword began planning to release its own line of disposable lighters, under the Scripto brand name.

By the end of that year, however, Wilkinson Sword had instead found new owners itself. In May 1973, following several months of negotiations, Wilkinson Sword announced that it had agreed to be purchased by British Match for £19.4 million. That company traced its origins back to 1843 and the founding of Bryant & May, which had begun importing matches in the 1850s. Bryant & May formed a partnership with Masters, owned by Swedish Match, in 1927, forming British Match Corporation. Then, in 1953, British Match acquired Bryant & May, as well as Swedish Match's U.K. holdings, a move which gave the Swedish concern a 33 percent stake in British Match.

Following the Wilkinson Sword acquisition, the enlarged company renamed itself as Wilkinson Match.

Wilkinson Match proved no match for its U.S. competitors, however, and by the middle of the 1970s, the company had decided to pull out of the U.S. market and focus instead on its stronger position in the European market. Wilkinson Sword as a brand began to dwindle, and its market share, once nearly 8 percent in the United States, slipped to below 1 percent by the 1980s.

Nonetheless, the company caught the eye of Pittsburgh-based Allegheny International, which had begun a diversification drive in the late 1970s. In 1978, Allegheny bought up Wilkinson Match, breaking it up into its component businesses, including the Scripto and Wilkinson Sword units.

Under Allegheny, however, Wilkinson initially fared little better. By 1980, the company had been stripped of its own sales force, and marketing was placed under Scripto instead. Lacking marketing support, Wilkinson Sword's market share continued to slip into the mid-1980s. By 1984, the company appeared to have hit rock bottom, after Scripto was sold off to Japan's Tokai. That move left Wilkinson Sword with no sales and marketing support at all.

A new era for the company began in 1986, however, when Allegheny sold Wilkinson Sword to Swedish Match. Two years later, that company was itself acquired by Stora Kopparberg, also based in Sweden, which, in 1989, sold off the Swedish Match consumer products division, including Wilkinson Sword, to the Netherlands-based consortium, Eemland Holdings. One of Eemland's main partners was Gillette, which had taken a 22 percent stake in Eemland in what was seen as an attempt to gain control—and bury—Wilkinson Sword.

Yet Wilkinson Sword's future was rescued in 1992 when a mergers and monopolies commission ordered Gillette to dispose of its stake in Eemland. The following year, Eemland sold Wilkinson Sword to Warner-Lambert, which had owned the Schick razor brand since the 1970s.

Ownership Changes for the New Century

Throughout its ownership upheavals, Wilkinson Sword had continued to develop new products, including its successful Ultra Glide line of shavers in the late 1980s. The company also launched a line of disposable lighters under the Cricket brand name, although that operation was sold off in 1990.

In the 1990s, Wilkinson Sword—which by then had shed its gardening tools business to Fiskars—began to focus its growth efforts on the personal care market, developing new razor lines, as well as other products, including manicure and pedicure sets. The company also continued to develop new razor technologies, resulting in 1999 with a new diamond coated blade, the FX Diamond. Under Warner-Lambert, Wilkinson Sword was combined with Schick, forming Schick-Wilkinson Sword.

In this arrangement, the company's products were marketed under the Schick name in North America and elsewhere, including Japan, where Schick maintained a strong market presence, while Wilkinson Sword became the group's brand name for its core European market. The new entity claimed the world's number two spot in the razor market, with an 18 percent share of the global market and sales of more than $620 million by 2001.

Wilkinson Sword's ownership changes had not ended. In 2000, Pfizer acquired Warner-Lambert in a hostile takeover. Although Pfizer continued to invest in Schick-Wilkinson Sword, its interests clearly lay elsewhere, and in June 2002, the company announced its interest in finding buyers for the division. In the meantime, Wilkinson Sword maintained its tradition as one of the world's pre-eminent sword makers, crafting the ceremonial sword for the Queen Mother's Jubilee celebration that year.

The search for new owners reached an end in March 2003, when Energizer Holdings, makers of the Eveready and Energizer brands, agreed to pay $930 million for Schick-Wilkinson Sword. For Energizer, formed in 2000 from a spinoff from Rahlston Purina, the moved marked its first diversification effort. For Wilkinson Sword, the new ownership promised a new era as one of the world's leading shaving and personal care products manufacturers. Still, Wilkinson Sword remained true to its heritage as a cutting-edge innovator. In May 2003, the company launched its latest development, the four-bladed Quatro safety razor system.

Principal Competitors

Gillette Company; Wella AG; BIC SA; Fiskars Oy; WKI Holding Company Inc.

Further Reading

De Jonquieres, Guy, "Facing Up to the Costs of a Close Shave," *Financial Times*, October 22, 1992, p. 21.

"Energizer to Buy Schick-Wilkinson Sword for $930M," *St. Louis Business Journal*, January 21, 2003.

Jones, Richard, "A Cut Above," *People Management*, July 15, 1999, p. 40.

"Looking Sharp: The Wilkinson Sword Story," *Western Daily Press*, January 3, 2003.

Roskin, Gary, "A Wilkinson Sword for the Queen's Jubilee," *JCK's High-Volume Jeweler*, May 2002, p. 62.

"Wilkinson Sword Plans Four-Blade Razor Launch," *Marketing Week*, May 15, 2003.

—M.L. Cohen

William Grant & Sons Ltd.

Phoenix Crescent
Strathclyde Bu
Bellshill ML4 3AN
United Kingdom
Telephone: (+44) 1698 843843
Fax: (+44) 1698 844788
Web site: http://www.glenfiddich.com

Private Company
Incorporated: 1886
Employees: 915
Sales: £400 million ($700 million)(2002 est.)
NAIC: 312140 Distilleries

William Grant & Sons Ltd. is one of the world's leading producers of Scotch whisky, ranking number four overall. Yet its flagship Glenfiddich brand is the undisputed leader in the more exclusive single-malt category, claiming nearly 40 percent of all single malt Scotch sales worldwide. While Grant's competitors include some of the world's largest diversified drinks groups, including Diageo and Seagrams, the largest part of the company's operations remain focused on its whisky production, which, in addition to Glenfiddich, include the 100-year-old The Balvenie brand of Scotch whiskey and, since 2002, Canada's Gibson's Finest blended whisky. The company also produces private label Scotch whiskies, a market which provides approximately 20 percent of the company's revenues. Despite its emphasis on whisky, Grant has diversified its portfolio somewhat at the turn of the 20th century, buying three rum brands from Diageo at the end of 2002 and launching a fourth, Sailor Jerry, in 2003, and acquiring Iceland vodka group Polstar. The company also hold a 30 percent stake in Scottish rival Highland Distillers and its Famous Grouse and Mac Callan brands. Wholly owned by the founding Grant Gordon family, William Grant & Sons remains a resolutely private company. Sales have been estimated to top £400 million ($700 million) in the early 2000s. In 2003, CEO Patrick Thomas—who had been the first CEO from outside the Grant family in the company's history—stepped down from the post, as the family once again decided to assume control of the group's operations.

Founding Scotch History in the 19th Century

Born in 1839 in Dufftown, Scotland, William Grant first went to work at the age of seven herding cattle on lands belonging to the Duke of Fife. Grant went on to apprentice as a cobbler, but instead went to work as a clerk, before becoming a bookkeeper for the Mortlach distillery. It was there that Grant learned the art of distilling, remaining in the position for some 20 years, and eventually becoming the distillery's clerk and manager.

Throughout his career at Mortlach, Grant saved up his earnings—which reached no more than 200 pounds per year. Finally, in 1886, Grant had saved enough to go into business on his own. Together with his wife and their seven sons and two daughters, Grant purchased a plot of land in Speyside, near the River Fiddich. For a little less than 120 pounds sterling, Grant acquired a secondhand still and other equipment from the Cardhu Distillery. Construction began that same year, with all work being carried out by Grant, his sons, and a stone mason; by 1887, the distillery had begun production. Grant named his distillery Glenfiddich, Gaelic for "Valley of the Deer." The company's stag's head logo was later to become famous around the world.

Grant's whisky, using spring water from Robbie Dru, quickly achieved a popular following in Scotland, attracting other distillers to the Speyside region. While much of the Scottish market at the time consisted of blended whiskies, combining grain and malt whiskies, Grant's whisky remained a purely malted whisky, produced in small quantities in single barrels—almost a century before the creation of a true single-malt variety. The rising popularity of Scottish whisky in general led to a boom in the number of distilleries in operation as the 19th century drew to a close.

Grant too took part in the expansion of the Scotch market when, in 1892, he bought Balvenie Castle—previously owned by Grant's former employer, the Duke of Fife—and surrounding farmlands. Grant set to work converting the castle itself into a distillery, which began producing its own, unique whiskey in 1893. The Balvenie, as the brand became known, remained one of the only whiskies to boast not only having its own malting plant but also growing its own barley.

Until the end of the century, much of Grant's production was sold to third-party blenders, such as Pattison Limited, then the

Company Perspectives:

Not much has changed at the Glenfiddich Distillery since the first spirit ran from the stills on Christmas Day, 1887. It is still independent; owned and run by the fifth generation of the same family. Our founder, William Grant, aspired to create "the best dram in the valley". He achieved it, and we maintain it—through a single-minded dedication to craftsmanship and quality throughout every stage of production.

leading whisky blender and distributor in the country. Yet the huge growth in the number of new distilleries at the turn of the century had led the industry into over-production, resulting in financial collapse. Pattison itself was one of the early victims of the whisky market crash, declaring bankruptcy in 1898. By 1899, the crash had claimed a growing number of distilleries.

William Grant & Sons too was hit hard by the crash, losing its largest customer and finding itself saddled by debt. Yet Grant saw opportunity in the turmoil of the Scottish whisky market and decided to expand his business from a simple distillery to a complete wholesale, blending and distribution operation. Grant was joined by his sons, and also by son-in-law Charles Gordon, who became the company's sales agents. In 1903, the company set up a whisky storehouse in Glasgow, and by 1904, Grant had established its first export office, in Blackburn, in Lancashire, England.

One year later, Grant began exporting to Canada after discovering that the country's High Commissioner was a distant relative. After setting up an export office in Canada, Grant also opened an office in the United States. While John Grant was building up the company's North American operations, Charles Gordon traveled to the Far East on a year-long tour starting in 1909, introducing the Glenfiddich brand throughout India, Singapore, Hong Kong, Shanghai, and Japan, before turning to Australia and New Zealand. Gordon next brought the Glenfiddich brand to the European continent, opening sales offices in Rotterdam, Hamburg, and in Scandinavia. By 1914, the company had more than 60 sales offices, supporting its exports to 30 countries.

Rationing efforts during World War I coincided with increasing prohibitionist sentiment to cut into the growth of the Scottish whisky industry. A major blow, at least in the short term, was the passage of the Immature Spirits Act in 1915, which barred sales of whisky that had been aged for less than two (later three) years. While the Act spelled the end of large numbers of distillers, it would later provide one of the major selling points for Scottish whisky. Nonetheless, continued raw materials shortages during the war put an end to production in 1917.

Grant did not resume production again until 1919 and the following year faced a new threat to its business, as prohibition sentiment swept across many of its major markets. While Prohibition was enacted most famously in the United States, the ban on alcohol extended into Canada, most of Scandinavia, Belgium, and Russia as well. The drop in whisky sales nearly wiped out the Scottish industry; by the end of Prohibition, only six Scottish distilleries remained in operation, including both the Glenfiddich and Balvenie distilleries.

William Grant himself did not live to see the end of Prohibition. By the time of his death in 1923, a new generation of the Grant Gordon family, and in particular William Grant Gordon, had joined the company. The younger Grant Gordon persuaded the company to increase its production despite the drop off in sales. In this way, the company was prepared to meet the surge in demand as countries began dropping their prohibition efforts in the early 1920s. In this way, Grant not only edged out potential newcomers, it also was able to present a higher-quality whisky that had spent more years aging.

Postwar Market Leader

Grant opened a London office in 1927, and restored its Scandinavian export markets soon after. The repeal of Prohibition in the United States in 1933 brought a new peak in demand and the Glenfiddich brand had already begun to assert its dominance as the world's best-selling Scotch whisky.

World War II once again brought a halt to whisky production, with barley diverted as a crucial food crop. Yet Winston Churchill correctly recognized the importance of Scotch whisky as a valuable source of foreign currency, stating, in 1944: "On no account reduce the amount of barley for whisky. This takes years to mature and is an invaluable export and dollar producer. Having regard to all our other difficulties about exports, it would be most improvident not to preserve this characteristic British element of ascendancy." Through Churchill's intercession, distillers were once again given an allotment of barley, and production could continue. In order to counter the coal shortage, Grant took to burning peat—which in turn added a distinctive flavor to the company's wartime production.

The postwar period saw the emergence of a new and stronger worldwide demand for Scotch whiskeys. Faced with a fresh rise in the number of Scottish distilleries, Grant turned to marketing for the first time. In 1957, the company commissioned a new bottle for its flagship Glenfiddich brand. Designed by Hans Schleger, the new bottle featured a highly distinctive triangular shape that made it instantly recognizable among the host of whisky brands and other types of alcohol on the shelves.

The 1960s brought a fresh marketing coup. If most of the whisky sold in the world remained of the blended type, a growing number of connoisseurs had begun to discover the single-malt type preferred by the Scots themselves. While a blended whisky might be composed of whiskies from several different distilleries, a single malt was the product of a single distillery—and often from a single barrel. In 1963, William Grant & Sons recognized the marketability of this whisky type, and became the first to market its whisky on the export market under the new denomination.

Grant also sought to increase its control over its distribution network, and in 1964 the company acquired the U.S.-based distributor Popper Morson. In this way, Grant claimed to be the first Scottish distiller to own its U.S. import business. The company's export efforts were later acknowledged during the 1970s, as the Glenfiddich brand became the world's leading Scotch whisky brand.

Glenfiddich remained the company's flagship brand through the 1990s. In that decade, however, the company began stepping up its marketing efforts for its other brand, The Balvenie, which

Key Dates:

1886: Scotsman William Grant builds his own distillery, Glen Fiddich, and is joined by his seven sons.

1887: Glen Fiddich begins production of whisky.

1892: Grant buys Balvenie castle and converts it to a distillery, beginning production of The Balvenie whisky the following year.

1903: Grant enters blending, wholesale and distribution, opening storehouse in Glasgow.

1905: Exports to Canada begin; sales offices in Canada and the United States are established.

1923: William Grant dies; grandson William Grant Gordon convinces company to increase production in spite of Prohibition.

1957: Glenfiddich brand receives new and distinctive triangular bottle design.

1963: William Grant & Sons becomes the first to market its whisky as "single malt" to the export market.

1964: Company acquires its own U.S. importer and distributor, Popper Morson.

1990: New distillery in Kininvie is built to support third-label production business.

1998: Company acquires 30 percent stake in Highland Distillers.

2000: Patrick Thomas is appointed CEO, the first from outside the Grant Gordon family to lead the company.

2002: The portfolio diversifies with acquisition of three rum brands, a Canadian whisky brand, and Iceland's Polstar vodka brand.

2003: Patrick Thomas resigns, and Grant Gordon resumes management control of business.

had become the whisky connoisseur's favorite. At the same time, Grant had built up a strong business as a private label supplier for other brands. In support of this activity, the company built a new distillery, the Kininvie, located in Banffshire near Grant's historical Dufftown home. In the meantime, the company's private label sales encompassed not only blended whiskies, but other categories of alcoholic beverages as well. In this way, the company began producing the vodka for the launch of Virgin Vodka in the early 1990s.

By the mid-1990s, however, Grant had been confronted with the rapid consolidation of the global drinks industry, which saw the emergence of such major players as Seagrams, Diageo, Allied Distillers, and Remy Cointreau. Determined to maintain its status as a privately held, family-owned company, yet hoping to remain competitive, the secretive Grant began opening itself up to outsiders, taking on a number of directors from outside of the family. The company also moved to add to its product range, adding new labels, such as the 15-year-old Solera Reserve, and the 18-year-old Ancient Reserve, both under the Glenfiddich brand. Another new product was Grant's first single-malt whisky liqueur. At the same time, the company began looking for external growth opportunities. After talks to acquire a stake in publicly listed Burn Stewart Distillers failed

to result in agreement in 1997, the company instead acquired a 30 percent stake in rival Highland Distillers, in a partnership with the Edrington Group, which took the other 70 percent of the formerly public company, in 1998.

In 2000, the company appointed Patrick Thomas, from France, as the group's CEO, marking the first time someone from outside of the Grant Gordon family would lead the company. Thomas promptly led the group on a restructuring, and took the Glenfiddich brand into a successful new marketing campaign designed to update its image. Thomas, who had originally joined the company as a director in 1994, also began seeking opportunities for diversifying Grant's product portfolio.

Toward that end, Thomas oversaw a series of brand acquisitions. The first of these included three rum brands held by Diageo and Pernod Ricard, which was followed by the purchase of Gibson's Finest, a Canadian whisky owned by Diageo. At the end of 2002, the group added to its portfolio Iceland's Polstar and its line of flavored and premium vodkas. Following the purchase, the company began preparations to build a new vodka distillery for the brand.

Under Thomas, revenues at William Grant & Sons grew strongly, topping £400 million, with profits topping £40 million. Yet in 2003, the Grant Gordon family decided to take back managerial control, and Patrick Thomas resigned as CEO. As newly appointed chairman Charles Gordon told *The Herald:* "We wish to continue the transition of our family business towards a fully professional organization, focusing on the development of brands and leveraging the enormous advantages of the values and long-term perspective that the family can bring to the business." In this way, the company intended to maintain its tradition as a family company, even as it developed into a diversified drinks group in its own right.

Principal Subsidiaries

Highland Distillers Limited (30%); Maxxium Worldwide B.V.; William Grant and Sons Inc. (United States).

Principal Competitors

Diageo plc; Seagram Company Ltd.; Jim Beam Brands Worldwide Inc.; Irish Distillers Group plc; United Distillers and Vintners Ltd.; Remy Cointreau; Allied Distillers Ltd.; Cantrell and Cochrane Group Ltd.

Further Reading

Charles, Mathew, "A Family Business Shows its Spirit," *Herald Sun* (Melbourne, Australia), October 22, 2001, p. 26.

Fursland, Eileen, and Jane Pickard, "Breaking Tradition Takes Great Bottle," *People Management*, September 12, 1996, p. 34.

Powell, Robert, "Grant & Sons Cheered by Booming Sales," *Herald*, October 16, 2002, p. 21.

Walsh, Dominic, "Whisky Distiller Adds Frenchman to Mix," *Times*, October 25, 2000, p. 31.

——, "William Grant Adds to Range After Shake-Up," *Times*, October 5, 1998, p. 47.

—M.L. Cohen

Winchell's Donut Houses Operating Company, L.P.

2223 Wellington Avenue, Suite 300
Santa Ana, California 92701-3101
U.S.A.
Telephone: (714) 565-1800
Fax: (714) 565-1801
Web site: http://www.winchells.com

Wholly Owned Subsidiary of Shato Holdings, Ltd.
Incorporated: 1948 as Winchell Donut House
Employees: 1,300
Sales: $60 million (2002 est.)
NAIC: 722211 Limited-Service Restaurants

Winchell's Donut Houses Operating Company, L.P. runs a chain of more than 200 doughnut shops that are located in 12 states in the western United States and in scattered countries abroad. The bulk of its stores are in southern California, with more than half operated by franchisees. Winchell's offers more than 30 types of doughnuts, as well as cinnamon rolls, bagels, croissants, muffins, brownies, and cookies, and also serves coffee, juice, soda, and other beverages. The firm is owned by Vancouver, B.C.-based Shato Holdings, Ltd.

Beginnings

The first of Winchell's Donut Houses was opened on October 8, 1948 in Temple City, California, by Verne H. Winchell, a 33-year-old jukebox salesman who had majored in business at Pasadena City College. Though he had originally planned a drive-in hamburger stand, when an identical operation appeared across the street Winchell switched gears and opened a drive-in doughnut and coffee shop instead. A cup of coffee cost a dime and a doughnut was a nickel. Customers could watch doughnuts being made through the shop's windows.

Winchell's concept proved to be a successful one, and in 1949 he opened two additional restaurants in Huntington Park and South Gate, California. Each year afterwards, two or three more outlets were added, and in 1953 the growing chain established its headquarters in the city of Alhambra, along with a facility to prepare doughnut mixes.

In 1961, Winchell's stock began trading on the over-the-counter market; at the same time, the firm was starting to expand into Arizona and Colorado. Two years later, the company moved its headquarters and mix operation to a newly constructed building in South El Monte, California. By this time, Winchell's had begun franchise sales and was opening 30 to 40 new stores per year, while taking in annual revenues of more than $3.6 million.

The year 1964 saw the chain expand into the Pacific Northwest and introduce the apple fritter, a doughnut-like treat which quickly proved popular with customers. In 1966, the United Fruit Company courted the firm and made an offering to buy it for $19 million. However, the deal fell apart at the eleventh hour. By 1967, sales stood at $7.8 million, and annual earnings were more than $1 million.

Merger with Denny's in 1968

In 1968, the company, which now boasted a total of 255 outlets, merged with Denny's Restaurants, Inc. in a stock swap deal worth nearly $30 million. Verne Winchell would continue to manage the doughnut chain, as well as serving on Denny's board of directors. In 1971, Winchell's bought out its franchisees and converted all units to company ownership; the following year, Verne Winchell was named chairman and CEO of Denny's. In 1973, the doughnut division's headquarters and production center were moved to a site near the parent firm's home base of La Mirada, California.

Under Verne Winchell's leadership, both restaurant chains expanded dramatically, and during the 1970s Winchell's Donut Houses grew to 1,000 units. Stores were opened as far away as Japan, Spain, Holland, Korea, and the Philippines, and revenues reached an estimated $200 million per year.

By the end of the decade, some of the firm's locations had become unprofitable, and in 1980 it was announced that 150 of the 968 units then in operation would be closed. That same year, Verne Winchell left Denny's, and several years later he sold his ownership stake for a reported $600 million. In his eight years of managing Denny's, its sales had more than quadrupled, to $680 million. Winchell would go on to pursue interests in real estate and horse breeding, the latter a passion he had indulged as far back as the 1960s with a horse that bore the name "Donut King."

Winchell's Donut Houses' fortunes continued to deteriorate in the 1980s, and 1985 saw another round of store closures in which 91 outlets were shuttered in Illinois, Minnesota, Ohio, and Texas. The company also reintroduced its franchise program, though most sales would consist of conversions of existing units.

The typical investment required of a Winchell's franchisee at this time was less than $100,000, which included a $30,000 fee to the corporation. Six percent of gross sales were also paid back to the company for royalties and advertising. An average outlet grossed $225,000, which yielded a profit of 12 percent. Franchisees were required to take a six-week training program and subsequent refresher courses; they could expect visits from the company's regional consultants to monitor quality. Though 70 percent of Winchell's sales took place before noon, most restaurants remained open round the clock, with business in the overnight hours usually dominated by police officers. New outlets were typically located on a busy street on the side which saw the most traffic during morning rush hour.

In 1985, Denny's returned to private ownership in a leveraged buyout by its management, and the resultant debt led to a spin-off of the Winchell's division in December 1986. Fifty-eight percent of the unit's stock was offered on the New York Stock Exchange, with Denny's keeping a 42 percent stake and majority voting power. The move to a so-called Master Limited Partnership ownership structure was due in part to the tax benefits it offered. After the stock sale, which raised $84 million, the firm became known as Winchell's Donut Houses L.P.

The chain had by now shrunk to 720 company-owned and 22 franchised units, but it remained the second-largest doughnut chain in the United States after industry leader Dunkin' Donuts. It was also the largest on the West Coast, with 466 outlets in California alone. The company had recorded profits of $6.8 million on sales of $180 million for the fiscal year ended in June 1986.

In the months following the stock offering, Winchell's financial picture began to take a sharp turn for the worse. Though the company was introducing new products such as cinnamon rolls and bear claws, and had reached a deal to sell its doughnuts at 600 7-Eleven stores in Los Angeles, per-store sales were dropping and quarterly losses started to mount. In the summer of 1987, four of the firm's board members resigned, and the end of the year saw the departures of president Carl Hass and CEO Donald L. Pierce, who also served as president of Denny's. These events were taking place as Winchell's parent firm was changing ownership yet again, having been purchased by TW Services in July.

By January 1988, Winchell's stock had dropped from its opening price of $18 to less than $4, and 45 more stores were set for closure. As the firm was preparing to report annual losses of $11.5 million on sales of $158.5 million, several groups of investors filed class-action lawsuits against both the company and Denny's and its underwriters, alleging deficiencies in the offering materials.

In the spring of 1988, company veteran James C. Verney was named to lead the ailing Winchell's. One of his first priorities was to address sagging morale among the firm's employees, and he met with workers in groups of ten to listen to their concerns. The financial reports continued to be grim, however, and $12.8 million in losses were recorded on sales of $145 million for the year. By December, the chain had shrunk to 671 outlets in 15 states, 68 of which were franchisee-owned.

Winchell's problems appeared to stem from a variety of factors. While the company blamed increased competition, much of it from small mom-and-pop operators, some of its difficulties were internally generated, according to observers. Under Denny's ownership, the firm had allocated little money to modernizing its restaurants or advertising them, and much of its profits had allegedly been pumped into keeping the parent firm afloat.

Sale to Shato Holdings in 1989

In June 1989, Denny's owner TW Services was sold to Coniston Partners, which shortly afterward sought to jettison the stake it owned in Winchell's. A buyer was found in Shato Holdings, Ltd., a Vancouver, British Columbia-based firm controlled by Canadian multi-millionaire Peter Toigo. Shato owned Coca-Cola Bottling and Kentucky Fried Chicken franchises in British Columbia, a hotel and restaurant catering company, 31 White Spot restaurants, and other hospitality industry properties. After the deal was finalized, Winchell's shareholders would receive $3.80 per Class A share of stock, with Coniston agreeing to forgo compensation for the 1.6 million Class B shares it held.

In December 1989, shortly after the sale had been completed, Shato announced it was selling 263 Donut House stores to Pizza Hut, Inc., which would convert them to drive-through restaurants. The deal was worth nearly $40 million, close to what Shato had reportedly paid for the whole chain. In early 1990, the firm appointed a number of new executives, including a new president, Robert Galastro, who set about trying to improve Winchell's financial picture. Galastro had formerly served as operational vice-president for International House of Pancakes.

The company soon announced several new initiatives to boost revenues. These included adding menu items to expand the restaurants' business beyond the morning rush hour and acquiring a plant in northern California that would ship frozen dough to the chain's outlets, which had heretofore made it from scratch. The plant had been purchased along with the nine unit Rolling Pin Donuts, Inc. chain in March.

In October, a new prototype store was opened that offered seven types of sandwiches, four salads, and nine flavors of frozen Dannon yogurt. Dubbed Winchell's n' More, it featured

Key Dates:

1948: Verne Winchell opens his first doughnut shop in Temple City, California.

1953: A new headquarters/production facility is opened in Alhambra, California.

1961: The company goes public on the over-the-counter market and expands eastward.

1968: Winchell's Donut Houses is acquired by Denny's Restaurants, Inc.

1970s: The chain expands to more than 1,000 stores, including some abroad.

1980: 150 stores are closed; Verne Winchell retires.

1986: Master Limited Partnership is formed, with 58 percent of its stock sold on the New York Stock Exchange.

1989: Shato Holdings, Ltd. buys Winchell's Donut Houses; 263 stores are sold to Pizza Hut.

1992: Nancy Parker takes over the firm and begins to focus on foodservice and retail sales.

1997: Tom Dowling replaces Parker and returns the company's focus to doughnuts and coffee.

1999: "Warm 'N' Fresh" guarantee is introduced.

a redesigned interior. Initial results were held to be promising, and more such units were announced, but the effort was later abandoned. An earlier attempt to add sandwiches in 1983 had also been dropped after initial testing.

In May 1991, Galastro left the firm, and his replacement's tenure as president was brief as well. Winchell's fortunes were again looking bad when Nancy Parker, previously the firm's director of Human Resources, was named general manager on an interim basis in early 1992. Her assurance and professionalism impressed the company's board, and a few months later she was appointed president. Once in charge, Parker wrapped up the uncompleted transfer of outlets to Pizza Hut, began giving store managers more autonomy, and created a line of frozen doughnuts for sale both in retail stores and to foodservice accounts.

Return to Profitability in 1992

These new measures helped make 1992 Winchell's first profitable year since the mid-1980s, and the company's health continued to improve over the next several years. Sales for 1994 hit approximately $82.5 million, at which time the company had a total of 240 corporate-owned and 60 franchised outlets. During the mid-1990s, sales began to slip again, however, and dipped to an estimated $71 million in 1996.

In 1997, Parker was replaced by former Baskin-Robbins vice-president Tom Dowling, reportedly because Shato executives wanted the firm to focus on retail stores rather than packaged and foodservice sales. Shortly after his appointment, he rolled out a new concept called Winchell's Express, a service counter that could be placed in convenience stores or sandwich shops to sell doughnuts that had been partially prepared off-site. Seven such outlets were initially installed in Subway restaurants in Las Vegas.

The company was also experimenting with its product mix, adding bagels and new "flavored-dough" doughnuts which had fruit and other ingredients added before baking. Another addition took the form of shaped doughnuts that were prepared for certain holidays, including heart-shaped donuts for Valentine's Day and Mother's Day. The company had for years logged its annual sales peak on Halloween, when specially decorated doughnuts were featured.

In 1998, Michell's introduced a new, higher-quality blend of coffee called "Legendary Gold." Ads for the drink targeted the ubiquitous Starbucks chain, using copy that described it as a premium quality, cheaper alternative to "Big Bucks" coffee. The firm also abandoned its traditional Styrofoam cups for the more expensive, environmentally friendly "Perfect Touch" variety seen in gourmet coffee shops.

These moves all came as Winchell's was celebrating its 50th anniversary and declaring a renewed commitment to the firm's core product line of doughnuts and coffee. The company had simultaneously redesigned its stores and updated its logo. It was also making plans to expand to 500 locations by 2000. Moreover, the firm was addressing a chronic shortage of doughnut bakers by converting some underperforming outlets to "mother stores" where two bakers could supply four locations with doughnuts. During 1998, Winchell's spent $9 million on new stores and $4 million on renovations to others. Despite these efforts, sales continued to drop, sliding to an estimated $60 million.

One of the firm's biggest problems continued to be the influx of new competitors. In addition to sales that were being taken by an onslaught of gourmet coffee shops and grocery store bakeries, Winchell's turf was now being targeted by Krispy Kreme, the North Carolina-based doughnut chain that was on an aggressive campaign of expansion and from whom Winchell's had recently recruited its new vice-president of development. The eastern firm's stores showcased the process of making doughnuts, and in January 1999 Winchell's opened the prototype of a similar store in Pomona, California, called "Winchell's World," where customers could watch an automated doughnut production line through large windows. The initial store was co-branded with Blimpie Subs and Salads and offered that firm's sandwiches at a separate counter area.

By this time, the Winchell's food products division, which had grown under Nancy Parker, had been abandoned, a decision that was attributed to the public's preference for fresh, rather than frozen doughnuts. The firm had also scuttled a line of chicken dishes that had been offered under the Pollo Especial brand.

"Warm 'N' Fresh" Guarantee Announced in 1999

In June 1999, Winchell's took another major step back to basics, instituting a guarantee that all of its doughnuts would be "Warm 'N' Fresh" or free between 6 and 9 am. In a move taken from Krispy Kreme's book, a red flashing light would signal the emergence of a new batch of doughnuts, which would stay warm for 15 minutes.

The year 1999 also saw new partnerships formed to open more Winchell's Express outlets in 7-Eleven stores and at Lucy's Laundry Marts, a laundromat chain which offered food from the likes of Subway and Burger King. Sales were now rebounding and increased by nearly 18 percent for the year to an estimated $70 million.

In 2000, the firm announced it was abandoning the Winchell's World concept but would add 16 new stores in Los Angeles and was considering expansion to the Midwest and East. The company was also now working on increasing bulk sales to schools and businesses. In early 2002, a new television ad campaign was launched in Los Angeles, and in November of that year company founder Verne Winchell passed away at the age of 87. By this time, the firm was being led by a new president, Bob Zanolli.

After 55 years, Winchell's Donut Houses had come full circle back to its original concept of offering fresh doughnuts and hot coffee with personalized service. The firm's "Warm 'N' Fresh" program, launched in 1999, was helping it reclaim lost ground as it battled new competitors such as supermarket bakeries and gourmet coffee shops.

Principal Competitors

Allied Domecq Quick Service Restaurants; Krispy Kreme Doughnuts, Inc.; Starbucks Corporation; Panera Bread Company.

Further Reading

Bellantonio, Jennifer, "Winchell's Basks in New Glaze, Thanks to Rival," *Orange County Business Journal*, July 23, 2001, p. 1.

Cebrzynski, Gregg, "Winchell's Repositioning with New Image and Products," *Nation's Restaurant News*, November 9, 1998.

Dawson, Angela, "Filling the Hole: Winchell's Donut Houses Looks for Way to Boost Business during Afternoon Hours," *Los Angeles Daily News*, November 26, 1990, p. B5.

Deemer, Susan, "Hole-Istic Medicine," *Orange County Business Journal*, February 1, 1999, p. 3.

Deemer-Schaben, Susan, "Winchell's Drops Factory Concept, Eyes Midwest," *Orange County Business Journal*, February 28, 2000, p. 13.

"Denny's Inc. Spinning Off Winchell's Donut Houses to Raise Cash," *Los Angeles Times*, December 20, 1986, p. 12.

"Denny's to Close 150 Doughnut Shops," *Wall Street Journal*, August 6, 1980.

"Doughnut Chain Founder Winchell Dies at LV Home," *Las Vegas Sun*, November 29, 2002, p. 8.

Flass, Rebecca, "Winchell's Returns with TV Ads," *Adweek Western Advertising News*, January 14, 2002, p. 4.

Fried, Ian, " 'Half-Baked' Idea—Winchell's Sees Growth through Mini Stores, Fast-Food Partners," *Orange County Business Journal*, November 10, 1997, p. 1.

Kapner, Suzanne, "Risk-Taking Pays Off for Parker, Winchell's," *Nation's Restaurant News*, December 12, 1994, p. 7.

Liddle, Alan, "Winchell's Repositions for Better Image," *Nation's Restaurant News*, June 25, 1990, p. 1.

Mahoney, Sally Gene, "Winchell's: Full Circle Back to Franchises," *Seattle Times*, November 11, 1985, p. A11.

Martin, Richard, "Canadian Company Acquires Winchell's," *Nation's Restaurant News*, July 31, 1989, p. 1.

——, "Winchell's N' More: Not Just Doughnuts Anymore," *Nation's Restaurant News*, November 19, 1990, p. 3.

Norman, Jan, "Filling Holes at Winchell's—Troubled Doughnut Chain Takes on New President, Attitude," *Orange County Register*, March 29, 1988, p. D1.

Spector, Amy, "Winchell's World, Krispy Kreme in Battle for LA Doughnut Dough," *Nation's Restaurant News*, January 18, 1999.

Stanton, Russ, "Winchell's Tries to Get on a Roll by Diversifying," *Orange County Register*, October 4, 1990, p. C1.

Takahashi, Dean, "Winchell's Stock Plunges on Buyout," *The Orange County Register*, July 21, 1989, p. C1.

——, "Pizza Delivery Wars Get Hotter—Pizza Hut to Buy Winchell's Shops and Convert for Take-out," *Orange County Register*, December 22, 1989, p. C1.

"United Fruit Calls off Its Proposal to Acquire Winchell Donut House," *Wall Street Journal*, November 11, 1966, p. 3.

"Winchell Donut Sale to Denny's Approved by Holders of Both," *Wall Street Journal*, March 21, 1968, p. 23.

—Frank Uhle

WinCo Foods Inc.

650 Armstrong Place
Boise, Idaho 83704-0825
U.S.A.
Telephone: (208) 377-0110
Fax: (208) 377-0474
Web site: http://www.wincofoods.com

Employee-Owned Company
Incorporated: 1968 as Waremart
Employees: 7,400
Sales: $1.82 billion (2002)
NAIC: 445110 Supermarkets and Other Grocery Stores

WinCo Foods Inc. is a warehouse-type grocery chain with 43 stores in five western states: Idaho, Washington, Oregon, California, and Nevada. WinCo's goal is to be the low-price leader in every area they serve. The company began in 1967 with one store under the name of Waremart. In 1999, Waremart changed its name to WinCo.

Beginnings: 1960s–1970s

WinCo's history began in 1967, when Ralph Ward and Bud Williams opened Waremart, a discount warehouse grocery store in Boise, Idaho. Ward and Williams founded their store with the goal of providing a wide selection at very low prices. By the following year, the company had two stores. In 1972, a Waremart store in Vancouver, Washington, was completely destroyed by a tornado. This destruction in no way represented the future of Waremart, as it picked up the pieces and moved on to expand immensely.

In 1978, Bill Long, an employee since 1968, was named president of the company; in 1985, he was named CEO. Also in 1985, employees purchased the Waremart Foods Employee Stock Ownership Trust, an employee pension plan, from the Ward family. The company believed this would create more dedicated employees, since they would have a personal stake in the company's success.

Rapid Growth in the 1980s and 1990s

Between 1985 and 2000, Waremart replaced a majority of its retail stores with updated and expanded facilities, a majority of which became 85,000-square-foot facilities. In addition, new stores were built and sales figures rose dramatically. By 1987, the company had sales of $198 million and 850 employees. The following year, sales jumped to $212 million. By 1991, the number of employees doubled, to 1,750, with sales just under $300 million. In 1993, sales exceeded $350 million. By 1994, Waremart had 21 stores, 2,900 employees, and sales of $419 million. Waremart's formula for growth involved buying up sites, then waiting two to five years before putting the stores in. This allowed the company to grab the best sites without committing a store until the time was right. While a site was empty, Waremart monitored such factors as population growth and business growth to determine the best time to build the store.

Throughout the 1990s, Waremart also bought eight Cub Foods stores, a franchise from SuperValu, Inc. in the Pacific Northwest. By 1998, the Cub Foods franchise was running out and Waremart did not wish to make royalty payments for the name. At the same time, Waremart was considering changing its name, since they noticed customer confusion with other large ''mart'' stores, such as Kmart and Wal-Mart. The company decided to use the name ''WinCo,'' which stood for ''winning company.'' Some employees of the company suggested that the name be an acronym for the five states that had WinCo stores—Washington, Idaho, Nevada, California, and Oregon—but the first suggestion won in a vote. The company first tried the new name on a Cub Foods store in Reno and found that customers were accepting of the change. The corporate name change, which was enacted in 1999, was a costly one, requiring new bags, aprons, hats, in-store signage, as well as the large names on and in front of its 27 stores. Still, the company thought it was worth the expense, as large profits and a growing number of dedicated customers followed.

WinCo earned the loyalty of thousands of bargain shoppers. Because it bought in bulk, sometimes whole truckloads from factories, WinCo consistently saved up to 7.5 percent over what it would normally pay a distributor. Therefore, it could sell its products for significantly less than its competitors. Furthermore,

Company Perspectives:

WinCo has fostered a 35-year tradition of success by focusing on very large stores with a huge selection of national brands at prices below our competition. In addition, the very nature of having employee stockholders that have seen their Employee Stock Ownership Plan (Pension Plan) grow at a 19.3 percent annual compound growth rate creates extremely dedicated employees. This has made WinCo a very successful company.

unlike wholesalers such as Sam's Club and Costco, WinCo did not require a membership fee from its shoppers. Another difference between WinCo and warehouse stores was that WinCo customers were not required to buy in bulk. Other factors that contributed to WinCo's low prices included its bag-it-yourself system, with the customer bagging her own groceries, and its no-frills, warehouse-type stores. Other cost-saving policies were the fact that the company did very little advertising and did not accept debit or credit cards, which charge a fee per transaction.

In 1998, with sales around $900 million, the company ranked 281st on the *Forbes* list of the nation's largest 500 private companies. Sales had been growing 20 percent per year. At this time, the company opened a new 900,000-square-foot grocery and perishable distribution center in Woodburn, Oregon, with further construction around the corner. At the time, six new stores were being built: in Reno, Nevada; Sacramento, California; Eugene and Covallis, Oregon; and Idaho Falls and Boise, Idaho. The Idaho Falls store, employing around 170 people and costing $2.3 million to build, opened in 1999 to a large crowd of shoppers. At 85,000 square feet, the new WinCo was more than twice as large as the old Waremart it replaced. It featured a larger produce department, a delicatessen, and a 24-hour bakery. Still, not everyone was happy with WinCo's growth.

In 1999, union members from Sacramento's Central Labor Council and the Coalition for the Advancement of Working Women gathered in front of the Sacramento WinCo to protest. The union members claimed that WinCo abused its employees, especially working mothers who, the union claimed, were often fired without warning. They also protested WinCo's wages, calling them below average. In 2000, members of the United Food and Commercial Workers (UFCW) 588-Northern California—through leafletting stores, picketing, staging rallies, going door-to-door, and a phone campaign—persuaded WinCo to withdraw plans to build a store in Folsom, California. Union members claimed that non-union stores such as WinCo posed a threat to working people's wages, benefits, working conditions, and job security.

Continued Growth in the New Century

In 2000, WinCo did some protesting of its own when it filed a lawsuit against the Missionary Church of the Disciples of Jesus Christ, based in Covina, California. WinCo claimed that the church violated the company's no-solicitation policy from 1998 to 2000 and that customers had been complaining about being approached for donations. With 32 stores, each averaging

about $750,000 in sales a year, WinCo continued to expand. It opened a new store in Federal Way, Washington, as well as a 110,000-square-foot health and beauty, gourmet, and non-food distribution center in Myrtle Creek, Oregon. Total company sales for 2000 were in the $1 billion range.

Also in 2000, WinCo hired its first public spokesperson, Mike Read, a former corporate spokesperson for Albertson's Inc. This marked a shift for WinCo, which traditionally did not make public many of its business matters. At the same time, the company installed Image Data LLC's True ID service in six stores after a three-month test program of the service eliminated check fraud in a Portland, Oregon, store that previously had been plagued by fraudulent checks.

To end 2000, Winco sold $65 million of its shares to six investors who were eager to invest in the company. Strong management, WinCo's dominant market position, and its low-leveraged profile were among the factors that appealed to investors. The senior-notes deal had a seven-year final maturity.

In 2001, WinCo opened its 36th store, located in Richland, Washington. In 1999, Washington's governor initially voted against the deal to sell WinCo, for $2 million, the city-owned land the company pursued. There were worries about traffic congestion, as well as concerns that WinCo would conflict with the city's vision of a resort-style community. More than 100 city residents had signed a petition against WinCo, while 18 citizens spoke out against it in a town meeting. In the end, WinCo got the city's vote, and it opened its fourth Washington store. The 92,700-square-foot store opened its doors to hundreds of customers for its sneak preview, with a jazz band performing and employees giving out free food. The new store sported eighteen two-sided checkout stands, a concept of WinCo's that allowed one cashier to check out a new customer while the other bagged the customer's groceries.

Later in 2001, in Federal Way, Washington, UFCW members protested, vowing to keep picketing until WinCo left or joined the union. WinCo claimed the picketing did not hurt the store's profits, and they had no plans to join the union. Of its 35 stores at the time, only one—in Kennewick, Washington—had union workers. The protestors had no overall impact on WinCo's expansion, which continued full-throttle. In Roseville, California, the company began construction for a new store, while a Twin Falls, Idaho, WinCo expanded, adding 14,000 square feet to the store and several improvements, including a larger entrance, more checkstands, and greater space for shoppers to move around.

In 2002, WinCo began plans to build a new store in Brentwood, California. While the local planning commission first voted to approve WinCo's construction, it was later voted down after the local United Food and Commercial Workers Union appealed the project. The union claimed that WinCo's environmental impact report failed to fully comply with the California Environmental Quality Act. Yet, in the following month, after WinCo worked to fully comply with California's environmental obligations, the planning commission reinstated its approval of WinCo's construction. The 96,000-square-foot store, upon completion, became Brentwood's first discount warehouse supermarket, as well as its first non-union one.

Key Dates:
1967: Waremart is founded by Ralph Ward and Bud Williams.
1978: Bill Long is named president of the company.
1985: The company's employees buy Waremart Foods Employee Stock Ownership Trust from the Ward family.
1994: Waremart grows to 21 stores and 2,900 employees.
1998: The company ranks 266th on the *Forbes* list of the nation's largest 500 private companies.
1999: Waremart changes its name to WinCo.
2000: WinCo sells $65 million of its shares to six investors.
2002: A former employee charges the company with criminal racketeering.
2003: WinCo sales hit the $2 billion range.

Later that year, WinCo endured another legal difficulty when a former employee charged the company with criminal racketeering. Lino Paul, a Sudanese refugee, had been fired as a cashier in Boise, Idaho, when he sold beer to a customer at 5:59 a.m. The state enforced a nightly ban on selling retail alcohol before 6:00 a.m. Mr. Paul, who was black, claimed that another employee, who was white, authorized the sale. WinCo disputed that there was any racial bias involved in its decision, claiming that company policy required termination of any employee who did not comply with state alcohol laws. Paul had received money from the United Food and Commercial Workers International Union to help pay his lawyer fees. Part of Paul's complaint involved WinCo's employee association, which was set up to provide support to employees, independent of management. Paul claimed the association was a ''sham'' union working directly under management and that it did nothing to help him when he was fired.

Meanwhile, a new WinCo store opened in Stockton, California, drawing record crowds. As cars searched for empty spaces in the parking lot, customers waited at checkout stands for as long as an hour and a half. The store's 92,000 square feet far exceeded the second-largest store in the region, Raley's, at 62,000 square feet. The new WinCo was stocked with eighteen checkout stands—with dual conveyor belts—and 600 grocery carts. However, the cheap prices were the biggest crowd-drawer. The downturn in the economy since 2000 reportedly contributed to WinCo's success, as consumers sought ways to save money. By 2002, with an economy still suffering, WinCo had grown into a 37-store chain.

In 2003, WinCo continued its amazing growth. A new store, employing 200, opened in Modesto, California. The company also began plans to build a 720,000-square-foot food storage and distribution center in Ceres, California, further expanding its presence in the state. Distribution centers allowed the company to buy in bulk directly from food processors. This resulted in a reduced dependence on food brokers, thus decreasing buying costs and allowing WinCo to sell products cheaply. This was one way WinCo made the company more efficient and price conscious.

While planning construction for the Ceres distribution center, WinCo already had 11 stores in California. The distribution center, which was planned for completion by 2004, would employ 200 to 250 people. In the meantime, WinCo made plans to open several new stores throughout California, as well as in Nevada, which could increase the number of employees at the distribution center to somewhere between 500 and 600. Earlier in the year, WinCo's opening in Modesto, California, had attracted 2,850 phone applications for its 200 jobs. Similar interest was expected in Ceres. WinCo offered its full-time employees an above-minimum wage, as well as medical, dental, and retirement benefits and paid vacations. Meanwhile, the new distribution center would allow WinCo to expand beyond its previous borders, as far south as Los Angeles and San Diego and as far east as Las Vegas.

Further expansion plans in 2003 included a 93,000-square-foot store in Kent, Washington. The company also expressed interest in further expansion in the Puget Sound, Washington, area. The biggest obstacle in finding a new site there was size, as new WinCo stores ranged between 92,000 and 96,000 square feet (nearly twice as large as the average major grocery store).

With over 80 percent of the company owned by employees, WinCo was named the largest employee-owned company in the Pacific Northwest and the 21st largest in the country. WinCo prided itself on its community involvement, and the primary focus of its donation program, since WinCo's beginning, were local school districts.

WinCo filled an under-represented niche in the supermarket business by providing a large choice of goods at very cheap prices and eschewing the traditional grocery store's customer services. Others caught on to the idea, and competition began to rise. For instance, Top Food & Drug started expanding in Washington's Puget Sound area. Top Foods also sold at a discount, though perhaps not as much as WinCo, since Top Foods provided more services than the typical WinCo. For example, Top Foods' clerks bagged customers' groceries. Nevertheless, WinCo's rock-bottom prices brought in customers. One informal comparison found that WinCo beat its competitors' prices by more than a dollar on some items, while customers have claimed that, on average, WinCo's prices were between 50 cents and a dollar cheaper per item. This was the principal factor in WinCo's impressive growth since it opened its first store in 1968. By 2003, WinCo owned a total of forty-three stores, including eight in Idaho, six in Washington, 16 in Oregon, 11 in California, and two in Nevada, with total company sales looming in the $2 billion range.

Principal Competitors

Albertson's, Inc; Raley's, Inc; Safeway, Inc.

Further Reading

Anderson, Steven, ''Waremart Plans Meridian Store,'' *Idaho Business Review*, December 5, 1994.
——, ''Waremart to Switch Moniker to WinCo,'' *Idaho Business Review*, September 14, 1998.
Brown, Craig, ''Cub Foods to Be Renamed WinCo Foods,'' *Columbian*, September 30, 1998.
——, ''Marketplace Column,'' *Columbian*, June 21, 2000.

Carlson, Brad, ''Waremart Has Sites for More Stores, But Isn't Sure When They'll Be Built,'' *Idaho Business Review*, February 19, 1996.

——, ''WinCo Hires Albertson's Spokesman,'' *Idaho Business Review*, October 9, 2000.

Clements, Barbara, ''Grocery Workers Union Soon to Be in 2-front Battle Negotiations,'' *News Tribune* (Tacoma, Washington), March 19, 2001.

Coetsee, Rowena, ''Council Approves WinCo Despite Objections,'' *Contra Costa Times*, May 31, 2002.

Day, Julie Finnin, ''The Basket Chase $upermarkets Seek Market Niches as They Gear up for the Future,'' *Columbian*, November 22, 1998.

Gardner, Steven. ''WinCo Foods Considering Third Store, Near Evergreen Airport,'' *Columbian*, May 23, 2001.

——, ''WinCo to Build in Evergreen Area,'' *Columbian*, March 16, 2002.

Lewis, Jakema, ''WinCo Feeds Market Appetite,'' *Securities Data Publishing*, November 20, 2000.

——, ''WinCo Circles $65M Deal, Encounters Strong Investor Appetite,'' *Securities Data Publishing*, December 11, 2000, p. 1.

Orr, Patrick, ''Former Employee's Lawsuit Calls WinCo Union a 'sham,' '' *Idaho Statesman*, September 6, 2002.

Parish, Linn, ''Vandervert Wins Projects Worth $13.1 Million,'' *Journal of Business-Spokane*, June 29, 2000.

Phillips, Kelli A., ''WinCo Store Pressing Ahead,'' *Contra Costa Times*, May 24, 2002.

Ramsey, Jane, ''Brentwood to Welcome New Shopping Center,'' *Contra Costa Times*, January 4, 2002.

——, ''Appeal Set of Grocery Shopping Center in Brentwood WinCo Foods Has Won Planning Commission Approval for a Store,'' *Contra Costa Times*, April 7, 2002.

——, ''Unions Block WinCo Project,'' *Contra Costa Times*, April 12, 2002.

Rogoway, Mike, ''Shakespeare Wouldn't Care, But Customers Do,'' *Columbian*, December 26, 1999.

Szymanski, Jim, ''It's WinCo's Bag Discount Bag-It-Yourself Grocer with Distinctive Combination of Price, Variety Will Open 75,760 Square-foot Store Monday in Federal Way,'' *News Tribune*, June 11, 2000.

Trevison, Catherine, ''Waremart Inc. Takes Over Homebase Bid,'' *Portland Oregonian*, June 25, 1999.

——, ''East County Gets Two New Grocers,'' *Portland Oregonian*, May 23, 2001.

''Waremart Builds California Grocery,'' *Idaho Business Review*, June 19, 1995.

—Candice Mancini

Württembergische Metallwarenfabrik AG (WMF)

Erhardstrasse
D-73309 Geislingen (Steige)
Germany
Telephone: (49) 7331 25-1
Fax: (49) 7331 45-387
Web site: http://www.wmf.de

Public Company
Incorporated: 1853 as Metall-Waaren-Fabrik Straub & Schweizer
Employees: 5,492
Sales: EUR 578.1 million ($551.5 million)(2002)
Stock Exchanges: Frankfurt am Main
Ticker Symbol: WMF
NAIC: 339912 Silverware and Hollowware Manufacturing; 332211 Cutlery and Flatware (Except Precious) Manufacturing; 333294 Food Product Machinery Manufacturing; 332999 All Other Miscellaneous Fabricated Metal Product Manufacturing; 332439 Other Metal Container Manufacturing; 332214 Kitchen Utensil, Pot, and Pan Manufacturing; 327112 Vitreous China, Fine Earthenware, and Other Pottery Product Manufacturing; 327212 Other Pressed and Blown Glass and Glassware Manufacturing

Württembergische Metallwarenfabrik AG (WMF) is one of the world's leading manufacturers of commercial coffee makers and high quality solid silver and stainless steel cutlery, cookware, and tableware for private consumers and catering establishments. Headquartered in Geislingen, Germany, where the company's main production facility is located, WMF also manufactures in He Shan, China. WMF's consumer products, which account for roughly 70 percent of sales, are sold through the company's own 149 retail outlets in Germany and 16 WMF stores in Austria, the Netherlands, and Switzerland and through upscale department stores and special retailers all around the globe. Besides WMF AG, the WMF group of companies includes the German hotel and catering industry suppliers Gebrüder Hepp and Boehringer Gastro Profi, cutlery manufacturer Auerhahn, enamel cookware producer Silit, bake ware maker W.F. Kaiser, thermos and gift item manufacturer alfi Zitzmann, and the Swiss buffet system maker Hogatron. One third of WMF's ordinary shares is owned by Helvetic Grundbesitz Verwaltungs GmbH; Deutsche Bank AG, Munich Re, and Wüstenrot Stiftung e.V. own about 17 percent each.

Silver-plated Tableware in the 1860s

The history of WMF began in 1853. Daniel Straub, a miller's son with a strong entrepreneurial spirit, founded a metal-plating business in his hometown Geislingen, a small German town near Stuttgart. Having grown up at the dawn of industrialization, the 38-year-old who had married another wealthy miller's daughter put the two mills he owned to new uses. Within a decade, he transformed the water-powered mills from grain mills for local farmers into power-stations for his industrial ventures. In addition, the construction of a railway through the mountain town had not only earned Straub—who had invested his inheritance in the project—a considerable sum, it also connected him to the world.

In 1850, Straub established a mechanical workshop which soon grew into a factory for mill equipment such as big iron wheels and gears, pumps, and turbines. Straub's first company was later called Maschinenfabrik AG and eventually taken over by Heidelberger Druckmaschinen AG in 1929. In 1853, Daniel Straub, together with his childhood friend Friedrich Schweizer, founded a second business—the small metal-plating factory Straub & Schweizer. Schweizer, the son of a lathe artisan and metal turner, had gathered the crucial know-how in a new technology for silver-plating sheet copper while working in various regional tinware factories. He and his brother Louis oversaw the manufacturing of the silver-plated, richly decorated coffee and tea pots, candleholders, and boxes that were soon made at Straub & Schweizer by the company's 15 employees. The demand for such items was high in the second half of the 19th century, when the bourgeois class emerged as the leading force behind industrialization. Heavily influenced by the culture of nobility, nouveau-riche merchants and the emerging upper middle class wanted to decorate their living rooms as lavishly as noblemen did. Often lacking the funds to purchase solid gold or silver items, they chose the silver-plated imitations which created the same ''noble'' impression.

In 1862, Straub & Schweizer's elegant silver-plated serving trays, candleholders, and wine coolers received excellence awards at the World Exhibition in London. By the end of the 1860s, the company employed about 160, mostly experienced metal craftsmen such as metal chasers, brass workers, founders, and bronze painters, who soon had to be recruited from all over Germany. Straub & Schweizer's finely engraved and polished tableware was shipped as far as the Netherlands, Denmark, and Russia, while northern Germany emerged as one of the company's major domestic markets. The company's first sales office with a showroom was established in Berlin in 1868.

When Friedrich Schweizer abruptly left the company in 1866, Straub bought his business partner out. He managed the company until his son Heinrich, an engineer, became a co-owner of the business, which was renamed Straub & Son. For the next six years Heinrich Straub, who was also actively involved in his father's first enterprise, the machine works, helped his father oversee the continuous expansion of the silver-plating factory. However, in 1876 Heinrich caught a severe cold and contracted tuberculosis, from which he died. His son's early death devastated Daniel Straub, and his natural entrepreneurial drive came to a sudden halt. On top of that, a significant investment in a local ore mine in 1875 had put considerable debt into his company's balance sheet. Five years later, Straub's main creditor, the *Württembergische Vereinsbank,* or Wurttemberg Union Bank, urged him to merge his business with another nearby silver-plating factory: A. Ritter & Co.

Merger in 1880 Creates WMF

A. Ritter & Co. was founded by Alfred Ritter and chemist Carl Haegele in 1871. Initially established in Stuttgart, the company soon moved operations to nearby Esslingen, where there was more space to expand production facilities. The company not only started competing with Straub & Son but also lured away some of the company's experienced staff. However, A. Ritter & Co. focused on lavishly decorated, luxury items and used a different technology to make them. At Straub & Son, high mechanical pressure and heat were used to attach the silver layer to the sheet metal. At A. Ritter & Co., the metal was dipped in a bath of silver. With the help of an electrical current, it was covered with a fine, even layer of silver. This new method, which was called galvanization, was more flexible and economical and

could be applied to more complex items. When the company ran into serious financial difficulties in 1874, Hermann Ostertag replaced Alfred Ritter as a business partner. Four years later, the company had recovered somewhat but still carried considerable debt. By 1880, A. Ritter & Co. employed about 250 people. Around the same time, Straub & Son had roughly 200 employees. The latter company had established a name for itself and was financially successful. However, Straub & Son was still a huge workshop for craftspeople rather than a factory. On the contrary, A. Ritter & Co. had invested in a modern industrial production but was still a newcomer in the market.

In June 1880, the owners of Straub & Son and A. Ritter & Co. met with representatives of the Wurttemberg Union Bank and signed a merger agreement. The newly formed public limited company was called Württembergische Metallwarenfabrik AG, Wurttemberg Metal Goods Factory, or, in short, WMF. Wurttemberg Union Bank owned three quarters of the company's share capital. The remaining quarter was divided between Daniel Straub, Carl Haegele, Hermann Ostertag, and some bank managers. Soon afterwards, Gustav Siegle, the owner of a Stuttgart paint and dye factory and a member of Wurttemberg Union Bank's supervisory board, acquired the bank's majority share in WMF. Siegle knew all the owners of the two factories to be merged. Haegele had worked for him as an engineer, one of Ostertag's nephews was his son-in-law, and he went to college with Straub's son Heinrich.

Daniel Straub, however, was not happy with the merger. He refused to cooperate with Haegele, who had been appointed as WMF's managing director. Nevertheless, the reorganization of the two operations progressed fairly quickly. Geislingen turned out to be the better location and the equipment and staff from Esslingen were relocated there in the second half of 1881. In February 1882, Straub stepped back from his duties at WMF. A few days before the merger, he had founded a new holding company for his other businesses, such as the machine works, which gave him plenty to do. By the end of 1882, all the key management positions at WMF had been taken over by former A. Ritter & Co. employees.

Dynamic Growth between 1880 and 1897

After the merger, WMF entered a period of dynamic growth. This growth was driven by two major factors: expansion of production capacity and product range, mainly through acquisitions, and expansion of the company's distribution and sales network, domestically as well as internationally. In 1883, WMF established its own glass-making workshop to end the company's dependence on outside suppliers. The skilled workers from Bohemia hired for this job moved to Geislingen and started making the artistically engraved glass inserts for tea glass holders, butter and mustard dishes, salt and pepper shakers, and other tableware and decorative items.

Straub & Schweizer had made silver-plated cutlery for hotels and institutions since 1859. Thirty years later, with the takeover of Berlin-based cutlery manufacturer Alexander Katsch, WMF gained crucial know-how for a product range that later became the company's hallmark. Another step that advanced WMF's cutlery-making know-how came about with the acquisition of the Munich Galvanoplastic Art Institute, a major

Key Dates:

1853: The small metal-plating factory Straub & Schweizer is established.
1868: The company's first sales office opens in Berlin.
1880: Straub & Son is merged with competitor A. Ritter & Co. to form Württembergische Metallwarenfabrik AG (WMF).
1914: WMF starts making infantry cartridges and shells.
1920: The ''Silit'' line of cookware is introduced.
1927: WMF launches its first electric coffee maker for commercial use and a ''Cromargan'' stainless steel pan.
1936: The company once again switches to military goods production.
1969: WMF products are sold at department stores for the first time.
1981: WMF's brand-new logistics center opens in Geislingen.
1985: Lawyer Wolfgang Schuppli becomes the company's majority shareholder.
1992: Commercial coffee maker ''Programmat 4'' is launched.
2001: WMF's modular specialty coffee maker ''combiNation'' is introduced.
2003: Thorsten Klapproth succeeds Rolf Almendinger as CEO.

manufacturer of large and small statues for buildings, fountains, tombstones, and gardens in 1890. The institute's chemists developed a new galvanizing technology that made it possible to vary the thickness of the silver layer on any given object. This process was used to apply more silver to the parts of cutlery pieces that wore out the fastest. This in turn eliminated the otherwise necessary replacing of worn-off silver. The competitive advantage of WMF's ''patented silverware'' immediately turned into cash flow. Ten years later, sliver-plated cutlery had become one of the company's main product lines.

After the takeover of one of WMF's main German competitors, Berlin-based Deutsche-Industrie-Aktien-Gesellschaft, in 1889, the company established a silver-plating operation and a warehouse in Berlin to better serve customers in northern Germany. The retail stores that carried WMF items—mainly jewelers and a few housewares stores—were regularly visited by the company's traveling salesmen to inform them about new products. WMF's customers from rural areas were invited to central sales seminars. Carl Haegele was the driving force behind the company's effort to add a direct sales channel to the mix: WMF's own sales outlets. In 1880, the company took over A. Ritter's sales branch in Stuttgart and transformed it into a factory outlet store. In the following years, a network of WMF-stores was set up at highly frequented locations in major German cities. The company-owned stores gave the WMF-brand premium exposure and made it stand out among its competitors. The direct contact with customers also provided valuable information about their preferences and tastes. In the early 1890s, WMF stores began generating more sales than traveling salesmen did.

International expansion began in 1884, when WMF bought a stake in former A. Ritter & Co. associate A. Köhler & Cie in Vienna. The first WMF store in Vienna opened the same year. Two years later, another subsidiary was set up in Warsaw, which at that time belonged to the Russian Empire. Each of the two companies established a silver-plating operation that purchased sheet metal or unfinished goods from WMF. That way, WMF gained access to the Austro-Hungarian and to the Russian market without having to pay the high import duties for luxury goods. Within a short period of time, revenues from Russia accounted for about one fifth of WMF's total sales.

Major Supplier to the Military in 1914

The acquisition of another competitor—Göppingen-based Schauffler & Safft—in 1897 marked a new chapter in WMF's history. The company was founded in 1876 by two former employees of a Göppingen tinware factory, Hans Schauffler and Adolf Safft, and was the leading German manufacturer of nickel-plated metal goods such as cooking utensils, tea and milk urns, lanterns, tabletop stoves, and, later, coffee makers. Due to Hans Schauffler's exquisite sales skills, the company exported roughly half of their output. Nickel-plated items, which did not tarnish and were easier to clean, represented serious competition for WMF's silver-plated products. They could be polished by machines and therefore be made comparatively cheaply.

Less than one year after the takeover, WMF's supervisory board replaced Carl Haegele with Hans Schauffler as the company's new executive director. Schauffler focused on boosting sales, and within seven years revenues from the so-called ''Göppingen ware'' doubled, while the factory's workforce rose from roughly 500 to almost 1150. However, Schauffler's sudden death in 1904 left WMF without a leader. The supervisory board decided to establish a board of five directors, each of them with a clearly defined area of responsibility. In 1905, WMF bought another competitor, Cologne-based Orivit AG, a manufacturer of stylish metal tableware and decorative articles which were covered with a layer of brass, bronze, silver, or gold. WMF had paid a significant sum for Orivit. Nevertheless, the company's efforts to transform the financially struggling firm into a profitable operation eventually failed.

By 1914, WMF had become a leading supplier of silver-plated household items and the largest employer in the state of Wurttemberg. About 4,000 people worked for WMF in Geislingen and another 2,000 worked at other locations in Germany and abroad. There were more than 25 WMF sales outlets in Germany and cutlery accounted for roughly one-fifth of their sales.

The outbreak of World War I in the summer of 1914 brought WMF's first period of extensive growth to a sudden halt. Metal was a crucial ingredient for the German war economy and not available any longer for civil uses. Exports were halted. WMF's production in Warsaw was shut down and later sold. In addition, 760 WMF employees were called up by the military. In order to avoid the company's shutdown, WMF became a major contractor for the German army. Because of its patented process for making cartridges and shells from high-quality steel, the company became almost the sole supplier of these munitions during the war. An increasing number of female employees replaced the men drafted into the army. At its wartime peak, WMF employed about 8,000 workers and put out a total of roughly 200 million bullets and shells for the infantry. Meanwhile, the company's retail outlets sold products made by other firms.

Economic and Political Turmoil: 1919–45

The decade that followed World War I gave WMF only a short time for recovery between two severe economic downturns. The 1920s started out with two years of accelerating inflation, resulting in the financial ruin of the German middle class. When WMF tried to cut personnel cost by extending work hours in spring 1922, while the wages paid were not sufficient to cover the cost of daily living, a part of the company's workforce went on a three-month strike.

Despite the economic turmoil, WMF tried to stay on the leading edge of product design and quality for household consumer goods made from metal. Since the demand for decorative items declined due to widespread economic hardship, the company focused on cutlery, serving dishes and kitchenware such as metal graters, colanders, pots, casseroles, and frying pans. In 1920, WMF introduced a new line of cookware made from high-quality steel, which was called "Silit Steel." Seven years later, WMF launched three product innovations: the company's first "Siko" pressure cooker, WMF's first electric coffee maker for commercial use with two different brewing functions, and a non-rusting, acid-resistant, and "taste-free" pan made from Krupp's V2A stainless steel with a high chrome content. Soon after, a whole new line of this type of cookware was launched under the brand name "Cromargan."

In 1924, WMF's patent for its special silver-plating process for cutlery expired. Although many competitors immediately adopted the technology, WMF managed to expand its cutlery business. In 1926, the company started making solid silver cutlery. By 1928, cutlery sales accounted for roughly two-thirds of WMF's total revenues. In 1932, the company introduced a line of Cromargan cutlery.

The worldwide economic depression that was initiated by the New York Stock Exchange crash in late October 1929 reached Germany in the early 1930s. WMF's exports—which accounted for about one-third of the company's revenues—dropped by 67 percent between 1930 and 1933. Although WMF shut down all production plants except the one in Geislingen and laid off hundreds of workers, the company still found itself in the red for the first time. The National Socialist (Nazi) Party that came into power in 1933 launched a massive government-financed program designed to lift the nation out of the depression, resulting in a short period of recovery for WMF. While exports were down, the company greatly expanded its domestic network of sales outlets to 141 by the end of the 1930s. While the Nazi government's economic policy initially was a success, it soon became apparent that it had another agenda. In 1936, the leader of the National Socialist Party, Adolf Hitler, demanded that the German economy had to be ready for another war within four years.

In order to continue operations after World War I, WMF had certified to the Allied Control Commission that all the machinery that was used to produce ammunition had been sold or destroyed and that in the future WMF would not make any more war goods. However, immediately after Hitler's call for rearmament, WMF's executive director Hugo Debach once more set the course to become a military contractor. Two months after the beginning of World War II, in December 1939, he suddenly died.

Before and during the war, WMF struggled with increasingly severe shortages of raw material. Once again, the company became a major supplier of ammunition and manufactured parts for airplanes. Beginning in 1940 a growing number of prisoners of war—and later forced laborers—were employed by WMF. These workers, about half of whom came from the Soviet Union, lived in camps around Geislingen and accounted for about one-third of the company's total workforce by mid-1944. Beginning in February 1944, a separate concentration camp was established by WMF in Geislingen for hundreds of Jewish women from Hungary who were originally destined to die in Auschwitz. As the war came close to the end in April 1945, over 900 female concentration camp prisoners were set free by the American Forces that occupied Geislingen.

Postwar Growth and Diversification

WMF's plant in Geislingen survived the bombing raids during World War II, but the company lost twelve sales outlets to the war and 33 in the Soviet occupied zone. While Arthur Burkhardt, WMF's Technical Director and driving force behind a rigorous modernization program that started in the early 1940s, underwent a denazification process for former members of the NSDAP (National Socialist German Workers Party), the company manufactured everything that could be made with the raw materials available, such as tin milk cans and light metal pots and containers. Back at work after the currency reform in western Germany in 1948, Burkhardt initiated the automation of as many production processes as possible, starting with the silver-plating of cutlery. Production capacity was expanded, but the Galvanoplastic Arts Workshop closed down in 1953. Meanwhile, WMF tried to fill the Germans' seemingly insatiable demand for new silverware, tableware, and cookware in a more modern style. The cooperation with renowned design professor Wilhelm Wagenfeld during the 1950s won WMF new recognition as a design-oriented manufacturer of upscale consumer goods. During this time, Chromargan stainless steel replaced silver as the main surface material.

The end of the 1950s marked the end of the postwar consumption wave for basic household goods in Germany. To make up for the slowing sales to consumers, WMF focused more on institutional customers to whom the company had started marketing directly. New WMF sales subsidiaries were established in western Europe and North America to boost exports. As a cost-cutting measure, WMF's product range was cut back, the enamel cookware and pressure cooker line Silit was sold off in 1964, and a production facility was set up in Greece in the same year. On the other hand, the company started making forged blades for table knives which had previously been purchased from outside vendors. In the second half of the decade, the company marketed some of its products as promotional items to businesses, modernized its sales outlets, and launched a new brand for upscale tableware, "Marke Tischfein," which in 1969 made its way onto the shelves of selected department stores. However, after the cooperation with

Wagenfeld had ended, WMF fell behind in regards to design standards. By the end of the decade, the company had lost its image as a trendsetter.

After Burkhardt's departure in 1969, WMF's new management board decided to branch out into new fields to overcome the company's problems, including highly volatile prices for raw material, rising labor costs and an increasingly saturated domestic market. The electronic circuit boards that had been made in-house for WMF's line of commercial coffee makers were now also offered to others. In 1972, the company took on the selling of U.S.-made vending machines for hot beverages which were modified for the German market. However, the machines flopped in Germany and Europe at that time. Another "modern" invention from the mushrooming fast food chains across the Atlantic was throw-away plastic tableware, which WMF started making in 1972. Three years later, WMF once more set up a production facility abroad—this time in Singapore—after its plant in Greece had been closed due to political turmoil. In the same year, the company invested in a brand-new, fully automated warehouse and distribution center in Geislingen, which went into full operation in 1981.

Change and Renewal in the 1980s and Beyond

While Germany slipped into another recession with the onset of the 1980s, WMF underwent fundamental changes in ownership and management. The early 1980s were characterized by the streamlining and reorganization of the company's business. The production of glass was ceased, as was the contract manufacturing of circuit boards and the marketing of hot beverage vending machines. The business was organized into three divisions: one for cutlery, tableware and gift items; a second one for cooking utensils and household goods; and a third for all the company's products that were sold to the hospitality industry.

Up until the end of the 1970s, the descendants of Gustav Siegle held the majority of WMF's shares. Siegle's daughters had married into some of Wurttemberg's most influential noble families, who thereby gained a decisive influence on WMF's supervisory board. In 1979, the German metal conglomerate Rheinmetall AG acquired a majority stake in WMF from a number of Siegle heirs. However, in 1985 Rheinmetall sold its majority stake in WMF to the lawyer Wolfgang Schuppli for anti-trust reasons. Schuppli brought in Rolf Allmendinger, a former executive manager of the Einkaufsgesellschaft Nürnberger Bund, as WMF's new CEO. Allmendinger initiated a turnaround in an increasingly complex and competitive environment. To get the company back on a profitable track—in the 1980s WMF generated DM600 million in sales but almost no profits—he completed the process of focusing on the company's core business and initiated new growth through innovations and acquisitions. In 1993, Schuppli sold all but 27.9 percent of his WMF shares to investment subsidiaries of Deutsche Bank, Munich Re, and Wurttembergische AG Versicherungs-Beteiligungsgesellschaft.

When the Berlin Wall fell in November 1989, WMF immediately sent 50 salesmen to East Germany to scout suitable locations for new sales outlets, including the old stores that were lost after World War II. By July 1990, when East Germans ex-changed their money for the West German *Deutschmark,* there were already 252 specialty retailers in eastern Germany where they could purchase WMF silverware. Within three years, WMF grossed about DM100 million in the new German states that joined the Federal Republic of Germany in October 1990.

After this "inner-German boom," the reality of saturated markets, consolidation, and increasing global competition set in. WMF reacted with a number of acquisitions that were designed to develop the company into a leading supplier of kitchen utensils and tableware to both private consumers and commercial customers. In 1987, WMF bought thermos maker alfi Zitzmann, followed one year later by Pforzheim-based Hepp. Founded in 1863, Hepp had an international reputation as a manufacturer of upscale cutlery and serving utensils for hotels. Also in 1987, WMF acquired a 24.9 percent share in German porcelain manufacturer Hutschenreuther. In the 1990s, the company expanded its product range with three more acquisitions: Hogatron, the Swiss maker of buffet serving and storage systems for the restaurant industry, German cutlery maker Auerhahn, and the financially struggling cookware maker Silit, which again became part of the WMF group in 1998. Another addition to the WMF group followed four years later when German baking tin maker W.F. Kaiser & Co. was acquired.

To regain a leading edge in design, WMF started working with a number of freelance designers. Distribution was expanded to include a growing number of furniture stores, where WMF's latest lifestyle-oriented creations were presented around the themes coffee and tea, wine and bar, and breakfast. Long gone was the period in the early 1990s when one-third or more of WMF's total sales came from cutlery. Within a decade, that percentage had fallen to 23 percent. Most competitors had moved their production to Asia and price pressures increased. In 2002, WMF moved its Asian production plant from Singapore to China. Production there was forty times cheaper than in Geislingen, where most of the company's output still originates, and eight times cheaper than in Singapore.

In a shrinking domestic market, the company has set its sights abroad and invested in new and innovative products. WMF's Exports accounted for almost 45 percent in 2002. In that year alone, the number of WMF shops-in-shops in Japanese department stores tripled and reached 65. Korea emerged as the company's most important foreign market for cookware. One of the most promising future sectors for WMF, however, might be the booming worldwide market for specialty coffees.

Beginning in the late 1960s, the commercial coffee makers WMF's institutional division launched—from the first electronically controlled bulk-brewing coffee maker "Programmat" in 1969 to the "Bistro" model line launched in 1995 to WMF's latest modular specialty coffee makers "combiNation" introduced in 2001—increasingly gained acceptance in the national and international hospitality market. They are in use on cruise liners and trains as well as in hotels and fast food restaurants. Not surprisingly, the newly renovated WMF sales outlet in Dusseldorf was equipped with a little café. The company's new CEO, Thorsten Klapproth, who succeeded Allmendinger in mid-2003, was planning to revive consumer interest in upscale cutlery through a new, emotional advertising campaign but saw the highest potential for future growth in commercial coffee makers, which accounted for roughly 15 percent of total sales. In mid-2003, WMF acquired a 34-percent stake in the Swiss market leader M. Schaerer AG. Built on a solid financial basis, the company seemed well positioned to claim its stake in the global market.

Principal Subsidiaries

W.F. Kaiser & Co. GmbH; Gebrüder Hepp GmbH; Silit-Werke GmbH & Co. KG (96%); WMF Immobilienverwaltungs GmbH; alfi Zitzmann GmbH; Carl Zitzmann GmbH; Auerhahn Bestecke GmbH; WMF Gastronomie Service GmbH; Boehringer Gastro Profi GmbH; Silit-Werke Beteiligungs-GmbH; BHS tabletop AG (24.9%); WMF (He Shan) Manufacturing Co. Ltd. (China); WMF Manufacturing Co. Ltd. (China); Silit France S.a.r.l. (96.2%); WMF Belgium S.A.; WMF Española S.A. (Spain); WMF Italia S.p.A. (Italy); WMF Nederland B.V. (Netherlands); WMF Nederland Filialen B.V. (Netherlands); WMF in Österreich Ges. m.b.H. (Austria); WMF (Schweiz) AG (Switzerland); WMF of America Inc. (United States); WMF Flatware (Pte.) Ltd. (Singapore); WMF Singapore (Pte.) Ltd.; WMF Italia Gestione Immobiliare S.r.l. (Italy); WMF Hogatron AG (Switzerland); WMF France S.a.r.l.; WMF United Kingdom Ltd.; WMF Far East K.K. (Japan); WMF Japan K.K.; Kaiser Italia S.R.L. (Italy); Kaiser Bakeware Inc. (United States); Kaiser & Co. Polska Sp. z o.o. (Poland); Gastromedia Sp. z o.o. (Poland; 20%); G.T.I. Manufacturing Company Ltd. (China; 33.3%).

Principal Competitors

Wilkens Bremer Silberwaren AG; SEB S.A.; Guy Degrenne S.A.; WKI Holding Company, Inc.; Tchibo Holding AG; IKEA International A/S.

Further Reading

150 Years of WMF, Geislingen, Germany: WMF Württembergische Metallwarenfabrik Aktiengesellschaft, 2003, 166 p.

Forms of Success, Geislingen, Germany: WMF Württembergische Metallwarenfabrik Aktiengesellschaft, 2003, 8 p.

Iwersen, Sönke, ''Messer, Gabeln und Patronenhülsen,'' *Stuttgarter Zeitung*, February 15, 2003, p. 13.

Lehnen, Alexandra, ''WMF widmet sich dem Lifestyle,'' *Lebensmittel Zeitung*, February 25, 2000, p. 17.

''Die privaten Verbraucher halten WMF die Treue,'' *Frankfurter Allgemeine Zeitung*, February 21, 1994, p. 19.

''Schuppli gibt Mehrheit an WMF ab,'' *Frankfurter Allgemeine Zeitung*, December 15, 1993, p. 18.

''Schwache Inlandsnachfrage bremst das Wachstum der WMF,'' *Frankfurter Allgemeine Zeitung*, February 16, 2001, p. 22.

Stankevitch, Debby Garbato, ''WMF launches Grand Gourmet,'' *HFD-The Weekly Home Furnishings Newspaper*, May 2, 1994, p. 68.

''Von Besteck und Kochtöpfen allein kann WMF längst nicht mehr leben,'' *Frankfurter Allgemeine Zeitung*, September 19, 2002, p. 22.

''WMF--Von Württemberg in die weite Welt,'' *Lebensmittel Zeitung*, February 28, 2003, p. 67.

—Evelyn Hauser

Zindart
LIMITED

Zindart Ltd.

Flat C&D
25/F Block 1
Tai Ping Industrial Centre
57 Ting Kok Road
Tai Po, New Territories, Hong Kong S.A.R.
China
Telephone: (852) 2665-6992
Fax: (852) 2664-7066
Web site: http://www.zindart.com

Public Company
Incorporated: 1978
Employees: 10,638
Sales: $120.7 million
Stock Exchanges: NASDAQ
Ticker Symbol: ZNDT
NAIC: 323117 Books Printing; 323119 Other
    Commercial Printing; 339932 Game, Toy, and
    Children's Vehicle Manufacturing

Zindart Ltd. produces die-cast collectibles for other companies, such as miniature toy cars for Mattel Toys and Keepsake Ornaments for Hallmark Cards, Inc. Zindart also owns Hua Yang, a producer of specialty printing and packaging. Zindart's die-cast, plastic forming, and packaging capacity together allow the company to offer a turnkey manufacturing service. Zindart has invested in state-of-the-art equipment to streamline setup times and can handle large production runs of up to 30 million units. Based in Hong Kong, Zindart has two plants in mainland China and offices in the United States and the United Kingdom.

Hong Kong Origins

Zindart Industrial Co. was founded in Hong Kong in 1978 by George K.D. Sun. Its production facilities were relocated to the new Zhong Xin factory in nearby Guangzhou, China, in 1982, and a second plant, called Xin Xing, opened there five years later. At this time, certain entities of the People's Republic of China acquired a controlling interest from Zindart's founder,

management, and The Ertl Company. In 1993, two investment groups, ChinaVest Limited of Hong Kong and San Francisco and Boston-based Advent International, acquired a 76 percent controlling interest in Zindart from shareholders in the People's Republic of China.

Zindart was starting to turn its focus away from the toy market, which was very trend-conscious, making planning for large production runs difficult. More detailed replicas aimed at adult collectors were one area of expansion. Zindart attained net income of $3.7 million on revenues of $35.6 million in 1994.

A new plant, the Dongguan Facility in Guangzhou, was begun in 1994, though it would not be fully complete for another four years. Zindart was also setting up a research and development center in Singapore. The company posted a profit of HK$40 million on turnover of HK$330 million in the fiscal year ended March 1996. Hallmark Cards, Inc., a customer since 1983, and The Ertl Company each accounted for a quarter of revenues. Earnings and sales had averaged more than 20 percent annual growth for the previous ten years, according to Henry Hu, Zindart chairman and CEO.

In 1996, the company sought to raise HK$100 million ($18 million) for expansion in Southeast Asia. Zindart was going public on the Singapore Stock Exchange as it was perceived as being more accommodating to industrial stocks than the Hong Kong exchange, reported Singapore's *Business Times*. Zindart CEO Henry Hu was the founder of Wah Shing, a soft-toy manufacturer that had recently gone public on the Singapore exchange.

Another attractive bourse for Zindart was the NASDAQ in the United States, which had more liberal listing requirements than the Hong Kong stock market and tended to see higher valuations of initial public offerings. It also afforded companies access to more than $5 trillion in U.S. equity capital, reported the *South China Morning Post*.

Going Public in 1997

Zindart Industries Co. Ltd. had its initial public offering (IPO) on the NASDAQ in March 1997, listing 1,725,000 Amer-

Company Perspectives:

The Company's strategy calls for further penetration of global collectible markets by achieving greater critical mass and presence in the global sectors it serves through marketing to a broader range of collectible customers as well as highly selective investments in the collectible industry. The Company addresses the market need for vendors that can manufacture high-quality products in the required volumes and in a timely and cost-effective manner. The Company provides a turnkey manufacturing service that enables it to satisfy customers' requirements at every stage in the production process, including component sourcing, product engineering and model making, computer-aided mold design and production, and manufacturing and packaging of the finished product. This coordinated, one-stop production process provides the Company's customers with shortened lead times from design to production, a single participant in the manufacturing process instead of multiple participants, and increased efficiency, resulting in lower per-unit costs. The Company's customers include many well-known marketers of die-cast and injection-molded giftware and collectibles, as well as packagers and publishers of books. The Company has successfully developed long-term relationships with many of its principal customers.

ican Depository Shares priced at $10.00 each. It chose the ticker symbol ZNDTY, later shortened to ZNDT. Proceeds from the offering were used to fund the completion of a third factory in Guangzhou, which would triple the company's capacity.

Zindart posted record results for the fiscal year ending March 31, 1997. Net sales rose 33 percent to $72.2 million, while net income of $5.7 million was up 23 percent. Fueling these figures were record sales for both Hallmark's Keepsake Ornaments and The Ertl Company's die-cast toys. Die-cast replicas accounted for more than half of Zindart's business. Molded plastic giftware accounted for another quarter, with the remainder coming from toy plastic figurines. Zindart Manufacturing consolidated its operations from three factories into the main Dongguan Facility in 1997.

Hua Yang Printing Holdings Co. Limited, a manufacturer of "pop-up" books and specialty packaging, was acquired in February 1998 for $35 million and up to a million new shares of Zindart stock. Hua Yang supplied packaging to two of Zindart's largest customers, Hallmark and Mattel Toys; it also had two principal shareholders in common with Zindart, ChinaVest and Advent, which acquired a majority holding in Hua Yang in 1995. Headquartered in Hong Kong, Hua Yang employed 2,500 people at its facility in nearby Shenzhen in mainland China.

Hua Yang had its start as a small, family-run business printer founded by C.M. Chan in Shanghai in 1935. It was relocated to Hong Kong in 1949, and in 1953 it became known as Hua Yang Printing Company Ltd. Packaging operations began in the 1960s with the acquisition of a two-color offset printing press. C.M. Chan's son Karl became head of the company in 1970. Four-color presses were added in the 1980s, and the company

entered the labor-intensive business of producing pop-up books in 1989. Six-color presses were added in 1995, when Hua Yang consolidated its manufacturing in the PRC, while keeping headquarters in Hong Kong.

Hua Yang had annual sales of about $33.5 million in the fiscal year ended March 31, 1997. Zindart passed $100 million in annual revenues with the Hua Yang purchase.

George Sun retired as chief executive of the company he founded in 1998. He was succeeded by Alex Ngan, a partner in ChinaVest. Peter A.J. Gardiner became chairman of the board in September 2000, succeeding Robert Theleen. Gardiner had previously been CEO of Veriflo, a supplier of semiconductor materials, and the U.S. arm of British multinational Dalgety plc.

Gardiner told the *Wall Street Transcript* that the book publishing business had become vertically integrated, eliminating the role of the book packager. As a consequence, Hua Yang began to call directly on publishers in both London and New York. Significant clients included Penguin Putnam Inc. and Scholastic Inc.

By this time, Zindart was making more than model cars. It contracted to produce wind-up radios and flashlights for a company called FreePlay Group. Zindart expanded its relationship with Mattel by producing board games based on the TV show *Survivor*. Board games manufacture called upon Hua Yang's specialized printing experience and also required production of molded plastic pieces.

Corgi Acquired in 1999

Zindart acquired Corgi Classics Limited, a classic British manufacturer of collectible, die-cast model cars and planes, in July 1999. Based in Leicester, Corgi employed 54 people in Great Britain and Hong Kong at the time and had sales of $30 million (£18.7 million) a year. Corgi products were distributed in Europe, North America, and Asia. Zindart paid $46.4 million (£29 million) for the company.

In November 1999, Corgi acquired the rights and tooling to produce Lledo products, the second largest collectible brand in the United Kingdom. Also, a subsidiary of Corgi was set up in Chicago in 1999 in order to develop the brand's own distribution network in the United States. Zindart also soon began marketing a miniature, working steam train under the Bassett-Lowke brand.

Corgi's origins dated back to the 1930s. It began producing die-cast car replicas in 1956. A management-led group had acquired the company from Mattel for £13 million in 1995. Its new owners, which included the British investment group Cinven, backed an aggressive expansion strategy, reported the *European Venture Capital Journal*. In the late 1990s, Corgi had a 55 percent market share in the United Kingdom. Over the years, Corgi had developed a considerable international following, and the value of its brand name was of key interest to Zindart. The Corgi connection was expected to open new opportunities in Europe, as well as raising Zindart's profile as an original equipment manufacturer, as Zindart chairman Robert A. Theleen told the *South China Morning Post*. Theleen was also chairman of ChinaVest.

Key Dates:

1935: C.M. Chan's printing business is founded in Shanghai.
1949: Chan's printing company is relocated to Hong Kong.
1953: Chan's printing company is renamed Hua Yang Printing Company Ltd.
1978: Zindart is founded in Hong Kong.
1982: Zindart production moves to Guangzhou.
1987: Hua Yang opens a plant in Shenzhen.
1993: Investment groups ChinaVest and Advent acquire control of Zindart and Hua Yang.
1997: Zindart goes public on NASDAQ.
1998: Hua Yang is acquired by Zindart.
1999: Corgi Classics Limited is acquired.
2001: Hua Yang enters the perfume packaging business.
2003: Zindart announces the sale of Corgi to management.

After being acquired by Zindart, Corgi introduced Premier Models, which incorporated details not found in most die-cast car replicas. Corgi also rolled out Unsung Heroes, its tribute to Vietnam era personnel and vehicles. Corgi had been producing collectible cars based on James Bond films since 1965, and in 2001 continued the tradition with a unique bundling deal with book and video distributor Baker & Taylor. Baker & Taylor packaged its James Bond DVDs with Corgi's models of the vehicles driven by Agent 007 in each particular film. This gave Corgi exposure in markets it had not traditionally served, boosting its North American presence.

Corgi licensed other well-known brands for its collectibles. It brought out a line of miniature Budweiser delivery vehicles in 2002. In the same year, a line of die-cast collectibles celebrated the 25th Anniversary of the *The Muppet Show,* including Miss Piggy driving a pink convertible. In September 2003, Zindart announced the pending sale of Corgi to a group of its managers.

Company Enters Perfume Packaging in 2001

Hua Yang entered the complex perfume packaging business in 2001 with an order to package Christian Dior perfumes for sale in duty free shops. Printing operations were moved into a new, larger, and more efficient factory in Shenzhen in spring 2002. State-of-the-art printing and cutting machines were installed. The company also opened an office in London to serve as a liaison with publishers there in developing new products. Hua Yang had recently won a contract to produce an edition of the popular Cranium board game.

Zindart Limited posted net income of $8.4 million on sales of $120.7 million in 2002. In 2003, Zindart Manufacturing

contracted to produce two lines of miniature vehicles, Stars 'n Stripes and Muscle Machines, for Funline Merchandising Co. It was also producing small home improvement and consumer electronics items.

Principal Subsidiaries

Bassett Lowke Ltd. (United Kingdom); Bassett Lowke (Railways) Ltd. (United Kingdom); Blow-ko Ltd. (United Kingdom); Dongguan Xinda Giftware Co. Ltd. (China); Guangzhou Jin Yi Advertising Co. Ltd. (90%; China); Hua Yang Holdings Co. Ltd. (Cayman Islands); Hua Yang Printing Holdings Co. Ltd. (Hong Kong); Icon Collectibles Ltd. (United Kingdom); Lledo Collectibles Ltd. (United Kingdom); Luen Tat Model Design Co. Ltd. (British Virgin Islands); Luen Tat Mould Manufacturing Ltd. (51%; British Virgin Islands); Onchart Industrial Ltd. (55%; British Virgin Islands); Shenzhen Huaxuan Printing Product Co. Ltd. (China); Wealthy Holdings Ltd. (British Virgin Islands); Zindart Ltd. (Bermuda).

Principal Divisions

Hua Yang; Zindart Manufacturing.

Principal Competitors

Action Performance Companies, Inc.; Enesco Group, Inc.; Hasbro, Inc.; RC2 Corporation.

Further Reading

Ang Wan May, "HK's Zindart Seeks S'pore Listing," *Business Times* (Singapore), April 1, 1996, p. 17.

"CEO Interview: Peter Gardiner—Zindart Ltd. (ZNDT)," *Wall Street Transcript,* July 9, 2001.

Gopalan, Nisha, "Firms Turn to Nasdaq; Exchange Pushes for Foreign Listings," *South China Morning Post* (Hong Kong), Sun. Money Sec., September 14, 1997, p. 2.

Kelly, Catherine, "Zindart Will Pop Up as Owner of Hua Yang," *Printing World,* December 1, 1997, p. 24.

Kosman, Josh, "ChinaVest Kicks Off $200 Million Fund," *Venture Capital Journal,* September 1, 1997.

Lu Ning, "ChinaVest Eyeing S'pore Bourse," *Business Times Singapore,* March 7, 1996.

Thomson, Andy, "Cinven Nets a Double," *European Venture Capital Journal,* September 1, 1999.

Wong, Douglas, "HK Firm to Raise S$18M from S'pore Share Offer," *Straits Times,* April 1, 1996.

Yu, Kai Peter, "Control of Brand Names Lauded as Key Tool to Growth," *South China Morning Post* (Hong Kong), Bus. Sec., July 30, 1999, p. 3.

"Zindart's Division to Produce Packaging for Christian Dior Products," *Asia Pulse,* May 7, 2002.

—Frederick C. Ingram

INDEX TO COMPANIES

Index to Companies

Listings in this index are arranged in alphabetical order under the company name. Company names beginning with a letter or proper name such as Eli Lilly & Co. will be found under the first letter of the company name. Definite articles (The, Le, La) are ignored for alphabetical purposes as are forms of incorporation that precede the company name (AB, NV). Company names printed in bold type have full, historical essays on the page numbers appearing in bold. Updates to entries that appeared in earlier volumes are signified by the notation **(upd.)**. Company names in light type are references within an essay to that company, not full historical essays. This index is cumulative with volume numbers printed in bold type.

INDEX TO INDUSTRIES

Index to Industries

CONTAINERS

DRUGS/PHARMACEUTICALS

ENGINEERING & MANAGEMENT SERVICES

ENTERTAINMENT & LEISURE

FINANCIAL SERVICES: BANKS

FOOD PRODUCTS

FOOD SERVICES & RETAILERS

HEALTH & PERSONAL CARE PRODUCTS

HEALTH CARE SERVICES

LEGAL SERVICES

MANUFACTURING

PAPER & FORESTRY

PUBLISHING & PRINTING

TEXTILES & APPAREL

WASTE SERVICES

GEOGRAPHIC INDEX

Geographic Index

United States

NOTES ON CONTRIBUTORS ⎯⎯⎯⎯⎯⎯⎯⎯⎯⎯⎯⎯⎯

Notes on Contributors

BRENNAN, Gerald E. California-based writer.

COHEN, M. L. Novelist and business writer living in Paris.

COVELL, Jeffrey L. Seattle-based writer.

DINGER, Ed. Bronx-based writer and editor.

FIERO, John W. Writer, researcher, and consultant.

GREENLAND, Paul R. Illinois-based writer and researcher; author of two books and former senior editor of a national business magazine; contributor to *The Encyclopedia of Chicago History* and *Company Profiles for Students.*

HALASZ, Robert. Former editor in chief of *World Progress* and *Funk & Wagnalls New Encyclopedia Yearbook;* author, *The U.S. Marines* (Millbrook Press, 1993).

HAUSER, Evelyn. Researcher, writer and marketing specialist based in Arcata, California; expertise includes historical and trend research in such topics as globalization, emerging industries and lifestyles, future scenarios, biographies, and the history of organizations.

HENRY, Elizabeth. Maine-based researcher, writer, and editor.

INGRAM, Frederick C. Utah-based business writer who has contributed to *GSA Business, Appalachian Trailway News,* the *Encyclopedia of Business,* the *Encyclopedia of Global Industries,* the *Encyclopedia of Consumer Brands,* and other regional and trade publications.

KEPOS, Paula. Manhattan-based editor and writer.

LEMIEUX, Gloria A. Researcher and writer living in Nashua, New Hampshire.

MANCINI, Candice. Montana-based writer.

STANFEL, Rebecca. Writer and editor living in Montana.

STANSELL, Christina M. Writer and editor based in Farmington Hills, Michigan.

TRADII, Mary. Writer based in Denver, Colorado.

UHLE, Frank. Ann Arbor-based writer; movie projectionist, disc jockey, and staff member of *Psychotronic Video* magazine.

WOODWARD, A. Wiconsin-based business writer.

657